SCOTTISH HISTORY SOCIETY

SIXTH SERIES

VOLUME 22

Scottish Witchcraft Narratives and Tracts

Scottish Witchcraft Narratives and Tracts

Edited by

Julian Goodare

SCOTTISH HISTORY SOCIETY
2026
BOYDELL PUBLISHING SERVICES

First published 2026
ISBN 978-0-906245-52-1

A Scottish History Society publication
supported by Boydell Publishing Services
Boydell Publishing Services is part of Boydell & Brewer Ltd
and of Boydell & Brewer Inc.
website: www.boydellandbrewer.com

Boydell & Brewer's Authorised Representative for product safety in the EU is Easy Access System Europe – Mustamäe tee 50, 10621 Tallinn, Estonia,
gpsr.requests@easproject.com

A CIP catalogue record of this publication is available
from the British Library

Printed and bound in Great Britain by
TJ Books, Padstow, Cornwall

CONTENTS

THE EDITOR

Julian Goodare is Emeritus Professor of History, University of Edinburgh. He has recently co-edited the companion volume to the present one: Julian Goodare and Liv Helene Willumsen (eds.), *Scottish Witchcraft Trials* (Woodbridge: Scottish History Society, 2025). His other books include *The European Witch-Hunt* (London, 2016). His edited book *The Supernatural in Early Modern Scotland* (Manchester, 2020; co-edited with Martha McGill) was runner-up for the Katharine Briggs Prize of the Folklore Society. He is Director of the online Survey of Scottish Witchcraft.

ACKNOWLEDGEMENTS

My greatest debt is to my long-time colleague Louise Yeoman, with whom I have often worked on many aspects of Scottish witchcraft. Her knowledge of manuscript sources is immense, and she is also a leading expert on the experience of Calvinist spirituality among other things. Her advice has been particularly welcome in the Bargarran and Pittenweem cases below, but has been felt throughout the book. I also owe many debts to Martha McGill in my understanding of Scottish witchcraft; her advice on the Bargarran case has been particularly helpful. It was she who drew my attention to the newsletter in NLS MS 3278, and she is also a fount of erudition on the intellectual understanding of demonic possession. I have also benefited from discussions with Hollie Baddick on medical aspects of the Bargarran case, and with Alasdair Raffe on its ecclesiological aspects. Dr Raffe has also kindly advised me about aspects of Sir James Turner's essays.

I have received welcome advice about Sir George Mackenzie's 'Pleading' from Leslie Dodd, John Finlay and Michael Wasser. Dr Wasser and Laura Doak, two leading experts on the justiciary court records, have also advised me on the search for Mackenzie's still-enigmatic 'Maevia'. Kath McSweeney has kindly advised me about the Irvine *Trial*.

Thank you to Jackie Gulland for reading and commenting on a draft of the Introduction.

Special thanks go to Alasdair A. MacDonald for invaluable guidance on Latin translations.

I am grateful to the British Library for permission to reproduce the text of Sir James Turner's two essays. The newsletter from NLS MS 3278, edited below as an appendix to the 'Bargarran Witches' Manuscript, is reproduced with the permission of the National Library of Scotland. The 'Bargarran Witches' Manuscript itself is copyright ©CSG CIC Glasgow Museums and Libraries Collection: The Mitchell Library, Special Collections. I am grateful to the National Records of Scotland for permission to publish material from its JC series of public records. The assistance of the staff at all four institutions has been appreciated.

Kelsey Jackson Williams, General Editor of the Scottish History Society, has provided welcome support throughout the editing process.

ABBREVIATIONS

ESTC	English Short Title Catalogue, 1473–1800, online.
Golden (ed.), *Encyclopedia*	Richard M. Golden (ed.), *Encyclopedia of Witchcraft: The Western Tradition*, 4 vols. (Santa Barbara, Calif., 2006).
NLS	National Library of Scotland, Edinburgh.
NRS	National Records of Scotland, Edinburgh.
ODNB	*Oxford Dictionary of National Biography* (2004).
SD	*Sadducismus Debellatus: or, a True Narrative of the Sorceries and Witchcrafts Exercis'd by the Devil and his Instruments upon Mrs. Christian Shaw, Daughter of Mr. John Shaw, of Bargarran in the County of Renfrew in the West of Scotland, from Aug. 1696 to Apr. 1697* (London: H. Newman and A. Bell, 1698).
SHS	Scottish History Society.
SPCR	Scottish Privy Council Records Database (Universities of Stirling and Dundee, 2024), online.

INTRODUCTION

Witchcraft was a live issue in Scotland during the sixteenth, seventeenth and early eighteenth centuries. Trials for witchcraft sometimes became headline news, and news of specific trials also raised general intellectual questions about the nature of witchcraft. Everyone wanted to make sense of the strange magical events that witches were said to take part in, and intellectuals wanted to use witchcraft to contribute to debates about how the world should be understood. This volume collects a number of written *narratives* about specific trials, and written *tracts* that discuss witchcraft in a more general or theoretical way. It complements a recent volume, *Scottish Witchcraft Trials*, also published by the Scottish History Society; that volume collects a number of records of witchcraft trials themselves.[1]

The idea of witchcraft, as a crime involving both magical harm and a pact with the Devil, arose in Europe in the early fifteenth century and spread gradually throughout the Continent during the remainder of the century.[2] In Scotland, there were occasional trials for witchcraft from the late fifteenth century onwards. Witch-hunting became more common after the Reformation; the Scottish parliament passed an act against witchcraft in 1563.[3] Narratives and tracts of the kind collected in the present volume began to be written in the 1590s, a time of national panics over witchcraft. Further such works continued to appear until even local panics began to subside in the 1700s.

INTRODUCING NARRATIVES AND TRACTS

Witchcraft was a shocking and sensational crime, and it attracted wide attention. The period in which witchcraft prosecutions first rose and then declined

1 Julian Goodare and Liv Helene Willumsen (eds.), *Scottish Witchcraft Trials* (Woodbridge: SHS, 2025). A document omitted from the *Trials* volume is edited in an appendix below, as explained later in this Introduction.

2 Julian Goodare, *The European Witch-Hunt* (London, 2016), 31–54.

3 For a survey of scholarship on Scottish witchcraft and witch-hunting, see Julian Goodare, 'Witchcraft in Scotland' in Brian P. Levack (ed.), *The Oxford Handbook of Witchcraft in Early Modern Europe and Colonial America* (Oxford, 2013), 300–17. The classic account of the subject, though dated, remains Christina Larner, *Enemies of God: The Witch-Hunt in Scotland* (London, 1981).

was also the period in which news media, especially printing, developed and became more sophisticated.[4] Scotland was hardly a leading country for the development of printing, but eventually, at least by the later seventeenth century, the Scottish printing industry was active enough to be able to issue quite a few cheaply-printed but topical narratives and tracts – including several about witchcraft.[5] The slowness with which Scottish printing developed may be connected to the curious fact that most of the Scottish narratives and tracts about witchcraft appeared only when the rate of prosecution of witchcraft was already declining. The earliest narrative edited below, from 1618, may even represent a *failed* project to produce a printed pamphlet. However, at this point it may be helpful to say a little more about the terms 'narrative', 'tract' and 'pamphlet', as these relate to works discussing witchcraft.

The term 'narrative' is used in this book to describe a written text by an author telling the story of a specific witchcraft prosecution or a bewitchment. Today such an author might well be a journalist. Narratives of specific witchcraft cases can be similar to the trial records for those cases, and sometimes incorporate extracts from trial records, but they are also distinctive. Trial records, written by the legally trained clerk of the court, focus on information necessary to establish the court's own authority, the correctness of its decision-making procedure, and the nature of the evidence for the accused person's guilt or (occasionally) innocence. Narratives address a broader, public readership. They aim to tell a continuous story, and they sometimes point morals or draw broader conclusions.

Narratives of specific witchcraft cases are sometimes described as 'pamphlets', a term focusing on their size and format rather than their content. Scholars of English witchcraft have made extensive use of such pamphlets, which compared with Scottish ones constitute a larger proportion of the available source material – England has more pamphlets and fewer surviving trial records. Scholars of Scottish witchcraft have focused more on the trial records, which in Scotland are more abundant – but they should also make as much use of the pamphlets as they can. Detailed work on the English pamphlets has shown that they benefit from being reprinted in scholarly editions.[6] This

4 For a discussion of witchcraft as news throughout Europe, see Wolfgang Behringer, 'Witchcraft and the Media', in Marjorie E. Plummer and Robin B. Barnes (eds.), *Ideas and Cultural Margins in Early Modern Germany: Essays in Honor of H. C. Erik Midelfort* (Farnham, 2009), 217–36.

5 Adam Fox, *The Press and the People: Cheap Print and Society in Scotland, 1500–1785* (Oxford, 2020).

6 Two one-volume editions of selected English pamphlets are Barbara Rosen (ed.), *Witchcraft in England, 1558–1618* (2nd edn., Amherst, 1991), and Marion Gibson (ed.), *Early Modern Witches: Witchcraft Cases in Contemporary Writing* (London, 2000). There is a six-volume edition of photographic reprints, with editorial commentary, of witchcraft pamphlets and longer demonological works: *English Witchcraft, 1560–1736*, 6 vols. (London: Pickering & Chatto, 2003). Individual volumes are: 1. *Early English Demonological Works*, ed. James Sharpe; 2. *Early English Trial Pamphlets*, ed. Marion Gibson; 3. *The Matthew Hopkins Trials*,

edition aims to bring the Scottish pamphlets into a similar state of accessibility and interpretation. However, the term 'pamphlet' is used here only for those narrative works that are of pamphlet length and that were, or could have been, printed as free-standing works. More generally the term 'narrative' is preferred.

The term 'tract' is used in this book for works addressing witchcraft as a topic of intellectual enquiry. As part of the genre of writing known as 'demonology', these works seek to prove that witches exist, and to explain the powers of witches and of the Devil.[7] Each tract tends also to have a distinct agenda of its own. Some of the works edited here, for instance, aim to use witchcraft to score points in a contest to defend orthodox Christianity against a perceived rise of deism and atheism. Like trial records, the tracts often discuss questions of accused witches' guilt or innocence, but in a more theoretical way, looking at the types of evidence that are required. This edition includes two general accounts of witchcraft, a general account of magic, and a published speech in the court of justiciary.

There are some overlaps between the categories of 'narratives' and 'tracts'. Some of the works categorised here as 'narratives' also discuss general issues, while some of the works categorised here as 'tracts' also cite specific cases. This is particularly so for the longest work in the present edition, *A True Narrative of the Sufferings and Relief of a Young Girle* (1698), which is constructed around the narrative of a specific case but which also includes sections of general discussion. These overlaps help to justify the inclusion of all this material within a single edition. More will be said about this later in the present Introduction.

Most of the documents edited below were printed at the time. Most of those that were printed – all except the first and third of the Pittenweem pamphlets – have also been digitised by Early English Books Online or Eighteenth Century Collections Online. The accessibility of page images of printed books in these digital collections is a boon to scholarship. However, these documents are difficult texts to understand, and sometimes even to read. Obscure expressions need to be explained, and contextual references need to be identified. Details of authorship and date are not always correct in digital editions or library catalogues. The present edition provides introductions to each document, and a scholarly apparatus that should facilitate their interpretation by the reader.

---

ed. Malcolm Gaskill; 4. *The Post-Restoration Synthesis and its Opponents*, ed. Peter Elmer; 5. *The Later English Trial Pamphlets*, ed. Peter Elmer; 6. *The Final Debate*, ed. James Sharpe.

7 The classic account of European demonology is Stuart Clark, *Thinking with Demons: The Idea of Witchcraft in Early Modern Europe* (Oxford, 1997). Two important recent works are Jan Machielsen (ed.), *The Science of Demons: Early Modern Authors Facing Witchcraft and the Devil* (London, 2020), and Julian Goodare, Rita Voltmer and Liv Helene Willumsen (eds.), *Demonology and Witch-Hunting in Early Modern Europe* (London, 2020).

DOCUMENTS INCLUDED IN THIS EDITION

The brief summaries here offer an overview of the contents of this edition. In addition, each document has its own fuller introduction preceding the text.

Trial, Confession, and Execution of Isobel Inch, John Stewart, Margaret Barclay and Isobel Crawford, for Witchcraft, at Irvine, anno 1618

This is a narrative account of the prosecution of four witches at Irvine in 1618. Two died in custody, and the other two were tried and executed. The narrative, almost uniquely in Scotland for this period, is similar to the more numerous genre of English witchcraft pamphlets. It was evidently written by someone closely involved in the investigation, and may well have been intended for publication. The suspects' confessions include remarkable details of visits to fairyland, of visions, of demonic conspiracy, of an animal-like or fairy-like familiar, and of image magic and other secret rituals in a deserted house and at the seashore. The narrative candidly relates details of imprisonment and torture.

Sir James Turner, 'Of Magicke' and 'Of the Jewes Cabale', *c.*1670

The royalist soldier Sir James Turner is best known for his 'Memoirs' and his publications on military matters. He also wrote a manuscript volume of essays on various subjects, and his essay 'Of Magicke' exemplifies the views of an educated layman of the period. His second, shorter essay on the Kabbalah is a spin-off from the main essay, or continuation of it. Turner's discussion ranges over various branches of ceremonial magic and witchcraft, mainly in traditional vein but adding some thoughts from the recent scientific discourse of the period. He regards magic as a reprehensible intellectual pursuit deriving from ancient times, and places witchcraft within this broader context.

Sir George Mackenzie, 'For Maevia, Accused of Witchcraft', 1672

This is a speech delivered in the court of justiciary by Mackenzie as defence advocate for 'Maevia', his fictionalised name for an accused witch. It was published in his *Pleadings in some Remarkable Cases before the Supreme Courts of Scotland, since the year 1661* (1672). Mackenzie is of interest for having discouraged witchcraft prosecutions when he was king's advocate from 1677 onwards. In this earlier defence speech, while not denying the existence of witchcraft, Mackenzie attempts to narrow the grounds on which witches may be convicted, and attacks belief in witches' flight and shape-shifting.

Witch-Craft Proven, 1697

This anonymous demonological tract presents an enthusiastic conspectus of demonological views on witches and learned magicians. The author clearly knows some Hebrew; he shows a particular interest in biblical languages, and in traditions of ancient magic and divination. He gives a lurid account of the witches' sabbat, and describes a range of idiosyncratic techniques for identifying witches.

A Relation of the Diabolical Practices of Above Twenty Wizards and Witches of the Sheriffdom of Renfrew, 1697

This publication is a narrative of the trials of a number of witches said to have caused the bewitchment of Christian Shaw, daughter of the laird of Bargarran. It prints several documents connected with the pre-trial investigations. The anonymous author took part in the early stages of the trial of the accused witches in the spring of 1697, and his work is particularly valuable for this stage in the proceedings. It is largely independent of the next two documents about the same case, the 'Bargarran Witches' manuscript (1697) and the *True Narrative* (1698), also edited below.

The 'Bargarran Witches' Manuscript, 1697

This composite manuscript, now in the Mitchell Library, Glasgow, is connected to the famous *True Narrative* edited below. It contains an earlier version of the 'Narrative' itself – the story of Christian Shaw's demonic possession and the witches that had allegedly caused this – with revealing differences that can shed light on the narrative's process of compilation. The manuscript also includes other material, including a number of documents submitted to, or produced by, a commission of enquiry early in 1697. The most striking document collected in the manuscript is a tract by James Williamson, 'Vindication of the Witches', making erudite demonological criticisms of the evidence used to convict the witches. The compiler of the 'Bargarran Witches' manuscript clearly supported the trials, but the information that he compiled showed that not everyone agreed. Finally, an appendix is added – a newsletter with an even earlier, variant version of part of the text.

A True Narrative of the Sufferings and Relief of a Young Girle, 1698

This composite publication is the longest single document in the present volume. The central part of it consists of a narrative of daily events connected with the bewitchment of Christian Shaw, daughter of the laird of Bargarran, in 1696–7, and with the trials of a number of witches said to have caused her bewitchment. Seven witches were eventually convicted; they were executed in Paisley in June 1697. The central 'narrative' of Christian's bizarre behaviour comprises about two-fifths of the text. The remainder consists of a long introductory discussion of witchcraft, documents connected with the trials, and other related material. Two long demonological speeches by the prosecuting advocate, Francis Grant, are included. Printed in 1698, the *True Narrative* aims to revive the prosecutions and to achieve more executions.

Five Pamphlets on the Pittenweem Case, 1704–5

This is an edition of the following five pamphlets:

1 *An Account of the Wicked and Terrible Confederacy of Betty Laing* (1704).

2 *A True and Full Relation of the Witches at Pittenweem* (1704).

3 *An Account of a Horrid and Barbarous Murder* (1705).

4 *An Answer of a Letter from a Gentleman in Fife to a Nobleman* (1705).

5 *A Just Reproof, to the False Reports ... Dropt in Two Late Pamphlets* (1705).

These anonymous pamphlets discuss the investigation and prosecution of a group of alleged witches in Pittenweem during 1704 and 1705. The first two pamphlets narrate the alleged doings of some of the witches. However, the privy council intervened to order the release of all the suspects in October and November 1704 (although one had already died in prison). One of the accused witches, Janet Cornfoot, was then lynched by a crowd on 30 January 1705, making the case a *cause célèbre*. Two more pamphlets were published at this point; they criticise the local authorities for procedural malpractice, for encouraging the prosecutions and for failing to restrain the crowd. Finally, a fifth pamphlet, almost certainly by Patrick Cowper, minister of Pittenweem, replies to the criticisms and defends the authorities.

[John Bell,] *The Tryal of Witchcraft*, *c*.1705

This anonymously published demonological tract was probably written by John Bell, minister of Gladsmuir. The tract tries cautiously but determinedly to establish the reality of witchcraft in the face of scepticism. The focus is on practical arguments of the kind that might be made to stand up in court. Unusually, the bulk of the citations are to English works, making some aspects of the tract curiously distant from Scottish witchcraft discourse. Most of the cited works are also old; Bell is not up to date with the debate, either in England or on the Continent. The tract is thus a noteworthy specimen of the decline of demonology.

Appendix: Alloa and Related Witches, Clackmannanshire, 1658–61

This is part of a trial record, relating to the trials of twelve accused witches that took place in 1659 during a local panic in the Alloa area. It belongs with a much larger group of documents that were published about this case in the companion volume to this one, *Scottish Witchcraft Trials*. As explained in the introduction to the document itself, it was omitted from that volume because the National Records of Scotland were unable to produce the manuscript until after the volume had been completed.

OTHER WRITINGS ON SCOTTISH WITCHCRAFT

In addition to the works edited in the present volume, several other Scottish witchcraft writings can be mentioned here. The discussion that follows has three related purposes. First, it makes specific mention of all important Scottish narratives and tracts on witchcraft that have been excluded from the present edition, giving overviews of their content and reasons for their exclusion. Second, it surveys recent scholarly studies that have discussed these writings. Third, it sets these primary and secondary works within the broader context of other secondary works discussing aspects of demonology as it was understood in Scotland.

There have been many scholarly publications on Scottish witchcraft. Few have focused primarily on demonology, although many works discuss some demonological ideas in context of investigating other topics, notably witchcraft prosecution or popular belief.[8] Works discussing specific narratives or tracts are discussed elsewhere in this Introduction, or in the introductions to individual works below. Here are some notes on the few scholarly works that focus specifically on Scottish demonology.

All subsequent scholars are indebted to the meticulously compiled analytical list of the nineteenth-century bibliographer and book collector John Ferguson. Ferguson identified most of the extant printed works discussing Scottish witchcraft, and sorted out many problems of dating and attribution.[9]

[8] Julian Goodare, 'Bibliography of Scottish Witchcraft', in Julian Goodare (ed.), *Scottish Witches and Witch-Hunters* (Basingstoke, 2013), 234–45. See also the bibliographical essay that concludes Julian Goodare (ed.), *The Scottish Witch-Hunt in Context* (Manchester, 2002), 218–19, and Stuart Macdonald, '*Enemies of God* Revisited: Recent Publications on Scottish Witch-Hunting', *Scottish Economic and Social History*, 23 (2003), 65–84.

[9] John Ferguson, 'Bibliographical Notes on the Witchcraft Literature of Scotland', *Proceedings of the Edinburgh Bibliographical Society*, 3 (1895), 37–124. This work was also issued as a separate

The modern study of Scottish demonology as an intellectual concept begins with Christina Larner. In her PhD thesis of 1962 she devoted a chapter to the medieval background (still relatively unexplored by subsequent Scottish scholars), a chapter to John Calvin on the grounds that Scottish demonology was Calvinist, a chapter each to King James VI, Sir George Mackenzie and George Sinclair (on whom more in a moment), two chapters to the various works connected with the Bargarran case of 1697 (including *Witch-Craft Proven*, on the plausible assumption that it had such a connection), and a chapter to *The Tryal of Witchcraft* of *c*.1705. All in all, Larner had at least something to say about most of the texts edited below. She did not know the Turner or Bargarran manuscripts; her focus on intellectual demonology meant that she had little interest in the Irvine *Trial* and the Pittenweem pamphlets; and 1962 was a very long time ago in witchcraft studies. Her thesis nevertheless addressed questions with which scholars of demonology are still concerned.[10]

Very few other scholarly works survey the whole of Scottish demonology. One that does do so is my own recent study of ideas about witches' flight. This draws on most of the works edited below, as well as several of those not edited but mentioned in the remainder of the present Introduction. Witches' flight was a key demonological concept; if demonologists could prove that witches flew, they had an unanswerable case for the reality and importance of witchcraft. Partly as a result of this, the idea of flight was one of the earliest to evoke intellectual scepticism, and seems to have contributed in the later seventeenth century to a decline in the credibility of witchcraft.[11]

I now turn to a partly thematic but mainly chronological survey of specific demonological works and groups of works.

Scotland's early chroniclers and historians, from the fourteenth to the early seventeenth centuries, narrated supernatural episodes from time to time. Further study of their use of witchcraft and demonology is needed, but there has been a relevant study of the way in which they used folklore, often engaging with the supernatural.[12] A study of the witches in the chronicles'

---

offprint from this journal, and has additionally been reprinted in Brian P. Levack (ed.), *Witchcraft in Scotland* (New York, 1992). Ferguson's own book collection is now held in Glasgow University Library.

10 Christina Larner (*née* Ross), 'Scottish Demonology in the Sixteenth and Seventeenth Centuries and its Theological Background' (University of Edinburgh PhD thesis, 1962). She later revised her discussion of *Witch-Craft Proven* and *The Tryal of Witchcraft* for publication as Christina Larner, 'Two Late Scottish Witchcraft Tracts: *Witch-Craft Proven* and *The Tryal of Witchcraft*', in Sydney Anglo (ed.), *The Damned Art: Essays in the Literature of Witchcraft* (London, 1977), 227–45. Larner's later and more famous book *Enemies of God* draws on her thesis from time to time, but for the most part is an independent work based on research done in the 1970s.

11 Julian Goodare, 'Witches' Flight in Scottish Demonology', in Goodare, Voltmer and Willumsen (eds.), *Demonology and Witch-Hunting*, 147–67.

12 Juliette Wood, 'Folkloric Patterns in Scottish Chronicles', in Sally Mapstone and Juliette Wood (eds.), *The Rose and the Thistle: Essays on the Culture of Late Medieval and Renaissance Scotland* (East Linton, 1998), 116–35.

narratives of prophecy shows that prophetic 'witches' were very different in character from the witches actually prosecuted in early modern Scotland; not all prophetic witches were human, for instance.[13]

William Hay, in about 1530, outlined scholastic demonology as it was then understood, as part of his course of theology lectures on the seven sacraments, given at the University of Aberdeen. His discussion of witchcraft came within his lectures on the sacrament of marriage; he felt it necessary to explain witchcraft at some length as a possible impediment to intercourse. Hay's lectures have been published in the original Latin, with a parallel translation into English.[14] Hay has recently been discussed in connection with his reference to the visionary cult of the 'seely wights', fairy-like beings.[15] However, his broader place in demonology remains to be assessed.

The Reformation brought major changes to Scotland's religious culture, even though Protestantism retained the Augustinian basis of demonology. There have been two demonological studies of John Knox, Scotland's leading Reformer. One of these surveys Knox's general engagement with demonological concepts, arguing that his writings show him as an activist and preacher rather than as a systematic theologian, but that he nevertheless acquired an awareness of the demonic pact in Geneva in the 1550s.[16] A further study gives more detail on the biblical basis of Knox's ideas.[17] Knox was on the committee that seems to have been responsible for drafting the 1563 witchcraft act, and his limited legal knowledge may well have fed into the inept way in which the act seemed to treat 'witches' as publicly identifiable practitioners with clients.[18] An important study of the role of the Devil in Scotland brings out the specifically Protestant uses of the Devil. Even in a religious culture emphasising the sovereignty of God, the Devil was frequently invoked as a mechanism for internal self-scrutiny by those seeking godliness.[19] Further recent studies of the supernatural in Scottish Protestantism, on sermons and on divine providence, provide context for Scottish witchcraft writings.[20]

13 Julian Goodare, 'Witchcraft and Prophecy in Scotland', *Journal of the Northern Renaissance*, 12 (2021), online.

14 William Hay, *Lectures on Marriage*, ed. and trans. John C. Barry (Edinburgh: Stair Society, 1967), 120–9.

15 Julian Goodare, 'The Cult of the Seely Wights in Scotland', *Folklore*, 123 (2012), 198–219; Julian Goodare, 'Seely Wights, Fairies and Nature Spirits in Scotland', in Éva Pócs (ed.), *Body, Soul, Spirits and Supernatural Communication* (Newcastle, 2019), 218–37.

16 Julian Goodare, 'John Knox on Demonology and Witchcraft', *Archiv für Reformationsgeschichte*, 96 (2005), 221–45.

17 Stuart Macdonald, 'John Knox, the Scottish Church, and Witchcraft Accusations', *Sixteenth Century Journal*, 48 (2017), 637–52.

18 Julian Goodare, 'The Scottish Witchcraft Act', *Church History*, 74 (2005), 39–67.

19 Michelle D. Brock, *Satan and the Scots: The Devil in Post-Reformation Scotland, c.1560–1700* (Farnham, 2016).

20 Michelle D. Brock, 'Fallen Spirits and Divine Grace: Sermons and the Supernatural in Post-Reformation Scotland', and Martha McGill and Alasdair Raffe, 'The Uses of Providence

The present edition does not include Scotland's best-known witchcraft tract, King James VI's *Daemonologie* (1597), as this has been published in three modern scholarly editions. That by James Craigie for the Scottish Text Society is a variorum edition collating early printings with the surviving manuscripts. It is valuable, not only for this, but also for unravelling textual problems presented by typographical errors in the original publication.[21] Lawrence Normand and Gareth Roberts' edition may be the most accessible, giving a single text in modernised spelling. It has a detailed introduction, and copious footnotes explaining difficult words or commenting on aspects of the text.[22] Neil Rhodes, Jennifer Richards and Joseph Marshall have produced another accessible modern edition, with useful reference notes and a glossary.[23]

James's *Daemonologie* was a compact but general and comprehensive account of demonology.[24] It was couched as a dialogue between the questioning Philomathes and the learned Epistemon, in which Philomathes raised some of the standard objections to witchcraft belief but readily allowed himself to be persuaded. James began with an account of learned magic and magicians in order to establish the powers of the Devil and the operations of the demonic pact, before introducing witches themselves, the harm they did, and their relationship with the Devil. He included a distinctive section on fairy belief and visions, insisting in conventional manner that ignorant people perceived a variety of different spirits, but that these spirits were all really demons. Finally

in Early Modern Scotland', both in Julian Goodare and Martha McGill (eds.), *The Supernatural in Early Modern Scotland* (Manchester, 2020), 144–59, 160–77.

21 King James VI and I, *Daemonologie*, in *Minor Prose Works of King James VI and I*, ed. James Craigie (Edinburgh: Scottish Text Society, 1982), pp. xvii–xxi, 1–56.

22 Lawrence Normand and Gareth Roberts (eds.), *Witchcraft in Early Modern Scotland: James VI's 'Demonology' and the North Berwick Witches* (Exeter, 2000), 327–426. For a discussion of the principles of their edition see Lawrence Normand, 'Modernising Scottish Witchcraft Texts', *EnterText*, 3 (2003), 227–37.

23 King James VI & I, *Selected Writings*, eds. Neil Rhodes, Jennifer Richards and Joseph Marshall (Aldershot, 2003). *Daemonologie* is at pp. 10–12 (introduction), 149–97 (text).

24 There is an extensive secondary literature on *Daemonologie*. The most incisive discussion of James's theoretical ideas remains Stuart Clark, 'King James' *Daemonologie*: Witchcraft and Kingship', in Anglo (ed.), *The Damned Art*, 156–81. A recent overview is provided by P. G. Maxwell-Stuart, 'A Royal Witch Theorist: James VI's *Daemonologie*', in Machielsen (ed.), *The Science of Demons*, 165–78. The editions of *Daemonologie* by Craigie and by Normand and Roberts, mentioned above, are important. They are informed by a pioneering work establishing a connection between the first draft of the manuscript and some of the witches of North Berwick: Rhodes Dunlap, 'King James and Some Witches: The Date and Text of the *Daemonologie*', *Philological Quarterly*, 54 (1975), 40–6. A recent historical discussion of *Daemonologie* is Lizanne Henderson, *Witchcraft and Folk Belief in the Age of Enlightenment: Scotland, 1670–1740* (Basingstoke, 2016), 154–62. For literary discussions see Jacqueline E. M. Latham, '*The Tempest* and King James' *Daemonologie*', *Shakespeare Studies*, 28 (1975), 117–23, and Daniel Fischlin, '"Counterfeiting God": James VI (I) and the Politics of *Daemonologie* (1597)', *Journal of Narrative Technique*, 26 (1996), 1–27. The latter work was also published in Graham Caie *et al.* (eds.), *The European Sun: Proceedings of the Seventh International Conference on Medieval and Renaissance Scottish Language and Literature* (East Linton, 2001), 452–74.

he called for witches to be punished, emphasising the power of divinely appointed rulers and magistrates. He encouraged the use of an unusually wide range of evidence against witches, including the swimming test that most demonologists had rejected. He claimed in his introduction to be writing in refutation of the sceptical publications of Johann Weyer and Reginald Scot, but this introduction may well have been written afterwards; there is at any rate no specific engagement with either author in James's text. James wrote his first draft in direct response to the North Berwick panic of 1590–2, presumably not long afterwards, and revised and published it in direct response to the subsequent panic of 1597. His defence of the swimming test, in particular, was probably a response to criticism of the test's use in the 1597 panic.[25]

Another well-known work excluded from the present edition is the pamphlet *Newes from Scotland* (*c.*1591), about the North Berwick panic of 1590–2. This pamphlet too has received a modern scholarly edition in the Normand and Roberts volume mentioned above.[26] *Newes from Scotland* is to some extent an English pamphlet, having been published in London for an English readership, but it is of course about Scotland, and it derives from a Scottish text written probably by James Carmichael, minister of Haddington.

Intellectual demonology needs to be set in context of fictional literature on witchcraft.[27] Several 'elrich' (otherworldly) poems were written in the late fifteenth and early sixteenth centuries. Not many of them explicitly include witches. However, demonology covered a broad field of relations between humans and demons. Roule's 'Devyne poware of michtis maist' (also known as 'Roule's Cursing') parodies the Catholic form of excommunication, while 'Lord Fergus Gaist' is a poetic mock-conjuration of a spirit that may be a demon.[28] The best-known and most extravagant 'elrich' poem, Alexander Montgomerie's burlesque 'Flyting with Polwart' (*c.*1580), includes a wide variety of witches and other supernatural beings, and has been analysed by Jacqueline Simpson.[29] Three witches, two of them based on real women

25 For connections between *Daemonologie* and the panics of the 1590s see Christina Larner, 'James VI and I and Witchcraft', in Alan G. R. Smith (ed.), *The Reign of James VI and I* (London, 1973), 74–90; Julian Goodare, 'The Scottish Witchcraft Panic of 1597', in Goodare (ed.), *The Scottish Witch-Hunt in Context*, 51–72; Julian Goodare, 'The Framework for Scottish Witch-Hunting in the 1590s', *Scottish Historical Review*, 81 (2002), 240–50; and Brian P. Levack, 'King James VI and Witchcraft', in his *Witch-Hunting in Scotland: Law, Politics and Religion* (London, 2008), 34–54.

26 Normand and Roberts (eds.), *Witchcraft*, 290–326.

27 For fictional works that include Scottish witches see Julian Goodare, *Weird Sisters: Scottish Witches in the Literary Imagination* (Edinburgh, 2026, forthcoming).

28 These and other relevant works have been edited in *'Duncane Laideus Testament' and other Comic Poems in Older Scots*, ed. Janet Hadley Williams (Edinburgh: Scottish Text Society, 2016). For further discussion see Janet Hadley Williams, 'The Elrich Poems: The Supernatural and the Textual', in Goodare and McGill (eds.), *The Supernatural in Early Modern Scotland*, 25–38.

29 Jacqueline Simpson, '"The Weird Sisters Wandering": Burlesque Witchery in Montgomerie's *Flyting*', *Folklore*, 106 (1995), 9–20. The 'Flyting' is a composite work; the witch-related part

although heavily fictionalised, also feature prominently in the harder-hitting satirical poem 'The Legend of the Bishop of St Androis Lyfe' (*c.* 1584), probably by Robert Sempill, which has been discussed by David Parkinson.[30]

The later seventeenth century was another period in which several works relevant to broader supernatural topics were written in Scotland. Robert Kirk's treatise *The Secret Common-Wealth* (1692) is an erudite reconstruction of ideas about angels, second sight and supernatural communication; it has been edited with a number of other related works by Michael Hunter.[31] Another pamphlet from this period is Andrew Telfair, *A True Relation of an Apparition* (1696).[32] The pamphlet narrates an episode of haunting by what would now be called a poltergeist, in the stewartry of Kirkcudbright. Thus it is not specifically about witchcraft, but falls within the broader topic of magic.

Scotland's longest published work discussing witchcraft was George Sinclair's *Satans Invisible World Discovered* (1685).[33] Sinclair, a presbyterian natural philosopher, wrote to prove the existence of witches and demons, and by so doing to combat the perceived problem of fashionable atheism. He also attacked Cartesian natural philosophy in his introduction.[34] His ultimate aim was theoretical – to prove the existence of witches and spirits. He set out to do so by assembling narratives of individual cases as empirical evidence. His

is known as the 'Secund Invective'. See Alexander Montgomerie, *Poems*, 2 vols., ed. David J. Parkinson (Edinburgh: Scottish Text Society, 2000), i, 143–54.

30 David J. Parkinson, '"The Legend of the Bishop of St Androis Lyfe" and the Survival of Scottish Poetry', *Early Modern Literary Studies*, 9.1 (May 2003), online. For the poem's text see James Cranstoun (ed.), *Satirical Poems of the Time of the Reformation*, 2 vols. (Edinburgh: Scottish Text Society, 1891–3), i, 346–90. For the main real witch in the poem, the visionary Alison Pearson, see Julian Goodare, 'Emotional Relationships with Spirit-Guides in Early Modern Scotland', in Goodare and McGill (eds.), *The Supernatural in Early Modern Scotland*, 39–54.

31 Michael Hunter (ed.), *The Occult Laboratory: Magic, Science and Second Sight in Late Seventeenth-Century Scotland* (Woodbridge, 2001). For recent discussion of Kirk's ideas see Julian Goodare, 'Between Humans and Angels: Scientific Uses for Fairies in Early Modern Scotland', in Michael Ostling (ed.), *Fairies, Demons, and Nature Spirits: 'Small Gods' at the Margins of Christendom* (London, 2018), 169–90, and Lizanne Henderson, 'Fairies, Angels and the Land of the Dead: Robert Kirk's Lychnobious People', in Pócs (ed.), *Body, Soul, Spirits and Supernatural Communication*, 238–57.

32 Alexander Telfair, *A True Relation of an Apparition, Expressions and Actings, of a Spirit, which infested the house of Andrew Mackie in Ring-Croft of Stocking, in the paroch of Kerrick, in the stewartry of Kirkcudbright, in Scotland* (Edinburgh: George Mosman, 1696). This pamphlet has been reprinted in Charles K. Sharpe, *A Historical Account of the Belief in Witchcraft in Scotland* (London, 1884), 229–54, and in Thomas Davidson, *Rowan Tree and Red Thread* (Edinburgh, 1949), 257–70.

33 George Sinclair, *Satans Invisible World Discovered* (Edinburgh: John Reid, 1685). For a recent discussion of Sinclair's work see Martha McGill, *Ghosts in Enlightenment Scotland* (Woodbridge, 2018), 54–9.

34 Michael Wasser, 'The Mechanical World-View and the Decline of Witch-Beliefs in Scotland', in Julian Goodare, Lauren Martin and Joyce Miller (eds.), *Witchcraft and Belief in Early Modern Scotland* (Basingstoke, 2008), 206–26. Sinclair's anti-Cartesianism is expounded by Alasdair Raffe, 'Intellectual Change before the Enlightenment: Scotland, the Netherlands and the Reception of Cartesian Thought, 1650–1700', *Scottish Historical Review*, 94 (2015), 24–47, at pp. 37–41.

project was inspired by the writings of Joseph Glanvill and Henry More, two of the so-called 'Cambridge Platonists' – particularly Glanvill's *Saducismus Triumphatus* ('Denial of Spirits Defeated'), an influential book assembled and published in 1681 by More from notes made by Glanvill before the latter's death. Sinclair repeated several of Glanvill's cases. *Satans Invisible World Discovered* comprises a large number of 'Relations' of specific episodes, most of which are neither Scottish nor about witchcraft.[35] Inclusion of it here would thus have unbalanced an edition of texts about Scottish witchcraft, as well as making the edition unmanageably long. Sinclair's book was reprinted in 1871 with additional material.[36] A modern scholarly edition of Sinclair would be a desirable project to complement the present edition.

Finally, mention may be made here of the witchcraft chapter that the advocate and academic lawyer William Forbes included in his legal textbook of 1730.[37] By this date, witchcraft prosecutions were almost vanishingly rare, and the intellectual credibility of witchcraft had also declined. Nevertheless the 1563 Witchcraft Act was still on the statute book, so Forbes dutifully expounded it, while narrowing the range of acceptable evidence in a way that would have made convictions very hard to achieve. In an appendix he dropped a heavy hint that he himself did not believe in witchcraft, and looked forward to a change in the law. That change did in fact come in 1736, when the English and Scottish witchcraft acts were eventually repealed.

CONNECTING NARRATIVES AND TRACTS

Let me return to the question of 'narratives' and 'tracts', beginning with George Sinclair's book as an example. Sinclair wanted to communicate

35 Among Sinclair's 36 numbered 'Relations', the following concern Scottish witchcraft (the dates are Sinclair's): Relation 1 (bewitchment of Sir George Maxwell of Pollok by Bessie Weir, Margaret Jackson and Marjorie Craig, 1684); Relation 3 (Agnes Sampson, North Berwick, 1591); Relation 9 (Hob Grieve, Lauder, 1649); Relation 11 (bewitchment of Gilbert Campbell, Glenluce, by Alexander Agnew, 1655–6); Relation 13 (bewitchment of King Duff, medieval); Relation 15 (Bessie Graham, Kilwinning, 1649); Relation 17 (Sandy Hunter or Hamilton alias 'Hattaraik', no date); Relation 21 (Isabel Heriot, Ormiston, 1680s); Relation 25 (William Barton and his wife, Kirkliston, 1650s); Relation 33 (Janet Douglas, discoverer of the witches of Pollok in Relation 1); Relation 34 (Helen Elliot, Culross, no date, and related cases). An unnumbered 'Postscript' relates the case of Major Thomas Weir and his sister Jean Weir, Edinburgh, 1670.

36 George Sinclair, *Satan's Invisible World Discovered*, ed. Thomas G. Stevenson (Edinburgh, 1871). This edition adds a biographical and bibliographical note concerning Sinclair himself, some additional 'relations' that had been appended to the original by an enlarged reprint of 1764, and various further accounts of witchcraft and magic in Scotland.

37 William Forbes, *The Institutes of the Law of Scotland*, 2 vols. (Edinburgh: Watson and Mosman, 1722–30), ii, 32–41 (main chapter), 371–3 (appendix). Forbes's chapter was influenced by the witchcraft chapter in Sir George Mackenzie's treatise on criminal law of 1678; that chapter is discussed later in this volume, in the introduction to Mackenzie's speech of 1672. Forbes is discussed by Larner, *Enemies of God*, 176–7.

a general message about demonology and witchcraft, to deepen people's understanding of how 'Satan' operated in the human world, and to show how natural philosophy could explain the interaction of spirit and matter. But his chosen strategy to achieve this was to publish a collection of case-studies, or 'relations' as he called them – relations that were presented in narrative form. If 'tracts' expound general principles, while 'narratives' tell particular stories, then there is evidently a connection between them.

It is helpful to treat 'narratives' and 'tracts' as ideal types, which can be analysed in principle but which are not found in their pure form in actual discourse. Real texts on witchcraft are made up of elements of both types. So real texts can be thought of on a spectrum. To take two examples from this edition, the Irvine *Trial* is close to being a pure narrative, with little or no general discussion of principles; Turner's 'Of Magicke' is close to being a pure tract, with little or no telling of the stories of specific witchcraft cases or discussion of the trajectory of such cases. How can Irvine and Turner be connected?

The narrative of the Irvine *Trial* concentrates exclusively on the case at hand, and never pauses to offer general reflections on witchcraft. Yet it is still underpinned by general assumptions about the powers of witches, the motives of witches (they are either vengeful or they wish to avoid poverty), the rituals that witches perform, the Devil's appearance, how witches relate to the Devil, and so on.

As for Turner, although he mainly deals in generalities, he gives *examples*, most of which are biblical or classical, like the so-called witch of Endor. He mentions these examples only briefly, but the reader needs to understand them as narratives. In the Bible, the witch of Endor is a character in a story. Under attack by the Philistines, King Saul seeks to know what his fate will be in the approaching battle, and visits a prophetic woman – a 'woman that hath a familiar spirit at En-dor', as the Authorised Version of the Bible describes her. She summons the apparition of the dead prophet Samuel, who correctly foretells Saul's defeat and death. This story was endlessly cited by witchcraft writers because it was the nearest thing that the Bible could provide to a *story* about a witch. The story was so well known that Turner and other authors needed only to allude to it, not to narrate it – but it was still understood as a series of events that unfolded over time.[38]

So Turner foregrounds general principles and keeps his narratives in the background; the Irvine *Trial* foregrounds specific events and keeps its general

[38] See Charles Zika, 'The Witch of Endor: Transformations of a Biblical Necromancer in Early Modern Europe', in F. W. Kent and Charles Zika (eds.), *Rituals, Images, and Words: Varieties of Cultural Expression in Late Medieval and Early Modern Europe* (Turnhout, 2005), 235–59; Charles Zika, 'The Witch of Endor Before the Witch Trials', in Louise Nyholm Kallestrup and Raisa Maria Toivo (eds.), *Contesting Orthodoxy in Medieval and Early Modern Europe: Heresy, Magic and Witchcraft* (Basingstoke, 2017), 167–91; Charles Zika, 'Endor, Witch of', in Golden (ed.), *Encyclopedia*, ii, 308–10.

principles in the background. They are at opposite ends of a spectrum, but they do both contain these two types of material. For an example in the middle of the spectrum, we may turn to the second of the Pittenweem pamphlets, *A True and Full Relation of the Witches at Pittenweem*. Half of the text does indeed narrate recent events in Pittenweem, as the main title promises – but the other half, as a subtitle announces, consists of 'An Essay for Proving the Existence of Good and Evil Spirits'. This 'essay' is a miniature demonological tract, complete with biblical citations (the witch of Endor duly appears), and asserting stridently that the truth of witchcraft is confirmed by witches' confessions. These confessions are themselves narratives, yet they reaffirm general principles.

In this book, perhaps the hardest document to categorise in these terms is Sir George Mackenzie's speech 'For Maevia'. This is a document from a trial, at least in its original context – but Mackenzie himself removed it from that context by publishing it without the rest of Maevia's trial documents, by omitting to mention the outcome of her trial, and simply by placing his text in the hands of readers who were not members of the court. His book of 'pleadings' (defence speeches) resembles Sinclair's book in the way that it seeks to make general points by means of case-studies. And each of the speeches seeks to apply general principles of law to a narrative of factual events.

Narratives of individual cases provide a way of understanding witchcraft prosecutions, when we analyse their development on a timeline from initial suspicion to ultimate execution. We can understand some aspects of witchcraft through analysing systems of belief and social structures, but these systems and structures are dynamic ones when they operate on actual individuals.[39] The Bargarran case, the most prominent one in this book, displays all sorts of different attitudes to different accused witches at different times. The young demoniac Christian Shaw, and those around her, begin by suspecting just two witches; then they start to think that there is a 'Crew' of witches. Arrests and interrogations begin. Some of the members of the 'Crew' confess to having attended witches' meetings but are switched to a category of innocent victims, so that they can testify for the prosecution as star witnesses. And so on. Indeed the Bargarran case includes at least two separate narratives: the story of Christian's possession and bewitchment, and the story of the witches' investigation and prosecution. A general theory can explain these changes over time, but only a narrative can show them.

The individuals from whom we hear most in this book are the educated theorists and prosecutors, developing their ideas about witches and the Devil. Yet witchcraft was a contested subject, and not every theorist agrees with the prosecutions. In the 'Bargarran Witches' manuscript, the minister Thomas

[39] Cf. John P. Demos, *Entertaining Satan: Witchcraft and the Culture of Early New England* (Oxford, 1982), pp. vii–ix.

Blackwell preaches that there are many more witches out there, and urges his congregation to identify them – but then James Williamson learnedly demolishes the very evidence on which the prosecutors have been relying (or might have demolished it, if the prosecutors had listened to him). As for the accused witches themselves, we sometimes hear their voices in the book too – particularly in the Irvine *Trial*, under the harrowing circumstances of interrogation under torture. Even when their voices are silent, we may still be able to reconstruct what is being done to them in the name of godliness.

CONCLUSIONS

The documents edited below require detailed study, which the present edition hopes to facilitate. So 'conclusions' may be premature. Nevertheless, here are some preliminary reflections on patterns that can be perceived in the documents, and questions that can be asked about them. I will begin with questions about narratives, and then turn to questions raised by broader principles of demonology.

The basic pattern of village witchcraft was structured as a narrative. It began with a quarrel between two parties, and was followed by misfortune to one of the parties that they interpreted retrospectively as bewitchment by the other party. Sometimes the quarrel had included a threat or a curse. Bitter quarrels and curses can be found at the beginning of all three of the main narratives in this book, those of Irvine, Bargarran and Pittenweem. Many witchcraft trial records show that this could be enough to achieve a conviction for witchcraft.

However, this basic pattern is not enough for our narrators. After the curse, each narrative then takes off into a more elaborate story. All three narratives tell of collective, ritual malefice by a group of witches, and image magic in which the witches use ritual objects to attack their victims. The Irvine witches make model ships and sink them; the Bargarran witches place various objects around the house as 'charms'; the Pittenweem witches make a magical doll to represent their victim. Or so the narratives tell us.

The Irvine *Trial* is an articulate, detailed and in places elaborate work, deftly weaving together several narrative strands in a single text. However, some of the events it narrates are impossible to take literally, and today's readers have to ask themselves which episodes are true and which are fantasies – and, if fantasies, whose fantasies. The Bargarran story is more disjointed in this book; the *True Narrative* is no longer the single authoritative version now that we have the earlier manuscript with which to compare it, and the multiplicity of stories in this exceptionally complicated case is difficult to grasp. As for the Pittenweem case, the early pamphlets tell fairly straightforward stories of bewitchment, even though they are hard to take literally, but once the panic collapses we start to hear alternative versions of the events. Eventually the final pamphlet, the *Just Reproof*, lashes out at everyone, repeatedly contradicts the critics of the prosecution, and well-nigh destroys any sense of coherence that the sequence of events might have possessed. Care and patience is needed with all these narratives, to work out which of the events are plausible in today's terms, and which events – including the supernatural events – carried credibility for the people at the time. And it must constantly be borne in mind that people at the time did not all agree about what had happened, or about what was supernatural.

Overall, then, these narratives do not represent typical bewitchments: they represent *remarkable* bewitchments. That does not diminish their value; on the contrary, we need to understand how people viewed remarkable bewitchments. The narratives in this book provide the intense emotional drama, eye-catching colour and nightmarish horror that made witchcraft such a compelling idea.

The fact that people did not all agree about supernatural events can be used to introduce the question of demonology. People wanted to understand the role of magic in their everyday lives, the role of God and the Devil, and the powers of witches in the cosmic struggle between God and the Devil. The tracts and tract-like texts in this book address these demonological questions.

Demonology was a Europe-wide enterprise, as any assessment of demonological writings in just one country must recognise. Scotland produced some demonology, as this book shows, but not enough to create a continuous demonological tradition. Not even King James VI's *Daemonologie* created a national tradition. Later Scottish writers cited the royal treatise from time to time, but *Daemonologie* did not dominate the discussion, nor did it make a distinctive contribution to the way in which later writers understood witches. Perhaps this is a tribute to James's skill in synthesising existing witchcraft scholarship. He did not *want* his book to be original or distinctive; he just wanted it to be correct and persuasive.

James's one distinctive contribution to demonology was the word 'demonology' itself, which seems to have been his own coinage (from Latin '*daemono-logia*', science of demons). Other writers coined similar words in their titles, such as 'demonomania' (craze for demons; Jean Bodin, 1580) or 'pneumalogy' (science of spirits; Sébastien Michaëlis, 1583). The word that caught on was 'demonology', being used in the titles of several other books in the seventeenth and eighteenth centuries.[40] But that was in Europe as a whole. The Scottish authors edited below did not take up the king's new word.

Instead, later Scottish writers gathered their demonological ideas from all over Europe – from a variety of places, and a variety of times. The following

40 Timothy Chesters and Thibaut Maus de Rolley, 'Le Diable dans la bibliothèque: la classification des traités de démonologie dans les catalogues bibliographiques aux XVIe et XVIIe siècles', *Early Modern French Studies*, 39 (2017), 2–16, at pp. 2–3.

brief summary mentions the national origins and publication dates of the main demonological writers from whom writers in this book drew in an identifiable way. Sir James Turner relied mainly on Cornelius Agrippa (Germany, 1530), though he also cited King James VI and Jean Bodin (France, 1580). Sir George Mackenzie mainly used Martin Delrio (Flanders, 1599–1600), and also cited Bodin, Jacques D'Autun (France, 1671), William Perkins (England, 1608) and Paolo Grillando (Italy, *c.*1524). John Wilson, who wrote the preface to the *True Narrative*, used Joseph Glanvill (England, 1681), though his disagreement with Glanvill on the separability of soul and body during life indicates that he had some other source of information. Francis Grant, the prosecuting lawyer in the Bargarran case, derived most of his demonological ideas from Delrio, though he also cited King James VI. John Bell relied mainly on Richard Bernard (England, 1627) and on Perkins.[41]

Overall, the most useful of these authors was probably the encyclopedic Delrio. Nobody seems to have used the *Malleus Maleficarum* ('Hammer of Witches') of 1486, which today has become the most notorious demonological work and which was indeed influential in its own day. Grant did cite the *Malleus*, but his citation to it was almost certainly at second hand, via Delrio. Delrio himself had refurbished the *Malleus*'s own arguments in a way that proved more useful in the seventeenth century. William Hay's early account of demonology in *c.*1530, mentioned above, may well have been influenced by the *Malleus*; further research would be desirable on this.

'Demonology' was not a self-contained topic. The lawyers Grant and Mackenzie, in particular, looked beyond it; many of their ideas came from writings on criminal law. The ministers like Wilson and Bell drew ideas from theology; they tended just to cite the Bible, but they probably used biblical commentaries as well.

The intellectual level of these Scottish writers varied. Sir James Turner plagiarised almost the whole of his second essay from Agrippa, while John Bell made an egregious error in copying a second-hand citation. Sir George Mackenzie may have been the most knowledgeable, and Francis Grant may have tried hardest to produce original ideas. James Williamson was ingenious in deftly turning demonological reasoning against the prosecutors. However, this is not said in order to award points for cleverness to some writers and to disparage or downgrade others. All these writers were important in their own way. Witchcraft ideas were successful when they operated across different intellectual levels. In Europe as a whole, there were a few original thinkers who produced new ideas, a perhaps larger number of synthesisers who included the new ideas in broader systems of thought, and a far greater number who

41 Of these writers, there are entries for Agrippa, Bodin, Delrio, Glanvill, Grillando, James VI and Perkins in Golden (ed.), *Encyclopedia*, and for Bodin, Delrio, James VI and Perkins in Machielsen (ed.), *The Science of Demons*.

summarised, simplified and repeated the most *usable* ideas. Usable witchcraft ideas were ideas that could support a case in court, or ideas that could enable ordinary people to understand their problems in terms of bewitchment.

One might expect lawyers to be conservative, expounding the law as it stood and consciously avoiding originality. To some extent we do find this – but lawyers can be innovative when they address the facts of a specific case. Grant explains how the Devil can make witches invisible: he not only blocks the light coming directly from the witch to the spectator, but also fills the gap that this would cause by refracting light *around* the witch so that the spectator sees the objects behind the witch. At a time when cutting-edge scientific experiments were being carried out with lenses, mirrors and prisms, this could seem persuasive.

Overall, though, the late-period demonology that is gathered in this book is no longer cutting-edge. Most of our writers' ideas had already appeared in the sixteenth century or earlier. When Bell defined witchcraft as being about the witch, the Devil, and divine permission, he was using the same formula as the *Malleus Maleficarum*. Christina Larner, who pointed this out, commented: 'It is not clear just how Bell came by his formulation, but it is unmistakable: here in the eighteenth century, at the birth of the age of reason, we find a clear echo of fifteenth-century Scholasticism.'[42]

These works do not show precisely how demonology lost its credibility. We may think that the Scientific Revolution left it high and dry; in the long run this is surely true, but at the time it was not obvious that the 'science of demons' was going to be inherently unscientific. Grant's idea about the Devil refracting light was inherently unscientific in that it was untestable by experiment, but that may not have seemed a crucial weakness at the time. And the intellectual sledgehammer that Williamson wielded against witchcraft evidence was also inherently unscientific, relying just as much on traditional assumptions about the Devil as his opponents. Williamson disbelieved in the Bargarran 'spectral evidence', not because the Devil's preternatural powers were incredible, but because the Devil was a powerful *deceiver* whom we should distrust. Perhaps demonology destroyed itself from within.

Demonology of some kind was essential to witch-hunting, but the connection between ideas about witchcraft and the prosecution of witches is not simple. One useful distinction can be drawn in demonology between 'prosecuting' and 'non-prosecuting' demonology. Some writers discussed witchcraft simply as an abstract intellectual idea, while others also demanded that this idea should be applied in the world. The prosecuting demonologists were those who actively demanded that witches should be executed.[43]

42 Larner, 'Two Late Scottish Witchcraft Tracts', 242.

43 For this distinction in Europe as a whole see Julian Goodare, 'Connecting Demonology and Witch-Hunting in Early Modern Europe', in Goodare, Voltmer and Willumsen (eds.), *Demonology and Witch-Hunting*, 345–81, at pp. 366–72.

How can this distinction be applied to the writers edited here? Sir James Turner is the most obvious non-prosecuting demonologist. He disapproves of magic and witchcraft, and expounds the powers of the Devil and the relationship between the Devil and wicked humans. But he makes no demand for prosecution, and shows hardly any interest in the kind of evidence that might be produced in court. At the other end of the spectrum, in the *True Narrative*, John Wilson and Francis Grant both direct their demonological ideas towards the specific goal of achieving convictions in the Bargarran case.

Prosecuting demonology was itself a debate, which could be argued on both sides. Sir George Mackenzie thus belongs in this category. He is not primarily interested in abstract ideas; he is deeply engaged with the debate about whether witches should be executed. But he reaches different conclusions in the debate. The same can be said for James Williamson, whose tract is included in the 'Bargarran Witches' manuscript. The Pittenweem pamphlets are immersed in a debate about specific witches' guilt or innocence, but some of them discuss broader demonological principles. Patrick Cowper, the probable author of the final *Just Reproof*, comes over as a keen witch-hunter with a dogmatic certainty about the validity of the prosecutions, impotently furious at the collapse of the panic and the refusal of the central authorities to support it.

Witch-Craft Proven is a curious mixture in this respect. Much of it is non-prosecuting, following intricate lines of linguistic analysis. Its catalogue of learned magicians is partly written in the past tense, with no sense that these men should be prosecuted or that they are necessarily even still alive. Yet the tract concludes with a section on how to detect a witch, which aligns the tract with prosecuting demonology. Most of the discussion does not focus closely on real evidence that might be used in court, and the author describes several eccentric methods of detection that were never mentioned in Scottish courts. Nevertheless, this tract's tone of dogmatic certainty about witches and what must be done with them is grimly familiar. By contrast, John Bell is interested in prosecutions, but lacks the confidence to demand executions. Like Williamson, he warns that some apparent evidence of witchcraft might be false because of the Devil's deceptions.

The lateness of most of these texts means that they return again and again to the question of demonic possession. This was not completely new; in his *Daemonologie* James VI included an entire chapter on the subject, describing demoniacs' typical symptoms and weighing up Catholic and Protestant dispossession practices.[44] That chapter did not raise the question of witches causing possession, but elsewhere James told of a trial sparked off by 'a young lasse, troubled with spirites, laide on her by witchcraft ... she saw the shapes of diverse men and women troubling her', and those she named were

[44] James VI, *Daemonologie*, in his *Minor Prose*, 48–50 (book 3, chapter 4).

convicted.[45] More research is needed on earlier possession cases, but they were rare at the time; most witchcraft cases did not involve possession. In the 1690s and afterwards, demonic possession came to dominate the discussion in a way that it had not done before. One reason for this is the extraordinary evidence generated by Christian Shaw's possession in the Bargarran case. Even the Bargarran witches were accused of other malefices, some of which might have been thought to be more serious – they were said to have killed several people, including a minister and a laird. But demonic possession provided a compelling spectacle. Whether it was literally true that 'Thousands in this Countrey have been Eye and Ear Witnesses' to Christian's performances, as the *True Narrative* asserted, there is no doubt that members of the elite flocked to Bargarran, and that Christian became a celebrity.

Behind the Bargarran case lay the sensational witchcraft panic at Salem, Massachusetts, in 1692, which also involved demonic possession. The present edition of documents from the Bargarran case may facilitate investigation of the connections between the two. The editorial commentaries on the 'Bargarran Witches' manuscript and on the *True Narrative*, below, discuss various ways in which Salem may have influenced Bargarran. Here, though, a broader point may be made. The Salem panic was controversial even while it was in progress, and led to public recriminations afterwards. One lesson that Salem could teach was that witchcraft panics involving demonic possession were a bad idea.

And although news of Salem witchcraft surely influenced the Scots, there was more to it than that. Witchcraft news crossed the Atlantic in both directions. Robert Calef, a merchant in Boston, Massachusetts, gathered and published evidence of the recent excesses at Salem. In the preface to his book, this is how he replied to a possible objection to its publication:

> But here it will be said, what need of Raking in the Coals that lay buried in Oblivion. We cannot recall those to Life again that have suffered ... Truly I take this to be just as the Devil would have it, so much to fear disobliging men, as not to endeavour to detect his Wiles, that so he may the sooner, and with the greater Advantages set the same on foot again ... *And if Reports do not (herein) deceive us, much the same has been acting this present Year in Scotland.*[46]

Calef dated his preface at Boston, 11 August 1697, which was just two months after the seven witches were executed in Paisley. A transatlantic voyage took about two months, so he seems to have been sent news about Christian Shaw's bewitchment even before anything was printed about it, and very likely before

45 James VI, *Daemonologie*, in his *Minor Prose*, 55 (book 3, chapter 6). This 'young lasse' has not been identified. James did not specify whether she was Scottish.

46 Robert Calef, *More Wonders of the Invisible World* (London: Nathaniel Hillar and Joseph Collyer, 1700), sig. A2 (preface). Emphasis added.

the witches' trial had concluded. Calef himself was totally unconvinced by the story of bewitchment, and expected his readers to agree. Perhaps the story that crossed the Atlantic was already a sceptical one. It might be added that Calef's broader point remains relevant for everyone today. We need to understand the injustices of the past in order to avoid, or to remedy, the injustices of the present.

So there is a final point to make about the fact that much of the material in this book comes late in the period of witch-hunting. These narratives and tracts may enable us to reconstruct the growing doubts that the prosecutors themselves faced. Witchcraft prosecutions relied on certainty: not only was witchcraft certainly the ultimate wickedness, but also the specific person who was being accused was certainly guilty. Many of the texts in this book proclaim both of these certainties, but they do so in the face of scepticism and doubt. There may be human values other than godliness; there may be less harsh ways of expressing godliness; and executing people who might actually have been innocent is not a godly deed.

EDITORIAL CONVENTIONS

The texts have been transcribed letter by letter, with the following provisos. The obsolete letters thorn and yogh have been transcribed as 'th' and 'y' respectively; ampersand has usually been transcribed as 'and' except in titles, in Latin passages, and in the word '&c'. The letters i/j and u/v, where scribal and typographical practice often depended on placement within the word, have normally been modernised. Printed 'vv' has been transcribed as 'w'. Letters in square brackets have occasionally been added to aid comprehension, e.g. 'of[f]', 'the[e]'. Capitalisation is given as in the original, except that personal names (including 'the Devil') and place names, and opening words in sentences, have always been capitalised. Punctuation is given as in the original, except that some full stops or commas have been added if this was desirable for clarity. Italics are given as in the original, except that Latin words have been italicised, with translations in footnotes, and a few long passages that were printed in italics (such as introductions to pamphlets) have been converted to roman. Square brackets in originals have been converted to round brackets; thus all square brackets below are editorial. Main titles of printed works have been standardised in format, with no attempt to reproduce the variety of font styles and sizes, capitals and italics, found on the original title pages. Abbreviations in manuscripts have been expanded silently. Scribal additions to manuscript texts (words inserted above the line or in the margin) are shown \thus/. Unimportant scribal self-corrections in manuscripts have been ignored, but important additions or deletions have been noted in footnotes. Where a manuscript is damaged or illegible, the nature and extent of the problem has been indicated in square brackets or in a footnote. Folio or page numbers of the original documents have been added in curly brackets after the first page, thus {*fo. 2r.*} {*p. 3*}. Further editorial matters relating to individual documents are discussed in the introductions to those documents below.

1. *TRIAL, CONFESSION, AND EXECUTION OF ISOBEL INCH, JOHN STEWART, MARGARET BARCLAY AND ISOBEL CRAWFORD, FOR WITCHCRAFT AT IRVINE, ANNO 1618*

INTRODUCTION

This is a pamphlet-length narrative about the investigation and trial of four witchcraft suspects in Irvine in 1618. The author was evidently an eyewitness of, or participant in, the investigation. His access to pre-trial confession documents suggests that he may have been one of the ministers or others involved in the interrogations. The pamphlet is similar to many English witchcraft pamphlets of this period. It also bears comparison with the best-known Scottish witchcraft pamphlet, *Newes from Scotland* (*c.*1591). It may well have been written for publication, though no contemporary published version is known.

The narrative initially concerns Margaret Barclay, the wife of Archibald Dean, burgess of Irvine. In 1617 she brought a slander case before the kirk session against John Dean, a skipper, her brother-in-law, who had called her a thief. The case was ended by a reconciliation. However, on John Dean's next voyage, late that year, his ship was wrecked at Padstow in Cornwall; he and five others, including the burgh's provost, were drowned. It turned out that the sinking had allegedly been foretold in Irvine by a wandering magical practitioner, John Stewart, known as 'the Juglour', who was arrested in April 1618 and interrogated. Stewart's detailed confession implicated Barclay, who had allegedly cursed the ship vengefully; she too was interrogated, and confessed under torture. Stewart's and Barclay's confessions drew in two more suspects, Isobel Inch – whom Stewart picked out of an identity parade – and, later, Isobel Crawford – whom Barclay named. Crawford eventually confessed under torture also. Further colourful evidence was provided by Inch's 8-year-old daughter, Margaret Taylor.

From these confessions an extraordinary tale gradually emerged, of Stewart's visits to fairyland, of visions, of demonic conspiracy, of Crawford's animal-like or fairy-like familiar, and of image magic, demonic sex and other secret rituals in a deserted house and at the seashore. Some of these rituals may really have been carried out, but at least some aspects were fantasised, and further study would be necessary to unravel the conflicting and sometimes impossible testimonies. Some testimony also related to more mundane family quarrels and curses. Barclay's reproach to her unsupportive husband, 'ye haif been over-long in comyng', was made at a dramatic moment. The prosecution was initiated by the burgh magistrates, but others soon became involved. Interrogators and prosecutors included David Dickson, minister of Irvine, several other ministers from the area, several burgh councillors and officials, a local nobleman and one or two local lairds. These local prosecutors obtained two successive commissions of justiciary from the privy council.

One point of interest in the pamphlet is the way in which it places the various confessions and other negotiations into a continuous narrative. It also candidly narrates circumstantial details of torture and of pricking for the Devil's mark – details that would normally have been omitted from an official trial record. Some of these details may have been exaggerated; Stewart's pricking upon the forehead with 'ane greit preyn' (pin) seems improbable. The pamphlet nevertheless relates several first-person conversations connected with the interrogation and torture. It also relates, though in less detail, the two trials and executions that ensued, those of Barclay and Crawford.

A theme that emerges clearly from the narrative is that the suspects' confessions did not all agree with each other or with the statements of Inch's daughter. Several instances of arguments about this are given. Moreover, Barclay and Crawford repeatedly alternated between confession and retraction. This led to some discussion, and reasons had to be given for accepting confessions that had been retracted. At one point the magistrates of Ayr sent their own witchcraft suspect, Janet Bous, to be investigated as a possible associate. In the end, Stewart committed suicide in prison, Inch died after falling from the church roof in an attempt to escape, and Barclay and Crawford were brought to trial, convicted and executed.

The present edition, unusually, is taken, not from an original manuscript, but from a printed version of about 1855. This is a rare pamphlet, almost entirely without editorial commentary, entitled *Trial, Confession, and Execution of Isobel Inch, John Stewart, Margaret Barclay & Isobel Crawford, for Witchcraft, at Irvine, anno 1618*. The title page adds 'From the original manuscript', and, at the foot, 'Herald Office: A. Guthrie, Printer, Ardrossan and Saltcoats.' It is unclear whether the title derives from the manuscript or whether it was added by the 1855 editor, but there seems no reason not to retain it for the present edition.

The date of 1855 – or, strictly, 'about 1855' – comes not from the pamphlet itself but from the bibliographical scholar John Ferguson in 1895.[1] He gave no reason for the dating, but there is no reason to doubt him, nor is the precise

1 John Ferguson, 'Bibliographical Notes on the Witchcraft Literature of Scotland', *Proceedings of the Edinburgh Bibliographical Society*, 3 (1895), 37–124, no. 120.

date crucial. The imprint 'Herald Office' links the pamphlet to the *Ardrossan and Saltcoats Herald* newspaper, which began publishing in 1853 from an office in Saltcoats, with Arthur Guthrie as the editor, publisher and printer.[2] The adjacent towns of Ardrossan and Saltcoats are near to Irvine, where the events narrated in the document took place.

Sir Walter Scott had previously discussed the document at length in his *Letters on Demonology and Witchcraft* (1830). He wrote that 'A copy of the record of the trial, which took place in Ayrshire, was sent to me by a friend who withheld his name, so that I can only thank him in this general acknowledgement.'[3] It seems, therefore, that Scott did not have the original manuscript. Scott's quotations from his document largely conform to the 1855 version, and occasionally clarify the latter's readings. The 1855 version did claim to be 'From the original manuscript', which may well be correct, as we shall see; unfortunately no archive of relevant papers from the *Ardrossan and Saltcoats Herald* in this period is known to exist.[4] As for Scott's copy, the provenance of the original manuscript is lost in the failure of Scott's correspondent to supply his name. It may perhaps emerge in future. Perhaps a contemporary printed edition may even be found; the text certainly reads as if it was intended for publication. In the meantime, analysis of the present text has much to teach us.

The 1855 edition seems to be a fairly good *literatim* transcript, but care has been required in establishing a coherent text from it. Numerous apparent misreadings have been corrected in the text below, with the 1855 readings being indicated in footnotes. Some readings have been retained even when doubtful, e.g. 'apperiance' where 'appeirance' would be more likely (p. 10), partly because of uncertainty about the original scribe's intentions; he seems to have been modifying his own Scots orthography in the direction of standard English, as we shall see. The repeated misreading of 'Insch' as 'Justh', while bizarre at first sight, in fact tends to confirm that the transcriber was looking at a contemporary manuscript; that is indeed what this word might look like to an inexpert transcriber.

As well as problems of transcription, the 1855 edition contains errors of typography. A few words are run together without spaces, or spaces have been added (e.g. 'deny it behir' has been printed for 'denyit be hir', p. 3; 'treatieand' for 'treatie and', p. 10); these errors are corrected silently. A few more such errors, where there is no reasonable doubt about the meaning, have also been corrected silently (e.g. 'Quhilh' has been corrected to 'Quhilk', p. 3; 'tallit' corrected to 'callit', p. 15). Punctuation has not generally been changed, but

2 *Ardrossan Herald* website, <http://www.ardrossanherald.com>.

3 Sir Walter Scott, *Letters on Demonology and Witchcraft* (London, 1884; orig. 1830), 255–64; quoted footnote at p. 255.

4 Email correspondence with North Ayrshire Heritage Centre has ascertained that neither they nor Ayrshire Archives hold such papers (May 2017).

a few obvious errors have been corrected silently (e.g. 'James, Stevenson,' p. 4). Some full stops need to be read as commas or semicolons, since the sense continues into the next sentence. The 1855 edition has one editorial interpolation, explaining the word 'sched' (p. 5), and there is an asterisk on p. 11 apparently to indicate a reference note explaining the word 'burrioes' (the note, however, does not appear). Some punctuation, particularly apostrophes, may have been added by the 1855 editor or typesetter.

The language is mainly middle Scots, but the process of transition to standard English has begun. There are gerunds in Scots '-and' ('professand himself', p. 4) but more in English '-ing' ('destroying and doun-putting', p. 3). On the other hand, there are past tenses in English '-ed' ('assythed', p. 4) but more in '-it' ('contractit', p. 3). There are many more instances of Scots 'quh-' than of English 'wh-' ('quhairupon', p. 3), but a hybrid 'Qwhat' (p. 8), like a hybrid past tense 'finishet' (p. 16), are signs of transition.

TEXT[5]

Trial, Confession, and Execution of Isobel Inch, John Stewart, Margaret Barclay and Isobel Crawford, for Witchcraft, at Irvine, anno 1618

{*p. 2 blank*} {*p. 3*} Heir is set doun at greit length the grund of the deadly malice contractit by Margaret Barclay, spous of Archibald Dein, burges of Irvine, against Johnne Dein, younger, skipper, burges of the said burgh, her ain guid brother, and Janet Lyll, his spous, quhairupon the devilish practices afterspecified, in destroying and doun-putting of the said Johnne Dein, skipper, Andro Tran,[6] provost of the said burgh, Abraham Howe and Johnne Barclay, merchants; Alex. Baillie and James Stevenson, mariners; and of the ship herself and hail[7] equipage of the same ensuit; togedder also, with the hail form, process, and deduction thereof, and evident presumption, whereupon the said Margaret Barclay and her associates under-written war apprehendit, with their hail particular confessions.

In the first, for the better clearing of the foresaid deidly malice contractit by the said Margaret against the said John Dein Younger, hir brother-in-law, and the said Janet Lyll, his spous, as is so to be understandit; like as it is of veritie that there was process and action of slander, intentit and depending, before the kirk session of the said burgh of Irvine, at the instance of the said

5 Source: *Trial, Confession, and Execution of Isobel Inch, John Stewart, Margaret Barclay & Isobel Crawford, for Witchcraft, at Irvine, anno 1618* (Herald Office: A. Guthrie, Printer, Ardrossan and Saltcoats, n.d. [*c*.1855]).

6 1855 'Traw'.

7 'hail': whole.

Margaret, against the said Johnne Dein, her broder-in-law, and his said spous, for the alledgit slandering of hir, of sum particular theft. Quhilk action and process dependit thrie or four severall dyettis before the session. Quhairupon before the final end and conclusion of the foresaid process, the said Johnne Dein, skipper, was urgit to go on his voyage towards France, so that the foresaid proces restit and saisit[8] for ane tyme, and until the said Johnne his return therefra.

And at the making sail of the said Johnne Dein upon his said voyage, the said Margaret Barclay, pursuer of the said slander, uttered thir words of imprecation following, God, let neither sea nor salt wattir bear the said Johnne Dein above, but that the partans[9] eat him in the bottom of the sea for the slandering of her guid name. Quhilk words of imprecation being dilatit[10] by the said Andro Tran, provost, as being an elder and member of the session, and ane of the owners of the forsaid ship; he then being at hame; and the said Johnne Dein, skipper on his said voyage; and the said Margaret citit before the session thairfor, and denyit be hir the said words of imprecation utterit by hir. In manner forsaid wer sufficientli verified and provin, and the said Margaret ordanit to be punishit thairfor, as the particular actis of session and haill proces led thairintill proposes.

After the return of the quhilk Johnne Dein from his said voyage, the forsaid proces and action[11] of slander of the forsaid theft was of new wacknit[12] *{p. 4}* and dependit then two or three dyettis before the session. So that for avoiding of further trouble, the saids parties were reconciled by the session. But[13] prejudice always of the punishing of the forsaid imprecation.

Quhilk reconciliation being so maid the said Margaret Barclay utterit in face of session, that although thay war reconciled for obedience of the session's ordinance, yet she haid not nor never would pardon nor remit the said Johnne Dein and his said spouse from the bottom of hir hairt. The said Johnne Dein, his next voyage making, and making saill towards France, the same being in the end of the month of November, sixteen hundred and seventeen years. The said Margaret Barclay, notwithstanding of the foresaid reconciliation, of new upon her bare knees utterit the former imprecation in this manner – God, let never sea nor salt water bear thame above that had injurit me, but that the partans eat thame in the bottom of the sea, and to

8 'saisit': ceased.
9 'partans': crabs.
10 'dilatit': reported, accused.
11 1855 'acton'.
12 'wacknit' (wakened): revived.
13 'But': without.

haive my hairt sufficientlie assythed[14] upon thame, I wold be content that my saull war saithan[15] in the cauldroun of hell.

After the departir of the quhilk ship towards hir said voyage, the said Johnne Dein, skipper thereof, the saides Umquhil[16] Andro Tran, provost, quho was dilaitor and upgiver of the foresaid first imprecation, and haill remanent merchandis and owners of the said ship, particularly after nominate being on their voyage, it is of verite that thair come ane vagabond called Johnne Stewart (as he himself declarit) professand himself to have skill in juglorie and palmestrie, within the dwelling hous of the said Umquhil Andro Tran, provost in the said burgh of Irvine, about the space of fourteen days after the making saill of the said ship, and after conference had be him with the servant of the said Umquhil Andro's hous, declairit that the guid wyfe of the hous was ane widow, and that hir bairns war fatherless, and that the guidman of the hous was deid upon the coist of France, or betwixt and thair, and reported the same in sundrie other partes[17] of the town. Quilck words being kepit close be the servants of the said Umquhil Andro's hous and sic otheris personnes to quhome he haid spoken the same. Laist thay sould haif grevit the said Umquhil Andro's wyfe and sic otheris quho had interest in the said ship.

At last the trouth and verite of the death of the said Andro, and of the said Johnne Dein, skipper, Abraham Howe, and Johnne Barclay, merchandis; Alexander Baillie, and James Stevenson, mariners, and of the haill equipag of the said ship being fund so to be after return of Robert Thomson and James Stevenson,[18] younger twa of the said ship's companie, quho war savit by the admirable providence of God, quha declarit that upon the fourth day of December, being the eight day after their making saill, their ship, skipper, haill merchantis, owners, and mariners perishit, and was cassin away at Padstow, upon the coast of England, and thay twa war only in lyf. After the quhilk report and declaration truely maid by the said twa boyes; incontinent[19] the words utterit be the said Johnne Stewart, vagabond, touching the declarations of the said Andro's death, being the space of ane month before the return of the said twa boyes, was then maid manifest and openlie declarit be the servant of the said Umquhil Andro's hous, and sic utharis to quhome he had declarit the same.

Quhairupon the said Johnne Stewart, vagabond, being upon great suspicion upon quhat[20] foreknowledge he had forespokin the said Umquhil Andro's

14 'assythed': compensated.

15 'saithan': seething.

16 'Umquhil': deceased, late.

17 1855 'parties'.

18 It seems that there were two James Stephensons. Quite possibly they were elder and younger, in which case the text here should read 'James Stevenson younger, twa'.

19 'incontinent': immediately.

20 1855 'quha'.

death, as also that he was hanter and frequenter of the said Margaret Barclay's companie, quho utterit the foresaids horrible imprecations. The said Johnne Stewart, vagabond, having cum privatlie under {*p. 5*} cloud of night upon the last day of Apryll, 1618 yeris last bypast, to the said burgh of Irvine, to the dwelling hous of the said Margaret Barclay. He upon the morn thairafter was upon certain information maid be the provost and bailies of the said burghe, tymouslie apprehendit and put be thame in sure captivity and prisonny [*sic*] conform[21] to the Actis of Parliament sett doun against vagabounds. And being examined be thame upon quhat fore knowledg he had fore spoken the said Umquhil Andro Tran's death. He at the first, notwithstanding of quhatsomever probation in the contrair constantli denyit the afore speaking of the Umquhil Andro's death and denyit him to haiv any kynd of skill of these maters but onlie in doing and using of sum practices usit be juglers. Quhill in end about the space of twentie four houris thairafter he being more strictly examined thairupon be Allan Dunlop, ane of the baillies of the said burghe, and upon quhat acquaintance and occasion he addrest himself under cloud and silence of nyght to the said Margaret Barclay's hous, and by quhat means he attaint to the pretendit knowledge of palmestrie, he not being ane scholler, but the forme of ane sturdie vagabond.

He then confest that he had declairit in the said Umquhil Andro Tran's house that he was deid upon the coast of France, or betwixt and thair, and that about the space of twa yeir syne the said Margaret Barclay cum to him in the town of Kilwinning, and gave him ane pynt of aill at the brigend, craivand ernestlie of him that he, as being ane skillet man quho plaid practices, wold help hir be quhat meane she might get geir, kyis milk,[22] love of man, and her hartis desire on sic personnes quho had done hir wrong; and that she might get the fruit baith of sey and land, etc.; and after drinking with her, she convoyed him ane myll of[f], and that thay sched[23] at the brig of Lugdor,[24] which is ane myll dystant from the burgh of Irvine, and that at their departing, the said Margaret gaiv him ane half merk piece. And as he declarit to the said baillie, he refusit to grant to hir desyr, and that his answer was to hir, he could not do these things, and had no skill thairof.

As also the said Johnne confest publicly to the said baillie and aldermen of the burghe, that the said Margaret Barclay notwithstanding of his former refusal maid to hir of hir petitioun forsaid, com to him within the said burghe, about the space of twa monthis befor the maiking saill of the said ship, and insisted ernistlie with him to get hir sum meane and to learne hir quhat way she sould be avengit of the grait scandal and wrong she had gottin ather be

21 1855 'confirm'd'.
22 'kyis milk': cows' milk. 1855 'geir thyis milk'. Scott 1830 reads 'gear, kye's milk'.
23 The 1855 editor adds '(separated, parted)' here, which is the meaning of 'sched'.
24 Probably a bridge over the Lugton Water, north of Irvine.

sey or land, becaus she had not gottin hir intent befor the session, but rather punishment. In so far as she was dilatit for hir imprecation be the provost and that every man had hornis (as it was) in hir syd. Quha as he himself refusit to help hir as having no skill, etc.

Lyk[25] as also he confest to the forsaid baillie that he com to the said burghe the tyme of the maiking saill of the said ship, and accidentilie (as he declairit) went up to the said Margaret Barclay's hous, within the quhilk he declares the said Margaret, uther twa wemen, and ane mayd was makand muill[26] pictures and portraittis of clay, representing the figuris of men, quhairof thair was ane maid with (as it war, a bony face and a brown baird) quhilk the magistrates of the said burgh incontinent apprehendit to be the figur of the said Andro Tran, provost, dilaiter[27] of the said imprecation, and that the said Margaret and her said associates mixt the saides figures of men maid of clay with reid things lyk reid plowmes and things lyk naills of haddockis, and that ane of the wemen, being {*p. 6*} ane aigit woman, with a sheir clippit ane lock of his quhit hair abune his lug,[28] and mixt the said pictures of clay thairwith; and that he saw thame mak ane meikill schip and ane litle boat of clay, and that at the making of the said work the Devill apperit among thame in the similitude and lyknes of ane black litle quhalp, lyk unto ane lady's bonny black messen,[29] as he termit it, and spack unto thame, saying, Be all my servants, and obey me, and renounce God, and I assure you ye and ilk ane of you sall have ritches and gear aneuch and your hartis desyr in all thingis both be sey and land, and that thay all answerit – It sall be so.

After the quhilkis, the said Johnne Stewart, vagabound, declarit that the said Margaret and hir said associatis tuik the remanent of his said hair and singit it at the fyr, and thairafter cuist the same to the said black little quhalp – quhilk being done the said Johnne declarit that the said Margaret Barclay and hir said associats went altogether up the gait and enterit ane great hous, quhar na man dwelt, the black little quhalp ever following upon them, and that thair entrie was in the said hous in the tym of the night, and had thair sundrie meittingis. And tuik the provost and baillies of the said burghe for the furder clearing of his said declaration to ane greit waist hous[30] in the Briggait of the said burghe, last possest be Robert Burns, affirming confidentlie that was the hous, and that after thair meittings and consultations had thairin, the said Margeret and hir said associatis went thairfra directly to the sey syd after aught houris at evin (the same being in the hinder end of November, the Devil in similitude of the said black quhalp following on thame, he himself

25 1855 'Lyll'.
26 'muill': earth, possibly earth from a graveyard.
27 1855 'dilaite'.
28 'abune his lug': above his ear.
29 'quhalp' (whelp): young dog; 'messen': lap-dog.
30 'waist hous': empty house.

being now hard by, and cuist in the sey the schip of clay, and little boat of clay, quhilk had in the end thairof as he declarit lang thingis lyk hornis) with the foresaid muill figures and pictures of men, together also with sum litle reid stones the cullour of orangeirs [*sic*], and that the sey, after incasting thairof, radgit, roarit, and swallit up, and becum reid like reid madder litt,[31] and tuick the magistrates of the said burghe to the said Margaret Barclay's hous, and declarit constantlie that the Devill was raisit in hir[32] back hous at the soll of the window.

After the quhilk confession the said Margaret Barclay was incontinent thairefter, apprehendit and put in captivitie, be the said Allan Dunlop, baillie, and being examinat be him first upoun the last hynous and horibill imprecation maid be hir on hir bair kneyis, in maner foirsaid, asking that God sould never let sey nor salt watter beir thame above quho had sclanderit and injurit hir, etc., and that she wold be content to haiv hir hairt assythit, that hir soull war seithand in the caldroun of hell, and thairefter upoun the haill remanent divlish practises above rehersit. The said Margaret at the first confidentlie with ane pairt[33] countenance denyit the forsaid horribll imprecation maid immediatelie befoir the last making saill of the said schip, and forsaid haill divlish practises – yet, notwithstanding quhairof, in respect of the said Robert Thomson, quho was ane of the boyes of the ship quha returnit saif by the admirable providence of God, his compearance before the said baillie, affirmand constantlie him, befoir his going in the said ship to be ear witness to hir said horribill imprecation and divlish wish of hir saull to be sethand in the caldroun of hell, &c. She confest that poynt, alledging the saim to haif been spoken be hir in the grat graiff and malice of hir hairt, &c.

As also, the said Margaret, being examined be the said baillie at the ernest desyr of her nychtburs, quhat was her meaning, quhen she lost {*p. 7*} her purs, to say, 'My purse is lost; thair is both silver and gold thairintill, but thairof I regard not, but thair is sumthing within the saim quhilk gif I want I will go mad.' She denyit she utterit these words (I will go mad), but confessit it was true hir purs was lost upon the ane day, and was on the morne thairefter laid tymously be four hours in the morning to her dur, out of quhilk she wantit nothing except onlie ane litle piece of cannell.[34]

And for furder tryall of the verite of the said Johne Stewartis former declaration, the said Allan Dunlop, baillie, convenit sundrie of the inhabitantis, wemen, useris of the said Margaretis hous, befoir the said Johne, in so far as he declarit he knew not the said wemen's names quho was with the said Margaret at the foirsaid work, but would know thame gif he saw thame. Quho, being

31 'reid madder litt': red dye from the madder plant.
32 1855 'his'.
33 'pairt': pert, bold.
34 'cannell': cinnamon.

convenit befoir him he repellit sindrie, and at last the said Johnne tuik ane of the said wemen be the hand quhais name was Isobell Insch[35] spous of Johnne Tailyeour, indweller in the said burgh, quho was born in Innerkip, and sayd to hir thou was thair fra the begynning to the ending. Quha constantlie denyit that ever she saw him befoir, or was ever in companie with him. Quhairupon the said baillie quhile[36] furder tryall and clearing of the forsaid divlish practises, causit commit hir to ward in the bell hous of the kirk, dystant from the said Margaret's warding place, quhilk was in the tolbuith. Till in end Margaret Tailyeour dochter to the said Isobell Inch, of the age of aught yeir old, being quyetlie[37] examinat be the said Allan Dunlop, baillie, in presence of the aldermen of the said burgh, gif she knew ony thing of the divlish practises above specifeit other as being, or as keeper of the said Margaret Barclay's bairns and rocker of the creddill. The said Margaret Tailyour, dochter to the said Isobell Insch[38] of the age forsaid, as being present with hir said mother at the forsaid divlish practices, and quho ressavit dailie intertenment in the said Margaret Barclay's hous, maid hir confession in manner underwritten:–

In the first, She declarit in presence of the said baillie and aldermen of the said burghe that the forsaid jugler was three tymes befoir in the said Margaret Barclay's, and that her mother drank with him thair, and that ane nyght at evin the said jugler got ane chopin of beir[39] fra the said Margaret, he being sittand upon ane cyst[40] in the hall, and that thairefter immediatlie the said Margaret tuik hir plaid about hir, and fillit thair plaitts full of wattir, and cuist the saim bak over hir heid, and said thir wordis. This is a pastime, and the said Margaret and the forsaid jugler went up the gait; she being present with thame led in the said Margaret's hand (John and Hew, quhilk twa bairns, being left be the said Margaret for keeping the hous till hir return),[41] and broght furth the said Isobell Insch,[42] hir mother, out of hir hous, and tuik hir up the gait with hir and left the said jugler and hir said mother in the briggait (being the way to the forsaid waist hous), commanding thame to stay thair quhile she returned to thame bak, and declarit that the said Margarett[43] to the tunheid, she being in hir hand, and brocht ane woman out of ane hous at the Tounheid with hir, and causit hir stay apairt quhile she and the said woman com to hir; and that after the said manner, and that the

35 1855 'Justh'.
36 'quhile': until.
37 1855 'guyetlie'.
38 1855 'Justh'.
39 'chopin of beir': tankard of beer.
40 'cyst': chest.
41 *Sic.* The meaning seems to be that Taylor herself accompanied Stewart and Barclay, with Barclay holding her hand, while Barclay's children John and Hugh (whom Taylor was employed to look after) were left in the house.
42 1855 'Justh'.
43 *Sic.* Perhaps 'went' has been omitted here.

foirsaid woman dwelt at the tuneheid. Their cuming to hir, thay thrie went all doun the gait directlie to the briggait quhair they met the said juggler and hir awin muther, quha was stayand upon thame,[44] and that the juggler askit at thair meitting at the said Margaret – Haiv ye dune and gottin that woman ye went for? and thay answered, yes, we haif gottin hir, and that immediatly thairafter the {*p. 8*} said jugler oppint the forsaid waist hous dur, within the quhilk he himself, the said Margaret Barclay, the said Isobell Insch[45] hir ain mother, the said woman quhilk dwelt at the Tunheid, ane mayd of the age of fourteine yer old, quhome she knew not quhais head was coverit with ane gairgill,[46] and she hirself enterit in, and went first up directlie to ane heigh loft within the said waist hous havin brocht with thame twa boitts of clay, quhilk the said bairn[47] declairs was maid of the remanent of the clay of ane bak of an chymney laitlie biggit[48] be the said Margaret befor; and that they satt all in pairrs together in this manner, viz., the said jugler and Margaret Barclay, the said Isobell Insch,[49] hir ain muther, and the woman of the tunheid, and the said mayd of the age of fourteen years, and she hirself togither, and that black doig cum among thame. But of the quhilk the bairn declaires thair com furth a blak man, and cuist liht to thame lyk glanses of fyr of hys mouth, and that his eyes schynit lyk candills, and demandit at them, "Qwhat now haiv ye done, and ar ye reddy?" and they answered, – We are doand; and that befoir thair depairting out of the said waist hous, the said Jugler had carnall deall with the said Margaret Barclay in the heich loft, thay all beholdand and luikand on, the black doig being present and standing besyd, and that immediately thairefter the said Jugler and the said Margaret Barclay, the sayd mayd of the age of fourtein yeirs, and hirself, went directlie along the brig to the sey (the said Isobell Inch, hir mother, and the said woman of the tunheid being lockit in the said waist hous till thair return). She being led in the said Margarit's hand, be reason of the mirknes of the nyht, the said blak doig following on; and thair the said Juglour and the said Margaret cuist in the sey the foresaid twa boittes of clay and sum reid stanes, and that of new the said Margaret cuist bak the plaitts full of wattir bak ovir hir heid, and that the sey ragit and barmit[50] up and becum like reid bluid – sayand thir wordis after incasting thairof. The turn is now dune, and that they all returnit a bak fra the sey directlie to the foirsaid waist hous, within the quhilk hir mother

44 'stayand upon thame': waiting for them.

45 1855 'Justh'.

46 The woman of the Townhead would later be identified as Isobel Crawford. The maid of fourteen years seems never to have been identified by name. The word 'gairgill' has not been found in dictionaries.

47 1855 'bairns'.

48 'biggit': built.

49 1855 'Justh'.

50 'barmit': frothed.

and the woman of the tunheid was lockit in, and that the said Joglour oppint the Lock of the waist hous dur, and let thame twa furth. Quhilk being done, the bairn declarit that thay went altogether directlie fra the said waist hous doun the gait to Margaret Barclay's hous, the said black dog and black man following them, and that they sched[51] befoir Margaret Barclay's[52] hous; at the quhilk plaice the bairn declares the Jugler tuik a lock of his hair and cuist it to the blak dog, quhairwith he departit with the said blak man from thame, and that thairafter Margaret Barclay and her associate, the bairn hir self being present, went up and drank in the said Margaret's bak chalmer, quhill neir hand midnight, she being rokand the bairn. And for forder confirmation of the veritie of her haill narration forsaid, the bairne being demanded at quhat inspraith[53] saw she in the forsaid waist hous, whose answer was, that thair was ane bed full of Lint in ane of the beddis of the chalmer in the said waist hous, and confidentlie avowit her haill former narration to be true, and confrontit her ain mother, who was warded in the bell house, sayand – Mother, ye did nothing but stayit in the loft until we returnit, and avowit the same to be true in Margaret Barclay's face, poynt be poynt, not alterand thairfra in any sort; and that the said Margaret Barclay prommeist to hir ane pair of new schone not to tell of their proceedings; as also, that hir awin mother commandit hir that she tauld not any bairne quhat she had sein. Lykas, also, the said bairne being brocht befoir the Juglour, he utterit thir wordis. {*p. 9*} That saim litle nackett[54] was thair; and in respect of the bairn's denomination of the Rid stane to be callit the maister's stane.

And for the moir perfyt tryall of the foirsaides devlish practises, and confronting of the said Juglour, the bairn, Isobell Inch hir mother, and Margaret Barclay, thay were all convenit befoir the Ministrie and bretheren of the presbitrie of Irvine. Lyk as thair the Juglour and the bairne confidentlie avowed thair haill former confessions as in face of the said Margaret and Isobell – quha with brassin countenances (being severallie confrontit) denyit confidentlie as of befoir thair haill divlish practises, and evrie particular, poynt, and circumstance thairof – the said Margaret alledging confidentlie not onlie the forsaid haill devlish practices to be altogether false and fenyeit,[55] but also the haill form and manner of hir first acquaintance with him, and craving of sic kynd of help of him, and the said Margaret being thairafter examinat be the said Ministrie, quhat was hir meaning to haive a pickill woll and piece of rowan tree and sundrie culours of threid in her purs, quilk was fund thairintill be the magistratis of the said burgh, the tym of hir captivitie. She answerit thairof, that hir kow gaiv not hir milk in the accustomed maner she wont to

51 'sched': parted.
52 1855 'Esatti's'.
53 'inspraith': household furnishings.
54 'nackett': youngster.
55 'fenyeit': feigned. 1855 'fenzai'.

do, and that in hir concept the fusionn and substance thairof was tane away in so far as she declarit hir milk was in the over scruiff – thairof starny lyk unto starnis of meltit buttir,[56] and that for remeid thairof and bringing agane of her kowis milk, she was informit the sewing in hir taill of the forsaid woll rowin trie and cullerit thried, the same wold restore hir to hir milk.

After the confronting of the quhilkes persons[57] in presence of the ministrie, the said Johne Stewartes being examined be the said ministrie upon his bygane lyf, and by quhat meane he profest himself to have skyll of thingis to cum, and to reid fortunes, as he callit it, the said John confest that about the space of twenty sax yeirs syn tharby, he being travelling on an Hallowein betwixt the toun of Monygoiff and Clary, in Galloway. He forgetherit with the King of Pharie and his company, and that the King of Pharie gave him a straik with ane quhyt rod on the brow, at the quhilk tyme the power of his tung and his ane ey was tane frae him, and that he wantit the said power and sicht be the space of three yeirs; and that the said was[58] restorit agane to him be the said King of Pharie and his companie on ane Hallow Evin at the town of Dubling in Ireland; and that everie Setterday at evin he was with them all that night sensyn, as also on everie Hallowevin, and declarit thay met everie Hallowday, sumtyme in Lanark Hill and sumtyme in Kilmaurs Hill, and was lernit be thame; and for tryall of the stroke gottin be him on the brow fra the King of Pharie (as he callit him). Being demandit quhat pairt of the brow he gat the forsaid straick, he publickly poyntit furth with his finger, tuching the same, saying – In this pairt he straick me. Quhilk pairt was immediately thairefter (his eyes being closit) prickit with ane greit preyn,[59] and the same left stickand thairuntill, quhairof he had no sence nor feeling, and declarit that he saw with the King of Pharie sundrie personnes quhois names[60] he rehersit particularlie; and that all sic personnes quho war tane away by suddane death went with the Pharie.

Lykas, upon the morn thairefter,[61] Isobell Inch, mother to the bairn, being ernestlie delt with be the said Allan Dunlop, baillie, and Adam Cunyngame, of Meckinsth,[62] for reveilling and oppening up of the truth quhairof thair was so mony probabilities, and that so meikill the rather that God had mervelously,

56 *Sic.* Perhaps the dash indicates an omitted or illegible word. 'Fusionn': goodness or nutritive quality; 'scruiff': scurf or hard crust; 'starny, starnis': starry or star-shaped, stars. The meaning may be that the milk had hardened into a crust with star-shaped patterns.

57 1855 'personn'.

58 1855 'wus'.

59 'preyn': pin.

60 1855 'name'.

61 1855 'theirefter, I,'.

62 *Sic.* This person appears to have been a cadet of the Cunninghams, lairds of Auchenharvie near Irvine. In 1614 there is mention of Adam Cunningham, son of the late Adam Cunningham of Auchenharvie: *Register of the Great Seal of Scotland*, vii, no. 986. He is designated in March 1617 as Adam Cunningham of 'Chapeltoun', then of 'Markinche': ibid., no. 1615.

by expectatioun[63] of all man, oppenit the mouth of hir awin {*p. 10*} bairn to be witness against hir quha constantlie unto the end abaid be hir haill former narratioun. After long treatie maid then with hir, and prayer maid be sum of the ministrie to hir, quho gaiv to thame ane dilatour[64] answer, promissing at nicht to reveill, so far as she knew, of these materis, and unto the quhilk tym she wold diclair nothing. At the quhilk tym appoyntit be hir, the said Allan Dunlop, baillie, Adam Cunynham, of Meckinsth,[65] and Jn. Blair, late baillie, went to hir, and after new ernest treatie and invocation of God's name, she began and utterit thir wordis – Wo be unto the[e] Margaret Barclay, quho has brocht me innocentlie to this poynt. Thou art ane evill woman. Thou is in the haill caus heirof, and God can never forgive thee for that quhilk thou has done; and that the maner how she was brocht on that purpois was, That upon ane nicht at evin, Margaret Barclay cum to hir to hir awin hous in Irvine, and desyrit hir to go with hir and help hir to bring ane caldroun[66] from the hous of Sibella Wallace, quho dwelt at the brigend of the toun, and she should not stay, and that upon plane simplicitie she having satisfiet Margaret's desyr, not knowing betwixt hir and God of any other purpois. The Juglour was standand in the briggait, quhilk was the hie way to the said Sibella Wallace's, and went and opinit the waist hous dur, last possesst be Robert Burns[67] and that he and the said Margaret enterit in thairat, and that the said Margaret urgit hir to enter in, quhilk she refusit to do, and that she enterit no forder in the said waist hous except onlie within the utter dur thresheld, and stuid at the bak of the portell dur, and that she saw nothing quhat Margaret and the Juglour did, and that they twa theirefter went directlie to the trig ward, (quhilk is the hie passag and direct way to the sey), and that Margaret said unto hir, We are going to Sibella Wallace's, at the brigend, and will not stay, and that thay causit hir stay at the forsaid waist hous dure unto thair return, and that it was half ane hour and moir befoir thay returnit. And being demandit at quhither gif or not thay went to the sey, she answerit, she could not tell, but thay stayit longer space then thay micht lauchfulie haif gane to the sey syd. And prommiest to the said Allan Dunlop, baillie, gif he would put her to libertie, that he sould not mak ane evill voyage, but haif ane guid success both be sey and land, and that upon the morn she wuld declair all uthir things she knew in that matir. And in token of her faithful prommeis, gaiv to the baillie her hand. Betwixt and the quhilk tyme she brak ward, and cum furth at the bak window of the bell-hous, and cum doun the sclaittes of the kirk, thair being yron boltis, lockis, and yron fettirs on hir, and was apprehendit

63 'by expectatioun': against the expectation.

64 'dilatour': delaying, dilatory. 1855 'dilatr,'.

65 *Sic*. See the previous note concerning Adam Cunningham.

66 This is not a witches' cauldron, but an ordinary item of cooking equipment.

67 1855 'Isobel Burns', but Robert Burns was mentioned earlier. This may have been an error by the original scribe.

immediatlie efter hir fall and breking of ward be the watches of the burghe, appoyntit that nicht for watching, and efter the said Allan Dunlop, baillie, his cumming to hir, and demand maid be him quhat was the occasion she brak ward, and be that mean intendit to falsifie hir awin promeis maid to him upon the nicht befoir tuching the reveilling of the truth. Hir answer was in this maner – Guid baillie, I can not tell, but in cais ye had been present with me within this hous, my hart was opinit and laid in braid band, I sould haif shawn you all thingis, but now both my hart and braist is closit. I can tell you nothing, and fra thenfurth ever to hir deathe, continuallie denyit the haill forsaid devlish practises, as also that her former haill assertion was fals and fenyeit,[68] and departit this present lyf within the space of fyve dayes thairefter without ony furder confession, and was poisonit[69] be all apperiance as the magistratis and haill inhabitantis of the said burghe apprehendit.

Be vertue of the quhilck commission,[70] his hieness four justices in that part,[71] {*p. 11*} creat[72] clarkis, serjands, demsteris,[73] and all utheris, membris of court, and causit summond ane[74] inquest of personnes, of[75] the four halfs round about, and leist suspect be passing upon the assys of the Juglour and the said Margaret Barclay, quho was then only in captivitie,[76] and upon that same day of the assys and justice court, my Lord and erle of Eglintoune (quho dwellis within the space of ane myle to the said burghe,) having cum to the said burghe at the ernest request of the said justice, for giving to them of his lordships countenance, concurrence, and assistance, in trying of the forsaid devilish practices, conform to the tenor of the forsaid commission.[77] The said Johne Stewart, for his bettir preferring to the day of the assys, was put in ane lockfast buith, quhair na maner of persoun might haif access to him quhil the doonsitting of the justice court, and for avoyding of putting violent handis on

68 1855 'fewyeit'.

69 1855 'pissonint'.

70 There seems to be a discontinuity here. This phrase assumes that this commission has been discussed before, but this is the first time that it appears in the present text. On 2 June 1618 the privy council granted a commission of justiciary to John Peebles, former provost of Irvine, Alan Dunlop and James White, burgesses of Irvine, and John Blair, former bailie of Irvine, for the trial of John Stewart and Margaret Barclay for witchcraft. The sunk ship was named as the *Gift of God*. It was noted that Stewart had confessed but that Barclay had so far refused to do so: *Register of the Privy Council of Scotland*, xi, 366–7.

71 'justices in that part': judges in that case.

72 'creat': appoint. 1855 'great'.

73 A sergeant was a court's security guard and messenger; a dempster was a minor ceremonial official who announced (but did not decide) the verdict.

74 1855 'and'.

75 1855 'or'.

76 'quho was then only in captivitie': who was the only person then remaining in captivity.

77 Alexander Montgomery, sixth earl of Eglinton, was a local magnate. He had converted from Catholicism through the influence of David Dickson, minister of Irvine: Edward M. Furgol, 'Montgomery, Alexander, Sixth Earl of Eglinton (1588–1661)', *ODNB*.

himself, was verie strictlie gairdit and flitherit[78] be the airms, as us[e] is, and upon that same day of the assys, about half ane hour befoir the doun sitting of the justice court, Mr David Dickson, minister at Irving, and Mr George Dunbar, minister of Air, having went to him to exhort him to call on his God for mercie for his bygane wicked and evil lyf, and that God wold of his infinite mercie, lowis him out of the handis of the Devil quhom he had servit thir mony years by gane He acquiescit to their prayer and godlie exhortation, and utterit thir wordis – I am so straitlie gardit that it lyis not in my hand to get my hand to tak off my bonnett, nor to gett bread to my mouth. And immediately after the departing of the two ministers from him, the Juglour being sent for at the desyr of my Lord of Eglintoune, to be confrontit with ane woman of the burghe of Air, callit Janet Bous, quha was apprehendit be the magistratis of the burghe of Air, for witchcraft, to the burghe of Irving purposlie for that effect.[79] He wes fund by the burrow officers, quho went about him stranglit and hangit be the cruik of the dur, with ane tait[80] of hemp (or a string maid of hemp, supposit to have been his garten, or string of his bonnett) not above the length of twa span long, his kneyis not being from the grund half ane span, and was brocht out of the hous, his lyf not being to[o] layt expellit; but notwithstanding of quhatsomever meines usit in the contrair for remeid of his lyf, he revievit not, but so endit his lyf miserablie by the help of the Devill his maister.

And becaus, thair was then onlie in lyf the said Margaret Barclay, and that the personnes summondit to pass upon her assys and upon the assys of the Jouglour, quho by the help of the Devill his maister, had put violent hands on himself, war all present within the said burghe; thairfoir, and for essewing[81] of the lyk, in the person of the said Margaret, our soverane Lords Justices in that part particularly abovenamit, constitut be commission, efter solemn deliberation and advys of the said nobill Lord, quhois concurrence and advys was cheifly requirit and tane in this mater, concludit with all possible diligence befoir the doun sitting of the Justice Court, to put the said Margaret in torture. In respect the Devill by God's permission had maid hir associatis, quho war the lichtes of the caus to be thair awin burrioes,[82] and usit the tortour underwritten, as being the most safe and gentill (as the said

78 *Sic.* The meaning is evidently 'fettered'.

79 1855 'effer'. Scott 1830 reads 'affair', which is also possible. The participation of the burgh of Ayr is noteworthy; it may be connected with the involvement, noted in the text, of George Dunbar, minister of Ayr. The burgh accounts of Ayr record expenses in connection with several other witches or suspected witches for 1617–18, but Bous's name is not mentioned, nor is there any other record of a prosecution of her: *Ayr Burgh Accounts, 1534–1624*, ed. George S. Pryde (Edinburgh: SHS, 1937), 267–8.

80 'tait': tuft or string.

81 'essewing' (eschewing): avoiding.

82 'burrioes': butchers or slaughterers. The 1855 editor adds an asterisk at this point, presumably intending to add a note explaining the word.

noble lord asswrit the said justices, be putting of hir twa bair leggis in ane pair of stockis, and thairafter be ourlying[83] of certane yron gaddis[84] severally ane be ane, and thair eiking and augmenting the weht be laying on mae[85] gaddis and in easing of hir be aftaking of the gaddis of yron, ane or mae, as occasion offerit, quhilk yron gaddis war but litle schort gaddis, and brak not the schynne of hir leggis") [*sic*]

After using of the quhilk kind of gentill tortour, the said Margaret began {*p. 12*} according to the incress of the payne to cry, and for God's caus to tak of[f] hir schinnis[86] the forsaid yrons, and she sould declair trulie the hail mater. Quhilk being removit, she began at hir former denyall, and being of new assayit in tortour as of befoir, she then utterit thir wordis – Tak af, tak af, and befoir God I will schaw[87] you the haill forme.

And the saides yrones being of new upon hir faithful prommies removit, she than desyrit my Lord of Eglintoun, the said four justices, and the saids Mr David Dickson, minister of the burghe, Maister George Dunbar, minister of Air, and Mr Mitchall Wallace, minister of Kilmarnock, and Mr Jn. Cunnynghame, minister of Dalry, and Hew Kennedy, provost of Air, to cum be thame selfis, and to remove all utheris, and she sould declair truelie, as she sould answer to God, the haill mater. Quhois desyr in that being fulfillit, she maid hir confession in this maner, but[88] ony kind of demand freilie without interogator,[89] (God's name by ernest prayer being called upon for opining of hir lipis, and easing[90] of hir hairt that she by rendering of the truth miht glorifie and magnifie his holie name, and disappoynt the enemy of hir salvation.)

Margaret Barclay's confession – In the first, She confest being tuichit mervellouslie in hart; that the first tym she maid her acquaintance with Johnne Stewart, Juglour, was by the ernest persuasion of Isobell Inch, from quhom thair was ane pair of plaiddes stollin, and that she was directit be the said Isobell, to try at him quho had tane the same; and that efter inquisition maid be hir at him tuching the away taking and steilling of the saidis plaides, that the said John Stewart his answer was, that at that tym he could not tell, and tuik it to advizment, quhill first he spak with the Pharie with quhom he declairit he met ilk Seterday at evin, and that according to promeis, efter the Seterday at evin in the oulk[91] thairefter. He cum to hir to hir awin hous, and assurit hir that the plaids war away to Irland in a bote; and also confest that

83 'ourlying': over-laying. 1855 'onlrying'.
84 'yron gaddis': iron bars.
85 'mae': more.
86 1855 'schnnis'.
87 1855 'wall scha'.
88 'but': without.
89 'interogator' (interrogatory): formal question.
90 Scott 1830 reads 'easing'. 1855 'causing'.
91 'oulk': week.

gif he had not tauld her that answer and respons, that the said Isobell Inch and she was both resolvit to ane man, callit Cunyng, quhom she supponit[92] had ane buik that could rais the Devill.

The said Margaret confest also, but ony interogator in grait humilitie of hart, that the said Juglour, efter his return with his answer concerning the saids plaids, prommeist to hir gif she wold use his ways, that she sould get geir aneuch, and that she demandit quhat ways ar these of yours, and that he answerit, It is to go with the Pharie as he did.

As also, she confest that efter ernest treaty maid with the Juglour be hir by quhat means she miht get hir hart assythit, ather by sey or land, aganes these quho had injurit hir in sic sort as she particularlie maid him acquent with. That he upone ane new proppit[93] and affixt be him, brocht in his bag upon his back twa schipis of clay to hir hous, the said umquil Isobell Inch and the bairn hir dochter being present, and that her suitt was, to caus twa of the schipes companie die.

As also the said Margaret declarit that she demandit – Can ye caus the twa die, but ony harm to the rest; and that he answerit, Yes; and being inquyrit at be hir quhat way could he do that, she declares he answerit, I sall caus these twa[94] leipt over buird in the sey, and drown thame selffis.

And the said Margaret being ernestlie and straitlie examinat tuching the number of hir associatis, in so far as the bairn, quho was then brocht befoir hirself, the Juglour, Isobell Insh, and the bairn [*sic*]; yet, in respect of the bairne's confident assertion in hir face, uttering thir wordis, Margaret, ye ken ye brocht ane woman out of the Tounheid, and causit me stay at the {*p. 13*} smyddie bar quhill ye returnit and brocht hir with you, and that woman satt with my mother in the waist hous, and stayit in the loft of the waist house quhill we com from the sey syd.

Efter the quhilk assertion maid mervellouslie be the bairn, the said Margaret declarit, Thair was ane woman with us quha dwellis at the Toun heid, quho had ane dochter with me, and was my owin servant be the space of twa yeires, and quha hes ane sone callit Johne Leith, quho is Johne Symsone, the smiths prenteis, quhois name was Isobell Crawfurd, quhoim she gat in ane hous above the dwelling hous of James Thomsonne at the Toun heid; and that that woman brocht with hir the tym that I fetchit hir ane thing under hir plaid, quhilk was visioun facit[95] lyk ane aip or ane schitt, quhilk was black

92 'supponit': supposed, believed. 1855 'suppoint'.

93 *Sic*. Perhaps this should read 'upone ane new day proponit' (on a new day, proposed).

94 1855 'wa'.

95 The online Dictionaries of the Scots Language, s.v. visioun, quotes this phrase to illustrate the meaning 'A person seen as a dream figure or apparition; an incorporeal or ghostly being'. However, this whole passage about the 'thing' under Crawford's plaid is slightly obscure; perhaps the original scribe had difficulty in rendering Barclay's meaning, or perhaps the 1855 transcriber has gone astray in a way that is no longer recoverable, and the word is

dyn cullourit; and that the said Isobell held it under hir plaides; and that at thair meitting that thay luikit all under hir plaides to it; and that the[96] said Isobell callit the same to hir ane Pharisie as she callit it, and that the said Isobell Crawford was better skillit then the Juglour was, and reprovit[97] him quhen he brocht the schipis of clay, that he maid not thame fassionit lyk schips; and that the Juglour answerit to hir, The schips ar well aneuch[98] maid, and that at thair meitting and concluding of the foirsaid materis, the said Margaret declarit sche gat onlie but ane vote in the caus, and that efter the voiting and finall conclusion, she declaires they went all directlie to the sey; and that the Juglour cuist in the sey the saids twa boittes of clay and one litle rid stane out of his purs the quantite of ane plowm,[99] quhilk was callit and termit to him to be the maister ston.

And the said Margaret being demandit at and ernestlie delt with, to declair nathing but the trouth, and that quhilk she wold byd be.[100] She answerit with teares shed in gret abundance saying, Gif that woman war heir she cannot nor will not deny; and she wald tell you all mair perfytlie then I can: and for my awin pairt althocht I denyit constantlie, and ever sayd, as ye knaw in my denyall; quhen[101] I am away, God will cleir thir thingis, and my pairt will be kent, and it is not now sa; I will not lie now nor heip synn upon syn, but I was aschamit of thir thingis, I being but ane young lass, and was not of intention to die obstinate, and declairit befoir God thar was not ony mayd with thame except the little bairn,[102] and prayit ernestlie the ministrie to pray to God to pardonn hir, hir great and hynous offence.

Isobell Crawfurd's apprehending. – And the said Isobell Scheirar, alias Crawfurd, efter the foisaid declaration maid by the said Margarit, being incontinent sent for, and brocht in, out of the Walrix, quhair she was werdand [*sic*] lint, quhilk is distant half ane myle from the said burghe. Immediately at her up cumming the tolbuith stair, the said Margaret hearing the noyse and clamor of the people, she demandit at the Ministrie, May she do me any evill; and being in great feir, trembling, and qualking, she sayd to the Minister of the said burghe of Irvine, Minister of Air, and remanent Ministrie quho was confortand hir – For God's caus suffer not hir to cum neir hand me, and being put upon that grund, that the said Isobell had not power to do hir ony harme. She then prayit to God to saif hir from that woman; and the said

---

not 'visioun' at all. The phrase 'lyk ane aip or ane schitt' would be more likely to indicate ugliness than ghostliness.

96 1855 'she'.

97 1855 'reprobit'.

98 1855 'aneuth'.

99 'quantite of ane plowm': size of a plum.

100 'byd be': abide by.

101 1855 'quehen'.

102 This evidently refers to the earlier mention of a maid of fourteen years; her presence is now being denied.

Isobell being then brocht befoir her, demanding, Quhat now Margaret was I with you; God forgive you, and tak it not on your soull. Quha answerit in this manner: Isobell, how can you deny ye wur thair. I got you in the hous above James Thomsonne's, in the Tounheid, and ye brocht with you under your plaides, be the bak of the smyddie bar, the thing that ye callit to me ane pharisie, quhilk was blak dyn cullourit, lyk unto ane {*p. 14*} aip or ane schitt, and reprovit the Juglour that he maid not the schips of clay, fassionet lyk schipis, quha then replyit to the said Margaret as of befoir with exclaimationes, Margaret, God forgive you.

Efter the quhilk confession maid be the said Margaret, and hir willingness, as she hirself declarit, to suffer thairfor, the Justice Court quhilk was of befoir due tymin lauchfullie fensit,[103] satt doun, and the assys sworn, and admitted of the said Margarettis awin consent, and sche remanand constant uponn hir former haill confession in greit humilitie. Quhill[104] the cummyng[105] of Archibald Dein, hir husband, with William Flemmyng, his procurator, haifing demandit at hir quidder gif or not he sould compeir for hir. She answerit as ye pleas, for all that I haif confest was in tortour, and befoir God all that I haif spoken is fals and untrue. But ye haif been over-long in comyng.

Yet, notwithstanding of hir new denyall, in respect it was earnestlie knowin to the assessor[106] that hir confession was maid ingeneously,[107] being releivit out of all tortour with tearis, greit humilitie, and submissioun of mynd,[108] and that she proceedit sua ordurlie in hir confessioun in mony poyntis; but interogatur[109] and in respect of the greit presumptionnes and probabilities in the caus, she being removit, and ane Chancellour chosin as us[e] is; thay all in ane vote, but variance,[110] Fyllit hir[111] of the haill poynts[112] of the dittay;[113] and found hir worthie of death, conform to the Laws of the Realm.

Efter the quhilk conviction and furthgiving of dome[114] againes her, she, in presence of the houll Assys, utterit thir words – Now ye haif fyllit me; befoir God I am innocent, and all that I haif spokin is fals.

[103] 'lauchfullie fensit': formally constituted (as a court).
[104] 'Quhill': until.
[105] 1855 'Cumming'.
[106] 'assessor': judge.
[107] 'ingeneously': ingenuously, truthfully.
[108] This passage helps to clarify that, in many trial records when a confession is said to be given 'without torture', this can mean that torture *was* used to extract the confession but that the suspect then repeated or confirmed the confession afterwards.
[109] 'but interogatur': without questioning. This phrase indirectly acknowledges that many confessions were shaped by coercive leading questions.
[110] 'but': without. 1855 'vote, variance'.
[111] 'Fyllit hir': found her guilty.
[112] 1855 'poynt'.
[113] 'dittay': indictment, list of accusations.
[114] 'dome' (doom): judicial sentence.

In consideration quhairof, the Ministrie foirsaid, finding her to be turnit, and that pairtlie for schame of hir husband and neir friend quhom[115] she beheld, and that the Devill had gottin entrie of new, they removit from hir, hir husband and friends, and ernestlie delt with hir of new, in greit sinceritie, because the hour of execution approchit, quha then as of befoir ratified her haill former confessioun to be trew in everie poynt, and utterit thir wordis to the[116] assys – I tak it betwixt me and God and be the death I am going to, all that I haif spockin is trew, and pray for me all; and desyrit that Barbara Montgomerie, relict of Umquhill Andro Tran, provost, Janet Lyll,[117] relict of Umquhill John Dein, skipper, and haill remanent weidowes, being in the haill sevin in number, sould be send for.[118] Quha being sent for, she satt doun on hir bair kneyis desyrand[119] thame, for God's cause, and as they wold God sould forgiv thame, to pardon hir fra thair hairtes for the greit wrong she had done to thame. Quhilk sevin weidowes, haifing all frielie pardonnit hir desyrand[120] God, to pardon hir, sche thairefter, efter depairting of the said weidowes, desyret to speik with hir husband, and no sooner beheld him but than forbad him to tak ony thocht of hir. In so far as notwithstanding quhatever sche had spokin, all wer fals betuixt hir and God; and sua remannit continuallie obstinat quhill the verie last and uttermost moment, at the quhilk tym sche desyrit Mr David Dicksonn, minister, to publiclie intimat that all that sche had confest of befoir was trew, and that malice was the grund of all, and desyrit the magistratis to do no hairm[121] to Isobell Crawfurd, quho[122] was in the Tollbuith, and sua utterit thir wordis – God's blessing and myne be among you all, and pray for me; and hir braith chokit be the executioner, hir handis being up to the heavins, uttering thir wordis – Lord ressave my saull in his mercie. {*p. 15*}

Eftir the death and execution of the quhilk Margaret Barclay, the provoist and baillies of the said burghe, upoun certane[123] greit evidencis, presumptiones, and probabilities notour to thame, both tuiching the said Isobell Scheirer, alias Crawfurd, hir former liff, greit suspicion and brute[124] of the countrie, the bairnes' taking of the said Magistrate to her house at the Tounheid as being the house out of the quhilk Margaret Barclay brocht out the woman

[115] 1855 'qhom'.
[116] 1855 'the to'.
[117] 1855 'Kyll'.
[118] The mention of seven widows may be an error. The document has twice listed six names of drowned men, the first occasion being its opening sentence: John Dean, skipper, Andrew Tran, provost, Abraham Howe and John Barclay, merchants, and Alexander Baillie and James Stevenson, mariners.
[119] 1855 'beforehand'.
[120] 1855 'beforeand'.
[121] 1855 'harim'.
[122] 1855 'quo'.
[123] 1855 'cerane'.
[124] 'brute': rumour. 1855 'brate'.

to the perfytting of the former devlish practis. The said Margaret, hir awin dilating of hir in maner foirsaid, sche then being tuichit in the greittist sence of hir hynous offence, and feir tane be the said Margaret of hir, the tym of hir demanding may she do me ony skayth.[125] Hir constant affirmatioun thairof in hir face, and how sche careit the thing quhilk she termit to be callit the Pharisie; obtenit new commission of the Lords of his majesteis most honourable Privie Council, for taking tryall, and gif neid were to tortour hir.[126] And upon the day of the assys, Maister David Dickson, minister of the said burghe, enterit with hir, and maid ernest prayeris to God for oppnyng hir obdurit and closit[127] hairt, and that God wold caus hir out of her awin mouth reveill the secret of that matter, quhairof by all evident appeirances sche was culpable. Eftir ending of the quhilk prayer, the said Isobell was put in tortour in the same maner, with yron gaddies on hir bair leggis, as was done with Margaret Barclay, quha admirablie,[128] without ony kind of payne, dyn, or exclamation, sufferit above threttie stanes of yron to be laid on hir leggis,[129] never schrinking thairat in ony sort, but remaining as gif it was studieing;[130] quhill in end the said yrons war hallielie removit and tane af hir, and ane uther pairt of hir schynnis being of new assayit with the foirsaid gaddis of yron, thair not than being thrie stane of yron led on, gaif horrible loud cryis, crying in this maner – Tak af, tak af, and I sall tell all. And all being removit – Johne[131] Peibles of Knogerhill, lait provost; Allan Dunlop, and James Quhyt, present baillies; and Johne Blair, late baillie, his friends, justices, Mr David Dickson, minister, and sundrie uthairs of the burghe being present, – maid hir confession in maner[132] underwritten:–

Isobell Crawfurd's Confessionn. – In the first sche confest that Margaret Barclay come to hir ane night at evin, betwixt sevin and aught hour at evin, and desyrit hir to go with hir, and that Margaret sould pleis hir, and that Margaret had the twa schips of clay with hir, and sayd – We all are reddie, and only wayting on you; and that thay went doun the gate[133] directlie, and thair thay forgetherit with Isobell Inch and the Juglour, the Devill being

125 'skayth': harm.

126 On 2 July, the council granted a further commission of justiciary to the magistrates of Irvine, plus John Peebles and John Blair, for the trial of Isobel Shearer alias Crawford, for assisting the late John Stewart and Margaret Barclay in witchcraft: *Register of the Privy Council of Scotland*, xi, 401.

127 1855 'closi'.

128 'admirablie': astonishingly.

129 30 stones' weight was about 300 kilos. My osteoarchaeologist colleague Kath McSweeney has confirmed to me that this weight would have been plausible. It would have been very painful and would have caused a number of fractures.

130 *Sic.* Scott 1830 reads 'remaining, as it were, steady'. The most likely reading is 'remaining as gif it war studieing', meaning 'remaining as if she was considering'.

131 1855 'Johhne'.

132 1855 'mater'.

133 'gate': street.

among thame, quho assurit thame that work could not be done without ane virgine;[134] and that thay enterit all in the said waist hous in the briggait, the bairn being present with thame; and that thair thay satt and concludit, and fassonit[135] schips of clay bettir, and that the Devill, in similitude of ane black man, demandit – What now haif ye done, and are ye reddy? and that thay answerit – We are doand; and that he sayd – Be all my servands and ye sall want nothing; and that thay all answerit – We sall be so; as also that the Devill cuist light to thame out of his mouth, the hous being mirk.

And sic lyk confest that efter thair furthcoming out of the said hous, that sche accompaniet thame to Sibella Wallace's at the brigend, whilk is the direct way to the sey, and that sche went no forder.

And being examinat tuiching that poynt of Margaret Barclay's accusation, in bringing with hir that thing callit the pharie or pharisie, as she termit it, under hir plaid, she confest that the Devill had given hir that to keip sax weeks befoir the ending and perfyting of that work thay had in hand; and that sche keipit the same in hir bed, and that it spak to hir, but {*p. 16*} ressavit nather meit nor drink; and that quhen their work was finishet it then went and vanishit away, and saw no sensyn, and declarit that the twa personnes quhomat Margaret Barclay had spaciall malice and evill will at was Andro Tran, proveist, and Johnne Deyn, skipper. But simpliciter denyit that there was ony mae at the actioun except the Juglour, Margaret Barclay, Isobell Inch, the bairn, Isobell Inch's dochter, and hirself, and that she hirself went not to the sey, and did no evill.

And forder, she being earnestlie insistit with tuiching the commouning and consultation with the Devill; she declarit that Margaret's suit[136] was that the Devill wold execut that practies onlie aganes Andro Tran and John Dein, and that she demandit at him quhidder he could caus this twa leip over buird in the sey or not without the rest, and that he answerit, he could hardlie do that, and that she replyit, it was the wars of that.[137]

And in respect of hir greit brute[138] and suspicioun in the countrie sche was the moir ernestlie delt with, tuiching the maner and forme of hir first acquentance with the Devill, and what space it was sensyn.[139] Quha declarit that ane night at evin, about fyv yeir syn, he com to hir at Patonnes Thorn, at the tounheid of Irvin, in similitude of ane blak colt or fole, and thairefter com to hir awin dur in similitud of ane blak man, and prommeist gif sche wold be his servand, sche sould haiv geir aneuch,[140] and sould not want. Quhairunto sche was ever

134 Again this may well allude to the maid of fourteen years who was mentioned earlier.
135 1855 'fasonint'.
136 'suit': request. 1855 'suik'.
137 'it was the wars of that': so much the worse for that.
138 1855 'brite'.
139 'what space it was sensyn': how long it had been since.
140 'geir aneuch': enough goods.

reddy to accord. Since the quhilk tym sche declarit sche was ever scharp,[141] and has not as sche wont to haiv, and being ernestlie delt with quhat pairt he markit hir, sche denyit ever she was markit. And in the meyntime of all thir questions and answers, she started as gif she had bene prikit, and luikit about hir as gif sche had amaised,[142] and being put upon that resolution, without production of his mark, that thair was no salvation for hir, sche then declarit the Devill tuik hir but by the sleive and tuichit not hir flesh. Yit being moir straitlie delt with, sche then publicklie schewd the Devill's mark, quhilk was lyk ane braid dyn spott, in the inner syd of hir left thie, about ane handbraid under hir lisk,[143] quhilk being visiblie sein and knawin. Hir eyes was coverit, and ane greit lang preyne put thairintill half ane inch, she was altogidder fund to be insensible, and in takin[144] thairof; the preyn was left stickand thairintill a long space, and causit hir tak it out with hir awin hand.

Eftir the quhilk haill confession and assaying of the foirsaid Mark, and thanks giving to God for the manifestatioun of the trouth, the Justice Court being gone to and ane assyss sworn, sche in presence of the assyss, poynt be poynt, confest all, and desyrit the Magistratis to pray for hir and be guid to hir sone, and to caus gie him that quhilk was addebtit to hir in the countrie. Quhilk being done upon hir awin voluntar confessioun to the assyss, sche was convict and dome pronouncit.

Efter the pronouncing of dome sche immediately within half ane quarter of an hour thairefter past fra simpliciter hir haill former confessiounnes, and sua endit this lyf with ane absolute denyall of all, and without ony kynd of repentance dew to ane ordiner synner, ever making interruptioun to the minister in his prayer, and absolutlie refuisand to pardon the executioner.

141 'was ever scharpe': always suffered hardship.
142 *Sic*. Probably read 'had been amaised'.
143 'lisk': groin.
144 'takin': token. 1855 'taking'.

2. SIR JAMES TURNER, 'OF MAGICKE' AND 'OF THE JEWES CABALE', *c*.1670

INTRODUCTION

This text is a linked pair of demonological essays by the royalist soldier Sir James Turner (*c*.1615–*c*.1689).[1] Turner is best known today for his military career and his 'Memoirs' describing this.[2] He was a graduate of the University of Glasgow; his father was a minister and hoped that his son would follow him in the ministry, but Sir James instead became a military officer. No precise date can be given for his essays, which were never published, but they are likely to have been written in the period between 1668 and 1681, when he was in retirement from military service and is known to have written several other works. The work for which he was best known in his lifetime, *Pallas Armata*, published in 1683, was stated on the title page to have been written in 1670 and 1671.[3]

Turner's essays cover a variety of topics, most of which relate to public, political life more closely than his essays on magic. In the manuscript, he listed the titles of his collected essays as being of 'Dueties of soveraigns and subjects', 'The supreme pouer in all republicks', 'Monarchie', 'Aristocracie', 'Democracie', 'Orators, and preachors', 'Magick', 'The Jews Cabale', 'Friendship', 'Externall evills, and misfortunes', 'Imprisonment', 'Anger', 'Revenge', 'Duells' and 'Crueltie' (fo. 34v.). His work has some similarities to academic dissertations, but such dissertations would normally cover a narrower field. He belongs rather to the genre of essayists following Michel de Montaigne and Sir Francis Bacon. Within this genre, Turner is closer to the public-minded Bacon than the introspective Montaigne.[4]

The essay 'Of Magicke' must postdate 1658, as it cites a work by Sir Kenelm Digby published in that year. It may also predate 1677, as we shall see later

1 For his career see David Stevenson, 'Turner, Sir James (b. *c*.1615, d. in or after 1689)', *ODNB*.

2 Sir James Turner, *Memoirs of his Own Life and Times, 1632–1670*, ed. Thomas Thomson (Edinburgh: Bannatyne Club, 1829).

3 Sir James Turner, *Pallas Armata: Military Essayes of the Ancient Grecian, Roman, and Modern Art of War* (London: Richard Chiswell, 1683).

4 See for instance G. Douglas Atkins, *Reading Essays: An Invitation* (Athens, Georgia, 2008).

in this introduction. The shorter essay 'Of the Jewes Cabale', which follows 'Of Magic', is to some extent a continuation of the previous essay. It cites its predecessor and was evidently written at the same time. Both essays were underpinned by a common set of assumptions about the powers of angels and demons, the latter of which were called 'Divells'. Turner's interest in plural demons as well as a singular Devil is noteworthy. His mention of 'our Europæan Witches' indicates the breadth of context within which he thought.

In his magical essays, Turner partly employed traditional biblical arguments, and partly drew on newer scientific ideas. Among the latter was the idea that ignorant people might regard the unusual achievements of learned people as being witchcraft. Sir Thomas Urquhart criticised pedantic and ignorant scholars along these lines in 1652: 'By which meanes, mathematicall thaumaturgies, opticall magick, secrets of nature and other philosophicall mysteries, being esteemed to be rancke witchcraft, they ruine the best part of learning and make their own unskilfullnes supreame judge'.[5] Turner's own scientific interests reflected his military background, citing gunpowder as an example of an invention requiring 'great skill in naturall Magicke'. The interest he expressed in Sir Kenelm Digby was also military; Digby published experiments claiming to prove the scientific basis of the 'weapon-salve' whereby a wound was cured at a distance by applying a 'sympathetic powder' to the bloodstained weapon.

Turner's disdain for popular ignorance extended to aspects of traditional witch-belief. In his 'Memoirs' he wrote of a storm that his army had encountered in Ireland in 1642:

> Our sojors, and some of our officers too, (who suppose that no thing that is more then ordinarie can be the product of nature,) attributed this hurrikan to the devilish skill of some Irish witches; and if that was true, then I am sure their master [i.e. the Devil] gave us good proofe that he was reallie prince of the aire.[6]

Turner clearly felt himself to be above the credulous idea that witches might bring storms. However, his essays show that he was far from dismissing the Devil's power altogether.

In his text, Turner's main non-biblical citations are to Cornelius Agrippa, Jean Bodin and King James VI. He may have read more widely in demonology, but probably not much more widely. His main source is Agrippa, and it is worth pausing to discuss why this is so and what Turner found so fascinating

5 Sir Thomas Urquhart of Cromarty, *The Jewel*, eds. R. D. S. Jack and R. J. Lyall (Edinburgh, 1983), 249.

6 Turner, *Memoirs*, 22.

about him.[7] Heinrich Cornelius Agrippa von Nettesheim (1486–1535) was a celebrated German magical scholar who published numerous works but was particularly known for two: *De Incertitudine et Vanitate Scientarum et Artium* ('The Uncertainty and Vanity of the Sciences and Arts'), first printed in 1530, and *De Occulta Philosophia* ('On Occult Philosophy'), first printed in 1531–3 but mostly written and circulated some years earlier. Agrippa was controversial but much discussed, with his works providing a learned, compendious and accessible storehouse of magical information. They were frequently reprinted throughout the sixteenth and seventeenth centuries.

Turner relies mainly and perhaps solely on Agrippa's *De Vanitate*. First published in Latin, *De Vanitate* was also translated into English and other languages, and often reprinted.[8] Turner seems to have used a Latin version and perhaps an English one too; he mentions that Agrippa 'fell in a relapse' after his 'recantation', which could have come from the preface to the English version, but he professes to be translating Agrippa from Latin, and quotes a verse in Latin along with what seems to be his own translation of it. Turner treats *De Vanitate* as a 'recantation' of what he takes to be Agrippa's promotion of magic in his other book, though today it is regarded more as a paradoxical statement of Pyrrhonian scepticism (by which *nothing* could be known for certain) and of the primacy of faith over human reason.[9] Although *De Vanitate* has fewer details on magic than *De Occulta Philosophia*, it has enough for Turner's purpose. Its sceptical tone is also easy for Turner to adapt.

However, Turner does not follow Agrippa unthinkingly. In particular, Turner draws a firm conventional distinction between legitimate 'natural magic', which he regards as compatible with contemporary scientific understanding, and illegitimate 'ceremonial magic', which involves relationships with spirits. Turner regards these spirits as demons. Yet Agrippa downplays this whole distinction. He sometimes agrees that it is wrong to deal with demons, but he is less interested in legitimacy and more in efficacy.

Turner's debt to Bodin is much smaller, but again he is not uncritical. On shape-shifting, he writes that people only *seem* to be transformed into animals; 'I doe not fancy that the Divell himselfe can worke reall transformations'. He explicitly contradicts Bodin who had argued for real transformations.

7 For overviews of Agrippa see Brian P. Copenhaver, *Magic in Western Culture: From Antiquity to the Enlightenment* (Cambridge, 2015), 284–91; Christopher I. Lehrich, 'Agrippa von Nettesheim, Heinrich Cornelius (1486–1535)', in Golden (ed.), *Encyclopedia*, i, 22–24.

8 I have mainly used Henricus Cornelius Agrippa ab Nettesheym, *De Incertitudine et Vanitate Scientiarum Declamatio Invectiva* ('Invective Declamation on the Uncertainty and Vanity of the Sciences') (Cologne: Theodor Baum, 1575) and Henrie Cornelius Agrippa, *Of the Vanitie and Uncertaintie of Artes and Sciences*, trans. James Sanford (London: Henrie Bynneman, 1575).

9 Barbara C. Bowen, 'Cornelius Agrippa's "De Vanitate": Polemic or Paradox?', *Bibliothèque d'humanisme et renaissance*, 34 (1972), 249–56.

In the essay 'Of the Jewes Cabale', Turner continues his discussion of magic, presenting Kabbalah as a magical tradition constructed from false, misapplied and superstitious learning. This essay is even less independent than his main one; it is almost entirely a précis of Agrippa's chapter on the subject in *De Vanitate*.[10] Turner shows no awareness of current issues, such as the debate on the recent readmission of the Jews to England.[11] The readmission covered Scotland too, though hardly any Jews came to Scotland in Turner's time.[12] Indeed Turner is less interested in the Jews as such than in magic, though if he had looked beyond Agrippa he might have found out more about Jewish magic and Kabbalah's place in it.[13] Still, Turner's account of Kabbalah, superficial and derivative though it is, provides necessary context for his broader views on magic. His idea that the Hebrew language may be uniquely 'significative' may be connected with Renaissance Neoplatonism and attempts to identify the language of Adam and Eve.[14]

Turner's views may seem conventional; indeed they *were* conventional. But they were not universally held in his day. There was considerable elite and intellectual interest in mystical and occult ideas – in astrology, prophecy, freemasonry, Rosicrucianism, alchemy and other such topics.[15] In attacking the roots of such ideas, Turner was firmly orthodox, but also taking part in a real contemporary debate.

Turner participated in one specific magical debate: that arising from the alleged bewitchment of Sir George Maxwell of Pollok in 1676, and the witchcraft trials that ensued in Paisley in 1677. The witches had been detected

10 Agrippa, *De Incertitudine*, sig. I.7 (chapter 47, 'De Cabala'); Agrippa, *Of the Vanitie*, trans. Sanford, fos. 60r.–62v. (chapter 47, 'Of Cabala').

11 Barbara Coulton, 'Cromwell and the "Readmission" of the Jews in England, 1656', *Cromwelliana: The Journal of the Cromwell Association* (2001), 21–38. For Scottish aspects of the debate see Arthur H. Williamson, '"A Pil for Pork-Eaters": Ethnic Identity, Apocalyptic Promises, and the Strange Creation of the Judeo-Scots', in Raymond B. Waddington and Arthur H. Williamson (eds.), *The Expulsion of the Jews: 1492 and After* (New York, 1994), 237–258; Jeremy Fradkin, 'Protestant Unity and Anti-Catholicism: The Irenicism and Philo-Semitism of John Dury in Context', *Journal of British Studies*, 56 (2017), 273–94.

12 Kenneth Collins, 'The Jews in Scotland', in Colin MacLean and Kenneth Veitch (eds.), *Religion* (Scottish Life and Society series, vol. 12: Edinburgh, 2006), 256–80.

13 See for instance Gideon Bohak, 'Jewish Magic in the Middle Ages', in David J. Collins (ed.), *Magic and Witchcraft in the West: From Antiquity to the Present* (Cambridge, 2015), 268–99; Elliot R. Wolfson, 'Kabbalah', in Golden (ed.), *Encyclopedia*, iii, 605–7.

14 Cf. Richard Kieckhefer, *Magic in the Middle Ages*, 3rd edn. (Cambridge, 2022), 175.

15 More study of this is needed, but see Michael B. Riordan, 'Scottish Political Prophecies and the Crowns of Britain, 1500–1840', and Jane Ridder-Patrick, 'Astrology and Supernatural Power in Early Modern Scotland', both in Julian Goodare and Martha McGill (eds.), *The Supernatural in Early Modern Scotland* (Manchester, 2020), 107–26, 127–43; David Stevenson, *The Origins of Freemasonry: Scotland's Century, 1590–1710* (Cambridge, 1988), 77–124; Marsha Keith Schuchard, *Restoring the Temple of Vision: Cabalistic Freemasonry and Stuart Culture* (Leiden, 2002), 447–737. For the interest taken in mystical and occult ideas by Turner's contemporary Robert Leighton, bishop of Dunblane, see David Allan, *Philosophy and Politics in Later Stuart Scotland: Neo-Stoicism, Culture and Ideology in an Age of Crisis, 1540–1690* (East Linton, 2000), 180–1.

by a mute girl, Janet Douglas, whose powers were much debated. She claimed the power of 'second sight', so what was this, and was it demonic?[16] In 1677, the trainee minister Robert Knox wrote a detailed discussion of various possibilities, including the idea that Douglas's spirits might be harmless intermediate spirits.[17] Knox mentioned that 'Mr Gray, one of the ministers of the city of Glasgow' thought that Douglas's spirits were non-demonic visions – and added that 'This Master Gray exchanged several discourses in writ with Sir James Turner, concerning her.'[18] If those 'discourses in writ' were ever to come to light, they would no doubt add to our knowledge of seventeenth-century understanding of spirits, and of Turner's contribution to the debate. Turner's essays do not seem to allude to the Janet Douglas question, which may indicate that they were written before 1677.

The text is a neat copy, clearly written, though it is not always clear whether the scribe intends an initial letter to be a capital.

TEXT[19]

Of Magicke

As the word, Tirant, is now commonlie taken for a prince who oppresseth his subjects, in their goods, lives, or consciences, whereas originallie, it signified onlie a king, and not a Bad one, except with ane adjection, so Magicke in the originall Imports no more then \ane/ exact knowledge in philosophicall things, bot now is taken for that unlaufull art which is practised by the helpe of evill spirits. Magus was a Persian word, which signified a wise man, a priest, and a philosopher, and such were these three, who by the direction of the starre,

16 On Janet Douglas and second sight, see Domhnall Uilleam Stiùbhart, 'The Origins of Highland Second Sight', in Goodare and McGill (eds.), *The Supernatural in Early Modern Scotland*, 178–203, at pp. 191–3. On the Maxwell case overall, see Richard L. Harris, 'Janet Douglas and the Witches of Pollock: The Background of Scepticism in Scotland in the 1670s', in Steven R. McKenna (ed.), *Selected Essays on Scottish Language and Literature: A Festschrift in Honor of Allan H. MacLaine* (Lewiston, 1992), 97–124. For the trial records in the case, see Julian Goodare and Liv Helene Willumsen (eds.), *Scottish Witchcraft Trials* (Woodbridge: SHS, 2025), 504–28.

17 On intermediate spirits in this and other cases, see Julian Goodare, 'Between Humans and Angels: Scientific Uses for Fairies in Early Modern Scotland', in Michael Ostling (ed.), *Fairies, Demons, and Nature Spirits: 'Small Gods' at the Margins of Christendom* (London, 2018), 169–90.

18 Charles K. Sharpe, *A Historical Account of the Belief in Witchcraft in Scotland* (London, 1884), 138–43. 'Mr Gray' was John Gray (1646–1717), minister of St Mungo's, Glasgow, from 1672 until 1684.

19 Source: Sir James Turner's Memoirs and Essays, from the British Library Collection, Add. MS 12067, fos. 86v.–91r.

came to worship our savieour. Magick ordinarlie is divided in naturall, and Mathematicall, or Ceremoniall.

Naturall Magicke is that science, by the helpe whereof men contemplate all naturall causes in the mooveable heavens, and in the foure elements, and by a narrow search haveing found out their simpathie one with another, and attaind to the knouledge of the hidden pouers of Nature, by a fit and mutuall application of naturall things, produceth such effects that ofttimes are accounted Miracles, the causes of them being knowne onlie to these, who have by great studie attained to it, and yet nothing bot Naturall for these naturall Magitians, being excellent explorators of naturall causes, doe ty the superior with the inferior, and applyeth active things with passive, in so fit a manner and measure as is requisite, that they often produce things before the ordinarie time, which seeme to the ignorant, Miraculous, as to produce a rose in the month of Februare, to make a herbe grow up to a plant in a few hours, and sometimes to doe farre greater matters, as to procure raine and thunder, which those profound Naturalists, averre can be done with naturall causes whereof they undertake to give demonstrative reasons, yet it seemes, such things cannot be done without the helpe of the prince of the Aire.[20]

By the description which I have given of Magicke, everie philosopher is not a Magitian, bot everie naturall Magitian, must be a philosopher, neither must he onlie be perfite in that philosophie, which is ordinarlie taught in the schooles bot he must be endued with an accurate knouledge of all the hidden pouers of Nature wherby he may be able to produce these admirable effects. The Vugar[21] is deceaved who thinke any thing that is done more then ordinarie to be done by the helpe[22] of uncleane spirits, {*fo. 87r.*} for if all other effects of this Naturall Magicke, were as common, as the effects of gunpouder, they would be esteemed no more unnaturall then it, the invention wherof was not without great skill in naturall Magicke. The Egiptians, Indians, Persians, and Chaldæans were excellent in this knouledge. The three Magi who came to adore the savieour of the world were Chaldæans. Hermes, Zoroaster, and Numa Pompilius were all of them exquisite Naturall Magitians. Unless we will say, that the last of them had too much helpe of the Nimph Ægeria, who \no/ doubt was a she Divell.[23]

Mathematicall or Ceremoniall Magicke goes a greater length, and may justlie make the laufulnes of it suspected, in regard it produceth its wonderfull effects without naturall causes, onlie by Mathematicall Disciplines, and the

20 'The prince of the Aire': the Devil (cf. Ephesians 2:2). Throughout his text, Turner employs a wide range of different phrases to denote the Devil.

21 *Sic.* 'Vulgar': uneducated.

22 Conjectural reconstruction of damaged words: 'don[...]he helpe'.

23 Numa Pompilius, a legendary king of Rome, gained secret wisdom from the goddess or nymph Egeria: Stuart Clark, *Thinking with Demons: The Idea of Witchcraft in Early Modern Europe* (Oxford, 1997), 625.

strict observation and application of the heavenlie Influences, by which these Magitians pretend they can doe strange things, as to make Inanimate Bodies walke, or speake As Mercuries statue which spoke and the Brazen heade of Albertus, which spoke articulatlie.[24] These Magitians by their hatefull ambition striveing to Imitate the Almightie, may with some reason be thought to have assistance from the Archmagitian, who in all ages hath shoune himselfe to be Gods Ape.[25] Some doe referre Veneficiall Magicke to the Naturall one, bot unjustlie, in regard naturall reasons can not be given for the effects of it.[26] It is ane art, which produceth its effects, By philters, Drinkes, words, crosses, Incantations, signes, sighs, sobs, speeches, figurs, numbers, sounds, many times by looks, and most of these are comprehended under the generall name of Charmes; Wherby they averre, they can doe and produce many Naturall things by a simpathie of these corporeall or Incorporeall causes with that passive thing, to which they are applyed, as Orpheus did once calme a storme at sea, by singing a himne, And some women in Italie, by giveing men a kind of Cheese to eate, turnd them to Oxen, and when they had done their worke with them, restord them to their former shape, among others, one father Proestantius was thus used, as Augustine witnesseth.[27] Such a storie, we reade of Circe, that famous Witch.[28] And our daylie examinations of all our Europæan Witches furnisheth us with stories of such transformations. Bot thogh these who have that art, can doe, no question, very strange feates, yet I doe not beleeve, that the Divell himselfe can transforme any creature, bot onlie deludeth the fancy or Imagination, in makeing the parties beleeve that they are transformed, thogh Bodin in his Demonomanie, maintaine reall

24 From the fourteenth century onwards, a legend circulated that the scholar Albertus Magnus (*c.*1206–80) had made a metal head that spoke and imparted special knowledge with the aid of astral science. Versions of the legend had previously been narrated about other scholars, notably Gerbert of Aurillac, who eventually became Pope Sylvester II (r. 999–1003). See E. R. Truitt, *Medieval Robots: Mechanism, Magic, Nature, and Art* (Philadelphia, 2015), 69–95.

25 The Devil, who 'apes' (imitates) God.

26 'Veneficiall' originally referred to poison, but poisoning was often understood as wicked magic, and Turner is using the word in this latter sense. Here he distinguishes between 'Veneficiall Magicke' and legitimate 'Naturall' magic. At the outset of this paragraph he drew a similar distinction between natural magic and 'Mathematicall or Ceremoniall Magicke'; he may regard the latter as synonymous with 'Veneficiall Magicke'. His use of the phrase may indicate that he was using a Latin edition of Agrippa, in which chapter 44 was entitled '*Magia Veneficia*', rather than the English translation, in which this chapter was entitled 'Witchcraft'.

27 For the stories of the women and the cheese, and of Proestantius, see Augustine, *City of God*, book 18, chapter 18. Turner could find both stories in Agrippa.

28 Circe turned Odysseus' companions into pigs in Homer's *Odyssey*. For her role in demonology see Marianne Closson, '"Et ce que dict Homère de la sorcière Circé": Place et enjeux des références littéraires dans les traités démonologiques du XVIe siècle', in Martine Ostorero and Julien Véronèse (eds.), *Penser avec les démons: Démonologues et démonologies (XIIIe–XVIIe siècles)* (Firenze, 2015), 293–312, and Marina Montesano, *Classical Culture and Witchcraft in Medieval and Renaissance Italy* (Cham, 2018), 11–16, 241–6.

transformations.[29] I know that Nebuchadnezzar was turnd to ane Oxe, and after seven years time, recoverd his Manlie Shape; Bot that was done by Him {*fo. 87v.*} to whom nothing is Impossible, neither ought we to be Curious to know, whether it was done by naturall, or supernaturall Causes, for his word was sufficient to make it done. We reade in some stories, that Evill Merodach, after his father Nebuchadnezzars Death, gave his corps to the vultures to be eaten, for feare he sould returne from Death to Life for he thoght that as easie for him to doe, as to returne from the shape and condition of ane Oxe to that of a Man.[30]

We may justlie conclude then, that Veneficall Magick doth not at all belong to Naturall Magicke, bot is indeed a Diabolicall art, the effects of it haveing no naturall Causes, or if they have any, they may well be knoune to the old serpent whose agile and spirituall nature so many Degrees above the capacitie of Man, assisted with the long experience of neere sixe thousand yeares, may understand, and know them, bot are hidden, and keepd up from the knouledge of the most learned, and long livd, philosopher among the sonnes of Men. Wherfor it is very requisite that Naturall Magitians, who studie hidden, abstruse, and obscure naturall causes, sould *sapere ad sobrietatem*,[31] and not be a mad and restles curiositie endeavor to know more, then humane reason can reach to, and so give that Uncleane Spirit occasion to present them with his assistance to find out that, which of themselves they are not able to doe, for that Enemie of Mans salvation is apt enough to collor his Deceit with the show of Naturall causes, by the helpe wherof, he will undertake to these curious searchers to attaine the end of their Desirs, that he may likewise obtaine his end, which is the perdition of the soules of these his unhappie schollars.

Ceremoniall Magick comprehends these arts, which are called Goetia, and Theurgia. Goetia is that execrable and abhominable Magick, which ordinarlie is called the blacke Art, and which worketh by the assistance of evill spirits, the professors wherof are descrived thus by the poet

Gens Invisa Deo, maculandi callida coeli,
Quos genuit Natura, mali Qui sidera mundi,
Iuraque fixarum possunt pervertere rerum
Æthera sub terras adigunt, montesque revellunt.

A people hatefull unto God, to whom the pouers given
By strange and execrable charmes, t-obscure the face of Heaven

29 For Bodin's unorthodox view see Jean Bodin, *On the Demon-Mania of Witches*, trans. Randy A. Scott, intro. Jonathan L. Pearl (Toronto, 2001), 122–9 (chapter 2, title 6).

30 The biblical story of Nebuchadnezzar's transformation (Daniel 4:30–7) was often discussed by demonologists, including Agrippa.

31 'think soberly'.

Who makes the glistring stars to fall, who mixeth heavns with hells,
And doth all naturs works pervert by their Infernall spells.[32] {*fo. 88r.*}

They are divided in tuo sorts, the first are those, who by a mutuall compact or contract, gets the assistance of uncleane spirits for the promotion of their designes, on condition, that the partie contracting renounce their part in their Creatour, and in the workes of Christ their savieour, And these are properlie our Witches, who covenants with the Divell, to be his servants to get his assistance for fullfilling their lusts, ambition, avarice, revenge, or other passions of their uncleane hearts. The second sort are those, who pretend[33] to Invoke, and command the evill spirits to do what they list, by useing the Holy name of God, and by the pouer of the Divine attributes, thinke they can conjure and force these wicked spirits to doe as they please, and to ansuere them in all their impious curiosities. Certainlie they are given over to strong delusions, who Imagine they can command these pouers and principalities, who refused to obey the commands of the Allmightie, who created them. These Divells seeme to obey these presumptuous creatures, and to doe that by pouerfull constraint, which they doe most willinglie, that they may prey upon the soules of their Invokers, wherin they are seldome deceaved. Necromancers are of this last kind, (for Necromantie is Divination by the dead) and these take upon them to raise the dead, and force them to satisfie their demands, and obey all their Commands. These Geotici, cary about with them their familiar spirits, in glasses, boxes, rings, or in the shapes of liveing creatures whom these miserablie deluded Wizards fancy they have pouer to confine

32 This verse is from Agrippa, *De Incertitudine*, Chapter 45, 'De goëtia et necromantia':

> *Gens invisa Deis; maculandi callida coeli*
> *Quas genuit natura, mali qui sidera mundi;*
> *Juraque fixarum possunt pervertere rerum.*
> *Nam nunc stare polos, et fulmina mittere norunt*
> *Aethera sub terras adigunt montesque revellunt.*

Turner has omitted a line. The translation appears to be his own. James Sanford had previously translated the verse thus:

> A people hateful to the Lorde
> wel skilde to staine the skie,
> Which naught by nature be, and eke
> they can the things on hie
> Subuerte, as Starres and powers of thinges
> which firme and stable are.
> For they know how to staie the poles
> and slashing flames sende farre,
> They driue the aire down vnder earth
> and mountaines rent and marre.

Agrippa, *Of the Vanitie*, fo. 57v. (chapter 45).

33 'pretend': claim.

in these places as they please. The pithonist of Endor was one who excelled in this art of Necromancie, who at wicked Saul-s desire brought Samuell to speake with him, and told, that to morrow be that time he sould be with him;[34] Bot whether this was the reall Bodie of Samuell, or a phantasticke one, or if it was his reall Bodie, whether it was informed by his oune soule, or by ane Uncleane Spirit, is a question not yet decided, thogh it seemes, it was the old Deceaver, who onlie seemd to be the true Samuell, for it is not like, that the soule of that blessed prophet wold leave the Joyfull mansions to satisfie the curiositie of that Impieous king who, he knew, was rejected of God, neither is it probable, that the Lord wold permit ane uncleane spirit to enter in the bodie of so pretieous a saint, for it is said of them that after their separation from their soules, they rest from their labours yet this storie recorded in holy writ, hath perhaps given occasion to the Antients, to fancy that the soules of the dead might be recalled to the Bodies, or informed by other spirits, before a yeare went about, and therfor causd bury them in holy ground, and watch them with tapers and Lampes, and their graves waterd and besprinkled with holy water, for many of them thought[35] {*fo. 88v.*} the soule remaind a yeare on earth, after its separation from the Bodie. Bot these are opinions not probable, nor warrantable from scripture. These Geoticians and Necromantians pretend for their authoritie some Antient bookes written of their art, by Adam, Enoch, Salomon, Paul, Honorius, Ciprian, and others; yea by the Angells Rizioll and Raphael, and the tutelar Angells of Adam and Evias.[36] Bot these are *Aniles fabulæ*,[37] these names bot borroued, and the bookes written by Impieous Men, Inspired by the Prince and father of lyes.

The second part of Mathematicall or Ceremoniall Magicke is Theurgia, which is a science to produce wonderfull, and and allmost Miraculous effects, by the helpe of good Angells, whom they have pouer to Invoke, when they please. The professors of it, maintaine it to be Laufull, and so no doubt it wold be, if it could be proved that God had given command to these blessed Angells to compeare, when ever they sould be calld on by Man, or that God had commanded Men to Invocate Angells to assist them in either their Laufull, or Unlaufull designes, or satisfie them in all their Curiosities. And, no doubt, they are rightly servd, when the Divell appears to them, after they

[34] The biblical story of Saul and the witch of Endor (1 Samuel 28:7–25) was often discussed by demonologists. Turner's preferred interpretation – that the apparition of the dead Samuel was a demon in Samuel's shape, rather than Samuel's actual spirit – was conventional but not universal. His refusal to adopt a dogmatic position in the debate is noteworthy, though he could simply be following the undogmatic Agrippa.

[35] Likely reading. The final letter of this word is damaged in the MS.

[36] This list derives from Agrippa, chapter 45 (Latin sigs. I.5–I.6, English fo. 58r.).

[37] 'old wives' tales'.

have invokd ane Angell of light.[38] And they well deserve by their disavoueable boldnes to be deluded by that Spirit of Error.

It is matter of both sport and pitie, to heare who this[39] Deluded soules, use such strange rites and ceremonies, most wherof consists in the neatnes, and cleannes of their Bodies and all the members of it, of their apparell, their houses, and utensills, and of their sacrifices, whereby they conceave they dispose the heavenlie pouers to be propitieous and favorable to their designes, and to appeare to them, for their assistance, in any thing they desire. And by these ceremonies they wold have us beleeve, that uncleane spirits are banishd farre from them, and that none, bot the pure and holy angells can make their addresse to them. Bot wretched soules, they litle remember of the uncircumsision of their oune hearts, and affections, which makes them fit habitacls for wicked and uncleane spirits.

Illusions and Jugglings belong also to Mathematicall Magicke, when the sight or any other of the sences are deceaved by the seemeing appearances of these things that are not, and thogh some be of opinion, that the sence may be deluded by Naturall meanes, as by Suffumigations, Vapours, and lights, or perturbing the medium or middle of the sence, as the aire or water, as many times it is done in the Machines of your great Masks[40] {*fo. 89r.*} yet certainlie most of them are done by the assistance of evill spirits and by such Spells, and Incantations, as the professors of them have learned of their blacke Master, as are the seeming transformations of Creatures as of a Man in a bucke, a woman in a cat (for I doe not fancy that the Divell himselfe can worke reall transformations) or transportations, as to be carried in a nights time three or foure hundreth miles, and backe againe, the fantasie being stranglie deluded, without naturall causes. To this Art doth not belong these tricks, which are used by the puppite players and these we ordinarlie call Juglers; who doe them meerlie by Dexteritie and slight conveyances of hand. The fierie Chariots, which the prophets servant did see at his Masters prayer, to encourage him, were not fantasticall, for it is not to be supposed, that God deludes the eyes or sences of any man[;] they were reall, which for a time had a true existence by Gods appointment, and by his order were reduced againe to nothing. By what hath beene said, it may be easilie concluded, that all kinds of Magick, except the Naturall one are Unlaufull, and Naturall Magick itselfe hath great need to have limits and bounds to be set to it, least these who too curieouslie search after the perfite knowledge of it, fall in the bottomles gulph of the Mathematicall and Ceremoniall one. The Simpatheticall Pouder, is not to be accounted Magicall, thogh the effects of it, may seeme strange, even above

38 Cf. 2 Corinthians 11:14.

39 *Sic*. Presumably an error for 'how these'.

40 'Masks': masques (stage spectacles), which often used machinery to create remarkable visual effects.

ordinarie fancy, it being applyed to the blood of the partie wounded, to cure even at a very great distance, may be thought miraculous, bot the daylie experience of it, made by severalls, and the learned Discourse, which Sir Kenelme Digbie hath made of it, evinceth it to produce its admirable effects, by no other causes, then these which are naturall.[41]

The Naturall Magitians are bound to be perfite in all the parts of Naturall Philosophie, in Medicine, and Astronomie especiallie, and all Magick, whether naturall or Mathematicall, is at best, bot a medley or hodgepodge, of Astrologie, Idolatrie and Superstitieous Phisicke for that which is done with the helpe of evill spirits, can not bot be condemned by all who make profession of the name of Christ, neither can I bring any authoritie to condemne it, more authenticall, nixt to that of the holy scriptures, as that of Cornelius Agrippa, the most famous Magitian of his time, who Lived in the raigne of the Emperor Charls the fifth, and who had writ three bookes of the art, which he calld, *de occulta philosophia*. The words of his recantation in his booke *de Vanitate Scientiarum*, are these, if I english them right. Bot I myselfe, (sayth he) when I was young, wrote three bookes of Magick, which I termed {*fo. 89v.*} Occulta Philosophia, wherin, what ever I wrote amiss, being misled by my curiositie in my young yeares, I doe hereby recant, for I spent both much time and means, in the search of these vanities, bot the profite and gaine I made is, that I know by what pouerfull reasons to divert others from the like studies, for whosoever shall by the Illusions of the Divell, or operations of evill spirits, Divine or Prophecie, use exorcismes, Incantations, or such like, or by Magicall art show Phantomes or other delusions, now that Miracles according to Gods Word are ceased, shall all be tormented with the eternall fire of hell, with Iannes, Iambres, and Simon Magus.[42] Bot notwithstanding of this his recantation this unhappie Cornelius Agrippa, fell in a relapse, and not onlie studied, but exercised, that blacke Magick, which he had condemned, and fell to be lyable to that punishment himselfe speakes of, if God were not mercifull to him. That Simon Magus, he speakes of, is he mentiond in the Acts of the Apostles by Nation a Samaritan, a notable Magitian, and did such wonderfull feats, that at Rome he had a statue erected to him, with this inscription. SIMONI DEO MAGNO.[43] As the sorcerers of Egipt Imitated Moses his Miracles, so the Ecclesiastick storie tells us, that this Simon did Imitate these Miracles were

41 This is a reference to Sir Kenelm Digby, *A Late Discourse Made in a Solemne Assembly of Nobles and Learned Men at Montpellier in France; By Sr. Kenelme Digby, Knight, &c., Touching the Cure of Wounds by the Powder of Sympathy* (London: R. Lowndes, 1658). See Seth Lobis, 'Sir Kenelm Digby and the Power of Sympathy', *Huntington Library Quarterly*, 74 (2011), 243–60.

42 Iannes and Iambres, named in 2 Timothy 3:8, were traditionally taken to have been the names of Pharaoh's magicians. The Geneva Bible identified them as such in its gloss to Exodus 7:11. For the biblical story of Simon Magus, see Acts 8:9–24.

43 'To the Great God Simon'.

done[44] at Rome by the Apostles Piter, and Paul. Bot at length in the sight of thousands of the people, he was caught up hie in the Aire, by the pouer of his familiar evill spirit, bot was let fall of himselfe, with such force, that he was crushed all in peeces.[45]

Of Magick King James the Sixh [*sic*] writes in his Demonologie, Bodin in his Demonomanie, and of all the kinds and species of it, and extreamlie well. {*fo. 90r.*}

Of the Jewes Cabale

Many of the Hebrews did, and most of the Jews doe constantlie averre that upon Mount Sinai, God by his voyce did teach Moses this hidden art, which they call Cabala, and is as much to say, as as [*sic*] a tradition taught by word of mouth from man to man, and from age to age, without letters or writeing. They say, that since Moses time, it hath beene keeped among them, and is yet by the care and Industrie of these who learnd it from their fathers and elders, and taught it to succeeding ages, ane art which comprehends great Misteries, and not fit to be taught to the Vulgar, for to the perfite knouledge of it, few even of the wisest doe attaine. It is divided in tuo parts, the first is called, Brefith, or Cosmologia, which is ane accurate knouledge of all naturall things, as well the celestiall as sublunarie Bodies, wherin it is probable Salomon did excell, haveing written a booke of the nature of trees and herbes from the Cedar to the hissope.

The second part of the Cabala is called Demercana, and they Divide it in tuo speces. The first they call Arithmantia, which is a [*sic*] Accurate knouledge of the Naturs, of ficacies,[46] essences, pouers, vertues, names, signes, and significations of the Blessed Angells, and of the Divells also, as likewise of the soules of Men, whether in the Bodie, or after their separation from it. The second spece of their Demercana they call Theomantia, wherby they know the misteries, secrets, emanations, properties, vertues, and operations of the Divine Majestie, by vertue of which last, who ever can attaine unto it, can, they say, worke all manner of Miracles. By it Moses wrought all his wonders in Ægipt, and the wildernes, By it Joshuah commanded the sun to stand still,[47] By it Elias brought doune fire from heaven, and destroyd the king of Israells Captaines and their fifties.[48] And by it, the Impieous Miscreants averre, that our Lord and Savieour Jesus Christ, wrought all his Miracles, whill he was on earth. They say, Salomon had also this art, and by it composed

44 *Sic*. Read 'these Miracles that were done'.
45 This 'Ecclesiastick storie' appears to be from a combination of the apocryphal Acts of Peter and the Acts of Peter and Paul.
46 'ficacies': efficacies.
47 Cf. Joshua 10:12.
48 Cf. 2 Kings 1:2–15.

aneother, against the pouer, efficacie, and Incantations of Divells and Maligne Spirits. They tell us, they attaine to both the speces of Demercana, by the simbolicke application, Division, Conjunction, or separation of the Hebrew words, accents, letters, sillables, lines, punctums, {*fo. 90v.*} that are contained in the old Testament. The first part of the Cabala, which they call Brefith, or Cosmologia, is nothing els bot Naturall Magicke, according to its description in the forgoeing discourse,[49] and so if it exceed not its limits, not unlaufull. The second part with both its speces, is nothing bot a Necromanticall or Theurgicall Magicke, or worse, and so all together Impieous, blasphemous, and unlaufull.

If this Art had beene given by God to the Jews, or any of them, as necessare, either for his oune worship, or the salvation of mens soules, the edification of his Elect, or to the perfection of life, we must not doubt bot God wold have revealed it to his Church under the Gospell, which is ignorant of nothing that is necessare for these, or any of these ends, bot is amplie enough instructed in them by the spirit of truth in Gods written Word. It is then nothing bot a superstitious, Impieous and Idolatrous rapsodie of words, sillables, and accents, according to the vaine Imagination of him, who applies himselfe to that Studie, applyed to such expositions, as his cureious braine endites to him, and may with as great Confidence be denyed to beare that sence the Cabalist imposeth on them, as he pertinaciouslie averrs them to have. Neither are we to beleeve that there is any more Inherent Sanctitie, or more efficacie or vertue to produce such admirable sciences, in one language then another. Thogh it be undenyable, that some tongues are more significative then others are, and perhaps the Hebrew more then any other,[50] yet hence it will not follow that by the division, or conjunction of words, letters, sillables or accents scatterd in the severall Chapters, pages, and places of the old[51] testament, such misterious Interpretations sould be Imposed on us, as these Dreameing Rabbies wold gladly doe, for they are indeed nothing els, bot the effects of a long, vaine, and ane Idle Studie, extorting and wresting sences which pleaseth their capricieous humors best, from these places, words, or accents, which they conferre together, being there is no question, bot the contrare sence might with as much probabilitie be draune from other Chapters, pages, words, and sillables of the same old testament by any who is perfite in the Hebrew tongue, and wold cast away so much of his time idlie. And all the world knoues, that from the severall words, lines, sillables, sentences of any prophane writer, scatterd and dispersd thorough all his papers, such a sence may be composed, as the Author never Intended.

49 Turner's own previous essay, above.

50 This point in favour of the Hebrew language is not found in Agrippa's chapter.

51 The scribe originally wrote 'new', then crossed it out and wrote 'old' above the line.

In imitation of this Superstitious and Magicall Cabala of {*fo. 91r.*} the Jews, some Heretikes of the Christian Church, as the Ophitæ, and Valentinians,[52] composed aneother in the Greeke language, draune out of the new testament by the Cabalisticall art, in fitlie applying, and conjoyning scattered words, sillables, and letters of the greeke language, wherby they say, they have composed a *Corpus Veritatis*, a Bodie of truth, as they call it, without which these Impudent Blasphemers averre, the truth can not be found in all the foure evangells, being, say they, they differ one from aneother, and are allmost repugnant, They assert the true sence and meaneing of the words of most of the new testament, is hid from these who know not this their art, and is not to be knoune bot by it, and that this Cabala of theirs was left by our Savieour not by letters, or writeing, bot by word of mouth, and a Vocall pronuntiation. This, say they, is that Arithmeticall, and Alphabetarie Theologie, wherin the great misteries of the Christian religion are containd, which were not communicated to the Vulgar, bot to such, as it seemd good to our Lord Jesus to impart them, particularlie and secretlie to his Apostles, and from them to be devolved to others who succeeded them, and so were taught that Cabalisticall art, wherby they might find out these *Arcana*,[53] wherof Saint Paul sayth, he doth not speake bot among the perfite.[54]

This Art is in itself wicked, false, and blasphemous. It hath no warrand or ground out of Gods Word, and hath its rise from the impertinentlie curieous braines of these, who are given over to Strong delusions, because they wold not beleeve the truth. The knouledge of these Misteries, which they say, cannot be attaind to without this art, was either necessare or not necessare for all the members of Christs Misticall Bodie. If necessare, it is great blasphemie, and hie impietie, to say, Christ wold have them conceald from his poore members, who could not be Savd without them. If not necessare, why sould we thinke, that our Saviour wold teach ane art to his Apostles, wherby he might give to them occasion of Arrogance, and presumption, and to others of needles[s] Curiositie to pry in the knouledge of these things, which did not \at/ all concerne either their oune, or other mens salvation.

52 The Ophitae and Valentinians were two Gnostic sects in early Christianity.
53 'secrets'.
54 Cf. 1 Corinthians 2:6.

3. SIR GEORGE MACKENZIE, 'FOR MAEVIA, ACCUSED OF WITCHCRAFT', 1672

INTRODUCTION

This document is a speech made in the court of justiciary by an advocate defending an accused witch. It was published in 1672 by its author, Sir George Mackenzie of Rosehaugh, as one of a collection of his 'pleadings' or speeches in court.

During his career, Mackenzie engaged with the crime of witchcraft in three distinct roles: as a judge, as a defence advocate, and eventually as king's advocate, in charge of the legal system as a whole.[1] His earliest and formative witchcraft role was as a judge, and this should briefly be noted. He was a justice depute between 25 July 1661 and 8 December 1663, responsible for acting as a judge in criminal trials and in particular witchcraft trials. His tenure of office coincided with the largest and last of Scotland's national witchcraft panics, beginning in April 1661 and continuing until it faded slowly during the spring and summer of 1662.[2]

Mackenzie's biographer Andrew Lang, who outlined his career at this point, assumed that he already held the sceptical view of witchcraft that he urged in his later writings. Lang quoted a letter by Mackenzie boasting of having 'killd hundreths' and called it 'unintelligible', but it seems clear that Mackenzie was referring to convicted witches whom he had sentenced. The number of his death sentences may have been significant, even if 'hundreths' was an exaggeration.[3] Mackenzie may well have been influenced by witnessing judicial excesses during the 1661–2 panic, and most of the sceptical anecdotes that he later related about particular witches probably arose from his experiences at

1 Brian P. Levack, 'Mackenzie, Sir George (ca. 1636–1691)', in Golden (ed.), *Encyclopedia*, iii, 690–1.

2 Brian P. Levack, 'The Great Scottish Witch-Hunt of 1661–2', in his *Witch-Hunting in Scotland: Law, Politics and Religion* (New York, 2008), 81–97.

3 Andrew Lang, *Sir George Mackenzie, King's Advocate, of Rosehaugh, His Life and Times, 1636(?)–1691* (London, 1909); see the chapter on 'Mackenzie as a Defender of Witches', pp. 39–47. Quotation at p. 46. Maevia is discussed briefly on p. 44.

this time. However, the only specific evidence of him *expressing* early scepticism is the speech for Maevia itself, the date of which is not precise.

The speech for Maevia, edited below, was given in Mackenzie's second witchcraft-related role: as a defence advocate. The profession of advocate was his basic occupation, and he could have continued working as an advocate even while he acted as a justice depute; both these occupations were essentially part-time, and the courts had long vacance periods.[4] So Maevia's trial may have occurred during the witchcraft panic of 1661–2, a period that saw many more witchcraft trials than did the following decade.

It may be helpful before proceeding further to take brief notice of Mackenzie's third, later, witchcraft-related role: the role of king's advocate, to which he was first appointed in 1677. Brian Levack has argued that Mackenzie used this role to tighten prosecution procedures in witchcraft cases, contributing to the decline of Scottish witch-hunting.[5] Shortly after his appointment, in 1678, Mackenzie published his major work *The Laws and Customes of Scotland in Matters Criminal*.[6] This book contained a chapter on the crime of witchcraft that made a number of the procedural points studied by Levack, and also commented on the range of evidence that he thought acceptable. At over twice the length of the present pleading, Mackenzie's chapter covered the topic much more broadly. There is little direct overlap between his two texts, but the shadow of the pleading may be detected in the later chapter from time to time when he makes similar citations. The two works have been compared by a recent study of the idea of witches' flight, and further study of the similarities and differences

4 In Mackenzie's letter quoted above, he wrote that during his time as justice depute 'I lost a hundreth pounds sterling yearly by wanting the employment of ane advocat': Lang, *Mackenzie*, 46. This might mean that he had no employment at all as an advocate, but it might instead mean that he lost a portion of his business worth £100 per year. There was no known rule prohibiting the holding of these posts concurrently. I am grateful to John Finlay for a discussion of this subject.

5 See the references given above, and also Brian P. Levack, 'The Decline and End of Scottish Witch-Hunting', in Julian Goodare (ed.), *The Scottish Witch-Hunt in Context* (Manchester, 2002), 166–81, and Brian P. Levack, 'Judicial Torture in Scotland during the age of Mackenzie', in *Stair Society Miscellany Four*, ed. Hector L. MacQueen (Edinburgh: Stair Society, 2002), 185–98.

6 This has been published in a modern scholarly edition, identifying Mackenzie's citations and commenting on his legal approach: Sir George Mackenzie, *The Laws and Customs of Scotland in Matters Criminal*, ed. Olivia F. Robinson (Edinburgh: Stair Society, 2012). The witchcraft chapter (part 1, title 10) is at pp. 66–86. Mackenzie had completed a first draft of this book (which survives in manuscript) in 1672: J. D. Ford, *Law and Opinion in Scotland during the Seventeenth Century* (Oxford, 2007), 380.

between the pleading and the chapter would be desirable.[7] Mackenzie also mentioned witchcraft briefly in two later works.[8]

In publishing his pleading, Mackenzie anonymised his client's case using the name 'Maevia', although he gave real names for most of his other cases. He also anonymised, as 'A. B.', the person whom Maevia was said to have bewitched. Mackenzie also anonymised the next case in his book, a case of wife-beating by a man whom he called 'Titius'. 'Maevia' and 'Titius' were standard generic or placeholder names in legal discourse. One difference between these cases was that criminal trials like Maevia's were in principle matters of public record, whereas the wife-beating case was heard before the privy council, which was not a public court. Mackenzie's reason for anonymising Maevia's case is unclear.

From Mackenzie's own text we can learn the following things about Maevia, about her trial, and about the content of the accusations against her. She was tried in the court of justiciary in Edinburgh (one of the 'supreme courts of Scotland'). The trial took place between 1661 and 1672 inclusive. It must have been after 10 September 1661 – the date of Margaret Hutchison's trial, which Mackenzie cites. (Hutchison in fact had two trials, 20 August and 10 September; Mackenzie quotes from the second one.) This cuts out a large number of cases from the early stages of the panic of 1661–2. Mackenzie does not tell us the outcome of Maevia's case, but this is ominous; in other cases he mentions favourable decisions, and he says on his title page that decisions are included. Maevia may well have been convicted and executed.

As for Maevia herself, we may note that she was a woman, which reduces the field of possibilities, if only a little. She faced three accusations: first, of having laid a 'distraction' on a woman neighbour by whispering in her ear, and then, second, of having taken it off by means of a plantain leaf and a paper with the written name of Jesus. Third, it had been 'deponed by two dying and penitent Witches, that she flew like a Dove with them to their meeting places': thus she had been named by two previous witches in their demonic confessions. She herself had not confessed, or so we may infer from there being no mention of a confession being used against her. There is no indication of where she lived.

7 Julian Goodare, 'Witches' Flight in Scottish Demonology', in Julian Goodare, Rita Voltmer and Liv Helene Willumsen (eds.), *Demonology and Witch-Hunting in Early Modern Europe* (London, 2020), 147–67, at pp. 155–7.

8 Sir George Mackenzie, *The Institutions of the Law of Scotland* (Edinburgh: John Reid, 1684), 379 (book 4, title 4); Sir George Mackenzie, *Observations on the Acts of Parliament* (Edinburgh: Heir of Andrew Anderson, 1686), 166. These works add little to Mackenzie's views on witchcraft as such, but they have contributed to a discussion of his changing views on the classification and nature of crimes in general, and the place of witchcraft therein: O. F. Robinson, 'Law, Morality and Sir George Mackenzie', in *Stair Society Miscellany Six*, ed. Hector L. MacQueen (Edinburgh: Stair Society, 2009), 11–27.

So Maevia was part of a small group. She herself was a third suspect, and she was preceded by two connected suspects, presumably all from the same place, probably all convicted and executed. The group might have had further members, but Mackenzie mentions no others, so a group of just three seems likely. It may in due course be possible to find surviving manuscript records of Maevia's case.[9]

In the meantime, there is much to be learned from Mackenzie's pleading as it stands.[10] The text as we have it is a fully written-out version, with citations to juristic and demonological writings, and with quotations in Latin of which a few are lengthy. He probably gave a simplified version as a speech in court, and then handed the written version to the judge for his further perusal.[11]

9 In the justiciary court records in the National Records of Scotland, there are three main places where the case might be recorded. The Books of Adjournal, JC2, are the court's main formal records. The Minute Books, JC6, are preliminary and less formal versions of the texts that would later be written up for the Books of Adjournal; they sometimes have omissions, but sometimes include extra material. The related Process Notes and Supplementary Process Notes, JC26 and JC27 respectively, both consist of bundles of miscellaneous documents that were used or collected in the course of the administration and hearing of cases. These records mostly cover the whole period 1661–72 within which Maevia might be found, though the Minute Books have a gap between July 1659 and June 1662 (thus omitting almost all of the witchcraft panic of 1661–2), and the Process Notes and Supplementary Process Notes are so miscellaneous that no estimate of their completeness can be made. A preliminary search was made by page-turning JC2 and JC6, looking for Mackenzie's name in connection with the witchcraft cases, but this failed to find Maevia, probably because very many cases do not name a defence advocate.

The JC26 and JC27 bundles constitute a voluminous and potentially very useful source, often containing fuller versions of documents that were abbreviated for the Books of Adjournal, as well as further material. There are about eighteen boxes of these bundles for this period. But they are not sorted or indexed in much detail, with the contents of many bundles being jumbled. The Survey of Scottish Witchcraft research team went through all this material, so in theory it might be possible to compile a list of all the witchcraft material in JC26 and JC27 from the Survey database. The online database is not really set up for such a task, however, nor are the bundles consistently described within the boxes, so in practice it might well be necessary to comb through every box. Without knowing name, date or place, the task would be intricate, but a future researcher using these boxes may be able to find Maevia using the indications I have given here.

I am grateful to Laura Doak and Michael Wasser for advice on the manuscript justiciary court records.

10 Two detailed discussions of Mackenzie's pleading have been published: Christina Larner, *Enemies of God: The Witch-Hunt in Scotland* (London, 1981), 186–9, and Andrew R. C. Simpson and Adelyn L. M. Wilson, *Scottish Legal History, Volume One, 1000–1707* (Edinburgh, 2017), 358–60. Mackenzie's witchcraft views are placed in context of his political views by Clare Jackson, *Restoration Scotland, 1660–1690: Royalist Politics, Religion and Ideas* (Woodbridge, 2003), 188–90, and of his neo-Stoic philosophical views by David Allan, *Philosophy and Politics in Later Stuart Scotland: Neo-Stoicism, Culture and Ideology in an Age of Crisis, 1540–1690* (East Linton, 2000), 190–205.

11 For the defence advocate's role in general see Michael B. Wasser, 'Defence Counsel in Early Modern Scotland: A Study Based on the High Court of Justiciary', *Journal of Legal History*, 26 (2005), 183–201. I am grateful to Dr Wasser for his advice on this case. This was a period in which pleading in writing alone was increasing, at least in civil procedure: David R.

The present pleading was thus addressed principally to the judge rather than to the assize (the jury). In a criminal trial, the judge presided and made decisions on law; the assize heard the arguments and made decisions on facts. The assize's eventual verdict of guilty or not guilty was essentially a decision about whether the prosecution's facts were true or not. But a criminal trial also involved the legal question of whether these facts constituted a crime or not, and this was for the judge to decide.

A criminal trial can thus be understood as passing through two stages, of which the present pleading belongs to the first. In the first stage, the prosecution would present its accusing 'dittay' or 'libel' (Mackenzie uses the word 'lybel' or occasionally 'endictment'): a statement that the 'panel' (accused person) had committed certain specified facts and that these acts constituted a specific crime under the law. The defence, at this stage, could argue before the judge against the 'relevancy' of specific items in the libel. To argue against the relevancy was to argue that the facts alleged by the prosecution, even if true, would not prove the crime as this was legally understood. The prosecution would reply with its own contrary arguments, and then the judge would make a ruling on relevancy. This ruling could include striking out certain items from the libel as irrelevant, or even dismissing the whole case. Striking out certain items could be important for accused witches, who sometimes faced long lists of separate charges – three in Maevia's case. Mackenzie in his pleading argues explicitly that the first article against her is 'not relevant' in two separate ways. He does not repeat this phrase in his arguments against the other two charges, but he continues to argue in a similar way, at least against the second charge.

At the second stage, once the judge had made his ruling on relevancy, the defence would have a further opportunity to put the panel's case, this time by arguing before the assize that the prosecution's facts were not true. The present pleading was not addressed to the assize, but the members of the assize would be likely to be present at the earlier stage and so would have heard its arguments.

These considerations are relevant to an analysis of the present pleading in two ways. First, did Mackenzie argue for Maevia on law, on facts, or on both? His arguments, as will be seen, were on both, and the two were sometimes hard to disentangle; further detailed analysis would be desirable. Second, what logical forms did he use in his reasoning? Prosecution arguments, by convention, were organised in 'syllogistic' form, a structure of formal logic containing three 'propositions' of which the first two were 'premisses' and the

Parratt, *The Development and Use of Written Pleadings in Scots Civil Procedure* (Edinburgh: Stair Society, 2006), 22–9. However, Mackenzie in the introduction to his book on pleadings emphasised oral delivery, and it seems clear that the present document operated in both oral and written forms.

third was a 'conclusion'. Thus the 'major premiss' would be that such-and-such facts were a crime; the 'minor premiss' would be that the accused person had done such-and-such facts; the 'conclusion' would be that the accused person, therefore, had committed a crime. But Mackenzie's view was that the defence should not be tied to this rigid form, and indeed it will be seen that the present pleading flows more freely in the way that its statements are organised.[12]

Mackenzie began his arguments by affirming his own belief in witchcraft, in order to secure his position against criticism. This indicates the unusual, contested and perplexing nature of witchcraft as a crime; no lawyer would have had to affirm his own belief in murder, for instance. However, supporters of witchcraft prosecutions sometimes attacked their critics by alleging that their criticisms of specific aspects concealed a deeper lack of belief in witchcraft, and Mackenzie clearly wanted to head off such an attack.[13]

He then concentrated his arguments on the naturalness or not of the events alleged, arguing that if (for instance) a cure with a plantain leaf *might* be natural then it could not be proved to be unnatural. This was an argument on law, at least in the first instance; an argument on facts would have claimed that Maevia had not used a plantain leaf at all, or that the leaf had had some other purpose. However, the argument also contained at least an implicit commentary on the facts. If a cure with a plantain leaf was a 'natural thing' then the cure really worked directly by the coldness of the leaf. The prosecution's alternative understanding of the facts was that the plantain leaf had no power of its own to effect a cure, and so the cure must have been worked invisibly by the Devil on the witch's behalf.

In his pleading, Mackenzie allowed his disapproval of most witchcraft prosecutions to appear, but he had to be careful. Maevia was part of a group of three accused witches, of whom the two others had been convicted and executed already. He was not in a position to attack their prosecutions. He thus constructed part of his defence of Maevia by arguing for a distinction between her and these two others. They had confessed to attending a sabbat, which was standard evidence for their own guilt – but, he argued, their naming of Maevia as also having been present 'amounts to no more, but that they dreamed that my Client was there: and were it not a horrid thing, to condemn innocent persons upon meer dreams' (p. 195). The argument here was based on the assumption that even a guilty witch was not *bodily* present at the sabbat, for a guilty witch experienced the whole sabbat through dreams or illusions, but that these dream-experiences were themselves wrought by the Devil with whom the witch had made a pact. There was an alternative

12 Parratt, *Written Pleadings*, 14–20. This passage includes an exposition of Mackenzie's own discussion of this topic in the essay that opened his book on pleadings.

13 For an example of such an attack later in the present volume, see the conclusion to the *Just Reproof* (1705), the last of the Pittenweem pamphlets.

demonological view that witches were carried bodily to the sabbat by demons, but Mackenzie did not mention that.[14]

Keen witch-hunters had no doubt that confessing witches could accurately name other witches whom they had seen at the sabbat, but Mackenzie's argument to the contrary was at least plausible in demonological terms. It was common in Scottish witchcraft prosecutions for evidence like this against Maevia to be used as a reason to *arrest* and *interrogate* the person, so that by the time they came to trial their own confession could be used as evidence against them.[15] It was less common for the prosecution to bring forward, at the trial of a suspect who had not herself confessed, evidence of her having been seen at the sabbat by another witch – but this was what Maevia's prosecutors did. It is likely that this evidence weighed less heavily against her than the evidence of her having caused the neighbour's 'distraction'. In arranging the components of a pleading in order, Mackenzie recommended that it was 'most natural to urge the weakest Arguments first'.[16] He may well therefore have thought that the prosecution's case against Maevia was strongest concerning the 'distraction', with which he began, and weakest concerning her flying to the sabbat, with which he concluded his defence of her.

Returning to the distinction between law and facts, it will thus be seen that Mackenzie's arguments on the first two items of Maevia's libel – the causing of the 'distraction', and the curing it – were based on law. On the third item – flying to the sabbat – he argued principally on the facts: she was not there, and indeed could not have been there since the facts libelled were impossible. This might suggest that his arguments here were directed principally at the assize rather than the judge. However, he probably also hoped that the judge would agree that this item was 'ridiculous', as Mackenzie called it, and would rule it irrelevant.

Mackenzie wrapped up his pleading with a final peroration, in which he departed from the specifics of Maevia's case and launched an attack on the severity and injustice of many witchcraft prosecutions in Scotland and elsewhere. Thus, for instance, although Maevia had not confessed, he denounced

14 For an overview of the sabbat in the context of broader demonology see Julian Goodare, *The European Witch-Hunt* (London, 2016), 71–9; for a detailed study of one debate see Walter Stephens, '"In the body": The Canon *Episcopi*, Andrea Alciati, and Gianfrancesco Pico's Humanized Demons', in Goodare, Voltmer and Willumsen (eds.), *Demonology and Witch-Hunting*, 86–106. Mackenzie did not use the word 'sabbat', but this has become conventional among historians studying demonology.

15 Numerous examples are given in Anna Cordey, 'Reputation and Witch-Hunting in Seventeenth-Century Dalkeith', in Julian Goodare (ed.), *Scottish Witches and Witch-Hunters* (Basingstoke, 2013), 103–20. This paper discusses some cases in which Mackenzie himself is likely to have acted as a justice depute.

16 Sir George McKenzie, *Pleadings in some Remarkable Cases before the Supreme Courts of Scotland, since the year 1661* (Edinburgh: George Swinton *et al.*, 1672), 13. He added that a 'young Pleader' who needed to establish his credibility before the judge should reverse this order.

the methods by which confessions were commonly obtained in witchcraft cases – torture, often by sleep deprivation. This passage has often attracted attention from witchcraft scholars, as indeed it should. The present edition translates his long final Latin quotation and identifies its source – a discussion of a fifteenth-century witchcraft panic in Arras, in the then Burgundian Netherlands, that had become notorious as a miscarriage of justice.

TEXT[17]

For **Maevia,** *accused of Witchcraft*

XVI. PLEADING.

I am not of their opinion, who deny that there are Witches, though I think them not numerous; and though I believe that some are suffer'd by providence, to the end that the being of Spirits may not be deny'd; Yet I cannot think, that our Saviour, who came to dispossesse the Devil, who wrought moe Miracles in his own time, upon possesst persons, then upon any else, at whose first appearances the oracles grew dumb, and all the devils forsook their temples; and who promised, *John* 12. that the Princes of this World was now to be cast out, would yet suffer him to reign like a Soveraign, as our fabulous representations would now perswade us.

This person for whom I appear, stands endicted as a Witch, upon several Articles, the first whereof is, that she did lay on a Disease upon *A. B.* by using a Charm. 2. That she took it off by another. 3. That it is deponed by two penitent Witches, that she and they did flee as Doves to the meeting place of Witches. {*p. 186*}

As to the imposing or taking off of diseases by Charmes, I conceive it is undenyable, that there are many diseases whereof the Cures, as well as the Causes, are unknown to us; Nature is very subtile in its operations, and we very ignorant in our inquiries; from the conjunction of which two, arises the many errors and mistakes, we commit in our reflections upon the productions of nature: to differ then from one another, because of these errors, is sufferable, though to be regrated; but to kill one another, because we cannot comprehend the reason of what each other do, is the effect of a terrible distraction; and if this were allow'd, the most Learned should still be in greatest danger, because they do oftimes find mysteries which astonish the ignorant; and this should give occasion to the Learned to forbear deep searches into natural mysteries, lest they should loss their life in gaining knowledge, and to persecute one another: for every Physitian or Mathematician, who is emulous of another,

[17] Source: Sir George McKenzie, *Pleadings in some Remarkable Cases before the Supreme Courts of Scotland, since the year 1661* (Edinburgh: George Swinton, James Glen and Thomas Brown, 1672; ESTC no. R19287), 185–97.

but cannot comprehend what his rival doth, would immediatly make him passe for a Wizard. It is natural for men to think that to be above the reach of Nature, which is above theirs. If this principle had taken place amongst our predecessors, who durst have us'd the Adamant?[18] For certainly, nothing looks liker a Charm, or Spell, than to see a Stone draw Iron; and men are become now so wise, as to laugh at these who burnt a Bishop, for alledging the World was round, so blind and cruel a thing is ignorance:[19] And if this principle, of believing nothing whereof we do not see a cause, were admitted, we may come to doubt, whether the curing of the *Kings Evil* by the touch of a Monarch, may not likewise be called charming.[20] This then being generally premised, to curb the over-forwardness of mankind,

It is alledged, that the Lybel[21] is not relevant, in so far as it is founded upon my Clients having threatned to do her neighbour an evil turn, that she went in to her house, and whispered something into her ear, whereupon she immediatly distracted: {*p. 187*} for, though threatning, when mischief followes, hath been too much laid weight upon by us, yet the Law hath required, that many particulars should concurre, ere this be sustained, as that the person who threatned did ordinarily use to threaten, and that mischief constantly followed her threatnings, *minae ejus quae solita est minas exequi*,[22] that these threatnings appeared rather to be the product of a settled revenge, then of a boiling and airie choller, which doth oftimes, especially in women, occasion very inconsiderat extravagancies. 2. It is required, that the threatnings were specifick, as if she had promised that she should cause her distract, and the distraction accordingly followed: but it were too lax, to ascribe every accident to a general threatning, as is clear by *Dallrio, lib. 5. sect. 3.*[23] Lawyers likewise

18 'Adamant': magnet.

19 This seems to derive from a passage in Burton's *Anatomy of Melancholy*, a book in which Mackenzie took an interest as a neo-Stoic. During a discussion of the shape, size and composition of the Earth, Burton mentioned that '*Virgil* sometimes Bishoppe of *Mentz* was therefore called in question, because he held *Antipodes* [i.e. believed that there were people living on the other side of the Earth] ... and contradicted that opinion of *Austin*, *Basil*, *Lactantius*, that held the earth round as a trencher, but not as a ball': 'Democritus Junior' (Robert Burton), *The Anatomy of Melancholy* (Oxford: Henry Cripps, 1621), 320.

20 After the Restoration (1660), Charles II energetically revived the practice of touching for the King's Evil (the disease of scrofula). Royalist writers and preachers frequently contrasted the king's divine power of healing with the rebellion and disorder of witches and parliamentarians: Peter Elmer, *The Miraculous Conformist: Valentine Greatrakes, the Body Politic, and the Politics of Healing in Restoration Britain* (Oxford, 2013), 116–24.

21 'Lybel': the dittay (indictment), listing each of the criminal actions which the accused person was formally alleged to have done.

22 'the threats of her who is accustomed to make threats'.

23 Delrio's book was first published in 1599–1600, and often reprinted. I have used Martin Del Rio, *Disquisitionum Magicarum Libri Sex* (Lyon [Lugduni]: Cardon, 1608) ('Delrio, *Disquisitiones Magicae*'). The title of book 5, section 3 is: 'The best indications whereby a judge may proceed safely to try this crime'. For an abbreviated translation see Martín Del Rio, *Investigations into Magic*, ed. and trans. P. G. Maxwell-Stuart (Manchester, 2000), 193–202.

consider, if the occasion of the quarrel was so great, as might have provockt to so cruel a revenge as that which was taken; whereas here the occasion was very mean, not exceeding two pence. And though all these do concurre, yet *Farin. Quaest. 5.* [*sic*] *num. 37.*[24] acknowledges, that these are not sufficient to infer the crime of Witchcraft, but only to load the person accused with a severe presumption, or to infer an arbitrary punishment; and in the Process against *Katharine Oswald*, the 11. of *November*, 1629. those threatnings, though the effect followed, were not found sufficient to infer Witchcraft, but only to be punishable *tanquam crimen in suo genere*,[25] that is to say, as an unallowable and scandalous kind of railing.[26]

The second defence against this Article is, that it is not relevant to the Lybel, that the malefice was occasioned by my Client, except it were condescended[27] by what means it was occasioned; for in Law, when I am said to have produced any effect, there must be a necessary contingency shewed betwixt what I did, and what followed, for else, the very looking upon her might have been said to have been a cause, and when sicknesses are alledged to have been occasioned by Witches, the {*p. 188*} ordinar signs given, are, that the disease be in it self such as cannot be occasioned by nature, as the vomiting up of nailes, glasses, and other extraordinar things; that the person maleficiat do go in an instant, from one extremity to another; as from being extreamly weak, to be immediatly extreamly strong; or use extraordinar motions, which cannot be occasioned by Nature,[28] as *D. Autum*. in his discourse of Witchcraft doth most learnedly observe.[29] But so it is, that neither of those can be observed here; for distraction is a very natural disease, and has oftimes fallen upon a man in an instant, especially upon an excesse of fear; and who knows, but this Woman, who by her Sex and Humour, is known to be very fearfull, might have been so surprized at my Clients coming into her, after the threatning, that this excesse of fear might have thrown her into that distraction, under

24 Prospero Farinacci (Prosperus Farinacius), *Praxis et Theoricæ Criminalis* ('The Practice and Theory of Criminal Trials') (Frankfurt: Palthenius, 1622), 773 (question 50, no. 37), argues that prior threats do not constitute strong evidence to prove the commission of a crime.

25 'as a crime of its own sort'.

26 For Oswald's case see *Selected Justiciary Cases, 1624–1650*, 3 vols., ed. S. I. Gillon and J. I. Smith (Edinburgh: Stair Society, 1954–74), i, 130–40. Oswald's defence lawyers tried to argue that some of the charges against her were not relevant because the alleged harm had not been preceded by threats. However, the judges found all the charges relevant, and Oswald was convicted, so Mackenzie's use of her case is questionable. Mackenzie returns to the topic of prior threats, using the same citations as here, in *Matters Criminal*, 74–5 (part 1, title 10, para 8).

27 'condescended': specified.

28 Here Mackenzie is comparing the victim's 'distraction' with demonic possession. The behaviours he describes are those of a demoniac. His argument is that the victim's behaviour in this case was different and thus natural.

29 Jacques D'Autun, *L'Incredulité Scavante et la Credulité Ignorante au sujet des Magiciens* ('Learned Incredulity and Ignorant Credulity concerning Magicians') (Lyon: Jean Molin, 1671), 480–1 (part 2, discours 7).

which she now labours; and yet my Client might have had no influence upon her as the cause, but as the occasion only of this her distemper.

All conclusions in criminal cases should be very clearly inferr'd, since the crime is so improbable, and the conclusion so severe. And therefore, Lawyers are of opinion, that if the inferences be not demonstrative, and undenyable, *conclusio semper debet sequi debiliorem partem*,[30] that which but may be, may not be, and Lawyers do constantly conclude, that we must only conclude that in crimes to have been done, which could not but have been done. And who can say, that this necessarily was done by her here, which could not but occasion this Distaction [*sic*], and therefore, *Perkins, cap 6.* do's assert, that no malefice can be a sufficient ground to condemn a Witch, except she either confess, or that it be proven by two famous[31] Witnesses, that she used means that might have produc'd that effect.[32] And though where Charms and other means expressly discharg'd are used, these unlawful means are by the Judge repute, as if these means might have been effectual, *in odium illiciti*,[33] and that the users have only themselves to blame in that case, who would use these {*p. 189*} Charms, Spells, and Incantations, of which the Law is jealous: yet where none of these are used, but a simple whisper, the effect in that case cannot be said to have flow'd from it, nor do's any severe presumption lye against a thing that is ordinar. And *Bodin. lib. 4.* concludes, that *in capitali judicio ex praesumptionibus veneficas non esse condemnandas, ut si sagae deprehendantur egredientes ex ovili cum ossibus, bufonibus, vel aliis instrumentis magicis instructae licet oves statim moriantur.*[34] All conclusions must be necessar or presumptive; but so it is, that this conclusion

30 'the conclusion should always follow the weaker party': a legal maxim.

31 'famous': reputable.

32 William Perkins, *A Discourse of the Damned Art of Witchcraft* (Cambridge: Cantrel Legge, 1608), 211–19. This passage is found in Perkins' chapter 7, not 6.

33 'with the condemnation appropriate to a crime'.

34 'in capital cases witches are not to be condemned from presumptions, but if witches are caught coming out of the sheepfold in possession of bones, toads, or other magical instruments, and the sheep die immediately.'

Jean Bodin's *Démonomanie* was first published in 1580 in French, often reprinted, and translated into Latin, German and Italian. Mackenzie seems to be translating and paraphrasing freely, probably from a French edition. He gives another Latin version of the same passage, making different choices of vocabulary and word order, in *Matters Criminal*, 76 (part 1, title 10, para 9).

Bodin's French text is as follows: 'Si donc la Sorciere est trouvee saisie de crapaux, ou lezars, ou hosties, et autres ossemens, et graisses incogneues, si elle a le bruit d'estre Sorciere, telles presomptions sont tres-violentes et urgentes: ou bien si autrefois elle a esté reprise de justice, et non justifiee: c'est une presomption bien fort urgente: ou bien si on l'a veue sortir de l'estable ou bergerie de son ennemy et puis apres le bestiail de la bergerie mourir'. Jean Bodin, *De la Demonomanie des Sorciers* (Antwerp, 1586), 348 (book 4, ch. 5). Translation: 'If then a witch is seized in possession of toads, lizards, communion wafers, or other strange bones and ointments, and if she is rumoured to be a witch, such presumptions are very strong and compelling. Or if in the past she was brought before the courts, and never cleared, it is an extremely compelling presumption. Or if she has been seen coming out of the stable or sheepfold of her enemy, and then later the livestock of the sheepfold dies': Jean Bodin, *On the Demon-Mania of Witches*, trans. Randy A. Scott, intro. Jonathan L. Pearl (Toronto, 2001), 210.

is not necessar, since all these remedies might have been used, and yet the user might have been innocent: for, a necessar conclusion is *à qua veritas abesse non potest*;[35] and if this inference be only presumptive, it is as undenyable, that Witchcraft cannot be inferr'd from such a presumptive conclusion, as is clear by *Farin. quaest.36. num. 11.*[36] *Perkins, Bodin.* and others above-cited: and if it were otherwise, Judges might condemn upon guessing or malice, and so moe would be in danger to die by injustice, then by Witchcraft; and may you not as well punish such as stay bleeding by applying a Stone, or who prevent abortions by girding the woman with a Belt, now much in fashion? And therefore it is very remarkable, that by the 73. Act, 9 Par. Queen *Mary*, Witchcraft, Sorcery, Negromancy, and sicklike arts for abusing the people, are only forbidden;[37] nor can it be subsumed that any Art, or exterior thing, whereby people use to be abused, were here used, and therefore this Article cannot be said to fall under the prohibition of the Act of Parliament.

The second Article is, that my Client did cure the said person whom she had formerly distracted, by applying a *Plantane* leaf[38] to the left side of her head; and binding a Paper to her Wrest,[39] upon which was write the name of *Jesus*. Which being done by her who was an ignorant person, being done to the person who formerly distracted upon her whisper, and the Cure being perfected in lesse time, then Nature uses to take for {*p. 190*} composing such gerneral [*sic*] and horrid distempers, might necessarily infer, that this Cure was performed by Witchcraft.

Against which Article, it is alledged, that the conclusion here should demonstrat, that necessarily this cure was performed by no natural cause, whereas the mean here used, *viz.* the applying of a Plantane leaf, is a natural thing, and may cure in a natural way, it being known that there is nothing so cold as a Plantane leaf, and so it might have been very fit for curing such a distraction, which is the most malignant and burning of all feaverish distempers. Or who knows, but that this distraction having been occasioned by the excessive fear she had of my Clients revenge, but that how soon she was

---

The 1581 Latin translation, for comparison, reads: 'Si igitur Sagas bufonibus, Iacertis, hostiis, ossibus, pinguibusque ignotis instructa deprehenditur, et famosa est rerum magicarum nomine, presumptiones sunt validissimae: si aliquando reprehensa in iure, nec absoluta est, vehemens est presumptio: si ex stabulo inimici aut ovili visa suerit egredi, postea'que pecudes moriantur'. Jean Bodin, *De Magorum Daemonomania libri IV* (Basel, 1581), 388–9 (book 4, ch. 5).

35 'one from which the truth cannot be absent'.

36 Farinacci, *Praxis et Theoricæ Criminalis*, 559–72 (question 36), deals with indications that may be sufficient to order judicial torture.

37 'are only forbidden': only these arts are forbidden, and no others. The act being cited is the Witchcraft Act of 1563.

38 This was one of two related plants, the greater plantain or the ribwort plantain. Both were traditionally recognised as having healing qualities, particularly for the treatment of wounds, and do in fact contain astringent chemicals: Richard Mabey, *Flora Britannica* (London, 1996), 320–3.

39 'Wrest': wrist.

reconciled to her, and that she had by the same strength of fancy which made her sick, conceived that she would likewise restore her against that sicknesse, her distraction might have abaited with her fear? 2. The Law-givers having punished crimes, because these crimes are destructive to their subjects, and Common-wealth, have for the same reason only punished such indifferent inchantments, as did either kill men, or ensnare them to unlawfull lusts, but not those Arts, where the health of man and the fruits of the ground were secured, against diseases and tempests, as is clear, *Per l. 4 Cod. de Malef & Math. Eorum est scientia punienda, & severissimis merito legibus vindicanda, qui magicis accincti artibus, aut contra hominum moliti salutem, aut pudicos ad libidinem delexisse animos detegentur, nullis vero criminationibus implicanda sunt remedia, humanis quesita corporibus, aut aggrestibus locis, ne Maturis vindemiis metuerentur imbres, aut ventis grandinisque lapidatione quaterentur: innocenter adhibita suffragia, quibus unius cujusque salus, aut existimatio lederetur, sed quorum proficerent actus, ne divina munera & labores hominum sternerentur.*[40] Which law being a Statute made by *Constantine*, who was a Christian Emperor, being conceived in so devote terms, and insert by *Justinian*, who was a most Christian Prince, amongst his own Laws, cannot but be a {*p. 191*} Law very fit to be observed in a Christian Common-wealth. And though it be alledged, that this Constitution was abrogat by *Leo, nov. 65*. yet, it is very remarkable, that this Constitution made by *Leo*, is not insert in the Basilicks, so that it seems it has been thereafter abrogated.[41]

It is not probable, that the Devil, who is a constant enemy to mankind, would employ himself for their advantage; and the name of *Jesus* being used, so much respect ought to be had to it, that the user should not be punished with death, except it could be clearly proved otherwise, that she had received this Charm from the Devil; in which case, the Author, and not the thing, occasions the punishment, or else, if she had been discharged by the Church, or any Judicatory, to use that Cure, as that which was in it self dangerous; but to burn a poor ignorant woman, who knew not that to be evil which she used, were to make ignorance become Witch-craft, and our selves more criminal, then the person we would condemn. And all these Laws and Citations which

40 This is from the Code of Justinian, book 9, title 18, 'De maleficiis et mathematicis et ceteris similibus' (Concerning poisoners, diviners, and other criminals of the same description). Mackenzie quotes paragraph 4. The edition he used is not known, but there appear to be one or two typographical errors in his text as it is printed. A modern translation of the paragraph is: 'The knowledge of those who, by means of magic arts, plot against the health or lives of men, or turn chaste minds to licentiousness, should be punished, and repressed by the severest laws. Those, however, who seek remedies for the ailments of humanity, or, while in the country, innocently exert themselves to preserve grapes from showers, or from the effects of rain or hail, ought not to be liable to criminal accusations, as their efforts are directed not to the injury of the health or reputation of mankind, but to prevent the gifts of God and the labors of humanity from being destroyed.' *The Code of Justinian*, trans. Samuel P. Scott (Cincinnati, 1932), 9.18.4.

41 Mackenzie returns to this topic in more detail in *Matters Criminal*, 77 (part 1, title 10, para 10).

can be brought to prove, that magical Incantations are punishable by death, though imployed for the well-fare of mankind, must be interpret so, as to relate only to some of these unlawful cases above-related. And I admire,[42] that those who inveigh so much against this Constitution of *Constantine*, have never taken notice, that these Charms are only allowed, even for the wellfare of man and beast, *ubi sunt innocenter adhibita suffragia*,[43] where devotion was used, though erroniously, as in this case. And we know, that a whole Family in *Spain* pretend to be able to cure Diseases by the toutch, as being descended from *St. Katherine*, and are therefore called, *Saludadores*;[44] and that another family in *France*, who alledge they are descended from *St Hubert*, do cure such as are bitten by mad Dogs, and yet neither of these are punished by any Law, since they ascribe their cures to Devotion:[45] And there are but few men who have travelled any where, but use some Charm or other, out of innocence or railery; and to burn these, or the {*p. 192*} common people, who think they may follow their example, were an act of great cruelty. And since the Cross is allowed by the Canonists to be applyed to any part of the body, *per c. non licet. 26. quaest.*[46] I see not why the Name of *Jesus* may not be applyed, in the same way: Nor can I think that the Devil would allow the using of that sacred Name at which he is forc'd to tremble, and by the very naming whereof, all Ecclesiastick Histories tell us, that the Devil has been dispossesst, and therefore, *Ghirland. de sortil. num. 23.* gives it as a general rule, that *ubi alia nomina ignota ultra Dei nomina inveniuntur, tunc superstitiosa dici possunt & ita puniri.*[47] *Cassiodorus* relates, that *multis efficax remedium fuit, trina recitatio versiculi,* Psal. 115. *dirupisti vincula mea, &c.*[48] and *Bartholinus* in his Anatomy,

42 'I admire': I am astonished.

43 'where they are requests for benefits, innocently made'.

44 In Spanish popular tradition, *Saludadores* (the word roughly means 'healers') were men with the power to cure diseases, especially rabies, and to perform other extraordinary feats. *Saludadores* supposedly acquired their powers from being born as seventh sons, or on Christmas Eve or Good Friday. They carried a mark on their bodies that was said to be the 'wheel of St Catherine'. See María Tausiet, *Urban Magic in Early Modern Spain: Abracadabra Omnipotens*, trans. Susannah Howe (Basingstoke, 2014), 99–123.

45 There was a tradition that rabies could be cured by a St Hubert's Key, an iron nail-like device sold at the shrine of St Hubert in the diocese of Liège. See Jolanta N. Komornicka, 'Man as Rabid Beast: Criminals into Animals in Late Medieval France', *French History*, 28 (2014), 157–71, at p. 166.

46 This is a citation to the *Decretum*, Causa 26, q. 5, c. 3, which begins 'Non liceat …', and which says that it is lawful to use the sign of the Cross ('symbolo divino') when gathering medicinal herbs. See *Corpus Iuris Canonici* (2 vols.), vol. i: *Decretum Magistri Gratiani* (Graz, 1959), part 2, causa XXVI, q. V, c. 3 (p. 1028).

47 'where other unknown names, not those of God, are found, then they can be said to be superstitious, and so be punished'. The reference is to Paolo Grillando (Paulus Grillandus), *Tractatus de Hereticis et Sortilegis eorumque Poenis* ('Treatise on Heretics and Witches and their Punishments') (*c.*1524 and later editions).

48 'for many things, a powerful remedy was a threefold recitation of the verse of Psalm 115: "thou hast loosed my bonds"'. Cassiodorus was a sixth-century Roman writer and statesman.

defends, that these Verses repeated with a loud voice in the ear of one affected with the Epilepsie, will cure him,

Gaspar fert mirham, thus Melchior, Balthasar aurum,
Haec tria qui secum portabit nomina regum,
Solvitur à morbo, Christi pietate caduco.[49]

And though some have disallowed even pious Sentences, or Names, when joyned to superstitious circumstances, as when they are only to be writ upon Parchment, and cut too in such a figure, or bound by so many threeds only, yet to condemn the users as Witches, when they are used simply,[50] as here, seems to be the other extream.

In things that are abstruse and dubious, the Law should still favour that which tends to the good of the Common-wealth: yea, and though it sometimes may punish Charms, when used to the disadvantage of men, though it know them not certainly to be unlawfull; yet, it doth not follow, that it should punish that which may tend to their advantage, except they know it to be certainly unlawfull. And though our Act of Parliament punishes such as seek help by unlawfull meanes of Sorcerers, or Necromancers, yet they must first be prov'd {*p. 193*} to be Sorcerers, or Necromancers, who make a trade of abusing the people, as that Statute sayes,[51] which cannot be drawn at all to a dubious Cure used in one case, and by the application of natural means; and therefore, though *Drummond* was burnt as a Witch, albeit he had never committed any malefice, but had only cured such as were diseased, yet having in a long habit and tract of time, abused the people, and used Spells and Incantations, which had no relation at all to Devotion; and having continued that trade, albeit he was expresly discharged, his case was very far different from this, and deserved a far more severe punishment.[52] The same may be likewise answered to the condemnatory Sentence pronounced against *John Burgh*, who was convicted of Witchcraft in *anno*, 1643. for pretending to cure all diseases, by throwing into water an unequal number of pieces of Mony, and sprinkling the patients with the water; so that it may be justly said, that these died rather for being

---

This 'verse' is Psalm 115:7 in the Vulgate, and Psalm 116:16 in the Authorised Version.

49 'Caspar brings myrrh, Melchior incense, and Balthasar gold. The one who carries with him these three names of the kings, is protected against the falling sickness [i.e. epilepsy], through the mercy of Christ'.

The physician Thomas Bartholin or Bartholinus (1616–80) published several works with the word 'Anatomy' in the title. Mackenzie may be referring to Bartholin's best-known work, *Anatomia*, published in various Latin editions in the 1650s and in English in 1665. The quoted verse does not seem to appear in the English edition, however.

50 'simply': ignorantly, without education.

51 The Witchcraft Act of 1563.

52 Alexander Drummond, a magical practitioner from Auchterarder, was executed for witchcraft in 1629. The documents concerning his case are edited in Julian Goodare and Liv Helene Willumsen (eds.), *Scottish Witchcraft Trials* (Woodbridge: SHS, 2025), 127–83.

publick cheats & *falsarii*,[53] then for being Witches, & *venefici*.[54] Upon which account *ars Pauliana* [*sic*] also is punishable, by which some Cheats pretend to cure diseases, by Spells and pious Characters, revealed (as they pretend) to S. *Paul*, when he was caryed up to the third heavens; for, here the foundation makes the cures known to be cheats.[55]

I might likewise alledge here, that it is against the confest principles of all Criminalists, that *una venefica non potest esse ligans & solvens in eodem morbo*,[56] cannot both put on, and take off, a disease; for, it seems that the Devil thinks, that it were too much to bestow such favours upon one of his favourits, so that he is juster then those, who affect plurality of Benefices;[57] or else he thinks it would lessen too much the esteem of those faculties, if one could exerce both; or else it is not probable, that she who had the malice to lay on the disease, would condescend to serve in the taking it off. But however, I

53 'cheats'.

54 '*venefici*' could mean 'witches' or 'poisoners'; the first meaning is intended here. For Burgh's case see *Selected Justiciary Cases*, iii, 597–603. Burgh was charged with having cured various diseases, not of having 'pretended' to cure them; this was presented as witchcraft, not fraud.

55 The '*Ars Paulina*' ('Paul's Art') was the title of one of several seventeenth-century magical manuscript books containing instructions on how to gain knowledge by elaborate invocations of angels: Lynn Thorndike, *A History of Magic and Experimental Science*, vol. ii (New York, 1923), 282. This work was attributed to the Apostle Paul, but it was more common to ascribe such works to King Solomon. Orthodox critics claimed that the spirits invoked were really demons, not angels. See Julien Véronèse, 'God's Names and their Uses in the Books of Magic Attributed to King Solomon', *Magic, Ritual, and Witchcraft*, 5 (2010), 30–50.

56 'one witch has not the power both to bind and to loose in the same sickness'. This was not a standard view; many demonological works and trial records show individual witches removing their own bewitchments. Mackenzie cites the case of Margaret Hutchison in 1661. Andrew Birnie, her defending counsel, had argued that '*una et eadem persona non potest esse saga ligans et solvens* [one and the same person cannot be a witch who binds and looses], which two offices are always bestowed by the Devill on distinct persons': *Records of the Proceedings in the Justiciary Court, Edinburgh, 1661–1678*, 2 vols., ed. W. G. Scott-Moncrieff (Edinburgh: SHS, 1905), i, 6–9, 11–13 (quotation at p. 12). Mackenzie returned to Hutchison's case in his *Matters Criminal*, citing it repeatedly throughout his witchcraft chapter. The quotation given above reappears there, using the word '*saga*' instead of '*venefica*' for 'witch', on p. 81 (part 1, title 10, para 19).

The *Malleus Maleficarum* (1486) briefly described 'three kinds' of witches: 'those who harm but are unable to heal, those who cure and do not harm as a result of a particular agreement entered into with a demon, and those who harm and heal': *The Hammer of Witches: A Complete Translation of the 'Malleus Maleficarum'*, 2 vols., ed. and trans. Christopher S. Mackay (Cambridge, 2009), ii, p. 233 (translation), fo. 95C (question II.1.2); see also p. 151, fos. 58C-D (question I.9), and pp. 358–9, fos. 155C-D (question II.2, introduction). In practice, the *Malleus*, like most demonological works, generally regarded witches as being able both to harm and to heal.

57 An anticlerical joke, comparing the Devil's actions with those of clergymen who hold more than one benefice.

find much weight hath been laid upon this principle, by those who did debate *Margaret Hutchesons* Process, and so let it have its weight.[58] *{p. 194}*

The third Article of my Clients endictment is, that it is deponed by two dying and penitent Witches, that she flew like a Dove with them to their meeting places.[59]

This Article seems to me very ridiculous; for I might debate, that the Devil cannot carry Witches bodily, as *Luther*, *Melanchton*, *Alciat*, *Vairus* and others assert,[60] because it is not probable, that God would allow him the permission constantly to work this miracle, in carrying persons to a publick place, where they joyn in blaspheming His Name, and scorning His Church.[61] Nor is it proper either, to the nature of heavy Bodies to flee in the air, nor to Devils who are spirits, and have no armes, nor other means of carrying their Bodies: but I may confidently assert, that he cannot transform a woman into the shape of a Dove, that being impossible; for how can the Soul of Woman inform and actuat the body of a Dove, these requiring diverse Organs, and administrations; and to believe such transmutations, is expresly declared Heresie by the Canon Law, and to deserve excommunication, *cap. Episcopi*, 26. *quaest.* 5.[62] and is condemned by St. *Augustin*, *lib.* 18. *de civit. Dei*,[63] *delrio lib.* 2.

58 Margaret Hutchison, from Duddingston, was tried twice for witchcraft, on 20 August and 10 September 1661. She was acquitted on the first occasion and convicted on the second. Mackenzie quotes from her second trial. See the last but one reference note.

59 For a discussion of Mackenzie's ideas about this in context of other ideas about witches' flight, see Goodare, 'Witches' Flight in Scottish Demonology', 155–7.

60 All these writers could plausibly be quoted as having taken a moderate or sceptical view on aspects of witchcraft. See Matteo Duni, 'Alciati, Andrea (1492–1550)', in Golden (ed.), *Encyclopedia*, i, 29–30; Jörg Haustein, 'Luther, Martin (1483–1546)', ibid., iii, 676–77; Jörg Haustein, 'Protestant Reformation', ibid., iii, 936–38 (on both Luther and Philipp Melanchthon); Michaela Valente, 'Weyer, Johann (1515–1588)', ibid., iv, 1193–1195.

61 By calling witches' flight a 'miracle', Mackenzie was undermining it further. Only God could work miracles, and it was usual for Protestants to argue that miracles had ceased. The conventional demonological view in favour of witches' flight was that flight was a 'wonder' rather than a miracle, and that the Devil was able to work wonders.

62 This was the famous Canon *Episcopi*, a central text in the debate on witches' flight. Its meaning was debated, but it was often used in the sceptical sense in which Mackenzie employed it here. See Goodare, *European Witch-Hunt*, 71–3, and Edward Peters, '*Canon Episcopi*', Golden (ed.), *Encyclopedia*, i, 164–65. The text of the Canon *Episcopi* is at *Corpus Iuris Canonici*, vol. i: *Decretum Magistri Gratiani*, part 2, causa XXVI, q. V, c. 12 (pp. 1029–31). For a translation see Alan C. Kors and Edward Peters (eds.), *Witchcraft in Europe, 400–1700: A Documentary History*, 2nd edn. (Philadelphia, 2001), 60–3.

63 In his *City of God*, book 18, chapter 18, Augustine discussed the power of demons to create illusions. These illusions were often understood as imbued with demonic power, but Mackenzie uses the passage to argue that the illusion of transmutation into a dove is simply false. For St Augustine and demonology generally see Jörg Haustein, 'Augustine, St. (354–430)', in Golden (ed.), *Encyclopedia*, i, 68–9.

quest. 18[64] *Girland.* §. 7.[65] and though the Scripture tells us, that *Nebuchadnazor* was transformed from a man to a beast by God, yet it follows not that the Devil hath that power; or as some Divines assert, he did but walk, feed, and cry like a beast, and had brutish thoughts.[66]

We must then conclude, that these confessions of Witches, who affirm, that they have been transformed into beasts, is but an illusion of the fancy, wrought by the Devil upon their melancholy brains, whilst they sleep; and this we may the rather believe, because it hathe been oft seen, that some of these confessors were seen to be lying still in the room when they awak'd, and told where, and in what shapes they had travell'd many miles: Nor is this illusion impossible to be effectuated by the Devil, who can imitate nature, and corrupt the humours, since melancholly doth ordinarily perswade {*p. 195*} men, that they are Wolves (*Licanthropi*[67]) Dogs, and other Beasts.

Since then these confessions are but the effects of melancholy, it follows necessarily, that the depositions of these two Witches amounts to no more, but that they dreamed that my Client was there: and were it not a horrid thing, to condemn innocent persons upon meer dreams, as is concluded by *Frans. Ponzan. tract, de lamiis. cap.* 1. *num.* 52. *Sunt illusae, ergo non est standum ipsorum confessionibus: confessio enim haec deficit in suis principis, & est contra naturam, & ita impossibilis.*[68] I confess, that such confessions may be a ground to condemn the confessors, because though they were not actually where they dream'd, at these meetings, yet it infers that they had a desire to be there, and consented to the Worship, and believed that transformation to have been in the Devils power; but all these are but personal guilts in the confessors, and cannot reach others. And besides this, it is very clear, that the depositions even of confessing and

64 Delrio, *Disquisitiones Magicae*, 172–5; Del Rio, *Investigations into Magic*, ed. and trans. P. G. Maxwell-Stuart, 98–102. The title of book 2, section 18 is: 'Can magicians transform the bodies of one species into those of another?' Delrio's answer concentrates on the question at issue here, whether a human can be transformed into an animal. He explains that genuine transformations are impossible, but that the Devil (and thus also witches, drawing on the Devil's power) can create the illusion of such a transformation that will convince not only the person themselves but also those around them. Maevia's prosecutors, in arguing that she flew 'like a Dove', are making this same point, and Mackenzie's citation of Delrio against them is a misuse of Delrio's argument.

65 Grillando, *Tractatus de Hereticis et Sortilegis*.

66 The biblical story of Nebuchadnezzar's transformation (Daniel 4:30–7) was often discussed by demonologists.

67 'werewolves'.

68 'They are illusions, therefore there is no confirming them via the confessions of these same people; for such confession is deficient in its very principles, is against nature, and thus impossible'. The reference is to Gianfrancesco Ponzinibio, *Tractatus Subtilis, et Elegans, de Lamiis, et Excellentia Utriusque Juris* ('Subtle and Elegant Treatise on Witches, and the Excellence of Both Civil and Canon Laws') (1519–20), an Italian legal treatise that denied the reality of witches' flight and attacked the procedures commonly used in witchcraft prosecutions. See Dries Vanysacker, 'Ponzinibio, Giovanni Francesco', in Golden (ed.), *Encyclopedia*, iii, 912–13.

penitent Witches, are no concluding probation; for they are *sociae criminis*,[69] and such ought not to be believed; and they can give no sufficient *causa scientiae*[70] and reason of their knowledge, the want of which doth in Law enervat the deposition of a Witness: and with us, the depositions of dying Witches were repell'd, in the case of *Alison Jolly, pen. Oct. 1596.*[71]

Divines, whose punishments reach no furder then Ecclesiastick censure, may punish not only certain guilt, but scandal; yet Lawyers, being to inflict so severe a punishment as Burning, and loss of all their moveable Estate, should not punish that guilt, till it be convincingly prov'd. For, though this woman were guilty, yet if she be so, she will suffer by the sting of her conscience here, and will be reserv'd for a greater fire hereafter, then you can ordain for her; whereas if she be innocent, your sentence cannot be reformed. And why should you take pains to {*p. 196*} augment the number of the Devils servants in the eyes of the world?

Nor doth the Civil Law punish alwayes what Divines condemn; for thus, though it be murder by the Divine Law to kill a Wife taken in the act of adultery, yet the Civil Law allowes it: and though it be unlawfull by that Law to cheat our Neighbour in buying or selling, yet the Civil Law allowes all such bargains, except the cheat amount to the value of the half. Thus, the one of the Laws respecting mainly the good of Souls, and the other the good of Commerce, as they have different ends, so they take different measures; and therefore it is, that politick Lawes, have allowed cures even by suspected means; which principle is also allowed by *Bartol. Salicet. Azo:* and others, *ad dict. l.* 4.[72] and even according to the principles laid down by Divines, except there were a paction prov'd, or confest, all remedies should rather be ascribed to nature, then to Witchcraft.

Consider how much fancy does influence ordinar Judges in the trial of this crime, for none now labour under any extraordinar Disease, but it is instantly said to come by Witch-craft, and then the next old deform'd or envyed woman is presently charged with it; from this ariseth a confused noise of her guilt, called *diffamatio*[73] by Lawyers, who make it a ground for seizure, upon which she being apprehended is imprisoned, starved, kept from sleep, and oft times tortured: To free themselves from which, they must confess; and having confest, imagine they dare not thereafter retreat. And then Judges

69 'associates in crime'.

70 'ground for (their) knowledge'.

71 In the trial of Alison Jolly on 30 October 1596, the prosecuting advocate produced a confession made by the late Janet Stratton, who seems recently to have been executed for witchcraft. Jolly herself, however, was acquitted: Robert Pitcairn (ed.), *Criminal Trials in Scotland, 1488–1624*, 3 vols. (Edinburgh: Bannatyne Club, 1833), i, II, 397–9.

72 Bartolomeo da Saliceto and Azzone da Bologna ('Azo') were medieval Italian jurists. Each was the author of several works, and it is not clear which Mackenzie has in mind.

73 'evil reputation'.

allow themselves too much liberty, in condemning such as are accused of this crime, because they conclude they cannot be severe enough to the enemies of GOD; and Assisers are affraid to suffer such to escape as are remitted to them, lest they let loose an enraged Wizard in their neighbour-hood. And thus poor Innocents die in multitudes by an unworthy Martyredom, and Burning comes in fashion; upon which account I cannot but recommend to your Lordships serious {*p. 197*} consideration, that excellent passage of a Learned lawyer, *Baldwinus, ad § Item lex Cornelia justit: de publ. jud. Sed quo gravius, & ab hominis ingenio magis alienum est hoc malum, eo major adhibenda est cautio, ne quis ejus praetextu ab adversariis temere obruatur, facile enim hic quid vis consingere potest ingeniosa simultas, ut & multitudinem credulam statim emoviat, & judices irritet adversus eum quem cum demonibus rem habere mentietur. Ante annos sexaginta, sensit infoelix nostra patria, magno suo malo, hujusce generis calumniis, magna erat Waldentium mentio, quos adversarii jactabant nescio quid commertii habere cum innumeris spiritibus, hujus criminis praetextu optimi quique statim opprimebantur, sed tandem senatus Parisiensis, causa cognita, vidit meras esse sycophantias & infoelices reos liberavit.*[74]

[74] This passage is from: Fran[ciscus] Balduini (François Baudoin), *Commentarij in libros quatuor Institutionum Iuris Ciuilis et eiusdem libri duo ad Leges Romuli, & Leges 12. Tab.* ('Commentaries on the Institutes of Civil Law [of Justinian] in four books, and on the Laws of Romulus and the Twelve Tables, in two books') (Paris: Jacques Dupuys, 1554), 774 (book 4, title 18). Either Mackenzie or the typesetter has made several errors of transcription. The original reads:

Sed quo gravius & ab hominis ingenio magis alienum est hoc malum, eo maior adhibenda est cautio, ne quis ejus pretextu ab adversariis temere obruatur. Facile enim hic quiduis confingere potest ingeniosa simultas, ut & multitudinem credulam statim commoueat, & attonitos iudices irritet aduersus eum, quem cum demonibus rem habere mentietur. Ante annos sexaginta sensit infoelix nostra patria magno suo malo, huiusce generis calumnias. Magna erat Valdensium mentio, quos adversarij iactabant nescio quid commercij habere cum immundis spiritibus. Huius criminis praetextu, optimi quique statim opprimebantur. Sed tandem Senatus Parisiensis, causa cognita, vidit meras esse sycophantias: infoelices reos liberavit.

Translation: 'But inasmuch as the more serious and more foreign to the human mind is this evil, by so much is there a need to apply greater caution, lest by pretence thereof anyone be brought by chance to ruin by his adversaries, for it is easy for that which you wish to attest [to be] a clever plot, so that he may at once drive away the many believers, and may whip up the judges against the man whom he falsely claims to have dealings with demons. Sixty years ago, our unhappy country underwent its own great evil and calumnies of this kind: there was great talk of the *Vaudois*, whose adversaries alleged that they had I know not what dealings with innumerable spirits; under pretext of this crime all the worthiest of people were being oppressed, but at length the *Parlement* of Paris, the case having been heard, saw that it was mere lies, and freed the wretched accused.'

This refers to the notorious panic over witchcraft in Arras in 1459–60, known as the *Vauderie* of Arras. The *Parlement* of Paris overturned the convictions, mostly posthumously, in 1468. 'Vaudois' was a French word, originally referring to an adherent of the medieval Waldensian heresy, that had come to be used as a synonym for 'witch'. See Franck Mercier, *La Vauderie d'Arras: Une chasse aux sorcières à l'automne du Moyen Âge* (Rennes, 2006); Gordon A. Singer, 'Arras', in Golden (ed.), *Encyclopedia*, i, 58–9.

4. *WITCH-CRAFT PROVEN*, 1697

INTRODUCTION

This tract includes one of the most lurid accounts of the witches' sabbat in the whole of Scottish witchcraft writing.[1] It is also among the most theoretical – and detached from practicalities of Scottish witchcraft experience as this appeared in witchcraft prosecutions. The anonymous author claims that his account is based on 'the most Authentick Authors, Divine and humane, Ancient and Modern'. He has clearly read widely, but his citations are almost entirely to the Bible. The only non-biblical authors explicitly mentioned are Moses Maimonides and Abraham ibn Ezra, both medieval Jewish philosophers. The author's interest in the Hebrew and Chaldean languages is notable. He may well have been a minister, since the opening pages and the two concluding paragraphs are full of the kind of practical Calvinist divinity that ministers were accustomed to employ in their sermons. The material on ancient languages may have come from a biblical commentary rather than from specialist study.

The tract is up to date in focusing on demonic possession – a topic that appears as soon as witchcraft proper becomes the sustained focus (pp. 10–11). The discussion at that point may well allude to the Bargarran case of 1697. News of this case may have prompted the author to write or at least to publish his tract; perhaps he was even one of the numerous ministers who were drawn into the case. We do not know when in 1697 the tract was printed, but its Glasgow printer may indicate an author in the west. There is a mention of a possessed person pulling cloth from the garments of their 'tormentor' (p. 11), something that had been reported at Bargarran. The tract's repeated use of the otherwise rare word 'wizards' calls to mind the first of the published Bargarran tracts.[2] There is nevertheless no explicit mention of the Bargarran case.

1 This point, among others, was made by Christina Larner, 'Two Late Scottish Witchcraft Tracts: *Witch-Craft Proven* and *The Tryal of Witchcraft*', in Sydney Anglo (ed.), *The Damned Art: Essays in the Literature of Witchcraft* (London, 1977), 227–45. She also established that *Witch-Craft Proven* could not have been written by John Bell, to whom it has often been attributed. Bell probably did write *The Tryal of Witchcraft* (*c.*1705), edited below in the present volume. The author of *Witch-Craft Proven* is unknown.

2 *A Relation of the Diabolical Practices of above Twenty Wizards and Witches of the Sheriffdom of Renfrew* (1697), edited below in the present volume. Here the word 'Wizards' occurs only

The tract is notable for its lengthy discussion of how to detect a witch (pp. 14–16). This gives a sophisticated theological analysis of the Devil's mark, the witch's inability to shed tears, the swimming test, the mark in the eyes, and several other more unusual methods – most idiosyncratically, the idea that a witch will be forced to urinate if salt is burned, and the idea that witches have a distinct smell. These methods are presented as practical, but only the Devil's mark was at all common in actual trials in Scotland, and even that had become controversial by the late seventeenth century. Some of the other methods may have been used from time to time; the witch-pricker John Kincaid had claimed to detect witches by their smell.[3] Strikingly, though, there is nothing in the tract about witches' confessions, one of the most common types of trial evidence. Confessions may be alluded to indirectly, since there is a brief mention of torture – it is said that not even torture can make witches shed tears (p. 15) – but that is all. Even more conspicuously absent is the idea that witches may be named by their neighbours – the other standard type of evidence routinely used by the courts.

The author is in fact more interested in learned magicians and necromancers than in ordinary village witches. He catalogues different types of magicians (pp. 5–10) and methods of divination (pp. 12–13) in detail. Here he often uses the past tense, emphasising the historical nature of his discussion, and also indicating that he has little or nothing to say about whether learned magicians are still active. As for village witches, they were usually known for their malefices – but here, apart from 'tormenting' possessed persons, the only mention of witches' malefice comes indirectly, when witches at the sabbat are made to report the 'horrible villanie' that they have perpetrated (p. 5).

Overall, then, the author's interest in witches stems from their relationship with the Devil. His discussion of why most witches are women focuses on this relationship (p. 12). His account of the witches' sabbat is one of the most colourful and elaborate such accounts in Scottish demonology (pp. 4–5). The Devil preaches from the pulpit of the church; there are black candles; there is feasting and music, and sexual orgies with plural demons – 'Incubusses' and 'Succubusses'. Much of this, and most explicitly the idea that the rich feast is 'but in show', draws on the idea of inversion, whereby the Devil's actions are understood and reconstructed not just as bad actions but as the specific *opposite* of good actions.[4]

in the title, which might have been added by the London printer, but that could still have influenced our author. The Bargarran trial records call male witches 'warlocks', a more common term.

3 Julian Goodare and Liv Helene Willumsen (eds.), *Scottish Witchcraft Trials* (Woodbridge: SHS, 2025), 498.

4 Cf. Stuart Clark, *Thinking with Demons: The Idea of Witchcraft in Early Modern Europe* (Oxford, 1997), 69–79.

TEXT[5]

Witch-Craft Proven, Arreign'd, and Condemn'd in its Professors, Professions and Marks, by diverse pungent, and convincing Arguments, excerpted forth of the most Authentick Authors, Divine and humane, Ancient and Modern

By a Lover of the Truth.

Deut. 18.9. *When thou art come into the land, which the Lord thy God giveth thee, thou shalt not learn to do after these Abominations.*

Vers. 10. *There shall not be found among you any one that maketh his Son or his Daughter to pass through the Fire, or that useth Divination, or an Observer of times, or an Enchanter, or a Witch.*

Vers. 11. *Or a Charmer, or a Consulter with Familiar Spirits, or a Wizard, or a Necromancer.*

Exod. 22.18. *Thou shalt not suffer a Witch to live.*

Glasgow, Printed by *Robert Sanders*, One of His Majesties Printers. *Anno Dom.* 1697. *{p. 2}*

Witch-Craft Proven, Arreign'd, and Condemn'd in its professors, Profession, and Marks, by diverse pungent, and convincing Arguments, excerpted forth of the most Authentick Authors, Divine and Humane, Antient and Modern.

That there be Spirits, the Word of God, the light of Nature, the truth of History, and dayly experience, do clearly demonstrat, and that joyntly? [*sic*] as with one breath, so that they must needs be wretchedly infatuat,[6] and senselesly benumm'd, who suffer themselves (against so evident testimony) to be led aside to the contrair Opinion: Yet such bewitched miscreants and miserable Catives[7] there are, and in all Ages there has been (call them Deiests or Atheists as you list) who have made bold to impugne so notour a Truth, either out of a curious affectation in crosing the common sentiment to be reputed singular, or else from an Judicial blindness and case-hardness of Spirit,[8] in being given over to a Reprobat sense (by gain-standing the Truth) to receive a lie, whose case is more to be pitied than imitated, and their blinded Judgment more to be spurned at, and to be rejected with scorn, than kindly and amicably to be embraced.

5 Source: *Witch-Craft Proven* (Glasgow: Robert Sanders, 1697; ESTC no. R232480).

6 'infatuat': senseless or foolish.

7 'Catives': wretches.

8 'Judicial blindness' is a judgement from God, as punishment for a person's sins, making a person unable to perceive the truths of God. 'Case-hardness of spirit' is similar: having a hardened conscience and being unaware of one's sinful state.

For if there be no Spirits, then (not to speak of a multitude of vile absurdities, and gross horrid Blasphemies, that would natively[9] follow therupon) there is no Eternal Death, Life, nor Resurrection to be expected, nor any Locall place of Punishment for the Damned to be Tormented in, by the instruments of His Wrath, in the execution of Justice upon unrepenting Sinners, nor any Heavenly Joy and Solace to be expected by the truly Godly after this Life; which were manifestly to Raze two of the most Glorious and Divine *{p. 3}* Attributes of God both at once. For 1*st*, How can the glory of His rich mercy appear to the Elect, but by a declaration of the Glory of His severe and deserved Justice towards the Reprobat. 2*ly*, For what end is conviction of Sin both in the good and bad, if it be not to Reclaim the one in undeserved Mercy for Obtemperating,[10] and to Reprobat the other in deserved Justice, for declining and not harkening unto the Heavenly, and Divine Call. 3*ly*, Whence pray are these inward frights, and terrours of a troubled Conscience, bred in the stoutest Atheist, either upon their departure forth of the World: or while they be going forward in a full Bensile[11] and carier[12] of all imaginary[13] wickedness, and be in health and soundness both in Body and Mind, that a quick stop and discharge is put thereto, by a sudden roaring of an allarmed and awakned Conscience; whereby sometime sooner, sometime later, an inrood hath been made upon the Kingdom of Darkness, by an immediat, supream, and irresistable Divine power, to the recovery and reclaiming of not a few, to the praise and glorious manifestation of the ineffable riches of his grace towards the poor lost Sons of *Adam*; witness hereunto the joynt testimony of the Elect of God through all ages of the World, the Heavenly Quier of Angels, and the glorious company of the triumphant Saints.

Hence then it appears, by undenyable evidence, and by a perpetual chain of Divine Providence (whatever the grosly prophane brag in the contrair) that what vain thoughts soever the Sons of men may idlely entertain in the heat of lust, and youth, anent the falshood and vanity of such doting, and fanciefull opinions (as they in their joylie[14] and merrie fits be pleased to term them) they shall sooner, or later, feel the testimony of their Conscience as a witness within them, constraining them seriously to comply with the truth of what they formerly mocked at in the days of their vanity; when at the last hour they shall be either trysted[15] with inexpressible fears, Terrours, and Agonies, of a troubled mind for their past life, by way of conviction and condemnation; or with unconceivable joy, peace, and composour of Conscience, upon a

9 'natively': plainly.
10 'Obtemperating': obeying.
11 'Bensile': determination or impetus.
12 'carier': career.
13 'imaginary': imaginable.
14 *Sic*. Perhaps read 'jolly'.
15 'trysted': met.

sealed pardon and absolution, to their eternall and unspeakable satisfaction and solace both here and hereafter.

So that by a genuin confession and universal consent of the {*p. 4*} better sort of all Men, of all conditions, and in all ages, yea and of all religions;[16] how different soever in opinion other ways the former opinion of the Subsistance of Spirits hath been generally received for an undoubted Truth, specially by Divine Penitents; upon whom the Grace of God hath mightily prevailed, with an irresistable, and Supream Divine power: Now if there be Spirits, there must needs be some good, set apart for the service of the truely Elect, and some Bad who be Ministers of Justice for execution of Divine vengeance upon all the ungodly Reprobat of whose service, converse, and familiarity among the Sons of men in obedience to their respective charges there is so full and clear mention made as well in Sacred as prophane Story, as that I Hope none will be so impudent to deny much less to gainsay so notour a Truth, to Wit, that there be Familiar Spirits, and that Men and Women make League and Compact, and intimately converse with them. *Joannes* and *Jambres*,[17] *Pharao* and *Balaam*,[18] *Manasseh* and King *Saul*, with the Endor *Witch* be pregnant instances hereof from Divine Story;[19] and *Zeroaster*, *Michael Scot*,[20] *Faustus*, *Major Weir*,[21] St. *Giels* of Brittain High Constable to *Charles* the Seventh King of *France*,[22] *Bladud* Son of *Lud* King of *England*,[23] our own Mc *Baith* and *Natholicus* Kings of Scotland[24] with *Liodorus* that famous Sicilian Wizard,[25] and innumerable others beside be recorded for confirmation of the Truth hereof, in Humane Story.

16 The author may have the Jewish religion in mind here, since he later displays interest in Jewish writers.

17 Iannes and Iambres were the traditional names of Pharaoh's magicians.

18 For Balaam, see Numbers 22:21–35.

19 For Manasseh, see further below. For Saul and the witch of Endor, see 1 Samuel 28:7–25.

20 Michael Scot (d. *c.*1235) served the Emperor Frederick II as an astrologer.

21 Major Thomas Weir was executed for incest in 1670. Stories of witchcraft were told about him. See Michael F. Graham, 'The Afterlives of Thomas and Jean Weir', in Martha McGill and Alasdair Raffe (eds.), *The Scottish State and the Experience of Government*, c.*1560–1707: Essays in Honour of Julian Goodare* (Edinburgh, 2025), 259–76.

22 Gilles de Rais, marshal of France, was executed in 1440 for sodomy, necromancy and murder. See Ben Parsons, 'Sympathy for the Devil: Gilles de Rais and his Modern Apologists', in Barbara I. Gusick and Matthew Z. Heintzelman (eds.), *Fifteenth-Century Studies*, 37 (Woodbridge, 2012), 113–37. In 1697, the year in which *Witch-Craft Proven* was published, the story of Gilles de Rais was refurbished by Charles Perrault as 'Bluebeard' in his *Tales of Mother Goose*.

23 Bladud was a legendary king of Britain who taught necromancy and died in an attempt to fly, according to Geoffrey of Monmouth (*c.*1136).

24 In the histories of Scotland by Hector Boece (1527) and George Buchanan (1582), Natholocus and Macbeth were kings who consulted with diviners and witches. See Julian Goodare, 'Witchcraft and Prophecy in Scotland', *Journal of the Northern Renaissance*, 12 (2021), online.

25 Heliodorus of Catania, a legendary necromancer.

Nor has there been wanting some in all Ages, who by the special grace and goodness of God to them, upon their giving over, and falling off, from such detestable, and Devilish practices, hath remitted to Posterity, the manner of entering into that cursed Profession, with the Ceremonies thereto belonging: Namely, how the Wizards, and Witches, warned[26] by an Officer give their Personal suit and Presence[27] in one Shape or other, at time and place, to attend the pleasure of their Lord, which is mostly in the night-time, nor is any place so piacular[28] or sacred, but that the Devil and his Creatures (by permission) may meet therein, nay even the verie Churches themselves, where he makes bold to mount the Pulpit, black candles with a blew Low,[29] burning all the while, both about the Pulpit, and Binch,[30] and in several other parts and quarters throughout, and in all places wherever they meet, {*p*. 5} He gives his Hellish advice to his miserable Catives, and they confess to him what horrible villanie they have perpetrat since their last meeting, receiving his praise and applause accordingly, the most profligat and notorious wretches be always by him had in the highest esteem, and when they be thus met, they be often richly feasted (tho' but in show) with meat, drink, and musick of the best, or with whatever else may ravish and captivat the senses, the *Incubusses* also serve to satisfie the lust of the Witches, and the *Succubusses* the lust of the Wizzards: at their meeting and departing they pay their accustomed reverence to *Lucifer*, and perform all worship to him, and by anointing themselves with certain oyntment, compounded at the command of the Devil, they are carried in Spirit through the Air, hither or thither, by one mean, or other: and when any be to be entred, they be recomended, and presented by the Society, whereupon giving their right hand to Satan, and renouncing the Christian Faith, and Sacraments, and upon transferring the Dominion of themselves, Soul and Bodie to him for ever, with a promise to worship Him as their Lord, they are sworn and solemnly admitted, and then have given them on[e] Hellish imp or moe, for their Titular and Gardian, (by way of Spirit Familiar) to direct and guide them throughout all the passages of their time, whereby they perform afterwards all their lewd and wicked deeds.

Now since from what is said, it manifestly appears that their [*sic*] be wicked Spirits, and that there be who are in Covenant and League with them, such as the *Judicial Astrologer*, *Monethly-Prognosticator*, *Sooth-sayer*, *Magician*, *Sorcerer*, Necromancer, Charmer, and Wizard, all comprised in the prohibition under the name WITCH,[31] it will not be a miss to tell you what every one of the

26 'warned': summoned.
27 'suit and Presence': a legal phrase denoting formal participation in a feudal court.
28 'piacular': sinful, requiring expiation; the opposite of sacred.
29 'Low': flame.
30 'Binch': bench.
31 *Exod*. 22.18. (Footnote in original.)

said Professors of Witchcraft be, wherein they differ and agree one with another, of these in order. And,

First, An Astrologer, is either taken in a good sense, for such as contemplate the Stars and Face of Heaven, that they may therein view the incomparable Glorie, Wisdom, Power, Goodness and Providence of God, discovered and shining forth in them,[32] which formerly was, and still ought to be the practice of the truly Godly in all times according to the Precept,[33] and the end of their creation,[34] in this first {*p. 6*} sense it may more fitly be termed Astronomie than Astrologie. But when it is taken in an evil sense for such as gaze upon and view the face of Heaven, that they may read and divine by the Position of the Stars, the Fates, or Fortunes of States, and Persons in relation to Life, Death, Felicitie, Adversitie, and the like, as to their circumstantial events in good or evil; it is called *Astrologie Judicial*, and for the causes fore-mentioned, not without pregnant and sufficient ground, deservedly condemned:[35] hence as the *Hebrews* affirm the *Radix*, *Term*, or *Thema*, comes from an Arabick word signifying to decide, which seems to point at such as take upon them to determine things of future Contingencie, by the view of the Sky, as says *Isaiah*,[36] upon which account they were held in venerable esteem, and were highly respected by the *Babylonians*, *Chaldeans*, and other Nations,[37] as also with the ungodly *Jews*, *Isaiah* 47.11. And therefore where mention is made of them, they be ordinarly joyned with Star-gazers, Monethly-Prognosticators, Magicians, Sorcerers, Chaldeans, Sooth-sayers and Wise-men, as in *Isaiah* and *Daniel*, in the fore-cited places appear.

Secondly, the Monethly-Prognosticators whereof mention is made by *Isaiah*[38] were such as did instruct, give notice, or make known before hand the several aspects of the Sun, Moon, and other Planets amongst themselves, with their influences, revolutions, and common effects, naturally following thereupon, as to the various Occurrences that were to fall out throughout each moneth of the year: which is much in kind to the Astronomie or Astrologie in the better part, mentioned in the preceeding §: and in so far only is to be disproven,[39] as it dipps into Astrology Judicial, whereof formerly.

Thirdly, Sooth-sayers, or according to the old Scots Dialect, Truth-tellers, were such as observed the Clouds, Planets, and the flying of Birds, whereby they pretended to foretell all future Events in all humane actions, as to good

32 *Rom.* 1.18,–22. *Psal.* 8.1,3: 19.1.–3. & *Psal.* 104. (Footnote in original.)

33 *Isa.* 40.26. (Footnote in original.)

34 *Gen.* 1.14. (Footnote in original.)

35 For the decline of astrology in this period see Jane Ridder-Patrick, 'Astrology and Supernatural Power in Early Modern Scotland', in Julian Goodare and Martha McGill (eds.), *The Supernatural in Early Modern Scotland* (Manchester, 2020), 127–43.

36 *Isa.* 43.12. (Footnote in original.)

37 *Dan.* 1.20. 2.2. 4.7. 5.7. 2.10. (Footnote in original.)

38 *Isa.* 47.13. (Footnote in original.)

39 'disproven': disapproved.

and bad Luck; which at first took place in the East, and from thence was communicat to other Nations.[40] Hence in the Original the word is derived from HAANAN a Cloud, for that by the chattering or flight of Birds in the Air they pretended to know things to come: others fetch the word from HAAJIN an eye making them to agree, and to be the same with the Astrologer {*p. 7*} Judicial fore-said, which without all naturall and divine ground or reason, pretended to know seasonable and opportune times, for the doing of matters, by viewing the Sky, Signes, Planets, and other Stars:[41] some again there be, who derive it from the former word HAANAN, a Cloud, for that by enchantments, and such like wicked Arts they deceived the sight, making the Spectators otherways look upon things then in truth they were, and in this they were in kind to the Magician, whereof afterwards, such were *Joannes* and *Jambres*, who by their lieing wonders which they wickedly brought to pass by their Enchantments sought thereby to belie the true miracles wrought by the hand of *Moses*, at the command of the Lord[42] the greatness of whose Crime is palpable from the severity of the Judgement mentioned in the Law,[43] which is to be duely execute in full and deserved punishment upon them without all pity or compassion.

Fourthly, Magicians, Such were in high esteem among the Nations[44] and pretended to be well seen,[45] and to have great skill in the nature of things, even of the highest Import and Concern: and seems to have been the same with the Diviner, whom they used to consult in all weighty Cases, as did the *Philistines*[46] and the King of *Babylon*[47] which was an abomination to the Lord,[48] because perpetrat by unlawful and wicked means[49] as by Sand, Iron, Stones, &c. Some by lying on the ground, and some by a walking-staff: Hence says *Hoseah*[50] *My People ask Counsel at their Stocks, and their Staff declareth unto them*: Such ordinarily professed skill in telling secrets, and future events, by observation of Stars (wherein they agreed with the Judicial Astrologer) and by the unlawful use of such like superstitious circumventing means of fraud and deceit, Satan either suggested to them, that which was desired to be known, or otherwayes by crafty and ambiguous answers concealed his ignorance of that he could not reveal as by these following Oracles appear.

40 *Isa*. 2.6. (Footnote in original.)
41 *Isa*. 47.13. (Footnote in original.)
42 *Exod*. 7, 8, 9, 10, 11. (Footnote in original.)
43 *Levit*. 20.6. (Footnote in original.)
44 *Dan*. 2.2. 5.7,8. *Exod*. 7, 8, 9, 10 *ch*. (Footnote in original.)
45 'pretended to be well seen': claimed to be proficient.
46 *Sam*. 6.2. (Footnote in original.)
47 *Ezek*. 21.21. (Footnote in original.)
48 *Sam*. 15.23. (Footnote in original.)
49 *Sam*. 28.8. (Footnote in original.)
50 *Hos*. 4.12. (Footnote in original.)

Aio te Æœcide, Romanos vincere posse,
Craesus Chalim penetrans magnum pervertet opum vim.[51]

The word *Chartummin* rendred Magician is not properly {*p. 8*} Hebrew, but Chaldaic, tho' in use with them[52] and is commonly rendred both by the *Greeks* and *Latines* Genethliacon or Interpriter (as says *Aben-ezra*[53]) from their taking on them to divine from the Nativity hour the good or bad luck of the Enquirer, by the *Greeks* they were properly called *Sophi*, and by the *Persians Magi* wisemen, whence they seem to fetch their name.

Fifthly, The Sorcerer, whereof there were two sorts, 1. Such as either deluded the outward senses, by *Legerdemeen*; or *2ly*, such as by their wicked art did great hurt, hence the punishment was diverse; whoso did ill by his wicked art, or witch-craft, was by the *Jews* Law to be stoned to death, but the Deceiver or Deluder was only to be scourged: the original word *Cashaph*, or foreseer, in the Hebrew signifies changing or turning, hence the Greek word *Bascaino*, and the Latine word *Fascino*, to bewitch: with the *Persians* they be termed *Magi*, wise, and for the affinitie of the name held vulgarly to be somewhat in kind to the Magician, whereof in the preceeding §: nor were they any whit in less esteem as the signification of the word *Magos*, wise, seems to import, which at first was taken in a good sense (as the word *Tyrannus* with the Latines and the word *Knave* with our Progenitors which two words were in old time taken for a King and a servant, but now bear a quite different signification as is obvious enough to all) even so, for that the *Ægyptians* and *Chaldeans* give themselves to the studie and Practice of Devilish arts, the word Magos began in time, to be taken in an evil and malignant sense, of this sort were the Sorcerers of *Ægypt*, mentioned by *Paul*[54] of whom we have spoken formerly.

Sixthly, The Necromancer was he that sought unto the dead, and enquired at them[55] expresly forbidden in the Law of the Lord[.][56] Such raised in appearance (by the help of a Familiar Spirit) the Dead, and asked Counsel

51 These were two of the notoriously ambiguous pronouncements of the Delphic oracle: 'I tell you, Pyrrhus, that you the Romans can conquer', and 'If Croesus crosses the River Halys he will destroy a great empire'.

52 *Dan*. 2.10. (Footnote in original.)

53 Abraham ibn Ezra (d. 1167) was a Jewish philosopher. The work alluded to here may be Jan Leusden, *Ionas illustratus per paraphrasin Chaldaicum, Massoram magnam, & parvam; et per trium præstantissimorum Rabbinorum Schelomonis Jarchi, Abrahami Aben Ezræ, Davidis Kimchi, textum Rabbinicum punctatum, nec non per varias notas philologicas* ('Jonah Illustrated by a Chaldean Paraphrase, the Great and Small Massorah, and by the Rabbinic text annotated by three most eminent Rabbis, Solomon Jarchi, Abraham ibn Ezra, and David Kimhi, as well as by various philological notes') (Utrecht, 1656, and later editions).

54 *Tim*. 3.8. (Footnote in original.)

55 *Sam*. 28.11,15. (Footnote in original.)

56 *Deut*. 18.11. (Footnote in original.) The original text runs on at this point ('Law of the Lord such raised ...'), but a new sentence seems to be required. The question mark at the end of that sentence is probably an error.

at them, as did the Witch of *Endor* for King *Saul* in distresse? [*sic*] Of the Necromancer it is said, that he made himself hungrie, and slept among the dead, or else that he put on proper Cloaths, and burned Incense, that he might have fellowship with, and advice from the dead; the partie consulter (it seems) behoved likeways to fast, as may be gathered from the first of *Sam.* 28.22. to the end. {*p. 9*}

Seventhly, A Charmer, Enchanter, or Conjurer, comes from the Hebrew word CHOBER, which signifies conjoyning or consociating, in Chaldee they be called RATIM, of mutering, or mumbling, the Greek word is *Emphaidon*, charming or enchanting, he speaks Words of a strange Tongue, and without sense, firmly believing that such words are profitable to cure, prevent, or remove sickness, and to cause to prosper; thus sometime they repeat verses out of the Bible and to that effect make the Bible medicine to the Body, which is the medicine and food of the Soul.[57] Such kind of Cattle[58] with Fortune-readers, and such wicked and unhallowed Stuff frequently abound amongst us, so that I need not tell you what they are, would to God we had not so frequent occasions and access of knowing them.

Eighthly, A Wizard mentioned in *Deut.* 18.11. Was one who took upon him to foretell things to come, without any solide ground of reason or divine Revelation; he differed from the Astronomer, and Judicial Astrologer, and Sooth-sayer, in that they fetcht their knowledge from external causes, but he from a secret impulse of the Devil, all of them agreeing in this, that their pretended skill was without any solide Foundation tho' generally they were much set by, and looked upon as famous in their generation and men of renown, for that they made show of great skill and cunning in disclosing hidden things, and foretelling future events: and be (when mentioned,) usually joyned with such as have Familiar Spirits; as well in Legal prohibitions[59] as in Historical relations[60] and in the Prophesie *Isa.* 8.19. Such professors as those fore-mentioned, eight[61] were by a general Name called *Chaldeans* from their mother Land wherein they at first were hatch'd, the Hebrew word JIDGNONI, whence the *Wizard* has his name, signifies knowledge or cunning, whereunto accords the Greek word GNOSTES a knowing one, or Prognosticator, hence the *Gnosticks* of old had their name, who laid claim to a greater knowledge than in Truth they had, and that without all warrand Divine or Humane: But in the *Chaldean* Tongue he hath his name of remembrance, from the word ZECURU because he revealed things worthy to be remembred, (as {*p. 10*} they verily thought who were by them deceived,) hence in the *Jew* traditions,

57 *Prov.* 3.22. (Footnote in original.)
58 'Cattle': contemptible people.
59 *Lev.* 19.31. 20.27. (Footnote in original.)
60 *Sam.* 28.3,9. 2 *Kings* 21.6. 23.24. 2 *Chron.* 33.6. (Footnote in original.)
61 This 'eight' refers to the eight types of 'Professors of Witchcraft' whose enumeration is now coming to an end. The comma before the word seems to be a typographical error.

he is describ'd to be one, who put in his mouth the bone of a Bird, called JADVANG, and burned incense, and did other works until he fell down as with shame, or modesty, and spoke things that were afterward to come to pass.

Thus did the Devil by his said Agents, or Instruments, so craftily carry, and demean himself, in the discovery of secrets by them, that it was verily believed by the greatest Kings, and Potentats, that there could be nothing so dark, and abscond,[62] that they could not reveal, *Dan*. 2.2,5. So that they were to them as the Prophets of old were to the Israel of God, the time of that ignorance God winking at; but why they should be trysted now (in the Meridian Sun-shin of Gospel-Ordinances,) with the same faith, and belief, (God now calling all men every where to repent, and turn from their former evil way, to walk in newness of Life, and to conform themselves to the example of His Son, whom he hath sent into the World, to destroy the works of the Devil, 1 *John*. 3.8.) is (without all controversie) justly astonishing, and surprising.

Having thus far run through part of my task, in describing the chief professors of Witch-Craft, and in shewing you wherein they agree with, and dissent one from another, some placing their skill in one thing, some in another, some being acted with a Spirit of Divination, and some being taken up with contemplation of the heavenly Orbs, of which they pretended to read all future events, and to tell, and disclose all secrets whatsoever.

It next rests that we shew unto you, what a Witch is, and what be the several Parts and *Species* of Witch-Craft, wherein we shall observe the same order as heretofore. *First*, Describing and defining what a Witch is, both from Scripture, and the Original; as also, what horrid guilt they underly who are guilty of the same, and then discourse to you what be the several Parts, and *Species* thereof: as also, we shall shew you what may probably be the reasons, why Satan so far unmaskes himself at this present, as to present to the tormented (by a sort of corporeal representation) the persons of their tormentors, in their various habits, gesturs, and actions, and in their present Posturs they are in for the time; so that the tormented {*p. 11*} shall be able to give an account of what they hear, see, and suffer by them, for the time; who, and what they are who trouble them, and how and by what means they be tormented by them, and yet all by-standers whatsomever, neither do hear, see, nor feel any thing, tho' the tormented be able to prove and confirm what they say by the surest tokens imaginable, as by pulling to them in open Air, part of their tormentors garments[63] (none either seeing persons nor vestments but the tormented only,) which how soon they lay hold on they from thence forth become visible, so that all know them to belong to such and such persons, who knew the said Suspected persons to use such habits

[62] 'abscond': hidden.

[63] In the Bargarran case of 1697, Christian Shaw was reported to have pulled some pieces of cloth from the sleeves of Jean Park, one of her 'tormentors'.

formerly: and last of all, I shall give some vive and shrewd Marks, and some unquestionable tokens, as they be recorded in the most approven Authors, how and by what means, a Witch (in League, and Covenant with the Devil) may be decerned to be so, that the innocent may not be condemn'd with the nocent,[64] but that Judgment may trot in an even path, and an easie way be opened for their discovery, either by Confession, Conviction, or Probation, to the Praise, and Glory of God. Thus when I have answered promise, by performance, I shall sum up all with a short Conclusion, and so end.

A Witch in Scripture-account is one who liveth in the dayly Practice, and habitual exercise of Devilish Arts, wherof mention is made in *Exodus* 22.18. *Lev.* 19.26. *Deut.* 18.10,11,12. and a pregnant instance thereof we find recorded[65] anent *Manasseh* King of *Judah*, who sold himself to do wickedly in the sight of the Lord, and for a long time lived in the Practice of Devilish Arts, condemned.[66] Which thing they also do, who are guilty of such horrid impiety: hence then it appears, in what a woful estate they are in, who thus live in continuall commerce with the Devil, in manifest opposition against God, and his Word, whose Sin fast ripens unto Judgement, witness *Pharao*, *Saul* and *Manasseh*; nor is the momentany[67] pleasure here, ever able to counterballance the loss hereafter, the Devil seldom gratifies the man but with the destruction of the Soul, hence is it that the truly Godly never trace these stops, for that they be ranked among the works of the flesh[68] and all such be severely threatned by God, that he will judge them, {*p. 12*} and be a swift witness against them,[69] whoever they be that be guilty of the same, either in professing skil, or using and practicing directly or indirectly, any of the parts and *Species* thereof, whither it be in going to any such for advice, or encouraging them in their Sin by harbour, supplie, or any other countenancing of them, whereby they may be encouraged in their sin; the Hebrew word *Mecashephah*, rendred commonly by us a Witch, signifies properly to deceive, as it were by *Legerdemeen* as did the Sorcerers of *Egypt* in their lieing wonders (whereof formerly) by locking the outward senses, and changing the appearances of things: in Greek it is rendred *Pharmacopeia*, *Gal.* 5.20. that is to say poysoning, or as our translators turn it bewitching; for that all poysoning is comprehended under murther, as a consequent of the same, by the Latins it's called *Fascino*, to deceive, hence you see the harmony of all three, with the reason, for that such Catives as they, not only deceive, poyson, and murther others, but themselves also, in that they be captivat by the Devil at his pleasure, and reserved (as Satan and his angels be) to the Judgment of the

64 'nocent': guilty.

65 *King.* 21 *compared with* 2 *Chr.* 33. (Footnote in original.)

66 *Lev.* 20.6, 27. 1 *Chr.* 10.13. (Footnote in original.)

67 'momentany': transient, momentary.

68 *Gal.* 5.20. (Footnote in original.)

69 *Mal.* 3.5. (Footnote in original.)

great day for their reward, and then shall all such know to their cost what it is to league and make compact with the Devil.

The word *Mecashephah* mentioned before is of the fœminin gender, either for that the woman was by Satan first deceived, or for that that Sex is more readily circumvented, or else for that moe of them than of men be thus deceived, altho there be not wanting men Witches as well as women Witches[70] whose Sin is as hainous, and their Judgement as grievous as is the Judgement and sin of the other: so that whoever they be without respect of Sex or quality, who are guilty of this great sin any manner of way whatsomever, most[71] needs be in a woful and lamentable estate, the black catalogue and roll whereof (that none may pretend ignorance,) be pleased to view as they follow in the several *Species* thereof, having spoken formerly of the Professors hereof.

First, *Hydromancie*, which is a divination by water. 2*ly*, *Aëromancy*, by Air. 3*ly*, *Pyromancy*, by fire. 4*ly*, *Geomancie*, by earth. 5*ly*, *Capniomancy*, by smoak. 6*ly*, *Alectriomancy*, by the crowing of Cocks. 7*ly*, *Psychomancy*, or *Necromancie*, that consult the Dead. 8*ly*, *Alphytomancy*, that divine by the inspection of wheat-flowr. 9*ly*, *Ictuomancie*, by fish. 10*ly*, *Libanomancie*, by Incense. 11*ly*, {*p*. *13*} *Cheiromancy*, by the hands. 12*ly*, *Phisiognomy*, by the face or countenance. 13*ly*, *Gastriomancy*, which is a divination by giving answers forth of the belly, by a familiar spirit, such a one was that *Pythonissa*, mentioned by *Paul*[72] who was acted by the spirit of *Python*, or Divination, throw the Instinct of the Devil, so called from *Pythius Apollo*, the original word *Ob*, signifies a bottle,[73] and is applyed to such as being inspired with a Familiar Spirit spoke with hollow voices forth of their belly, the maner whereof the Prophet *Isaiah* showeth to be with a hollow, slow voice[74] which *Maimonie* in his Treatise of Idolatrie,[75] *cap*. 6. *sect*. 1. Explaineth thus, that he that had this Familiar Spirit, or Spirit of *Python*, stood and burned Incense, and holding a rod of Mirtle-tree in his hand, waved it, and spoke certain words in secret untill he that enquired did hear one speak unto him, and answer him, touching that which he enquired, with words from under the Earth, and with a slow voice: Or else he took a dead mans skull, and burned Incense thereto, and used enchanting and charming words, till he heard a low and slow voice which was *Sauls* sin[76] for the which the Lord slew him[77] and hath threatned to cut of[f] all from among

70 *Lev*. 20.27. (Footnote in original.)
71 *Sic*. Read 'must'.
72 *Act*. 16.16. (Footnote in original.)
73 *Job*. 32.19. (Footnote in original.)
74 *Isa*. 29.4. (Footnote in original.)
75 Moses Maimonides, *De Idololatria Liber* ('Book on Idolatry'), edited and translated by Dionysius Vossius (Amsterdam, 1641, and later editions). Moses Maimonides (1135–1204) was a Jewish philosopher.
76 *Sam*. 28.7.–15. (Footnote in original.)
77 *Chr*. 10.13. (Footnote in original.)

his People, who do enquire of any such.[78] 14*ly*, There is a *Species* of Divination practised by the King of *Babylon*, which seems to have been in use among the Heathen mentioned by *Ezekiel*[79] which was done by inspection of Beasts intrals. 15*ly*, there is a kind of Witchcraft by enchanting spells, or charms, whereby Men, Women, Children, and Beasts, be in their persons, or Goods, hurt or poysoned.[80] 16*ly*, Jugling, when by the Devils conveyance, and a deception of the outward senses, diverse strange and wonderful things are done, not really, but by slight, and in appearance, or external show only.[81] 17*ly*, there is an usual way of fortelling things to come by *Horoscop*, very much in practice now a-days, (specially in *Padua*, and in diverse other places both in *Italie* and *Germany*) whereby they foretell, (by erecting a Sheam[82] of the Heavens, with respect to the Nativity of the Enquirer,) all Events whatsomever, in relation to the question demanded, at the least they give out that so they can do: all which *Species* of {*p. 14*} Divination and Witchcraft, with all that has, or any manner of way may relate thereto is expresly forbidden in the Law of the Lord[83] which is summarily comprised, *Exod*. 22.18.

As to the reasons, why Satan so far unmasks himself at this time, by so palpable and legible discovery of such as be in League and Covenant with himself; We shall shortly sum them up as follows, 1*st*, It may flow from the multitude of Witches, that may possibly be abounding amongst us, and Satans being willing to have such cut off in time, least by a preached Gospel, some be gained.[84] 2*ly*, It may flow from some whited Professors[85] of the truth, being engaged in his service, and his spite to the Gospel, that the immaculate truth might be scandaliz'd through them. 3*ly*, We say, that the shew of the Tormentors, to the tormented, in bodily sort, may be one of Satans Stratagems, whereby he may be afterward enabled, the better to cut off the innocent with the nocent, it being easie for him who is the arch Deceiver and Master-peice of all craft, to make the innocent Lambs of God appear in show among his own Wolves: although with this remarkable difference, that all the powers of darkness, be no way able to make such palpable discovery herein, by the tormenteds laying hold on their garments, as they readily do on the others: which verifies that of the Psalmist, *He that keepeth Israel, neither slumbers nor sleeps*.[86] For the presence of the one is meerly Phantastical, and the other more real, and while as they be not seen to all by-standers but to the tormented

78 *Lev*. 20.6. (Footnote in original.)
79 *Ezek*. 21. *vers*. 21. (Footnote in original.)
80 *Act*. 8.9,10. 19.13. *Eccl*. 10.11. (Footnote in original.)
81 *Exod*. 7, 8, 9, 10. (Footnote in original.)
82 'Sheam' (scheme): diagram or horoscope.
83 *Deut*. 18.10,11,12. (Footnote in original.)
84 The argument seems to be that the Devil wants his witches to be executed, fearing that they might otherwise be reconverted to Christianity through hearing sermons.
85 'whited Professors': persons falsely professing Christian belief. Cf. Matthew 23:27.
86 Psalm 121:4.

only, you must know that it's a[n] easie thing for Satan to open the eyes of one, and restrain the sight of another.

Now that we may draw to a close, we shall in the next place give you some vive and shrewd marks, or some evident and probable tokens, whereby a Witch, or such as have made express League and Compact with the Devil, may be decerned from all others.

The first whereof, is the insensible or dead nip of a blea[87] colour somewhat hard, and withall insensible, which for that it's known to many, I shall not insist much on it, only give me leave to say, that what way so ever, whither by accident, or otherways, such insensible marks be in the body, yet no such mark as theirs every circumstance considered, is to be found with any others but themselves, neither can ignorance how they come by it, or their getting of it when infant from their {*p. 15*} nurce, plead any excuse, it being no way probable that a Witch can have any such power from the Devil.[88]

The *Second* mark is, that such can by no means be drowned, tho' tyed hand and foot together, and thrown into a River; perhaps either for that they be destinat for another Element,[89] or els for that they having renunced Baptism, the external Sacramental sign whereof is water, they be rejected and spurned against by this Element, by a Divine Destination and a secret fence and Arreist of a supream overruling Providence, which contrair to a common Course of Nature, hath put a stop to that light and fluide Body of Water, whereby it by no means can receive into it the Body of a Witch, tho' in its self gravanimous[90] and heavie.

The *Third* Mark is, that there can nothing befall them in time, (how heavie and afflicting soever) no not though the torture it self were made use of,) draw from them the least tear, though to that end they often distort, throw,[91] and wring their faces, making as tho' they were weeping, which is the more remarkable, especially in Women, for that such ordinarily carrie a bowl of tears in their head, which in Crocadell form they can let fall, upon very slight and momentuous[92] occasion: God by special Providence denying them tears, the ordinary consequent and external sign of Repentance, to

87 'blae': dark blue or livid.

88 The argument is that the Devil cannot give a *witch* the power to place the Devil's mark on an innocent person. Usually it was thought to be the Devil himself who marked the witch, but here the context is a discussion of the possibility of an infant being dedicated to the Devil by their 'nurce'. The *Malleus Maleficarum* (1486) had argued that midwives who were witches could dedicate children to the Devil at birth; these children thereby acquired witchcraft powers, but were not strictly witches, and could be reclaimed by being re-baptised. See *The Hammer of Witches: A Complete Translation of the 'Malleus Maleficarum'*, 2 vols., trans. Christopher S. Mackay (Cambridge, 2009), ii, pp. 321–7 (translation), fos. 138C–141D (question II.1.13).

89 'another Element': the fire in which they will be burned in hell.

90 *Sic*. 'Gravaminous': cumbrous.

91 'throw' (thraw): twist.

92 'momentuous': momentary.

whom he hath denyed the internal Grace, altho' it cannot be denyed but that the wicked may seek a blessing, as did the prophane *Esau* with tears,[93] hence you see upon what account tears be denyed to Witches altho' not to other Reprobates, for tho' these be in some sense at an agreement with Satan, Sin, and Hell, yet is their Covenant and League not so express, as is the League and Covenant of the other.

The *Fourth* Mark is, the Balsilisk,[94] or Serpentine sight, wherewith they be endued to kill, poyson, and destroy, what, and whensoever they please, were it not that a Divine overruling providence doth often restrain and curb them, which sight is in them above all other men and women in the world most remarkable, for while as in the Aple of the Eye there is to be seen in all and every one, the Image of a man (commonly called the babe in the eye) with the head up and the feet down; the quite contrair is to be seen in them, to wit, the feet up, and the head down; God as it were hereby making open show {*p. 16*} to the World, that He who keepeth His own as the Apple of the eye,[95] taketh no such thought for the Slaves of Satan, but suffers the Devil whose Image they bear thus (by inversion) as an external Sign) [*sic*] to portray his Image in them, upon which account a Witch whither Man or Woman will not look on fixedly or stedfastly in the face, namely, if they be adverting.[96]

In the original Hebrew this Image in the Eye is called ISHON, the little man, or the black of the Eye. Or else it is called Bath or Babath the Apple of the Eye, or the Daughter of the Eye, both which be made mention of by the Psalmist David,[97] while as in other places one only of the said words be used as ISHON the little Man or Black of the Eye.[98] Babath or Bath the Apple of the Eye, or the Daughter[99] the Black being the only Organ of sight, and the Apple of the Eye the Daughter as it were of that Organ. For Bath or Babath signifies a Daughter, as said is, and it serves for a munition and defence to ISHON the little Man or Black of the Eye, the true Organ of sight; from hence is it that the Comparison is drawn of Gods defending and keeping his People as the Black or Apple of the Eye, while as of Satans imps he hath no such care, as said is.

The Fifth Mark is, that a Witch will by no means be perswaded to repeat, the heads of the Christian Religion, as they be summarly comprehended in

93 Cf. Genesis 27:34.

94 *Sic.* A basilisk was a legendary creature, a cross between a cock and a serpent, that could kill with its gaze.

95 Cf. Psalm 17:8.

96 'adverting': paying attention. From this point onwards, the text shifts to a much smaller typeface, the compositor evidently intending to cram all the rest of the text onto one page. This saved the pamphlet from exceeding sixteen octavo pages, the maximum that could be printed from a single sheet of paper.

97 *Psal.* 17.8. (Footnote in original.)

98 *Deut.* 32.10. *Prov.* 7.2. (Footnote in original.)

99 *Lam.* 2.18. *Zech.* 2.8. (Footnote in original.)

the Decalogue, Lords Prayer, and Belief,[100] but with severa[l] minchings,[101] eikings,[102] or inversions, which is certainly worth the marking; nor can their Ignorance, or Bashfulness, plead any excuse, for whether it be before a multitude, or a fewer number, they will neither of themselves, nor by following another, by any means be engaged to repeat the Words in Form and Order as they are.

The Sixth Mark is, That if you put any great or gross Salt in the Pipe of a Kye,[103] and put all into the Fire, upon hearing the crackling, and seeing the blewish low[104] thereof, which is like that of Brimstone, instantly they shall let go their Urine; but whither this flows from an inward passion and stupifaction of mind, that upon hearing the crackling, and seeing the Blewish Low foresaid they be brought to remember the horrible noise and Sulphurious burning that is abiding them in Hell, at the Judgment of the great Day, when Soul and Body shall be joyned together in one, and for ever and ever made lyable to the Wrath of the Everliving God, or on what other account as yet I know not, however as I am duely informed the mark is no less true than strange.

Seventhly, There are not wanting some who be bold to averr, that a Witch may be known from a peculiar sent or smell, which is to be found in them, beside[105] all other People in the World, and which neither flows from the nestiness of Cloaths, Vermine, or the like, but a contradistinct smell from any such thing, which may seem the more probable for that the five Senses being the Doors of the Soul whereby what is within is ordinarly disclosed, and the Devil being in full Possession of their Soul, must needs emitte his own sent even that of the Pit.

Now from what is said, it plainly appears, how watchfull and circumspect we ought to be, that we be not carried about with every wind of Doctrine, either to gainstand the Truth, or receive a lie, in this so guileful and perverse an Age, wherein notwithstanding of the manifold opportunities of Grace, Sin hath the ascendent over us, hence Impiety and Transgression of all kind, doth flow down as a mighty stream, to the great Scandal of our holy Profession, few giving themselves to the Exercise and Practice of Godliness, or bringing forth the Fruits thereof in newness of Life: Hence is it that Satan so mightily prevails amongst us, and still is like to do, except[106] we set our selves against his Wiles, and wicked Devices, by an Holy and tender Walk, in all Humility and

100 The 'Decalogue' was the Ten Commandments; the 'Belief' was the Creed, probably the Apostles' Creed.

101 'minchings': omissions.

102 'eikings': additions.

103 'Pipe of a Kye': a pipe-key was a metal key with a hollow stem, fitting over a pin in the lock. Here the hollow stem is used to contain the salt.

104 'low': flame. The author has previously mentioned the Devil's use of 'black candles with a blew Low'.

105 'beside': unlike, apart from.

106 'except': unless.

Godly Fear, putting on the Spiritual Armour, whereby we shall be enabled to quench all the fiery Darts of the Devil.

For this end let us beg from the Hand of our God, who is a liberal Giver, quickning and supporting Grace, in time of need, and to learn from the fall of others, that our standing is not in our selves, but in the free mercy and supporting Grace of God, who by a continual watching Eye of Providence, preserves us every moment, which is the only cause, why we are not consumed long ere now, unto whom let us in all Humility recommend our selves for Direction and Protection, that we may be safe and secure, while we be travellours of hope, passing through this vale of misery towards our end in eternal Felicity, where we shall be ever with the Lord, World without end, Amen. FINIS.

5. *A RELATION OF THE DIABOLICAL PRACTICES OF ABOVE TWENTY WIZARDS AND WITCHES OF THE SHERIFFDOM OF RENFREW*, 1697

INTRODUCTION

This is the first of three texts in this volume about the witchcraft trials that arose from the alleged demonic possession of Christian Shaw, daughter of the laird of Bargarran in Renfrewshire. Christian was aged 10 when in August 1696 she began to experience convulsions ('fits') and other bizarre behaviour. Over the next several months she named several people who were 'tormenting' her through witchcraft. Judicial investigations began early in 1697; eventually seven witches were brought to trial at Paisley in April and May. All were convicted, and executed on 10 June; an eighth suspect had previously committed suicide in prison. A more detailed discussion of the case is given in the introduction to the third and longest of the texts, the *True Narrative of the Sufferings and Relief of a Young Girle* (1698), below. The trial records themselves have been published in the companion volume to the present one, where a further discussion of the case will also be found.[1] The present introduction, meanwhile, focuses on the specific features of the *Relation of the Diabolical Practices* itself, and the ways in which it resembles, and differs from, the two texts that follow it in the present volume – the 'Bargarran Witches' manuscript and the *True Narrative*.

The *Relation* is much shorter than the better-known *True Narrative*, but it has its own independent value. It deals mainly with two specific early phases in the proceedings: the gathering of evidence against the suspects in February 1697 at Bargarran and Renfrew, and the beginning of the trial proceedings in April 1697 at Paisley. After seven or eight months, Christian Shaw's possessed behaviour was now coming to an end. The bulk of the *Relation* consists of copies of documents produced in February. The *Relation* then skates much more briefly over the later trial proceedings, though it does mention the convictions in May and the seven executions that ensued in June. Dated

1 Julian Goodare and Liv Helene Willumsen (eds.), *Scottish Witchcraft Trials* (Woodbridge: SHS, 2025), 567–635.

1697, it seems to have been printed soon after the executions, and expects that further trials and executions will follow. As an unpolished assemblage of documents, it gives the impression of having been rushed into print. It was issued by a London printer, but there seems to be little attempt to add local colour for a distant metropolitan readership. Even the word 'Scotland', though it appears on the title page, is absent from the text. The word 'Wizards', too, appears only in the title.

The author identifies himself as 'T. P.' He was clearly Scottish, despite the London publication of his work; his text contains Scotticisms such as 'other twa' and 'thir Words'. The main indication of his identity is that he was associated with the trial commissioners in some unspecified but probably junior capacity: he was 'with the Commissioners on the Tryall' (p. 3). Perhaps he was a servant or legal adviser to one of the commissioners.

This trial commission was the second of two commissions in the case. A previous enquiry commission had been appointed by the privy council on 19 January, not to hold a trial but to gather evidence and to report back.[2] As the *Relation* itself shows, the enquiry commission held two meetings at which written statements were taken: at Bargarran on 5 February, and at Renfrew on 18 February. The enquiry commission then made a 'verball report' to the privy council on 25 February, whereupon the council recommended the king's advocate, Sir James Steuart of Goodtrees, 'to Cause bring to Edinburgh all such persones as he Finds by the report from the Commissioners that he has sufficient probation of uitchcraft and malifice against', and to obtain written evidence from the enquiry commission, with a view to holding trials in the court of justiciary in Edinburgh.[3] However, this plan for trials in Edinburgh was soon changed. On 9 March the council instead issued a commission of justiciary to thirteen named commissioners who would hold the trial locally, with their first meeting to be at Renfrew on 18 March.[4]

The trial commission thus held a preliminary meeting to constitute the court at Renfrew on 18 March, as they had been instructed, but then moved the proceedings to Paisley. The first real business meeting of the court, with the accused persons present, was in Paisley on 14 April.[5] T. P., who seems to have been present at this meeting, calls it 'the first *Dyet* of the *Tryall*' (p. 3). He describes several events around this time as an eyewitness: interrogations of the suspects to get them to confess, and a session of pricking to find the Devil's mark. No confessions were extracted, but the prickers found marks on most of the suspects. T. P. takes particular interest in the stripping naked of Martha Sempill, a 'well *Favourd*' lass aged 17 or 18, for this purpose (p. 4).

2 SPCR, A1697/1/17.
3 SPCR, A1697/2/44.
4 SPCR, A1697/3/11.
5 Goodare and Willumsen (eds.), *Scottish Witchcraft Trials*, 571–2.

His account of pricking is unusually detailed. Later, however, T. P.'s account becomes more sketchy, and he may no longer have been present in person in May or June.

Only the first section of the *Relation* is T. P.'s own text – an introduction, or, as the publishing convention would have it, a covering letter. The bulk of the text consists of copies of six documents, all from February 1697. The first five of these had been produced by the previous enquiry commission. No doubt the enquiry commission's documents were available to the trial commission.

The *Relation*'s initial document is thus a report of the enquiry commission, narrating the evidence that they have gathered – a 'narrative of the precognitions taken by the commissioners', as the document should have been headed, since 'precognitions' were statements taken down from witnesses in connection with a forthcoming criminal trial. The London printer, presumably unfamiliar with the Scots word 'precognition', introduces confusion by calling the report a 'narrative of the recognition of the commissioners'. Still, it soon becomes apparent that the commissioners have examined a number of different suspects and other witnesses, several of whom have been confronted with Christian Shaw herself. The first such person mentioned is James Lindsay, but the commissioners soon shift their attention to Katherine Campbell, the maidservant whose curse had triggered the onset of Christian's fits. They then interrogate Elizabeth Anderson, and gather a large number of names of further suspects.

Katherine Campbell was always thought of as a witch, and she was eventually one of those executed. But only a small proportion of the testimony came from suspects like her. The other four documents from the enquiry commission came from three young people – 'the three *little Confessors*' as T. P. calls them (p. 3) – who were intially suspected as witches but who were converted into star witnesses for the prosecution. These were Elizabeth Anderson, aged about 15, 16 or 17, described as 'a very Useful Person in the said Enquiry' (p. 6), and her two cousins, James Lindsay, aged about 14, and his younger brother Thomas Lindsay. All three were indeed useful, because they could testify about having attended witches' meetings and having witnessed bewitchings, without being considered guilty themselves – a tacit agreement seems to have arisen that they had been coerced into particpating and had not made a pact with the Devil. But James Lindsay was only just old enough to testify on oath (the minimum age was 14, and the defence at the trial would object that James seemed to be younger), while Thomas Lindsay, though imaginative, was never thought to be old enough to do so. Elizabeth Anderson's detailed and articulate testimony, however, carried legal weight. She made her first confession to the enquiry commission at Bargarran on 5 February, and then a further confession at Renfrew on 18 February. This was followed by statements by James Lindsay and Thomas Lindsay. These statements constitute the *Relation*'s second, third, fourth and fifth documents.

Finally, as his sixth document, T. P. prints a letter from Christian Shaw's mother, Christian McGilchrist, to her husband, John Shaw of Bargarran, also dated 18 February 1697. This describes a recent episode of Christian Shaw's affliction. McGilchrist's letter reads like an early draft of an episode in the main 'Narrative' of the affliction, of which T. P. appears to have been unaware. A version of this 'Narrative', with an expanded version of this episode, would be published by the *True Narrative* in 1698, while another version of it is found in the 'Bargarran Witches' manuscript.

The *Relation*'s documents overlap in places with the 'Bargarran Witches' manuscript, which is edited below as the second of the three Bargarran-related texts in the present volume. This manuscript, as explained in the introduction to it below, was probably compiled during the proceedings by John Shaw of Bargarran. Among other things, the manuscript contains versions of four of the six documents printed by the *Relation*: the initial 'precognition', the second of Elizabeth Anderson's confessions, and the confessions of her two Lindsay cousins. The present edition prints all these documents in the *Relation*'s version, with footnotes giving variations and additional information from the manuscript version. The *Relation* itself is thus printed in full here. The 'Bargarran Witches' manuscript also has further material from the enquiry commission, which should be read alongside the *Relation*'s material.

There exists a third version of the report of the enquiry commission, which also overlaps considerably with the *Relation*. This is a 20-page manuscript in the National Library of Scotland, with the title 'Fallowes ane accompt of the precognitione taken by the commissioners appointed by the lords of his majesties privie cownsell for makeing inquirie anent the witches and witchcroft [*sic*] within the sheriffdome of Renffrew particularlie anent the afflicted case of Christen Shaw daughter to the laird of Bargarran'.[6] It comprises eight items: (1) the text of the commission itself; (2) a minute of the commissioners' meeting at Bargarran, 5 February 1697; (3) Elizabeth Anderson's first confession; (4) a minute of the commissioners' meeting at Renfrew, 18 February 1697; (5) Elizabeth Anderson's second confession; (6) James Lindsay's confession; (7) Thomas Lindsay's confession; (8) Christian McGilchrist's letter. This NLS version of the report is not edited here, as almost all of its contents are the same as the *Relation* or the 'Bargarran Witches' manuscript or both, with only small verbal differences.[7] However, the way in which this version combines its material is interesting. Its inclusion of Christian McGilchrist's letter shows

6 National Library of Scotland, Acc. 6687, no. 9.

7 These items are edited here in the *Relation*'s version, except for items numbered 1 and 4, which are absent from the *Relation* and are edited here in the 'Bargarran Witches' manuscript's version. Where the *Relation* and the 'Bargarran Witches' manuscript differ, NLS, Acc. 6687, no. 9 is usually closer to the *Relation*, though that does not necessarily make them more correct.

that this letter was formally submitted to the enquiry commission and was not just an extra document that T. P. added. One additional paragraph in the NLS version will be discussed later in this volume, in the introduction to the *True Narrative*, as it sheds light on the development of the 'Narrative'.

Turning now to a comparison between the *Relation*'s material and the 1698 *True Narrative*, we find that the latter includes some of the *Relation*'s material, but only in abbreviated form. The *True Narrative* gives abbreviated versions of the commission's report itself, of Anderson's second statement, and of the two Lindsays' statements. It omits Anderson's first statement and McGilchrist's letter. An analysis of the way in which the *True Narrative* selected and condensed its material might reveal something of its priorities, while the *Relation*'s more detailed account is clearly of value. The *Relation* names several names not found in the *True Narrative*. The *Relation* also pays less attention to Christian Shaw and more attention to the various other malefices of which the witches were accused.

It may thus be helpful to summarise these other alleged malefices. The witches were accused of having killed four children: those of William Fleming, minister of Inverkip, John Ritchie, minister of Kilpatrick, Matthew Park in Parkland, and James Miller in Erskine. They had killed John Hardie, minister of Dumbarton, who had died of a strange and violent disease in January 1696. And they had sunk the ferryboat of Erskine round about that time, drowning George Cunningham of Brighouse and the ferryman John Glen.[8]

The *Relation* has important information on this last point, telling that the young Thomas Lindsay described a witches' meeting to plan the sinking of the ferryboat. Lindsay's story was that a number of witches met to plan the sinking a few weeks before it happened. He listed 23 names of witches, of whom most but not all would reappear in the Bargarran case itself. However, Lindsay related that two of the witches, Janet Ker and Janet Wodrow, were then arrested, so that they were already in prison at the time when the other witches sank the boat. This story, though presumably a fantasy in its elaborated form, was constructed around at least some real events. It may help to sketch some of these events, in the hope that further research will be able to connect the Bargarran case with earlier witchcraft prosecutions in the area.

On 3 March 1696, the privy council granted a commission of justiciary to try Janet Wodrow in Kilmacolm for witchcraft. This commission did not specify the nature of her crimes beyond mentioning that she had 'comitted severall Malfices', but the assumption seems to have been that she would be found guilty and executed. The commissioners were William Cunningham of Craigends, Alexander Porterfield of Duchal, William Muir of Glanderston, Robert Sempill, sheriff depute of Renfrew, John Crawford of Milton, John

8 The fullest account of these malefices, fictionalised but well researched, is in Isabel Adam, *Witch Hunt: The Great Scottish Witchcraft Trials of 1697* (London, 1978), 77–85, 178–9.

Caldwell of that Ilk and Alexander Porterfield of Fulwood.[9] All of these men except Crawford would become involved in the Bargarran case.[10] When Wodrow was interrogated, she named several other names, so the presbytery lobbied the privy council for an extension to the commission of justiciary.[11] The council granted this on 7 May, authorising the commissioners to try, not only Wodrow, but also those whom Wodrow had named as witches. A limiting clause was added to the commission, requiring the commissioners to report back to the privy council before they put any sentence into effect.[12] No such report seems ever to have been made, which may indicate that the trials were never brought to a conclusion. Indeed, the presbytery complained on 22 July that several of the commissioners 'did not accept' their commission, thus frustrating the prosecutions at least temporarily.[13] On 28 July, at the presbytery's request, the council appointed some additional commissioners: John Alexander of Blackhouse, Thomas Crawford of Crawfordsburn and Gavin Cochrane of Craigmuir. One of the existing commissioners, Robert Sempill, sheriff depute of Renfrew, was required to be one of the quorum; he would later be one of those who tried the Bargarran witches, and may well have been important in co-ordinating the prosecutions.[14]

Two other earlier witchcraft suspects to bear in mind came from Elizabeth Anderson's family. Elizabeth's father, Alexander Anderson, features prominently in the *Relation*'s documents from February 1697, but he died shortly afterwards in prison; the trial record mentions him as 'umquhile [i.e. the late] Alexander Anderson in Bowes of Inchinand'.[15] Then there was Jean Fulton, also from the parish of Inchinnan, grandmother of Elizabeth Anderson and her two Lindsay cousins. She was under suspicion of witchcraft already on 5 February 1696, and the presbytery heard on 11 March that two ministers had gathered evidence concerning her.[16] The *Relation* shows that the enquiry commission heard a good deal about Jean Fulton, and was told that she had died about a year earlier in Paisley tolbooth while under suspicion of witchcraft; presumably this was not long after 11 March. So witchcraft fears had been ignited into prosecution initiatives in at least four Renfrewshire parishes – Inchinnan, Kilmacolm and (as we shall see in a moment) Greenock, as well as Erskine itself – shortly before Christian Shaw's fits commenced in Erskine parish. And malefices had been reported in other parishes too: Inverkip, and

9 SPCR, A1696/3/15.
10 Some of the Bargarran commissioners are discussed in Adam, *Witch Hunt*, 56–7.
11 NRS, Minutes of Presbytery of Paisley, 1660–1699, CH2/294/4, p. 223.
12 SPCR, A1696/5/19.
13 NRS, Minutes of Presbytery of Paisley, 1660–1699, CH2/294/4, p. 231.
14 SPCR, A1696/7/46.
15 Goodare and Willumsen (eds.), *Scottish Witchcraft Trials*, 604, 633.
16 NRS, Minutes of Presbytery of Paisley, 1660–1699, CH2/294/4, p. 223.

(north of the Clyde) Kilpatrick and Dumbarton. Further investigation of these earlier events might well reveal more of the background to the panic.

One of the key witchcraft suspects in the *Relation* is Mary Morrison, the wife of Francis Duncan, merchant and skipper in Greenock. As a 'gentlewoman', Morrison was an important suspect – but well-connected people were harder to prosecute. Most earlier prosecutions of 'rich witches' had failed in Scotland.[17] The prosecutors of 1697 seem to have intended to work their way up to Morrison gradually, beginning with other witches who were easer to prosecute. Morrison emerges first in the *Relation* as one of the witches in a gathering, as 'ane Gentlewife called by them Antiochia' (p. 10). The name 'Antiochia' seems to derive from Elizabeth Anderson's first statement, though it is T. P. himself who links it with Morrison's real name. The meaning of 'Antiochia' in this context is obscure; it seems to be a learned name rather than a product of folk culture, though it could be a learned misunderstanding of a word spoken by Anderson.[18] Neither the *True Narrative* nor the trial record mention the name, though it appears in the 'Bargarran Witches' manuscript. As for Morrison herself, T. P. seems to assume her guilt and to expect that she and others will soon be prosecuted. The *True Narrative* ostentatiously anonymised her, but also hoped to *encourage* further prosecutions, perhaps because the momentum had slowed by the time this latter work went into print.

Another way to compare the *Relation* and the *True Narrative* is to look at what the latter said about the former – or may have said about it. The editor of the *True Narrative* denounced a 'late Scurrilous Pamphlet, that has been printed in *England*', claiming aggressively but vaguely that this former pamphlet lacked 'good *Language*, *Sense*, or *Truth*'.[19] Was this pamphlet the *Relation*? When the *True Narrative* was being published in 1698, the *Relation* (dated 1697) is likely to have been available; and it had indeed been printed in England. And there is no other known candidate – no other extant pamphlet on the case (whether 'Scurrilous' or not) that the *True Narrative* could have been citing. On the other hand, the content of the *Relation* offers no clue as to why the *True Narrative*'s editor could have objected to it. Both works supported the recent prosecutions and hoped for more prosecutions, for instance. And the *Relation* was issued by the same London publisher, Hugh Newman, who

17 Louise Yeoman, 'Hunting the Rich Witch in Scotland: High-Status Witchcraft Suspects and their Persecutors, 1590–1650', in Julian Goodare (ed.), *The Scottish Witch-Hunt in Context* (Manchester, 2002), 106–21.

18 'Antiochia' was the Latin version of the placename Antioch, often mentioned in the Bible. However, it does not seem to have been a widely-recognised personal name. The name is further discussed by Joyce Miller, 'Men in Black: Appearances of the Devil in Early Modern Scottish Witchcraft Discourse', in Julian Goodare, Lauren Martin and Joyce Miller (eds.), *Witchcraft and Belief in Early Modern Scotland* (Basingstoke, 2008), 144–165, at pp. 155, 163–4.

19 See the edition of the *True Narrative*, below, at p. 2 of the original text. In addition, the preface to the *True Narrative* complained of 'such ridiculous Pamphlets as no doubt by the Instigation of Satan, have lately been sent abroad' (p. ix).

would later be employed by the *True Narrative*'s own promoters when the latter issued a revised version of their own work under the title *Sadducismus Debellatus*.[20] Perhaps the 'Scurrilous Pamphlet' was a different work, now no longer extant. The 'Bargarran Witches' manuscript, edited below, contains a tract by James Williamson that criticises the evidence used for the prosecutions; this is not known to have been issued in printed form, either in England or anywhere else, but it does show that critical voices could be raised. The 'Scurrilous Pamphlet' thus remains a mystery.

The *True Narrative*'s denunciation led Isabel Adam to the perhaps premature conclusion that T. P.'s *Relation* was a 'maverick' publication, to be contrasted with the 'official' *True Narrative*. This in turn led her to construct a speculative account of how T. P. acquired Christian McGilchrist's letter in an underhand way.[21] There is, however, no evidence that T. P. acquired the letter by underhand means, and indeed it is far from clear that his intentions were at variance with those of the *True Narrative*. The reader of the *Relation* and the *True Narrative*, indeed, must be struck by the similarities between the two works in their overall approach to the dramatic emergence of the threat of witchcraft in the west of Scotland.

In the edition below, a few unimportant typographical errors, such as 'Advocatrs' (p. 4), or 'where where' (for 'where were', p. 12), have been corrected silently.

TEXT[22]

A Relation of the Diabolical Practices of above Twenty Wizards and Witches of the Sheriffdom of Renfrew in the Kingdom of Scotland,

Contain'd, In their Tryalls, Examinations, and Confessions; And for which several of them have been Executed this Present Year, 1697.

London, Printed for Hugh Newman at the Grashopper in the Poultry. {*p. 2 blank*} {*p. 3*}

To Sir T. M.[23]

SIR, According to your Request, I send you Inclos'd the Proceedings of the Commissioners appointed by the Lords of His Majestys most Honourable Privy Councill, for enquiring into the *Witches* and *Witchcrafts* in the Shiriffdome

[20] The editorial introduction to the *True Narrative*, below, includes a discussion of *Sadducismus Debellatus*.

[21] Adam, *Witch Hunt*, 100, 241–2.

[22] Source: *A Relation of the Diabolical Practices of above Twenty Wizards and Witches of the Sheriffdom of Renfrew in the Kingdom of Scotland* (London: Hugh Newman, 1697; ESTC no. R3963).

[23] This person has not been identified, and may have had no direct connection with the case. It was conventional to present a published narrative as some kind of letter, and 'Sir T. M.' is merely the addressee of this imagined letter.

of *Renfrew*, of which I have had Opportunity of knowing more than many others, as having been with the Commissioners on the Tryalls; And shall add nothing here, save what passed at the first *Dyet* of the *Tryall*, which was at *Paislaw* [*sic*], where were Met of the Commissioners, my Lord *Blantyre*, my Lord *Halcraig*, Sir *John Maxwell* of *Polock*, Mr. *Francis Montgomery*, *Blackhall*, *Duchall*, with several others, to the Number of Eleven.[24] There was Deputed in the room of the King's Advocate, Three Advocates, *viz*. Mr. *John Menzies*, Mr. *Grant* and Mr. *Stuart*.[25] The *Panalls* being 21 in number, were frequently call'd to see if they could be brought to Confession; They were Confronted with *Bargarens* Daughter, and the three *little Confessors*, *Elizabeth Anderson*, and the two *Lindsays*. But they still deny'd all: which put the Court to Cull out 7 of them, against whom *Threatnings*, and some *Malifice* following could be proven. These were *Margaret Lang*, in *Cartinpan*, a Woman Famous for *Religion*, ever since the 60 year of God,[26] and really a Person of extraordinary *Gravity* and *Wisdom*; I know not whether to call it *Natural* or *Diabolical*; but I have never heard a Woman speak so *Gravely*, *Pertinently*, and *Religiously* both to the *Ministers* and *Judges* then she did. The other were *Katharine Campbell*, *Agnes Nasmith*, *John* and *James Lindsays*, *Agnes Fostur*,[27] and *Margaret Fulton*: This *Kate Cambell* is a young Well-favour'd Lass, 20 years of Age; but the rest most part Old, both Men and Women.

The Commissioners, after their first Assay to have them confess, before they brought them to a Formal Tryal, would have them Try'd by Pricking, which really to me seems strange, for there was not any of them, save *Margaret Fulton*, but *Marks* were found on them, which were altogether *Incensible*, That a Needle of 3 Inches length was frequently put in without their Knowledge, nor would any blood come from these places, and tho many, especially *Doctors*, ridicul'd these as *Storys*, yet after we cal'd Dr. *Bisbin* and *Baird*,[28] and let them

24 Twelve commissioners took part in the trial: Alexander Stewart, fifth Lord Blantyre, Sir John Hamilton of Halcraig, Sir John Maxwell of Pollok, Mr Francis Montgomery of Giffen, Mr John Stewart younger of Blackhall, John Alexander of Blackhouse, Alexander Porterfield of that Ilk (or of Duchal), John Houston of that Ilk, William Muir of Glanderston, Robert Sempill sheriff depute of Renfrew, John Shaw of Greenock and Mr James Smollett commissary of Edinburgh. See the trial record in Goodare and Willumsen (eds.), *Scottish Witchcraft Trials*, 571–2. A thirteenth commissioner, Mr John Kincaid of Crossbasket, advocate, had been named in the commission of 9 March but seems not to have acted.

25 The prosecuting advocates, named in the commission of 9 March, were Mr John Menzies, Mr Francis Grant and Mr James Stewart. Grant seems to have done almost all the work.

26 'the 60 year of God': 1660.

27 *Sic*. This name is evidently an error for Angus Forrester, one of the suspects against whom charges were dropped, so he should not appear in this list. Forrester is the 'Highland Body' who is later mentioned several times in the *Relation*. Here, however, T. P. has omitted John Lindsay in Barloch, one of the seven who *were* eventually prosecuted.

28 Dr Matthew Brisbane had previously examined Christian Shaw in Glasgow; 'Dr Baird' has not been identified. T. P.'s account of the pricking should be compared with the detailed official report about it, written by James Brisbane, minister of Kilmacolm: Goodare and Willumsen (eds.), *Scottish Witchcraft Trials*, 610–11. That report does not mention either of these 'doctors' as witnesses, but Matthew Brisbane did submit a separate statement in

see a Needle {*p. 4*} of a great length put into the top of one of the *Vertibræ* of the Back, and one into *Margaret Lang*, a handbreadth beneath her Ribbs in the Region of the Lower Belly, they both thought it wonderful, being in a place where, in another Woman, the Needle could not but peirce the Gutts: All the other 14 were also prickt and marks found in most of them. But I was most concern'd for *Martha Semple* Daughter to *Margaret Lang*, who was most exactly search'd twice, yet no mark found; tho the pricker mist not to search the very *Soles* of her *Feet* and other more *Secret Places*, for when there was any difficulty to find the mark they did quite uncloath them, but then it was in a Room, and not publickly, before one or two of the *Justices*, a *Minister*, one of the *Advocates*, and the *Clark*, my Lord *Halcraig* and I were only present with *Martha*; but realy she is as well *Favourd* and *Gentile* a Lass as you'l look on, and about 17 or 18 years of Age, I took up Mr. *Wylie*[29] to her to see if he could bring her to any Confession, he spoke long to her but she deny'd all notwithstanding of what you see in the Encloased paper, but she was the only person amongst them all that ever I saw Weep.

They were at last on the 15*th*. of *April* to have been brought to their Tryall, after 3 or 4 days trifling with them by pricking, and to bring some of them to Confession, but just as the Assize was constitute they mov'd to have a little more time to provide themselves *Advocates*, which the *Justices* yeilded to, and adjourn'd to the 2*d*. *Tuesday* of *May*, and in this Interval the two Brothers did Confess,[30] and upon Examination said the same things that the two *Lindsays* and *Anderson* had declared, as you have it in the within Paper. Another Man also confes'd, But the *Devil* Strangled him in Prison, for he was found sitting in a Chair with a Cord about his Neck but slack and ty'd to no thing.[31] After the Adjournment the *Judges* met again, and having Sufficient Evidence of several *Mallefices* done by each of the Seaven above-named, with the Testimonys of

---

which he mentioned having witnessed the pricking of Margaret Fulton: ibid., 596–7. T. P.'s statement that no mark was found on Fulton is contradicted not only by this statement but also by the official report itself. However, neither of these documents mentions Martha Sempill, so it seems that T. P. is correct in stating that no mark was found on her.

29 Robert Wylie, minister of Hamilton, was 'witness to their proceeding' at this investigation, and later wrote a long letter defending the prosecutions: David Laing (ed.), 'An Original Letter to the Laird of Wishaw (now presented to the Museum), relating to the proceedings against James Aikenhead "the Atheist," and the trial of witches in Paisley in 1696', *Proceedings of the Society of Antiquaries of Scotland*, 11 (1874–76), 438–45, at p. 440.

30 This might refer to the two brothers who were eventually executed, James Lindsay alias Curate and John Lindsay alias Bishop. However, there seems to be no other reference to their having confessed. Perhaps T. P. has confused them with the young brothers James Lindsay and Thomas Lindsay, but they are mentioned separately as 'the two *Lindsays*' later in this same sentence. A perhaps more likely source of confusion is that the court did receive late confessions, around this time, from Janet Rodger and Margaret Rodger, who were sisters. The court added their confessions to those of 'the two *Lindsays* and *Anderson*' in the way that T. P. describes here, and T. P. himself groups them together later in his text.

31 This was John Reid, who hanged himself in prison on 21 May. There is more about him in the 'Bargarran Witches' manuscript and the *True Narrative*, later in the present volume.

the five Confessing *Witches*,[32] all concuring in the same Acts, Sentenc'd them to be burn'd the 10*th*. of *June*, which was accordingly Executed. The other 14 being Respited till the *Kings* Advocates Pleasure, among whom is one *Morison* Wife to *Francis Duncan in Greenock* call'd in the paper the *Devils Gentlewife Antiochia*, on whom many marks are found; of which you'l receive further Information by the Incloas'd to which I referr you, and am, Sir,

Your much oblig'd Humble Servant, T. P. {*p*. 5}

A NARATIVE Of the *RECOGNITION*[33] Taken by the *Commissioners*, Appointed by the *Lords of His Majesties Privy-Council*, for Enquiring into the *Witchcrafts*, and *Witches*, in the *Shirrifdom* of *Renfrew*; with Relation to the Afflicted Case of *Christian Shaw*, Daughter to the Laird of *Bargarren*. At the Place of *Bargarren*, *Feb*. 5. 1697.

Present, the Lord *Blantyre*, &c.[34]

The said *Christian Shaw*, being Confronted with one *James Lindsay* (whom *Elizabeth Anderson*, one of the Confessing *Witches* Under-written Declared, Was one of the said *Christians* Troublers in her Fits) Did, upon {*p*. 6} Touching the said *James*, take a very Violent Fit, Leaping, Starting and Staring, with such a Stiffning of all her Joynts, that it was hard for the Assistants to keep her from Falling, and, at last, fell, as quite Dead, and Senseless, for some time; and, after Recovery, being Confronted with one *Catherine Campbell*, who being once Servant to her *Father*, for a Mis-representation of her to her Mistress, *Curst her*; and is the Aledg'd Instrument of all the said *Christian* her Trouble. The said *Katherine* being by the said *Commissioners* Interrogate on several Points, in the Hearing of the said *Christian*, she Deny'd all, and particularly her Accession to the said *Christian* her Trouble, or the Rise thereof. But the Child still Charging her, Conjured her to tell the *Commissioners*, Why she would never Pray, *That God would deliver her from that Ill, and Restore her well again*. *Katherine* did not disown her Refusal, but shifted about for frivolous Excuses which the *Commissioners* bearing home on her, as a Great Argument of her Guilt; and finding she could hardly evade the Force of it, *Katherine* offers to run at the Child (they being then at some distance from one another) and the Child did all she could to shun her Touch. *Katherine* Complain'd; saying, *Now I would Pray for her, but she will not let me*. But the Child being forc'd to suffer her Touch by the By-standers, tho most Unwillingly, and with great

32 These are Elizabeth Anderson, James Lindsay, Thomas Lindsay, Janet Rodger and Margaret Rodger, who had originally been suspected of witchcraft but who were converted into star witnesses for the prosecution.

33 *Sic*. The correct word would be 'precognition', a Scots law term meaning a statement taken down from a witness before a trial.

34 The 'Bargarran Witches' manuscript (at p. 21) lists the commissioners present: Alexander Lord Blantyre (presiding), Sir John Houston of that Ilk, Gavin Cochrane of Craigmuir, William Cunningham of Craigends and Robert Sempill sheriff depute of Renfrew.

Fear, she immediately after fell down, in a most Violent Fit, as before, on *James Lindsay*'s Touch: But thereupon *Katherines* Tongue was loosed, and she said, *The Lord Bless her, The Lord Deliver her*; which nothing could Oblige her to do before: And the Child her self declared, after that Fit, and *Katherines* Prayer, she now found her self free of all Fear to Touch the said *Katherine*, or any other of her Tormentors.

The *Commissioners* were then Earnest with *Katherine*, to tell why she would, or could *not Pray* before she Touch'd the Child? But, to this, she could give no Satisfactory Answer.

Afterwards the *Commissioners* call'd a *Young Damsel*, Nam'd *Elizabeth Anderson*, whom they found a very Useful Person in the said Enquiry, as being many times admitted by her {*p. 7*} *Father*, and other *Friends*, to their Meetings with the *Devil*, as her Confession hereto Subjoyned does Evidence, to which you are Referr'd. As also the *Commissioners* having Examin'd *Christian Shaw*, about the Persons Represented to her as her Tormentors in those Fits; and finding her Testimony Confirmed by *Elizabeth Anderson* her Confession, with relation to many of the Persons Accused by *Christian*. The *Commissioners*, on that Evidence, Ordered them all to Prison, (viz.) *Alexander Anderson*, Father to the said *Elizabeth*, *Agnes Nasmith*, *John Lindsay* in *Barrcloch*, John Lindsay in *Formachin*, *James Lindsay* his Brother, *Agnes Foster*,[35] *Margaret Fulton*, and the said *Katherine Campbell*, where they are to lie till farther Orders. But the said *Christian Shaw* knows and remembers another Person, whom she declares she has not the Power to Name: And she has many times attempted it, but is still seized with Fits when she Assays to Express it; She came, at last, to say, for her first Name, *Margaret*, or *Pincht Margaret* (a Name given her by the *Devil*, from a Pincht Cross-Cloath, ordinarily worn on her Brow) But cannot express her Patronimick, or Surname. The *Commissioners* were so concern'd at this, that they urged her to Write it, which being loth to try for fear of Torture, she nevertheless essayed it; And beginning to Write other Names, she was desir'd to try that too, but could Write no more save *Margaret*, and the Letter *L.* of her Sirname, being presently taken with a most Violent Fit, the Pen falling out of her hand, and she falling Dead, as above, with Groans, heavier and sorer then ordinary. Within a while the *Commissioners* having caus'd her to take a little of a Julip,[36] after her Recovery, some Ministers standing by, Presented her with a Bible, desiring her to Read a Passage in it, which they pointed to her; but no sooner had she cast her eyes on the Book, but instead of Reading, she fell to Sing a very Melodious Tune, such as is used in *Opera*'s; and, within a little while after fell in her Fits again, and even then the Musick ceas'd not, tho she appear'd as one dead, with her Mouth open, but neither her Lips nor Tongue stirring, She remain'd long in the Fit,

35 *Sic.* The 'Bargarran Witches' manuscript (at p. 22) has 'Angus Foster' here.
36 'Julip' (julep): a sweetened medicinal drink.

till one of the *Commissioners*, {*p. 8*} desir'd the Book might be Clos'd; which done, she Immediately came to her Self; and being Askt what she meant by Singing, when she was desir'd to Read, she was not sensible she had Sung, and declar'd she did not remember it.[37]

Bargarren-Place. Febr. 5. 1697.

Elizabeth Anderson, Daughter to *Alexander Anderson*, Aged 17 years, or thereby, Declared that about 20 days ago, she was Invited by her Father, to go along with him to *Bargarrin*'s Yeard, about Twelve a Clock in the Day, who went both together; and having come there, they met with ane Black Man, who had ane Bonnet on his Head, and a Band about his Neck, whom her Father, and *Agnes Nasmith*, then present, told her, He was the *Devil* And that there was in Company with that Black Man, whom she thought was the *Devil*, the Persons following; viz. the said *Alexander Anderson* her Father, *Agnes Nasmith* in Park of *Erskin*, *John Lindsay* in *Formaken*, call'd, The *Bishop*, *James Lindsay* his Brother, *Margaret Fulton*, Spouse to *Robert Wallace* in *Kilpatrick*, and Sister to the Grandmother of the said *Elizabeth*, who Dyed in *Paislay* Tolbooth, Accused of *Witchcraft* above half ane Year since, or thereby. And that their Discourse was at that time concerning *Christian Shaw*, Daughter to the Laird of *Bargarren*, who was then not well, and whose Life they all promis'd to take away by Stopping of her Breath; and that she saw the *Devil* several times before in her Fathers House, in Company with her Father, and several others. And that the *Devil*, with the Company foresaid Danc'd all in the said Yeard the time foresaid. And that her Father Discharged her to tell any thing she saw, or else she would be Torn {*p. 9*} in pieces; And that she was more Affraied of the forsaid Persons, then she was of the *Devil*. And being Examin'd whether or no any Person in the Company foresaid Desired her to Ingage in the *Devil*'s Service? She declared, That both the *Devil* and her Father Invited her several times to the *Devil*'s Service, Promising to Reward her for her paines But that she altogether refus'd to Ingage therein: And that notwithstanding thereof, she went along to the foresaid Yeard, to the said Meeting with her Father; Where she heard the *Devil* say, That no body would see them: At which the forsaids Persons then present did Laugh. And being asked, If she was Affraid when she saw the *Devil* in the Yeard? She Declared, She was Fear'd not, because she had seen him several times before.

Elizabeth Andersons Additional Confession, who Compear'd, and being Examin'd upon the Point of *Witchcraft*, Declared the Particulars following.

[37] For a different version of this document, see the appendix to the 'Bargarran Witches' manuscript, below.

Renfrew, Feb. 18. 97.[38]

That about Seven years since or thereabouts, the said *Elizabeth Anderson* was with the Deceas'd *Jean Fulton*, her Grandmother; and playing about the door of the House she saw ane Black grim Man go into the House to her Grandmother; who abode with her a considerable space, talking with her; and afterward she came to the door, and desired the said *Elizabeth Anderson* to come in; and upon her incoming, desired her to take the Gentleman (as she named him) by {*p. 10*} the Hand, and she would give her ane Bony Black new Coat, which accordingly she did; which seemed to her very cold: whereupon she was affraid, and immediatly he vanished and went away. About a Month after her Grandmother and she were both in the House together, when the aforesaid Gentleman appeared to them, (which the said *Elizabeth* then suspected to be the Devil) and he and her Grandmother fell a talking together, by rounding[39] in others Ears, but understood not what they said; and afterward her Grandmother desired her to take the Gentleman by the hand, but she refusing, saying, It was the Devil, which her Grandmother denying, said, It was a Gentleman a Friend of hers; and she still insisting and threatning her if she would not take him by the hand, she would get none of her Cloaths, but the said *Elizabeth Anderson* would not be perswaded to do it, but saved her self from him, saying, the Lord be between me and him, whereupon her Grandmother said, she need not fear for it was no ill thing, and upon that the Devil went away in a Flight, she knew not how; and declares, for a long time after, she was no more troubled with the said Gentleman. Till one time her Father *Alexander Anderson* desired her to go with him through the Country to seek their Meat;[40] to which she replyed, she need not go seek her Meat, seeing she might have Work: But her Father pressing her, she went with him, where he took her to ane *Muir* in Kilmacolme, where were gathered together, before they came, *Agnes Nasmith*, *Margaret Fulton*, *John Lindsay*, called *Bishop*, *James Lindsay*, called *Curat*, ane *Heighland Body*, *Katherine Campbel*, ane *Gentlewife* called by them *Antiochia*, *Thomas Woodrous's Wife* in *Carslup*, *Margaret Lang* in *Cartinpan*, and her Daughter, *Martha Semple*, *John Read*[,] *Smith*, *John Stuart*[41] and his *Wife*, *Annable Read*, *Margaret Sherer*, *Margaret Rodger* in *Park*, *Janet Rodger* her *Sister*, *Robert Wallace* in *Kilpatrick*, [*1 word blank*] *Allason* there, *Thomas Birkinyers* Wife in

[38] The 'Bargarran Witches' manuscript (at p. 24) lists the commissioners present: Alexander Lord Blantyre, Sir John Houston of that Ilk, Gavin Cochrane of Craigmuir, Alexander Porterfield of Fullwood, Robert Sempill sheriff depute of Renfrew and William Muir of Glanderston.

[39] 'rounding': whispering.

[40] 'seek their Meat': beg for their food.

[41] The 'Bargarran Witches' manuscript (at p. 21) has 'John Stewart' here. This seems to be a small instance of anglicisation by the London publishers.

Stamne-butts,[42] and several others whom she does not know or remember, when the aforesaid Gentleman who appeared to her formerly, came to the said *Elizabeth Anderson*, bidding her Renounce her Baptism, promising her if she would consent thereto, she should be better then she was then, and she would get better Meat and better Cloaths, and she would {*p. 11*} not need to beg. But (as she declared) she would not Consent to him; And he enquired of her, What brought her thither? then she replied, That she came with her Father. Whereupon the Devil and her Father went together, and talked to one another; but she knew not where-about: And declares that the cause of her meeting at that time (as she said) was about the forming of a Picture, of Mr. *William Flemings* Minister at *Innerkeppe* his Child, who at that time effected the same; the Main Actors being, her Father, *Agnes Nasmith*, *Margaret Fulton*, *Isabel Cochran*, and some others, who at that time put in Pins both small and great; but their Master told them they behoved to have some other thing before it could take Effect. As also she Confesses, she was present at ane Meeting with that Crew, above the Town of *Kilpatrick*, where were present her Father, Mother, and Sister, *Margaret Lang* and her Daughter, *Margaret Fulton*, *Agnes Nasmith*, *Margaret Rodger* and her Sister *Janet*, *Margaret Sherer*, *Robert Wallace* in *Kilpatrick*, with the foresaid Gentleman, whom they called their Lord; where they formed ane Picture of Mr. *John Ritchie* Minister of *Kilpatrick* his Child, and they all Stabed Pins in the same, both great and small; and heard the said *Margaret Rodger* say, stay a little till I stop ane Pin in the Heart of it, which accordingly she did. And declares, she went with her Father to the *Ferrie-Boat* of *Erskin*, where he took her on his Back over the Water to *Kilpatrick* in a Flight.[43] Farther Confesses, To have been present at the Drowning of *Brighouse*, and the *Ferrier* of *Erskin*,[44] where was present in the Boat, the Devil, her Father and Mother, *William Miller* at *Formakin*, the *Ferriers Mother-in-Law*, *Margaret Fulton*, and some others; and there were on *Erskin* side of the Water *John Lindsay* the *Bishop*, *James Lindsay*, the *Curat*, *Margaret Cochran*, [*1 word blank*[45]] *Tarbet*, *Jennet Waugh*, *Margaret Shearer*, *Margaret Lang*, and her *Daughter*, *John Stwart* [*sic*], and his *Wife*, the *Highland Body*, *Catherin Campbel*, and several others, with her Self; and heard them say, That they would have saved one of the Horse, but they could not get it done, unless they had saved also one of the Men which were Drounded, and which she believes was *John Glen*, {*p. 12*} had not his Mother-in-Law prevented it. Moreover she declares,

[42] *Sic*. These names later appear, more correctly, as 'Birkmire' and 'Stainie-butts'.

[43] The 'Bargarran Witches' manuscript (at p. 25) adds here 'and also declares that the words that her father spoke when he toke her on his Back and flew with her, Mount and flee'. In the present *Relation*, these words appear instead towards the end of Elizabeth Anderson's confession.

[44] The witches were accused of having sunk the ferryboat of Erskine, drowning George Cunningham of Brighouse and the ferryman John Glen, about a year previously.

[45] The 'Bargarran Witches' manuscript (at p. 29) mentions Elizabeth Tarbet in Newark.

she was present at the putting down of a Child of *William Montgomries* in *Bargarrans Land*, where were present Margaret Fulton in Kilpatrik, *Agnes Nasmith*, her *Father Mother* and *Sister*, *John* and *James Lindsays*, Bishop and Curat, *Margaret Lang*, in *Cartinpan*, *Janet Waugh*, *Margaret Sherer*, *Thomas Woodrouse's Wife* in *Carsslup*, *Thomas Lindsay*, *James Lindsay* his *Brother*, *John Reid*[,] *Smith*, and several others whom she does not know or remember, with the Black Man whom they called their Lord, about two a Clock in the Morning, where they Strangled a Child with a Sea Napkin: The Main Actors, being *Agnes Nasmith* and *Margaret Fulton*, who opened the Door of the House, and after they were entred, went to the Fire and lighted ane Candle, which was blacker nor your Candles usually are, somewhat blewish; and none in the House ever stir'd or wakened, and they stayed all in the House upwards of ane Hour; And declares, that she heard *Agnes Nasmith* say, What if the People of the House awake? To which *Margaret Fulton* replyed, You need not fear. Lyke as confessed, That upon *Wednesday* about five Weeks since or thereby, her Father brought her out of his House with him, and come all the way with her on her foot to *Bargarren* out-Yeard,[46] where they come in by ane Shap[47] in the Yeard to ane Meeting, where were present *Agnes Nasmith*, *Margaret Fulton*, *John Lindsay* Bishop, *James Lindsay* Curate, *Agnes Foster*, the *Highland Body*, *Janet Waugh*, *Margaret Sheirer* in *Eskingram*, *Margaret Lang*, *Margaret Cunningham* Spouse to *Thomas Woodrow* in *Carsslap*, *John Read*, *Smith*, *John Steward* and his *Wife*, *Thomas Birkinyers* Wife, *Thomas Lindsay*, *James Lindsay* his Brother, and *Alexander Anderson*, the Declarant, her Father; Where was also present the *Devil*, who had on ane Black Coat, ane Blew Bonnet, ane Blew Band, who Played on a Pipe, and they all Danced. At which Meeting they were Contriving and Consulting with the foresaid Black Man, whom they called their Lord, about the Destroying of *Christian Shaw*, Daughter to the Laird of *Bargarren*; where some of them were for Stabbing her with a Touck;[48] particularly, *Agnes Nasmith*, *{p. 13}* *Margaret Fulton*, *Margaret Rodger*, *Thomas Woodrouse* Wife, *Margaret Sheirer*, and others, were for Hanging her with a Cord, particularly the *Highland Body*, *John Read*, and his Daughter; and others for Stopping her Breath, and Choaking her, and particularly *Janet Waugh*, *John Lindsay* Bishop, *James Lindsay* his Brother, and the Gentle Wife, whom they called *Antiochia*, as also Declared that she heard some of them say, That if ever they should have a Meeting again, they should have her out of the House and destroy her: But fearing they would be taken before they should have ane other Meeting, their Lord, as they called him, gave them ane piece of ane Unchristned Bairns Liver to eat, except her, and the other Two,

46 *Sic*. The 'Bargarran Witches' manuscript (at p. 25) has 'orchard' here, probably more correctly.
47 *Sic*. The 'Bargarran Witches' manuscript (at p. 25) has 'slap' here. A 'slap' or 'slop' was a gap in a wall.
48 'Touck': sword.

who has Confessed, viz. *James* and *Thomas Lindsayes*, telling them, that though they were Apprehended, they should never Confess, do to them what they would. And farder declares, That several of them were feard, That the said *Elizabeth Anderson* should Confess and tell of them, in regard she had done it formerly. They threatned her, if she did, They would Tear her all in pieces, if ever they got their hands on her, and particularly *Margaret Lang*, who Threatned her most. And farther declares, that against the next Meeting, they intended, if they were not Apprehended, To Forme the said *Christian Shaws* Picture, and then they would gett a gett[49] of her; And when the Meeting was ended, which continued upwards of Two houres, or thereby, they went all away in a Flight, except the said *Elizabeth Anderson*, who went home on her foot. Farder Confesses, That one Night her Father raised her out of her Bed, and took her to the Ferry-Boat of *Erskin*, where he took her on his Back, and, in a Flight, carry'd her over the Water, and went from that both together to *Dunbarton*, to the Yeard of Mr. *John Hardy*, Minister there, where were present *Agnes Nasmith*, *Margaret Fulton*, *Robert Wallace* her Husband, *Margaret Lang*, and her Daughter *Martha Semple*, *Alexander Anderson*, *Thomas Woodrous* Wife, *James Lindsay*, *Thomas Lindsay* his Brother, [*1 word blank*] Mc. *Killops*, Mother-in-Law to *John Glen* the Ferrier, *Katherin {p. 14} Campbell*, the *Highland Body*, *John Lindsay* Bishop, *James Lindsay* Curat, *William Miller* in Formakin, the Gentlewoman called by the Crew *Antiochia*, and the foresaid Black Man, whom they called their Lord; where the foresaid *John Lindsay* Bishop, Played on a Pype, and all Danced; at which Meeting they Formed the Picture of the said Mr. *John Hardy*, which was made of Bees-Wax, Hair, and other Materials, and Dabbed it full of Pins small and Great, and thereafter put it amongst Water and Ale Mixed, and then put it on a Spit, which *Agnes Nasmith* and others told her, they Roasted at the Fire, the Main Actors were, the said *Agnes Nasmith*, and *Margaret Fulton*, who made the Same Picture,[50] and when they had done they went all away in a Flight, except her Father, and her self, who come upon their Feet to the Ferry again, and carry'd her over, in a Flight as foresaids: And Declares, That the foresaid *Agnes Nasmith* got the Picture in Custody when they parted; And also Declares, That the Words that her Father spoke, when he took her on his Back, and Flew with her, were *Mount and Fly*; And also Declares, That no Person promised her any good Deed, or Reward, to make the said Confession.

49 *Sic.* The 'Bargarran Witches' manuscript (at p. 26) has 'get a gate' here. A 'gate' was a road, so this phrase means 'find a way'.

50 'the Same Picture': the aforementioned picture or image.

Feb. 18. 97.[51]

James Lindsay being examined Confesses as follows, (Aged 14 years, or thereby,) That one day he met with the Deceas'd *Jean Fulton* his Grandmother at her House in *Inchannen*, wher she took from him a little *Round Cap* and a *Plack*, But being loath to part with the same, required them from her again; which she refusing, he cal'd her *an old Witch* and run away; upon which she follow'd him and cry'd, that she would meet him another time with an Ill turn: about {*p. 15*} 8 days therafter, as he was begging thorough the Country near to the Town of *Inchannen*, he met again with his Grandmother at the Back of the yard of that House at the head of the Causey, where there appear'd to him *ane Black Grim Man*, with black Cloaths, ane black Hat, and blew Band; his *Grandmother* desiring him to take the *Gentleman* by the Hand, (as she term'd him) who accordingly did as he was desired, whose hand seem'd to the said *James* to be exceeding cold, and gript him very straitly; whereupon the said Gentleman enquir'd at him, If he would serve him, and he would give him a Bonny black Coat and a black Hat, and several other things? to which he reply'd, *yes I'le do't*; and continuing there a litle time they parted, when the said Gentleman (which he knew thereafter to be the Devil) and his Grandmother went away together from him, but he knows not how. This the said *James Lindsay* declares was the first time that ever he saw the *Devil*, or engaged with him; and thereafter confesses he was frequently at Meetings with him and others, and particularly the Meetings after specify'd, besides many others: *Viz*. That about 5 Weeks before *Jennet Ker* was Apprehended he went with her to a Muir in *Kilmalcolme* Parish upon a Hill to a Meeting there about 4 a Clock in the afternoon, where were present whom he knew (besides several others whom he does not know or remember:) The said *Jennet Ker*, *Jennet Woodrow*, *Margaret Alexander*, *Margaret Cochran*, [*1 word blank*] *Tarbett*, *Alexander Anderson*, and his *Wife*; *John Lindsey* Bishop, *Agnes Nesmith*, *John Lindsay* in *Barclough*, *Jennett Waugh*, *Margaret Sheirer*, *William Miller* in *Formaken*, *Margaret Lang* in *Carterpan*, *Martha Semple* her *Daughter*; *Kat. Ferrier* at *Craigtownburne*, *John Reid*, *John Stuart* and his *Wife*; *Patrick Lindsey* in *Formakin*, *Katherin Campbell*, ane *Highland Body*, cal'd by the Crew their Drudg; and ane White-haird Man which he says was *James Lindsay* Curat, who play'd upon a Fiddle to them and they all Danc'd with the first Gentleman, whom they cal'd their Lord, who came to the said *John Lindsay*, and took him by the Hand and forbad him to tell, at which time they were contriving about the Drowning of *Brighouse*,

[51] The 'Bargarran Witches' manuscript (at p. 26) confirms that this statement was taken at Renfrew on 18 February. It also adds subscriptions of the commissioners at the end: Alexander Lord Blantyre, Sir John Houston of that Ilk, Gavin Cochrane of Craigmuir, Alexander Porterfield of Fullwood and Robert Sempill sheriff depute of Renfrew. Robert Alexander, a notary who acted as clerk to the enquiry commission, also signs (p. 29). Alexander wrote a newsletter of his own about this time, which is edited below as an appendix to the 'Bargarran Witches' manuscript.

{*p. 16*} when he should come over the Ferry of *Erskin*, (the foresaid *Jennet Ker* being the main Instigator) where he heard their *Lord* say, That if they could not get him out by the Hairs of the Head, they would sink the Boat and all therein, and *Jennet Woodrow* reply'd, That if they could get *Brighouse* Drown'd alone they would be content, *John Glenn the Farrier* were sav'd,[52] but [*1 word blank*] *Mckillops*[53] Mother-in-Law to the said *Farrier* (who was also present) said in regard he had put her out of the House a little while before the Meeting, she should have him Drown'd also. And likewise Confesses, That at the Comitting of the said Fact, the heal[54] forenam'd persons were present with several others, except the said *Jennet Woodrow* and *Jennet Ker*, who were then at that time in Prison; and that the *Devil* was at the Head of the Boat, and *Alexander Anderson*, *William Miller*, *the Farriers Mother-in-Law*, and *John Steward*, and his *Wife* were in the middle of the Boat, and the rest of the Crew abovenam'd with himself and several others upon *Erskin* side of the Water.

As also Confesses, he was present at the putting down of a Child of *Mathew Parks* in *Parkland*, with the Persons abovenam'd, and several others, as *Thomas Lindsay* his Brother, *Elizabeth Anderson*, Daughter to *Alexander Anderson*, where was present with them ane Black-haird Man, bare-headed, in ane black Coat and a long blew Cravat, which was don late at Night about 12, when the whole Family were asleep except ane Servant-lass, who waited on the Child, who at this time went to the Door a little, and in the Interim before she return'd they put a Cord about the Childs Neck and Strangled it; the main Actors of the Fact being *Margaret Fulton*, and *Agnes Nesmith*, and when the Lass came in again to the place where the Child was, they heard her cry these words, *Mathew, O Mathew! Mathew! The Bairn is Dead*;[55] whereupon they all went away.

Note, That the foresaid *Elizabeth Anderson* another Confessant, agrees in her Confession to this Article, that the {*p. 17*} Bairn was in the Cradle when the Fact was Comitted, and that when they had don they took the Cord with them. Likeas Confesses, he was present at the Strangling of a Child of *William Montgomerys* in *Bargarrins-land*, with *Martha*[56] *Lang* in *Cartanpan*, *Martha Semple* her Daughter, *Thomas Lindsay his Brother*, *Margaret Rodger*, *Alexander Anderson*, and his Wife and two Daughters, *Jane and the said Elizabeth Anderson*, *John Lindsay*

52 That is, if they could only get Brighouse drowned they would not mind if John Glen was saved.

53 The 'Bargarran Witches' manuscript (at p. 27) has 'Margaret Mckillop' here.

54 'heal': whole.

55 Both Matthew Park himself, and his wife Margaret Lyle, related a version of this story, and the 'cry' seems to have been thought important. However, in their version of the story, the child was found dead in the morning, and it was then that 'his wyff cryed to him O Mathew Mathew the child is gone': Goodare and Willumsen (eds.), *Scottish Witchcraft Trials*, 599, 631. This is not at all the same as a servant discovering the dead child 'late at Night about 12', and uttering a 'cry' that the witches (who are presumably invisible) hear themselves.

56 *Sic*. NLS, Acc. 6687, no. 9, p. 13, has 'Margat'.

Bishop, *James Lindsay Curate*, and *Patrick Lindsay* his Son; *Agnes Nesmith*, *Jennet*[57] *Lindsay* in *Barloch*, *Jennet Waugh*, *Margaret Shearer*, Crooked *William Millar*, *Kath. Ferrier* in *Craigtown-burne*, *John Steuart* and his *Wife*, *Kath Campbel*, and the *Highland-body* their Drudge, and several others, whose Names he does not know or remember; Where was present the foresaid Black-hair'd Man, nothing on him but ane black Shirt, and a black Hood, cald by the Crew their Lord, where they Strangled the Child with ane Sea Napkin, and heard *Agnes Nasmith* cry *draw the Lowp*,[58] and at theyr entring to the House *Agnes Nasmith* opened the door and went in, and the rest followed her to the Fyre syde, and lighted a Candle tending to a blewish colour, where they stayed a considerable space upwards of ane hour, and during that time none of the House awakned, for he heard one of them, to wit *Agnes Nasmith*, say, she wold keep them from Wakening; the main Actors were the foresaid *Agnes Nasmith* with *Alexander Anderson* and another Woman whom he did not know, and who is condescended on[59] by the other twa Confessants, viz, *Thomas Lindsay* his *Brother*, and the said *Elizabeth Anderson*, to be *Margaret Fulton* in *Kilpatrick*. Furder Confesses, That upon a *Wadensday* about fyve weeks since or therby, he was taken on a sudden in a Flight, wher he was begging near to the place of *Inchannen*, from that to *Bargarrens* Orchyeard, to a Meeting with the Crew, where were *Agnes Nasmith*, the foresaid *Margaret Fulton*, his Brother *Thomas*, *John Lindsay* Bishop, *James Lindsay* Curat, the Highland Body, *Jennet Waugh*, *Margaret Sheirer*, *Margaret Lang* and her Daughter *Martha Semple*, *Thomas Woodrow*'s *Wife* in *Cairslop*, *John Reid* Smith, *John Stewart* and his Wife, *Thomas Birkmire* in *Stainie-butts* and his Wife, *Alexander Anderson* {*p. 18*} and his Wife and twa Daughters, ane *Gentle Wife* called by their *Lord* his Wyfe *Antiochia*, and several others whome he does not know or Remember; wher the Devil theyr Lord, as they called him, played upon a Pype and they all danced; at which Meeting they ware advyseing and consulting the destroyeing of *Christian Shaw* Doughter to *Bargarren*, wher some of them ware for distroyeing and pulling down of the House upon her, some for Choaking and Stopping in[60] Pins in her Throat, others for hanging her with a Cord, some for seeing if they could get her out of the house and distroy her. And Confesses, They all agreed to the *Forming of her Picture* against the nixt Meeting if they ever should have ane; but fearing they showld be apprehended ere that tyme; theyr Master gave them all ane peece of ane Unchristned bairns Liver, excepting himselfe and other twa, viz. *Thomas Lindsay* his Brother, and *Elizabeth Andersone*, they telling them though they ware apprehended they would never Confess doe to them never so much.

57 *Sic*. NLS, Acc. 6687, no. 9, p. 13, has 'John'.
58 'draw the Lowp': tighten the noose.
59 'condescended on': specified, agreed upon.
60 'Stopping in': pushing in.

Lykeas Confesses, Being in Bed in the house of *William Killoch* in *Davistown* late at Night he was taken out of his Bed in a Flight, wher he never knew till he was in *Dunbartown*, in the yeard of Mr. *John Hardie* Minister there, where were present at the Meeting of the Crew, *Agnes Nasmith*, *Margaret Fulton*, *Robert Wallace*, *Margaret Lang*, *Marthew* [*sic*] *Semple*, *Alexander Anderson*, his *Wyfe* and *Daughter Elizabeth*, *Thomas Lindsay*, his Brother who agrees to his Confession; [*1 word blank*] Mc. *Killops*, Mother-in-Law to *John Glenn*, *Farrier*, *Kathrin Cambel*, the Highland Body, *John Lindsay* Bishop, and *James* his Brother, *Thomas Woodrow's Wyfe*, *William Miller* in *Formaken*[,] ane Gentle Wyfe, called by theyr Lord his Wyfe *Antiochia*, with several others whome he knows not or remembers; where the forsaid *John Lindsay* Bishop played on a Pype, and they all Danced, at which Meeting they framed the Picture of the said Mr. *John Hardie*, and dabbed it full of Pins small and great, and therafter put it in Water and Ale mixt and then Roasted it at the Fyre, the Main Actors being the said *Agnes Nasmith* and *Margaret Fulton*, who formed the same; and when they had ended theyr Meeting, declares {*p. 19*} he was taken back to his Bed again in a Flight, as said is And declairs, *Agnes Nasmith* got the Picture in Custody when they parted. Furder Confesses, he hes several tymes appeared to the Chyld (whyte in the foot)[61] both in *Glasgow* and *Bargarren*, tho Invisible to Spectators, with others as *Agnes Nasmith*, and *Alexander Anderson*, the Highland Body, (in *John Davisons*) and *Margaret Lang* tormenting the Child,[62] wher he declares, he and the foresaid Persons and some others were the Occasion of the foresaid *Christian* her putting out the *Coales*, *Cinders*, *Bones*, *Hay*, *Fire*, *Sticks*, and other trash which they put in her Mouth, intending to Choak her. And furder acknowledges, That he and the foresaid Persons and others did oftimes Prick and Stab her as if it had been don by Pins, and the way and manner how he had don it was his having a Needle, which if he put in his Cloathes, her Body would be prickt and Stab'd in that place where he Stab'd the Needle, and if he should put it in his Hair, that part of her Head wher he put the same would be Stab'd. And further declares, He was present when the said *Christian Shawe* put Pins out of her Mouth, which he and the aforesaid persons and others had put in, and also at the time of his doing these Arts, the said *James* cry'd thir Words, *Help John Davison*, who was also then present; and also when the Minister began to pray in *Bargarrens* House, the Devil, he and the rest immediatly went away. And also declares, There was no Person promis'd him any Reward for making the foresaid Confession, and declares he cannot Write. And also declares, That the Devil and the rest of the Crew cal'd *John Lindsay* Bishop, *The Post*.

[61] *Sic*. The 'Bargarran Witches' manuscript (at p. 29) has 'whyle in her fitt' here, probably more correctly. NLS, Acc. 6687, no. 9, p. 15, has 'whyte in the feet'.

[62] The 'Bargarran Witches' manuscript (at p. 29) has 'with others as Agnes Easmith, Alexander Anderson, the Hieland body, the Gentlewife and John Davidson and Margaret Lang Tormenting the Child' here.

Thomas Lindsay declares,[63] That one Night lying in Bed in his Grandmothers House *Jane Fulton*, late at Night there came in a Black Man, with black Cloathes, ane blew Band and black Hat, into his Grandmothers, but he being asleep at the time, she awaken'd him, desiring him to take the Gentleman by the hand, and she would give him a Black Coat, which accordingly he did, whose {*p. 20*} Hand seem'd to be very Cold, and enquir'd at him, *If he would serve him, and be his Man*, and he would give him a Red Coat, which he said *he would do*; And thereafter he declares, The Gentleman, which he knew thereafter to be the *Devil*, went out the Broad side of the House: And Declares farther, That when he gave his Consent to *serve the Devil*, he Nipt him in the Neck, which continu'd Sore Ten[64] dayes space. Thereafter, one day, coming by his Grandmothers House (she then being dead) as he thought, she Appeared to him, Clapping his Head, Desiring him to be a good Servant to the Gentleman to whom she had Gifted him, and forbidding him to Reveal it. And thereafter she Evanisht out of his Sight. Likeas Confesses, one Night Lying in Bed in the House of *Robert Shaw* in *Barscobe Hill*, late at Night, he was Awaken'd out of his Sleep, and taken away in a Flight, to the House of one *Mathew Park* in *Parkland*, to the Murthering of a Child of his; where were present, *Jennet Ker*, *Alexander Anderson*, and his Wife, and Daughter *Elizabeth*; *John Lindsay* Bishop, and *James Lindsay* Curate, *Agnes Nesmith*, *Margaret Fulton*, *John Lindsay* in *Barloch*, *Jennet Waugh*, *Margaret Sherer*, Crooked *William Miller*, *Margaret Lang*, her Daughter *Martha Semple*, *Katharine Ferrier*, *John Reid*, *John Stuart*, *Anaple Reid* his Wife,[65] *Katharine Campbell*, the *Highland Body*, *James Lindsay* his own Brother, *Jane Park* in *Paisley*, [*1 word blank*] *Ross*,[66] her Mother, and the said Gentleman, whom they call'd their Lord; where they Strangled the Child with ane Small Cord, while the whole Family were Asleep, except a Lass who Waited on the Child, who at that time went to the Door; and before she return'd, *Jennett Ker*, and *Margaret Sherer*, put the Cord about the Childes Neck, and Strangled it, and after they had done, they all went away in a Flight: And Declairs, he was brought to his Bed in the same maner again. As also Confesses, another Night being in Bed in the House of *Walter Alexander* of *Ersken Kirk*, he was taken away in a Flight to a Meeting at the House of *William Montgomry* in *Bargarrens* Land, with the Crew, where {*p. 21*} they Strangled his Child about two a Cloak in the Morning, being there present *Margaret Fulton*, *Agnes Nesmith*, *James Lindsay* his Brother, *Alexander Anderson*, and his Wife and two Daughters; *John Lindsay* Bishop, *James Lindsay* Curat, *Margaret*

63 The 'Bargarran Witches' manuscript (at pp. 30–1) confirms that this statement, like the previous ones, was taken at Renfrew on 18 February. It also names the commissioners present: Alexander Lord Blantyre, Sir John Houston of that Ilk, Gavin Cochrane of Craigmuir, Alexander Porterfield of Fullwood and Robert Sempill sheriff depute of Renfrew.

64 The 'Bargarran Witches' manuscript (at p. 30) has 'two' here.

65 The 'Bargarran Witches' manuscript (at p. 30) has only 'John Stewart and his wife' here.

66 The 'Bargarran Witches' manuscript (at p. 30) has 'Jean Ross her mother' here.

Lang and her Daughter, *Jennet Waugh*, *Margaret Shearer*, *Thomas Woodrow's* Wife in *Cousslop*,[67] *Kathrin Campbel*, the Highland Body, and several others, with the forsaid Gentleman whom they called their Lord; the Main Actors being *Agnes Nesmith* and *Margaret Fulton*, who opened the door of the House, and when they were entred the House went to the Fires side, and lighted a Candle which was blacker then other Candle but somewhat blewish; and none of the house ever stirred or awaked, and heard the said *Agnes Nesmith* say, What if the People of the House awaked? to which *Fulton* replyed you need not fear, which was in the mean time whilst they Strangled the Child with ane sprekled Sea-Napkin, and after committing of the Fact they all went away, the said *Thomas* was brought in a flight to his Bed again.

Likeas Confesses, About five Weeks since or thereby, coming by *Finlastown* about Twelve a Cloak midd day, was taken in a sudden Flight, when he never knew, till he was in *Bargarrins* Ortchyeard, where were present *Margaret Fulton*, *John* and *James Lindsays* Bishop and Curat, the Highland Body, *Jennet Waugh*, *Margaret Shearer*, *Margaret Lang* and her Daughter, *Thomas Woodrow's* Wife,[68] *John Reid* Smith, *John Steuart* and his Wife, the *Gentle Wife* called by the Crew *Antiochia*, *Thomas Birkmyres* Wife, *James Lindsay* his own Brother, *Alexander Anderson* his Wife and two Daughters, *John Lindsay* in *Barloch*, and the foresaid Gentleman whom they called their Lord, who played on a Pipe and they all Danced, and after the merry fit they fell a consulting about the destroying of *Christian Shaw* Daughter to *Bargarrin*, where some of them were for Stabbing her with Pins, some for Stabbing with a Tuck, some for hanging her with a Cord, some for geting {*p. 22*} her out of the House to destroy her, but declares he heard them all consent to the making of her Picture against the next time, but fearing they should be apprehended ere the time. Their Lord gave them ane peice of ane Uncrissened bairns Liver, except himself his Brother and *Elizabeth Anderson*; And he told them tho they were apprehended they should never confess, after the eating of that, do to them never so much. And after the Meeting was ended, which continued about two hours space the said *Thomas Lindsay* was caried back to the verry same place from which he was taken away. {*p. 23*}

THE Copy of a Letter SENT, From *Bargarrens* Lady to him, being then at *Ranfren*,[69] dated *Febr*. 18. 1697.

My Dear, I Thought it fit to give you ane Account of *Christians* Condition, this day about two a Clock in the Afternoon she said she saw the *Devil* in likness of a Man, she seemed to be somewhat feared, and I desired her to say

67 The 'Bargarran Witches' manuscript (at p. 30) has 'Margaret Cunningham spouse to Thomas Wodrow in Carslap' here.

68 The 'Bargarran Witches' manuscript (at p. 31) has 'Margaret Cunningham' here.

69 *Sic*. Renfrew is meant. This may be a typographical error for 'Ranfreu'.

The Lord Rebuke thee Satan, but the use of her Tongue was taken from her, yet recovering it in a short space she asayed[70] to speak, but was presently seised with a Fit, and when that was over she went about the Room deaf and blind as you your self have seen her before, but still speaking, as to a Bumbee,[71] said, *With the Lords Strength thou shalt not put Straw nor Stiks into my Mouth*, houlding her hand fast on her Mouth all the while, then walking a litle faster {*p. 24*} she cryed out, the *Bumbee is Stinging me*, and sitting down looked on her Leg where was the Impression, very deep of finger Nails. The *Devil* appeared to her again in the Bed like a Gentleman, she standing at the Bed-side reasoned with him after this maner; *Thou thinks to make me a Witch but through God's Strength thou shalt never be the better; I charge thee in the Name of God to be gon and thy Papers too, for I will have non of them, I will not fear thy ill, stand here see if thou dare come one step nearer me: I think thou art feareder for me then I for thee*; then turning she went up and down the Room as before, and again was bitten with Teeth in the hands very deep, and Impressed with Nails of Fingers more then twenty four times, which made her cry aloud every time she received them, and shewing the place where she was hurt by getting her hand upon it; but we neither saw nor heard any thing about her. She continued in this Fit from two a Clock till past five at night, she said in the Fit *Margaret Lang* had given orders to Torment her, so by the Lass you will get a fuller account; till meeting; I remain

Your, *&c. Sic Subscribitur*,[72] *Christian M'gilchrist*. FINIS.

70 'asayed' (essayed): tried.
71 'Bumbee': bumblebee.
72 'Thus it is subscribed'.

6. THE 'BARGARRAN WITCHES' MANUSCRIPT, 1697

INTRODUCTION

The composite manuscript edited below bears many resemblances to the better-known *True Narrative of the Sufferings and Relief of a Young Girle*, published in 1698, which is edited as the subsequent text in the present volume. However, the manuscript also contains revealing differences, of three types. First, it contains additional documents that are not included in the *True Narrative* – most strikingly, a tract by James Williamson criticising the evidence used in the witchcraft trials. Second, it omits some of the documents published in the *True Narrative*. Third, there are intriguing differences in some of the documents that are common to both texts. For instance, both texts contain the central narrative of Christian Shaw's demonic possession, but in two noticeably different versions. These differences may reveal much about how the narrative was compiled, and help us to understand the bizarre events that it related. At the end of the edition, a further short document is added as an appendix: a contemporary newsletter relating yet another version of some of these events.

The manuscript: description, date, purpose

The 'Bargarran Witches' manuscript, as it is known by its present holders, the Mitchell Library, Glasgow, is an untitled foolscap volume in original binding containing the texts of a number of documents relating to the Bargarran witchcraft case. The manuscript was bought in London for the Library by George Neilson, who published one of its documents in 1910 – a sermon by James Hutchison, minister of Kilallan, that he preached in Paisley on 13 April 1697 to the commissioners of justiciary trying the accused witches.[1] Neilson noted internal evidence that the volume had been in the possession of the Shaw of Bargarran family in the eighteenth century, and it seems reasonable

[1] James Hutchisone, 'A Sermon on Witchcraft in 1697', ed. George Neilson, *Scottish Historical Review*, 7 (1910), 390–9.

to assume that John Shaw of Bargarran, Christian Shaw's father, was probably responsible for compiling it.

The manuscript has 36 leaves, with a modern pencil numbering (pp. 1–72). Two further leaves have been cut out at the beginning, about a dozen at the end, and four or five between pages 64 and 65. The leaf comprising pp. 65–6, on which the last few lines of the Williamson tract are written (p. 66), has been partly cut away, leaving only a slip. The same has been done to the leaf comprising pp. 39–40, on which the end of the 'Continued Accompt' (on which more in a moment) is written. This *partial* cutting indicates that these texts were still considered important when this was done. We cannot know what was cut out, but there is no direct indication that any text from 1697 has been removed. The beginnings and endings of the text are intact at both ends of the volume, and every 1697 document seems complete.

All of the 1697 documents appear to have been written by a single scribe, on several different occasions. He left several blank pages. The manuscript was probably compiled gradually during the first few months of 1697, when the judicial enquiry and later the criminal trial were proceeding. The last datable document relating to 1697 consists of notes about the witches' execution on 10 June (p. 43); up to that point in the manuscript, all the individual documents are written more or less in chronological order. On later pages, perhaps at a later date, the scribe added two further documents that had originally been composed earlier: the sermon mentioned above by James Hutchison, preached on 13 April, and a 'Prefatorie Discourse' – effectively a sermon – apparently delivered on 28 March by Thomas Blackwell, in connection with a fast held by the presbytery.

Then there is the remarkable 'Vindication of the Witches' by James Williamson. The scribe separated this tract from all the other documents by placing it at the other end of the volume, turning the book over and writing backwards from the end towards the middle. As a result there are fewer clues to its dating. The separation may well indicate the tract's very different message from the other documents.

The volume does not seem to have been written as a working document for the prosecution, of the kind that would have been on the table when a group like the presbytery of Paisley, the enquiry commission or the trial commission met; it covers too many different phases of the process. Nor does it feed directly into the printed *True Narrative* as a copy-text for the compositors; there are too many textual differences. It is probably a file copy that was compiled, for his own information and use, by one of the men involved in the prosecutions. This could have been one of the ministers or lawyers, but internal evidence of the manuscript's later possession by the family at Bargarran supports a view that the compiler (though not necessarily the scribe) was John Shaw of Bargarran himself.

Several items have been added to the volume since 1697. The miscellaneous nature of these led Isabel Adam, the only scholar since Neilson to have discussed the manuscript in print, to describe it as John Shaw's 'commonplace book'.[2] However, the volume is not really a commonplace book in origin; it was clearly compiled in 1697 with the single topic of witchcraft in mind. The present edition omits this later material. It also omits Hutchison's sermon, as this has already been published. And it omits four documents that were printed in *A Relation of the Diabolical Practices of Above Twenty Wizards and Witches of the Sheriffdom of Renfrew* (1697); these documents appear instead in the edition of that work above in the present volume, with substantive differences between the printed and manuscript versions being noted in footnotes.

A list of the manuscript's contents is given here, with additional page numbers that are found below in the present volume, and with items not edited below being *italicised*:

- Pages 1–15: 'Informatory Accompt ... of the Trouble of Christine Shaw', August 1696 to 14 February 1697 (below at pp. 138–56).
- Page 15: Enquiry commission's proceedings, Renfrew, 18 February 1697 (below at pp. 156–7).
- Page 16: Text of the enquiry commission, 19 January 1697 (below at p. 157).
- Pages 17–19: Declarations by Matthew Brisbane, physician, and Henry Marshall, apothecary, Glasgow, 31 December 1696, 1 January 1697 (below at pp. 157–60).
- *Page 20: blank.*
- *Pages 21–2: Enquiry commission's investigation of James Lindsay and Katherine Campbell, Bargarran, 5 February 1697. Edited above as part of the 'Relation'.*
- Pages 22–3: Enquiry commission's investigation of Elizabeth Anderson, James Lindsay and Thomas Lindsay, Renfrew, 18 February 1697 (below at pp. 160–2).
- *Pages 24–6: Elizabeth Anderson's second confession, Renfrew, 18 February 1697. Edited above as part of the 'Relation'.*
- *Pages 26–9: James Lindsay's confession, Renfrew, 18 February 1697. Edited above as part of the 'Relation'.*
- *Pages 30–1: Thomas Lindsay's confession, Renfrew, 18 February 1697. Edited above as part of the 'Relation'.*
- Pages 31–9: 'Continued Accompt of the Trouble of Christine Shaw', 18 February to 28 March 1697 (below at pp. 162–70).

[2] Isabel Adam, *Witch Hunt: The Great Scottish Witchcraft Trials of 1697* (London, 1978), 129, 243–4.

- *Page 40: blank.*
- Pages 41–2: John Reid's confession, and report of his death in prison, Renfrew, 21 May 1697 (below at pp. 170–4).
- Page 43: Report of the executions of the seven witches, Paisley, 10 June 1697 (below at pp. 174–5).
- *Page 44: Arithmetical calculations. Not edited here.*
- *Pages 45–52: Sermon by James Hutchison, 13 April 1697. Edited by George Neilson in the 'Scottish Historical Review', 1910. Not edited here.*
- Pages 53–6: 'Prefatorie Discourse' to the presbytery's fast, by Thomas Blackwell, Paisley, 28 March 1697 (below at pp. 175–9).
- *Pages 57–61: Notes of an essay on meditation. Not edited here.*
- *Pages 62–3: Notes of early Christian martyrs, dated 1725. Not edited here.*
- *Page 64: Arithmetical calculations. Not edited here.*
- *Page 65: blank.*
- Pages 66–71: James Williamson's tract 'Vindication of the Witches' (below at pp. 179–85).
- *Page 72: Draft financial accounts. Not edited here.*

In the 'Informatory Accompt', the 'Continued Accompt' and elsewhere, the scribe has transcribed various signatures, sometimes trying to indicate the form of a signature. In the present edition, these signatures are left as they are written, with no expansion of abbreviations. The scribe sometimes uses an extraordinarily high level of capitalisation, even for the seventeenth century, e.g. 'she being brought back to the Chamber Lay for a Considerable Space, and when Recovered she Declared That thair were' (p. 6); 'will not faill To Introduce The Lykenes of any' (p. 69). Most of these capitals have been eliminated in the interests of readability and historical comprehension.

The manuscript 'Narrative' and the printed 'Narrative'

The two 'Narratives' of Christian Shaw's behaviour, manuscript and printed, differ noticeably in form and style – and also in substance. The manuscript is rougher in style, with individually-numbered paragraphs that rarely flow together, and is in two separate parts: a main 'Informatory Accompt', covering August 1696 to 14 February 1697, and a supplementary 'Continued Accompt', covering 18 February to 28 March 1697. The printed *True Narrative* splices the two parts together and revises the text throughout, smoothing it out into a more continuous and readable narrative. The manuscript gives names of witnesses at the end of most paragraphs; the printed *True Narrative* omits these.

As well as these differences of presentation, there are differences of substance, which raise questions about the veracity of the printed *True Narrative* and indeed about the broader motives of the promoters of the witchcraft prosecutions. Two small initial examples will show that the editors of the *True Narrative* sought to improve the story that they were telling, and were willing to depart from literal truth in order to achieve this. First, the manuscript said in paragraph 19 that Katherine Campbell 'never appeard to the Child' after she was imprisoned, but the *True Narrative* added a story about her having later appeared on specific days when she was let out of prison. The idea here was that witches lost their powers once they were apprehended by governmental authorities, since these authorities had divinely-legitimated power against which the Devil could not prevail.[3] The *True Narrative* was evidently trying to drive this idea further home. A version of the story of Campbell's subsequent appearance was also related by the prosecuting advocate, Francis Grant, in his summing-up speech to the assize.[4] Second, the manuscript said in paragraph 21 that Christian 'stript her self of all her cloaths that were upon her and left not her very shirt upon her body', but the *True Narrative* changed this perhaps embarrassing story, saying instead that she tried to do so but was prevented. The manuscript shows that the local ministers Andrew Turner and James Brisbane, who contributed to the editing of the *True Narrative*, witnessed this episode in person; so, if they were involved in changing it, they really knew what they were doing.[5]

Two spectacular passages in the printed *True Narrative* described episodes, one in late November or early December and the other on 24 January, in which Christian Shaw confronted and argued with the apparition of a witch, who was invisible to all the others present. In the first episode the witch was Katherine Campbell, whose curse had set off Christian's troubles. Christian, with Bible in hand, quoted and expounded scripture to 'Katie' at considerable length, reproached her for tormenting her, accused her of hypocrisy, and predicted that she would suffer damnation. The second confrontation episode was similar, except that a different, unnamed witch was being confronted. Yet both these passages are completely absent from the manuscript 'Informatory Accompt', and have clearly been spliced into the narrative as subsequent additions. How should we understand this?

There are three possible explanations for these confrontation episodes. One is that accounts of the episodes were written down at the time like all the others, but were then somehow mislaid temporarily when the manuscript was being compiled, and were restored to their proper place in the printed version.

3 Cf. Stuart Clark, *Thinking with Demons: The Idea of Witchcraft in Early Modern Europe* (Oxford, 1997), 560–71.

4 Printed in the *True Narrative* at its pp. 4, 6 (pp. 269, 272 below).

5 The introduction to the edition of the *True Narrative*, below in the present volume, discusses how the narrative was assembled.

The similarity between the two episodes makes this less likely; these are not random omissions. A second, contrasting explanation is that the accounts were not written until later, and were deliberate fabrications. Neither of these explanations can be ruled out entirely. However, a third explanation is preferred here, a modified version of the second one. The accounts were indeed written later, but were not so much deliberate fabrications as exercises in reconstruction of Christian's likely past behaviour.

Towards the end of the manuscript version of the narrative, on 1 February, there is a *retrospective* mention of conversations with apparitions: 'Note here That severall moneths before this tyme she was distinctly heard to give thir replyes to some as discoursing with her thoe unseen and unheard by spectators about her' (p. 9). So, in February, perhaps some 'spectators' were remembering, or being encouraged to remember, these early conversations. By this time, the written narrative must have been taking shape, as the compilers assembled the initial written fragments into a single draft text. As the compilers worked, they might well have talked to the witnesses, who would explain or comment on the written notes that they had made at the time. This 'Note here' may have been included retrospectively on 1 February, out of its proper chronological order, because nothing had been written down at the time; all that the compilers had to go on was the witnesses' recollection in February of a conversation with an apparition 'severall moneths before this tyme'.

The manuscript contains two further hints on how to understand this episode. Its earliest *dated* mention of a conversation with an apparition is in the statement of the apothecary Henry Marshall on 1 January (p. 19). Marshall described a visit to Bargarran on 20 November during which he had witnessed Christian talking to the apparition of Katherine Campbell. In Marshall's account, Christian did not expound scripture; rather she was trying to protect herself from Campbell who was about to stab her with a sword. The first confrontation episode in the *True Narrative* would have been around that date, and may well be an improved version of this event. The second hint comes in the notes of the witches' executions, which records that a minister asked Katherine Campbell 'if she did not remember the godly discourses and gracious admonitions which Christine Shaw while in a fit gave her' (p. 43). This was when Campbell was waiting for the verdict in her trial, on 19 May, so the improved version of the story must have taken shape by then. Indeed it had probably taken shape before then, since her recorded reply, that she did remember, indicates that she had already been told about it.

The manuscript gives no comparable hints as to the origin of the second confrontation episode, on 24 January, but its similarity to the first episode is striking. However, this time Christian was addressing, not Katherine Campbell, but an unnamed witch who, she said, had become a witch only three nights previously. This was an orthodox idea in demonology, but it was an idea without a broader purpose in Christian's psychodrama, and it was not mentioned again. Still, it might have been harder to invent than the remainder of Christian's speech in this episode, which consisted of conventional pieties. This second confrontation episode is thus even harder to interpret than the first one, but it may have had its origin, at least, in something that Christian had really said.

The reason for adding these episodes to the narrative is clear enough: confrontations with invisible apparitions were part of the classic behaviour of a demoniac. Well-informed people in Scotland in 1697–8 had access to other accounts of demoniacs, and they wanted to shape their account of Christian's behaviour to conform to such accounts. For instance, Hugh McLachlan and Kim Swales have observed that Deodat Lawson's pamphlet about witchcraft and possession in Salem, Massachusetts in 1692 has similarities to the printed *True Narrative*.[6] The confrontation episodes are particularly notable here. In Lawson's pamphlet, Ann Putnam senior has a fit during which she argues with the apparition of Rebecca Nurse ('Goodw. N.'), and quotes scripture to her:

> She then began to Complain of, and as it were to Converse personally with, Goodw. N., saying, *Goodw. N. Be gone! Be gone! Be gone! are you not ashamed, a Woman of your Profession, to afflict a poor Creature so? what hurt did I ever do you in my life! you have but two years to live, and then the Devil will torment your Soul* ... After this, she seemed to dispute with the Apparition about a particular *Text* of Scripture. The Apparition seemed to deny it, (the Womans eyes being fast closed all this time) she said, *She was Sure there was such a Text*; and she would tell it; and then the Shape would be gone; for said she, *I am sure you cannot stand before that Text!* then she was sorely Afflicted ... at last she broke forth and said, *It is the third Chapter of the Revelations*.[7]

This is comparable with Christian Shaw's first confrontation episode, in which (among other things) she was said to have quoted 'many places of Scripture thorow the Revelation and Evangelists'. Moreover, there were other published accounts of demonic possession from which the compilers of the *True Narrative* could have drawn. In the widely-circulated English *Witches of Warboys* narrative, one of the possessed children, Joan Throckmorton, had long confrontations with a spirit.[8] Various other aspects of the reported behaviour of previous demoniacs could have influenced the narrative of Christian Shaw's

6 Hugh McLachlan and Kim Swales, 'The Bewitchment of Christian Shaw: A Reassessment of the Famous Paisley Witchcraft Case of 1697', in Yvonne G. Brown and Rona Ferguson (eds.), *Twisted Sisters: Women, Crime and Deviance in Scotland since 1400* (East Linton, 2002), 54–83, at pp. 70–2.

7 Deodat Lawson, *A Brief and True Narrative of some Remarkable Passages relating to Sundry Persons afflicted by Witchcraft, at Salem Village* (Boston: Benjamin Harris, 1692), 6.

8 *The Most Strange and Admirable Discoverie of the Three Witches of Warboys* (London: Thomas Man and John Winnington, 1593), sigs. N–N3. This work would later be discussed at length by John Bell in *The Tryal of Witchcraft* (c.1705), as will be seen below in the present volume.

possession, and further research may shed more light on this.[9] Some other passages in which the *True Narrative* expanded upon the manuscript version are noted in footnotes to the *True Narrative*, below. Further comparison of the two texts would be revealing.

The accounts of Christian's biblical knowledge in these confrontation episodes are not implausible in themselves. Scottish children's education focused heavily on the Bible. And the local ministers would have been neglecting their duty if they had not, once Christian's fits began, explained to her and to her family the religious framework within which such afflictions should be understood. Indeed the *True Narrative* stated that many ministers 'kept days of Humiliation and Prayer weekly in the Family, and sometimes in the Parish Church with the Congregation' – naming fourteen ministers from several presbyteries who had taken part (p. xxxvii). The account of the first confrontation episode specified that Christian quoted one of these ministers' recent 'lectures' – though the minister's name seems to be wrong, another small indication that the account was not written down at the time. So the likelihood that Christian would have had the knowledge to enact these confrontation episodes does not constitute proof that these episodes have been accurately reported. The editors of the *True Narrative* commented, both on Christian's good understanding of scripture in her discourses with the apparitions, and on the assistance that she had received from the Holy Spirit (p. xiv). Perhaps they themselves experienced the guidance of the Holy Spirit as they piously reconstructed what they believed that her words had been, or could have been.

Other items in the manuscript

Much that the *True Narrative* does publish is not found in the manuscript, notably the *True Narrative*'s introductory essay, and the two detailed speeches in court by the prosecuting advocate Francis Grant. Here, however, some notes can be given of further items where the manuscript adds to our knowledge.

The printed *True Narrative* omitted or abbreviated several of the documents submitted to, or produced by, the commission of enquiry in January and February 1697. Several of the commissioners' own examinations of witnesses were omitted, and the statements of the physician and apothecary were abbreviated. The manuscript gives these in full. The physician's and apothecary's statements were also printed in full in *Sadducismus Debellatus*, the revised

[9] One example would be the possession of the Goodwin children in Boston, Massachusetts, narrated in Cotton Mather, *Memorable Providences relating to Witchcrafts and Possessions* (Boston: R. P. and Joseph Brunning, 1689). This began when a 13-year-old girl accused a laundress of stealing some linen, and her mother cursed the girl (pp. 2–3); the children had some ease from their symptoms when the woman was arrested (p. 7). Both these motifs would reappear in Christian Shaw's case.

London version of the *True Narrative*, making a few minor textual changes from the manuscript version edited here; the manuscript version may well be closer to the originals. (The relationship between *Sadducismus Debellatus* and the *True Narrative* is discussed further in the introduction to the latter work, below in the present volume.) The edition of the manuscript below thus includes all of the enquiry commission's documents that it contains, with the exception of four that are given instead in the edition of *A Relation of the Diabolical Practices* (as discussed above). The manuscript also includes a fuller version of the confession and suicide of John Reid, and a slightly different version of the account of the execution of the witches; these documents are edited below and can be compared with the *True Narrative*'s versions.

The manuscript also includes two sermons: James Hutchison's sermon, published in 1910, and Thomas Blackwell's 'Prefatorie Discourse', edited below. Blackwell was preaching to introduce a public fast throughout the presbytery, at the time when the criminal trial was getting under way. Like Hutchison's sermon, it is an example of how ministers preached to their congregations about the threat of witchcraft. Blackwell clearly hopes that the accused witches will be convicted, and seems to regard their not having confessed as an indication of guilt. He declares that there are probably many more witches within the congregation, and hints that anyone who does not support the public fast may be a witch. He urges the congregation to pray 'that God would discover all others that are guiltie and are not apprehended'.

The manuscript's most striking addition to the documents that were printed at the time is a tract by James Williamson making erudite demonological criticisms of the evidence used to convict the witches. This tract deserves its own introductory discussion.

James Williamson's 'Vindication of the Witches'

The author of this tract, James Williamson of Chapelton, was a minor laird in Dunbartonshire. He is not known to have written any other works, but he appears in 1700 as a signatory to a petition to parliament in favour of trade.[10] His tract addresses an educated readership; he makes a parade of terms like 'postulate' and 'corollary' that are used in formal logic, and includes a word in Greek. He deploys many of the assumptions of conventional demonology to undermine the prosecutions. On the surface he may seem to make only tangential reference to the Bargarran case, and he avoids naming names – but his tract is in fact carefully constructed to attack the specific range of evidence that the prosecutors presented in court in Paisley.

[10] Records of the Parliaments of Scotland (www.rps.ac.uk), A1700/10/28. Chapelton was not very near Bargarran; it was in the parish of Cumbernauld, in the detached eastern part of Dunbartonshire. See Joseph Irving, *The Book of Dumbartonshire*, 3 vols. (Edinburgh, 1879), ii, 397.

Williamson begins, as many demonologists did, not with witches but with the Devil. He presents the Devil in an unusual but not unorthodox way: as a prosecutor in God's court. The Devil accuses certain humans of being sinners, and seeks God's permission to inflict punishment (God's 'vengeance') on these sinners. As well as being a prosecutor, therefore, the Devil is also an active agent in the world, inflicting the punishment himself in response to God's judgments. Some of the accusations of sinfulness that the Devil makes are true, while others are false; Williamson implies that God grants permission to the Devil when the human really is a sinner. However, he refrains from stating this explicitly, perhaps because in Christian theology God's purposes are held to be ultimately unknowable, or because *all* humans are held to be sinners. At any rate, the Devil is doing God's work by acting as a functionary in his court. Williamson adds that God does not *need* the Devil for this purpose; good angels also inflict punishment on sinners. But the Devil is definitely an active agent in the physical world.

A second point about the Devil, running through the whole tract, is also an orthodox one: the Devil is a liar and deceiver. In particular, the Devil assumes the likeness of other people, or creates the apparitions of other people – and these other people are not necessarily witches. Indeed the Devil may deliberately cause the apparitions of innocent people to appear, in order to incriminate them. This point had previously been made by Sir George Mackenzie in his 1672 'pleading' (edited above in the present volume), and by the 1690s it had become a mainstream position, adopted even by some who favoured witchcraft prosecutions.[11] Yet this point was capable of fatally undermining some of the central evidence for the Bargarran prosecutions. No matter how many confrontations Christian Shaw had with the apparition of Katherine Campbell, and no matter how many fits she had when Campbell touched her, this would not prove Campbell to be guilty; the Devil caused the fits, and caused Campbell's likeness to appear, for his own deceitful purposes.

Williamson sees demonic possession as a punishment for sin; the 'damsel' and her parents are being afflicted because they are sinners. He adds, 'in charity', that they are probably not greater sinners than those around them, but he explains that sometimes ordinary sinners are still singled out for extraordinary punishment. This forms a contrast with the attitude of the witch-hunters, who were much more keen to see Christian as an innocent victim.[12]

Witches, as well as the Devil, certainly exist in Williamson's view. What witches do is to accuse other people before human tribunals, just as the Devil does before God's tribunal, 'sometymes truely sometimes falslie'. Thus, witches who confess, naming other people as witches, cannot be trusted to name the

[11] Stuart Clark, *Vanities of the Eye: Vision in Early Modern European Culture* (Oxford, 2007), 144–53; the Bargarran case is discussed at p. 152.

[12] On this point, the preface to the *True Narrative* declared that 'There is no just ground to reflect on *particular* Persons or Families upon account of such troubles', citing some of the same biblical passages as Williamson but drawing different conclusions (p. vii).

guilty and not the innocent. This point was capable of fatally undermining more of the Bargarran evidence: the confessions of the three young star witnesses, Elizabeth Anderson, James Lindsay and Thomas Lindsay, who had named numerous people whom they had seen at witches' meetings. Williamson calls them 'Litle Imps', and explains at length why their testimony is not credible.

Williamson then turns to another form of evidence: the Devil's mark, which he regards as an insensitive spot on the skin. The Devil's mark had been in disrepute in Scotland ever since the most prominent witch-prickers had been disgraced in 1662;[13] yet the prosecutors of 1697 revived it, finding marks on many of the accused witches. Williamson explains in detail that the Devil's mark is not convincing evidence, because innocent people have natural marks.

The question of the Devil's intentions in all this is of interest to Williamson. Why, he wonders, does the Devil get his 'instruments' (the witches) to reveal some other witches truly? He suggests three answers. Perhaps it is so that they will go to hell sooner. Or perhaps the witches thus revealed have been troublesome to him or to other witches. Or perhaps, by speaking truth, he may be able to recruit other Christians. This kind of elaborate reconstruction of the Devil's intentions may be characteristic of the demonology of this period; the prosecuting lawyer Francis Grant did a good deal of it in his speeches in court (published in the *True Narrative*). But Williamson's conclusions are anti-demonological – or rather, anti-prosecution.

Perhaps Williamson was fortunate that, in taking careful aim at the most notorious Bargarran evidence, he did not have to confront some of the other types of evidence commonly used in witchcraft trials. Witches cannot credibly incriminate others – but can they confess, truly and reliably, that they *themselves* are witches? Williamson's main reason for rejecting the testimony of Anderson and her cousins is in fact that they themselves are witches, 'in a Compact' with the Devil. He does not explain why he thinks this, but presumably he believes their confessions at least to this extent. Elizabeth Anderson, James Lindsay and Thomas Lindsay had been named as accused witches in the initial trial commission in March;[14] only later were the charges against them dropped so that they could operate as prosecution witnesses. None of the seven witches who were executed confessed, so the main evidence against them was Christian's 'spectral' evidence plus the confessions of the three young witnesses.[15] Williamson's critique of this evidence was cogent, but it is not clear what would he have said about accused witches who *did* confess to having made a pact with the Devil.

13 Brian P. Levack, 'The Decline and End of Scottish Witch-Hunting', in Julian Goodare (ed.), *The Scottish Witch-Hunt in Context* (Manchester, 2002), 166–81, at pp. 174–5.

14 SPCR, A1697/3/11.

15 The confession of John Reid (edited below) also named several witches, but it was recorded on 21 May, too late to be used in the trial of the seven Bargarran witches, which had concluded on 19 May.

As for witches who curse their neighbours and cause misfortune to them, this too was a common form of evidence in Scottish witchcraft trials, but did not attain the same prominence in the Bargarran case, because of the notoriety of Christian Shaw's possession. Yet the Bargarran witches were accused of causing ordinary misfortune too, as shown by both the trial record and the *Relation*. Williamson does not discuss this.

Much of Williamson's argument is a form of the distinctive 'Protestant demonology' identified in a celebrated essay by Stuart Clark.[16] Protestant pastoral demonologists endorsed belief in witchcraft, but warned their congregations that misfortune might be a punishment from God for one's own sin, or a test of one's faith, rather than the result of bewitchment. The biblical story of Job was important here: God permitted the Devil to afflict Job, not because Job was a sinner, but because he wished to test Job's faith. Williamson does not develop the idea of suffering as a test of faith, but the Devil as a prosecutor in God's court may well be derived more from Job than from anything else in the Bible.

So Williamson's critique is to some extent an old-fashioned argument – or, to put it another way, an argument with a long pedigree. He certainly does not engage with the latest anti-demonological philosophy. Europe in the 1690s saw a widespread and bitter controversy about this, provoked by the works of Balthasar Bekker. Using Cartesian philosophy, Bekker claimed that the Devil and other spirits, being spirits, were unable to affect the physical world; only God, being beyond spirit and matter, was able to do so. Biblical accounts of the Devil's activity were to be understood metaphorically and figuratively; to take them literally, as demonologists did, was superstitious.[17] Williamson, whose arguments rest on traditional theology and not on natural philosophy, shows no sign of interest in such views.[18]

Williamson's broader religious views are intriguing and would repay further study. He was evidently a keen episcopalian; he would later, in 1709, be active in supporting the episcopalian controversialist and future bishop Archibald Campbell.[19] His tract shows him to be interested in apostolic succession and

16 Stuart Clark, 'Protestant Demonology: Sin, Superstition, and Society (*c.*1520–*c.*1630)', in Bengt Ankarloo and Gustav Henningsen (eds.), *Early Modern European Witchcraft: Centres and Peripheries* (Oxford, 1990), 45–81.

17 For the Bekker debate see Jonathan Israel, *Radical Enlightenment: Philosophy and the Making of Modernity, 1650–1750* (Oxford, 2001), 375–405.

18 Further study may be able to place Williamson in the range of English and British demonological views, which have been studied by various scholars. See Ian Bostridge, *Witchcraft and its Transformations,* c.*1650*–c.*1750* (Oxford, 1997); Peter Elmer, *Witchcraft, Witch-Hunting, and Politics in Early Modern England* (Oxford, 2016); Michael Hunter, *The Decline of Magic: Britain and the Enlightenment* (New Haven, 2020).

19 NRS, letters from Williamson to Campbell, 2 April and 30 May 1709, CH12/12/312. Cf. Rowan Strong, 'Campbell, Archibald (*c.*1669–1744), Scottish Episcopal bishop', *ODNB*. For presbyterian and episcopalian culture in this period see Alasdair Raffe, 'Presbyterians and Episcopalians: The Formation of Confessional Cultures in Scotland, 1660–1715', *English*

the authority of the true church, in the primitive church, and in 'schism'; he wishes for a 'return to Catholick unity' (by which he does not mean Roman Catholic). He has a particular dislike of the New England Protestants. A presbyterian could object to the New Englanders' congregationalism, but would hardly have been likely to use Williamson's provocative word 'heresy' about them.

Overall, then, Williamson is a witchcraft sceptic, but his scepticism is not about the existence of witches. Nor does his scepticism relate to judicial procedure, such as the use of torture to gather evidence. Yet he is radically sceptical about the theological basis for evidence of witchcraft. He even says that he wants the genuine witches to be punished – but this must not be by the use of evidence that might incriminate the innocent. And all the evidence he has discussed is evidence that might incriminate the innocent. The true remedy for witchcraft and possession is repentance for sin and turning to God, within a framework of legitimate Christian authority.

It would be interesting to know whether Williamson's tract was circulated during the Bargarran witches' trial, with the intention of influencing the outcome, or afterwards, as a critical comment on it. After the trial, as the printed *True Narrative* makes clear, pressure for further prosecutions continued, and this tract could well have contributed to the debate on that topic. The *True Narrative*, in its concluding 'Advertisement', denounced a plan to publish a pamphlet opposing the prosecutions. It would be fascinating to know whether Williamson's 'Vindication' was intended to be that pamphlet or part of it. But the *True Narrative* envisaged a pamphlet about Mary Morrison, while Williamson does not engage with arguments about individuals.

Williamson's 'Vindication' was at any rate not the only critical voice to be raised about the Bargarran prosecutions. A 'Treatise on Witchcraft' written about this time by the presbyterian John Bell, who in 1697 was minister of Broughton in Lanarkshire, generally endorsed belief in witchcraft, but was scathing about

> the sorceries exercised upon the Laird of Bargarran's daughter, anno 1697, a time when persons of more goodness and esteem than most of their calumniators were defamed for witches, and which was occasioned mostly by the forwardness and absurd credulity of diverse otherwise worthy ministers of the gospel, and some topping professors [i.e. persons professing exceptional Christian piety] in and about the city of Glasgow.[20]

Historical Review, 125 (2010), 570–98; for specific disputes see Ben Rogers, 'Religious Comprehension in Scotland, 1689–1695', *Journal of Ecclesiastical History*, 74 (2023), 774–800.

20 Quoted by Charles K. Sharpe, *A Historical Account of the Belief in Witchcraft in Scotland* (London, 1884), 173. This manuscript treatise is now lost, surviving only in three extracts quoted by Sharpe at his pp. 173, 208–9, 216–17. See Christina Larner, 'Two Late Scottish Witchcraft Tracts: *Witch-Craft Proven* and *The Tryal of Witchcraft*', in Sydney Anglo (ed.), *The Damned*

One may wonder who these 'persons of ... goodness and esteem' were; perhaps they included Margaret Laing, who was executed, and Mary Morrison, who survived. One may also wonder which of the 'otherwise worthy' ministers in the Glasgow area Bell had in mind as the principal promoters of the prosecutions. The aftermath of the trials is discussed more fully in the introduction to the *True Narrative*, below. In the meantime, though, returning in conclusion to the 'Bargarran Witches' manuscript itself, historians can at least be grateful to John Shaw of Bargarran for having preserved Williamson's 'Vindication', with its fresh perspective on the witchcraft debate – even if Shaw remained unpersuaded by its arguments.

The Appendix

After the end of the edition of the 'Bargarran Witches' manuscript itself, an edition is given of two short documents with related material, both of which originated from the enquiry commission in February 1697. The first is a copy of a newsletter from Robert Alexander, the clerk to the enquiry commission, reporting some of the commission's proceedings.[21] This newsletter reads like an early version of what would become paragraph 37 of the 'Informatory Accompt'. The second document, which was probably enclosed in Alexander's letter, narrates some episodes of Christian Shaw's behaviour in early February. Much of this narrative is the same as paragraphs 33 to 36 of the 'Informatory Accompt', but again it is evidently an earlier version, with several differences. The published *True Narrative* has been adapted from the 'Informatory Accompt' to form a more persuasive narrative of demonic possession, but even the 'Informatory Accompt' has been adapted in some ways.

TEXT[22]

Ane Informatory Accompt of the Beginning, Progress and Circumstances of the Trouble of Christine Shaw Daughter to John Shaw of Bargarran.

1. The Laird of Bargarran having a daughter whose name is Christine Shaw, a very hopefull and sensible chyld of the age of 11 yeirs. About the

Art: Essays in the Literature of Witchcraft (London, 1977), 227–45, at pp. 227–32. The wording of the second of these extracts (Sharpe's pp. 208–9) is the same as part of one of Francis Grant's speeches in court (in the *True Narrative* at its p. 13); neither Sharpe nor Larner comment on this, and in the absence of Sharpe's manuscript it seems impossible to say more about it.

John Bell's extant tract, *The Tryal of Witchcraft* (c.1705), is edited below in the present volume.

21 Robert Alexander was also sheriff clerk of Renfrew, and is described in the commission's own documentation as a 'writer' (lawyer) in Glasgow. He also appears in the 'Informatory Accompt' as a notary witnessing several signatures.

22 Source: Mitchell Library, Glasgow, 'Bargarran Witches' manuscript.

letter end of August last Ther wes a woman servant in the house whose name was Katrine Campbell against whom the Child alledged That she had stollen and drunk some milk, Wpon quhich the said Katrine fell into a rage, and in presence of the Lady and the rest of the family, did in the Childs face 3 tymes hydeously imprecat the heavie curse of God upon her, and lykewayes at the same tyme and with the same breath had this horrid expression to the child thrice repeated, The Devill harle your soull through hell; This wes declared judicially before the Church session of Erskine, as upon oath by famous witnessis. Quhich is hereuith produced.

2. This falling out on the Munday; Upon the Fryday morning thairafter, about the rysing of the sun, one Agnes Easmith[23] meeting the Child in Bargarren Closs with another of her sisters, enquyred how the Lady and the young child wes; and of quhat age the young child wes. To quhich the said Christine replyed: that she did not know. Then the said Agnes enquyred how she wes her self? and quhat age she wes off? To quhich she answered she wes well and going in 11 yeiris. Witnessis hereto Agnes McCashly and Jean Kerr servants. *Sic subscribitur*[24] Agnes McCashlen.

3. Wpon the morrow being Saturday she going to bed at night in perfect health fell a strugleing in her sleep crying help help. And immediatly afterward suddenly gott up, and flew over the top of a resting bed (on quhich she wes lying) to the admiration[25] of her father, mother and other spectators when in appearance she had bein brained, If providentially a woman had not being standing thair calling for some coalls to the chamber fyre. Wpon quhom the force of the child (fleeing out as said is) came with such violence as the woman had neither had bein able to resist nor preserve the Child, if the door had not bein at her back, and having thus prevented the child in her arms, brought her into another bed, quhair she lay for the space of half ane hour stiff and insensible, as if she had bein dead, and slept none for 48 hours thairafter But cryed out of violent pain throw her whole body, and quhair she fell any way drowsie she fell into great frights and cryed out help, help. Witnessis thereto Jean Allexander in Killellan and Agnes McCashlen servants in the house. *Sic subscribitur* Jean Allexander, Agnes McAshlen.

4. After which tyme the pain fixed in her syde which wes attended with such violence, that her body bended so up, that she would have stood as a bow upon her feet and neck, and thus she continued for 8t[26] days without power of speech During which tyme she had scarce half ane hours intermissione att once, the fitts coming instantly on by a swerfe[27] and going instantly off

23 This name is given as Agnes Nasmith in most other documents concerning the case. The trial record calls her 'Agnes Easemith or Neasmith'.

24 'Thus it is subscribed'.

25 'admiration': astonishment.

26 *Sic*. Read '8'.

27 'swerfe': swoon.

by a swerfe, she being perfectly well and sensible in the intervales. Witnessis hereto The Lady Northbarr, John Whyt apothecary in Pasley, Archibald Ballantyne of Kelly and his Lady. *Sic subscribitur* Jonet Aikine, John Whyt, Arch: Ballantyne, Jonet McGilchryst.

5. Wpon all quhich the parents called for the said Easmith and threatned her as having bein the occasion of thair Childs trouble, and thairafter she had six days Intermissione. *Sic subscribitur* Cristine Aikine, John Whyt.[28]

6. After this about the middle of September she fell in fitts differing from the former, during quhich the strenth of 4 men, could scarce hold her in her fits[29] strugleing so as if she had bein strenuously defending her self from {*p. 2*} [*about 4–5 words damaged*] any person about touched any part of her body she [*1 word damaged*] vehemently cry and screek, as if they had bein assaulting her [*about 3 words damaged*] but could speak none. Witnessis hereto The Lady Northbar, Lady Kelly, Mr Andrew Turner minister and John Mcgilchrist wryter in Glasgow. *Sic subscribitur* Jonet Aikine, Jonet Mcgilchryst, Andr: Turner, J°McGilchryst.

7. About this time her parents called for physicians viz. Dr Johnstoun and John Whyt apothecary in Pasley, who applyed seaverall things but had no effect upon the patient either to the better or worse, all the whyle her belly extraordinary ryseing and falling, as it had bein a pair of bellowes, and her body in such strange motions as would have made the whole bed shake To the consternation of beholders. Witnessis hereto Lady Northbar, Lady Kelly, Mr Andrew Turner minister and James M^{c}gilchrist of Northbar. *Sic subscribitur* Jonet Aikine, Jonet Mcgilchryst, Andr: Turner, JM^{c}Gilchryst.

8. Someday thairafter her fitts altered again, in that she got speaking during the tyme of the fits, and thairin fell a crying, That the forsaid Katrine Campbell, and Agnes Easmith were cutting her syde, and other parts of her body, which parts in that tyme were violently tormented, and quhen the fitt removed she still averred, that she had sein the same persons doing the same things, of quhich she cryed whyle in the fitt. In the intervale being still as well and sensible as ever, and would not beleive but the bystanders saw them as well as she, In this condition she remained with some intervales (with some but not very considerable variety) for the space of a moneth, Witnessis hereto Lady Northbar, John Walkinshaw in Erskine and James Mcgilchrist of Northbar. *Sic subscribitur* Jonet Aikine, JWalkinshaw, JMcGilchryst.

9. After quhich tyme she wes carried to Glasgow quhair Dr Birsbane by Mr Hendery Marshell apothecary made applicatione of medicine to her, after quhich she had a 4tnights intermissione, after quhich her fitts returned after this manner, She knew quhen the fitts were a coming by a pain in her syde quhich she felt before they came, quherin her throat wes prodigiously drawn

28 This paragraph would later be omitted from the published *True Narrative*.
29 Conjectural reconstruction of damaged word: 'f…'.

into her breast, and her tongue back in her throat, her whole body becoming stiff and extended as a dead corpse without sense and motion, And sometymes her tongue wes drawn out of her mouth over her chin ane extraordinary lenth, Her teeth would have checked together upon it, that bystanders were forced to thrust something betwixt her teeth for the preservation of her tongue, and it wes still observed that her tongue wes so tortured as this when she essayed to pray. And thus she continued with sensible intervales, quhairin she had perfect health, and could give a full accompt of quhat she wes heard utter whyle in the fitt. Witnessis hereto the Lady Northbarr and John Walkinshaw abovenamed. *Sic subscribitur* Jonet Aikine, J Walkinshaw.

10. Again she being brought back to her fathers house about the 12th November (and, the former fitts continueing with some variatione) she put out of her mouth some parcells of hair, some curled some plated, some knotted of different collours, and that in large quantities. Thus she continued to doe 4 or 5 days in swarfeing at every quarter of ane hour. Witnessis hereto The Lady Northbar, Janet Jamison her servant and Mr Andrew Turner minister. *Sic subscribitur* Jonet Aikine, Andr: Turner, R Allexander nottar at the Command of Janet Jamison who declares she cannot wryt.

11. And being again carried to Glasgow for the space of 3 days in her former swerfeing fitts, and at the end of every quarter of ane hour, she put out of her mouth coall: cinders about the bignes of chesnuts, some quherof were so hot that bystanders could scarce handle them: Then for the space of 2 days in her swarfing fitts as formerly she put furth of her mouth straw folded up together, and when put out returned to its lenth, and that in great quantities. Then she put out of her mouth bones of various sorts and syzes as bones of foules and small bones {*p. 3*} of the heads of kine,[30] and then some small candle firr sticks about 3 or 4 inch long, which when any upon the sight either of bones or such took hold of them to pull them out, They found them horribly drawn back into her throat, particularly the Laird of Kellie observing a bone in her mouth lyke a duck shank, and essaying to draw it out, he declares that he found something as drawing it into her throat, so that it took his full strenth to pull it out. After this she put out of her mouth some quantities of unclean hay, as if it had bein taken out of a dunghill with intermixt dung, quhich was so stinking that the Child could not endure the taste of her mouth, but still after outputting of the same was necessitat to reinge her mouth with water, Then for a night and a day she put out of her mouth a considerable number of wild foull feathers, after that a gravell stone which to the judgment of spectators had bein past by some in a gravell fitt, at some more litle small whyt stones, and a whole galse[31] wher with they use to dye, together with lumps of candlegrease and eggshells, During quhich

[30] 'kine': cows.

[31] *Sic.* The published *True Narrative* has 'whole nut gall'.

tyme she continued in her swerfeing fitts, with small intervales as formerly, quhairin she wes in perfect health. Witnessis hereto Kelly and his Lady, Lady Northbar, Rebeckah Marshell servant, Dr Birsbane and Mr Hendry Marshell attestatione producit. *Sic subscribitur* Arch: Ballantyne, Jonet M^c^Gilchryst, Jonet Aikine, RAllexander nottar at the comand of Rebeckah Marshell who declares she cannot wryt.

12. Sometyme after the outputting of such things she fell into more than ordinarly violent fitts with lamentable crying, four persons, being hardly able to keep her from climbing up the walls of the chamber or from hurting her self otherwayes, ane extream pain being in her back, and throw the rest of her body, having no power of her speech, but in her sensible intervales she declared that 4 men Allexander and James Andersones, and other two (of whom she gave grave marks[32] but knew not thair names) were Tormenting her. It is to be observed that many of thes she names are known among us to be of ill fame, and thair is this remarkeable instance that for some tyme she knew not the name of the said Allexander Anderson till he came on[e] day a begging to the door quhair the child wes, She cryed out that, that wes he quhom she saw amongst the crew, and in this condition she continued 4 or 5 days. Witnessis hereto the Lady Northbar, Christian Aikine and Janet Jamison servant. *Sic subscribitur* Jonet Aikine, Christine Aikine, RAllexander nottar at the Command of Janet Jamison who declares she cannot wryt.

13. After this she fell into other fitts quhairin she saw the forenamed persons with some others and heard and saw seaverall things that were among: particularly she wold have told, quhen she would take her fits? How often she would take them, off what continuance they would be; which ordinarly fell out accordingly with some discourses among them relating to her self and others, Witnessis hereto the persons abovenamed and John M^c^gilchryst wryter in Glasgow. *Sic subscribitur* Jonet Aikine, Cristine Aikine, J^o^M^c^Gilchryst, RAllexander nottar at the Command of Janet Jamison who declares she cannot wryt.

14. About the 8^t^ of December being brought home again from Glasgow, having had 6 or 7 days intervale she fell into frighting fitts, The occasion of which she declares is her seeing the Devill in prodigious and horrid shapes threatning to devour her and to take her witts from her, and then she falls dead and stiff with all the parts of her body extended and straight as a dead corpse without sense or motion, which fitts as they come suddenly on without her knowledge, so instantly she recovers and grows perfectly well, and ordinarly they come when she essayes to pray. Witnessis hereto, The mother of the Child, Mr Andrew Turner and Mr James Birsbane ministers. *Sic subscribitur* Christian Mcgilchryst, AndTurner, JBirsbane. {*p. 4*}

[32] 'grave marks': detailed descriptions.

15. In which tyme also she takes other fitts more sensible knowing when they are a coming, how long they will stay, when they will return, In quhich her eyes strangely alters and turns in her head to the admiratione of beholders with a continuall painfull working about her heart, sometymes her joynts complicat and drawn together, which fitts she takes by a swerfe, her head being draun about forcibly toward her shoulders, and instantly recovers after the same manner, During this tyme the fitts alters as to the tyme of thair coming and duration, sometimes endeavouring to byte her oun fingers, or any thing else that comes in her way, her seeing the persons beforementioned moe or fewer about her, her poynting thame out to bystanders thoe by them unseen; sometyme declareing that she hath a grip of them by thair cloaths, particularly December 17t she wes in a sore fitt and cryed out of saveralls that were Tormenting her, she being in the bed grasped toward the foot thairof and cryd out that she had got a grip of the sleeves of one Joan Parks girkinale[33] which wes as she said duddie[34] at the elbow, and instantly the Childs mother and aunt being holding her in the fitt heard a cloath rent but saw nothing but found in every one of the childs hands a peice of red cloath, off which kynd of cloath thair wes none in the roome nor about the whole house. Another particular is that she tells that thair is such or such ane one among the Crew going to prick her tongue, quhairupon it is instantly pulled back in her throat and she lyes dumb a considerable tyme, sometymes upon her recovery she tells that she hears seaverall things among thame, but she dare not make thame knoun, yet when by her mother or others she is prevailed at to tell them, Instantly the torment falls out as she told it wes threatned. She says further That they appear to her ordinarly with lights and strange sorts of candles quhich is fearfull to her. Witnessis hereto Lady Northbar, Mr Andrew Turner and Mr James Birsbanes ministers, Lady Kellie, and the Chylds mother. *Sic subscribitur* Jonet Aikine, Andr: Turner, Jbirsbane, Jonet Mcgilchrist, Christian Mcgilchrist.

16. Thus she continues not only in the fitts forementioned with some alteration, but falls by swerfeing in light fitts, quhairin she continues for two or three hours, sometymes more, sometimes less with very short intervales, and in the fitts she doth not much complain of pain, but hath a strange and unaccountable motion, and palpitation sometyme in her breast, sometyme in other parts of her body, which continues sometymes greater sometymes less during the quhilk tyme of her said fitt, quhairin she is not so solid as at other tymes there, in the intervales she is as composed as ever, as she uses to be in the intervale of \all/ other fitts which (with the rest) comes instantly on and goes instantly off by a swerfe. Witnessis hereto the persons abovenamed. *Sic subscribitur* Jonet Aikine, Jonet Mcgilchrist, Andr: Turner, JBirsbane.

33 'girkinale': jerkin, jacket.
34 'duddie': ragged.

17. 1° It is to be observed that the forsaid Agnes Easmith being brought by the parents a 2^{d} tyme to see the Chyld; wes desyred to pray for her, She prayed that the Lord God of heaven and earth might send the Child her health and try out the verity. And that thoe the said Agnes had bein formerly very troublesome to the Child yet the child declares that from that tyme furth she did no more Torment her but appears to her apprehension[35] defending her from the fury of the rest, Witnesses Lady Northbar and Lady Kellie. *Sic subscribitur* Jonet Aikine, Jonet M^{c}gilchrist.

18. 2° It is to be observed that the forsaid Katrine Campbell could by no means be prevailed with to pray for the Child but upon the contrary quhen requyred by the minister and others cursed him, and all the family of {*p*. 5} Bargarren, and particularly the child and all that belonged to her and wished and said The Devill let the chyld never grow better, nor any that belongd to her be in a better condition nor the child wes in, untill such tyme as she should be repaired of the scandall that they had raisd upon her. Witnessis hereto Mr Andrew Turner minister, Gavine Walkinshaw of that Ilk, John Duncan schoolmaster in Erskine. *Sic subscribitur* Andr: Turner.

19. 3° It is to be observed that Bargarren having prevailed with the sherriff by the presbitries recommendation to imprison her, from the tyme of her imprisonment she never appeard to the Child thoe formerly she had appeared ordinarly as one of her most violent Tormentors. Witnessis Lady Northbar and Lady Kellie. *Sic subscribitur* Jonet Aikine, Jonet M^{c}gilchrist.

20. 4° To be observed that at the tyme quhen the child put out of her mouth the hair and other trash abovenamed, Katrine Campbell being in custody as said is, Ther wes found in her pocket a ball of hair of seaverall collours which wes afterwards thrown into the fyre, And it is lykewise here to be observed that the child after this put no more hair out of her mouth. Witnessis The parents of the Child. *Sic subscribitur* JoShaw, Christian M^{c}gilchrist, Katrine Deans ther servitrix.

21. January 1 about 10 of the cloack at nyght she fell by sudden swerfes into fitts differing from the former, In that after her swerfe was over she lay quiet, and as if she had bein slumbering made no motione at all with her body in the bed, yet at the same tyme the minister and others present heard her mournfully repeat (but scarce above her breath) and talk of seaverall stories in meeter, and as we thought were expressions of the ryse and progress of her oun trouble, and thus she continued (still naming of some of the forementioned persons) till her parents and others offered[36] to rouse her, by touching and moving her body, upon quhich instantly she uttered horrid screeks, and cryed as if she had bein peirced thorow with small swords, and assaulted for her life, and after fell a singing, leaping and dancing for a long tyme, and laughing

[35] 'to her apprehension': as she experiences it.
[36] 'offered': attempted.

with ane unusuall and loud voice, Tearing doun the curtaines of the bed, and pulling off her head and neck-cloaths, and was acted with such force and strenth in thes extravagancies that the minister and her father could not hinder her in her dancing and leaping thoe they joyned their whole strenth to prevent her, and after prayer the minister finding her composed, Enquyred if she remembered what she had done whyle in the fitt? She replyed that she did distinctly remember her miscarriadges[37] and particularly her singing and dancing, she also declared that the witches ther encloseing her in a ring and dancing and singing about her wes the occasion of her dancing which she gladly then performed with the rest. Thus she continued for some days in fitts after this manner with some variatione, And it is here to be observed that when in one of the fitts she wes tearing off her head clothes, her parents resolving to see what would be the event, did not resist her but gave her way, whereupon she stript her self of all her cloaths that were upon her and left not her very shirt upon her body. Witnessis Lady Northbar, Mr Andrew Turner and Mr James Birsbane ministers. *Sic subscribitur* Jonet Aikine, Andr: Turner, JBirsbane.

22. After this about the 11ᵗ or 12ᵗ of January she fell again into fitts different from the former, in that she would have bein on a sudden carried away from her parents and others that were about her throw the chamber and hall down a long stair towards the Tower Gate with such swift and unaccountable motion that it was not in the power of any to prevent her, her feet not touching the ground to the apprehension of spectators, but she going from them as it were in a flight, and in her motion wes heard to laugh in ane unusuall manner. But throw the divine providence the gate being shutt She {*p. 6*} [*1 word damaged*] thair: till such tyme as some of the family could overtake her who endeavouring to lift her and carry her back found her instantly fall dead and stiff, and in this posture she being brought back to the chamber lay for a considerable space, and when recovered she declared That thair were about the number of 9 or 10, who had carried her away as said is, in a shue[38] (as she termed it), quhairin she then took pleasure, her feet not at all touching the ground to her apprehension. Witnessis Lady Northbar, Robert Montgomery and Janet Jamisoune servitors. *Sic subscribitur* Janet Aikine, RAllexander nottar at the Command of the saids Rob: Montgomry and Janet Jamison who declares they cannot wryt.

23. The night following she was suddenly carried away as said is throw the chamber and hall from her parents and others who were about her toward the top of the house 16 steps of a stair quhair she saw nothing but darknes, and had the apparition of strange and unaccountable things, But wes carried doun again as she thought in a shue, and she asserted after her recovery out

37 'miscarriadges': misconduct.
38 'shue': swinging motion.

of the fitt that she mett upon the stair the number of 6 women and 4 men (some of quhom she named, and gave grave marks of others) and by them wes carried toward the gate again as said is. And accordingly was found thair, the gate being shut as formerly, and wes carried up dead and stiff with all the parts of her body extended, she still declareing when composed That she endeavoured to oppen the gate in her fitt, and that thes about her were helping her to oppen it with a designe to droun her in the well, Quhich she said she heard amongst them, As lykeways that then the world would beleeve she had destroyed her self. It is to be observed here that one tyme she wes prevented with the gate in the former posture, even there the gate wes not barred and that at that tyme they could not get the gate oppened, thoe both she and they were endeavouring to get it up. Witnessis the persons abovenamed. *Sic subscribitur* Jonet Aikine, RAllexander nottar at the Command of Rob: Montgomry and Janet Jamison who declares they cannot wryt.

24. In about this tyme she again was carried from them in the former manner, on a sudden doun the stair toward the cellar nixt adjacent to the chamber, quhair were her brother and sister providentially with a lighted candle quhich she soon put out, but they crying and holding her by the head cloaths quickly discovered quhair she was, upon quhich Mr Allexander King minister at Bonnill being in the chamber made haste doun stairs quhair he found her in the forsaid posture but free of the grips of her sister, The occasion quhairof was her loosening her head cloaths, and the said Mr Allexander having prevented and keept her in his armes till the candle wes lighted, and endeavouring to bring her up did declare that he found something forcibly drawing her doun stairs, but being recovered she fell dead and stiff upon the staire and wes in this posture carried up and laid in bed, quhair she lay as said is a considerable space, It is to be observed here that quhen some fitts in this kind were ready to seize her she gave advertisement thairof to spectators, and gave signes of her earnest desyres of thair help to prevent her motion which for ordinary wes practised and took good effect. Witnessis Lady Northbar and the said Mr Allexander King. *Sic subscribitur* Jonet Aikine, Allexr King attests the abovenamd paragraph.

25. After this she fell into fretting and angry fitts as she termed them In which her humour wes cross to all that those about her could either say or doe, nothing proving satisfactory but displeasing to her, her former fitts now and then seizing her. But when recovered and in a right composure of mynd, declared that her Tormentors about her gave her advice and still suggested to her to goe to such and such remote places of the house {*p. 7*} her allone, and bring with her a snood or cravat or some such thing, promising her rough allmonds, and some such sweet meats, which they specified and named to her, and for that end desyred her to bring her apron with her to hold them,

with a snood to tye up her hair. Accordingly the damsell when seized[39] again with fitts, in this kynd endeavoured resolutely to repair to thes place having a snood or a cravat and her apron with her, and would suffer none in her company, so that her parents and others about her found them selves under a necessity to keep and detain her by force, and she being thus prevented uttered hydeous screeks and crys of which in thir sort of fitts she is[40] scarce free. Witnessis John Walkingshaw in Erskine, Margaret Campbell Indweller in Glasgow and Rebeckah Marshell servant. *Sic subscribitur* J Walkinshaw, Margret Campbell, R Allexander nottar at Command of Rebeckah Marshell who declares she cannot wryt.

26. Upon Thursday January 14^{t} at night, a young Lass appeard to the Chyld with a scabbed face among the rest of her Tormentors who told her that she wes to the house to morrow, forbidding the Child to reveall it. The nixt day January 15^{t} The Child earnestly enquyring at her mother and the rest of the family what beggars came to the gate that day? off what countenance and visadge they were? But the family not knowing her intention by such a question, gave no heed therunto, But she still insisting and being in company with her mother and another Gentlewoman about 4 aclock in the afternoone, said to them that she thought she might tell them somequhat that she was forbidden to reveall (the tyme being now past) quhilk she endeavouring to doe, presently fell a crying that she was tormented, and pricked throw her whole body, yet recovering out of the fitt Told the thing that she had to reveall was that the scabbed faced Lass who appeared to her yesternight should have bein at the gate this day at ten a clocke, Quhairupon the servants being questioned did declare that accordingly at that tyme thair had bein such ane one at the gate, and had received her almes. Witnessis The Childs mother, Margret Campbell abovenamed. *Sic subscribitur* Christian McGilchrist, Margret Cambell.

27. January 16^{t} and 17^{t} She put out of her mouth when recovered of her swooneing fitts, a great number of pins, Quhilk she declared Jean Park forced into her mouth, as also did another in the habit of a Gentlewoman, who had bein allwayes one of her most violent tormentors, and much after this manner she continued till January 21^{t}. Witnessis the persons abovenamed. *Sic subscribitur* Christian McGilchrist, Margret Cambell.

28. Att which tyme her fitts again altered, she falling and continueing in them with heavie sighs and groans and hydeous outcrys, telling thes who were about her that catts, ravens, owles and horses, were destroying and pressing her doun in the bed, at this tyme her mother and another Gentlewoman being in the roome with her did declare that Immediatly after the taking her out of the bed in this condition they did see something moving under the bed

[39] Word damaged. The published *True Narrative* has 'seiz'd'.

[40] The published *True Narrative* has 'was'. The present tense in the manuscript indicates early compilation.

cloaths about the bignes of a Catt. Witnessis these persons. *Sic subscribitur* Christian McGilchrist, Margret Cambell.

29. The same day in the morning in the intervale of her fitts The Child did declare she overheard the witches about her (still naming Allexander and James Andersones, Jean Park and others) suggesting to one another that the Devill had promised and engadged to them to carry her over the hall window that so they myght droun her in the wall[41] and therby the world would beleeve that she had destroyed her self, and that same day and seaverall tymes thairefter, when seized with fitts did attempt to goe over to the windou with such force and resolution, That thes who were about her could scarce with all thair strenth prevent her. Witnessis, Kelly and his Lady and John Walkingshaw. *Sic subscribitur* Arch: Ballantyne, Jonet McGilchrist, JWalkinshaw. {*p. 8*}[42]

30. Note here That in and about this tyme quhen she essayed in her light fitts to read any part of the scripture, repeat any of the psalms or answer any questions of our Catechisme she wes suddenly struck dumb stiff and dead and this continued for a long tyme tearing all about her.

2do note That when the minister went to prayer she recovered of her fitts and wes ordinarly free of them during the tyme of prayer, even thoe seized of them before, albeit sometymes when prayer began, she made disturbance by idle lowd talking, especially singing, particularly January 22^{d} she was more turbulent and troublesome then she used to be, continueing some space after the minister began to pray, singing and making a hideous noise, stryking with her feet at the minister in prayer, spitting in his face, uttering reproachfull talk of him, calling him dog &C: She being composed, and out of the fitt before prayer wes ended. The minister quhen he had done, finding her sober and in a right composure of mynd, did enquyre why she made such disturbance, To quhich she replyed she was forced to doe it by the hellish Crew about her and that she thought that thair were none of her oun words that she uttered, Declaring also she had some that suggested to her but that they had threatned to torment her, if she should offer to make it knoun, and accordingly she essaying twice to express her mynd, was cast into two tormenting fitts successive quhairin she cryed out of violent pain, all the parts of her body being rigid and extended lyke a corpse, two men being scarce able to resist her strenth, and when recovered She again essaying to express her mynd twyce by wryt fell suddenly into two other greivously tormenting fitts, quhairin she was struck deaff dumb and blind, her tongue being draun a prodigious lenth out of her mouth and quhen touched in any part of her body, uttered horrid screeks and outcrys and quhen recovered of the fitt declared that the forenamed persons viz. the Andersones, Jean Park,

41 *Sic*. The published *True Narrative* has 'well'.

42 Page 8, uniquely, has a set of lines ruled round it to create margins in which paragraph numbers are entered.

ane Gentlewoman, one John Davieson, with the rest of the hellish Crew, were Tormenting her, as also that thair had bein 15 of them about the house all the last night and were now all gone save one who was to stay about the house, till she was out of the fitts, and accordingly her brother and sister did declare, that they saw about the same tyme a woman in the garden with a red coat about her head at the root of ane aple tree, but knew her not, but the Laird being in Church with the most of the servants, the thing was not further searched. Witnessis the said Mr Andrew Turner and Margaret Campbell. *Sic subscribitur* Andr: Turner, Margret Cambell.

31. In and about this tyme the Chyld being in bed, her parents and others being about her cryed out that she was smitten severly by some of the forenamed persons thair hands, and thos who were about her did distinctly hear the noise of the stroak when she cryed, and the same night or the night before she sitting with the rest at the chamber fyre she cryed out something was wounding her thigh, Quhairupon instantly her mother putting her hand in the Childs pocket, found her folding knife opened quhilk had bein folded when put in her pocket, But her uncle not trusting the thing did again put up the knife and leave it folded in her pocket, and instantly the Child cryed out as said is The knife was cutting her thigh being oppened by the means of Jean Park and others, upon quhich her uncle searching her pocket again found the knife opened as formerly it had bein, This twice or thrice fell out after the same manner to thair admiration, Witnessis her uncle and Margaret Campbell. *Sic subscribitur* JMgilchrist, Margret Cambell. {*p. 9*}

32. Munday, January 25^t^ She Continueing all this whyle in her [*about 2 words damaged*] quhairof she hath but small intervales for ordinary wes often seized of her former swooneing stiff fitts with this remarkeable variation, her throat was sometymes prodigiously extended, and sometymes prodigiously contracted and canvelled,[43] with great pain and difficulty of breathing. In thir fitts she appears in palpable danger of being choaked, and throw the violence of pain in her throat strugles with her feet and hands as if some were actually about to strangle her, and can speak or cry none, with fitts of this kynd she was frequently seized for seaverall days and in the intervales did declare that the forementioned persons with others quhom she could get named were endeavouring to stranggle her, she did declare lyke wayes that the occasion of her not having power to speak or cry in fitts of this kynd wes a bunch in her throat like a pullets egg quhich allmost choaked her. Witnessis Lady Kelly and Mr Andrew Turner. *Sic subscribitur* Andr: Turner, Jonet M^c^gilchrist.

33.[44] February 1st She endeavouring as formerly to make known what she was forbidden to reveall wes instantly seized with a sore fitt, and in the

43 'canvelled' (more usually 'convelled'): wrenched.

44 The newsletter edited as the appendix below (pp. 186–90) gives an earlier version of paragraphs 33 to 37.

intervale said she could not understand, why such restraints were laid upon her except by charme, quhich she thought myght be found out, as she overheared amongst some of the hellish crew, by searching for it beneath the bed quhair she lay, quhich having quickly done her self, found beneath the forsaid bed, ane intire egg shell to the apprehensione of spectators, being oppen in the end, quhich being presently throun into the fyre, did melt away lyke wax without any noise, after this the chyld said she would not be Tormented as formerly, quhen essaying to reveall quhat she had being forbidden to tell, but her tongue would be draun doun her throat, quhich according happened. As also she made knoun many things she had not access to doe before, particularly that they had frequently sollisted her to be a witch herself, promiseing her great rewards, and perfect health also, to induce her thairunto; Quhilk tentatione she throw the infinit mercy of God resisted, telling them (she naming the forementioned persons) That the Devill promised that, that he could not perform, and granting he could full fill thes promises to her yet she was sure from the scriptures, that hell and the wrath of God was the finall reward of all such that yeelded to this wickednes, To quhilk they replyed that hell and the wrath of God so much talked of, was not so formidable as is represented, This paragraph attested by her father and the forsaid Margaret Campbell. *Sic subscribitur* JShaw, Margret Cambel.

34. Note here That severall moneths before this tyme she was distinctly heard to give thir replyes to some as discoursing with her thoe unseen and unheard by spectators about her, she lykewayes at this tyme did declare That they frequently urged her to give them her consent to take away the life of her young sister upon her mothers breast, which tentation she also (throw the mercy of God) still resisted, Telling them she would never yeeld to that, which replyes spectators heard her distinctly utter as to some in conference with her thoe they saw nothing. She did lykeways declare that thair had bein a charm laid upon the top of the house quhair her young sister was a nursing, and that they did therby design her life, and that this wes the reason why she had so often for some moneths before desyred her mother to bring home her sister, telling her mother that the infant would daylie decay as long as she stayed thair, and accordingly her parents observing the daylie decay of the infant even to skin and bone, brought her home quhair she recovered, attested by the Lady Kelly and Margret Campbell. *Sic subscribitur* Jonet M^c^gilchrist, Margret Cambel. {*p. 10*}

35. February 2^d^ The chyld being in her chamber with her mother, the minister and others, on a sudden fell a trembling upon the sight of one John Lindsay in Barcloch talking with her father in the hall, did declare to her mother that the said John Lindsay wes one of the crew that Tormented her, whom she knew, wherupon she wes desyred to goe to the hall, and in a way unknown to him, touch some part of his body, which she having at some aversation done, wes instantly seizd with a Tormenting fitt, after which her

father and the minister thought themselves oblidged to make known the thing to the said John Lindsay, and interrogat him thairupon, but he giveing no satisfying answer, The minister and childs father and mother desyred him to take the child by the hand himself quhich he being urged to doe, the Child wes again seized with a Tormenting fitt, her eyes turning in her head and all the parts of her body rigid and stiff, flew upon the said John Lindsay. Note here that the spectators who had come in with him to Bargarran did also take the chyld by the hand, but no such effect followed. This attested by Mr Andrew Turner minister, John Walkinshaw and Margret Campbell. *Sic subscribitur* Andr: Turner, JWalkinshaw, Margret Cambel.

36. The said day about 4 a cloack at night ther came ane old hieland fellow to Bargarren kitchine calling himself a wearie traveller, and said he behooved to lodge thair that night, quhilk the servants refuseing gave him some thing by way of almes, att this tyme the Child being in the chamber, with her mother and Margret Campbell her coosine, said that to the best of her apprehensione she thought ther wes one of the Crew in and about the house at that tyme, Quhairupon her mother made hast[e] with her daughter toward the kitchine, and finding thair unexpectedly the forsaid hieland fellow, the Child did declare he wes one of her Tormentors, wherupon her mother desyred the said hieland fellow to take the Chyld by the hand, Quhilk he being constrained to doe instantly wes seized with a violent fitt as formerly in the caice abovementioned, This falling out of the divine providence the Childs father thought himself concerned to secure him, and the nixt morning the minister being in Bargarren, the mater was imparted to him, called for the said hieland fellow, and having questioned him to and again[45] about this matter without any satisfyeing answer, brought the chyld out of the chamber, covering her face and allmost her whole body with his cloack and giving signes to the said hieland fellow, to touch her, as he had ordered him before, without the Childs knowledge, and in this posture he having touched her she not knowing of his touch wes instantly seizd with a violent fitt, others at the same tyme tyme touching her, but no such effect followed; and when recovered of her fitt sought leave of the forsaid hieland fellow to tell of some that haunted and molested her whom he had forbidden her to make known, at which the old hieland fellow, looking upon her with ane angry countenance, the Childs mouth was instantly stopt, But she being desyred by spectators to speak her mynd freely whether he would or not, replyed she durst not, yet notwithstanding Orbistoun, Dargavell, Porterfeild of Fullwood[46] and severall other Gentlemen thair present urging her to essay it, she was struck on a sudden with a violent fitt, her eyes turning in her head, her body falling in all parts

[45] 'to and again' (like 'to and fro'): in different ways.

[46] William Hamilton of Orbiston, John Maxwell of Dargavel, and Alexander Porterfield of Fullwood.

of it rigid and stiff {*p. 11*} lyke a corpse. Note here that Elizabeth Anderson who confessed[47] acknowledged fellowship with the Devill, amongst others she delated[48] active instruments in the chylds trouble, gave (before she saw this fellow in custody) grave marks of him, but declares she knew not his name when she saw him in a randevouze with the Devill and the rest in Bargarrens orcheard, and when after delation she was brought to the place, quhair he wes in custody, did declare in his face before spectators he was the person she spoke of. Witnessis Mr Andrew Turner minister, John Whyt apothecary in Pasley, Allexander Porterfeild of Fullwood and John Walkinshaw in Erskine. *Sic subscribitur* Andr: Turner, John Whyt, APorterfeild, JWalkinshaw.

37. Note here that the persons delated by the said Elizabeth Anderson who confesses fellowship with the Devill to have bein active instruments of the Childs trouble and consulting thairanent with the Devill in Bargarren orcheard, viz. her father Allexander Anderson, Agnes Easmith, Margret Fulton, James Lindsay the Curat &C: were accused to thair face by the child before my Lord Blantyre and the Gentlemen commissionated by the lords of his majestys privie councill to make inquyrie in the said affair, and they having also seaverally having also touched her before the said Lords Commissioners she wes in thair presence at each of thair touches severly tormented, others then present tuching her also, but no such effect followed. Note furder Katrine Campbell, being prevailed with in presence of the saids Commissioners to touch the chyld, the same effect followed, but more violent, than acompanied the toutch of the forsaids persons, and quhen the child recovered of her fit did declare she heard some thing as saying to her she was now lowsed, after Katrine Campbell had touched her, and that she might now touch any of the accused persons or they her after this, which accordingly upon tryall fell so out.

38. February 6[t] Continueing in her light fits for ordinary, she was now and then seized with more violent and painful fits, quhairin she lay dead, and all the parts of her body extended, and when recovered a litle was seen to have something in her mouth to the judgment of beholders lyke \the peice of/ ane orange pile[49] confected, which she seemd to be chewing, and having got doun her throat (as the spectators thought) fell again dead, as if she had bein choaked, her throat being prodigiously extended, and strugleing with her hands and feet, as if she had bein at the last gasp, to the affrightment of spectators, and quhen recovered thoe in the light fit said it was a very sweet orange pile, she got from the Gentlewoman, and did confidently affirm it wes ane orange pile confected, declaring also thair were present with the Gentlewoman, some of the persons abovenamed particularly one Margaret, L, whose surname she could not get exprest for fear of being Tormented as

47 Conjectural reconstruction of damaged words: '…ho conf…'.
48 'delated': accused.
49 'orange pile': (confectionery made with) orange peel.

wes threatned. Witnessis Elizabeth Kennedy spouse to Mr Andrew Turner, Margaret Aikine in Northbar, and Margaret Campbell abovenamed. *Sic subscribitur* Elizabeth Kennedie, Margret Aikine, Margret Cambell.

39. Thursday 11th February about 6 a clock at night thair were present in the house Mr Patrick Simpson minister and his wife, Lady Northbar and the parents of the Child discoursing and conferring upon the caice of the said Child wher she was present her self who in the tyme of thair conference told them that she would reveall to them something if she durst for her Tormentors, and essaying to doe the same {*p. 12*} was[50] instantly seized with a violent fit, quhairin she leaped even up and appeared as if she had been choacked, That spectators could scarce get her holden, after recovery the minister went to family worship and expounding the 110 psalm, and speaking of the limited power of the adversaries of Christ from the letter part of the first verse, She wes instantly seized with another fit, quhairin she put some blood out of her mouth, that raisd some grounds, of jeallousie[51] in the mynds of spectators, that somthing in her mouth had bein the occasion of it, but could not get her mouth oppened, thoe they used means to effect the same and after recovery they enquyred What was the occasion of her putting out of blood, and if she found any thing thairin that was the occasion thairof, Replyed she did not know for she found nothing but opening her mouth, they found one of her double teeth newly drawn out, she being recovered as said is, the minister proceeding again upon the forsaid subject, quhairat he was disturbed, she was instantly again seazed with another fitt. Witnessis the persons namd thairin and John M^{c}gilchrist. *Sic subscribitur* Jonet Aikine, Pat: Simpson, J^{o}McGilchrist.[52]

40. Thursday 12th February[53] Margaret Lang and her daughter Martha Semple came to Bargarran who had bein dilated by the forsaid Elizabeth Anderson and other two, viz. James and Thomas Lindsays, to have bein active instruments of the Childs trouble, consulting thairanent with the Devill, whom the Child could now name after the said Margaret Lang wes delated as said is (thoe when she essayed to doe it before wes Tormented) whom quhen the Chyld saw, said she was now bound up, and durst not declare before the said Margaret Lang, That she was one of her Tormentors, at the same tyme, the child desyred some of thes, who were about her, to seek some parts of her body, which they having done, found the parts of her body they touched contracted and canvelled,[54] as if it had bein by cords, and accordingly being questioned by the said Margaret Lang and her daughter did positively declare, That she had frequently seen her daughter, but declyned from fear (as she said) to accuse her self, notwithstanding of which the chyld being urged,

50 Word damaged. The published *True Narrative* has 'was'.
51 'jeallousie': suspicion.
52 The 'Witnessis ...' clause has been squeezed in by the scribe as an afterthought.
53 Thursday was 11 February. This is evidently Friday 12 February.
54 The published *True Narrative* has 'contracted and drawn hard together'.

by Mr Patrick Simpson and Mr James Hutchison ministers, then present, to tell her mynd freely, whether or not the said Margaret Lang was one of her Tormentors, quhairupon the child replyed yes, Quhilk being scarce pronunced, she was struck with a fearfull fitt, and after recovery essaying to \say the/ same thing again, and saying only the word Tint[55] wes suddenly struck with another fitt, after her recovery going to the chamber, Margaret Lang sitting near the hall doors spake after her Lord bless the[e], and ding[56] the Devill out of the[e], after quhilk quhen the said Margret was gone she could and did positively affirm the thing and lykewayes declared, the occasion of her being so restrained in her presence wes her laying a charme upon her, by the said Margret her letting fall a parcell of hair, Quhich accordingly was found at the back of the door, which was the occasion of her saying the word Tint in her former fit, thoe none saw the said Margaret lay the said hair doun thair. Witnessis the said Mr Patrick Simpson and Mr Andrew Turner ministers. *Sic subscribitur* Pat: Simpson, And: Turner.[57] {*p. 13*}

41. After this she was seized with many sore fits the said day, and particularly about 8 a cloack that night was so violently Tormented in her fitt, that her parents could scarce hold her, with her whole strenth she strugleing as if she had bein choaked. Att the same tyme thair was seen in her mouth a pin which with difficulty was got out, about a quarter of ane hour she continued in this manner, after this she fell a litle quiet, and had not much pain, and wes distantly heard conversing as with some about her thoe invisible to others, and the replys givine by her heard by the persons present, gave them ground to think that she was tempted, to sett her hand to a paper, then presented to her, by promise, That she should never be troubled any more, upon her yeelding thairunto, as also that she should get sweet meats, a drink of seck, a bony coat with silver thairon, att the tyme she was heard distinctly say as resisting the tempter, Thow art a filthie sow, should I obey ye, This wes not the end of my Creation, but to glorifie God, and thow promises what thow canst not performe; and when she recovered of her fitt wherin she continued near two hours thus reasoning did declare That it wes the Devill who presented him self to her, and tempted her as aforsaid, as lykewayes that she was violently urged by him to renunce her baptisme, argueing against the validity therof, saying it was done by a Curat, and useing severall other arguments, promising her such and such persons in mariadge if she would consent thairunto, which she throw divine mercy resisted, and wes distinctly heard reply, what art thow but a Sow, upon which he instantly appeared in the shape of a sow, as also she did declare when out of her fitt it had bein

55 'Tint': lost.
56 'ding': strike, drive.
57 The minister named earlier in the text of this paragraph was James Hutchison, not Andrew Turner.

suggested to her that one of her Tormentors would be at the door tomorrow, This attested by the Lady Northbar and John Mcgilchrist. *Sic subscribitur* Jonet Aikine, Pat: Simpson, J°M^c^Gilchrist.

42. And accordingly being February 13th she being in a sore fit about 12 a cloack of the day differed from the former fits, In that she continued thairin for more then 2 hours space both deaf and blind, so that she neither saw nor heard any about her, thoe her parents oft tymes cryed to her at a lowd voice, and touching her hand, and other parts of her body, but all to no purpose, she making a constant and unaccountable motion with her body walking to and froe, thorow the chamber, and uttering horrid screeks, and outcrys when any by force hindered her motion, still crying for her father and mother, and some others to come and take her home, supposing her self not to be in her fathers house, when the chyld was in this condition ther came one Margaret Rodger to her door, and her parents suspecting the said Margaret Rodger upon thair remembring what the Child had told the night before, that one of them should be at the door the day following, brought the said Margaret quhair the Chyld was, and before she had well entered the door, the Child presently discovered her (thoe she saw none else about her) and clapping her hands ran to her, crying Maggy Maggy wher hes thow bein; will thow take me home, flew upon her back *{p. 14}* desyring her to carry her home, wherupon Bargarren and his Lady and other spectators being astonished causd the said Margaret speak to the Child, which she having done, the Child answered her every word, but neither saw nor heard any about her, at which tyme also, sent for the 3 persons Confessing fellowship with the Devill, viz. Elizabeth Anderson, James and Thomas Lindsays, to try if the Child could hear or see them also, and accordingly they being brought into the roome, quhair the Child was she also ran upon them lawghing upon the sight of them as if she had bein over joyed, note here that the forsaid three persons, did then declare in the said Margaret Rodgers face, that she was at the meeting with them in the orchard of Bargarren, consulting with the Devill and the rest about the Childs ruine, attested by the Lady Northbar, John Walkinshaw and John McGilchrist all within named. *Sic Subscribitur* Jonet Aikine, JWalkinshaw, J°M^c^Gilchrist.

43. The sabbath following being February 14th, after some intervales she had sore fitts, and in one of the fitts said Margaret Lang and her daughter, were Tormenting her and cutting her throat, her words being scarce above her breath, and upon the nameing of them she wes lyke to be shaken in peices, her head shaking in a formidable manner, and she made to stand lyke a bow upon her head and feet at once, and when recovered of the fitt declared That the forsaid Margaret Lang said to her that she would give her a Tostie[58] as she

[58] The published *True Narrative* has here 'she would give her a Tosty (which imports hot and severe handling)'.

namd it, because she had made mention of her name, attested by the Lady Northbar and John McGilchrist. *Sic Subscribitur* Jonet Aikine, J°M^c^Gilchrist.

Additionall note for January 12^t^ Last

44. Mr Patrick Simpson being come thither to Bargarren for prayer and two of the Elders of that paroche present viz. Walter Paterson of Craigton and Robert Love in Maines of Erskine, after some shorter fitts before prayer began, in the time of singing she took a sore continueing fit first laughing then singing, and lastly turning very outragious, so that her father could scarcely get her holden, with his whole strenth, after her recovery from which she wes quiet all the tyme of prayer, lectureing and singing, and composedly attentive untill the whole religious exercise wes endit, and till some refreshment was taken, after the same: att the end of which she told the company she had something to say that she heard among her Tormentors saying but durst not reveall it, but the minister and her mother urging her not to obey the Devill but to be free, she told she would round it[59] to her mother, and in removing from her place, and coming in betwixt her mother and aunt she began to whisper in her mothers ears, before she got a sentence fully pronunced, she took a violent fit that her mother and spectators could scarce hold her, and when her mother (at her coming out of the fitt) told that her daughter was speaking of a meeting and a feast they had told her of in the yeard of Bargarren but was able to say no more, and then her mother desyring her to {*p. 15*} tell the rest of it, she began to heark to her again but wes [*2–3 words damaged*] nothing till she was seizd with another lyke fit, Quhairupon the minister perceiving her torment desyred them to forbear any furder troubling her. Attested by the persons thairin named, Pat: Simpson, WPaterson.

It is observable that according as the Child had told, that thair were a feast and a meeting of the Crew in the yeard, so the same is acknowledged and declared by 3 of the Crew that were thair, viz. Elizabeth Anderson, James and Thomas Lindsays, the very same day and tyme quhilk she condescends upon.[60]

It is lykewayes to be observed, that albeit all the forsaid persons now imprisoned, were her ordinary Tormentors, yet since thair imprisonment, she declares never any of them appears to her to torment her, but that her ordinary tormentors now are strangers whom she never saw before, except ane Gentle woman whose name she dare not reveall for fear of torment, This attested by me Andrew Turner and Bargarren. *Sic Subscribitur* Andr: Turner, JShaw.

Att Renfrew the 18^t^ February 1697

The quhilk day In presence of Allexander Lord Blantyre, Sir John Houston of that Ilk, Gavine Cochrane of Craigmuire, Allexander Porterfield of Fullwood and Robert Semple shereff deput of Renfrew, Commissioners appoynted

[59] 'round it': whisper it.
[60] 'condescends upon': specifies.

by the Lords of his majestys privie Councill for taking Inquyrie anent the witches and witchcraft Relating to Christine Shaw daughter to the Laird of Bargarren, Conforme to the said Commission dated the 19 day of January last, Allexander Lord Blantyre preses, Compeired the rexive[61] witnesses to the paragraphs preceiding, amounting to the number of 44 paragraphs and Consisting of 10 Leafes[62] and owned and subscribed the same. *Sic subscribitur* Blantyre preses. {*p. 16*}

Follows the double of the Commissione[63]

Att Edinburgh the 19th January 1697

The Lords of his Majestys privie Councill being informed off seaverall flagrant grounds of suspition of witches and witchcraft within the shyre of Renfrew, Especially from the afflicted and extraordinary condition of Christine Shaw daughter to John Shaw of Bargarran, Doe therefor hereby grant power and commission to Allexander Lord Blantyre, Sir John Maxwell of Pollok, Sir John Houstoune of that Ilk, Sir John Shaw of Greinock, William Cuninghame of Craigends, Allexander Porterfeild of Duchall, Glanderstoune, Caldwell,[64] Gavine Cochrane of Thornliemuire, Allexander Porterfeild of Fullwood and the shereff deput of Renfrew or any fyve of them as ther quorum, To make all lawfull enquyrie anent the said witches and witchcraft, and to cite and examine witnessis and take all lawfull probation, but without oath, for discovering of the same, and as they shall find cause to give order for imprisoneing, or otherwayes secuireing the persons justly suspect untill farder order, and the forsaids persons are hereby requyred to give ane accompt of thair dilligence and proceedings in the said matter to the Clerks of privie Councill betwixt and the tenth day of March nixt to come. *Sic subscribitur* Polwarth cancellar, Argyle, Leven, Forfar, Raith, Belhaven, JaStewart, Wanstruther, Ahope, Jo: Maxwell, Ro: Sinclair. Extract beiris. *Sic subscribitur* Gilb: Eliot *Cls: Sti: Cons:*[65] {*p. 17*}[66]

Declaratione be Dr Mathew Birsbane anent the Caice of Christine Shaw Daughter of the Laird of Bargarran.

About the 24^{t} or 25^{t} day of October last the Lady Bargarran brought a daughter of hers (a child of elevine yeirs old or therby) to this toun to take

61 'rexive': respective.

62 This phrase shows that the commissioners were not using the Bargarran manuscript itself, but another copy. The 'Informatory Accompt' in the Bargarran manuscript has 44 paragraphs, but covers only 7 leaves.

63 This text of the commission can be compared with the version in the council's minutes: SPCR, A1697/1/17.

64 William Muir of Glanderston and John Caldwell of that Ilk.

65 '*Clericus Secreti Consilium*': clerk of the privy council.

66 The last part of p. 16 is blank. In the margin opposite the blank space is written 'Margaret Lang'.

advyce of phisicians (as she said) for her. When I was at first brought to see her, I could hardly be perswaded that thair was any need of me, or any man else of my professione, the Child appeared so brisk, and vigorous in motion, of so florid good collour, so chearfull and in a word in outward appearance, every way healthfull: But it was not long till I found my self obblidged to alter my thoughts of her, for I had not been above 8 or 10 minuts in the roome by her, till she arose from her seat, and advertised the company, that she was instantly to be seizd of a fit, so being streight carried to her bed, I observed a considerable stiffness and distention in her left hypochondre:[67] which in a trice falling the patient was foorthwith taken with horrid convulsive motions of most parts of her body (her back and neck especially) and heavy groans at first, whilk was afterward turned (so soon, as she was able to frame words), into a kind of expostulatory mourning against some women, (two quhairof she allwayes named (for I have seen her afterwards in seaverall such fits) one of them Naismith (as I remember,) and the other Campbel.

All thes symptomes (I thought) were very reduceable to the freaks of hypocondriack mellancholly: and thairfor putting her in such a course, as I thought proper, against that kind of malady, I was in absolut security the Child having continued free from all the abovementioned symptoms for the space (I think) of a week in this toun, and some 8 or 10 days more in the countrey, till I was alarmed[68] by a friend of the Lady Bargarran's who told me that the Child was returned to the toun again, and worse then ever, for now she was in frequent hazard of choaking with mouth-fulls of hair, that she apprehended the women abovenamd to be pressing doun her throat, had not she her self her oun hand pulld it out.

Having read many such histories in authour, and heard the lyke from other hands too, but never seen any such thing my self, I was the more earnest to see the Child again, and for some weeks, that she stayd in this place, I was frequently with her and observed her narrowly. And I'me confident she had no humane correspondent to subminister hair, straw, coalls, cinders, hay, feathers, and such lyke trash to her: all which upon several occasions, I have seen her put out of her mouth in considerable quantitys, sometymes after severe fits, and at other tymes, without any trouble at all, evine in the very tyme she was discoursing with us. And for the most part she put out all thes things without being wet in the least: nay rather as if they had bein dryed with care and artifice; for one tyme I remember when I was discoursing with her and she with me, She gave me a cinder out of her mouth, not only dry, but actually hot, much above the degree of the naturall warmth of a mans body, during the time she was thus exercis'd, though she had dayly, not only light convulsive motions, but to a high degree strong convulsions and

[67] 'left hypochondre': the left side of the upper abdomen.
[68] 'alarmed': notified.

rigidity of the whole body (such sometymes that we call Tetanoi, sometymes hopisthotanus[69]) yet she never fancied, as at other times, that she saw any such people (as have been already named) {*p. 18*} about her, but the upcasting, or rather outputting of the things above mentioned, did noe sooner cease, but, in all her fits, when she was able to speak any, she allways cryed out, that they were pinching or pricking her. Thes fits were both more severe and more frequent than before, and folloud with a whyles alienatione of mynd. I have seen her to[o] when otherwayes free of all fitts, suddenly seazd with dumbnes, her tongue being strangely contracted that it appeard to her self, as she expressd it, as if people were drawing it doun her throat. This I declare in conscience, and in most solemne manner, is what I have seen, and handled, and, were it not for the hair, hay, straw, which things, *toto genere*[70] contrary to humane nature, I should not despair to reduce all the other symptomes to their proper classes in the catalogue of humane diseases. Writtine and signd at Glasgow this 31st of December 1696 By me, *Sic Subscribitur*, MBrisbane MD.

Declaratione be Mr. Henery Marshell apothecary

Being desired by John Shaw of Bargarran to declare what I know of his Daughter Christine her condition, I doe it as follows.

About the 29th of October last she was sent hither to have Doctor Brisbanes advyce to her, to quhom I was imployed as Apothecar. The Child was about eleven years of age, of a good habit of body, so far as I could judge, but now and then fell into convulsions, swoons, and little lightness, and when recovered out of thes she would be well again. By the use of the means the doctor used, she seemd to be alltogether freed of thes, wherefor she was taken back to the countrie, but she had not been long there, till she fell worse than before, and was sent hither to be treated again by the Dr., and then after her fits she takes out of her mouth, without any press of vomiting, tuftes of hair, straws long and folded together, burnt coalls, peices of bones, leather, spealls[71] of timber, and several other things, divers of which she has taken out and given to me, whyle I was speaking to her and she with me, And on the 20 of November last, I went to see her, I find her in a swerfe, wherinto she had fallen as I was entering the house, when she had lyn, a litle tyme in that, she arose in a great rage, and beat all about her, frowning with her countenance, and uttering a great deal of unknoun languadge, in ane angry manner, then she put the tuft of a hieland belt, wherwith she was girt, into her mouth, and pulled with her hand, so hard, that if we had not cut the belt with a knife, she had in all probability pulled out her teeth, and then she teared the tuft all to

69 'Tetanoi' (today 'tetanus') and 'hopisthotanus' (today 'opisthotonos') are both conditions involving muscular spasms.

70 'in their whole class'.

71 'spealls': chips.

wooll with her teeth, then she fell a tearing her cloaths, her shoes quhich she pulled of[f] her feet, and every thing she could get into her hands, Then she fell into a dumb fitt (as she termed it) quherin all her body was so canvelled, and distorted, that I endeavouring to put her arms in a better posture found them so rigid and stiff that I would have broken them sooner than reduce them,[72] Then she arose out of that, and went up and doun the roome, and would have gone as throw the wall, muttering the former unknoun languadge, Then she fell head long on the ground, as if {*p. 19*} she had been throun down with violence, quher she lay for some tyme as dead, Then she arose as if she had bein somewhat recovered, and fell a reasoning very distinctly thus. Keti what ails the[e] at me, I am sure I never did the[e] wrong, why would thow wrong me, Come let us gree, Let thair be no more difference betwixt us, Let us shake hands together (putting furth her hand as if she would take her by the hand), Then taking in her hand again, she said well Keti, I cannot help it, ye will not gree with me: Imediatly having thus said, she \cryed and/ fell into another swerfe, and out of that into another rage, quhairin she bitt her oun fingers and tore her hand upon pins, that were in her cloaths, at which being as if she were angry she pulled out all the pins and threw them away, and after she had been thus tortured for more than half ane hour without any intermission she recovered and became perfectly well, And then I asked her how she was, she told me she had just now a very bad fit, for all this tyme she knew no body, neither took any notice of me, thoe I spoke often to her and tosted her body,[73] I asked her quhat she saw in it,[74] she told me she saw Kati Campbell, Nansie Nesmith, Sandie Anderson, and many more that she did not know, I asked her quhat Kati Campbell was doing, she told me she was going to thrust a sword into her syde, quhich made her so desirous to be agreed with her, And when she had told me this, instantly she fell into another swerfe, and reacted all that is before said, and much more, quhich I have partly forgot, And in each of thes 2 fits she continued large halfe an hour. All this I declare in conscience and in most solemn maner to be a truth, in testimony quherof I have writ and subscribed this at Glasgow, this first day of January 1697 yers. *Sic Subscribitur*, He: Marshall Chyr:[75] Apothecar. {*p. 22*}[76]

Att Renfrew the Eightein day of February 1697 yeris, in presence of Allexander Lord Blantyre, Sir John Houstoun of that Ilk, William Muire of Glanderston, Gavine Cochran of Craigmuire, Allexander Porterfeild of Fullwood and

72 *SD*, p. 42, has 'so stiff, that I could not bring them to their Natural Posture without breaking them'.

73 The word written here as 'tosted' might be a copying error for 'touched'. *SD*, p. 42, has 'though I moved her Body, and spoke often to her'.

74 *SD*, p. 42, has 'what she saw in her Fits?'

75 'Chyr:' is short for 'chirurgeon' (surgeon).

76 Pages 20–2 contain material not included in this edition. See the introduction, above.

Robert Sempill shereff deput, Commissioners appoynted by the Lords of his majestys privie councill for taking Inquyrie anent the witches and witchcraft concerning the Laird of Bargarrans daughter, conforme to the Comissione thairanent daited the nyntein day of January last bypast. Alexander Lord Blantyre preses. {*p. 23*}

The Commissioners having conveened before them the persons following viz. Elizabeth Anderson daughter to Allexander Anderson, James and Thomas Lindsays sons to Mathew Lindsay sometyme in Blackhall, Quhilk three persons are grandchildren to umquhill Jean Fulton, who died about ane yeir since or thairby in the tolbooth of Pasley, being accused of witchcraft. Quhilks persons being examined saverally by the said Commissioners anent what they knew, and relation to that affair concerning Christian Shaw daughter to the Laird of Bargarran, and anent what other passadges they knew, relating to witchcraft, Who declared and confest in manner as is particularly mentioned in thair rexive confessiones, which are wryttine in papers a part, wnto which the Comissioners refeirs. Lykewayes compeired John Shaw of Bargarran and Mr Andrew Turner minister of Erskine, who in obedience to the former act produced before the said Comissioners ane long narrative or matter of fact consisting of 20 pages, in quhilk ther are many odd and strange passadges and circumstances containd, relating to the said Christine Shaw, which were all attested by the rexive witnesses thair present, and subscryved thairto. As also by the said preses[77] to which lykewayes the Commissioners remitts. And the Commissioners finding that thair are seaverall persons delated by the said Christine Shaw and by the said Elizabeth Anderson and James and Thomas Lindsay, and which persons delated as aforsaid viz. Margaret Lang spouse to William Semple in Cartinpen, Jean Anderson \daughter/ to Allexander Anderson, Martha Sempill daughter to Margaret Lang, John Lindsay bishop, Margaret Shearer in Erskine Green, William Miller in Gatesyde of Formakine, John Rid smith in Inchennan, John Stewart in Bowhouse of Inchenan, Anable Reid his spouse, Katrine Ferrier in Craigtoun burn, Margaret Cuninghoun [*sic*] spous to Thomas Woodrow in Carslop, Margaret Rodger in Whyt hill, Janet Rodger her sister, Margaret Ewing spous to Thomas Birkmyre in Stainiebutts, Margaret McKillop weadow in Bonnill, being under bad fame, The Commissioners ordered them to be apprehended and conveined before them, who having compeired one by one, and being confronted with the said Elizabeth Anderson, James and Thomas Lindsays, and the saids three persons confessing as aforsaid being interrogat by the saids Commissioners whether or not the particulars containd in ther lexive[78] confessiones relating to the rexive persons above dilated were true, they owned the same in thair presence, Therfor the Commissioners ordered them to the Tolbooth of Renfrew wher

77 The 'preses' (president) was Lord Blantyre.
78 *Sic*. Read 'rexive' (respective).

they remain till furder order, In testimony of the truth of the premisses the saids Comissioners and Robert Allexander wryter in Glasgow whom they have elected \thair clerk/ thairto have subscribed the same at day yeir and place forsaid. *Sic Subscribitur* Blantyre, PHoustoune, GCochrane, JPorterfeild, Ro: Sempill, RAlexander. {*p. 31*}[79]

A Continued Accompt of the Trouble of Christine Shaw Daughter to the Laird of Bargarran, Frae Thursday the 18th February 1697 at which tyme the Commissioners appoynted for taking inquyrie in the said affair mett at Renfrew the said day.

The said day about 2 acloack in the afternoon the Child being in the light fit said the Devill now appeared to her in the ordinary shape of a man, quhairupon she being in great feare and consternation wes desyred by her mother to pray The Lord Rebuke the[e] Satan, quhich the Child having essayed to doe, presently her tongue being drawn down her throat, lost power of speech, And again essaying to say the same thing wes seized with a greivous fitt, quhairin she strugled with feet and hands for some tyme, and then was hurryed with violence to and froe thorow the roume deafe and blind, yet seeking with the gentlewoman (who had bein alwayes one of her most violent Tormentors, and quhom she now gets named in the intervale of the fitt) in the lyknes of a bombee[80] and saying with the Lords strenth thow shalt not put in straw nor sticks in my mouth, and being at this tyme as said is hurryed to and froe in violence thorow the roume, cryed with a lowd voice The bombee hath stingd me, and presently sitting down and lowseing her stokine put her {*p. 32*} hand to that part of her leg quhich was affected as said is, quhairupon spectators did visibly see, the livele marks of naills of fingers, deeply imprinted on her leg. After this the Devill appeared to her again in the shape of ane ordinary Gentleman, against whom she reasoned after this manner, Thow thinks to tempt me to be a witch, but throw Gods strenth thow shalt never be the better, I charge the[e] in the name of God to be gone and thy papers too, for I will have none of them, I will not the[e], I will stand here and see if thow canst come one step nearer me, I think thow fears me more than I feare the[e], Then turning herself again wes hurryed with violence to and froe as said is, crying she wes bitten with teeth in the hands very sore, and nixt with the naills of fingers above 24 tymes quhich constrained her to utter horrid skreeks and outcrys at every tyme she received them, shewing the part of her body quhair it was nipt and bitten as said is, putting her hands thereon, but neither saw nor heard, any about her, and in this caice she continued from 2 till 5 in the afternoon, and quhen recovered she said the Gentlewoman aforsaid told her in the fitt That Margaret Lang (now in custody) had ordered her to treat

79 Pages 24–31 contain material not included in this edition. See the introduction, above.
80 'bombee': bumblebee.

the said Christine after this manner, and that the said Margaret Lang had a comanding power over the forenamed Gentlewoman, witnesses hereto Janet Aikine relict of umquhill Donald McGilchrist of Northbarr, Christiane Aikine weadow in Glasgow, and Margaret Campbell indweller thair. *Sic subscribitur* Cristine Aikine, Margret Cambell.

Fryday and Saturnday thaireftir she continued in hir fitts being violently bitten and nipt in her craig[81] and hands and other parts of her body, the marks of the teeth both upper and lower being visibly seen with the spittle and slaver of a mouth thairupon together at the marks of the naills of fingers, witnesses hereto Mr Andrew Turner minister at Erskine, John McGilchrist wryter in Glasgow and the within named Christine Aikine. *Sic subscribitur* Andr: Turner witnes to the marks of the naills of fingers, J°M^c^Gilchryst witnes to the whole, Cristine Aikine witnes to the whole.

The forsaid days the spectre of a crookit fellow appeard to her Tormenting her having his two feet deformed, the broadsyde of them outmost and his two heells near together as he moves, upon the appearance of this fellow Tormenting her her feet were put in the very same posture, as his were during the tyme of his Tormenting her, witnesses hereto the saids Janet and Christine Aikine and John McGilchrist. *Sic subscribitur* Cristine Aikine, J°M^c^Gilchrist.

Note here that the minister of Killmacolme declares thair is such a fellow swae[82] deformed in his feet as said is near to his own house, who hes bein of evill fame, It is lykewayes to be noted here that one of the confessors declares the forsaid fellow in Killmalcolme wes at the meeting in Bargarren orchard with the rest of the Crew.

In fitts of this kind she continued for seaverall days thaireftir, naming Jean Ross, the forsaid crooked fellow, and Margaret Allexander in Pasley, (quhich two women are delated by the three Confessors) who were tormenting her, particularly Sunday the 21 February and Munday following, the said Jean Ross greivously vexed her, telling her she wes comissionated so to doe, being that the Gentlewoman had a pain in her head at that tyme, and wes not able to come furth.

Note here that the child declares that the forsaid Gentlewoman about 2 days thairefter, appeard to her with her head bound up with a cross cloath, she not appearing to the Child formerly in that posture, witnesses hereto the said Janet and Christine Aikine and Margret Campbell. *Sic subscribitur* Cristine Aikine, Margret Cambell.

Upon Thursday thairefter she continueing in the former fitts but with sore weeping and crying of pain in her two sydes, she said in the intervale of the fitts she wes that night to be in greivous fitts, and that they were resolved to choack her by putting pins in her mouth, which accordingly fell out (she

81 'craig': neck.
82 'swae': so.

having emptied herself of all the pins in her cloaths before[)], In quhich fitt she wes blind and deafe, and jumped up and down in ane extraordinary manner with her body, pulling down what ever she felt with her hands, in this posture she continued for some days putting out a great quantity of small broken pins which she declared Jean Ross had put in her mouth, witnesses hereto the saids Christine Aikine {*p. 33*} and Margaret Campbell. *Sic subscribitur* Cristine Aikine, Margret Cambell.

The last of February about 4 aclock in the afternoon, she fell in greivous fitts, hydeous laughing, jumping and running with violence to and froe and thairafter weept sore, crying out of pain that a litle hieland man (who had bein Tormenting her for some days before) had broken her leg, which she scarce could get expresst in the fitt, and putting her hand to the place asserted, spectators lowsed her stokine, and saw visibly a sore bruise in her shin bone, which when toutched affected her so, that she uttered horrid screeks and outcrys, thorow pain, and when recovered, did declare The forsaid litle hieland fellow had given her that bruise. After this she put out of her mouth a crookit pin, quhich she said the forsaid hieland fellow had put in with a designe to choack her, witnesses hereto, the saids Mr Andrew Turner and John McGilchrist. *Sic subscribitur* Andr: Turner, J^{o}McGilchrist.

The first 8^{t} days of March she had litle variation of trouble but continuing in her former fitts, putting out of her mouth a great number of small pins, often fainting and falling dead upon the ground on a sudden, strugleing with feet and hands after lying in this posture as said is, (her naturall spirits being much weakened and exhausted) sometymes also she offered[83] to goe in into the fyre; she used at this tyme also, when ministers and other Christians mett in the family for prayer, to make great disturbance in the entery of that work, particularly March 2^{d}, which day was sett apart for fasting and prayer in the family, she being at first some what composed in tyme of prayer yet a blast of wind arysing on a sudden, which forced oppen the hall windows; she was at the same tyme instantly seized of a violent fitt when the minister was offering her up in prayer to God, in which fit she being both blind and deaffe, and also without sense of feeling was hurryed with violence to and froe throw the hall, sometyme falling on the ground as one dead (the members of her body rigid and extended[)], sometimes singing and making a hydeous noise, some tymes naming the Gentle woman, Margaret Archibald, Margaret Williamson her daughter and others whom she said were thair present afflicting her, standing and sitting in such particular places of the roume, as \she/ then condescended upon; and when recovered of her fitt, said she saw the Gentlewoman and the hieland man come in with the blast of wind that forced the oppening of the windows as said is.

[83] 'offered': attempted.

This falling out on the Teusday as said is she continued in the light fitt without any intermission till the sabbath thaireftir without being seizd of any sore fitt, and having gone to the Church on the Lords day following, was perfectly well for the most part of the day, yet averred she saw Janet Wauch in one of the windows of the church in her ordinary habit, she not being seen thair by any other.

Munday thairefter being March 8^{t}, for the most part of that day she inclyned to sleep, and could scarce be keept from it, But so soon as sleep seemd to seize her, fell a crying Mother, Mother, will ye not waken me for Ile be destroyed, and when awakened did fret and murmur at bystanders who had wakened her, In this condition she continued for the most part of this week. {*p. 34*}

Teusday being March 9t, her mother and Margret Campbell her cousin took the damsell with them to walk in the orchard, and coming in to the house again, her mother entering the Tower gate first, the damsell at her back, Margret Campbell standing a litle at the Tower Gate, and her mother going into the kitchine thinking they had bein both at her back, the damsell was suddenly carried away in a flight up stairs with so swift and unaccountable motione, that they did not in the least suspect her absence, But her mother turning about, and missing the damsell, cryed wher Christine, Margret Campbell, and instantly she getting out of the gate and her mother running up stairs, to look for the damsell, heard a noise, and following the noise found her daughter leaping and dancing upon on[e] of the stairs, seazd with violent fitts, and when recovered she said Jean Park had carried her away from her mothers back as she entered the kitchine door as afor said \her feet not touching the ground to her aprehension/[84] and that with a designe to strangle her with the roaps, on which cloaths usd to hang thair \in the wardrop/, But that the said Jean could get her no further then the place she was in, and did therfor leave her in such a violent fitt.

Sabbath thaireftir being March 14^{t} her fitts altered again, in that her mouth and nose were prodigiously distorted and turned about (whyle in the fitt) her face being strangely and horridly deformed. The same day she being in the Church the forenoon, and her gloove falling from her in the seat, the same was again given her, and put into her hand by some invisible agent to the consternatione of others.

Note here she hath not bein this long tyme free of some invisible spirit haunting her on all occasions, and suggesting many things unto her unheard by others, both concerning her self and other persons.

On the forsaid Lords day between sermons, she said she was to be violently Tormented in the afternoon, with the forementioned fitts, and therfor could not goe to church again, naming Janet Keir in Northbar in all the said fitts,

[84] The passage in oblique strokes is inserted above the line. Is this an early attempt to improve the supernatural quality of the narrative?

whom she had seen the forenoon, in the church (thoe invisible to others) and was the occasion of thir kynd of fitts, accordingly that afternoon she was extreamly afflicted and Tormented, crying in the fitts if the forenamed Janet Keir were not sent for she would grow worser and worser, accordingly the parents of the damsell in the evening sent for the said Janet Kerr [*sic*], (she all the whyle continueing in the fitts worser and worser) telling and threatning her, if the damsell were any furder troubled with her, she should be seized with others, Quhairupon she was no more troubled with hir nor thir kind of fitts \till Fryday thairefter/. The forsaid persons without being desyred in the chylds presence, being at the tyme in the fitt prayed God might send her her health, Quhairupon instantly she recovered.

Teusday thairefter being March 16t she was again seazed with her other sort of fitts, all the parts of her body being stiff and rigid, strugleing with feet and hand sometyme on the ground, sometymes in thir fitts she wes heard, conversing with the Gentlewoman, as she calld her, vindicating her self of what she then alledgd the Gentlewoman had charged her with Viz: That she had accused a person of honour and credit as one of her Tormenters, telling the Gentlewoman distinctly she was a liar, and that it was she herself and noe other ever mentioned any such thing. {*p. 35*}

Till the Fryday therefter she was never free of the light fitts and nou and then falling into swerfes and appeared to be allmost choacked by the means of some charmes and inchantments invisibly conveyed in her mouth, which inchantments and charmes were visibly seen in her mouth, and to the apprehension of spectators were as if it had been peices of chesnuts, orange piles, whyts of eggs of a yellow and whytish collour, and were duly seen when occasionally she oppened her mouth in the fitt, and when spectators essayed to get them out of her mouth, she keept her mouth closs, her teeth closeing hard together that noe strenth could oppen them, and when recovered of the fitt said Luckie Miller had put them in her mouth.

Wpon the Fryday being March 19t she was violently Tormented in sore fitts, wherin her neck was distorted, and bent back towards her healls lyke a bow, strugleing sometymes with feet and hands, sometyme stiff blynd and deaff, and without sense of feeling, putting out of her mouth a great number of small pins, which she said Luckie Miller had put in her mouth.

And about 6 of the Clock that night being violently Tormented fell a crying that if the Gentlewoman were not apprehended that night it would be in vain to seize her to morrow, for I have much to suffer at her hands,[85] betuixt 12 and ane in the clock in the morning. At this tyme she lifting up her eye lid with her hand, and looking upwards said what art thow that tells me the shereff and my father is coming here this night, a litle after this

[85] The word 'tomorrow' is crossed out at this point.

Bargarran and the shereff and James Guthrie meacer,[86] lighted at Bargarran gate, and came up stairs to the consternation of spectators remembring what the damsell had said before, The damsell continueing all the whyle blind and deafe neither hearing nor seeing, any body, yet was in the hearing of the shereff, her father, James Guthry and others discoursing with some invisible spirit about her, saying, Is the shereff come Is he besyde me, and putting out her hand to feell if any body were about her, and the shereff putting his hand in hers \she/ said to some invisible beeing as discoursing with her I cannot feell the shereff, how can he be here, how can I have him by the hand, as thow says seeing I feell it not. Thow says he hes snuff colloured cloaths, red plush breatches with black strips, ane floured musline cravat, and an embroydered sword belt, Thow says thair is ane old gray haird man with him, and ane ring upon his hand, I see and feell none of them, are they come to apprehend the Gentlewoman, Is this thair earand indeed. Note here, that the forsaid persons had that afternoon, got ane order from the Lords of the Justiciary, to apprehend the forsaid Gentlewoman, and were upon the way to put it in execution, against the morrow morning, but seeing the Torment of the chyld, and hearing what she had told if the Gentle woman were not apprehended this night, it would be in vain to seize \her/, took horse about 9 in the clock that night, to put the warrand to execution. {*p. 36*}

As the damsell continued to be violently and in ane extraordinary manner Tormented, sometymes lying with her neck and other parts of her body upon the ground, as if they had bein disjoynted, offering to throw herself into the Fyre,[87] about 10 in the clock she continueing in the fitts, her parents went to family worship, and her father reading a chapter, she repeated the words after him thoe in the blind and deafe fitt, which made spectators apprehend that the damsell had the sense of hearing in thir kynd of fitts, at least that she heard when the Scriptures were read. Therfor her father to try the truth of the thing did forbear to read any furder, which thoe he did yet the damsell continued to repeat the following verses of the chapter, thoe none in the roome were reading and she herself had no book, nor could see any, saying to some invisible spirit about her, will thow teach me a part of the old testament as well as the new.

The damsell still continueing in the forementioned fitts, and acted as aforsaid, oftentymes throwing her self into the fyre if she had not bein prevented by spectators, Telling us that now it was 12 of the clock, oh it is past now twelve, and some tymes throw the violence of her pain, and the decay of her naturall spirits, and want of breath, lay as if she had bein quyt dead, sometymes again recovering seemd to be willing to express somewhat

86 A macer was a sheriff's officer. One of his duties was to carry out arrests.

87 The words 'Telling us that now it was 12 of the clock, oh it is now past 12' are crossed out at this point. These words reappear, presumably more correctly, in the next paragraph.

which she could not get done, but put out of her mouth, a great number of crookd pins, all the parts of her body being prodigiously distorted, crying out hydeously of pain. Thus she continued till half ane hour after 12 anight, when on a sudden she recovered of the fitts to the admiratione of her parents and minister (then present) and others, Telling them she might now goe to bed, for she heard just now that the shereff and the other gentleman were lighted at the gentle womans house in Greinock, and accordingly the damsell went to bed, and was no further troubled that night, and accordingly the shereff and the meacer the nixt morning when they came to Bargarran, declared that it was about half ane in the morning when they lighted at Greinock.

Saturnday 20 March about 10 in the clock myd forenoon she was seizd with fitts on a sudden, falling doun dead, her eyes being closed \sometymes oppening and turning in her head/,[88] saw nor heard none about her, but was hurryed to and froe with violence throw the hall, now and then screiking and making a hydeous noise \when any by force hindered her motion/, she being in this posture and depryvd of the senses of hearing, feeling and seeing, James Lindsay one of the Confessors was brought into the roume, who so soon as he entered the door was seen by her, and she laughing and seeming to be somewhat glad ran towards him saying, wher hes thow bein Jamie this long tyme, how does thow, and answering him distinctly, every word he spoke, thoe at the same tyme other spectators, cryed with a lowd voice in her ears, yet she heard none, nor could perceive any object presented to her senses, Instance[89] one in the roome held before her eyes whyle she was {*p. 37*} conversing with the Confessor ane tobacco box and other objects but she did not discern it, which nevertheless so soon as it wes put in the hands of the forsaid James Lindsay, she did at the same instant presently discover it in his hand, and said, Jamie wher hes thow gott this box, she being in this posture the shereff, minister and Bargarren thought fitt to confront the Gentlewoman (then in the house in a roome above them) to try if the damsell could see her as she had done James Lindsay, And accordingly so soon the said Gentlewoman enterd the door, the Child being in the fitts as said is, fell a laughing and said I see the Gentlewoman[90] (thoe the damsell had never seen her personally all her life before except her spectre in the fitts), she lykeways heard her when she spoke to her and telling her distinctly[91] she had seen her the other night in her fitts \upon the Gentle womans enquyring when she had seen her/ Quhairupon the Gentlewoman on a sudden without being desyred prayed The Lord send the[e] thy health \or help this poor daft chyld/ and rebuke the Devill, which words were no sooner uttered, Then the damsell fell doun dead and stiff as

[88] About thirteen words, now illegible, have been crossed out here, and these seven words added in the margin.
[89] 'Instance': for instance.
[90] Three words, now illegible, have been crossed out here.
[91] The words 'Telling her' have been crossed out here.

she useth to doe before recovery of all her fitts, and in this posture carried to another roume instantly recovered of the blind and deaff fitt, and also of the light fitt, becoming presently well, and continueing \so/ for some space. Wpon her recovery of the fitts, being perfectly well and sensible, was enquyrd whom she had seen in her last fitt, replyed that thoe the Gentlewoman had bein in the roume above her yet she had seen her in the fitt, The damsell at this tyme not knowing that the Gentlewoman had bein brought doun stairs to her whyle in the fitt and had bein personally present in the hall with her.

Note here that about 2 hours therefter the Commissioners of Justiciary came to Bargarran, the damsell falling into another fitt, the said Gentlewoman wes again confronted with the damsell, in their presence, as in the caice above sett doun, and upon her praying the damsell recovered as aforsaid.

Sabbath following she fell into swerfeings and swooneings, not complaining of any pain except about her heart, falling doun dead both when she recovered, and when seazed of the fitts, sometimes singing after ane unusuall manner, telling spectators that Luckie Miller constrained her to it and that her oun lips were not moving, which spectators saw to be true, only her tongue was moving: For the preventing of which she frequently put her oun hand in her mouth. Att this tyme she was violently Tormented, when either she her self or thos about her essayed to read any part of Scripture, telling them that if she did but so much as hear the word of God read that day she would be extreamly tortured, especially when essaying to read Heb. 11 chap. v. 2^{d}, and v. 4^{t} the last part of it, and verse 6^{t} the last part of it, As also Isay chap. 40 and Psalms 3^{d}, at which tyme also she uttered horrid screeks and outcrys that she was nipt, and accordingly the marks of the naills of fingers, were visibly seen on her arms, she being thus nipt and bitten 4 seaverall tymes with such pain and violence, that the skin was teared from these parts of her *{p. 38}* arms, and fingers, wher the steads[92] of the teeth and marks of the nails of fingers were seen, so that throw the deepnes of the wounds the forsaid parts affected as said is bled, the blood being both seen and handled by spectators. She being in this condition seemd to be extreamly affected and opprest with sicknes as if she had bein in a fever, crying sometymes Take away thes dead childeren out of my sight, from 6 till 9 in the morning; she thus affected with the painfull sicknes as said is, and throw the rest of the day continueing in the forsaid fitts: charmes and inchantments were put in her mouth as formerly, which were visible to spectators. By means wherof she seemd to be allmost choaked: The damsell spitting on the ground, fell down on a sudden, and putt her hand to the spittle, and lifting some trash that had bein in her mouth, threw it from her, which spectators heard fall to the ground, with some noyse, but neither saw it in her spittle, nor after she threw it from her, thoe whyle

92 'steads': marks.

in her mouth they visibly saw something lyke orange piles, whyts of eggs, peices of chesnuts.[93]

Teusday March 23^{d} about 3 of the clock in the morning, she being asleep in her bed with her mother was on a sudden wakened (after a whyles strugling in her sleep) with much fear and consternatione, and wes seizd of her blind and deafe fits, and gripping fast by her mother in the bed, telling her and her father that the Devill was assaulting and standing by her in the bed, and cryed on a sudden, God almighty keep me from thy meetings, Ile die or[94] I goe to them, Ile never renunce my baptisme throw the grace of God for Ile goe to hell if I doe it, thow says Ile goe to hell however because I am a great sinner, but I beleeve what the word of God saith, thoe I have many sins yet the blood of Christ cleanseth from all sin, and I will not add that great wickednes to my other sins, Its no wonder thow make a lie to me, seeing thow was bold to lie in Gods face, I know thow art a liar from the beginning, the red coat thow promises me, is but the fyre of hell; perfect health and great riches thow promises me, But thow canst not perform what thow promises, Thoe I should never be whole Ile never renunce my baptism, it is God that hes keeped me all this whyle from being a witch, and I trust he will keep me of his grace and not because of any thing in me, and that same God that hes keeped me hitherto will yet keep me out of thy hands, This conference and thir replys her parents and others were witness to for the space of near ane hour, and after recovery the Child declared, That it had bein the Devill who had appeared to her assaulting her as aforsaid in the shape of a naked man, with a shirt, rough hands, and rough faced lyke birres. {*p. 39*}

Till Sunday following March 28th she continued in the light fitts, but with sore fitts every morning and evening, still naming, Luckie Miller, the Gentlewife, Elizabeth Tarbet in Newark, [*1 word blank*] Colquhoune ane hieland wife were Tormenting her.

The said day in the morning she recovered of all her fitts and also of the light fitts becomeing perfectly well and sensible and as composed as ever and still continues to be so, but how long God Knowes. FINIS. {*p. 40 blank*} {*p. 41*}

John Reds Confession
Renfrew May 21 1697

John Red in Inchennan prisoner here having desir'd to speak with the minister did upon his coming first privately to himself and afterward before Baylie Scot, Mr Andrew Cochrane clerk, and me John Verner declare as followeth.

First Being enquired how and when he was engag'd in Satans service and after what forme he appear'd unto him, he said that about a year agoe when

[93] After this paragraph, the scribe has left a gap of about five or six lines.
[94] 'or': before.

he had gone from his own house about midnight and was going about break of day by Balgavel moss he appear'd unto him there in the forme of a gray horse and went a gay piece[95] with him but spake none to him, and a 2nd time some while after he appeard to him also in the same place about the same time of day in the same forme and going about him gave him a byt or nip in his loyn which he found painfull for 14 days after. That the 3d time he appear'd to him was at Easter Southbar wood foot and being enquir'd in what forme he answer'd in the form of a black man, with black cloaths and a cape upon his head and fasses[96] about it and a blew craig cloath or cravat about his neck, and at that time he confest he spoke to him to engage him in his service and that then it was he renounced his baptism and gave up himself to the Devils service putting the one hand to the crown of his head and the other to the sole of his foot. After which tyme the pain of the byte or nip ceas'd. He confest also that he mett with him a 2d time shortly after \in/ the same place and in the same forme, at both which there were none others present with him and that then he drew the said John unto him and said he should be his freind, and being ask'd him [*sic*] what mov'd him to engage in that service, He answer'd It was that he might get gear and comfort in the work and that the Devil had promised him that he should not want any thing that he sought in his name, but said he perform'd ill and that he was a liar from the beginning.[97] Again the said John being enquird if he was at any meetings with the Devil afterwards, he said he warranded he had been at a duzen of meetings, but being particularly interrogat he specified only two that were in Bargarren yeard, the first of which was in harvest in the tyme of fruit in the nyght tyme where were present Margaret and Janet Rogers, John and James Lindsay bishop and curat, and the 2 boyes James and Thomas Lindsays, and Elizabeth Anderson, Agnes Nesmith and Mary Morison, and one in Carsdykes whom he call'd Pock or Bock or some name like that, And that there he bad[e] them pluck fruit, And being ask'd what he did then, he was as busie as the rest, and the nixt meeting in Bargarren yeard which he said was in the day time was about the time when there was a fast for Christine Shaw, all the company he nam'd were there present, And being interrogat how many he thought would be at the said meeting he said he warrand' there were threescore, but he did not see them all distinctly, only there was a litle body who was call'd the drudge, And being ask'd if the Devil was there at thes 2 meetings, he said he was nearby, in the same kind of garb as when he first engag'd with him; he said the first meeting in the night time they had a blew candle, and he granted there had been musick and dancing both the times and that John Lindsay was the pyper

95 'a gay piece' (gey): a considerable distance.
96 'cape': cap; 'fasses': tassels.
97 This biblical phrase (from John 8:44) is more likely to have come from the interrogators, a small indication of the influence that they exert throughout this formulaic text.

and plaid the one tune with a bitt stick and the other tune with a kaill runt.[98] Being ask'd if they had any consultation about doing harm to any person, he granted they were then contryving Christin Shaws death, aither to worry her or drown her in the wall &c.[99] Being enquird if they were not fear'd to be heard or seen, he granted that some of them were; bot the Devil said he should warrand them, that they should neither be heard nor seen, he granted also that the Devil should keep them ever from confessing, to which end the Devill gave every one of them a litle bitt of flesh to eat which he call'd ane unchristened bairns liver, and said who ever eat it should never confess, He granted he got a bitt of it but \said he/ lett it fall and did not eat it. Being enquired if he had seen any other persons there then he had allready named, {*p. 42*} He said they might have been there for him for he did not see them all, but he saw all whom he had expressly nam'd; Being enquird if when the Devil engag'd any in his service he did not give them names, he said he usually did so, himself he call'd Swift foot, and the litle body, he call'd Drudge, some Jack, som Tom. Being enquird anent Mary Morison, he said he saw her a lustie a woman[100] with cockups[101] who was call'd Antiochia.[102] Being enquird how he knew that that which appeard in the forme of a horse was the Devil, he said That horse appeard sometimes bigger, sometimes less came to him, he knew not how it evanish'd out of his sight.

To all this above writtine the minister, Baylie Scot and me John Vairner, were witnesses.

After his first confession to the minister, he was content to confess the same before witnesses, and while he was making the forsaid confession, he desired that what he said might be noted down, that he might be called again to remembrance of them, least he should forget, which accordingly was done by me John Verner in presence of himself and the rest of the witnesses and afterwards read \over/ to him.

Immediately therefter in presence of the Laird of Jordanhill,[103] the minister, Mr Andrew Cochran clerk and Baylie Paterson,[104] owning his former confessions, and being enquird by Jordanhill how they were advertis'd of their meetings, he said that ordinarly at their meeting the nixt time of the meeting was appoynted, and for particular warning there appear'd a black grew dog[105]

98 'bitt stick': piece of stick; 'kaill runt': stalk of kale.

99 'worry': strangle; 'wall': well.

100 *Sic.* Probably read 'a lustie woman', i.e. a vigorous woman.

101 'cockups': pads added to the coiffure.

102 For a discussion of this name, see the introduction to *A Relation of the Diabolical Practices of Above Twenty Wizards and Witches of the Sheriffdom of Renfrew*, above in the present volume.

103 Lawrence Crawford of Jordanhill.

104 This name has been altered, and the reading is uncertain.

105 'grew dog': greyhound.

with a chain about his neck, and being interrogat if the dog spake any, he said he only tinkled the chain and they were to follow.

The posture of John Reds death

Afterwards he being \in/ the upper prison where he was keept allone Baylie Scot declared that the said John call'd out from the window to him being on the street to keep that old body Angus Forester who had been his fellow prisoner and not let him go but keep him sure. The minister being abroad all the rest of that day and having desird some elders to keep conference with him by intervals, spoke to the said John after 9 aclock at night, the Bailie being present when he adhered to his former confession. And being enquir'd by the minister if he did wholly renounce the Devil and all engagments with his service and give up himself to Jesus Christ and did desire to find mercy of God through him: He assented thereto. And being enquird if he desird company, or would be affraid to be allone: he said he had no fear of any thing. And being left alone and \none/ having gone to him till after 12 aclock the nixt day being Saturnday May 22 that the minister came frome his study, to visit him; which the minister finding upon inquiry and being dissatisfied therwith, went up in company with the baylie and jaylor and when the door was opend and his name called upon and none answering, he was seen in a very lamentable posture. But the room being dark becaus a brod[106] that covered the light of the window had been set up, the minister desird it to be taken down, that he with the rest might distinctly perceive the posture quherin he was (which brod was not over the light of the window, when they had left him the night before) viz: sitting upon a stooll which was upon the hearth of the chimney with his feet upon the floor, in an ordinary posture of sitting, with his body streight upwards, his shoulders touching the lintel of the chimey [*sic*] and his neck ty'd up with his own craig cloath, with the knott of it behind, and the two ends of it tyed upon a bitt stick thrust into the cleft above the lintell of the brace betwixt and the building above, which was a stick the former prisoners had struck in there to hing some of their utensils upon; which the minister thinking it might have been but newly down,[107] and he not fully dead, caused cutt hard by the said stick; and quhen it was cut his body only leaned a litle aside to the corner of the chimney brace, And then the minister feeling his hands which was hinging down before him found him cold and stiff dead: whereby they concluded it had been done in the night. But by them quho first saw him, and all others that did observe all the particulars narrowly both before and after, the shereff came (who was imediately advertised therof[])] and John Campbel a chyrurgeon with him, it was certainly concluded that he could not have perpetratyd that fact himself: The craig cloath that was about

106 'brod': board.

107 *Sic*. Probably read 'newly done'.

his neck having no runloup,[108] but only an ordinary knot behind, and that not very strait,[109] but appeard only as if the knot that used to be tyd before had been turned behind his neck; and the stick whether for length or bigness which supported his head having no strength to bear any weight of his body so as to strangle him; and serving to no more purpose but to keep his body streight and upright from falling down one way or another, nor could have born the throwings and convulsions of death, But finding his body streight upwards as was said, and his head only bowing a litle forward with his bonnet upon it, and covering his \fore/ head, and his hands lying down before him one upon another, It was justly judged if he had by some other hand or power put[110] to death, and only left in that posture in which he could never have left himself if he had been the actor. Subscribd by me Pat: Simson minr: Walter Scot baylie, John Hall Jailor. {*p. 43*}

Confession of Margaret Lang at the stake

Margaret Lang confessed as follows, 1. That she had receivd the insencible marks found upon her body frae the Devil who apear'd to her in the likeness of a black man, and that when he first apear'd to her, she knew him not to be the Devil till afterwards. 2. That she was a real witch and in compact with the Devil, and had been a great hypocrit which she exorted spectators at the stake to guard against. 3. That beside other more frequent meetings[111] with the Devil, she had been above 80 times in privat conferences with him. 4. That the Devil requir'd the giving up of herself to him in a covenant and the engaging of her self in his service, which she said, she yeilded to. 5. Being enquird by a near relation of her own, anent her being in Bargarrens house tormenting Christin Shaw, she answerd in these words, The Devil having an absolut power and dominion over me, carried my shape whether[112] he would. And lykewayes she confessd unnatural Lust.

As John Lindsay Bishop was going to the stake to be burnt he was overheard say to his brother James Lindsay, Now Brother It is time that we should confess since our keeping it up will serve us to no purpose, To which the other answered That they should never do that.

And sicklyke Agnes Nasmith at the said tyme told the minister That her heart and tongue was bound up in such manner that she could not express what she would.

[108] 'runloup': slip-knot.
[109] 'strait': tight.
[110] *Sic*. Probably read 'been put'.
[111] 'more frequent meetings': meetings attended (frequented) by more witches.
[112] 'whether': whither.

As to Kathrine Campbel, ane minister discoursing her before her doome[113] was pronounced, enquired her if she did not remember the godly discourses and gracious admonitions which Christine Shaw while in a fit gave her at a certain time, and instanced her some particulars therof, Her answer was with heavy groans, yes I remember, and being urgd furder to confess the rest, she finding her self graveld[114] by her answer retracted all, and when her doom was given out against her she got out these words, That the doom pronounced on her was most just and that she could not free her self of witchcraft.

Thir five persons with John Lindsay in Barcloch and Margaret Fultoun in Kilpatrick were burnt at Pasley the 10^t^ June 1697. {*p. 53*}[115]

A Prefatorie Discourse in reference to a fast appoynted by the Presbitrie upon the 31 of March 1697[116]

My frindes we have bein \somtime/ preaching of Christ to yow, we are now to speake of the Devil to yow; the greatest enemie that our Lord and his kingdom hath in the worlde; the thing that I am about to intimat to you is this. The members of the Presbitrie having taken to their consideration how much Satan doeth rage in thir lands and quhich is indeed very observable in our bounds, and in our's only, quhich no doubt hath a voice to Ministers and Elders and Masters of families, and in a word to all conserned in thir bounds, they have thought fitt to apointe a day for fasting and humiliation that soe he who is the Lion of the tribe of Juda[117] may appear with pouer against him who is the angle[118] of the bottomless pit and throw him doun, who is now come out in grate wrath! O that it may \be/ because his time is short.

As to the causes of the fast, I shall hint a few things to yow, the thing being soe weell knoun in the bounds. The Presbitrie did not think it needfull to be any wayes large or formall in drauing up of causes, however, \in/ the first place, the causes of our preceeding fasts remain yet not sufficiently mourn'd over, so that tho we have no other causes but these formerlie named we have

113 'her doome': her judicial sentence (which had been delivered on 19 May).

114 'graveld': confounded.

115 Pages 44–52 contain material not included in this edition. See the introduction, above.

116 The first two-thirds of the text of this 'Prefatorie Discourse' has been printed, in a modernised version, in *A History of the Witches of Renfrewshire* (Paisley, 1877), 216–19. No source is given, but small textual differences suggest that some source other than the 'Bargarran Witches' manuscript has been used. The introduction to the document (p. 216) states that the 'Discourse' was delivered in Paisley by Thomas Blackwell, minister of Paisley, on Sunday 28 March 1697. This may well be correct; the presbytery of Paisley, on Wednesday 24 March 1697, ordered a fast to be held 'Thursday come eight days' (Thursday 1 April), with intimation to be made in parishes on the sabbath preceding (Sunday 28 March): NRS, Minutes of Presbytery of Paisley, 1660–1699, CH2/294/4, p. 258. Further investigation of this and other proceedings of the presbytery would be desirable. In the edition below, paragraph breaks have been added editorially to Blackwell's numbered points.

117 Cf. Revelation 5:5.

118 'angle': angel (in this case the Devil, a fallen angel).

ground to observe more fasts then on[e] or tuo. But yet a littell more closs to the purpose that Satan is greatly rageing in our bounds, he hath in all probabilitie enjoyd a long and old stock of subjects even among the hearers of the gosple; it may be some of them are hearing me just now, conscience being best judge of that matter, and now he hath come that lenth no doubt being permitted by God that his pouer is not only to be perceived in keeping many hearts from closing with Christ, but alsoe in tormenting and afflicting of a familie extraordinarly in our bounds, soe that it is seen to be the Devel and his instruments and none els. Therefor that Satan who is rageing and who hath gotten manye in all probabilitie to devote themselves soul and bodie to him and his service that such may be delivered out of his snare and that such may be discovered here, is one reason for calling for a solem fast again.

2^ly^ There is the impenitencie and obstinacie of persons supposed upon severall accounts {*p. 54*} trewlye to be guiltie, their continueing obstinatt and impenitent and refusing to confess in that matter, that God who hath the pouer of conscience, that he by the power of his spirite in the use of other means laufull for the finding out of the truth may make these means effectuall and may win in upon ther consciences by the pouer of his spirite to make them conffess they are guiltie.

3^ly^ The greate affliction of that poor childe and the familie in quhich she is soe nearly interrested: none of us knous hir afffiction[119] and hir parentes soe as it is in it self, it is easie to look upon one so tormented as she is in respect of quhat it would be to be soe tormented our selfes; or yet one in our families, we would remember them that are in bonds, as bound with them: and therfor lett our petitions have a speciall respect to the affliction of that familie that is sett up as a beacon upon the top of a mountain for all to take warning.[120]

4^ly^ Another reason is the misteriousness and difficulty of the process of witchcraft,[121] soe that it is the process, of all others, that requirs most prudence, soliditie, and severall other things quhich to name manie of yow would not understand me, but in a word it requirs much of the presence of Gods spirit to guide the Judges and worke upon the hearts and consciences of the pannals[122] so the truth may be found out and judgment accordingly execut. Thus we offer to yow severall reasons why it is necessar for us to observe a day of fasting and humiliation before God.

And now my freinds all I add is this, in the first place, I ame sure Ministers and I am sure the godly are calld to be very importunat with God in this matter; would ye know my freinds why we preach in vain to them that have devoted themselves to the Devel; it is them that maketh the gosple soe barran

119 *Sic*. Read 'affliction'.
120 Cf. Isaiah 30:17.
121 The process of trying witchcraft in a criminal court.
122 'pannals': accused persons in a criminal court.

and who knous but in this congregation there be maney who have these many years hence bein under vowes to Satan, and as for yow that are the people of God ye pray in vain for the success of the gosple to them, for til once[123] they be brought to see their sin and be convinced of the evil thereof and to loath themselfs upon the acount of the same, neither will your prayers nor the gosple doe them anie good, soe it is Ministers and the people of God's deuty and intrest to pray not only that God would find out the guilty among these *{p. 55}* that are apprehended, but that God would discover all others that are guiltie and are not apprehended, that the kingdom of Christ may run and be glorified and the kingdom of Satan destroyed.

The last word I say is this, I would fain hope that this congregation will in some measure be exemplarie to others in observing this fast. We intreate that all in this congregation, as they would Vaunt their Zeall for the advancement of the kingdom of Christ and the destruction of the kingdom of Satan, may prepare their hearts by prayer in secret before God in order to ther being in a more spirituall and serious \frame/ in this publick work; and if anie person or familie will slight soe great a dewty and promising opportunity especially when call'd to it upon such sufficient grounds and reasons, I will not take upon me to say they are witches or warlocks, but I'll take upon me to say they have not sincere respect to the advancement to [*sic*] the kingdom of Christ or destruction of the kingdom of Satan if soe be they be diverted by every triffell from it.

And now my freinds to detain yow no longer there are are [*sic*] a word or tuo by quhich we would introduce this dayes work, and the first of these is this, I think when we consider the designe of this days work, viz. the seeking of the destruction of the kingdom of Satan, it may be expected that one and all of us shuld be fund exceeding Zealous in this days work; have we forgotten Sathan's deceiving our first parents and soe diging hell for the reprobat? Have we forgotten his getting Sodom and Gommora brunt with fire and brimston?[124] Have ye forgotten the many fold persecutions he hath reased against the church of Christ in all ages[?] Have we forgotten how manie times he hath sett his foot or a spar to hinder the gosple from a people? Have we forgotten these evidences of his malice, and will we not be serious with God for the destruction of his kingdom and for the advancement of the kingdom of our Lord Jesus Christ.

Brethren may I address my self to yow, quhatever others doe in this days worke who knous not nor belives his enmitie, doe ye not remember how long he keped yow strangers from Christ and strangers to the sueetnesse of communion and felowship with him. May ye not remember how long he made some of yow work the will of the gentiles and keept yow as soe many

123 'til once': until at last.
124 Cf. Genesis 19:24.

slaves under his bondage and pouer, even after Christ had invited yow to come to him, and have ye forgotten Believers when ye wer brought to close with {*p. 56*} Christ how he reased up the plagues of your heart and made yow bemoan yourselfs with exclaming[125] that ye wer as a bullock unaccustomed to the yock[126] and wer oblidged to crye to God to break the plagues of your heart that soe ye might gett turning to him indeed? Belivers have ye forgotten the many excellent frames that Satan hath spillt to yow and the many excellent deuties, the performance of quhich he hath greatly marred? Have ye forgotten these things all together, and have ye forgotten the manyfald fierie darts, assaults and tentations with quhich he hath besett yow? Or doe ye remember these? If ye remember them, Belivers, pray Lett the sinceritie and fervencie of your prayers to God demonstrat soe much this day: and if ye remember them pray come out with David in the name of the Lord of hostes with great couradge and a noble countenance against this Golliaht[127] who is the Angle of the bottomless pitt. I say, belivers, let it not be said that ever yow will complain of quhat Satan hath done after this if soe be, ye be coldrife[128] in this days work. God gives yow a fair meetting with Satan and a fair occasion to put up with all your might to him who is the prince of the kings of the earth,[129] that he may be throen doun among us both to these that are his visible and as to these that are his invisible subjects.

The second word is this. I would have yow consider the voice of the same occasion of this fast. Quhat is the voice of abounding witchcraft? Quhat is thes [*sic*] voice of of a raging Devel? Its voice is this: we are a generation that have refused to covenant with Christ and therfor no wonder tho God give us leave to covenant with Satan, soe I say the voice of this occasion would in the first place be very seriously considered. Quhat is that? It seems we have contemn't Christ and refused to devote our selfes soul and body to him, otherwise it should not be soe among us, that we shuld have been soe lost to the lusts of our oun hearts and the counsell of our oun will, as that we should have devoted our selfes soule and body to the Devil. O my freinds, such ane occasion as this for a fast where we are a people under covenant with God, and a people that have been at the table of the Lord, at least the most \part/ of us, and a people that enjoyes the Light of the gospell, and yet for us to have the occasion of a fast upon the acount of abounding witchcraft! O this is astonishing.

Such as are judicious among yow, we hope these words will not be as water spilt upon the ground, but that they will in some measure Let yow see ther

125 Word altered; reading uncertain.
126 Cf. Jeremiah 31:18.
127 *Sic*. For the story of David and Goliath, see 1 Samuel 17.
128 'coldrife': somewhat cold.
129 In context this must be the Devil, who is called the 'prince of this world' in John 12:31. However, Jesus is called the 'prince of the kings of the earth' in Revelation 1:5.

is need of seriousness this day and need for a spirit of grace and supplication to wrestle with him that hath all pouer in heaven and earth, hell and the sea [*sic*], that he would destroy him that hath the pouer of darkness and the pouer of death, of whom God willing ye shall hear more. Finis. {*p. 71*}[130]

Double[131] of a paper drawn be James Williamson of Chappeltoun in Vindication of the Witches.

Postulato 1mo

That Satan the grand enemy of man's salvatione goeth to and froe up and doun the Earth, as ane explorator to spy out mens faults; That he tempts and seduces to sin; That he accuses and impleads before the Tribunall of God, sometymes truely sometymes callumniously: That he craves such as he accuses to be delivered up to him for vengeance, and inflicting of limited punishments, which he also frequently obtains. Thoe also sometymes it is not improbable that good angells may be by, and appoynted executioners of his vengeance as in the caice of Heliodorus and Maccabees chap 3^{d}.[132] But in that caice not Satan but the high preist did implead: Is a postulato which needs not be begged, being a true climactericall[133] propositione demonstrable from the scriptures, both in the old and new Testament as in the caice of Job whom he falslie accuses, and also by the wise allowance of God obtains; as in the caice of St Peter whom he craves to be delyvered up to him that he may winnow him as wheat,[134] and ommitting many other passadges of Scripture wherin this truth is either insinuat, or expressly sett doun, in the sentence of excommunicatione, the formall and direfull delyvering up to Satan with the dreadfull effect; Especially in the primitive Church following therupon, such as the inflicting of incurable diseases, at least by the use of physick, or naturall means except by the sincere repentance of the party delyvered up,[135] Together with the prayers, and absolutione of the Church, sometymes of death itself, besydes being infested with invisible apparitions, and corporall possessions till the party were reformed and released in manner as said is.

130 Pages 57–65 contain material not included in this edition. The text of the tract that follows is written from the back of the book towards the middle, so its page numbers are in reverse order, beginning at p. 71.

131 'Double': copy. The wording of this title is such that the phrase 'Vindication of the Witches' could have come from the compiler rather than Williamson himself.

132 In 2 Maccabees 3, an angel prevented Heliodorus from desecrating the treasury of the temple of Jerusalem.

133 'climactericall': decisive.

134 Cf. Luke 22:31 (the word is 'winnow' in the Geneva Bible and 'sift' in the Authorised Version).

135 The point here is that when a disease is inflicted by the Devil on a person as a punishment for the person's sin, it cannot be cured by medicine, but can be cured by the person's repentance for their sin.

Postulato 2do

2^{ly} as Satan transformes himself into ane angell of light[136] that he may the more powerfully deceive, so he also assumes the persons, or represents the lykenes either of good or bad, dead or living, as may most conduce to his great end, the ruine and destruction of mankynd: the verity of which may be also proved both from the scripture and humane records, as in the case of Sawll and Samuell at Endor,[137] and from the practise of magicians and necromancers, who as his delegats have thair power from him who can exhibit, produce or represent the lykenes, and to the eyes of the beholders the very same person of one who died a hundred yeirs agoe, or is then living (may be) at a thowsand myles distant, or of one who may be is not yet born, and yet when come to the age about which he is represented, appears to be the very same person.

From which 2 postulats thus confirmed, the following corrolaries, seems natively[138] to follow. 1° That Satan nor his instruments can inflict no disease, neither infest, haunt, trouble or {*p. 70*} corporally possess, any person till he have once impleaded him or her before God; and have the person delyvered up to him, as God in his wisdom, justice and mercy sees meet: 2° That the true phisick or exorcisme in such caices is the sincere reformation of the party greived together with the effectuall fervent prayers and absolution of the Church, upon good evidence and tryall of thair repentance, dispensed by such hands as have cannonick and apostolick authority for that effect according to the advyce of St James in his Catholick Epistle.[139] It may be also woorthie of the pains of the learned to search and enquyre whether, or noe in the caice of some demoniacks, especially that poor afflicted damsell, before the eyes and in the mouths of all, wher in charity it cannot be judged that she or her parents are greater sinners then others, who live round, especially in ane age and season wher impietys of all sorts, and schisme (which is voluntary secessione from the unity of the church and putting thes who are guilty under a tacite sentence of excomunication) abounds. I say thes things considered, whether the present caice may not be ane example and signe mixed with justice and mercy to this land, as the Galileans whose blood Pilate mixt with the sacrifices, and the 18 upon whom the Tower of Siloe fell, who were no greater sinners then the rest of or at Jerusalem,[140] to that people that unless we repent we shall all lykewayes perish, unless we return to Catholick unity

136 Cf. 2 Corinthians 11:14.

137 The so-called 'witch of Endor' summoned the apparition of the dead prophet Samuel at the request of King Saul: 1 Samuel 28:7–25. Williamson takes the conventional view that the apparition was really the Devil.

138 'natively': plainly.

139 Cf. James 5:13–16. The phrase 'Catholick Epistle' refers, not to Roman Catholicism, but to the fact that James's epistle was addressed to the faithful in general, not to a specific congregation.

140 For these stories see Luke 13:1–5. Williamson's point is the same as one that is made in a marginal note to this passage in the Geneva Bible: 'We must not rejoice at the just punishment

and turn Christian in practise, we shall all be as excomunicants from God and his church be given up[141] to Satan to tyrranize over us. This be the by.[142]

3°

Seeing Satan is calumniator and *Lictor publicus*[143] before Gods Tribunal and accuses and impleads Christians, sometymes truely sometimes falslie, then it is not inconsequentiall to beleeve that amongs thes who are in a Compact with him he may and doeth excite, and hand out[144] some to supplie his will and perform his part which himself cannot personally doe, who according to thair proposition to thair master doe accuse and implead mortalls sometymes falsely sometymes truely of thair oun crymes before humane Tribunalls, and if this be so then it will be reasonable to beleeve that thes Litle Imps, emissaries of his,[145] who are produced as evidences in the caice of the present demoniack, are sent by him to the very same purpose, to callumniat the innocent, as well as to accuse the guilty; from which corrollary it will then follow that such instruments of his may not at all be regarded or received as witnesses, because they are the Devills deputies and callumniators, and being acted in ther masters spirit who hes all malice to mankynd, will be in thair spliene and proportion so lyke wayes, but abstract from this other is another reason which irrefragably barrs them from being capable of bearing witnes and that is, besides the knoun and presumed integrity of the person who is received as witnes in any matter of weight, the religion of the oath of God is the firme ground, upon which the testimony is supposed valid. But thes Imps can have claime to none of thes, for first being childeren and servants of thair master who is the father of lies, ther ought no credit to be given them, and being atheists or at best apostats and infidels are not capable of the religion of ane oath, and thair testimony can amount to no more nor no less then thair oun condemnation being {*p. 69*} αυτοκατακριται self condemned.[146]

The 4ᵗ Corrolary will be that seeing Satan will personat any man or woman he pleases, the apparitions which are visible to the demoniack, whether meerly fantoms in the imagination or the objects of her externall senses,[147] either reall or by allusions, will be no argument that either such persons are really as present or are in Compact with the Devill, and from

of others, but rather be instructed thereby to repentance.' The phrase 'the rest of or at Jerusalem' may have been slightly garbled by the scribe.

141 *Sic*. Probably read 'and be given up'.

142 'be the by': by the way.

143 'public accuser' or prosecutor.

144 *Sic*. Probably read 'hound out', a phrase that appears later.

145 This must refer to the young Elizabeth Anderson, James Lindsay and Thomas Lindsay, who confessed to having participated in witches' meetings but were converted from accused witches to prosecution witnesses.

146 'αυτοκατακριται' means 'self-condemned' in Greek.

147 The pronoun 'her' indicates that Williamson is thinking of Christian Shaw.

this also followes that the declaration of witches against thair complices, can be of noe validity even thoe themselves were truely present, and no suspicion of the disingenuity, for it is plain the Devill can hardly fall upon more taking[148] stratagems to seduce silly soulls[149] into Compact with him then represent to them the advantage of honourable and choyce company to whose Table, fellowship and intimat secrecy, in banqueting and revells they will be admitted, and that the expectatione may not be deceived will not faill to introduce the lykenes of any may please the fancy, yea it is not impossible, but the Devill may without any illusione really introduce some persons, who are not at all in the Compact with him, which may be in some sort evinced from the accompt of his tempting of Christ himself in the Gospell his charging up to ane hie mountain, and thence to the pinacle of the Temple,[150] But passing this from the 2 postulats it will natively enough follow that he may carry about with him the persons of such as he hath impleaded and obtained to be delivered up to him for some wasting sin; and thoe no Compact or course of sin obstinately continued in, or may it not be conceived that by his subtilities he may take the advantage of such who have a custome of ryseing in thair sleep called *Noctu Ambulatores*,[151] and doing extraordinary things, how easie a busines is it for him to decoy such into his night Conventicles, and thoe the person doe his part in thair extravagancies, yet having returned and gone to bed again, may only look upon that he acted as a dream, Nay yet furder, it is not inconceivable that even innocent persons may effectually be present in thes Conventicles, for how possible is it for the Devill to cast on[e] into a profound sleep and having represented the sleepy person in the Conventicle may afterward, or even at the same instant, make so deep and firm impression, on his imagination, as might give him just ground to doubt if he were not personally present, And being accused and confronted by some of the Devill his emissaries might acknowledge as a true dead,[152] and this I call a Staticall[153] presence.

By what hath bein said, ther may also some accompt be rendered why the Devill by his instruments does truely disclose some that are in Compact with him, thoe they doe only but calumniat others which proceeds partly from thair ignorance in being themselves deceived with false representations, and partly of malice that they may be lyke thair master, and one reason possibly may be seeing all his aime is to precipitat men into eternall torment, when

148 'taking': attractive.
149 'silly soulls': (persons with) weak souls.
150 Cf. Matthew 4:5.
151 'sleepwalkers'.
152 'dead': deed.
153 'Staticall' alludes to a balance. If this word has not been miscopied here, the idea may be that the person is balanced between their false presence at the 'conventicle' and their true presence elsewhere.

he hath catched poor silly creatures he knows that the happines {*p. 68*} such as it is of thes is only ther being continued a litle space in the world. After which ther eternall torment abydes them, he is at pains even to cut that short that they may be by the so much the sooner miserable, and past hopes of mercy. Another reason possibly may be that such as are by his oun instruments disclosed, *Immorigere mentes*[154] and not so wickedly disposed or capable to perpetrat such attrocious peices of villany as he would have them instrumentall in, or may be thes have disoblidged some one or more of his most eminent servants and favorites, and so must fall as victims to thair malice. But a more considerable advantage and pregnant reason may be his subtility in speaking sometimes truth, that under collour thairof he may deceive, and with the greater advantage to his oun interest and prejudice to mankynd, for thes whom he hes not bein able to seduce or may be having impleaded them before God, did not obtain his designe against them, he assaults, with his new stratagem of callumniating, and even flatly accusing by his Imps and Emissaries excited and hunded out by him for that effect, and to the intent the callumny may be the deeper doe truely accuse some, and this proves a persecution no less sharp to generous soulls then death itself; how beit he hes the prospect of reaping this advantadge of them, that being extremely afflicted with the sense of thair wounded reputation and fame they may be tempted to doubt of the providences of God, of his goodnes and veracity; and so make them split upon this rock, whom he could not shipwrack other wise.

From the 2 grand postulats it will not be impertinent to take to consideration the character commonly called the witch or Devills-mark and both from thes argument rationally to weigh[155] how far it may be asigny *patho quo monitum*[156] of one in Compact with the Devill. 1° Therto constitut it such, it will requyre to be of such singularity as no naturall, externall or accidentall cause can possibly produce the lyke: other wayes, it cannot choise but be a very fallacious evidence, now the properties of it being to be a callous substance, or caruncle[157] of flesh without blood or sense if such ane one may be naturall, or adventitious, otherwise then by the impress of the Devill, then it will follow that necessary it is not ane evidencing, to ken of one's being in compact with him. Now it is plain enough to any any that hes but any smack of anattomy,[158] phisick or philosophy, nay any good stock of

154 This probably means '(having) disobedient or immoral minds'. The argument is that these witches are disobedient to the Devil.

155 Reconstruction of damaged word: 'we…h'.

156 *Sic.* It is not entirely clear whether the scribe has copied these four words correctly, nor which of them are intended to be Latin. The meaning seems to be 'a sign of suffering or harm, as a warning'.

157 'caruncle': small excrescence of flesh.

158 Initially written 'attomy' (which would mean 'skeleton'), presumably in error, and then altered.

common reason, that to produce such a callous substance, ther is no more necessity but the obstructing and extricating of capillary arteries, and small nerves, fibers, and presently emerges ane exsanguineous[159] and senseless peice of flesh, which in a small quantity may continue without either corruption or putriffaction, and that contrition, contusion,[160] and many other causes may produce the same. Ther is no doubt, nay it is very hard to know, if either naturally or accidentally the maist part of the bodies either of men or beast have not seaverall parts, which either have litle or none of *{p. 67}* either of blood or senses, but allowed to be not ordinarly produced but by the impress of the Devill, yet that will prove but very litle, for seeing by the first postulat, and seaverall places of scripture, and history, it is evident the Devill receives power to inflict diseases, and death, to scourge and harass poor sinfull mortalls, it will amount to the smallest part of thes to express such a character as may be the effect of ane Imp, or the smallest punsl[161] of contusion, And it is a maist ordinary thing for people to receive such marks, as are commonly called dead nips in thair sleep which does first smart, and after turnd livid, and then not improbablie turned callous, and yet they are so far from being reput devillish, That they are only lookt upon as friendly advertisements of danger instant and to be eschewed.

The great God delyver all such who are thus under the tyrrany of Satan, and grant such repentance unto men, and amity in his church, as may also prevaill with him to return, and so strenthen the hands of his servants, as by his grace they may be able to withstand the Enemie and the avenger, and give such wisdom to men as to disclose thes misterious compacts, and bring thes hellish Instruments to condigne punishment, by such save[162] means as the innocent be not ruined with the guilty, in and throw our king Imortall, and high preist the Lord Jesus, to whom with the father and the holy ghost be eternall praise, honor, glory, dominion, world without end, amen.

The new signe brought from New England[163] seems to be the greatest imposture of all viz: of the parties affected thair falling, or being corrept[164] with a fit or paroxisme upon the presence or toutch of any of thes persons who are represented to thair imaginations, and by them supposed to be thair

159 'exsanguineous': bloodless.

160 'contrition': grinding or bruising; 'contusion': bruising caused by a blow.

161 'punsl': not found in dictionaries, but may mean 'blow' or 'punch'. In this passage, Williamson argues that the Devil *can* produce an insensible mark, but that many people have such marks naturally, so no particular mark can be *proved* to have come from the Devil.

162 *Sic*. Perhaps read 'safe'.

163 This passage evidently refers to the witchcraft panic in Salem in 1692. The panic itself may no longer have been 'new' in 1697, but Williamson may have in mind some aspect of the subsequent controversy that it generated. The scribe's attention seems to have wandered at the end of this paragraph.

164 'corrept': rapt.

Tormentors, and this may first be demonstrated a possible way ordinar in nature without any concourse of the Devill, for if any shall but consider the knoun events of sympathy and antipathy, as they are ordinarly called, and the wonderfull effects of imagination, far exceeding the present caice, will not think it strange if a prejudiciat fancy have any aversation, and loathing at ane object so detestable and horrible as the troubled imagination represents it to be; but if this be not thought sufficient to solve the [*sic*]

Then from the \2/ forenamed principalls, it will be clear enough, and first then it would be considered that thair is not any such plentifull production in New England, as schisme, heresie and error, and then if the punishments and censures belonging to such be more plentifully seen and felt thair, then any wher else, it will be no wonder, viz: delyvering up to Satan, now Satan having obtained power to inflict diseases and it being his work to accuse and persecute, and being capable to represent any person; having so represented the persons; if he perceive his coming to be successfull, and to impose upon such men he will not faill to inflict the paroxysme upon the affected persons, when the other whom he had falsely represented to the imagination is truely present, wherfor we ought not to be ignorant of his devyces, which we suffer ourselves to be deluded by, conclamaty[165] *est de humano genere saltem de Christianis*,[166] and we shall so much as in us lyes resist Satan to overthrow the truth of Christs promise made to the Church that {*p. 66*} the gates of hell shall not prevaill against her,[167] and if this be so then all the secular power upon Earth, nor the burning all the instruments of Satan, really so or suspected to be such, cannot delyver till he who hes the keys of David, and oppens and no man shuts, and shuts and no man oppens,[168] doe the busines, either imediatly by his oun hand or by such to whom he hath delyvered the power of the keyes of the Kingdome by apostolick succession, acting according to the rules prescribed in the Gospell. FINIS.

165 'conclamaty': denunciation.

166 'is the nature of humans, or at least of Christians'.

167 Cf. Matthew 16:18.

168 Cf. Revelation 3:7.

APPENDIX[169]

[*Endorsed:*] Coppie of a Letter from Robert Allexander, Shereff Clerk of Renfrew to Alexander Finlayson, 1697

{*fo. 27r.*} A breiffe accompt of some things that past before the Comissione appoynted by the Privie Counsell for the takeing Inquiry anent the witchcrafts wsd[170] against Bargarrans daughter within the shereffdome of Ranfrew, written in a Letter from Robert Allexander shereff clerk to the said Comissione to his Comerad at Edinburgh.

Dated Munday the 8 of February 1697

Dear Billie, Ye shall know that at desyre of my Lord Blantyre I was persuaded to goe with his Lordship on Fryday last the 5th Instant to the place of Bargarran, wher ther was severall gentlemen of the shyre, viz. Houstone, Craigends, Craigmwre elder and the shereff deput, who with Blantyre made a quorum of Comissioners for makeing inquiry anent the witches and witchcraft within the shereffdome of Ranfrew,[171] and particularlie anent the case of Bargarrans daughter, who being all met with severall ministers on Frydayes morning at Bargarran, They caused adduce severall persones to the number of 7 or 8, whom Bargarrans daughter and one Elizabeth Andersone, aged 15 yeirs or therby had dilated to be guilty of witchcraft, This Elizabeth Andersone declared that about 20 dayes agoe she was inveatted by her father to goe with him to Bargarrans orchyard, about 12 acloake in the day, and having come ther they met with severall persones too tedeous here to name, with a black man haveing a black bonnat on his head and a blew band about his neck, whom her father and some of the rest told her was the Devell; and ther discourse was concerneing the killing and destroyeing of Bargarrans daughter, which they mutuallie promised to put in executione, This and severall uther things more she avoued in each of ther faces being confronted with them, one by one, among whom was her father named Alexander Andersone, when one [*1 word blank*[172]] Lindsay ane old fellow come in to the house, Bargarrans

[169] Source: National Library of Scotland (NLS), MS 3278, fos. 27r.–29r. Little is known about the provenance of this newsletter; MS 3278 is a bound volume of miscellaneous early modern documents. Newsletters were often copied and recopied; there is another copy of the first of these documents (the letter of 8 February 1697) in a box of miscellaneous early modern documents, NLS, Acc. 6687, no. 10. This copy omits the heading and Robert Alexander's name, but has one or two additional details, noted in footnotes below. Along with this copy, at NLS, Acc. 6687, no. 9, is a copy of the report of the enquiry commission; this is discussed the introduction to *A Relation of the Diabolical Practices of Above Twenty Wizards and Witches of the Sheriffdom of Renfrew*, above in the present volume.

[170] 'wsd' (used): practised.

[171] These commissioners were Sir John Houston of that Ilk, William Cunningham of Craigends, Gavin Cochrane of Craigmuir, Robert Sempill sheriff depute of Renfrew, and Alexander Stewart, fifth Lord Blantyre.

[172] This seems to have been James Lindsay alias Curate.

daughter cryd out aloud that he was one of her tormentors, who being desyred to touch him she instantly fell in ane violent fitt (efter tucheing him) In sua far as that she leapt wonderfully,[173] her armes being als stiffe as ane tree, This fitt being over, the[y][174] brought in ane Kathren Campbell whom Bargarrans daughter alleges to be her first instrument of her afflictione, and who was lykewayes the Lairds woman not long agoe, and having come in to the roume the Lassie seemed to be affrayed of her and rane from her, but Campbell being desyred to pray to God for the Lassie, she shiftd it till she gott the bairne in her armes, wherupon the chyld fell in ane uther violent fitt, and on the back of it Campbell prayd that God would deliver her, The chyld comeing to her selfe againe, repatted thir words, now I am lousd and can tutch them all without falling in ane uther fitt, and did actually tuch them without falling in ane uther fitt, Bot she declard that ther was one of her tormentors namd Margaret whom she knew verrie weell both as to name and surname, bot could not have power to name it. She called her sometymes Pincht Maggie, And being *{fo. 27v.}* desyred by the Comissioners to wryt it she took my pen and papper and wrot the word Margaret and the letter L of her surname, wpon wryting of quhich she was surprysd with ane most terable fitt and lape[175] and screichd wonderfully in sua far as the minister of Houstoun[176] and I being next to her, had difulty [*sic*] to hold her, her armes being als stiffe and hard as iron, which fitt being over, and she againe composd, they producd the Byble, quhich being opend they desyrd her to reade a part of it, viz. the 9th of Mark, bot sua soon as she cast her eyes on the Byble, her eyes turnd in her head, her face grew pale, and she sung a profane song (her lips not moveing) and then fell into screiching and cryeing, louping and such lyke till ye would have thought that she was dead, and even at the lowest, she sang as affoirsaid, This fitt conteinowd a long whyll, till it was movd that the Byble should be closd, quhich being done she imediatly recovered, and being askd whay [*sic*] she sang in stead of reading, she told she did not remember that she had done any such thing, This I would not have beleivd had I not beine both eye and ear witnes to all that I have written, It is verrie observeable in the last passage, that Sathan hath ane strange antipathie and hatrd at the word of God, in sua far as he will not suffer any (whom he can hinder) to look theron. Ther are severall uther passages anent that quhich I cannot not giwe yow ane accompt of bot efterward ye may, we are adjurnd till the 9th Instant In Ranfrew. In the meane tyme the Comission have securd 8 men and women.[177] *{fo. 28r.}*

173 'wonderfully': extraordinarily.
174 NLS, Acc. 6687, no. 10, has 'they'.
175 'lape': leaped.
176 Robert Taylor, minister of Houston, is mentioned in the *True Narrative*.
177 NLS, Acc. 6687, no. 10, adds 'in the tolbuith of Renfrew'.

Feb 2^{d}. The Child being in the chamber with her mother and others in the intervale of the fitts, and in perfect health, seemed to be somewhat surprised and struck \with/ feare upon the sight of \one/ John Lindsay talking in the hall with her father, she declaring to her mother the forsaid John Lindsay was among the rest of the Crue about her, whereupon she was desired by her mother to go towards him without fear and in a way unknown to him to lay her hands on some part of his body, which the Damsell having done, was immediatly seized with a violent fitt; this in Divyne Providence falling unexpectedly out, the Parents of the Childe and other spectators thought themselves concerned to make knoun the quholl matter to the said John Lindsay and likeways (to give further light in the thing) to[178] urge him to take the Childe by the hand quhich he having done, notwithstanding of the Childs aversatione therunto was imediatly struck with an extraordinary violent fitt, wherein she continued for some space, her eyes turning in her head, the parts of her body having become rigid and stiff.

Note that the Childe had given grave marks of the forsaid Lindsay before this fell out, as likeways that she had been all that day before in perfect health and in right composure of mynde.

Feb: first. The Childe essaying to reveall something she was forbidden to tell was seized with fitts, as she used to be in the like case, but in the intervale of the fitt said she could not understand how such restraints were laid upon her except by Charm, quhich she thought might be discovered by \makeing/ search beneath the bed where she lay, which she having quickly done her self, found in the Judgment of spectators ane egg shell, which instantly they having thrown in the fire did melt away like wax without any noise, after this, the Damsell said she would not be any further seized with rigid fitts, only her tongue would be drawn down her throat, when she should essay to make known what she was by them forbidden to tell, quhich at that time accordingly fell out, and likways without trouble got some things made known, she had not access to do before, Particularly she did declare, that she had been frequently urged and solisted by them to become a witch her self, promiseing her great rewards and perfect health also if she would yeeld thereunto. And when through the Infinite Mercy of God, she was helped to resist the temptation, telling them, that the Devill promised what he could not perform, and that supposing he could make good to her what he promised, yet she was sure from the Scriptures, that the Wrath of God, would be the finall reward of all those who yeelded to this Temptation. They replyed that Hell and the Wrath of God, so much talked of, was not so formidable as is represented.

[178] 'desyre' crossed out here.

Note here that frequently before this tyme, she was distinctly heard to give thir replyes, as to some discoursing with her on this subject, though none was heard talking with her at such times. {*fo. 28v.*}

She likways declared that she was frequently urged to give her consent to take away the life of her young sister upon her mothers breast, which temptatione she through the Grace of God still resisted and was distinctly heard say to some as discoursing with her, (though unseen and unheard by others) she would never yeeld to that.

Note here, that some months before this tyme, one day she told her Parents that there was a Charm she heard amongst them laid upon the top of the house where her young sister was a nursing, and that dureing the Childs abode there she would still decay, and therefore advysed her Parents, as they would preserve her life, to bring her home, quherupon the Childs Parents being before very sensible[179] of the Childs dayly decay, even almost to skin and bone, did accordingly bring her home, quhair the Child from that tyme recovered.

Feb: 2^{d}. Towards 4 a clock in the afternoon there came ane old fellow, but not in the habite of a begger, \to Bargarrans house/ telling them he behooved to lodge there that night, at this tyme the Damsell being in the chamber with her mother and others, said to her mother that to her best apprehension she thought there was now one of the hellish Crue in or about the house, quherupon her mother instantly repairing down stairs to the kitchine, found there unexpectedly the forsaid old fellow, who had the confidence to crave leave of her to lodge in the kitchine that night, being (as he said) on his way homewards, and gave no other reasons of his desires, but the Lady refusing him, made haste up stairs againe, and brought back with her her daughter, desireing her to take a look of the forsaid fellow, whom as soon as the Damsell saw, seemed as struck with fear, yet plainly did declare he was one of her tormentors, and that his spectre ordinarly was represented to her with the gentlewoman before named, who had been all along most cruell to her, quhereupon the Childs mother desireing the old fellow to take her daughter by the hand, quhich he being urged to do, instantly the Childe was seised with a fearfull tormenting fitt, and this falling out in the Divyne Providence, Bargarren thought himself concerned to secure the accused person (who is accordingly yet under custody). Feb. 3^{d}. The Child was scarce out of light fitts (quherin she is not so solide, as in the intervals) through the quholl day, yea, and had no intervals till this day \Feb. 4th/ about two a clock in the tyme of Prayer, falling also (as is usuall) into more violent fitts, and when recovered of them though in light fitts did declare, that the Gentlewoman (her most cruell enemy) had that morning given her a drink of sack, quhich

[179] 'sensible': aware.

she had actually taken, what truth was in this we know not,[180] however this is remarkable, that through the most part of the day thereafter, she fell and continued in great rage and fury, beyond what before had been observed, and could no ways be composed but once or tuyce fell a cursing and baning,[181] which was never heard before in her[182] but even \through/ the whole tract of her trouble very savory and religious expressions and evidences of piety.

Note here, that spectators at the same tyme took the Damsell by the hand after the forementioned persons had been urged to do it, yet no such effect followed as did upon the touch of the accused persons. {*fo. 29r.*}

That for the confirmatione of the abovementioned presumptions against the foresaid old fellow and to give further light in the thing, the minister covered the Childs head and face and almost her whole body with his cloak so as she was insensible and could not know who had touched her.

180 The story of this drink of 'sack' (white wine) is omitted from later versions.
181 *Sic.* 'Banning' meant 'cursing'.
182 'dureing' crossed out here.

7. *A TRUE NARRATIVE OF THE SUFFERINGS AND RELIEF OF A YOUNG GIRLE*, 1698

INTRODUCTION

This composite publication mainly narrates the events that transpired during and after the demonic possession of Christian Shaw, daughter of John Shaw of Bargarran. Shaw's tower-house of Bargarran was in the parish of Erskine, presbytery of Paisley and county of Renfrewshire. Christian Shaw, who was approaching the age of 11 when the events began, behaved in various bizarre ways between the autumn of 1696 and spring of 1697, and accused several people of causing her 'fits'. The 'Narrative' itself, at the heart of the tract, relates the story of Christian's behaviour.

The publication also contains further material. It goes on to discuss the trial, in Paisley in April and May 1697, of seven accused witches who were said to have bewitched Christian: Katherine Campbell, Margaret Fulton, Margaret Laing, James Lindsay alias Curate, John Lindsay alias Bishop, John Lindsay in Barloch, and Agnes Nasmith. All of these were convicted on 19 May, and executed in Paisley on 10 June. An eighth suspect, John Reid, hanged himself in prison on 21 May. Numerous further suspects had initial proceedings brought against them, and some of the promoters of the prosecutions sought to continue the trials for some time afterwards. The trial records themselves have been published in the companion volume to the present one.[1] During the trial, the prosecution produced detailed, learned and wide-ranging arguments combining demonology and law – arguments that the tract expounds and links to the case.

These events occurred during the later and declining stages of the Scottish witch-hunt. Executions on this scale attracted attention at the time, and the Bargarran case has often been discussed since.[2] It was the last local panic to result in significant numbers of executions in Scotland.

1 Julian Goodare and Liv Helene Willumsen (eds.), *Scottish Witchcraft Trials* (Woodbridge: SHS, 2025), 567–635.

2 The fullest account, thoroughly researched though fictionalised in presentation, is Isabel Adam, *Witch Hunt: The Great Scottish Witchcraft Trials of 1697* (London, 1978). For an account focusing on the scientific views of the prosecuting advocate, Francis Grant, see Tony

Structure and content

The text edited below, *A True Narrative of the Sufferings and Relief of a Young Girle*, was printed in Edinburgh in 1698. It is a composite work to which several hands have contributed. Because of the complexity of its structure, it may help to begin with a brief summary of the contents. Page numbers of the original are given, and then page numbers of the present volume below:

1 Preface. A general discussion of demonology (pp. iii–ix; below at pp. 208–19).

2 The 'Narrative' itself. A daily narrative of Christian Shaw's unusual behaviour and experiences, from August 1696 to March 1697 (pp. x–xxxviii; below at pp. 219–55).

3 Summary of the report of the enquiry commission, incorporating summaries of the confessions of Elizabeth Anderson, James Lindsay and Thomas Lindsay, February 1697 (pp. xxxix–xlii; below at pp. 255–60).

4 Summaries of statements by Matthew Brisbane and Henry Marshall, respectively physician and apothecary in Glasgow, 31 December 1696 and 1 January 1697 (pp. xlii–xliii; below at pp. 260–1).

5 Note of the confessions of Margaret Rodger and Janet Rodger, undated, perhaps April or May 1697 (pp. xliii–xliv; below at pp. 261–2).

6 Note of the confession, and suicide in prison, of John Reid, 21 May 1697 (p. xliv; below at pp. 262–3).

7 Account of the seven witches' execution, 10 June 1697, plus further commentary on their behaviour and guilt (pp. xlv–xlvi; below at pp. 263–5).

8 'Account of two letters', introduction to the two following documents (pp. 1–2; below at pp. 265–7).

9 'Letter 1': Summing-up speech to the assize at the trial by Francis Grant, prosecuting advocate (pp. 2–10; below at pp. 267–76).

10 'Letter 2': Speech replying to defence objections during the trial by Francis Grant, prosecuting advocate (pp. 10–21; below at pp. 276–93).

11 'Advertisement' against a planned rival publication (unnumbered final page; below at p. 294).

McAleavy, *The Last Witch Craze: John Aubrey, the Royal Society and the Witches* (Stroud, 2022), 195–210. The Bargarran case is placed in broader context by Michael Wasser, 'The Western Witch-Hunt of 1697–1700: The Last Major Witch-Hunt in Scotland', in Julian Goodare (ed.), *The Scottish Witch-Hunt in Context* (Manchester, 2002), 146–65.

There are thus 68 pages altogether. The first 46 pages are numbered in roman numerals, followed by 21 pages in arabic numerals and an unnumbered further page. The division in pagination is not explained, and seems unimportant; it presumably indicates that the two sections were printed separately. A fuller introductory account of each item in the *True Narrative* will now be given.

The author of the preface, unnamed in the publication itself, was John Wilson, minister of Largs in the presbytery of Irvine, who was commissioned to write it by the presbytery of Paisley.[3] Wilson had previously been one of the ministers who witnessed the pricking of the witchcraft suspects.[4] Other than that, he was presumably chosen for his knowledge of demonology in general.

Wilson acknowledges at the outset that his account will meet with scepticism. He attempts to establish common ground with the sceptics by admitting the difficulty of proving witchcraft. He even agrees with the sceptics that past witchcraft prosecutions have led to excesses. However, this display of up-to-date scepticism is merely the prelude to a detailed discussion of why the present case is different, and why it really constitutes witchcraft. Wilson is not especially well read in demonology, but he cites a few relevant works, including the fairly up-to-date Joseph Glanvill. As well as expounding relevant biblical passages, he explains (following Glanvill) that the Bible has only basic information on witchcraft and that more details need to be gathered by empirical enquiry, including the Bargarran case itself. The second half of the preface begins to resemble a sermon, and ceases to focus exclusively on demonology. But Wilson has not forgotten the Bargarran case. He openly hopes that more executions will follow those of June 1697: 'good things are hoped of our Magistrats, who have already so happily begun', and, even more explicitly, 'we wait execution of justice on the rest' (p. viii). The *True Narrative* is no merely theoretical exposition of demonology; it is a book deliberately designed to kill.

At the heart of the tract is the 'Narrative' itself. This consists of an account, often day by day, of Christian Shaw's unusual behaviour and experiences, from August 1696 to March 1697. A concluding commentary then asserts the truth of the narrative on the basis of the large number of respectable witnesses. The focus on Christian Shaw tends to obscure the fact that the witches at their trial were accused of several other malefices. The editor may have considered these malefices to be less convincing, or less extraordinary, than the bewitchment of Christian Shaw.[5]

3 *A History of the Witches of Renfrewshire* (Paisley, 1877), p. xxxiv.

4 Goodare and Willumsen (eds.), *Scottish Witchcraft Trials*, 610–11. The pricking seems to have taken place in Paisley in April 1697.

5 Wasser, 'Western Witch-Hunt of 1697–1700', 161. The trial records include more information on the other malefices; there is also more about them in *A Relation of the Diabolical Practices of Above Twenty Wizards* and Witches of the Sheriffdom of Renfrew, of which an edition appears above in the present volume.

The printed 'Narrative' is a revised recension of the manuscript 'Informatory Accompt' and 'Continued Accompt', edited above as part of the 'Bargarran Witches' manuscript in the present volume, with some additional material. There may well have been earlier versions also, and other intermediate ones. This final version retains traces of its earlier composite structure. In January, the printed narrative changes its format, with more dates mentioned, and the dates often given at the beginning of a paragraph. The end of the printed 'Narrative' outlines the previous structure: 'There is none of those Particulars mentioned in the Narrative, but had in the first Draught the Witnesses insert at the end of every particular Paragraph, and attested before the Commissioners for Enquiry at Renfrew, by the Subscriptions of the respective Witnesses' (p. xxxvii). As will be seen in the edition above, this is the structure of the 'Informatory Accompt' and 'Continued Accompt'.

After the 'Narrative', the next section of the published *True Narrative* collects various documents connected with the trial and execution of the seven convicted witches in Paisley in April, May and June 1697. Few of these derive directly from the trial record itself, but they complement that record in important ways. There is a summary of the report of a commission that gathered evidence for the trial. There are summaries of the confessions of Elizabeth Anderson, James Lindsay, Thomas Lindsay, Margaret Rodger and Janet Rodger, all of whom were initially suspected of witchcraft but then recategorised as innocent witnesses for the prosecution. There are summaries of reports by the physician Matthew Brisbane and the apothecary Henry Marshall, who examined Christian Shaw in Glasgow during her alleged possession. There is an account of the confession and death of John Reid, an eighth suspect who hanged himself in prison. The final document in this section consists of notes of events at the execution of the seven witches.

The penultimate section presents itself as two 'Letters' reporting aspects of the criminal trial in Paisley. The first of these is in fact the whole of the summing-up speech to the assize by the main prosecuting advocate, Francis Grant. The second is a speech made to the court by Grant during the trial, answering objections by the defence to various prosecution witnesses and to other aspects of the prosecution's case. Grant's speeches contain the most extended discussion of learned demonology, not to mention learned law, in the whole of the work. The speech replying to the defence advocate cites authorities in profusion. As well as being delivered orally it will have been handed to the judge in writing. It should be noted that, chronologically, this speech precedes the first one. The two documents purport to be 'Letters' written by someone who heard Grant's speeches, but this is a mere literary device to frame his words. Grant is sometimes suggested as the author of the entire *True Narrative* – certainly it is often attributed to him in library catalogues – but neither in the text nor in other contemporary sources is there any warrant for such an attribution. Grant clearly did not write the main 'Narrative', having become involved in the case only at the point when the events it narrated were coming to an end. As we shall see, there is a good deal of evidence as to how the 'Narrative' was compiled.

The final section is a brief 'Advertisement', on an unnumbered final page in much larger type. The editor of the *True Narrative* has heard of a plan to publish a rival pamphlet with contrary information; he indignantly threatens to expose the fraudulence of anyone who should do so. This rival pamphlet seems never to have appeared. The editor has earlier denounced a 'late Scurrilous Pamphlet, that has been printed in *England*' (p. 2). This may or may not have been *A Relation of the Diabolical Practices of Above Twenty Wizards and Witches of the Sheriffdom of Renfrew*, of which an edition appears in an earlier chapter of the present volume. The introduction to the *Relation*, above, has a further discussion of that work's relationship to the *True Narrative*.

Christian Shaw

Christian's condition and behaviour in 1696–7 were truly extraordinary, and her case has been discussed by several scholars. Here their various perspectives can be reviewed and drawn together, in the hope of producing a more rounded account that can assist in understanding the story told by the *True Narrative*. The *True Narrative* argued stridently that Christian's behaviour had been caused by the Devil; it was the Devil who sent witches to afflict her, and who had the preternatural power to manipulate objects, to give a young girl unusual strength, or to interfere with people's normal sense-perceptions. Such explanations are no longer accepted in conventional scholarship, so we have to ask: how can we understand Christian in present-day terms?

An initial approach to this question is to return to a medical framework of understanding, using medical knowledge unavailable to Christian's contemporaries. Her symptoms can be classified in various ways, and diagnosis and other interpretations can focus on different aspects. She experienced or performed specific *physiological* symptoms, including convulsions, and loss of hearing, sight or other senses. She experienced or performed specific *verbal or behavioural* symptoms, such as claiming to see invisible assailants (even engaging in arguments with such assailants), acts of self-harm, and regurgitation of objects. And her symptoms had a marked *periodicity*, with sudden alternations between periods of 'fits' and periods of normality.

Christian's convulsions and other strange behaviour were persuasively diagnosed by Stuart McDonald and colleagues in 1996 as having arisen principally from 'dissociative disorder', in which a person experiences distressing phases of disruption to their normal personality and behaviour, and 'conversion disorder', in which psychological trauma is 'converted' into physical symptoms.[6] Mental health diagnostic categories have been revised since 1996, and the term 'conversion disorder' is no longer used. The equivalent diagnoses today would be 'dissociative identity disorder' and 'functional neurological symptom disorder'.[7] Further research might use the details of these and related conditions, not as end-points to understanding, but as starting-points for fuller investigation of how Christian and those around her experienced and reported her condition.

In assessing Christian's state of mind, one of the hardest things to grasp (perhaps particularly for non-medical people) is the manipulative nature of some of her actions. Wild and uncontrolled antics in a trance-like, dissociative state may be recognisable, and acts of self-harm are familiar forms of psychotic behaviour. But some of her performances required careful planning in advance. She must have had to assemble and hide the materials that she would then claim to regurgitate, or the pieces of unusual red cloth that she would then claim to have torn from the sleeves of an invisible assailant. How can this be explained?

The diagnoses above, particularly functional neurological symptom disorder, regard such behaviour as involuntary rather than deliberately fraudulent. Most medical diagnostic systems attempt to distinguish between three patterns: straightforwardly genuine disorders, 'factitious' disorders (considered as involuntary), and 'malingering' (considered as deliberately fraudulent and ultimately non-medical). This topic is complex and contested, partly because of the difficulty of establishing intention when manipulative acts are identified.[8] However, a detailed case-study from the Netherlands brings out some behavioural patterns among modern clinical patients that seem applicable to Christian's case. Several patients were studied who were initially diagnosed

6 S. W. McDonald, A. Thom and A. Thom, 'The Bargarran Witch Trial: A Psychiatric Reassessment', *Scottish Medical Journal*, 41 (1996), 152–8. Observing that no historical diagnosis can be certain, they called their diagnosis 'tentative' and 'likely' (p. 157). A psychiatric interpretation had previously been put forward by Adam, *Witch Hunt*, 222–7.

7 American Psychiatric Association, *Diagnostic and Statistical Manual of Mental Disorders, Fifth Edition, Text Revision (DSM–5-TR)* (Washington: American Psychiatric Publishing, 2022), pp. 330–7 (for Dissociative Identity Disorder) and pp. 360–4 (for Functional Neurological Symptom Disorder). McDonald *et al.* used an earlier version of this work, DSM–IV, published in 1994.

8 See for instance Ken R. Welburn, George A. Fraser, Shelley A. Jordan, Colin Cameron, Lisa M. Webb and Dayle Raine, 'Discriminating Dissociative Identity Disorder from Schizophrenia and Feigned Dissociation on Psychological Tests and Structured Interview', *Journal of Trauma and Dissociation*, 4:2 (2003), 109–30; Christopher Bass and Peter Halligan, 'Illness Related Deception: Social or Psychiatric Problem?', *Journal of the Royal Society of Medicine*, 100 (2007), 81–4; Michelle R. Barth, Bethany L. Brand and M. Shae Nester, 'Distinguishing Clinical and Simulated Dissociative Identity Disorder Using the Miller Forensic Assessment of Symptoms Test', *Psychological Trauma: Theory, Research, Practice, and Policy*, 15:5 (2023), 846–52.

with dissociative identity disorder (DID), but were later found to have been faking at least some of their symptoms and 'imitating' the behaviour expected of a DID sufferer. However, they were not being dishonest; rather they had begun with identity problems of a depressive type, and had then discovered DID, which seemed to offer an explanation and solution for their problems. Other people around them, either laypeople or healthcare professionals, had encouraged these patients to understand their problems in terms of DID, and to expect DID-like experiences. Even if these patients did not have DID as such, they were genuinely suffering as they worked through its symptoms.[9] Similar processes probably operated for Christian Shaw.

However, the 'Narrative' tells of additional episodes not explicable medically, such as Christian's alleged flying. Nor are they explicable through fraud on Christian's part. Hugh McLachlan and Kim Swales have argued, persuasively, that there is no need to take all the accounts of Christian's behaviour literally; the writers are likely to have shaped them to their own purposes.[10] Comparison of the way in which the published *True Narrative* was adapted from the earlier narratives in the 'Bargarran Witches' manuscript strengthens this interpretation; the introduction to that manuscript, above in the present volume, has more details on this. Indeed, accounts of levitation that are even better supported by contemporary witnesses are not hard to find in early modern Europe, and such accounts were keenly debated at the time.[11]

Thus, the accounts of Christian's behaviour are partly stereotyped. To some extent they are accounts of real behaviour, but to some extent they are accounts of the behaviour that demoniacs were believed to exhibit. The narrators knew that Christian was a demoniac; they knew what demoniacs habitually did; and they shaped their accounts to display this standardised version of demonic possession. The fullest historical account of demonic possession, by Brian Levack, navigates cautiously between accusations of fraud and diagnoses of mental illness, but emphasises that Christian's reported behaviour, and that of other demoniacs in this period, were performances that conformed to culturally-recognised 'scripts' that were learned, repeated and then described by various commentators. These performances involved, not just the demoniac herself or himself, but also those around them as they shaped their own understanding of what they were witnessing.[12]

9 Nel Draijer and Suzette Boon, 'The Imitation of Dissociative Identity Disorder: Patients at Risk, Therapists at Risk', *Journal of Psychiatry and Law*, 27 (1999), 423–58.

10 Hugh McLachlan and Kim Swales, 'The Bewitchment of Christian Shaw: A Reassessment of the Famous Paisley Witchcraft Case of 1697', in Yvonne G. Brown and Rona Ferguson (eds.), *Twisted Sisters: Women, Crime and Deviance in Scotland since 1400* (East Linton, 2002), 54–83.

11 Carlos M. N. Eire, *They Flew: A History of the Impossible* (New Haven, 2023).

12 Brian P. Levack, 'Demonic Possession in Early Modern Scotland', in Julian Goodare, Lauren Martin and Joyce Miller (eds.), *Witchcraft and Belief in Early Modern Scotland* (Basingstoke,

A further perspective on Christian's behaviour, compatible with the model of cultural performance of 'scripts', arises from Scottish religious practices of the period. Psychological disturbance could be experienced and interpreted in terms of the Calvinist conversion experience – a transformative process that pious Christians were expected to undergo in Reformed Scotland. Ministers told their congregations vivid stories of the Devil's temptations and of the punishment for sin. A spiritually insecure person, often a child, might become terrified, believing that their evident sins would lead them to be damned. Ministers recognised these 'terrors' as a distinct phase in the experience, expecting the terrors to be overcome as the person attained assurance of Christ's grace and of their own salvation. Even normal religious 'terrors' could cause real trauma, though they were regarded as temporary and as non-medical. (Similarly, diagnoses of DID today must rule out behaviour that is part of a normally accepted religious practice.) However, the conversion process could go badly wrong, particularly if the person experiencing 'terrors' came to think in terms of bewitchment. This is what seems to have happened to Christian. Towards the end of the narrative, on 23 March, she was recorded as experiencing an apparition of the Devil and delivering a long, godly speech to him, perhaps indicating that she was beginning to overcome her terrors at last.[13]

The adults around Christian clearly believed in her demonic possession, and in bewitchment as its cause; they seem to have encouraged her to adopt and perform the identity of a bewitched demoniac. The narrative records no discussion about doubts or possible alternative explanations, beyond the formulaic statements of the medical men. The ministers who assembled at Bargarran almost certainly prayed 'that GOD might give an effectual Check to Satan's Rage and Dominion'; this would later be the stated purpose of the public fast held throughout the synod of Glasgow on Christian's behalf (described in the preface to the *True Narrative*). They occasionally staged tests, such as blindfolding her and getting her to identify a person, but by this time they were seeking to prove what they already knew. They could unwittingly have given her hints as to how to pass these tests – and passing the tests would have provided confirmation, both to the adults and to Christian herself, of the genuineness of her experiences.

2008), 166–84. Cf. Brian P. Levack, *The Devil Within: Possession and Exorcism in the Christian West* (New Haven, 2013), 19–31.

13 L. A. Yeoman, 'The Devil as Doctor: Witchcraft, Wodrow, and the Wider World', *Scottish Archives*, 1 (1995), 93–105. Christian Shaw's symptoms are discussed at p. 96. Other comparable cases are discussed in more detail in Louise Yeoman, 'Archie's Invisible Worlds Discovered: Spirituality, Madness and Johnston of Wariston's Family', *Records of the Scottish Church History Society*, 27 (1997), 156–86, and Louise Yeoman, 'Away with the Fairies', in Lizanne Henderson (ed.), *Fantastical Imaginations: The Supernatural in Scottish History and Culture* (East Linton, 2009), 29–46. For more on the Calvinist conversion experience see David G. Mullan, *Scottish Puritanism, 1590–1638* (Oxford, 2000), 85–110.

So Christian, encouraged by those around her, came to perceive herself as being 'possessed' by the Devil and as being subject to demonic assaults as a result. Demonic possession was not the same thing as witchcraft, but it could lead to accusations of witchcraft – and did so in this case. When Christian's fits began, in August 1696, she initially accused two people of causing them: Katherine Campbell, a maidservant in the Bargarran household, and Agnes Nasmith, an elderly beggar who had recently visited the house. Campbell and Nasmith would become two of the accused witches, and were both executed. But how and when did Christian and those around her first begin to think in terms of 'bewitchment'?

Readers of the *True Narrative* will have wondered what her parents, and indeed the medical practitioners, thought was causing Christian's symptoms in the early weeks and months. The line of argument that readers seem to have been expected to gather from the narrative could be summarised as: 'We initially assumed that this was a natural disease, so we consulted medical professionals. However, the practitioners from Paisley administered treatments that proved ineffective, and then we went to Dr Brisbane in Glasgow who informed us that it wasn't a natural disease at all. Suddenly, we realised that it must be witchcraft.'

However, this narrative seems to have replaced a previous story, in which Christian's parents immediately suspected witchcraft as soon as her fits began, and only called in the medical professionals to confirm this by ruling out alternatives. The earlier, manuscript version of the narrative, the 'Informatory Accompt', said that the parents threatened Agnes Nasmith, within days of the beginning of the fits, to get her to stop causing Christian's trouble, whereupon Christian had six days' relief from her symptoms. Tellingly, the published version omitted this episode. No doubt the earlier version is itself a construct, but, when we compare the two versions, we see editorial choices being made in the latter version, and strategies being adopted to shape the narrative into a form that the reader would find believable.

Only two witches, Katherine Campbell and Agnes Nasmith, were suspected in the first few months. But in December 1696, Christian and those around her began to develop the idea of a 'crew' of witches – an idea that enabled Christian to tell more elaborate stories of bewitchment. In early 1697, Christian herself gradually named further names, and Elizabeth Anderson, one of the early suspects who was converted into a star witness, also did so. Anderson is an important figure in the case; she was originally seen as a witch, but perceptions of her shifted so that she was seen as a victim of witchcraft. Comparable processes had operated during the recent witchcraft panic in Salem, Massachusetts, which may well have influenced the Bargarran case in this respect (and in other ways too).[14] For instance, Mary Warren began as one of the 'afflicted girls' accusing others of witchcraft, but then spent a period under suspicion of witchcraft herself, before re-establishing her position as an innocent victim of witchcraft.[15] Christian Shaw herself was never seriously suspected of witchcraft, but in the later stages of her possession she did report that the witches were *tempting* her to become a witch, an idea that to some extent replaced an earlier idea that the witches were trying to kill her. Further study of the trajectory of Christian's psychodrama – her own understanding and expression of what was happening to her – would be rewarding.

Authorship: compilation and editing

Who wrote the central 'Narrative' of Christian Shaw's behaviour? The original text, as the 'Informatory Accompt' and 'Continued Accompt' (edited above) show us more clearly, was assembled from a collection of fragments, each recounting an individual episode. This collection has then been through more than one process of revision, to which several different hands have contributed. It is presented as deriving from the accounts of various different eyewitnesses, so presumably the initial words describing each episode were written, either by one of those eyewitnesses themselves, or by someone near at hand who made notes from what the eyewitnesses said. These individual short passages, probably written on separate sheets of paper, were later compiled into a continuous narrative. The compiler or compilers presumably revised the original words, if only to present the various episodes in a standardised format. So we are looking for three types of 'author': the *initial writers* of individual episodes, the *compilers* who brought the episodes together, and the *revisers* who edited the work. Moreover, the processes of compilation and revision both seem to have occurred in stages. The idea of an 'author' or 'authors' is not a simple one.

Isabel Adam's view is that the authors were John McGilchrist (Christian Shaw's maternal uncle) and Francis Grant, though she gives no reasons to support this.[16] Hugh McLachlan and Kim Swales show in more detail that the 'Narrative' has been through a previous process of editing, co-ordinated by the local ministers Andrew Turner and James Brisbane.[17] This is convincing in

14 Information deriving directly or indirectly from the Salem panic may not only have influenced the observers' interpretations of Christian's behaviour (the point being made here), but may also have influenced what was said to Christian about how demoniacs behaved (as discussed above in the present introduction), and what was written about her behaviour afterwards (as discussed in the introduction to the 'Bargarran Witches' manuscript, above).

15 Emerson W. Baker, *A Storm of Witchcraft: The Salem Trials and the American Experience* (Oxford, 2015), 115–17.

16 Adam, *Witch Hunt*, 217–18.

17 McLachlan and Swales, 'Bewitchment of Christian Shaw', 68–70.

itself, and more will be said about it in a moment, but McLachlan and Swales have not examined the earlier version in the 'Bargarran Witches' manuscript, which brings us closer to the original authors of each section. Adam, who did examine this manuscript, may have noted that John McGilchrist's name appears in it from time to time, beginning in September 1696. The relationship between the 'Narrative' as published in the *True Narrative* and that given in the earlier 'Bargarran Witches' manuscript is discussed at more length in the introduction to the latter, above.

Two obvious candidates as compilers of the 'Narrative', and also as authors of at least some individual episodes, would be Christian Shaw's parents, John Shaw of Bargarran and Christian McGilchrist. They tend to remain in the background of the published 'Narrative', but Isabel Adam has argued persuasively that John Shaw was the moving spirit behind the prosecutions as a whole.[18] Shaw and McGilchrist were in the best possible position to know about their daughter's behaviour, and to influence what was written about it. McGilchrist's letter of 18 February 1697, printed in the *Relation* of that year (another document edited above in the present volume), described an episode of her daughter's recent behaviour; this description would later be expanded and worked into the published 'Narrative'.

Another plausible candidate to have made a contribution of some kind is Janet Aitken, Lady Northbar, Christian's maternal grandmother. In the 'Informatory Accompt' she appears as a witness to events within a week of the narrative's commencement, and goes on to witness more events than anyone else, usually as the leading witness. She seems to have been continuously present at Bargarran during the progress of her granddaughter's fits. Indeed one of Christian's episodes of fits takes place 'in her Grand-mothers house at *Northbar*' while she is on her way to Glasgow (p. xii). Aitken's late husband Donald McGilchrist of Northbar had been a Glasgow merchant, and the family's Glasgow connections could be investigated further.[19] The prominence of Aitken's name in the 'Informatory Accompt' may be part of a strategy to show that the witnesses were not *just* the girl's parents, but it is still thought-provoking. It is at any rate highly likely that the original authors of the individual episodes collected in the 'Informatory Accompt' and 'Continued Accompt' may be found among those that it names as witnesses, and that the compiler or compilers may also have been among those witnesses.

18 Adam, *Witch Hunt*, 234 and *passim*.

19 NRS, Testament of Donald McGilchrist of Northbar, late bailie of Glasgow, 12 August 1685, Glasgow Commissary Court, CC9/7/46. Janet Aitken's younger son John McGilchrist, another prominent name in the 'Informatory Accompt', was a 'writer' (lawyer) in Glasgow. Her elder son, James McGilchrist of Northbar, appears in the 'Informatory Accompt' from time to time, as does her other daughter, Janet McGilchrist, wife of Archibald Bannatyne of Kellie.

The presbytery of Paisley took an interest in the 'Narrative', and from the presbytery records we know the names of some of the compilers or revisers. The two most important were Andrew Turner, minister of Erskine (the parish in which Bargarran was located), and James Brisbane, minister of the neighbouring parish of Kilmacolm. Both had been frequent visitors to Bargarran and had witnessed several of Christian's fits, as the 'Informatory Accompt' shows. The presbytery commissioned Turner and Brisbane to 'take up a particular narrative' of the case on 30 December 1696.[20] Turner's and Brisbane's 'taking up' may well have involved compiling a connected narrative from initial fragments. Such a narrative in January 1697 would have been inconclusive, since Christian's fits were still continuing. The 'Bargarran Witches' manuscript shows the process of compilation at an intermediate stage; it presents two separate narratives, the first ending on 14 February and the second beginning on 18 February, that have not yet been combined.

This was the time when the enquiry commission was gathering evidence, and the minutes of the commission enable us to pinpoint one stage in the development of the narrative. The commission held two meetings, at Bargarran on 5 February and at Renfrew on 18 February. At the end of the proceedings on 5 February, the commissioners recorded this minute:

> The Laird of Bargarran haveing presented to the Commissioners ane long narative of matters relateing to the case of the said Christine Shaw, hes [*sic*] daughter, they recommend to the said Laird of Bargarran, and Master Andrew Turner minister of Ersken, to cause transcryve the same in paragraphs leaving ane distance betwixt each of them, and alsoe recommends to them to cause cite the rexive witnesses present att the particulars for approveing therof[21] att Renfrew the eightene day of Februarii instant, to which day and place the said commissioners adjourne themselves.[22]

This shows that John Shaw had presented, on 5 February, an earlier version of the narrative than any that is now extant. It consisted of continuous text, with no witnesses named, and perhaps not even paragraph breaks. It was the enquiry commission itself that asked for the witnesses' names to be added. The narrative was thus rewritten in the form preserved in the 'Bargarran Witches' manuscript in February, in between the two meetings of the enquiry commission, and it was John Shaw and Andrew Turner who gave it that form. The fact that the 'Informatory Accompt' continues up to

20 *A History of the Witches of Renfrewshire* (Paisley, 1877), pp. xxvii–xxviii.

21 'the rexive witnesses present att the particulars for approveing therof': the respective witnesses (who had been) present at each of the events described, for certifying them.

22 National Library of Scotland, report of the Bargarran enquiry commission, February 1697, Acc. 6687, no. 9, p. 4. Most of the enquiry commission's proceedings are documented in *A Relation of the Diabolical Practices of Above Twenty Wizards and Witches of the Sheriffdom of Renfrew*, above in the present volume.

14 February shows that they worked up to and including that day at least, and then presented a copy of that document to the commissioners on 18 February. Then, as Christian's fits continued, they felt it necessary to begin a further narrative – what would become the 'Continued Accompt'.

So the work on the narrative continued through the spring, as the investigations and trials unfolded. At some point, perhaps during the trial, the decision was taken to publish the narrative in print. Andrew Turner, Patrick Simpson, minister of Renfrew, and Thomas Blackwell, minister of Paisley, were commissioned to revise the narrative on 10 May. On that date, the members of the presbytery also read and approved the draft preface to the narrative that they had previously commissioned from John Wilson.[23] The *True Narrative* was already 'preparing for the press' on 16 June 1697, less than a week after the executions.[24] In the end it was not printed until 1698, mentioning in its own preface 'some *Accidents* which did retard it'.

The 'Narrative' of Christian Shaw's behaviour itself was only one component of the published *True Narrative*, comprising less than half of the text. There may well have been a single editor who assembled the various components for publication and saw the tract through the press in Edinburgh. That individual may or may not also have been responsible for the revised version, *Sadducismus Debellatus* (on which more in a moment). It may be tempting to try to identify that individual, but there is no direct evidence. Francis Grant is the person usually named, but his only detectable connection with the tract is that he provided the prosecution documents published as the two 'Letters'. John Shaw of Bargarran may be a more likely editor; he showed interest in compiling relevant documents in his 'Bargarran Witches' manuscript. However, this is no more than suggestive. We should recognise that the editor of the *True Narrative* wished to present his work to the public anonymously, and that he succeeded in that aim.

The tract was not only printed in Edinburgh, but also seems often to address an intended readership in that area. We are told repeatedly that the setting of events is 'in the West', beginning with the title page. The 'Narrative' itself is told *from* the west of Scotland, rather than from an Edinburgh perspective: 'Thousands in this Countrey have been Eye and Ear Witnesses' (p. xxxvii). After the end of the 'Narrative', however, we return to an Edinburgh perspective.

23 *A History of the Witches of Renfrewshire* (Paisley, 1877), p. xxxiv.

24 David Laing (ed.), 'An Original Letter to the Laird of Wishaw (now presented to the Museum), relating to the proceedings against James Aikenhead "the Atheist," and the trial of witches in Paisley in 1696', *Proceedings of the Society of Antiquaries of Scotland*, 11 (1874–76), 438–45, at p. 439. This long letter, by Robert Wylie, minister of Hamilton, defended the witchcraft prosecutions against London critics, and had much to say, both about these prosecutions and about the contemporary prosecution of Thomas Aikenhead (not 'James' Aikenhead) for blasphemy. The letter is discussed in the broader context of British intellectual debates by Ian Bostridge, *Witchcraft and its Transformations, c.1650–c.1750* (Oxford, 1997), 26–33.

There is mention of 'the whole Process', the trial record, 'which being extant upon Record, any who are Curious may have easy access thereunto' (p. 2). The idea of easy access to this record indicates an intended readership in Edinburgh.

The tract seems also to address a broader readership, beyond Scotland. The editor does not expect readers to understand Scots words such as 'harle', 'Snood', 'widder-shins', 'Tint' and 'ding' (pp. x, xix, xxvi, xxvii), none of which were particularly obscure. He may already have been aiming for a London readership. This aim was fulfilled when a London printer issued an anglicised version under the title *Sadducismus Debellatus*, of which an account will now be given.

Later editions

A revised version of the *True Narrative* was published in the same year in London, under the main title *Sadducismus Debellatus* (roughly translatable as 'Denial of Spirits Defeated').[25] This was substantially identical to the original text, but with numerous minor edits that were evidently intended to clarify the sense for an English readership. *SD* also introduced a few errors. Thus, for instance, 'Swerff' (p. xi) became 'Swoon' (*SD*, p. 2); 'a little round Cape and a plack' (p. xl) became 'a little round Cap, and a plack, or 1/3 of a penny' (*SD*, p. 39); 'Sheriff deput' (p. xvi) became 'under Sheriff' (*SD*, p. 10); 'Lord *Blantyre*, ... Sir *John Houston* of *That ilk*' (p. xxxvii) became 'Lord *Bantyre*, ... Sir *John Houston* of *Houston*' (*SD*, p. 37). The preface (unpaginated in *SD*) was rephrased in places; thus the final phrase of the original preface, 'the designed *Curtness* did occasion the wraping up of *much Matter* in *small Bounds*; and the punctual Exactness of *Truth* in every Circumstance was the *chief* Aim: So that other Defects ought to be the less quarrelled', became 'the design'd brevity occasion'd the wraping up of much Matter in few words; naked and Exact Truth in every Circumstance being our chief aim'. Other small cuts were made here and there. The final 'Advertisement', against the planned rival publication, was omitted.

The present edition of the *True Narrative* has not attempted to identify every variant reading in *SD*, since *SD* is a derivative and secondary text. However, some of the *True Narrative*'s obscure expressions have been clarified by reference, in footnotes below, to the equivalent expressions in *SD*.

Sadducismus Debellatus included one substantive addition to the text of the original *True Narrative*. The latter printed abbreviated versions of the written attestations by Matthew Brisbane and Henry Marshall, the physician and

[25] *Sadducismus Debellatus: or, a True Narrative of the Sorceries and Witchcrafts Exercis'd by the Devil and his Instruments upon Mrs. Christian Shaw, Daughter of Mr. John Shaw, of Bargarran in the County of Renfrew in the West of Scotland, from Aug. 1696 to Apr. 1697* (London: H. Newman and A. Bell, 1698; ESTC no. R215462).

apothecary who treated Christian Shaw in Glasgow. However, *SD* instead printed the full texts of both attestations. This shows that *SD* was produced by someone involved with the Bargarran case, and was not simply an unauthorised London copy. In the present volume, the full texts of the attestations are printed from earlier versions that were collected in the 'Bargarran Witches' manuscript, above.

The historical importance of the *True Narrative* has been recognised through its having repeatedly been reprinted as a historical document. The first such reprint was published in Paisley in 1775.[26] This was a straightforward reproduction of the 1698 text, with no editorial commentary. The language was modernised, and a few short passages, mainly Latin quotations, were omitted. A more influential and enlarged reprint was issued, again in Paisley, in 1809. For this edition, the *True Narrative* became the largest single item in a composite edition of documents on this and other cases, issued under the title *A History of the Witches of Renfrewshire*.[27] This edition was reissued with additional material in 1877.[28] A photographic reprint of the 1877 edition was issued, with further material and a new main title, in 2006.[29] These three editions have been valuable in drawing attention to the case and in the additional material that they have compiled. They do not, however, meet modern editorial standards as editions of the *True Narrative* itself.

The 1809 editor was John Millar, who identified himself on his title page as the 'Editor of the Paisley Repository'. His basic transcription was generally reliable, although he rephrased some of the grammar and made a few errors of transcription. However, much more seriously, he chopped up and rearranged much of the text, added and subtracted headings, and interpolated passages from other sources with inadequate editorial guidance. The structure of the work was thus obscured to an extent that modern scholarship cannot find acceptable. Readers of Millar's edition will find it almost impossible to ascertain which passages belong to the original 1698 publication and which are subsequent additions. Millar also silently abbreviated the 1698 text, omitting Latin quotations, several entire paragraphs, and the final 'Advertisement'. These shortcomings of 1809 were reproduced unaltered in the 1877 and 2006 editions.

These editions, however, have their own value in that they added further documents. The 1877 editor was the local historian James Dodds.[30] Between them, Millar and Dodds added a number of documents, some of which

26 *A Narrative of the Sufferings and Relief of a Young Girl* (Paisley: Alexander Weir, 1775).

27 *A History of the Witches of Renfrewshire* (Paisley: J. Neilson, 1809).

28 *A History of the Witches of Renfrewshire* (Paisley: A. Gardner, 1877).

29 *The Kirk, Satan and Salem: A History of the Witches of Renfrewshire*, ed. Hugh V. McLachlan (Glasgow: Grimsay, 2006).

30 His name was given only as 'J. D.' in the edition itself, but he declared himself as having edited it in the introduction to a later work that he also edited: *Diary and General Expenditure Book of William Cunningham of Craigends, 1673–1680*, ed. James Dodds (Edinburgh: SHS, 1887), p. xv.

widened the focus beyond the Bargarran case. Their additional primary sources on this case itself were extracts from the records of the presbytery of Paisley concerning it, extracts from the 1690s poll tax records of several of the people concerned in the events, and the text of a sermon by David Brown preached to the convicted witches on 9 June 1697, the day before their execution.[31]

The 2006 editor was Hugh McLachlan, a social scientist and philosopher who has made several other contributions to the history of Scottish witchcraft.[32] His edition was based on a photographic reprint of the 1877 edition, though a few pages were inadvertently omitted. His additional material included pamphlets concerning demonic possession at Salem, which Professor McLachlan suggestively argued had influenced the authors of the *True Narrative*, and a draft dittay of 1699 against a number of accused witches in the Renfrewshire region whose case was influenced by that of the Bargarran witches.[33]

Aftermath

The Bargarran prosecutions of 1697 led to seven executions and one death in prison – the last time in Scotland that a single witchcraft case claimed so many lives. The broader context of the case is also worth pondering. Brian Levack and Michael Wasser have noted the influence of the *True Narrative* on later Scottish cases.[34] One episode, particularly worth noting because it comes up later in the present volume, was in 1704, when Patrick Cowper, minister of Pittenweem, coached the young Patrick Morton on how to behave as a demoniac by reading the *True Narrative* to him.

A remarkable episode was reported in Antrim, Ireland, beginning in May 1698. A girl in the ninth year of her age was bewitched and rapidly exhibited similar behaviour to Christian Shaw. She regurgitated unusual items, experienced dramatic bodily contortions, and fell into fits in which she was not fully conscious of her surroundings. Like Christian, she was taken to a doctor in a distant town (Dublin) without effect. The witch who was accused of causing the possession was executed, but the fits continued because there were said to be two more witches involved. However, the girl was finally cured by a

31 Another extant sermon on the case was preached before the trial commissioners on 13 April: James Hutchisone, 'A Sermon on Witchcraft in 1697', ed. George Neilson, *Scottish Historical Review*, 7 (1910), 390–9. Brown focused on bringing the witches, as sinners, to repentance; Hutchison aimed to encourage convictions. For discussion of the two sermons see Christina Larner, *Enemies of God: The Witch-Hunt in Scotland* (London, 1981), 163–8.

32 Notably Christina Larner, Christopher H. Lee and Hugh V. McLachlan, *A Source-Book of Scottish Witchcraft* (Glasgow, 1977).

33 The 1699 case is discussed and placed in context by Wasser, 'Western Witch-Hunt of 1697–1700'.

34 Wasser, 'Western Witch-Hunt of 1697–1700', 159–61; Levack, 'Demonic Possession in Early Modern Scotland', 168–71.

'balsom' compounded of grease and hazel berries.[35] The narrative could well have been influenced by news of Christian Shaw's case, either through one of the publications connected with it or through direct contact between the west of Scotland and the Ulster Protestant community of Antrim.[36]

Even within the west of Scotland, the executions in Paisley on 10 June 1697 were not the end of the story. Several further suspects were still in prison at the time of the publication of the *True Narrative*. Its editor gave only initials, instead of full names, for these suspects, claiming that he did not wish to prejudice future legal proceedings against them.[37] In March 1699 there were renewed moves to have them and others tried, although in the end there were no further executions.[38] Two people were particularly prominent in these initials. 'M. M.' is the Greenock 'gentlewoman' Mary Morrison, who features prominently in the *Relation* edited above in the present volume. Morrison may well have been the sponsor of the intended rival publication against which the *True Narrative* directed its final 'Advertisement'.[39] 'J. P.' (or 'I. P.') is Jean Park; one important piece of evidence was the fragments of red cloth that Christian Shaw produced, claiming to have torn them from her sleeves. The use of these initials attracted the reader's attention to these people, an active reminder that these witches had not yet been prosecuted. The initials were mentioned explicitly for this reason in the aggressive final 'Advertisement'. Again we remind ourselves that the *True Narrative* was a book designed to kill.

Editorial conventions

The original printer renders most short quotations by italics, and longer ones by indented text with quotation marks at the start of every line. The latter quotations are represented in the present edition either by indented text, or else (with the long documents from the enquiry commission, pp.

35 Daniel Higgs, *The Wonderfull and True Relation of the Bewitching a Young Girle in Ireland* (n.p., 1699). None of the participants were named, making the narrative harder to investigate.

36 The Antrim case, with its Scottish links, is discussed in Andrew Sneddon, *Witchcraft and Magic in Ireland* (Basingstoke, 2015), 20–1, 40–1, 68–9.

37 The initials, as far as can be ascertained, stand for the following names. E. T. is Elizabeth Tarbet, in Newark; I. D. is the same as J. D.; I. K. is the same as J. K.; I. P. is the same as J. P.; J. D. (or I. D.) is John Davidson; J. G. is the same person as Luckie Miller (L. M.); J. K. (or I. K.) is Janet Keir, in Northbar; J. P. (or I. P.) is Jean Park, in Paisley; J. R. is Jean Ross, living near Bargarran; J. W. is Janet Waugh; L. M. is Luckie Miller, a woman living near Bargarran (this seems to be a nickname; she is the same person as J. G.); M. A. is Margaret Alexander, in Paisley; M. M. is Mary Morrison, wife of Francis Duncan, merchant and skipper in Greenock; W. R. (who is not an accused witch) is a neighbour of Mary Morrison, perhaps William Rowan, a member of the assize.

38 Adam, *Witch Hunt*, 219; Wasser, 'Western Witch-Hunt of 1697–1700', 152. A draft dittay of April 1699 named several suspects who had previously been connected with the Bargarran case, including Mary Morrison: *The Kirk, Satan and Salem*, ed. McLachlan, 336–63.

39 Morrison is stated positively to have been its sponsor by Adam, *Witch Hunt*, 216–18. This should however be treated as a probable conjecture. No rival publication appeared in the end.

xxxix–xliii) by ordinary text. It should be borne in mind that the original does not always indicate precise beginnings and endings of these quotations. The original printer usually represents intermissions in quotations in these indented passages by italics, retained in this edition. One extended quotation (p. xxxiii), given here as a single indented paragraph, was originally represented partly in italics and partly indented; another (p. xxxvi) was given entirely in italics but is here indented. Three short quotations (pp. xxxiv, xxxviii) were originally given with opening but not closing quotation marks; these have been reproduced in this edition. A few obviously typographical errors such as 'Darkuess' (p. iv) or 'the the shape' (p. 5) have been corrected silently.

TEXT[40]

A True Narrative of the Sufferings and Relief of a Young Girle; Strangely Molested, by Evil Spirits and their Instruments, in the West: collected from authentick testimonies there-anent. With a preface and post-script containing reflections on what is most material or curious; either in the history, or trial of the seven witches who were condemn'd to be execute in that countrey.

JOB 2.6. *And the Lord said unto Satan, behold he is in thine hand; but save his life.*

MATH. 15.22. *Have mercy upon me, O Lord, thou Son of David; my Daughter is grievously vexed with a Devil.*

ROM. 16.20. *And the God of Peace shall bruise Satan under your Feet shortly.*

EDINBURGH. Printed by JAMES WATSON in *Craig's Closs*, on the North-side of the Cross. M.DC.XCVIII. {*p. iii*}

PREFACE.

WISE Men do justly suspect, and are hardly brought to credit, the Accounts of *extraordinary* Stories; especially anent *Witchcraft*: Because the frequent impostures which the *Romanists* have obtruded on the World in their Miracles and Legends; the many *Relations* of odd things as done by Dæmons or Wizards, which yet, were either *false*, or the product of simple *natural causes*; the *ignorance* of several Judges and Juries, who have condemned silly Creatures *meerly* upon their ridiculous Confessions, or other slender proof; and the *difficulty* of conceiving the *Manner* or Philosophy, of some Operations and Appearances, tho undoubtedly true in Fact; are good *prejudices* against a *Sudden belief*, and *precautions* for an *exact Inquiry*.

[40] Source: *A True Narrative of the Sufferings and Relief of a Young Girle* (Edinburgh: James Watson, 1698; ESTC no. R213564). The text begins at p. ii.

But they are Men of *weak Souls*, destitute of *distinct* thoughts; who deny *all*, because they have discovered Error *in some*; or condemn as false, *all facts*, which they are *ignorant how* they came to exist: By the *same rule* of reasoning that, there are no *Enthusiasts*, because the best Men have been some times mistaken for these; nor are there any *Criminals*, in respect severals have suffered who were not truely such: considering, that many *Historys* are fabulous, therefore none is to be trusted: And all the *Phænomena's* in Nature, whose invisible causes they cannot comprehend, are meer Delusions.

The following narrative, as to the truth of Fact, is the best attested peice of History of this kind, that has occurred in many Ages: the most of the matters therein represented having gained the assent of *privat Scepticks*; and been proven before *publick Judges*. So that it's more surprising than the strange things of *Witchcraft* that any should seriously deny the *Beeing thereof*, and from thence discredit such useful Providences *at a distance*, when *Notoriety* has dispelled all Objections in the places where they did exist.

Many Authors have proven, at large, that there are Witches and witchcraft from *Reason*, *Scripture*, *Antiquity*, and *Experience* of all Nations and Ages in the World: And they have *solved the difficultys* which might obstruct the belief of this positive proof, by *possible Hypotheses* of Philosophy: Where it's to be observed, that tho any such explications of the natural manner of Phenomena's are subject to cavil, yet the existence of a thing which has so certain *positive Evidence* cannot be denyed in sound Reasoning; because, *Angels*, and *Men* not being made for civill converse together in *this* World, and all *communion* with *Devils* being interdicted us, the Scripture *needed* to unfold little of their way of acting; and still the *next* Age, may discover what *this* could not reach. As this has already unveiled what was thought unextricable in the *Last*: Unless *Impossibility* were presently *demonstrate*.

Herefore such a short hint, as may somewhat *Illustrat* the Events in the subsequent discourse, may suffice in the present Case: Especially since *Providence* does, by eminent occurrences, rather design our *practical instruction*, then a Subject of *notional Speculations*.

The Devil can assume a *corporeal Shape*, and *bespeak* Man out of it:[41] As he did to *Eve*, with our SAVIOUR, and in some *Heathen Oracles*: So that there is *Capacity* for their entring into *Contract*. Satan is *willing* thus to *ensure* mortalls of being enemies to Heaven, Earth, and their own Salvation; by his indefatigable malice against all the *three*: As Curiosity in *Witts*; Revenge, and Disclosure of Secrets in the *great*; covetousness in the *Wordling*[42] or *Poor*, and {*p. iv*} *pleasures in all* whom he thinks *needfull* (they being impregnable otherways) and is *permitted* by GOD, to attaque in this manner; does sufficiently blind them, to be *Susceptible* of his Proposals thereanent. We see dayly, how Criminals

41 'bespeak Man out of it': speak to humans, using his bodily shape.

42 *Sic.* Read 'worldling' (materialistic person).

lusts inflamed by Satan, divert their *Horrour* not only of eternal, but also of temporal *imminent* Torments: Perverting these instincts of *Nature* which might *fright* them from *surrender*. But further, he does *commonly* facilitate his conquest on Witches, by decoying them *Piece male*[43] to his Lure, through the mediation of Others from amonge Mankind that are already embarqued, till they be prepared and he get an opportunity of making with them an *explicit* Transaction.

That accordingly he has *defacto prevailed* in making Sorcerers and Witches, appears from the Testimony of the *Wisest* and *Best*, in all *States* and *Times*.

The *Heathens*, by Nature and Practice, discovering this truth, made *Laws* against *Maleficos* and *Mathematico's*[44] (these last tho they assumed the name of an art much encouraged by the Legislators; yet were known, under the Cloak thereof, to consult the Devil anent the fates of Men and States) which the *Roman* Senate and People did *execute*: And even the *Persians*, in some good Reigns, did the like. Under the *Old Testament*, the Magicians of *Egypt* and *Babylon*, who were baffled by *Moses* and *Daniell*;[45] *Balaam* and the Witch of *Endor*, with the success of both;[46] yea, *Jesabel*, *Manasseth*, and the ten *Tribes* their just Judgement for their Sorceries and Witchcrafts amongst other Crimes;[47] and the Laws made against such, as distinct from other Guilts: Under the *New Testament*, *Simon* Magus who bewitched the People of *Samaria*; *Elimas* the Sorcerer that was struck blind at *Paul's* Rebuke;[48] the *Pythonisse* who seems to have been possest of *consent*, because she was not *Tormented*, but got profit thereby; and such as *confessed*, *shewed their Deeds*, and *burnt their Books* in *Ephesus*:[49] Are undeniable instances hereof. Finally there are prophesies of False-Christs with *signs* and *wonders*, able to deceive, if posible, the very Elect: *General Councils* have made Canons against these Wretches: And the *experimental Knowledge* of injured Mortalls, with the publick Sentences which did vindicate the same; in subsequent Ages, are delivered down to us by the Writers thereof.

Hence *Gulielmus Linensis*, a Popish *Doctor*, was justly put to Death, even tho' he dyed *penitent*, he having confessed Witchcraft (whereof the written *Covenant* was found in his pocket) and that his share of the Devils Service was to *perswade* and *preach* that Witches were only silly deluded Melancholians,

43 'Piece male' (piecemeal): bit by bit.

44 This phrase indicates that Wilson is thinking of the Code of Justinian, book 9, title 18, 'De maleficiis et mathematicis et ceteris similibus' (Concerning poisoners, diviners, and other criminals of the same description). Justinian was a Christian emperor, but Wilson assumes, plausibly for his purpose, that this law had been handed down from pagan times.

45 For the magicians of Egypt, see Exodus 7:9–12. For the magicians of Babylon, see Daniel 2.

46 For Balaam, see Numbers 22:21–35. For the witch of Endor, see 1 Samuel 28:7–25.

47 For the punishments of Jezebel, Manasseh and the ten tribes see 2 Kings 9, 2 Kings 21 and 2 Kings 17 respectively.

48 Cf. Acts 13:8–11.

49 Cf. Acts 19:19.

whereby their *Confessions* were *no proof*. His success was such in this work of Darkness, that the People and Judges did *Slack*, and Witches were vastly multiplyed in few Years. *vid. Pet*: *Mamorius de Lamiis*, who gives an account of the Process, from authentick Records.[50]

Through these periods, it is observed, that Satan has oft shifted the *Scene*, and *turned* himself to many *Shapes*, as he found it most *accomodat* to his purposes: Whereby the manner of Apparition of Devils has been different, according to the *state of the times*. So *of old*, Satan appeared, and was worshiped, *as such* for deprecating his Mischeif: which is said to be retained in some of the most barbarous places of the *Indies* to this day. In the *darkness of Popery* he transformed into a more *innocent Spirit* (that pretended to fortell Deaths, reveal the Defuncts will, discover ocult murders, do other *friendly Offices*, &c. Which were subtile means of *inducing to him*, and *relying on him*) in the *Brounies* and *Phairies*.[51] These were *then* very frequent, he having *impudence* thus to appear openly proportional to the *knowledge* of Men, over whom his reign was so *universal*: As it is related to continue in the more Northern Regions at this day.[52] But since {*p. v*} *Light has broke out* in our Horison, he oftner works *externally* by Magicians and Witches, and *internally* on the lusts of Men, being *now mostly* restrained to his *own Sphere* or *Subjects*. Yet still he ensnares severals, partly, by *aping* the Ordinances of GOD; especially as they are corrupted in the Romish Church, whence so many *Monks* and *Nuns* as already prepared, have been found overcome. So he keeps with them publick *Assemblys in the Night* as of extraordinary *merit*: They formally *Worship* him by many *mimicall Gestures*: He *imprints* on them a kind of *Sacrament*: He inflicts *dreadfull Penances* on such as have not execute the commanded mischeifs: He teaches them *odd words* and *signes*, upon repeating of which *Exorcisms*, he (it being his *interest*) effectuats the *fore pactioned Operations* &c.

But though what he does *of himself*, or on the *Watch-word* or *Ensign* of Sorcerers or Witches, may, by *collection*, and *artful disposal* of *Matter* and *Form*;

50 'Gulielmus Linensis' (Guillaume Adeline) was a French monk and theologian in Evreux. In 1452 he attacked the emerging doctrine of demonology, preaching that the witches' sabbat was merely an illusion. He was arrested by the local bishop, forced to confess to witchcraft himself, and imprisoned for life. Adeline died in prison four years later (he was not 'put to Death'). His case was often cited to prove the reality of the witches' sect. '*Pet: Mamorius de Lamiis*' evidently refers to Pierre (Petrus) Mamoris, *Flagellum Maleficorum* (written *c.*1462; first printed *c.*1490). Mamoris was professor of theology at Poitiers. Wilson has garbled both his name and the title of his book, and the citation to it is probably a second-hand one. '*Flagellum Maleficorum*' means 'Scourge of Witches'; '*De Lamiis*' means 'Concerning Witches'. For Adeline and Mamoris see Martine Ostorero, 'Un prédicateur au cachot: Guillaume Adeline et le sabbat', *Medievales*, 44 (printemps 2003), 73–96.

51 James VI made a similar argument: James VI, *Daemonologie*, in *Minor Prose of James VI and I*, ed. James Craigie (Edinburgh: Scottish Text Society, 1982), 44–5 (book 3, chapter 2).

52 Wilson may have had in mind the much-publicised Swedish witchcraft panic of the 1660s and 1670s. For a Scottish account of this see George Sinclair, *Satans Invisible World Discovered* (Edinburgh, 1685), relation 28 (pp. 167–86).

appear surprising: Yet he cannot work *against Nature*; or so apply *Actives* to *Passives* as to overturn the *Course thereof*; since that is only competent to its *Author* who alon can do true Miracles,[53] or know immediatly, the thoughts of Man. Yea, after the *Fall* it is like, that even Satans *natural Powers* are come down below those of *good* Angels; and it is certain, that he is often *befooled* in his Designs by Providence: Notwithstanding whereof, he *retains* so much as (being permitted) is sufficient to bring about, by *unseen natural Means*, most of the extraordinary Appearances, that the Generality of the Learned have attributed to him: And particularly those in the subsequent Narrative: Many of which, tho' they are *beyond* the *Efficiency* of *Disease*, *Deceit*, or any *visible Cause*; yet may be the Effects of some such unperceived Means as follow.

There is no difficulty in Satan's *transmitting* in a short time an *Account* of Things which are *past*; since it's known he goes to and fro in the Earth:[54] Yea, he may have *certainly fore told* some future Events, as Alexander's Success against *Persia*,[55] &c seing he understands and may steal, the *great Revolutions* of the World, out of the *Prophets*; wherein they are so graphically circumscribed: Or he may discover his *own Resolutions* when-ever he is *commissioned* or *permitted* to execute a *Judgement*; which is the case of those whom, *for* seeking their Horoscops, GOD gives over to him to whom they do apply; and of *Saul*, who got so exact an account of his own End by the Philistines.[56] But without some such aid, Satan can only guess like the Phisician by the *Urine*, or Politician by the *Crisis* of States: which is the Cause that most of his Oracles are *ambiguous*.

His *transporting* of Witches is elsewhere explained. He can raise *Hurricanes* (as appears in *Job*) which are known to carry over Tracts of Sea and Land, very *ponderous Bodys*: As it's easy for him to *Condense* a part of the Vechicle: which may *protect the Breathing* and *yet cutt the Air*; like the *Fence* of Dyvers, and *beak* of a Sloop:[57] In which also he affects the magnifying of his *natural Powers* to be no less than of good Angels, who transported *Ezekiel* and *Elijah*. His covering of the Witches *from sight*, at some times, is also cleared, from the difficultys which seem to attend it, in another place: Where it appears very *possible* that his skill in *Opticks*, Reflection and *Refraction* of light &c. To

53 'its *Author*' is God, the Creator, who alone can work true miracles against the course of nature.

54 Cf. Job 1:7.

55 This may well refer to Alexander's visit to the Delphic oracle, as related by Plutarch. See *Plutarch: Hellenistic Lives*, trans. Robin Waterfield, ed. Andrew Erskine (Oxford, 2016), 19 (Alexander, chapter 14).

56 This is another reference to the story of the witch of Endor, who predicted Saul's fate (1 Samuel 28:7–25).

57 Swimmers when diving were advised to protect their necks with clasped hands: Christofer Middleton, *A Short Introduction for to Learne to Swimme* (London: James Roberts, 1595), sig. L4. The beak-head of a ship projected forwards above the water; it was the ship's bow that actually cut the water. However, the simile seems clear enough.

which his *Power* and *Agility* as a *Spirit* Subministrats[58] *Materials*: may effectuat all that can be proven to be true Fact in the Case.[59]

But *Glanvil*, *More* and others lay an other *Hypothesis* in *both. viz*. That the Soul is *separable* from the Body in some Cases, *without Death*: When by *God's Permission*, Satan, of the *parties Consent*, gets power over Soul and Body; whereby he may carry away the *one* from the Helm of the *other*, and sett it back again {*p. vi*} in it's Seat; *providing* the *vital Spirits* which make the Body a fit Receptacle, be well *preserved* by Ointments, that constrict the Pores, till the return of it's Guest: But Death ensues from a *Separation* when the Organs of the Body are rendred *altogether unapt* to obey the Soul's Commands in its Functions.[60] If such an opinion could be true, Satan might *place* this captivated Spirit to *actuat* any shape he thinks fit. But there needs not so much *Metaphysicks* to unridle the Appearances of Witches *as Beasts*, and the like: Since their *reall Persons* may be *covered* with a Vehicle; which by *disposal of the Rays* comming therefrom, may fascinat the Eyes by the same *Impressions* that come from the *true sight* of *such*. His power of representing another thing in lieu of that which is truly present; is so certain that its found he may make up the Image of persons who are not present at all: For it is undoubted that *Spiritual* Devils may some times be permitted to represent by *Phantoms* the most innocent and praise worthy Men, as Devils *incarnat* do traduce them.[61] He that accuseth the Brethren and imitats an Angel of *light*, may likeways *personat* the Children of *Light* by his Delusions: Yet the *Antecedents*, *Concomitants*, and *Consequents*,

58 'Subministrats': furnishes.

59 For the Devil's power over human senses, particularly sight, see Stuart Clark, *Vanities of the Eye: Vision in Early Modern European Culture* (Oxford, 2007), 123–60 and *passim*.

60 This probably derives from Joseph Glanvil[l], 'Some Considerations about Witchcraft', in his *Saducismus Triumphatus* (London: J. Collins and S. Lownds, 1681), 13–15 (sig. G4). Wilson cites 'Glanvil, More, and others'; Henry More contributed to *Saducismus Triumphatus*, so this may be Wilson's sole source. He may also have consulted Henry More, *The Immortality of the Soul* (London: William Morden, 1659), 267–85 (bk. 2, ch. 15). However, Wilson is not entirely convinced that the soul is separable from the body, and continues with an alternative line of argument.

61 This passage raises a question at the centre of the Bargarran evidence. When a bewitched person reports having seen the apparition of a person alleged to be a witch, does that prove the person to be a witch? Some people regarded these apparitions as proof of guilt, while others argued that the Devil might also cause the apparition of an innocent person to appear. Here, Wilson takes the latter view. However, this argument might undermine the Bargarran prosecutions and indeed the entire validity of Christian Shaw's reported experience, so in the remainder of this paragraph Wilson attempts to backtrack on it. First he argues that God will not permit the apparition of an innocent person to appear, before admitting that (as in the case of Naboth) sometimes he does permit it. For a perhaps more coherent discussion of this topic, reaching an opposite conclusion from Wilson, see James Williamson's tract 'Vindication of the Witches', edited above as part of the 'Bargarran Witches' manuscript.

The validity of 'spectral evidence' had been much debated at Salem: Wendel D. Craker, 'Spectral Evidence, Non-Spectral Acts of Witchcraft, and Confession at Salem in 1692', *Historical Journal*, 40 (1997), 331–58; Baker, *A Storm of Witchcraft*, 187–9. See also Clark, *Vanities of the Eye*, 144–53, in which the Bargarran case is discussed at p. 152.

of such providences, do readily *propale*[62] the *Falshood*; so as the just man, for the most part, shall not perish in his *Righteousness*, and GOD, in his *ordinary* Providence, will not laugh at the trial of the Innocent; tho sometimes it fall out, that the Sons of *Belial* may swear away the life of an *innocent Naboth*.[63]

There are several other things of less difficult Explication. Particularly, the Devil, or Witches might have been *heard* in converse by the Maid and not by Others; the same way as a *sound* directed through a *speaking Trumpet* does reach the *Ears* to which it is aimed without dispersing towards the intermediat, that are not in a streight line betwixt. The confederated Devil may, upon the Witches desire *infuse poisonous Humors, extracted* from Herbs of the same *Invisible Operation* with the *Steem* of *Madd-dogs*, or the *Pestilence*; which being joyned to the rapidous course of the Patient's own *Spirits*, *Humors*, and *Blood*, that Satan, by *ingyring himself*[64] *thereunto*, may, through the natural Means of *Pulsion*, set in *Carreer*: Can very well produce these *extraordinary Motions* which are mentioned in the *following Acount*.[65] They *delight* much in the Torture, or destruction, of *young Children*, in envy of CHRIST, who is tender of such *Little Ones*; and because the *Crime* is the *greater* the less the Patient has *offended*, or can *resist*. They use, or make others to repeat, *Scripture-words*, for gaining *Credit*, or *alleviating* the Terror, or to *disgrace* the *Word*, by such a *Mock-use*; as they did in time of our SAVIOUR, and therefore their *Testimony* was *rebuted*.[66] It's observable from many passages; that he *hastens*, sometimes, and *effects* their *Discovery*; by his *Malice* against their present *temporal Enjoyments*; *uncertainty* of their Continuance; and unsatiable *Desire* for their *full wreck*: Yet some of them, who, are *most maliciously bent*, he thinks fit to keep *here*, as *useful instruments*; and *Providence* permitts others to Live, that they, *wilfully filling up* their measure, under *Means*, may be finally *inexcusable*.

As to those whom, in *secret Judgement*, the Devil is permitted to torment; but, in *Mercy*, not to overcome: He may be carried thereunto from his design of *perverting* them by *Terror*, whereof he is at last disappointed: And *however*, the *defacing* of GOD's Image, and especially in despight of JESUS CHRIST Who honoured that Nature by assuming it, is his chief Delight: or he is *constrained* to make such stupendious Appearances against his *Will* (because he's most successful when he is least known) for a *visible* Testimony superadded to the greater Gospel-proofs, in *gross times*, that there are *Spirits* and a *Devil* to

62 'propale': publish. *SD*, preface (unpaginated), has 'discover'.
63 Cf. 1 Kings 21.
64 'ingyring himself': thrusting himself in.
65 Wilson argues here that demonic possession is caused by a transfer of poisonous vapours ('Humors' or 'steem') from the demon. This argument may well have derived from the way in which Glanvill had argued for a transfer of vapours from demon to witch, using the same analogy with infections transmitted by mad dogs: Glanvil[l], 'Some Considerations about Witchcraft', in his *Saducismus Triumphatus*, 21–4 (sig. G4). Cf. Julie A. Davies, 'Poisonous Vapours: Joseph Glanvill's Science of Witchcraft', *Intellectual History Review*, 22 (2012), 163–79.
66 This may refer to the mocking of Jesus in Matthew 27:29–31.

torment them, as it's observable that this was denied by Mr. *Aikenhead* (tho {*p. vii*} he died in full Conviction thereof) at the time when these things fell out in the Country.[67] Or Providence may tollerat such Sufferings, that they, tho' intended by the Devil for an instance of Malice, may, by their *Nottoriety*, be a mean of moving the Discovery, and bringing to Justice these Miscreants, whom he made use of as his Instruments in them; and who may have lived long in Rebellion against Heaven, and Destruction of Mankind by Malefices of the *same sort*; which fell out in this Case. Finally, the aboundant and efficacious *Grace of God* is conspicuous in enabling a young Girl to resist the bestlaid Assaults of the evil One to the utmost. As it is certain that he shews the greatest Malice in *Countries* where he is *hated* and *hateth* most; and the nearer his Reign be to an *End*.[68]

There are many other profitable Instructions which arise from this wonderful Providence, for such Dispensations have their own *Language*, and the Man of Wisdom shall *see* GOD's Name.[69]

The *usages* of Charmes for Men or Beasts, certain Characters, Words, Verses, and Spells: The *observation* of Times and Seasons as lucky, or unlucky: The *beleif* of having Success by carrying about some Herbs, Plants, or branches of Trees: And many the like *Superstitions*; which can have no natural *Causality* on the effects desired, are the very *Rudiments* of Witchcraft, and an *implicite* application to the Devil for *vertues* which GOD has denyed to things: Whence they are to be abhored as sinful in *themselves*, and introductory to *explicit* engadgment. So gross ignorance, prophane loosness, stupid forgetfulness of GOD, and neglect of his worship in Closets and Familys; Malice, Envy, Revenge, Discontent, oppressive fear of want, and distrustful anxiety of Spirit: Finally, a Libidinous Temper, Curses, Imprecations, and sinful Curiosity, are to be evited as *paving the way* to the same mischief.

Let none enveigh against a *profession of Religion*, because some under that specious covert have been found in League with the Devil. It's because of the glorious Lustre and Excellency of our Holy Faith that these Miscreants *paint* themselves with it; whereby like wise they may be less *suspected*, and more *able*, subtily to *gain* on others, and do their Masters work: So it was no stain on the Apostles that *One* of their number had a Devil, was a Traitor and Cheat: Nor that Satan transformes himself into an *Angel* of Light,[70] of

67 The parallel development of the Bargarran and Aikenhead cases is noteworthy, though this is the only mention of Aikenhead in the *True Narrative*. Thomas Aikenhead, a student in Edinburgh, was charged with blasphemy on 10 November 1696, convicted on 23 December, and executed on 8 January 1697. See Michael F. Graham, *The Blasphemies of Thomas Aikenhead: Boundaries of Belief on the Eve of the Enlightenment* (Edinburgh, 2008). In this work, the Bargarran case is discussed in the context of the aftermath of Aikenhead's at pp. 130–2.

68 Cf. Stuart Clark, *Thinking with Demons: The Idea of Witchcraft in Early Modern Europe* (Oxford, 1997), 335–45.

69 Cf. Micah 6:9.

70 Cf. 2 Corinthians 11:14.

design that the good ways of the LORD may be evill *spoken of*. Neither let us be under a *slavish Fear and Terror* of that Hellish Tribe, in truckling to their Humor, least they should do *Harm*, which savours of worshiping and paying homage to the *Devil*; whereas we ought only to make the *Lord of Hosts* our *Fear* and our *Dread*.

There is no just ground to reflect on *particular* Persons or Families upon account of such troubles. For no Man knoweth either Love or Hatred by *All* that's before them: All things come alike to *All*: And suppose ye that these were Sinners *above* all the *Galileans*, or above all that dwelt in *Jerusalem*?[71] The infinit wise GOD may thus try Faith, Patience, and Christian Fortitude. Job and our SAVIOUR were assaulted;[72] and seven Devils cast out of *Mary Magdelen* a chosen Vessel unto the LORD.[73] A Daughter of *Abraham* was bound by Satan for eighteen Years;[74] and his Messenger was sent to Buffet the great *Apostle* of the Gentiles.[75] The Woman of *Canaan*, *Math.* 15 c. 22. v. And the godly Man, *Mark* 9.24 v. Had their *nearest Relations* vext in this manner: And blessed be the LORD that has left such instances in *Record* for Prevention of stumbling; though it must be confessed that the same *Charity* which judges well of all things, cannot but alter it's *remark* when it's *proof* is sufficiently *clear* from the {*p. viii*} way in which the person affected did formerly *walk*, since *presumptions* do always cede to *Truth*, and Lawiers have a Maxim, that in *re clara non est locus conjecturis*.[76]

The *deaf Adder* that stopes the Eares at the charming *voice* of a Sun-shine *Gospel*, will, one way or other, fall into the charmes of Satan or his Instruments:[77] When Men *will have none* of CHRIST, he gives them up to their *own* Lusts, and power of their spiritual Adversarie; as, when *Israel* had *forsook* their GOD, he gave them up to *worship the Host* of Heaven. But how much ought we to be humbled, and how great *Diligence* ought to be used in the discovery, of so many *hid Achans* that are in the Camp of *Israel*![78] And what holy *caution* and pious use of our Baptismal Covenant, ought we to improve as the best *Amulits* against being either *Entysed* with the snares of the Devil, or *affected* by the attempts of his Instruments. Yet *Poverty*, *Age*, or *Features*, of any; yea nor *simple fame*, or the like slender grounds, which could not be worthy of being represented to a *Magistrate*; ought not to move us to *Suspition*, much

71 Cf. Luke 13:1–5.
72 Cf. the book of Job, and Luke 4:1–13.
73 Cf. Mark 16:9.
74 Cf. Luke 13:10–17.
75 This may refer to the Apostle Paul's encounter with the 'damsel possessed with a spirit of divination': Acts 16:16–24.
76 'In a clear matter there is no place for conjecture.' This traditional maxim is usually given as '*In claris non est locus conjecturis*', with substantively the same meaning.
77 Cf. Psalm 58:4.
78 Cf. Joshua 7.

less to *defame*: Since *Charity* hopes all things, and we ought to do to others, as we would be done by.

These things may meet with a very *different Reception*, especially in this unhappy Age and place of the World, where *Brittain* may be termed the *unfortunat Island*, *Africk* never having been more Fertile in the production of *Monsters*: since it's observed that through *All* the Successions of Men, there was never *before*, any *Society* or collective Body of *Atheists* till these dreggs of time; though there might have been here and there some *mishappen Births*. But wisdom is justified of her *Children*, and it's the Season for *Samson* to *awake* when *Delilah* gives the Alarum, that the *Philistens* are upon him.[79] What *peace*? so long as the *Whoredomes* of *Jesebel* and her Witchcrafts are so many.[80] But good things are hoped of our *Magistrats*, who have already so happily begun.

The Apostle said of *Job*'s Tryalls, ye have heard of the patience of *Job*, and have seen the *End of the LORD*.[81] So, in this Narrative you have a deplorable Schem of this Maids formidable *Fitts*, and of the *powers of Darkness* that combin'd, not only for ruining her *Body*; but also for murdering her *Soul*. In the mean time, the Hearts of many were *bleeding* for her, and much Application was made to *GOD* in her behalf: Diverse *solemn Fasts* were observed, both in her Fathers *Family*, in *the Paroch*, and throughout the bounds of the *Presbitry*, and *else-where*, her Case was expresly minded in publick Addresses to the Throne of Grace: Till at length there was a *general Fast* Religiously keeped in most parts of the *Synod*; that GOD might give an effectual Check to Satan's Rage and Dominion in the Countrey. *Boasting of Prayers* is to be abhorred, yet it is our *Duty* with all *Gratitude*, to acknowledge GOD the *hearer*, and to proclame to the World, the *Excellency*, of them; upon this very occasion: For He hath not turned away his Ear from *Us*; it being the comfortable *Result* of this History, that the Girle hath been perfectly well for many Months: And is not this a *Brand plucked out of the fire*;[82] and have not the *splintres wherewith* the Witches thought to have destroyed her, *recoiled* back upon some of themselves; and we wait execution of justice on the rest.

The *Devil could not* enter the Herd of Swine,[83] nor touch one Hair of *Job*'s Head, without *Permission* from Him *Whose Kingdom* ruleth *over all*: Whence though our Enemies be very *Indefatigable* and *Invisible*, yet we are under the Conduct of the *Watch-man* Who neither slumbers nor sleeps;[84] to *Whom* Darkness and Light are *both alike*; and *greater* is He that is in us, than he that is in the World: So that unless we wilfully forfeit our *Priviledges*, there is no fear {*p. ix*} of *Counter-poising* the wicked Ones, throwing down the *Gantlett*

[79] Cf. Judges 16:9.
[80] Cf. 2 Kings 9:22.
[81] Cf. James 5:11.
[82] Cf. Zechariah 3:2.
[83] Cf. Matthew 8:31–2.
[84] Cf. Psalm 121:4.

to all their Projects and Machinations; since neither Angels, Principalities, nor Powers, shall be able to *separat* us from the Love which is in CHRIST JESUS our LORD:[85] And though no Argument can be drawn from any *Merit* in us; yet we'll *carry the day* against all the Militia of Hell under the *Captain of our Salvation*; since he will *rest in His own Love. Is this the manner of Man, O Lord God*? yet a little while the Devil and his Accomplices, will be *cast* into the bottomless Pit, and we *transported* into *Imanuel*'s land.

It will not be a *natural sturdiness* of Temper, nor a *lifeless Mentioning* of the Name of GOD or CHRIST, that can shelter us from those Devourers, as appears in the Seven Sons of *Sceva*, *Acts* 19. but if the LORD be GOD then *folow Him*; for who is he that will harm you if ye be *Followers of that which is good*: he shall give His *Angels Charge* of thee to keep thee in all *thy Ways*: Great peace have they that love *Thy Law*, and nothing shall offend them: And they wrestle most successfully against Principalities and Powers who *fight* upon their *Knees*:[86] As resisting of the Devil is the way to make him *flee* from us.

Yet whom Satan cannot obtain to be tortured hereafter he will (when permitted[)] *torment* in this side of time; hence if *obsessions of Bodys* be so great a plague, how much worse is it to have him reign *Master* of our Souls?[87] Wherefore let us watch and pray against every Sin, the least of which is more Pleasing to *Him* and worse to *Us* then the being so corporally tormented.

If Satan as a Spirit may insinuat himself into our *Humors*; no wonder that by having such advantage in the *temper*, he can influence the Flegmatick to Slouth, the Cholerick to Anger, the Sanguin to Lust and sinful pleasure, the Melancholick to Despair, &c.[88] So they who think that they stand, have need to *take heed* lest they *fall*: And to pray that the Watch-man of *Israel* may make *an Hedge* about them and their House and about all that they have on every side.

Let this not only rouze our *Diligence* and stir up our *Gratitude* for not being affected alike: But let it also recall our *Admiration* and *love* of JESUS CHRIST who hath freed our *Souls* and *Bodys* from the power and Slavery of Satan: And finding our selves *too Weak* for him in awarding these deluding pleasures which procure our being *deserted* by GOD, and are Satans *Baits* to this fearfull Thraldom; let us run to the *Rock of Ages* for Protection and support, our *Sufficiency* being only of GOD.

85 Cf. Romans 8:38–9.

86 Cf. Ephesians 6:12.

87 *SD* (preface, unpaginated) renders this sentence as: 'If Satan's Possession of Bodies be so great a Plague, how much worse is it to have him reign *Master* of our Souls?' The switch from 'obsession' (being externally assaulted by a demon) to 'possession' (having a demon control one's inner processes) is intriguing. In England, some writers conflated the two terms, while others drew a distinction between them: Erika Gasser, *Vexed with Devils: Manhood and Witchcraft in Old and New England* (New York, 2017), 5–6. Scottish writers seem usually to have avoided this debate by using alternative terms like 'tormenting', but this edit in *SD* may indicate awareness of the debate.

88 These were the four 'humours' of classical medicine.

Seing there are Witches and Devils, there are also *immortal Souls* of the first, since the last does *contract for them*, and takes such *Pains* to *retain* them: So that the *Saducee*'s tho they have a judicial *blindness* in their *reason*, are hereby rendred inexcusable by *very sense*. *Evill Books* which stirr up and ensnare curious *Fantasies*, that are seldom accompanyed with accurrat *Judgments* (the Soul's looking *outward* diverting it from dyving *into* the deepths of truth) are to be restrained: And also such ridiculous Pamphlets as no doubt by the Instigation of Satan, have lately been sent abroad, of design to frustrat any good use which might be made of such rare Providences as are contained in the ensueing Narrative, by *Forging Others*, or *Disguising this*.

This has been delayed so long to be published; partly, that there might be the more *narrow* Scrutiny made into the Matters of Fact; and partly, by some *Accidents* which did retard it. In it the Reader is not to expect any Accuracy of *Stile*; because the designed *Curtness* did occasion the wraping up of *much Matter* in *small Bounds*; and the punctual Exactness of *Truth* in every Circumstance was the *chief* Aim: So that other Defects ought to be the less quarrelled. {*p. x*}

THE NARRATIVE

IT was about the end of *August* One Thousand Six Hundred Ninety Six, when the first Rise and Occasion was given, (so far as can be known) to these strange Things that befel the Child, who is the Subject of this Narrative; and the Manner was thus.

Christian Shaw, Daughter to a Gentleman of good account called *John Shaw* Laird of *Bargarran*, in the Parish of *Erskine*, within the Shire of *Renfrew*; a smart lively Girl, and of good Inclinations, about Eleven Years of Age, perceiving one of the Maids of the House, named *Catharine Campbel*, to steal and drink some Milk, she *told* her Mother of it; whereupon the Maid *Campbel* (being a young Woman of a *proud* and *revengeful* Temper, and much addicted to *Cursing* and *Swearing* upon any light occasion, and otherways given to *Purloining*) did, in a most hideous Rage, thrice imprecat the *Curse of GOD* upon the Child; and at the same time did thrice utter these horrid words, *The Devil harle* (that is *Drag*) *your Soul thorow Hell*. This past upon *Munday*, *August* 17. in presence of several Witnesses, who afterwards made Evidence of it.

Upon the *Friday* following, being August 21. about Sun-rising, one *Agnes Naismith*, an old Widow woman, ignorant, and of a *Malicious* Disposition, addicted to *Threatnings*, (which sometimes were observed to be followed with fatal Events) who lived in the Neighbourhood, came to *Bargarran*'s House; where finding the Child *Christian* in the Court with her younger Sister, she ask'd *How the Lady and young Child did*, and how old the young sucking Child was; to which *Christian* replied, *What do I know*? Then *Agnes* ask'd, *How her self did, and how old she was*; to which she answered, that *she was well, and in the eleventh Year of her Age*.

On the *Saturday*-night thereafter, being *August* 22. the Child went to Bed in good health; but so soon as she fell asleep, began to struggle and cry, *Help, Help*: And then suddenly got up, and did fly over the top of a Resting-bed, where she was lying (her Father, Mother, and others being in the Room, and to their great Astonishment and Admiration) with such violence, that probably her Brains had been dasht out, if a Woman, providentially standing by, and supported by a Door at her back, had not broke the force of the Childs motion; who being laid in another Bed, remained stiff and insensible as if she had been dead, for the space of half an Hour; but for Fourty eight Hours thereafter could not sleep, crying out of violent Pains thorow her whole Body, and no sooner began to sleep or turn drowsie but seemed greatly affrighted, crying still *Help, Help*. {*p. xi*}

After this the pain fixt in her left Side, and her Body was often so bent and rigid, as she stood like a Bow on her Feet and Neck at once, and continued without power of Speech, except in some very short intervals, for eight days; during which time, she had scarce half an Hours intermission together, the Fits taking her suddenly, and both coming on and going off by a Swerff or short deliquium,[89] but appeared perfectly well and sensible in the *Intervals*.

But about the midle of *September*, her fits returned in a manner *differing* from the former, wherein she seemed to fight and strugle with some thing that was invisible to spectators, and her Action appear'd as if she had been defending her self from some who were assaulting or attempting to hurt her, and this with such force that four strong Men were scarcely able to hold her; and when any of the People present toucht any part of her Body, she did cry and schreek with such vehemence, as if they had been killing her, but could not speak.

Before this time as she was seized with the trouble, her Parents had called for Physicians from Pasley, *viz. John Whyte* Apothecary a near relation, and afterwards Doctor *Johnstoun*; who took Blood and applyed several things both at first, and afterward, without any discernable Effect upon the Patient either to the better or worse: And she all the while of these Later Fitts being afflicted with extraordinary risings and fallings of her Belly; like the motion of a pair of Bellows! and such strange movings of her Body as made the whole Bed she lay on shake, to the great consternation of Spectators.

Some dayes thereafter was an alteration in her Fitts, so far, that she got speaking, during the time of them; and while she was in the fits, fell a crying, that *Katharine Campbel and Agnes Nasmith were cutting her side, and other parts of her Body*; Which parts were in that time violently Tormented. And when the fit was over she still averred, *that she had seen the same Persons doing the same things* which she complained of while under the fit (it being remarkable that in the intervals she was still as well and sensible as ever) and would not believe but

[89] 'Swerff' and 'deliquium' both mean 'swoon'.

that others present saw them at well as she! In this condition she continued with some but not very considerable variation either as to the fits or Intervals, for the space of a Moneth.

After which time she was conveighed to *Glasgow*, where Doctor *Birsbane* a Phisician deservedly famed for skill and experience, did by *Mr. Henry Marshell* Apothecary apply Medicine to her; after which having stayed in *Glasgow* about ten dayes and being brought home to the Countrey, she had near a fortnights intermission. But then her fits returned, with this difference, that she knew when they were acoming by a pain in her left side, which she felt before they came, and in these Fits her Throat was prodigiously drawn down toward her breast, and her Tongue back into her Throat; her whole Body becoming stiff and extended as a Dead Corpse without sense or motion: And some times her Tongue was drawn out of her Mouth over her Chin to a wonderful length, her Teeth setting together so fast upon it, that those present were forced to thrust something betwixt her Teeth for saving her Tongue. And it was oft observed that her Tongue was thus tortured when she essayed to *Pray*. And in this condition she was for some time, with sensible intervals wherein she had perfect health, and could give a full account of what she was heard to utter while in the Fit. For several dayes these Fits continuing with some variation, her Parents resolved to return her to *Glasgow*, that she might there have the more conveniency of being under the Doctors Oversight and Care, for further discerning the nature of her trouble and making use of the most probable natural remedies. But being on her way {*p. xii*} in her Grand-mothers house at *Northbar*, she did thrust or spit out of her mouth parcels of Hair, some curled, some plaited, some knotted, of different colours, and in large quantities: And thus she continued to do with several swooning Fits every quarter of an hour, both in her passage to *Glasgow* which was by Boat on *Thursday*, *Nor.* twelfth: And when she was in *Glasgow* for the space of three dayes ensuing she put as frequently hair out of her Mouth and in as great quantities, as the first day; her former swerfing or swooning Fits recurring as often thorow out the day as before: And thereafter from *Munday* to *Thursday* following she put out of her Mouth Coal-cinders about the bigness of Chasnuts, some whereof were so hot that they could scarcely be handled, one of which Dr. *Birsbane* being by her when she took it out of her Mouth, felt to be hoter then the heat of any ones body could make it. Then for the space of two days in these swooning Fits, as formerly, there was put or taken out of her Mouth straw in great quantities, tho but one straw at once folded up together which when put out returned to its length, was found to be both long and broad, and it was remarkable that in one of them there was a little small pin found. Thereafter were put out of her mouth bones of various sorts and sizes, as bones of Fowls and small bones of the heads of Kine,[90] and then some small sticks of Candle

[90] 'Kine': cows.

firr (a sort of Firr in this Countrey that burns like Candle) one of which was about three or four inches long; which, when any, upon sight of either bones or sticks took hold of to pull out, they found them either held by her Teeth set together upon them, or forcibly drawn back into her Throat; particularly *Archibald Bannatine* of *Kellie* younger[91] observing a bone in her mouth like a duck shank or leg bone, and essaying to pull it out, he declared he found something drawing it back into her throat; so that it took a deal of force to get it pulled out. It is to be noticed that she never knew how these things were brought into her mouth, and when they were got out of it she immediatly recovered of her fit, for that time. After this she put out of her mouth some quantity of unclean Hay intermixed with dung, as if it had been taken out of a Dunghil; which was so stinking that the Damsel could not endure the nauseating taste and vile relish those things produced in her mouth, which did necessitate her still to rinse her mouth with Water after the putting of that sort of matter out of it. Then for more then a days space she put out of her Mouth a number of wild-fowls feathers; after that a gravel-stone which in the judgment of beholders had been passed by some person in a gravel fit; with some small whitestones and a whole nut gall (wherewith they use to dye and to make Ink) together with lumps of Candle-grease, and egg-shells; during which time she continued as formerly in her recurring swooning fits with some intervals wherein she was in perfect health: Of all which there were many Famous[92] Witnesses who in that City (besides those who were continually with her) came frequently to visit her.

It is to be noticed, that the Damsel at the time of the putting out of her Mouth the Sticks abovementioned, being in Bed about eight a Clock at Night, told, she was to be grievously tormented with sore Fits that Night, which accordingly fell out: For a litle thereafter, she fell into a long swoon, wherein she had no use of any Sense, either of Hearing, Seeing, or Feeling, so as tho oft times the Beholders called to her with a loud Voice, moving also and tossing her body, all was to no purpose, and when the Laird of *Kelly* younger abovenamed, to try the Truth, gave her a very sore pinsh in the Arm, she had no Sense of it in the time. After recovery from the Swoon (but yet continuing {*p. xiii*} in the Fit) she fell a reasoning with *Katharine Campbel* after this manner,

91 Archibald Bannatyne of Kellie's wife was Janet McGilchrist, a sister of Christian Shaw's mother. Archibald himself was a local laird, a commissioner of supply for Renfrewshire in 1696: *Laws and Acts made in the Sixth Session of the First Parliament of our most High and Dread Soveraign, William* (Edinburgh, 1696), 9. He was designated 'younger' because his father James Bannatyne of Kellie was still alive (James had been a commissioner of supply in 1689: Records of the Parliaments of Scotland to 1707, online, 1689/3/189).

92 'Famous': reputable.

Thou sit'st there with a stick in thy Hand to put in my Mouth; but thorow GOD's strength thou shalt not get leave: Thou art permitted to Torment me; but I trust in GOD, thou shalt never get my Life, tho it's my Life thou design'st. *And at the time calling for a Bible and Candle, said,* come near me Katie, and I'l let thee see where a godly Man was given up to Satan to be Tormented: But GOD keeped his Life in His own Hand: And so I trust in GOD, thou shalt never get my Life, and all that thou shalt be permitted to do unto me, I hope thorow GOD's mercy, shall turn to my Advantage. This Man was Rob'd of All, and Tormented in Body, and had nothing left him but an ill Wife. Come near me Katie, and I'l read it to thee. *And reading that Passage of* Job, *when she came to the place where his Wife said to him* Curse GOD and Die, *the Damsel considering these words alitle, said,* O! what a Wife has this been, that bids her Good man *Curse God and Die*? she who should have been a comfort to him in his Trouble, turned a Cross to him?

Then after reading of the Chapter to the end, she lookt towards the foot of the Bed and said.

Now *Katie*, what think'st thou of that? Thou seest, for all the power the Devil got over *Job* he gain'd no Ground on him; and I hope he shall gain as litle on me. Thy Master the Devil deceives thee, he is a bad Master whom thou serv'st, and thou shalt find it to thy Smart, except thou Repent before thou Die; there is no Repentance to be had after Death: I'l let thee see *Katie*, there is no Repentance in Hell,

And turning over the Book citeing Luk: 16. Chap. *near the letter*[93] *end thereof, and reading the samen over, said,*

Katie thou seest, there is no Repentance in Hell, for this Rich Man besought *Abraham* to testify to his five Brethren, that they come not to the place of Torment, where he was; but Repent and turn to the LORD, for there is no winning out if once they come there; now *Katie*, thou hear'st this, what think'st thou of it? I'l let thee hear another place, which should pierce thy very Heart, *And turning over the Book, said she would read about* Adam *and* Eve *to her*, thou know'st *Katie*, the serpent the Devil thy Master, thought to have ruined Mankind at the beginning, his Malice was so great at that blessed State wherein they were then, seeing himself cast down from all hopes of Mercy, used all means possible for him to subvert their happiness, by suggesting to them fair Promises, and a prospect of Advantage to them before their Eyes, in causing them Eat of that forbidden Fruit; whereby they and their Posterity fell from that Estate wherein they were; and were made Subject to GOD's Curse for ever: But GOD did not suffer them to be at this stance, but of his infinit Mercy shewed to them a better way, whereby

93 'letter': latter.

> they might have Life Eternal by revealing to them that blessed Promise, *the Seed of the Woman shall bruise the Head of the Serpent*. Now *Katie*, what think'st thou of that Promise? But have mind of this, thou'lt get no Advantage by it, it's not made to thee, who hast renounced GOD's Service, and taken on with the Devil; thou art his Slave, thou deny'st this; but I know thou art a Hypocrite; for I remember, when thou wast in my Mothers House, thou bought a Catechism, upon a pretence to learn to Read, to cloak thy Sin: Wil't thou hear me, know'st thou the reward of the Hypocrit? I'l let thee hear it; I remember *Mr. William Gillies*[94] was Lecturing the other day upon the 23 of *Mathew*, where many a wo is pronounced against the Hypocrit, Eight dreadful Wo's here, *Katie*, and some of them belongs to thee: But I'l tell thee more, know'st thou the reward of the Hypocrit, they shall be cast into the Lake that burns {*p. xiv*} for ever, that's their Portion; do'st thou hear this now? Thou turn'st thy Back to me, when I am telling the truth; if I were reading a Story-Book, or telling a Tale to thee, thou would'st hear that. Remember it will be thy Portion too, if thou do not Repent, and Confess, and seek Mercy.

Again turning over the Book, she read about Pilat saying,

> Pilat he made a shew of cleansing himself of CHRISTS Blood, he wash'd his Hands and declar'd himself Innocent; but for all his washing, he had a foul Heart; he would not loss his Office for the saving of CHRISTS Life: He knew well enough that CHRIST was an innocent Person; but he preferred his Honour before CHRIST; Therefore to please the Jews, and to quench the strugling in his Conscience, he washt his Hands, and then delivered CHRIST to be Crucified by them.

Thus she continued for more then two Hours space, reasoning at this Rate, and exhorting her to Repent, quoting many places of Scripture thorow the Revelation and Evangelists. And when any offered to pull her Bible from her, she uttered horrid Schreeks and Out-crys, saying, *She would never part with her Bible as long as she liv'd, she would keep it in spight of all the Devils.*

Before we pass from this, it will be needful to give the Reader advertisement of some things. 1. That while she call'd for her Bible and a Candle she neither heard nor saw any of those Persons who were then actually and discernably present in the Room with her, and that *Katharine Campbel* to whom she directed her speech was not discernably present to any other Body but her self. And that pinch she got in her insensible fit, she found and complain'd of the pain of it in that part afterward, but knew not how she came by it, nor

94 No minister of this name is known. Perhaps this is a mistake for Neil Gillies, minister of the Tron Kirk, Glasgow, who is later mentioned as one of those who took part in prayers at Bargarran.

blamed any of her tormentors for it. 2. That these words set down as spoken by her, were the very same both for words and order as nearly as they could be gathered and remembred by the hearers, without any addition of their own. 3. That altho she was a Girle of a pregnant Spirit above her age, and had much of the Scriptures, and withal had pretty good understanding, above what might be expected of one of her years, of the foundamental principles of Religion taught in the Catechisms; yet we doubt not but in so strong a Combat, the Lord did by His good Spirit graciously affoord her a more then ordinary measure of Assistance, both now and at other times in the like debates.

Sometime after the putting out of her mouth the trash above-mentioned she fell into extreamly violent fits, with lamentable crying; four Persons being hardly able to withhold her from Climbing up the Walls of the Chamber, or from otherwayes doing her self hurt, mean time having no power of speech, while in the fit, but her back and the rest of her Body grievously pained: In which condition she continued four of five days with the usual sensible intervals: In which she declared, that four men *Alexander* and *James Andersons*, and other two (of whom she gave particular and exact marks, but knew not their names) were tormenting her. It was observ'd that many of these she named were known to be Persons of ill fame, as these two Persons last nam'd were: It is also remarkable, that for some time she knew not the name of the said *Alexander Anderson*, till one day he came a begging to the door of the house, where the Damsel was, whom she seeing, immediatly cryed out, *that was he whom she had seen among the Crew*.

After this she fell into other Fits, wherein she saw the forenamed Persons with some others, and heard and saw several things that past among them. Particularly, she sometimes told when she was to take the fits, how often she would {*p. xv*} take them, (which fell out accordingly) with some discourses that were among them relating to her self and others.

About the eight of *December*, being brought home again from *Glasgow*, and having had six or seven days respite from her fits, she afterwards fell into frightful and terrifying fits: The occasion whereof she declar'd to be, her seeing the Devil in prodigious and horrid shapes, threatning to devour her, and then she would fall dead and stiff with all the parts of her Body distended and stretcht out as a Corpse without sense or motion; which fits as they came suddenly on without her knowledge, so she did as suddenly recover and grew perfectly well; and they usually came on when she essayed to pray. In which time also other fits took her more sensibly, she knowing when they were a coming, how long they would continue, and when they would return: In which fits her eyes strangely altered, and turned in her head to the admiration[95] of Spectators, with a continual painful working about her heart, sometimes her joynts were complicat and drawn together, and her

[95] 'admiration': astonishment.

fore head drawn forcibly about toward her shoulders; which fits she took by first falling into a Swoon, and after her violent fits instantly recovered after the same manner. During this time the fits altered again as to their times of coming and continuance; in which she sometimes endeavoured to bite her own fingers, or any thing else that came in her way, also when she saw the Persons before mentioned, one or two of them about her, pointing them out to the Persons present with her, tho by them unseen, and sometime declaring that she had hold of them by their Cloaths. Particularly. *December*, 17, She being in a sore fit she cry'd out of several Persons that were tormenting her; and being in the bed, grasped with her hands towards the foot of it, and cry'd out, that she had got a grip of the sleeves of one J. P's. Jerkin (or Jacket) which was, as she said, duddie, (that is ragged or tattered) at the elbows: And in that very instant the Damsels Mother and Aunt heard the sound of the rending or tearing of a Cloth, but saw or felt nothing, only found in each of the Damsels hands which were fast closed when they got them opened, a bit of red Cloth, looking as torn off a Garment; of which kind of Cloath there had been none in the Room at that time nor in the whole house nor near it, that any knew of. Another particular she told was, that there was such an one among the Crew going to prick her Tongue, which thereupon was instantly pull'd back into her Throat, she lying dumb for a considerable space. Sometimes upon her recovery from her Fits she told that she heard several things spoken and communed among her afflicters, but durst not make them known; because they threatned to Torment her after this, or the other manner, if she should make them known, and accordingly when by her Mother or others she was prevailed with to begin to tell them instantly the Torment fell out as was threatned. She told further that her Tormentors appear'd to her usually with Lights and strange sorts of Candles, which were frightful to her to look to.

Thus she continued till the first of *January*. 1697, not only in the fits forementіon'd with some alterations, but fell likewayes by swooning into light Fits, wherein she continued for two or three hours together, sometimes more, sometimes less, with very short Intervals, in which Fits she did not much complain of pain; but had a great palpitation in her breast, and sometimes in other parts of her Body strange and unaccountable motions, which continued in a greater or lesser degree during the whole time of the Fit, wherein she was somewhat light, and not so solid in her mind as as at other times; tho in the Intervals {*p. xvi*} of these, as of all other fits she was sufficiently composed; which Fits, as all the rest, came suddenly on and went as suddenly off by a Swoon or Swerf.

Before we proceed further in the Relation, let it be noticed first, that the foresaid *Agnes Naismith*, being brought by the Parents a second time to see the Damsel, did (tho not desired) pray for her, *viz. that the Lord God of Heaven and Earth might send the Damsel her health and try out the Verity*: After which, the Damsel declared that tho the said *Agnes* had formerly been very troublesome to her;

yet, from that time forth she did not more appear to her, as her Tormentor; but upon the contrary, as she apprehended, defending her from the fury of the rest. 2. It is further here to be noticed that the fore nam'd *Katharine Campbel*, could by no means be prevailed with to pray for the Damsel, but upon the contrary when desired by some, cursed them and all the Family of *Bargarren*, and in particular the Damsel and all that belonged to her, withal adding this grievous Imprecation; *The Devil let her never grow better, nor any concern'd in her, be in a better condition then she was in, for what they had done to her*. Which words she spoke before diverse famous Witnesses. 3. That *Bargarren* having prevailed with the Sheriff deput of the Shire, to imprison the said *Katharine Campbel*; she from the time of her Imprisonment, never appear'd to the Damsel (tho formerly she had ordinarly appear'd as one of her most violent Tormentors) except once or twice, at which times it was found upon after enquiry, that she was not in the Tolbooth but either in the Jaylors house, or had liberty granted her to go out to Church.[96] 4. That at the time when the Damsel did put out her mouth the hair and other trash as above related, *Katrine Campbel* being taken into custody, there was found in her pocket a ball of hair of several colours, which was afterwards thrown into the Fire, after which time the Damsel put no more hair out of her Mouth. And it is to be further noticed that she said, she heard amongst the Crew, when tormenting her, that *Katharine Campbel* made that Ball of hair found in her pocket, of the hair of the Damsels head which had been cut when her trouble began, and which did agree in colour, &c. when compared.

Upon the first day of *January* about ten aclock at night, she fell by swoonings into Fits differing from the former, in that, after the swooning fit was over, she lay quiet, as if she had been dead, making no motion at all with her Body in the Bed; yet at the same time these present heard her mournful talking, but with a low and hardly audible Voice, and repeating several Storys in meeter which they thought to be Expressions of the Rise and Progress of her own trouble; and thus she continued (still withall naming some of the forementioned Persons) till her Parents and others offered to Rouze her, by Touching and Moving her body. Whereupon instantly she uttered horrid Schreeks, and cry'd as if she had been pierced thorow with Swords, and assaulted for her Life. After which she fell a Singing, Leaping, and Dancing for a long time, laughing with a loud Voice, in an unusual manner, tearing down the Hingings of the Bed, and pulling off her Head-cloaths and Neck cloaths; in which Extravagances she was acted with such Force and Strength, that her Father and Minister tho joyning their whole Strength together, could not get her Dancing and Leaping hindered. But after Prayer, the Minister finding her Composed, enquired if she remembered what she had done in time of the Fit; to which she reply'd,

96 This last clause, beginning 'except once or twice', is an interpolation not found in the manuscript 'Informatory Accompt'.

That she distinctly remembered her miscariages, and in speciall her Singing and Dancing, saying withall, that the Witches enclosing her in a Ring (or Circle) and Dancing and Singing about her, was the occasion of her Dancing, which *{p. xvii}* she then gladly performed with the rest. For some days after she had Fits much after this manner, with some variation: In one of which Fits, as she was tearing off her Head-dress cloaths, her Parents resolving to see what would be the event, did make no hinderance to her: Whereupon she stript her self of all her Cloaths that were upon her, not leaving so much as her Smock upon her Body, if that had been permitted.[97]

After this toward or about the Eleventh of *January*, she fell into Fits different from the former, in which she was suddenly carried away from her Parents and others that were about her, with a sudden flight, and in the first of these (to their great amazement) thorow the Chamber and Hall down a long winding Stair toward the Tower-gate, with such a swift and unaccountable motion, that it was not in the power of any to prevent her, her Feet not touching the Ground, so far as any of the Beholders could discern, being heard in her motion to laugh in an unusual manner: But by Divine Providence the Gate being shut, her motion was stopt till such time as some of the Family could overtake her, who endeavouring to carry her back, found her instantly fall as one dead and become stiff: In which posture, being brought back to the Chamber, she lay for a considerable space. And being recover'd she did declare, that there were about the number of Nine or Ten Persons who had carried her away in a Shue (as she term'd it, that is as one swinging upon a Rope) wherein she then took pleasure, her Feet not at all touching the Ground, to her apprehension.[98]

The Night following she was suddenly carried away, as before, from her Parents and others who were about her, thorow the Chamber and Hall, and sixteen large steps of a winding Stair up, toward the top of the House! where she met with Apparitions of strange and unaccountable things, but was carried down again as she thought in a shue or swing, asserting after her recovery that she met upon the Stair the number of six Women and four Men, and by them was carried toward the Gate again, where accordingly she was found, and was carried up as formerly, all the parts of her Body distended and stiff as one Dead; in which posture she lay for some time, and when recovering, declared, that both now and formerly, she had endeavoured to open the Gate, and that those she saw about her were helping her, with a design to get her to the Court to drown her in the Well, which she said she heard them saying among themselves, they intended to do, and that then the World would believe she had destroyed herself. It is observable that (these

[97] The phrase 'if that had been permitted' is an interpolation not found in the manuscript 'Informatory Accompt'.

[98] 'to her apprehension': as she experienced it.

kind of Fits continuing with her for some few dayes) in one of them she was stop't at the Gate, and found in the foremention'd Posture which was neither Locked nor Barred; yet could they not get it oppened tho both she and her Tormentors endeavoured it.

Before we proceed in the Relation, it is not to be omitted that as soon as the Damsels affliction was observ'd to be extraordinary and preternatural there were (besides times formerly set a part in a more private way) at the desire of the Parents and Minister, and by the Presbytries special order, a Minister or two appointed to meet one day of every Week at the house of *Bargarran* to joyn with the Family, the Minister of the Parish and other good Christians of the Neighbourhood, in Fasting and Praying which usually fell to be on the *Tuesday*. And upon the 12*th* of *January* it being the turn of Mr. *Patrick Simpson* a Neighbour Minister to be there; when he came to the house he found both the Minister of the Parish, and the Brother who was to joyn with him had been necessarly withdrawn; yet resolved to carry on the Work with assistance of three Elders, some other good People being present. When he first saw the Damsel {*p. xviii*} after he came to the house, he found her under some lesser Fits which came and went off quickly, and when Prayer began she was quiet and sober during the same, but in time of singing the 93 *Psalm*, she fell into a sore Fit, of greater continuance, first Laughing then making some sound like Singing, after that pulling her head Cloaths down over her Face, and lastly turning so outragious in her motions that her Father could scarce get her holden with his whole strength, but behoved to ly over upon the bed with her in his Arms untill the Fit abated: After her Recovery from which, she was quiet and composed all the time of Prayer; and while the Minister Lectur'd on *Mark*, 9. from 14 *verse* and forward to *verse*, 30. was very Attentive, carefully looking in her Bible the Scriptures quoted, so all along both in time of Prayer and Singing untill the whole Religious exercise was ended, and some Refreshment after the same taken, at the end of which she told the Company, she had something to tell which she heard some among her Tormenters saying, which she durst not reveal; But the Minister, and her Mother urging her to be free and not to obey the Devil, she said, she would tell it her Mother in her ear. Then coming from the other side of the Table, and placing her self betwixt her Mother and Aunt she began to Whisper in her Mothers Ear; but before she got a Sentence fully pronunced, she fell into a violent Fit, so as her Mother and those next her could scarcely hold her till the Violence thereof began to abate, and then her Mother told that she was speaking of a Meeting and a Feast they had spoken of in the Orchard of *Bargarran*, but was able to say no more, and after Recovery, her Mother desiring her to tell the rest of it, and she beginning to Whisper in her Ear, as before, could not get one word uttered till she was seiz'd again of a Fit, as violent as the former. Whereupon the Minister perceiving her Torment, desired them to forbear any further troubling of her. Notice, that accordingly there was a Feast and Meeting in that Orchard about that time, of the Crew, acknowledged, and declared afterwards by three of them that Confessed themselves to have been there. *viz. Elizabeth Anderson, James* and *Thomas Lindsays*, they not knowing what either the Damsel had Spoken, or one of them what another had Confest relating thereunto.

About or within a little after this time, she was again suddenly carried from them in the former manner down a Stair, which goes off from a Corner of the Chamber to a Celler just below it, where her Brother and Sister were providentially gone down a little before, to bring some drink from the Celler, and already near the stair Foot, with a lighted Candle, which she soon put out: But they crying and holding her by the Head Cloaths, quickly discovered to the rest where she was. Upon which Mr. *Alexander King* Minister at *Bonnil* (being then in the Chamber) made haste down Stairs where he found her, but her Brother and Sister had lost hold of her, she having loosed her Head-cloaths and let them go; yet Mr. *King* having caught hold of her, keept her in his Arms till a lighted Candle was brought, and endeavoring to bring her up Stairs, did declare that he found something forcibly drawing her downwards, but he still keeping his hold, she fell stiff as one Dead upon the Stair and was in this Posture carried up and laid in Bed, where she lay a considerable space. And when recovered of the Fit, she declar'd that the Occasion of her going down Stairs with such Force, was, that the Crew had suggested to her while she was in the light Fits, that the Devil was in the Meal Chist in the Celler, and that if she would go down and put out the Candle, she might force him out of it. Notice here first, that when some Fits of this kind were ready to seize her, she sometimes {*p. xix*} gave advertisement thereof to these present with her, giving signs of her earnest desire of their help to prevent her Motion, which usually proved to be of good effect, wherein the Divine Mercy toward her is much to be observed. 2. It is also to be noticed, that about the time when she was in these flying Fits, she used to utter horrid Screeks and Out cryes not like those of Rational Creatures: In which time there was heard for three nights together, when the Damsel was a sleep in Bed, Schreeks and Out-cryes of the same kind in the Court, when none of the Family was without Doors, to the great afrightment of those who heard them, being that they exactly resembled the Crys and Skreeks the Damsel used to utter in the Fits; who afterwards in one of her Intervals hearing some of the Family talking of those Crys and Skreeks, and alledging they had been uttered by some wild beast or other, said to them, they were mistaken, for it was *Margaret*. And two others of the name of *Margaret* call'd by the Crew their *Maggi's*, had uttered these Skreeks, the Devil having promised to them at that time to carry her out of the House to them, that they might drown her in the Well, where there were eighteen more waiting for her.

After this she fell into freting and angry fits (as she term'd them) in which her humor was cross to all that those about her could either say or do, nothing proving to her satisfaction, but every thing displeasing, (her former fits withal now and then seizing her) but when restored to a right composure of mind, she declar'd that her Tormentors about her did still suggest to her and advise her to go to such and such remote places of the house her alone, and bring with her a Snood (which is a head-lace such as Women ty up their hair with) or a Cravat or some such thing, promising her rough Almonds or some kinds of sweetmeats which they nam'd to her, and for that end, to bring her apron with her to hold them in, and accordingly when seiz'd again with fits of this nature did resolutly endeavour to repair to these places, having a Snood or Cravat and her Apron with her, and would suffer none to be in her Company, which put her Parents and others to a necessity of detaining her by force, and she being thus prevented, uttered hideous schreeks and outcryes, of which in this sort of fits she was seldom free.

Thursday, *January 14th*, at night a young Lass or Girle appear'd to her with a scabbed face amongst the rest of her Tormentors, telling her she was to come to the house to morrow about ten aclock, and forbidding her to reveal it.

The next day being *January 15th*, in the afternoon the Damsel earnestly enquired at her Mother and the rest of the Family what Beggars had come to the gate that day, and of what Countenance and visage they were? But the Family not knowing her design in such a question, gave no heed unto it; yet she still insisting and being in Company with her Mother and another Gentlewoman, about four aclock at night said to them, she thought she might tell them somewhat (the time being now past) she was forbidden to reveal; but beginning to tell she presently fell a crying that she was tormented and pricked thorow her whole Body; yet recovering from the fit, went on and told it; the thing she had to reveal was, that a scabbed fac'd Lass appear'd to her yester-night and was to be at the gate this day at ten a Clock. Whereupon the Servants being enquired at, what sort of beggers had been there that day, did declare among others, there had been a begger Wife at the door and a younger Woman or Lass with her who had Scabs on her Face, and receiv'd their Alms.

January, *16th*, and *17th*, When recovered of her swouning Fits, she put out of her Mouth a great number of Pins, which she declared *J. P.* {*p. xx*} had forc'd into her Mouth, and a Gentlewoman who had been always one of her most violent Tormentors.

January, 21. Her Fits altered again, after this manner, she would fall in them with heavy Sighs and Groans and hideous Outcryes, telling those about her that Cats, Ravens, Owles and Horses were destroying and pressing her down in the Bed: And at the same time her Mother and another Gentlewoman, being in the Room with her, did declare that immediatly after they had taken the Girle out of her Bed in this condition, they did see something moving under the Bed-cloaths as big as a Cat.

The same Morning in the interval of her Fits, she said, she heard her Tormentors Whisper amongst themselves, and suggest to one another, (naming *J. P.* the *Andersons* and others) that the Devil had promised and engaged to them, to carry her over the Hall Window, to the end they might Drown her in the Well which was in the court; and then they said the World would believe she had destroyed her self; and the same day and several dayes thereafter, when seiz'd with her Grievous Fits, did attempt with such force to get her self over that Window, that Spectators could scarce with their whole strength prevent her.

About this time, nothing in the World would so discompose her as Religious Exercises, if there were any discourses of God or Christ, or any of the things which are not seen and are Eternal, she would be cast into grievous Agonies; and when she assayed in her light Fits, to read any portion of the Scriptures, repeat any of the Psalms, or answer any Questions of our Catechisms (which she could do exactly well at other times) she was suddenly struck Dumb and lay as one stiff Dead, her Mouth opened to such a Wideness that her Jaw appeard to be out of joynt, and anone would clap together again with incredible Force. The same happened to her Shoulder blade, her Elbow, and Hand-wrists. She would at other times ly in a benum'd Condition, and be drawn together as if she had been ty'd Neck and Heels with Ropes; yet on a sudden would with such Force and Violence be pull'd up and Tear all about her, that it was as much as one or two could do, to hold her fast in their Arms: But when Ministers and other good Christians (seeing her in such intollerable Angoishes) made serious Application by Prayer to God, on her behalf, she got respite from her greivous Fits of this kind, and was ordinarly free of them during the time of Prayer, tho seiz'd of them before; and albeit usually when Ministers began to Pray she made great disturbance by idle lowd talking, Whistling, Singing, and Roaring, to drown the Voice of the person praying. Particularly *January* 22. She was more Turbulent then at other times she us'd to be, and continued some space after the Minister began to Pray, Singing and making a hideous Noise, fetching furious Blows with her Fist, and Kicks with her Feet at the Minister, uttering reproachful Talk of him, and calling him Dog, &c. Yet she being Compos'd, and her Fits being over before Prayer was ended, and the Minister when he had done, finding her Sober and a right Composure of Mind, enquired why she made such disturbance? To which she reply'd, she was forc't to do it by the Hellish Crue about her, and that she thought they were none of her own words that she uttered.

January 24th. She said some things relating both to herself and others had been suggested to her by her Troublers; but that they had threatned to Torment her, if she should offer to make them known. And accordingly she Essaying to express her Mind, was cast into two greivous Fits, in which she cry'd out of {*p. xxi*} violent pains; all the parts of her Body becoming Rigid and extended like a Corpse, her Head was twisted round, and if any offered by force to obstruct such dangerous Motion she seem'd to be upon, she would roar exceedingly; sometimes her Neck bone seem'd to be dissolv'd; and yet on a sudden became so stiff, that there was no moving of it; and when those greivous Agonys were over, she again Essay'd to express her Mind by Write, but to no purpose; for instantly she was cast into other two very greivous Fits, wherein she was struct Dumb, Deaf and Blind, and her Tongue drawn a prodigeous length over her Chin. And when the Fits were over, declar'd, the *Andersons*, *J. P.*, the Gentlewoman, and *I. D.* with the rest of the Hellish Crew, some of whom she could not name, had been Tormenting her in the Fits, and that there has been fifteen of them about the House all the last Night; but were now all gone, save one, who was to stay about the House till her Fits were over. And accordingly her Brother and Sister did declare; they saw that Morning a Woman in the Garden with a red Hood about her Head, sitting at the Root of an Aple-Tree; but *Bargarren* with most of the Servants being abroad, the Matter was not further search't.

The same day about Six at Night, she was seiz'd with variety of greivous Fits again, in which sometimes she lay wholly Senseless and Breathless, with her Belly swel'd like a Drum, as like a Woman with Child, her Eyes were pul'd into her Head so far, that Spectators thought she should never have us'd them more, sometimes when she was tying her own Neck-cloaths, her enchanted Hands would ty them so strait about her Neck, that she had strangled her self if Spectators had not given some Relief unto her; sometimes she was in hazard of burning her self in the fire, offering with violence to throw her self into the same. Divers time she did strick furious Blows at her near Relations in her Fits, she'd maintain Discourse with her Tormentors; and asking Questions concerning her self and others, received answer from them; which indeed none but her self perceiv'd: Reasoning particularly with one of them after this manner;

> O what ail'd thee to be a Witch! thou sai'st it is but three Nights since thou wast a Witch, O if thou would'st Repent, it may be GOD might give thee Repentance, if thou would'st seek it and Confess; if thou would desire me I would do what I could; for the Devil is an ill Master to serve, he is a Lyer from the beginning, he promises but he cannot perform. Then calling for her bible, she said, I'l let thee see where he promised to our first Parents, that they should not Die. *And reading the passage, said*, now thou seest he is a Lyer; for by breaking of the Commandment, they were made lyable to Death here and Death everlasting. O that's an Uncouth word; long Eternity never to have an end, never never to have an end: Had not GOD of his infinit Mercy ordain'd some to Eternal Life through JESUS CHRIST. The Devil makes thee believe thou wilt get great Riches by serving him; but come near,

and having uttered this word she lost power of Speech, her Tongue being drawn back into her Throat; yet beckning with her Hand to the Spectre to come near her, and turning over the Book, kep't her Eye upon that passage of Holy Scripture. *Job*. 27. 18. And pointing with her Finger at the place, and shaking her Head, turn'd over the Book again. And recovering Speech said,

> I'l let thee see where GOD bids us seek and we shall find, and reading over the place said, it is GOD that gives us every good Gift, we have nothing of our own, I submit to his will tho I never be better; for GOD can make all my trouble turn to my Advantage; according to his Word, Rom. 8. 28.

which {*p. xxii*} place she then read, and thus continued Reasoning, for the space of an Hour.

Sometimes she cry'd out of violent pain, by reason of furious Blows and Stroaks she had received from the Hands of her Tormentors, the Noise of which Stroaks bystanders distinctly heard, tho they perceiv'd not the Hands that gave them. One Night the Girle sitting with her Parents and others cry'd out. *something was wounding her Thigh*. Upon which, instantly her Mother puting her Hand in the Damsels pocket, found her folding Knife open'd, which had been folded, when put in her Pocket, but her Uncle not trusting the thing; did again put up the Knife and leaving it folden in her pock't, on a sudden she cry'd out as before, *the Knife was cutting her Thigh, being unfolded by the means of* I. P. and *others*, as she said: Upon which her Uncle searching her Pocket, again found the Knife open'd as formerly. This happened twice or thrice to the Admiration of the Beholders, tho they took special Notice that she nor any other visible Hand opened it.

January 25th. She was again seizd with her Swooning stiff Fits, with this remarkable Variation; her Throat was sometimes most prodigiously extended, and sometimes as strangely Contracted and Convel'd,[99] so that she appeard in palpable danger of being Choak't, and through the violence of pain in her Throat and difficulty of Breathing struggled with her Feet and Hands, as if some had been actually Strangling her, and could Speak or Cry none; with which kind of Fits she was frequently seiz'd for several days; and in the intervals did declare that the fore-mention'd persons, and others (whom she could not get then nam'd) were strangling her, and that the occasion of her not having power to speak or cry in the Fit, was a Ball in her Throat, which also was visible to Spectators; for they did clearly discern a Bunch in her Throat (while in the Fit) as bigg as a *Pullets* Egg which had almost Choak't her.

Sometimes she was kep't from eating her Meat; having her Teeth sett, when she carried any food to her Mouth. Diverse times also she was kept from Drinking, when at Meat; for no sooner could she taste the Drink, but she was in hazard to be Choak't thereby, and her self sometimes would have held the Cup so hard betwixt her Teeth, that it was not in the power of those

[99] 'Convel'd': wrenched.

with her to unloose it. And when any thing had fallen out amiss in the place where she was, as the falling and breaking of a Cup, and Body's receiving harm, and such like. She would fall a laughing and rejoyce extremely; which kind of Jollity was far from the Girl's temper when at her self.

February 1st. She Essaying to tell some things she had been forbidden by her Tormentors to make known, was handled with intolerable Torments. At the beginning of her Fits usually she would be kep't odly looking; sometimes toward the Chimney, sometimes towards other particular places in the Room, but could not always tell what she saw; yet for ordinary she'd Name such and such Persons, who, she said were then come to cast her into Fits. And when any desired her to cry to the LORD JESUS for help, her Teeth were instantly sett closs, her Eyes tuisted almost round in her Head, and she was thrown upon the Floor with the stiffness, and posture of one that had been some days laid for Dead: And on a sudden recovered again, and would weep bitterly, to remember what had befal'n her. The same day, when her Fits were over, she said, she now perceiv'd it was by the means of a Charm, that such Restraints were laid upon her that she could not tell what the Witches had forbidden her to make known, but the Charm might be found out (as she said) by searching for it beneath the Bed where she lay; and she having quickly done this her self, found (to the {*p. xxiii*} apprehension of Spectators) beneath the foresaid Bed, an inteir Egg-shell open in the end, which being instantly thrown into the Fire, did melt away after the manner of Wax, without any such Noise as Egg-shells use to make when burning in the Fire. After this the Girle said, she would not now be handled so severely, upon Essaying to make known what the Witches had forbidden her to tell, only her Tongue would be drawn back into her Throat, which accordingly happened. She did like ways inform her Friends of many things she had not liberty to do before the Charm was found out, particularly that her Tormentors had frequently solicited her to become a Witch her self, and promised her great Riches, and perfect Health also, to induce her thereunto. Which Tentation, she through the infinit Mercy of GOD still resisted, reasoning with them after this manner

> The Devil promises what he cannot perform, and granting he could fulfill his promises; yet I am sure from the Scriptures, Hell and the wrath of GOD will be the final reward of all such as yeild to this Wickedness.

To which she receiv'd this reply (which indeed none but her self perceiv'd) that

> Hell and the wrath of GOD so much talk't of, was not so formidable as was represented.

She also said, the Witches had Importunately urged her to give them her Consent, to take away the Life of her young Sister, who was at that time upon her Mothers breast; which Tentation also she was enabled thorow the Grace of God to resist. She told her Parents likeways, there had been a Charm laid upon the top of the House where her young Sister was (the Child having been sent out a nursing, by reason of the continued Affliction of the Family) and that the Charm had been plac'd upon the top of the House by *pinch'd Maggi*, who thereby did design the taking away of her Sisters Life; and that this was the Cause why she had so often for some Weeks before desired her Mother to bring home her Sister, constantly affirming, that the Child would daily decay as long as she stayed there: Whereupon her Parents observing the daily decay of the Infant; even to Skin and Bone, brought her home, where she recovered. And the Girle being asked how she came to the knowledge of these things? Reply'd, some thing speaking distinctly as it were above her Head, had suggested these and other things of that Nature to her.

February 2d. The Girle being in the Chamber with her Mother and others, was on a sudden struck with great Fear and Consternation; and fell a trembling upon the sight of *John Lindsay* in *Barcloch*, talking with her Father in the Hall. She said to her Mother, the foresaid *Lindsay* had been always one of her most violent Tormentors, and that she had been threatned with extreme Tortures, if she should offer to Name him; whereupon she was desired to go toward the place where he was, and touch some part of his Body in a way unknown to him, which she having done with some Aversation, was instantly seiz'd with extreme Tortures in all the parts of her Body. After which *Lindsay* was put to it, and Interrogat thereupon; but he giving no satisfying Answer, was desir'd to take the Damsel by the Hand, which he being unwillingly induc'd to do, she was immediatly upon his Touch cast into intolerable Anguishes, her Eyes being almost twisted round in her Head, and all the parts of her Body becoming Rigid and stiff, fell down in the posture of one that had been laid for some days Dead, and afterwards got up in a sudden, and tearing her Cloaths, threw her self with violence upon him, and when her Fits were over, Spectators did also take the Damsel by the Hand; yet no such effect followed. {*p. xxiv*}

About Six at Night there came an Old Highland fellow to *Bargarran*, who calling himself a weary traveller, said he behoov'd to Lodge there that Night, but the Servants refusing him Lodging, gave him something be way of Alms. At this time the Damsel being in the Chamber with her Mother and another Gentlewoman, said to her best apprehension there was one of the wicked Crew in or about the House at that time; whereupon her Mother made hast[e] with her Daughter down stairs toward the Kitchen. And finding there unexpectedly the Highland fellow, whom the Girle then accused as one of her Tormentors, she desired the Highland fellow to take her Daughter by the Hand, which he being urg'd to do, the Girle immediatly upon his Touch was grievously Tormented in all the parts of her body. And this falling out in divine providence, *Bargarran* caus'd secure him. The next Morning the Minister having come to *Bargarran* to visit the Damsel, and the matter being imparted to him, called for the Highland fellow, and having question'd him to and again[100] about this Matter without any satisfying Answer, brought the Child out of the Chamber covering her Face, and almost her whole Body with his Cloak, and giving signs to the Highland fellow to touch her in this posture, as he had ordered him before, without the Damsels knowledge, which he having done with great Aversion the Girle not knowing of his touch, was instantly cast into intollerable Agonys as formerly; yet others afterwards touching her, no such event followed. And when her Fits were over she besought the Highland fellow to allow her the Liberty for to discover and tell Persons that Haunted and Molested her, whom he had forbidden her to make known: Upon which the old Fellow looking at her with an angry Countenance, her Mouth was instantly stop't, and her Teeth sett: But being desired by those present to speak her mind freely; whether he would or not, at length reply'd, she fear'd to do it. And when thorow the importunity of the Lairds of *Dargavel* and *Porterfield* of *Fulwood*,[101] and some other Gentlemen there present, she Essay'd to declare her mind, she was seiz'd with her Fits again.

Before this time, the lamentable Case of the afflicted Damsel and Family had been represented to His Majesty's most Honourable Privy Council, who, upon serious Application made to them, worthily and piously granted a Commission to a Noble Lord and some worthy Gentlemen, to make enquiry into the same. By vertue of this Commission some suspected persons were seiz'd; particularly *February* 4. *Alexander Anderson* (an Ignorant, Irreligious Fellow, who had been always of evil Fame, and accused by the afflicted Damsel) by a special Order from the Commissioners for Enquiry, was apprehended and committed to Prison; as was also *Elizabeth Anderson* his Daughter, upon flagrant Presumptions of Witchcraft; for the other Year *Jean Fulton* her Grand-mother, an old scandalous Woman, being cited before the Kirk Session, and accus'd for hideous Cursing, and imprecating Mischief upon several persons, which had been followed with fatal Events; the fore-mentioned *Elizabeth Anderson* her Grand-child, who liv'd in the House with her, did declare before the Session, she had frequently seen the Devil in company with her Grand-mother, in the likeness of a small black Man, who usually did evanish on a sudden within the Walls of the House, when any Body came to the Door. Upon this Presumption was the said *Elizabeth Anderson* seiz'd with her Father, and committed to Custody; but at first most obstinatly denied accession any manner of way to the Sin of Witchcraft, until afterwards, when seriously importun'd and dealt with in the Prison by two Gentlemen, did, before she came to *Bargarran*'s *{p. xxv}* House, confess her Guilt, without *Bargarran*'s knowledge at that time. And that she had been at several meetings with the Devil and Witches, and amongst others, she did delate her own Father, and

[100] 'to and again' (like 'to and fro'): in different ways.
[101] John Maxwell of Dargavel and Alexander Porterfield of Fullwood.

the fore-mentioned High-land Fellow to have been active Instruments of the Girle's Trouble; and gave, before she was confronted with him, exact marks of this Highland body, and tho she declar'd she knew not his Name; yet when confronted with him did accuse him, and affirm he was the person she spoke of.

February 5th. A Quorum of the commissioners being met at *Bargarran*, and the persons then delated by *Elizabeth Anderson* to have been at Meetings with the Devil, and active instruments of the Damsels Trouble, *Viz, Alexander Anderson* her Father, *Agnes Nasmith, Margaret Fultoun, James Lindsay* alias Curat, *John Lindsay* alias Bishop, *Katharine Campbel*, were all of them (excepting *John Lindsay* alias Bishop, who was not then apprehended) confronted with *Christian Shaw* before the Lord *Blantyre* and the rest of the Commissioners at *Bargarran*, and several other Gentlemen of Note and Ministers then present, and accused by her as her Tormentors. And they having all severally touched her in presence of the Commissioners, she was at each of their touches seiz'd with grievous Fits, and cast into intolerable Anguishes, others then present also touching her the same way, but no such Effect followed. And it is remarkable, when *Katharine Campbel* touched the Girle, she was immediatly upon her touch seiz'd with more grievous Fits, and cast into more intolerable Torments then what followed upon the touch of the other accused persons, whereat *Campbel* herself being Damped and Confounded, tho she had formerly declined to Bless her, uttered these words; *The Lord God of Heaven and Earth Bless thee, and save thee both Soul and Body*; after which the Damsel when the Fits were over, in which she had lyen a most pitiful Spectacle did declare she was now loos'd, and that she might freely touch any of the accus'd persons, or they her after this without trouble, which accordingly upon tryal fell so out, and being enquired how she came to the knowledge of that, answered as formerly in the like Case, That some thing speaking distinctly as it were above her Head, suggested this to her; And likewise, usually gave her the knowledge of the Names of her Tormentors, and Places in which they liv'd.

February 6. The Girle being sez'd with sore Fits, some thing was seen in her Mouth, to the Judgment of Spectators like pieces of Orange Pills[102] invisibly convey'd into her Mouth, which she seem'd in her Agonys to be Chewing, and having got down her Throat, as those present apprehended, she did fall down Dead and stiff, as if she had been Choak't struggling with her Feet and Hands, as if at the last Gasp, her Throat swelling in a Prodigious manner; to the affrightment of Spectators, and when recovered, but yet in the light Fit; she'd say, O it was a very sweet Orange Pill which I got from the Gentlewoman, and did constantly affirm the same, declaring also that there had been others there present with the Gentlewoman, particularly *Margaret L.* or *pinch't Maggi*, whose Sirname she had neither Power nor Liberty to express, neither durst

[102] 'Orange Pills': (confectionery made with) orange peel.

she offer to do it, lest she should be Tormented as was threatned, and alwayes fell out when she Essay'd to do it, either by speaking or writing, which had appear'd the day before in presence of the Commissioners.

About this time, *Thomas Lindsay* a young Boy not yet Twelve Years of Age, was sez'd, upon flagrant Presumptions of Witchcraft; he had said before several credible Persons, the Devil was his Father, and if he pleas'd he could fly in the likeness or a Crow upon the Mast of a Ship, he sometimes caus'd a Plough stand {*p. xxvi*} and the Horse break the Yoke upon the pronouncing of some words, and turning himself about widder-shins; that is a turning himself round from the right hand to the left, contrar to the Natural course of the Sun. This he would do upon the desire of any Body who gave him a half-peny. Upon these and the like flagrant Presumptions he was apprehended, who at first tho he continued most obstinat in denyal; yet afterwards confess'd to the Minister in his own House before famous Witnesses, compact with the Devil, and that he had receiv'd the insensible mark from the Devil, which is visible upon his Body: As also, that he had been at several meetings with the Devil and Witches, where he said were present, his Brother *James* with others, and particularly those who had been delated by *Anderson*. This he confest, with some other wickedness of this kind before he was committed to Custody in *Bargarran house*.

After this *Bargarran* made diligent search for *James Lindsay*, elder Brother to *Thomas*, having been all along accused by the afflicted Damsel as one of her Troublers, whom she call'd the Glei'd, or squint Ey'd, Elff (as he was indeed) for that was the Name the Crue about her gave him, who when he was brought upon the place, tho' he did at first most obstinatly deny his Guilt, yet at length thorow the Endeavours of Mr. *Patrick Simpson*, a Neighbour Minister, ingenuously confessed the Guilt he was charged with, and in his Confession did agree in every material Circumstance with the other two, tho he knew not what they had confest, he having not seen them before his Confession, nor had he any occasion of Information in conference with others there-anent, being immediatly brought to the place from the Tolbooth of *Glasgow*, where he had been some Weeks before that time in Prison as a vagabond Begger, upon a design to have sent him to Forreign Plantations.

A more particular Account of what they freely Confess'd and Acknowledg'd before the Commissioners for Enquiry, we have for the satisfaction of the Reader subjoin'd to the Narrative; with an Abstract of the Report made by the Commissioners, to the Lords of His Majesty's most Honourable Privy Council, concerning the whole Affair.

February 11. There was by the Presbitry's appointment a publick Fast kept upon the Damsels account in the Church of *Erskine*, in which Mr. *Turner* Minister of the place begun the Work with Prayer, expounding *Rev.* 12. from Ver. 7. to Ver. 13. Mr. *James Hutchison* Minister at *Killellan* took the next turn of Prayer, and did preach upon 1 *Pet.* 5. 8. and Mr. *Simpson* concluded the Work, preaching upon *Mat.* 17. 20, 21. where the Girl was present all day; but before she came to Church that Morning she told, that while she was in one of her Fits the Night before, she heard the Devil speaking of that publick Fast, and what Ministers were to be there, and that old Man Mr. *James Hutchison* should stumble, and his Peruick fall off as he went up to the pulpit, and all the people should laugh at him, and he should break his neck in going home. And when she came out of the Church after the Forenoon's Work, she said, the Devil was a Liar, for no such thing fell out as he had threatned. She was all day very quiet in Church; altho being in some of her light Fits some Spectres appear'd in time of the publick Work, which she told of thereafter.[103]

About six at Night there were present in the Chamber with the Damsel, Mr. *Simpson* with his Wife, Lady *Northbarr* and others, discoursing and conferring about her Case; and while they were thus conferring together, she told them, she would gladly make some things known if she durst for her Tormenters; {*p. xxvii*} and afterwards essaying to do it, was instantly seiz'd with a violent Fit; in which she leapt straight up, and appear'd as if she had been choak'd, so that it was as much as one or two could do, to hold her fast in their Arms: And when the Fit was over, Mr. Simpson going about Family Worship, did expound *Psalm* 110. and speaking of the limited power of the Adversaries of our Lord JESUS CHRIST, from the latter part of Ver. 1 she was on a sudden seiz'd with another grievous Fit, in which she put out of her Mouth some Blood, which rais'd Grounds of Fear and Jealousy[104] in the Minds of Spectators, that something in her Mouth hurting her had been the occasion of it; yet they could not get her Mouth opened, tho they used means to open the same, her Teeth being closs set. And in the interval of the Fit she being ask'd, if she found any thing in her Mouth that had been the occasion of her putting out of Blood; she reply'd, she found nothing, nor knew the Cause thereof; but opening her mouth, those present found one of her double Teeth newly drawn out, but knew not what became of the Tooth; for tho' search was made for the same, it could not be found: After which the Minister proceeded upon the same subject, but was again interrupted by her renewed Fit, yet closed the Exercise with Prayer, after which, without more trouble, she was taken to her Bed.

February 12. *Margaret Laing* and her Daughter *Martha Semple*, being delated by the three Confessants,[105] and accused by the Girl to have been active Instruments in her Trouble, came of their own accord to *Bargarran*'s House, and before they came up Stairs the Girl said, she was now bound up, and could not accuse *Margaret Laing* to her Face: And accordingly the Girl's Mother

[103] This paragraph is an interpolation not found in the manuscript 'Informatory Accompt'.
[104] 'Jealousy': suspicion.
[105] Here and later, the 'three Confessants' are the three young star witnesses, Elizabeth Anderson, James Lindsay and Thomas Lindsay.

having desired some of those who were sitting by her to feel some parts of her Body, and they having done it, found her Body so stiff and inflexible, that there was no moving of it, and immediatly again found some parts of her Body contracted and drawn hard together, as if by Cords; after this *Margaret Lang* and her Daughter, having gone to the Chamber to the Girle, did in presence of the Ministers and others, desire the Damsel to come to her; for she would do her no Harm, and laying her Arms about her, spake very fairly to her, and question'd her if ever she had seen her or her Daughter amongst her Tormentors, to which the Girle did positively reply, she had frequently seen her Daughter; but declined thorow fear to accuse her self, saying faintly *No*; after which *Margaret* and her Daughter returning into the Hall, and the Minister enquiring at her why she said *No*, seeing she had accus'd her before, she answered, take me contrar, upon which she was seiz'd with a grievous fit; yet after her recovery being urg'd again by those present to tell her Mind freely, whether or not *Margaret Lang* was one of her Tormentors the Child thereupon Essaying to say *Yes*, and having half pronounced the Word, was cast into unexpressible Anguishes; and again in the interval of the Fit, she Essay'd to express the same thing, and saying only the word *Tint* (that is lost) was on a sudden struck with another fit, and when the fit was over, and the Child returned to the Chamber, *Margaret Lang* who was sitting near the Hall door, spoke these words after her. *The Lord bless thee, and ding (that is beat, or drive) the Devil out of thee*. A little after which words, *Margaret* going down stairs, the Damsel came to the Hall and said, her Bonds were now loos'd, and that now she could accuse *Margaret Lang* to her Face, and declar'd the occasion of her being so Restrain'd and Bound up while *Margaret* was present, was her letting fall a parcel of Hair at the Hall door as she came in; being a Charm made by her for {*p. xxviii*} that end, which also had been the occasion of her uttering the word *Tint* in the former fit: And accordingly a parcel of Hair had been found at the Hall-door, after *Margaret Lang* had gone straight from the Hall to the Chamber, which immediatly was cast into the Fire and burnt. And its remarkable, that it could be attested that there was no Hair, or any other thing else in that place before *Margaret Lang* came in, and the Girle being enquired, what way she knew *Margaret Lang* had laid the forementioned Charm upon her, replyed, something speaking distinctly to her as it were above her Head, had suggested that to her.

About Eight at Night she was severely handled in her Fits, much after the former manner, and while she was in her swooning Fits, there was seen in her Mouth a Pin, where with she seem'd almost Choak't; but by divine providence it was with great difficulty got out. After this she was somewhat composed, and did not much complain of pain; but was distinctly heard to entertain discourse with some invisible Creatures about her, and the Reply's given by her, and heard by those who took care of her, gave them ground to conclude she was tempted to set her Hand to a Paper then presented to her, with Promises that upon her yielding thereunto *she should never be troubled any more; as also that she should get sweet meats, a drink of Sack,*[106] *a bonny handsome Coat with silver Lace*: She was also distinctly heard say, resisting the Tempter, *Thou art a filthy Sow, should I obey thee; this was not the end of my Creation, but to Glorify GOD and enjoy Him for ever;*[107] *and thou promisest what thou canst not perform: Art thou angry at me for saying thou Sow, what should I call thee but thou filthy Sow? Art thou not the filthy Devil, for as brave as thou art with thy Silver and Gold Lace? Wouldst thou have me Renounce my Baptism? Dost thou promise to give me brave Men in Marriage, and fine Cloaths, and perfect Health, if I should consent thereunto? Dost thou say my Baptism will do me no good, because thou alledgest he was not a sufficient Minister that baptized me?*[108] *thou art a Liar, I'll be content to die ere I renounce my Baptism. O thorow the Grace of GOD I'll never do it.* And thus she continued Reasoning, being both Blind and Deaf, for the space of two Hours; and when she came to herself did declare it was the Devil, who first presented himself tempting her in the shape of a Sow, to Renounce her Baptism, as is hinted; and that he did chide her when she call'd him, *thou Sow*, and immediatly appear'd to her again in the shape of a brave Gentleman, as having Gold and Silver Lace on his Cloaths, still urging her to renounce her Baptism, which Tentation she thorow the special assistance of the Grace of GOD effectually resisted: she also said, that it had been suggested to her by the Spirit, speaking to her as it were above her Head, after the Combat with the Tempter was over, that one of her Tormentors would be at the House the Morrow.

February 13. She was seiz'd with a sore fit about Twelve a Clock of the day, in which she continued for more than two Hours space, both Deaf and Blind, Those in the Room with her crying to her with a loud Voice, and pinching her Hands and other part of her Body; but all to no purpose. And in this posture was hurried To and Fro with violence thorow the Room: And when any body by force offer'd to hinder the dangerous and violent Motion she seem'd to be upon, she'd Roar exceedingly, sometimes she'd desire her Father and Mother and others to come and take her Home (supposing her self not to be in her Fathers House) when the Girle was in this deplorable

106 'Sack': white wine. The newsletter edited above as an appendix to the 'Bargarran Witches' manuscript stated that Christian had actually received a glass of sack from the witches on 4 February. This story does not appear in the *True Narrative*. However, the *True Narrative* later quotes Francis Grant, in his summing-up speech to the assize ('Letter First'), as saying that Christian 'told, that her Tormenters were giving her a Glass of Sack, an Orange-pile, *&c*.' This may be connected with the *True Narrative*'s account of 6 February, which mentions orange peel but not sack.

107 The opening answer of the Westminster Shorter Catechism (the standard catechism used in the church of Scotland) was: 'Man's chief end is to glorify God, and to enjoy him forever.'

108 Christian had been baptised by an episcopalian minister before the Revolution of 1689: Adam, *Witch Hunt*, 94. The 'Bargarran Witches' manuscript says at this point: 'she was violently urged by him To Renunce her Baptisme, argueing against the validity therof saying It was done by a Curat' (p. 13). The published version has made various other changes to this passage, considerably lengthening it and adding first-person speech.

Condition, *Margaret Roger* who liv'd in the Nighbour-hood, came to the House of *Bargarran* enquiring for the Lady; and having come up stairs, the Parents of the {*p. xxix*} Damsel remembering what the Girle had said the Night before, that one of her Tormentors was to come that day to the House, brought *Margaret Roger* to the Chamber where the Girle was, and so soon as she entered the Door; the Damsel tho she could discern none of these who were present with her, nor answer them when they cry'd to her; yet presently saw her and ran towards her crying, *Maggi, Maggi, where hast thou been? wilt thou take me with thee, for my Father and Mother have left me*. Whereupon Spectators being astonish'd, caus'd *Margaret* speak to the Child, which she having done, the Girl distinctly heard and answered her every word. After this, the Three Confessants were also brought up to the Chamber where the Damsel was, and as soon as they entered the Door, she ran also to them laughing as if she had been overjoy'd, answering them when they spoke to her: and *Margaret Roger* there present, being confronted with the Confessants: They did declare, that she had been at Meetings with the Devil and Witches in *Bargarrans* Orchard, consulting and contriving *Christian Shaw*'s ruine.

The LORDS Day following, being *February* 14. After some short intervals she was again seiz'd with her fits, in which she said, *Margaret Lang and her Daughter Martha Simple, were Tormenting her and cutting her Throat*; which words thorow violence of Pain, and difficulty of Breathing, she uttered with a low and hardly audible Voice, and upon the naming of *Margaret Lang* and her Daughter, she was tost'd[109] and dreadfully Tormented in all the parts of her Body, being made sometimes to stand upon her Head and Feet at once, sometimes her Belly swelling like a Drum; and falling again in a sudden, and sometimes her Head and other parts of her Body were like to be shaken in pieces, so that Spectators fear'd she would never speak more. And when the fit was over, she declar'd, *Margaret Lang* said to her while in the fit, *That she would give her a Tosty* (which imports hot and severe handling) for naming her.

At this time she was seldom free of her light fits, which for most part were all the respite and ease she had from the unexpressible Agonys she endur'd in her more grievous fits; unless when asleep: and while she was in these fits, no Body could perswade her to pray, yet when in a right composure of Mind and perfectly at her self, she'd weep bitterly to remember this, expressing her fears, lest that might be any evidence GOD would forsake her.

February 18.[110] About two in the Afternoon, she being in the light fit, said, *The Devil now appear'd to her in the shape of a Man*; whereupon she being struck with great Fear and Consternation, was desir'd to Pray with an audible Voice,

109 *SD*, p. 30, has 'Tossed'. However, this word may well be related to the rare word 'Tosty', which is given, and explained, later in the present paragraph.

110 This paragraph should be compared with the letter of the same date, written by Christian Shaw's mother Christian McGilchrist, printed in the *Relation of the Diabolical Practices* (above in the present volume). The letter gives an earlier and briefer version of this episode.

The Lord rebuke thee Satan; which she Essaying to do, instantly lost power of speech, her Teeth being set, and her Tongue drawn back into her Throat, and she Essaying again, was immediatly seiz'd with another grivous fit; in which her Eyes being twisted almost round in her Head; she fell down as one Dead, strugling with Feet and Hands, and again getting up on a sudden, was hurried with violence Too and Fro thorow the Room Deaf and Blind; yet was speaking with some invisible Creatures about her saying, *with the Lords strength thou shalt neither put Straw nor Sticks into my Mouth*. After this she cry'd in a pitiful manner, the Bumbee[111] hath sting'd me, then presently sitting down and loosing her Stocking, put her Hand to that part which had been Nip't or Pinch't, Thereupon Spectators did visibly discern the lively marks of Nails of Fingers deeply imprinted on that same part of her Leg. And when she came to her self, she did declare, *That some thing speaking to her as it were above her Head*; told her it {*p. xxx*} was *M. M.* in a Nighbouring Parish (nameing the place) *that had appear'd to her, and pinch't her Leg in the likness of a Bumbee*. She likewise did declare, that the forementioned *M. M. instantly after this had been suggested to her, appeared in her own shape and likness as she us'd to be at other times*. Shortly after this being still seiz'd with her light fit, she whisper'd in her Mothers Ear, *The Devil was now appearing to her again in the shape of a Gentleman*: And being instantly seiz'd with her fits, in which she was both Blind and Deaf, was distinctly heard arguing after this manner. *Thou think'st to tempt me to be a Witch; but thorow GOD's strength thou shalt never be the better: I charge thee in the Name of GOD to be gone and thy Papers too, in the LORDS strength I'l not fear thee, I'l stand here and see if thou can come one step nearer me, I think thou fear'st me more then I fear thee*. Then turning her self again, she was hurried To and Fro with violence thorow the Room, as formerly saying, *she was Bitten or pinch'd very sore in the Hands with Teeth, and Nip't with Fingers, above Twenty four times*; which constrain'd her to horrid Schreeks, and out crys at every time she receiv'd them, shewing and pointing with her Finger on these parts of her Arm and Leg which had been Pinch't and Bitten; but neither saw not heard any about her. And accordingly Spectators did visibly discern the evident marks of the Teeth and Nails of Fingers upon her Arms and Legs. In this posture the Girle continued from two to five in the Afternoon, and when her Miserys were over, she said *M. M. told her in the Fit, that* Margaret Lang *then in custody, had ordered her to handle her after that manner. And that* Margaret Lang *had a commanding power over her*.

Friday and *Saturday* thereafter being *February* 19. and 20 she was frequently seiz'd with the foremention'd fits, and being violently Bitten Pinch't and Nip't in her hands neck and other parts of her body, so that the clear marks of the nails of fingers and steeds of teeth both Upper and Lower, with the spitle and slaver of a mouth thereupon were evidently seen by spectators. About this

[111] 'Bumbee': bumblebee.

time when seiz'd with her Blind and Deaf fits, a crooked fellow appear'd to her having his two feet deform'd his two heells wrying inward toward one another, and the fore parts of his feet outward from one another, so that the broadside of his feet mov'd foremost, and upon the appearing of this fellow her feet were put in the very same posture during the time he tormented her. It is to be noticed that there is a fellow in one of the neighbouring parishes, whose feet are exactly in that manner deform'd, who has been of a long time of evil fame, and given up by the confessants to have been seen at meetings with the Devil and the rest of the crew in *Bargarrens* Orchard.

Saturday being *February* 20. The whole family being gone to bed, they had left a great quantity of Peets (or Turf) beside the hall Chimney, which the next morning they saw them burnt to ashes, tho there had been no fire in the Chimney nor near them, so that the plaister and stones of the wall where the Peets or Turfe lay were in a great part turn'd to rubbish thorow the violence of the fire but no other damnage followed, the hall floor being laid with stones, and the Peets lying within the bosome of a large Chimney brace.

February 27th, The Chamber fire having been covered with ashes in the Chimney when the family went to bed, the next morning tho a good quantity of ashes had been left; yet they found all clean sweept away, and no appearance of ashes nor fire there at all, albeit none in the family that night nor next morning had been there after the fire was gathered, before this was observed.[112] {*p. xxxi*}

In fits of this kind she continued for several days thereafter, naming the forementon'd crooked fellow, *J. R.* and *M. A.* living in the neighbouring parishes, which two Women were delated by the three confessants to be amongst her tormenters, and particularly upon the Lords day being *February* 21. and the Munday following, the said *J, R,* appearing to her grievously vexed her, withall telling she was commissionated so to do. The Gentle woman *M. M.* having a pain in her head at that time, and so not able to come forth. Concerning which it is worthy of remark, that the Damsel declar'd *M. M.* to have appeared to her about two days thereafter with her head bound up with a Napkin (or handker-chief) in which like habite or posture, she did not formerly appear.

Upon *Thursday* thereafter being *February* 25 She continued in the former fits, weeping bitterly and complaining of pain in both her sides, she also told in the interval of her fits, that she was that night to be in very grievous and sore fits, her tormenters being resolved to choak her, by putting pins in her mouth, which (tho she emptied her self of all that were in her Cloaths) yet accordingly came to pass: In which she was both Blind and Deaf, leaping up and down in an extraordinary manner, pulling down what ever came to her

[112] This and the previous paragraph are an interpolation not found in the manuscript 'Continued Accompt'.

Hand, and this continued for some days putting out of her Mouth a great quantity of small broken Pins, which she declar'd *J. R.* had forc'd into the same.

Upon the Lords day being the last of *February*, about five a Clock in the Afternoon she fell into grievous fits, accompanied with Hideous or loud Laughing, Leaping, and runing with violence to and fro, and thereafter weept sore, crying out of Pain, that a little Highland Man, (whom she knew to be such by his habit and speech) was now breaking her Leg; which (because of pain) she scarce could get told in the fit, and putting her Hand to the part of her Leg affected, Spectators untying her stocking, distinctly observed a sore bruise in her Shin-bone; which when touched did so pain her, that she uttered horrid Schreeks and Crys; and when recovered did declare, that the little Highland fellow had given her that bruise. After this, she put out of her Mouth a crooked Pin, by which she told the fore said Highland fellow having forc't it into her Mouth, design'd to Choak her.

The first eight days of *March* she continued in her former fits; with little Variation, putting out of her Mouth a great number of small Pins, often fainting and falling as Dead upon the ground on a sudden, again strugling with Feet and Hands; by all which her Natural Spirits were much Weakned and Exhausted; sometimes also she Essay'd to go into the Fire. About this time when Ministers and other Christians met in the Family for Prayer, she us'd at the beginning of the work to make great disturbance, particularly *March* 2. which day being set a part for Fasting and Praying in the Family, prayer begun, she was for some time very composed, untill of a sudden, a strong blast of Wind forced open the Windows of the Room; upon which she was instantly seiz'd with a violent fit, the Minister in the very same time supplicating GOD that she might be delivered from Satans Bonds: In which fit she being both Blind and Deaf as to All, except her Tormentors, was hurried with violence to and fro the Room, sometimes falling down as one Dead, sometimes Singing and making a Hidious loud Noise, somtimes nameing *M. M.* and others, who she said, were there present Afflicting and Tormenting her, withall, nameing the particular places of the Room where she, saw them standing and sitting. After all which, when recovered out of the fit, she told that a Gentlewoman {*p. xxxii*} and a little Highland fellow came in with the blast of Wind, which forc'd open the Windows. This falling out upon the *Tuesday*, she continued in the light fit without any Intermission, till the Sabbath thereafter, not being seiz'd with any of her sore fits: And having gone to Church the Lords day following, was perfectly well for the most part of the day; yet affirmed she saw *Janet Wagh* and others in one of the Windows of the Church, tho invisible to all others.

Tuesday, being *March* the *9th*. Her Mother and *Margaret Campbel* her Cousin took the Damsel to walk with them in the Orchard; and returning back to the house, her Mother entring the Tower gate first, the Damsel being at her back and *Margaret Campbel* tarrying a little while at the gate; her Mother going into the Kitchen, suppos'd they had both been with her, whereas the Damsel was of a sudden carried away in a flight up Stairs with so swift and unaccountable motion, that her absence was not in the least suspected, but her Mother turning about and missing her, cry'd whither is *Christian* and *Margaret Campbel*? And instantly runing up Stairs to look for the Damsel heard a noise and following the same, found the Damsel Leaping and Dancing upon one of the Stairs being seiz'd with fits, out of which when she had recovered she told, that J. P. had carried her away from her Mothers back as she entred the Kitchen door (her feet not touching the ground to her apprehension) and that with a design to strangle her in an high wardrob with Ropes on which the Linning us'd to dry, but that the said J. P. could carry her no further then the place where she was found, and did therefore leave her in such a Violent fit.

Upon the Lords day thereafter being *March* 14. Her fits again altered, in that her Mouth and Nose were prodigiously distorted and turned about while in the fit, her face being thereby strangely and horridly deform'd. That same day she being in Church in the Forenoon, her Glove falling from her, the same was again put into her Hand by some invisible Agent, to the Amazment of beholders. To which we may add here, as that which is worthy of remark, that all this while an Invisible beeing, haunted her on all occasions, suggesting many things unto her, both concerning her self and others; but yet never heard by any but her self.

The same day betwixt Sermons, she told that she was to be violently Tormented in the Afternoon; which accordingly came to pass, and when in her fits she named one *J. K.* a Woman living in the Nighbouring bounds of whom she said, that she had seen her in the Church. As also, that she was Master of these kind of fits she was now afflicted with; withal asserting, that if the said *I. K.* were not sent for, she would grow worse and worse; which her parents finding to be true, sent in the Evening for the said. *I. K.* threatning her, if the Damsel was any further troubled with her, that she should be apprehended as others had been; after which the Damsel being in the mean time in a very sore fit, the forementioned *I. K.* prayed (tho not desired) that GOD might send the Damsel her Health; whereupon the Damsel was no more troubled with these kind of fits; but did instantly recover, by falling into a swoon as she us'd to do before recovery out of any of her fits.

Tuesday being *March* 16, she was again seiz'd with her other kind of fits, all the parts of her body being Stiff and Rigid; and sometimes in them was hear'd conversing with the Gentlewoman (as she call'd her) vindicating her self of what the Gentlewoman alledged against her, *Viz. That she had accused some innocent persons as her Tormenters.* To which the Damsel distinctly Reply'd, *That {p. xxxiii} she was a Lyer, saying, it was you your self, and none other ever mentioned any such thing.*

Thus she continued untill the Friday thereafter, being never free of the light fits, now and then also falling into swoons, and appear'd to be almost choaked by the means of some Charms and Inchantments, invisibly conveyed into her Mouth; which to the apprehension of Spectators, were as if it had been pieces of Chastnuts, Orange-pills, Whites of Eggs, or such like, all which were distinctly observed, when occasionally in the fit she opened her Mouth; and when Spectators Essay'd to get them out, she kep't her Mouth and Teeth so closs, that no strength could open the same. And when recovered out of the fit, she told *L. M.* a Woman living in the Neighbouring bounds had put them in her Mouth.

Upon Friday being March 19. She was violently Tormented with sore fits, in which her Neck was distorted, and bended back like a Bow towards her Heels, strugling with Feet and Hands, sometimes Stiff, Blind, and Deaf, putting out of her Mouth a great number of small Pins; which she said the forementioned *L. M.* had put in her Mouth. And about six a Clock that same Night being violently Tormented, fell a crying, *That if the Gentlewoman was not apprehended that Night, it would be in vain to apprehend her to morrow*: For, said she, *I have much to suffer at her Hands betwixt Twelve and One a Clock in the Morning*. After this the Damsel lifting up her Eye lids with her Hands, and looking upwards, said, *what art thou that tells me that the Sheriff and my Father are coming here this Night*? After which the Sheriff, her Father and *James Guthry* Meacer to the Justiciary Court instantly come up stairs, to the Amazment of those who remembered what the Damsel just now had said. The Damsel continuing all this while Blind and Deaf; yet was heard (the foresaid persons being present) distinctly to discourse with some invisible Beeing near to her, saying, *Is the Sheriff come, is he near me*? and streaching out her hand to feel if any were about her, the Sheriff put his hand in her's; notwithstanding of which, she said to the invisible Beeing discoursing with her,

> I cannot feel the Sheriff, how can he be present here? or how can I have him by the hand as thou say'st, seeing I feel it not? Thou say'st he hath brown coloured Cloths, red plush Breeches with black strips, flowred Musling Cravat, and an imbroidered Sword Belt: Thou says there is an Old gray Hair'd Man with him, having a Ring upon his Hand; but I can neither see nor feel any of them? what are they come to apprehend the Gentle Woman? Is this their Erand indeed?

And the Girle being enquired how she came to the knowledge of these strange things? Reply'd as formerly in the like case, something speaking distinctly as above her Head, suggested them to her. It is very observeable here, that the foresaid persons had that same Afternoon got an order from the Commissioners of Justiciary to apprehend the same Gentlewoman, and were so far on their way to put it to Execution against the next Morning; but being witnesses to the Damsels trouble, and hearing what she had told, to wit: That a delay in that matter would prove to her exceeding dangerous, they went straight on in their Journey that same Night to the Gentlewomans Habitation, and put their warrand to Execution.

As the Damsel still continued to be violently Tormented, sometimes lying with her Neck and other parts of her Body upon the Ground; as if they had been disjoynted, sometimes also Essaying to throw her self into the Fire. About Ten a Clock the same Night she continuing in the Fit, her Father (who had not gone with the Sheriff) beginning to read a part of the Word of GOD, she repeated {*p. xxxiv*} the Words after him tho Blind and Deaf in the mean time, which made Spectators apprehend, that the Damsel had the sense of Hearing in these sorts of fits, at least when the Word of GOD was read: To find out the truth of which, her Father did cease from reading, which tho he did; yet the Damsel continued to repeat the following Verses of the Chapter, while none in the Room were reading, and she her self had no Book: withal being heard say to some invisible Beeing about her, *Wilt thou teach me a part of the Old Testament as well as the New*.

The Damsel still continuing in the fore mentioned Fits, said unto the Persons present, that now it was Twelve of the Clock; Oh it is now past Twelve, sometimes lying as one dead thorow the violence of pain and decay of her natural Spirits, sometimes again recovering, essay'd to express somewhat, but could not; withal putting out of her Mouth a great quantity of crooked Pins, and the parts of her Body being prodigiously distorted, she complain'd of great pain: Thus she continued until half an hour after Twelve a Clock at Night; when on a sudden she recovered, to the admiration of Beholders, telling them, *She might now go to Bed*, being told by some invisible Informer, that the Sheriff and the other Gentleman, to wit the Macer, had now entred the Gentlewomans House; and accordingly going to bed, was no further troubled that Night. It is worthy of remark here, that the Sheriff and Macer at their return did declare, that it was just about that time they entred the Gentlewomans House, which the Damsel condescended upon.[113]

Saturday being *March* 20. About Ten a Clock in the Forenoon she was of a sudden seiz'd with fits falling down as dead, her eyes quite closed, sometimes again opening and turning in her head, she saw nor heard none about her, but was hurried with violence to and fro thorow the Room, crying with a loud voice when any by force would hinder her motion. She being in this posture and depriv'd thus of her senses, *James Lindsay* one of the three Confessants was brought into the Room, who no sooner entered the door but was perceived by her, and she smiling ran towards him, saying *Jamie* where hast thou been this long time; how is it with thee? And answered him distinctly to every word he spake, tho at the same time she neither heard nor saw any other in the Room, nor could converse with them albeit tryed by several experiments for that purpose, particularly a Tobacco Box being held before her Eyes by a person

[113] 'condescended upon': specified.

present in the Room, she did not see it, but as soon as it was put in the hand of James Lindsay she instantly enquired at him, "Where he had got that Box; she continuing in this posture, the Sheriff, her Father being present, thought it fit to confront M. M. who was now come, thereby to try if the Damsel would hear or see her as she had done *James Lindsay*, which accordingly they did. And as soon as M. M. entered the door the Damsel (tho still in the fit) presently smiled and said, I see the Gentlewoman now, tho formerly she had never seen her personally but only her spectre in the fits. She likewise heard her when she spoke to her answering distinctly some questions proposed by M. M., such as, When it was she had seen her tormenting her. To which she answered, she had seen her the other night in her fits, and further challenged her,[114] Why she had restrain'd her from making known the Highland Wifes name, as also saying unto her, Thou pretends thou knowest not what I say, thou knowest well enough. Upon all which; the Gentlewoman on a sudden (without being desired) prayed, That the Lord might send the Damsel her health saying, "Lord help thee poor daft Child and rebuke the Devil. Which words were no sooner uttered then the Damsel fell down as dead, and being in this posture carried to {*p. xxxv*} another Room instantly recovered of the Blind, Deaf, and also of the light fit becomeing perfectly well and continued so for some time, and being thus recovered and M. M. removed into another Room, the Damsel was enquired at whom she had seen in her last fit. To which she reply'd, she had seen the Gentlewoman, tho in the mean time she was altogether ignorant of the Gentlewomans ever being personally present in the Room with her.

The same day the Commissioners of Justiciary having come to *Bargarran*. M. M. and the Damsel were again confronted, upon which the Damsel (being in the light Fit) upon the first look of the forementioned M. M., was suddenly seiz'd with sore Fits, out of which when recovered, she accused her as being one of her most violent tormenters, particularly mentioning such and such times in which she had in an extraordinary manner afflicted her, as also what words she spoke in her hearing while in the Fit, and which is yet more remarkable, did question the Gentlewoman if she did not sometime in *December* last when she was tormenting her, remember how she went away from her in great haste, saying, she could stay no longer being obliged to attend a Childs burial at home. In confirmation of which it is very credibly informed that *W. R.*, a near neighbour of hers had a Child burried that same day, and that the Gentlewoman came not in due time to attend the Corpse to the burial place, but the Corpse being near to the Church yeard ere she reached the House from whence they came, she returned again to her own lodging, and so did not accompany the burial at all.[115]

114 This 'further challenge' is an interpolation not found in the manuscript 'Continued Accompt'.
115 Most of this paragraph is an interpolation not found in the manuscript 'Continued Accompt'.

The Lords day following being *March* 21, she fell into Swooning Fits complaining of no pain, except near to her heart, falling down as dead not only when the Fits seiz'd her, but also when she recovered, sometimes Singing after an unusual manner, withall informing Spectators that *J. G.* constrained her to that kind of Musick, her own Lips not at all moving in the mean time, which beholders saw to be true, only her Tongue, for preventing of which she frequently put her hand into her Mouth. And at this time when either she herself, or those about her, offered to read any part of Scripture, she was violently Tormented, declaring if she did but so much as hear the word of God read that day, she would certainly be extremely Tortured, in Confirmation of which when some essay'd to read *Hebr.* 11 2, 4, 6. *Isa* 40. *Psal.* 3. She uttered horrid Schreeks and Out cryes, Complaining that *She was Pinched*, in evidence of which, the Prints or Marks of the Nails of Fingers were distinctly seen on her Arms, and being thus pinched or bitten four several times with great violence and pain, the Skin it self was seen to be torn from off these parts of her Arms and Fingers where the Prints of the Teeth and Nails were observed; so that from the deepness of the Wounds the foresaids parts affected fell a Bleeding, which Blood was both seen and handled by Spectators. Moreover the Damsel while in this sad and lamentable condition seem'd to be extremely affected and oppressed with sore Sickness, as one in a Fever, crying sometimes to *Remove these Dead Children out of her Sight*; which she frequently repeated from six to nine in the Morning, and she still continuing thorow the rest of the day, it was observed that some Charms and Inchantments were put in her Mouth as formerly, of which the Damsel being very sensible,[116] fell down on a Sudden on the Ground putting her hand to some Spittle which she had put out of her Mouth, and lifted some Trash which she again cast down to the Ground, it making some Noise, but yet neither seen in her Spittle, nor else where by Spectators, tho while in her Mouth they distinctly observed something like Orange Pils, Whites of Eggs, and peeces of Chasnuts. {*p. xxxvi*}

Munday, Being *March*, 22, the fore mentioned *L. M.* or *J. G.* came to *Bargarrans* house, and being confronted with the Damsel, questioned her if ever she had seen her in any of her Fits, withal alledging that she *viz. L. M.* or *J. G.* could be none of her Tormentors, because the Damsel was not now seiz'd with a Fit, tho looking upon her as she us'd to be, when she look'd upon any of her other Tormentors when Confronted with them; upon which the Damsel being for sometime silent. *L. M.* or *J. G.* did again propose the same question to her, to which the Damsel distinctly reply'd *Yes*, upon which *L. M.* reply'd, perhaps, you have seen the Devil in my Shape.

As to this Conference there are several things exceeding remarkable, as first, that the Damsel upon her Answering, *Yes*, was immediatly seiz'd with a Fit. *2dly*, That however after *Katharine Campbel* had touch'd the Damsel

[116] 'sensible': aware.

in presence of the Commissioners, upon the 5*th*, of *February* last, she had ever since that time freedom to touch any of her Tormentors without being seiz'd with her Fits, as has been hinted, yet true it is, that in the room of that Charm a new one took place, *viz*. When any time she looked upon her Tormentors in the Face, at the very first look she was seiz'd with her Fits; which Charm she declar'd was laid by the means of the forementioned *L. M.* or *J. G.* And also taken off again by her that very Morning before she came to visit the Damsel, and this she said was suggested to her by some invisible beeing, speaking distinctly as it were above her head; and that therefore the Damsel now had freedom to look *L. M.* in the Face without being seiz'd with Fits, which for a considerable time before she could not do when confronted with any of her Tormentors. 3*ly*, It is yet more observable, that in the same Morning before ever *L. M.* came to visit the Damsel, it was told by the Damsel to several Persons in the Family, that L. M. had taken off that Charm, of her being seiz'd with Fits when looking any of her Tormentors in the Face, but withal that she had laid on another in its room, to wit, that as soon as the Damsel should by words confer with any of her Tormentors, so soon should she be seiz'd with a Fit, which accordingly was verified when she spoke to L. M. or J. G.[117]

Tuesday being *March 23d*, The Damsel being asleep in the Bed with her Mother about three aclock in the Morning was on a sudden awakned (having for sometime Struggled in her Sleep) in great fear and consternation, and being seiz'd with her Blind and Deaf Fits, took fast hold of her Mother, declaring to her Father and her, that the Devil was standing near to the Bed assaulting her, upon which she cry'd suddenly:

> God Almighty keep me from thy meetings. I'l die rather then go to them, I'l never thorow the Grace of God Renounce my Baptism; for I'l certainly go to Hell if I do it: Thou sayest I'l go to Hell however, because I am a great Sinner; but I believe what the word of God sayeth, tho I have many Sins; yet the Blood of Christ cleanseth from all Sin, and I will not add that great wickedness to my other Sins, which thou art tempting me to do. It's no wonder thou lie to me, seeing thou wast bold to lie in Gods Face. I know thou art a Liar from the beginning; and the red Coat thou promisest me, I know thou canst not perform it. And altho I should never Recover, I'm never resolv'd to renounce my Baptism, It is God who hath keeped me all this time from being a Witch, and I trust, he will yet by his Grace keep me, not because of any thing in me, but of his own great Mercy, and that he who hath keeped me hitherto from being devoured by thee, I hope will yet keep me.

[117] This paragraph and the previous one are an interpolation not found in the manuscript 'Continued Accompt'.

This Conference continued near the space of an hour, her Father Mother and others being ear Witnesses to the same. And after recovery the Damsel declared that it was the Devil, who {*p. xxxvii*} (in the shape of a naked Man with a Shirt, having much hair upon his hands and his Face like Swine Bristles) had appeard to her tempting her as aforesaid.

Untill Sabbath following she continued in the light Fit, but withal every Morning and Evening was still seiz'd with her sore Fits, continuing still to name M, M, (who was at this time set at liberty) the forementioned *L. M.*, *E. T.* an Highland wife, and others as being her tormentors. It is more then remarkable here that M. M. being set at Liberty upon Bail, the very day after she went home, she again appear'd to the Damsel tormenting her in her fits, and continued so to do several days thereafter, particularly upon the *Saturday* being *March* 27 after she was set at liberty: The which day the Damsel was heard name her in the fits and say to her, wilt thou say *God help me poor mad or foolish child as thou saidst the other day before the Judges: art thou wishing the Devil to take me? where is the Habite thou was cloathed with the other day.*[118]

On Sabbath Morning, being *March* 28. the Damsel thorow GOD's great Mercy towards her, was perfectly recovered, both of all her *Sore* and light Fits; becoming as Well, Sensible, and Composed as ever.

If it shall be questioned, how the Truth of all these strange Things is attested? There is none of those Particulars mentioned in the Narrative, but had in the first Draught the Witnesses insert at the end of every particular Paragraph, and attested before the Commissioners for Enquiry at *Renfrew*, by the Subscriptions of the respective Witnesses. But seeing the placing of them so now, would have occasioned the repetition of several persons Names over and over again, and would have made this Narrative swell too much in bulk; Therefore we judg'd it fittest now to set down the Names altogether at the end of the Narrative; and the rather that seing these things fell not out in a private Corner; but Thousands in this Countrey have been Eye and Ear Witnesses thereof to their admiration and raising of their Sympathy, and been fully convinced beyond all debate of a Diabolical influence upon the Affliction of the Damsel: We shall only now make mention of a few, *Viz*, beside the Father, Mother, Grand-mother, and nearest Relations of the Damsel, and servants of the Family, who were always present with her in her Fits: such of the Commissioners for Inquiry, and of Justiciary as had occasion to be on the place of the Events, particularly the Lord *Blantyre*, Mr. *Francis Montgomery* of *Giffen*, Sir *John Maxwell* of *Pollock*, Sir *John Houston* of *That ilk*, *Alexander Porterfield* of *that ilk*, the Laird of *Black-hall* younger, the Laird of *Glanderstone*, the Laird of *Craigens*, *Porterfield* of *Fulwood*, *John Alexander* of *Black house*, Mr. *Semple* Sheriff of *Renfrew*: And several other Honourable

[118] Most of this paragraph is an interpolation not found in the manuscript 'Continued Accompt'.

persons of good Sense and prying Witts; such as the Noble Earl of *Marshal*,[119] the Laird of *Orbiston*,[120] the Laird of *Kilmarnock*,[121] the Laird of *Meldrum*,[122] the Laird of *Bishopton* Elder and Younger,[123] *Gavin Cochran* of *Craigmure*, *William Denneston* of *Colgrain*, Dr. *Mathew Brisben*, &c. And many Ministers, who kept days of Humiliation and Prayer weekly in the Family, and sometimes in the Parish Church with the Congregation, *Viz*. Mr. *James Hutchison* Minister of the Gospel at *Kilellan*, Mr. *Patrick Simson* at *Renfrew*, Mr. *James Stirling* at *Kilbarchan*, Mr. *Thomas Blackwal* at *Paisly*, Mr. *James Brisban* at *Kilmacolme*, Mr. *Robert Tayler* at *Houston*; and of Neighbouring Presbytries, Mr. *Neill Gillies*, Mr. *James Brown*, Mr. *John Gray* Ministers of the Gospel at *Glasgow*, while the Damsel was there; Mr. *John Ritchie* Minister at Old *Kilpatrick*, Mr. *Alexander King* at *Bonnil*, Mr. *Archibald Wallace* at *Cardross*, Mr. *John Anderson* at *Drymmen*, Mr. *Andrew Turner* Minister of the Place, who was frequently there: besides Mr. *{p. xxxviii} Menzies* of *Cammo*, and Mr. *Grant* of *Cullen*, Advocates: who were Eye and Ear Witnesses to several important passages of the Damsels Affliction, and the convincing evidences of it's flowing from the Operation of the Devil, and his Instruments. The Truth whereof is further Adminiculat[124] by the Progress and Issue of the Tryal, at which were present at several Occasions, not only Sir *John Hamiltoun* of *Halcraig* one of the Senators of the Colledge of Justice, Sir *John Shaw* of *Greenock*, Commissar *Smollet* of *Bonnill*, Mr. *James Stewart* Advocat, who were concerned in the Commission with these others before mentioned: But also a great confluence of several Nobility and Gentry out of the Countrey, such as the Earl of *Glencairn*, the Lord *Killmares*, the Lord *Semple*, &c.[125]

And now we are sure, that after all the pregnant evidences of the truth of this Relation as to matter of Fact, they must be persons very hard of belief that can allow themselves to deny credite thereunto: And must needs conclude, that there is nothing credible in the World that ever hath been delivered to Mankind or posterity; and that they resolve to believe nothing though never so fully attested which they do not see with their own Eyes, and perhaps there are some hardned in their prejudicat conceits that will not believe even these so far as they may have influence to convince them of their Errors; but wisdom is and will be justified of all her Children.[126] And among all Ingenuous and sober Persons, We are hopefull this Narrative (which plainly relates things as

119 William Keith, ninth Earl Marischal.

120 William Hamilton of Orbiston.

121 William Cochrane of Kilmaronock. He represented the burgh of Renfrew in parliament. His title came from Kilmaronock in Dunbartonshire, not Kilmarnock in Ayrshire.

122 John Urquhart of Meldrum.

123 James Brisbane of Bishopton and John Brisbane younger of Bishopton.

124 An 'adminicle' contributes to proving a point without being itself a complete proof.

125 John Cunningham, tenth earl of Glencairn; William Cunningham, Lord Kilmaurs (later eleventh earl of Glencairn); Francis, tenth Lord Sempill.

126 Cf. Matthew 11:19.

they fell out without any kind of disguise) will obtain such entertainment[127] as it is truely design'd for, *Viz*. That we be hereby more and more confirmed in the Faith of the beeing of God and invisible Spirits, and admire and adore the wonderful works of God in the Depths of his Judgment, and that there is really a Hellish Hierarchy and Combination of Infernal Spirits enemies to God; and working all the mischief they can to Men; whereby also, there is an evident Testimony giv'n to the Truth of what is related in the Scriptures concerning the same, and withall to lament, that thorow the just displeasure of our Holy and Righteous GOD, those Devils get leave to break forth with so much Rage and Fury, and gets so many among profest Christians into a hellish confederacy with themselves to be the instruments of their Malice, and the actors of so many Tragedies in the Christian World: To stir us up also to bless and magnifie our GOD that those Devils and their Instruments are chain'd and limited that they cannot work all the evil they would, and as long as they will: and therefore to join in Thanksgiving to GOD for His deliverance of that afflicted Family and Damsel. Finally as we are to submit to such Afflictions as the LORD may think fit to measure out unto us, by whatsoever instruments as in the case of *Job*; so we are called to Watch and Pray that we enter not into Temptation while we have such Adversarys going about still seeking to devour us, and to rejoyce that we have a *strong protector* the blessed Captain of our Salvation, the LORD JESUS CHRIST who hath obtained the Victory over all the Devils in Hell, and hath promised all his Saints a share in His Victory, which they begin to have even in time, 1 Epistle *Joh*. 4. 4, And he hath given us hope through Grace of a speedy and certain accomplishment thereof. *Rom*. 16. 20. And therefore when we see all these things come to pass. *Luk*. 21. 28. "Let us lift up our heads because our Redemption draweth nigh. FINIS. {*p. xxxix*}

An Abreviat of the Precognition and Report made by the Commissioners appointed by His Majesty's Privy Council for *Enquiry*: And of the *Confessions* of *Elizabeth Anderson*, *James* and *Thomas Lindsays*, transmitted by these Commissioners to the Council before granting of the Commission for the *Trial*. To which is subjoined, the summ of the Confessions of *Margaret* and *Jannet Rodgers*, who did confess *during the Trial* of the rest, beyond Expectation. Together also with an account of the Confession and Death of *John Reid*, who made a Discovery conform to the former Witnesses, *after* the Trial was over. And finally, there are added some passages which fell out at the *Execution* of the Seven Witches who were Condemned.

[127] 'such entertainment': such a reception.

THE Commissioners for Enquiry having met at *Bargarran* in *February* 1697, did choose the Lord *Blantyre* Præses, and took the Confession of *Elizabeth Anderson*, aged about 17 Years, as follows.

That about seven Years ago she stayed with *Jean Fultoun* her Grand-mother, and playing about the Door, she saw a black grim Man go in to her Grand-mothers House: After which, her Grand-mother came to the Door, called her in, and desired her to take the Gentleman (as she nam'd him) by the hand; and which she did, but finding it very cold, became affraid; and immediatly he evanished. About a Month thereafter, her Grand-mother and she being in the House together, the said Gentleman (whom she then suspected to be the Devil) appeared to them, and fell a talking with her Grand-mother, by rounding[128] in one anothers Ears: Upon which the Grand-mother desired her to take him by the hand, being a friend of hers; but Elizabeth refusing, the Grand-mother threatened, that she would get none of the Cloaths promised to her, unless she should obey: Yet *Elizabeth* withstood, saying, *The Lord be between me and him*; whereupon he went away in a flight, but she knew not how. *Elizabeth* was not troubled for a long time thereafter, till her Father desiring her to go with him a Begging through the Countrey; and she saying, that she needed not seek her Meat, seeing she might have Work; her Father pressed her to go alongst, and took her to a Moor in *Kilmacome*, where were gathered together, at that and other subsequent Meetings, *Katharine Campbel*, *Margaret Fulton* (her Grand Aunt) *Margaret Lang*, *John Reid* Smith, *Margaret* and *Janet Rodgers*, the three *Lindsays* (beside the two Confessant ones) *&c.* and severals whom she did not know, and the foresaid Gentleman with them. He came to *Elizabeth*, bidding her renounce her Baptism, promising that if she would consent thereunto, she should get better Meat and Cloths, and not need to beg. But (as she declared) she would not consent. Then he enquired what brought her thither, she answered, that she came with her Father: Whereupon the Devil and her Father went and talked together apart, but she knew not where about. Declares, that in that Meeting was conferred the Tormenting of Mr. *William Fleeming* Minister at *Innerkipp* his Child. *Elizabeth* Confesses she was at an other Meeting with that Crew above the {*p. xl*} Town of *Kilpatrick*, with the foresaid Gentleman whom they called their Lord: And that she went with her Father to the Ferrie-boat of *Erskin*; where the Devil with the rest of the Band overturned the Boat and drowned the Laird of *Brighouse* and the Ferrier of *Erskine*, with several special Circumstances thereanent; particularly that some of the Crew would have saved the Ferrier, but one of them, *Viz.* His Mother in Law gainstood it, in regard he had expelled her out of his House a little while before the Meeting. Acknowledges she was present with them at the destroying of *William Montgomeries* Child, by strangling it with a Sea Napkin: where they having entred the House lighted a Candle which was

[128] 'rounding': whispering.

some what Blewish, and *Agnes Naismith* saying, what if the People a wake, *Margaret Fulton* replyed, ye need not fear: As also declares, that about five Weeks before the date, her Father brought her on foot to *Bargarrans* Orchard, into which they entred by a slop[129] in the Dyke, and where were present the persons before named, *&c.* and the Devil, who told that no Body would see them, at which they laugh'd. At this Meeting they, with their Lord, contrived the Destruction of Christian Shaw: Some being for Stobbing her with a Touck,[130] others for Hanging her with a Cord, a third sort for Choaking her, and some intended to have her out of the House to Destroy her; but fearing they might be taken before the next meeting to that effect, their lord (as they call'd him) gave them a piece of an unchristned Child's Liver to eat, (but the Declarant and the other two Confessants slipped the eating of it) telling them, that though they were apprehended they should never Confess, which would prevent an effectual Discovery:[131] And further, severals of them being affraid that the Declarant would Confess, and tell of them as she had done formerly on her Grand-mother, they threatened to tear her all in peices if she did so; and particularly *Margaret Laing* threatned her most. After two Hours, or thereby, they disappeared in a flight, except the Declarant, who went home on her Foot. Confesses likewise, That one Night her Father raised her out of her Bed, and they having gone to the Water-side, took her on his Back, and carried her over the River in a flight; from whence they went on foot to *Dunbritton*, and in Mr. *John Hardy* Minister his Yeard, the crew and their Lord being met, they formed the Picture of Mr. *Hardy*, and dabed it full of pins, and having put it amongst Water and Ale mixed, roasted it on a Spit at a Fire *&c*, After which her father and her self returned in the same manner as they went. Declares the particular persons that were imployed, and most industrious in the several Facts before-mentioned, *&c.*

James Lindsay (aged 14 Years) declares,

That one day he met with the deceast *Jean Fulton* his Grand-mother at her own House, where she took from him a little round Cape and a plack; but being grieved, he required them from her again, and she refusing he called her an *old Witch* and ran away, upon which she followed him and cryed that she should meet him with an ill turn. About 3 days thereafter he being a begging in the Countrey he met his Grand-mother with a black Grim Man, *&c.* Whom she desired him to take by the hand, which *James* did, but found it exceeding cold and was straitly griped, whereupon the said Gentleman (as she termed him) asked the declarant if he would serve him, and he should have a Coat, Hat, and several other things, to which *James* answerd yes, *I'le do it*, and after this the foresaid Gentleman (whom the declarant knew thereafter

129 'slop': gap.
130 'Touck': sword.
131 Several demonologists discussed spells for preventing confession.

to be the Devil) and his Grand-mother went away but knowes not how. Acknowledges he was frequently thereafter at meetings with the Devil and Witches, particularly these mentioned in {*p. xli*} *Elizabeth Andersons* confession: that their Lord came to *James* at the first publick meeting, took him by the hand, and forbade him to tell: that they contrived before hand at the said meeting the drowning of *Brighouse*, and concurrs with *Elizabeth Anderson* anent the design of saving the Ferrier which his Mother in Law did divert. He being Interrogat, declared he did not see *J. K.* and *J. W.* at committing of the foresaid Fact: (And indeed they were then in prison) that they with a Cord strangled *Mathew Park*'s Child; and that the Person who waited on the Child finding it stifled, cryed out *Mathew Mathew, the Bairn is Dead*: *Elizabeth Anderson* concurrs in this particular; and tells that when they had done, they took the Cord with them. Declares, that he was present at strangling *William Montgomeries* Child with a Sea Napkin, and heard *Agnes Naismith* say *draw the Loup* &c. That about five Weeks since he was carryed to them in *Bargarrans* Orchard, and concurrs with *Elizabeth Anderson* in what was treated there, anent distroying *Christian Shaw*, and the Charm against Confessing. Likeways the Meeting in *Dunbritton* anent Mr. *Hardy*, is acknowledged by him: And that he has several times appeared to *Christian Shaw* both in *Glasgow* and *Bargarran*, with the others that did Torment her and put in her Mouth Coal-cinders, Bones, Hay, Hair, Sticks, *&c.* Intending thereby to Choak her: That he and they did oft times Prick and Stob her in this manner, *Viz.* He had a Needle which if he put in his Cloaths, her Body would be pricked and stobed in that place where he fixt the Needle, and if he put it in his Hair, that part of her Head would be Tormented: That he saw her put out the Pins they had put in, at which time he cryed these words, *Help J. D.* who was also then present: That when the Ministers began to pray in *Bargarrrans* House at several occasions, the Devil and they immediatly went away *&c.*

Thomas Lindsay being below pupillarity, declares the same *Jean Fulton* his Grand-mother awaked him one Night out of his Bed, and caused him take a Black Grimm Gentleman (as she called him) by the Hand; which he felt to to be cold: And who having enquired if *Thomas* would serve him and be his Man, and he would give him a Red Coat, the declarant consented: And the Gentleman (whom he knew thereafter to be the Devil) gave him a Nip in the Neck which continued sore for Ten days.[132] Thereafter one day after his Grand-mothers decease, coming by her House, he thought she appeared to him clapping his Head, and desiring him to be a good Servant to the Gentleman to whom she had gifted him, and forbidding him to reveal it. Declares, that one Night lying in Bed in the house of one *Robert Shaw*, he was awakened out of his sleep and carried in a flight to *Mathew Parks* House,

[132] James VI discussed marks that remained sore for a period of time: James VI, *Daemonologie*, in *Minor Prose*, 23 (book 2, chapter 2).

where were present the particular persons named by him, and concurrs as to the manner of strangling of the Child with *James Lindsay* his Brother: And that another Night being in the House of *Walter Alexander*; he was brought to the strangling of *William Montgomeries* Child, and agrees likeways in the manner of it with his Brother; only he sayes the Sea-Napkin with which they committed the Fact was specled. He likewise concurrs as to the Meeting in *Bargarrans* Orchard about five weeks agoe, and what was acted therein: As also anent Mr. *Hardy*; with this Addition, *That himself turned the Spitt* whereon the Picture was roasted, *&c.*

It is to be noticed that as the three Confessants were separatly apprehended upon several occasions, so they (after the obstinacy to discover[133] was abated) did emit these confessions in several distinct places without Communication with, or {*p. xlii*} knowledge of, one anothers confessions in manner mentioned in the preceeding Narrative. The Commissioners did examine them upon *other* trying *questions* that were new, thereby to make experiment of their consonancy or disagreement: But still found them strangely to *accord*. The *Facts* did *fall out* in the manner declared by them, particularly the strangling of the Children, death of the Minister, drowning of those in the boat, and torture of *Bargarrans* daughter mentioned in the Confessions before exprest. Further, the Commissioners did confront them both with *Christian Shaw* the afflicted Girle, and the persons delated (whom they had caused apprehend) and both the Girle and Confessants did accuse these to their *Faces*, and bind them in *circumstances* with great steddiness and congruity tho separatly brought in. The Commissioners did also try some *experiments* annent the Girle her falling in Fits on approach of the accused, as is exprest in the Narrative; and *examined her*, with those who stayed *commonly* about her upon the particulars of her Sufferings: they tryed to cause her write (since she could not say out) the name of a person whom she first called *Margaret* or *pinch Maggie* and asserted to be one of her chief bourriers;[134] yet upon writing *Margaret* and the letter L, of her Sirname, the Girl was presently taken with a fearful convulsion, the pen being struck out of her hand and her self falling as dead, with groans heavier and sorer then ordinary: After some recovery whereof some Ministers pointed to her a passage of the Bible, but upon essaying to cast her eyes on it, she fell into vehement pangs; till one of the Commissioners desiring the Book might be closed, and that being done she immediatly came to her self, *&c.* Lastly, the Commissioners called before them those persons who *had signed* the passages of the several dayes in the written *Journal* of this Girles Sufferings: and having examined them thereupon, *transmitted* the same with the Declarations of the three Confessants, and several of the passages that

[133] 'obstinacy to discover': reluctance to confess.
[134] 'bourriers': executioners or torturers. *SD*, p. 40, has 'Tormenters'.

occurred in the precognition, to his Majestys Privy Council by whom they were appointed for that effect.

Besides this, the subscrived attestations of Doctor *Mathew Brisbane* Phisician, and Mr. *Henry Marshall* Apothecary in *Glasgow*, did influence the belief of an *extraordinary cause* of these events,[135]

The Doctor on the 31. *December* 1696 tells, that at first sight when he was brought, the Girle appeared so brisk in Motion, so florid in collour, so chearfull, and in a word every way healthfull, that he could hardly be perswaded she had need of a Physician: But within Ten Minuts he found himself obliged to alter his thoughts, for she rose from her Seat, and advertised she was instantly to be seiz'd with a fit, according whereunto he observed a considerable distention in her left Hypochondre, which in a Trace falling, she was forthwith taken with horrid convulsive Motions and heavy Groans at first; which afterwards as soon as she was able to frame words, turned into Expostulatory Mourning against some Women; particularly *Campbel* and *Nasmith*. Yet he thought those Symptomes were reducible to the Freaks of Hypochondriak Melancholy, and therefore put her in such a course as was proper against that kind of Malady. Upon which being freed, for some time: he was alarumed that the Child was returned to Town worse then ever for having his assistance. He then was frequently with her, and observed her narrowly; so that he was confident she had no visible correspondent to Subminister Hair, Straw, Coal-cinders, Hay, and such like trash unto her; all which upon several occasions he saw her put out of her Mouth without being wet; Nay rather as they had been dryed with Artifice, and actually Hot above the Natural Warmth of {*p. xliii*} the Body; sometimes after severe fits, and other times without Trouble when discoursing with him. When she had not only light Convulsive Motions, but to a high degree, such Rigidity of the whole Body, as we call τετανοί[136] she did not fancy as at other times, that she saw these persons already named about her: But the upcasting of the Trash abovementioned did no sooner cease, then in all her fits when she was able to speak any, she always cryed out that they were pricking or pinching her. He saw her also when free of fits suddenly seiz'd with Dumbness, *&c*. And this he solemnly declares himself to have seen and handled, and were it not for the Hay, Straw, *&c*. He should not despair to reduce the other Symptomes to their proper Classes in the Catalogue of humane Diseases. And in respect of these and some other Specialitys, the Doctor thereafter being adduced upon Oath in the Tryal, Depones, that in his Opinion these things did not proceed from Natural Causes arising from the Patients Body.

[135] The *True Narrative* here gives an abbreviated recension of these two attestations. For the full text of them, see the 'Bargarran Witches' manuscript, above in the present volume.

[136] 'τετανοί' (tetanoi): tetanus or muscular spasm.

Mr. *Marshall* the Apothecary, concurres with the Doctor: And gives some particular instances of his own Observation: And amongst the rest, That the Girle having fallen Head-long upon the ground, as she had been thrown down with violence, fell a reasoning very distinctly thus:

> *Katie* what ails thee at me, I'm sure I never did thee wrong, come let us 'gree, let there be no more difference betwixt us, let us shake Hands together (putting furth her Hand as if she would take another by the Hand, then taking in her Hand again, she said) well Katie I cannot help it, ye will not 'gree with me:

And immedatly she cryed, fell into a Swerff, and out of that into a Rage, wherein she continued without intermission for about half an hour; and perfectly recovered. Then she told him, that she saw *Katie Campbel, Nansie Nasmith*, &c. and many more; *Campbel* was going to thrust a Sword into her side, which made her so desirous to be aggreed with her; and when the Girle told him this, she instantly fell into another fit as formerly, in which she continued another half hour, *&c.* Dated 1. *January* 1697.

During the *Dependence* of the Trial, *Janet* and *Margaret Rodgers* confessed in this manner, The Commissioners had adjourned for two several dyets; and though they were to meet on the *Third*, yet it was not expected that they would proceed till providence might clear the prisoners guilt by *further testimonys* of those who might come to confess. The very morning of the third Term, the *Rodgers* did confess, which was a *Surpryse* to every one that came up to attend the Court, since these, as they were *Women*, and were not formerly *noticed* as others were; so they confessed of free motion, without any persons desiring it of them at the time; they had not such *means* of instruction as were administred to others: And the conjuncture of many circumstances were altogether *Singular*. Their confessions did coincide as to the *Meetings* and *things* acted therein, with the three former confessants, and the other evidences of the visible matters of Fact. Only they were so pointed as to condescend upon some of the pannals[137] whom they did not see at these rendevouzes; and great care was taken to compare their Testimonys with what had been already discovered, and to expiscate[138] their certain knowledge by new interrogators[139] when they were separate from one another *&c.* The whole Crisis had such an evidence that now the Commissioners, with the general approbation of the most intelligent of the Countrey, who came in to attend the Court, allowed the going on of the Process to debate of the *Relevancy*, and putting seven of the best known criminals, for whom an Advocat appeared, to the knowledge of an *Inquest*: According whereunto there were some days allowed for the

137 'pannals': accused persons.
138 'expiscate': to find out by scrutiny.
139 'interrogators': interrogatories, i.e. questions.

Pannals giving in their Informations {*p. xliv*} upon the relevancy: and at the Term; there was a great time spent in adducing the Probation, An account whereof is referred to another place.[140]

Upon the 21 of *May* 1697. After tryal of the Seven Witches, there is an Attestation Subscrived by Mr. *Patrick Simpson* Minister at *Renfrew*, *Walter Scot* Baillie there, *&c.* of this import. *John Reid* Smith at *Inchennan* prisoner, did in presence of the said persons and some others; Declare, that about a Year ago the Devil (whom he knew to be such thereafter) appeared to him when he was travelling in the Night time, but spoke none to him at the first encounter. At the second appearance he gave him a Bite or Nipp in his Loyn; which he found painfull for a Fortnight. That the third time he appeared to him as a Black Man, *&c.* Desired him to engage in his Service upon assurance of getting Gear and Comfort in the World; since he should not want any thing that he would ask in the Devils Name: And then he renounced his Baptism, putting the one Hand to the Crown of his Head, and the other to the Sole of his Foot; thereby giving himself up to Satans Service: After which the pain of the Bite or Nipp ceased. He told that hitherto there was none others present; but thereafter he was at several Meetings, particularly that in *Bargarrans* Yeard, about the time when there was a Fast for *Christian Shaw*, where the Devil appeared in the same kind of Garb as he first appeared to him, and they consulted *Christians* Death either by Worrieing[141] or Drowning her in the Well; and the Devil said, he should warrand them, that they should neither be Heard, Seen, nor Confess, to which end he gave every one of them a bitt of Flesh, that the Declarant got, but let it fall, and did not Eat it. Thereafter in presence of the Laird of *Jordanhill*,[142] the Minister, Mr. *Andrew Cochran* town Clerk, and Baillie *Paterson*, he owned his former Confessions: And being enquired of *Jordanhill* how they were advertised of their Meetings, he said that ordinarly at their Meetings the time of the next was appointed; but for particular warning there appeared a Black Dog with a Chain about his Neck, who tinkling it, they were to follow &c. And being enquired by the Minister if he did now wholly renounce the Devil (for he had formerly told how Satan had not performed his promise) and give himself to JESUS CHRIST, and desire to find mercy of God through Him: he assented thereunto. It is to be observed that *John Reid* after his Confession had called out of the prison Window, desireing Baillie *Scott* to keep that old Body *Angus Forrester*, who had been his fellow prisoner, closs and secure; whereupon the company asked *John* when they were leaving him on *Friday* night the 21 of *May*, whether he desired company or would be afraid alone, he said he had no fear of any thing: So

140 This is evidently the 'Account of Two Letters' (the prosecuting advocate's speeches in court), below.

141 'Worrieing': strangling.

142 Lawrence Crawford of Jordanhill.

being left till Saturdays Forenoon, he was found in this posture. *Viz.* sitting upon a stool which was on the Hearth of the Chimney, with his feet on the floor and his Body straight upward, his shoulders touching the lintel of the Chimney, but his Neck tyed with his own neck-cloath (whereof the knot was behind) to a small stick thrust into a clift above the lintell of the Chimney; upon which the Company, and especially *John Campbel* a Chyrurgeon who was called, thought at first in respect of his being in an ordinary posture of sitting, and the neck cloath not having any *run-loup* but an ordinary knot which was not very strait, and the sticks not having the *strength* to bear the weight of his Body or the struggle; that he had not been quite dead; but finding it otherways and that he was in such a *situation* that he could not have been the actor thereof himself, concluded that some extraordinary couse had done it, especially considering that the Door of the Room was secured, and that there was a *Board set* over the Window which was not there the night before when they left him. {*p. xlv*}

There shall little be added anent what past at the Execution of the seven Witches, because there is no *Subscribed* Attestation thereanent: And the design of the Publishers has been to advance nothing but what *stands Warranded* by Testimonies of known Credit beyond Contradiction. Yet this much is *Nottour*; that when they were going to the Stake, one of the Lindsays was overheard to say to the other, *Now Brother it is time that we should Confess, since our keeping it up will serve us to no purpose*, or the like Expression; To which the other Answered that they should *never* do that, *&c.* And *Margaret Lang*, before and about Execution, let drop at *Minuts* of the Devils Inadvertance,

> That when the Devil first appeared she knew him not to be such till afterwards; that he gave her the insensible Marks found upon her Body: She yielded to engage her self his Service by a Covenant, and besides publick meetings she had been above 80 times in private Conferences with him.

Being enquired by a near Relation of her own anent her being in *Bargarrans* House Tormenting *Christian Shaw*, Answered in these Words, the Devil having an absolute Power and Dominion over me carryed my shape wither he would; and it is known how she Confessed unnatural Lust, and profound Hypocrisy, *&c.* Tho truely it did appear from her concurring Mein and Circumstances, that these things fell from her at Seasons, when Natural Ingenuity and the vigour of Truth got the *Start* of Satan's *Manacles*. So *Agnes Naismith* &c. Frequently told the Minister, that their Heart and Tongue *were bound up* in such manner, that they could not express what they would: And sometimes it appeared by ocular Inspection of their Visage, that *convulsive Dampts*[143] did seize their Heads upon getting out the initial words of any such attempt.

[143] 'Dampts': stupefactions or trances.

There are two remarkable instances in the Case of *Katharine Campbel*, who was chief Instrument and Author of the Girles trouble. *Viz*. An Eminent Minister discoursing before famous Witnesses to *Katharine*, and enquiring if she did not distinctly remember the Godly Counsels, and gracious Admonitions; which *Christian Shaw* while in a fit mentioned in the Narrative, *Page*, 13.[144] gave her at a certain time, and instancing some particular thereof: Her answer was with heavy Groans, *Yes I Remember*. But being urged wherefore she would not Confess the rest as well as that passage; and finding herself thereby to be *Gravelled*:[145] She began to Retract and seemed Dampt, not being able to Extricat her Answer beforementioned. This occurred while she was in prison, before the tryal: And after it, she in presence of several Witnesses, did get out these words, *That the Doom pronounced on her was most just*, and that *she could not free her self of Witchcraft*: But upon such attempts she fell down Dead, strangly distended, and that six or seven times Successivly, with a Suddeness, that was both Surprising and Convincing to the Spectators: At which occasion it was observed, that immediatly before her falling into these fits; and upon her Essaying to speak when there were Charges laid Home on her *Natural Conscience*; her Mouth seemed to *Contract*: And she uttered heavy Moans; whereupon did follow her Convulsion: but after raising out of them, she turned to be Obstinat and Inflexible: And whenever there was any appearance of her being more *Plyant*, the foresaid fits did overtake her.

There is one thing further; which does astruct[146] the Credibility of what these Confessants averred, viz. That there are some others, both Men and Women in the Countrey, who have confessed and told the same things before some of the best Gentry and others, whose Care could proceed no further for want of *Authority*, which in due time will, no doubt, *not suffer these Witches to live*,[147] {*p. xlvi*} whom Divine and Human Laws have so justly ordained to be cutt off. Wherefore till the Event of a further Discovery, there shall only be added some passages which were omitted in the Narrative, tho they be attested by some of the same persons that were Witnesses to the other Matters mentioned therein.

Particularly, the Girle declares, that in one of her Conflicts with the Devil, he told her how a certain Minister (for whom she had a speciall respect) did Compile his Sermons through the Week, what Books he chiefly made use of, and several other Matters anent his Method of study in his Closet that no Mortal could know by ordinary Means: By which, no doubt, Satan did partly design (tho by a very false Argument) to raise the esteem of Books

144 Page xiii of the original publication.
145 'Gravelled': confounded.
146 'astruct': establish.
147 Cf. Exodus 22:18.

above Sermons collected out of them:[148] Concealing in the mean time, both the *Gift* of improving Helps, and the Blessing promised to the Hearer of the *word preacht*. When the Lady *Bargarran* received the two pieces of Red Cloath, that the Girle had torn from one of the Witches Sleeves as is above-narrated; she locked up the same and keeped the Key: Notwistanding of which Caution, some Friends having come to Visit the Girle, and being desirous to see the foresaids pieces of Cloath; she being in one of her fits, laughed, and told that her Mother needed not to seek for them in the place where they were locked up; the Witches having taken them away, and laid them in a Corner of the Celler; and accordingly being searched for, they were found in the particular place condescended on. There was another like passage which occurred to a Friend, who came in with *Bargarran* for soliciting an Commission from the Council: For he having brought alongst with him those pieces of Cloath, and buttoned his Pocket on them at Night; and put it in security as he thought; behold they are amissing in the morning; but after search are found in a good distance from the Pocket; though none visible had been in the Room to open it and carry them off. Finally, this Girle did in discourse, discover a great Sagacity; yet accompanied with extraordinary Modesty: And amongst other instances, she did observe the Doors and Windows open and shut again, upon the Witches entry thereat: There was at no time such a number of them about her as the Room might not very well contain, with the visible persons that were present therein: She observed them to shift their place with a great Agility, when any other came *into it* or *attacqued* upon her pointing them: And she often averred from the instance of the spirit that spoke to her above her Head, told their Names, and gave her other means of discovering of them, &c. That Satan does often contrive their Ruine, by the most *undiscernible Methods* he can, because an *open Deed* would scar others to undertake with so faithless a Master &c. {*p. 1*}

An Account of Two Letters Which Contain a Summary of What Appeared Most Material or Curious in the Trial of the Seven Witches Who Were Condemn'd to be Execute in the *West*.

The Truth of the strange Things mentioned in the preceeding Narrative was at first, carefully searched into only by *private Persons*: But at last became so *nottour*, that, upon Application founded on a *Journal* of these extraordinary Events, attested by many of the Gentry in the Country; the Council gave a Commission for enquiring thereanent.

148 Presbyterians argued for the superiority of their preaching over the allegedly uninspired written services of episcopalians. The implication here is thus that the Devil argues on the episcopalian side.

The Honourable Persons to whom this was recommended, did, with great Impartiality and Exactness, make a *Report*: which, in *Providence*, proved a *Mean* of moving the Government to notice the Execution of Justice on some of these Witches, who otherways, might have lurked without being discovered.

For, hereupon, the Council directed a second Commission, for *Trial* of those who appeared to them to be most loaded by the preliminary Probation adduced on the first. Several of these Judges were not only persons of *Honour*, but also of *singular Knowledge and Experience*: Conform whereunto they did proceed with *singular Caution*, and were so far from Precipitancy in the Affair, that, after *several Diets* of Court, they adjourned to a *long Term*, that, in the mean time, the Prisoners might be provided of Advocates.

Accordingly an Advocate compeared for them, and managed their Defence with all the Accuracy that could be expected. There were above *Twenty Hours* imploied, at one Diet, in Examination of Witnesses: And the Inquest being inclosed, did consume about *six Hours* in comparing the Probation. Whereupon Seven of the most notorious Criminals were Convict and Condemned.

The Crimes libelled and found proven against them, were not meer *spectral Imaginations*; but open and obvious *Facts*: *viz*. The *Murders* of some Children, and Persons of Age; and the *Torturing* of several Persons, particularly {*p. 2*} *Bargarran*'s Daughter: And *both* these, not at a *distance*, but *contiguously* by *natural Means* of Cords, Pins, and the like. *Besides* the other *ordinary Works* of Witchcraft, such as Renuncing *Baptism*, entering in *Contract* with, and *Adoring* the Devil under a Corporeal shape, *&c*. which could not but be sustained Relevant in Scotland, since there is an express Statute *Parl. 9. Act. 73: Queen* Mary, appointing the pain of Death to such.[149]

To make the Probation the more convincing, it was adduced orderly in *three Periods*. The First consisted of *unsuspected Witnesses*, who proved *Facts*: From whence it was necessarly inferred, That there was *Witchcraft* in the Case. The Second did include, *also unexceptionable* Witnesses, who deponed upon *Facts*; which made it *probable*, if not necessary, that the Pannals were *the Witches*. The Third did comprehend *six positive* Testimonies, of these who did *See* and *Hear* these Witches committing the Malefices libelled.

The only valuable Subject of Debate, was anent the Import of these *last* Testimonies; five whereof were by *Confessants*, who had been at the Meetings in which were committed the Crimes libelled; and the sixth of *Bargarran*'s Daughter, who was one of the Persons maleficiat. The *antecedent part* of the Probation was by Witnesses beyond exception: And the Judges upon a long Debate did sustain Four of these Six *only cum nota*,[150] and two of them to be Examined without Oath. So nice were they in favours of the Pannals Lives,

[149] The Witchcraft Act of 1563.
[150] '*cum nota*': with some reservation.

since some of these Witnesses might have been admitted in such a Crime without any *quality*, by the most scroupulous Judicatory in *Europe*. But all things were carried on in this Procedures with Tenderness and Moderation: For even the *Advocates*, who were sent to prosecute the Endytment by His Majesty's Council and Advocate, did not act with the Byass of *Parties*; but on the contrary, showed an equal Concern to have the Pannals assoilzied,[151] if it could be found compatible with Justice.

This is the Reason for which the Publisher doubts not, but the two following Letters (the one whereof gives a Compend of the Advocates Speech to the Jury, and the other, of their Answers to the Objections against the Confessant Witnesses) will afford a satisfying view of the chiefest part, of the Trial: since the Objections which were, or might have been made are therein Stated and Answered, or Anticipat and *Prevented*; and the intended Brevity would not permit to print at this time the whole Process, which being extant upon Record, any who are Curious may have easy access thereunto.

There is scarcely need to take notice of a late Scurrilous Pamphlet, that has been printed in *England*, and pretends to give an account of those proceedings: For any who reads it may easily find, that the Author has been either *Fool*, *Knave*, or *both*, there being neither good *Language*, *Sense*, or *Truth* in the most part of it.[152]

Letter First.

Sir, You having told me, that the odd Passages which occur in the *West*, have put many of your Neighbours and your self, upon reading all the Books you can get treating of Witchcraft: And therefore desired me to transmit to you my Observations at the *Court*: I shall not pre-occupy your Opinion {*p. 3*} by giving them in my own Form; but herein I send to you the exactest Duplicat of the Advocates Speech to the Inquest that I could obtain; and by the next Post you shall have something more Curious: *viz*. A Collection of their Answers to the Objections against the Six last Witnesses, that were adduced for concluding the Proof: Having these, you will want little that could be agreeable to such an accurat Gust[153] as yours is.

The Speeches to the Inquest Were of this import.

Good Men of Inquest,

You having sitten above Twenty Hours in over-hearing the Probation: And being now to be inclosed, where, it's like, you will take no small time

151 'assoilzied': acquitted. *SD*, p. 46, has 'to have the accused Persons absolved'.

152 This may or may not have been *A Relation of the Diabolical Practices of Above Twenty Wizards and Witches of the Sheriffdom of Renfrew*, published in an earlier chapter of the present edition. See the introduction to that chapter, above.

153 'Gust': sense of taste. *SD*, p. 46, has 'Pallat'.

to Re-consider and Compare it: We shall not detain you with summing up the same in *particular*; but shall only suggest some Things, whereof it is fit you take special notice in your perusal of it: *viz. 1mo.* The *Nature of your own Power*, and the *Management* thereof: *2do.* The *Object* of this Power which lies before you; wherein you are to consider, in the First place, Whether or not there has been *Witchcraft* in the Malefices libelled? And, in the Next place, whether or not *these Pannals* are *the Witches*?

As to your Power, it is certain, that you are both *Judges* and *Witnesses*, by the Opinion of our Lawyers and Custom: Therefore you are called out of the *Neighbourhood*, as presumed best to know the Quality of the Pannals, and the Notority of their Guilt or Innocence. Your Oath is, That you shall all Truth tell, and *no Truth conceal*; which does plainly imply, That you are to Condemn or Assoilzie, conform to your proper Conviction. Such is the excellent Constitution of Juries in *England*: and ought to hold more specially in this Circumstantiat Case, where there is such a *Chain* of different Kinds of Probation concurring against the same Pannals, as will appear by the Review thereof in its proper place.

We are not to press you with the ordinary Severity of threatning in Assyse of *Error*, in case you should *Absolve*; but wholly leaves you to the Conduct of GOD and your own Consciences, and desire that you proceed with all the *Care* of the *Pannals Lives* that is possible for you, as the Honourable Judges have set to you a desirable *Pattern*, in their great Caution thereanent.

As to the *Probation it self*; you see, that it is divided in Three Parts, *viz.* The *extraordinariness* of the Malefices: The *Probability of the* concurring *Adminicles*: And the Clearness of the *positive Probation*.

As to the First part, The Malefices, or *Corpora delicti*, are proven by *unexcepable Witnesses*, to have fallen out in such an odd and *extraordinary manner*, that {*p. 4*} it points out some other Cause, than the ordinary course of Nature, to have produced these Effects.

For clearing of this, particularly in relation to the Torments of *Bargarran*'s Daughter, you may consider not only the extraordinary Things that could not proceed from a Natural Disease, which ly proven before you; but also several other Matters of Fact, which is *nottour*; have been seen by some of your selves, and ly here in a Journal of her Sufferings: Every Article whereof is attested by the Subscriptions of Persons of entire Credit, before the honourable Commissioners appointed by His Majesty's Privy Council, for making Enquiry there-anent.

This Girl's throwing out of Hair, Pins, and Coals of *greater heat* than that of her Body or Blood; as also so *dry*, that they appeared not to have come out of her Stomack; nor had she any *press* of Vomiting at the time, that she declared the same to have been put in her Mouth by her Tormenters: Is deponed by Doctor *Brisban*, in his Opinion not to proceed from a Natural Cause.

She was not Tormented by any of the Pannals after their Imprisonment: Except two Nights by *Katharine Campbell*; which being a Surprise, it was thereafter discovered, that these two Nights the Jaylor's Wife had got out *Katharine Campbell* to Spin in her House.[154]

She having been speaking to one of her Tormenters as present (tho' Invisible to the By-standers) and asking how her Tormenter had got these clouted Red Sleeves; she suddenly gets up, takes hold of them, the Company hear a shreid,[155] and she pulls away two pieces of red Cloth, which all the By-standers beheld with amazement in her Hands: Nor was there any other peice of this kind of Cloth to be found in the Room at that occasion.

She told, that her Tormenters were giving her a Glass of Sack, an Orange-pile, *&c.* (thereby ensnaring her to accept of a Favour from them) and accordingly she was seen to *move* her Lips, and to have the Orange-pile betwixt *her Teeth*; tho' there was no visible Hand that could have done it.

She advertised before hand, that one of her Tormenters was to be at the Door at a particular Hour: And that another of them was in the Kitchin; before any did tell her thereof: which accordingly fell out: And these being brought to her presence, became obnoxious to the ordinary Means of Discovery.

When her Glove fell down from her, at a time that several persons were about her: it was lifted again by a Hand invisible to them.

She was not only transported throw the Hall and down Stairs, without perceiving her Feet to touch the Ground: But also was hurried in a flight *up Stairs*: And when a Minister endeavoured to retain her; he found a sensible weight, besides her own Strength, drawing her from him.

When she complained, that her Tormenters had bitten and scratched her; the *Steads*[156] of the Nails and Teeth were seen upon her Skin, with Blood and Spittle about the wounds, which were above Twenty four; while neither her own, or any others Teeth that were visible, could have done it.

She was most vehemently distorted, upon attempting to Tell, or even Write the Names of her Tormenters: yet that ceased as to any of them, how soon that person was aliunde[157] delated; and particularly she had liberty, after many painful Attempts, to Accuse *Margaret Laing*, how soon a Charm of Hair to restrain her, which *Margaret* had left behind the Door, was found and burnt; the Girle having told it to have been *tint*,[158] in manner mentioned in the Depositions. {*p. 5*}

154 Several demonologists wrote that witches lost their powers when lawfully imprisoned. For James VI's statement on this see *Daemonologie*, in *Minor Prose*, 35 (book 2, chapter 6).

155 'shreid': sound of tearing. *SD*, p. 47, has 'the Company heard the Noise of the cloaths tearing'.

156 'Steads': marks or imprints. *SD*, p. 48, has 'Marks'.

157 'aliunde': by another. *SD*, p. 48, has 'how soon that person was accused by any other'.

158 'tint': lost. *SD*, p. 48, has 'lost'.

She did throw out no more Hair after the finding of a Ball of Hair, of the same *Colour* and *Kind* with that thrown out by the Girle, in *Katharine Campbel*'s Pocket, with Pins in it, and the Burning of it.

After *Agnas* [*sic*] *Nasmith* had prayed for her, she did appear to her, but not *torment* her.

She foretold, that her Tormenters had conserted to throw her in a Fit, (whereof they did premonish, of design to fright her to Renounce her Baptism by the terror) at a certain *Hour*, and had left one of their Number to execute it: According whereunto, there was a Woman with a Red Coat seen under a Tree in the Orchard, and the Torment was brought on at the time appointed.

When she told, that there was something tormenting her under the Cloaths; the Spectators saw, the Bed-cloaths *move* in an extraordinary manner, after the Girle had been raised out of them.

When she complained that she was Beaten: the By-standers heard the *Noise* of the Stroaks.

She cried out at a time, that her Theigh was hurt: And one of the Company having searched her Pocket, found a Knife; but unfolded: However, having folded up the same, and put it in a second time; she cries of new: And upon the second search, it (tho' secured by the Spring) is found open, to the great wonder of the Beholders; since they did watch, that no visible thing could have possibly opened it.

She told of a Charm under the Bed: And accordingly it was found in the shape of an Egg, which melted away being put in the Fire: She told also, that her Sister that was boarded abroad, had Charms put above her in the House, and would not recover of the decaying Sickness till she were brought out of it: According whereunto, the Child being brought home, she straight way *recovered*.

She told of their meeting in the Yeard of *Bargarran*, for Consulting anent the destroying of her: And accordingly the Confessants have deponed, That they *did meet* and consult her Ruine in that place.

The Story anent her telling, That the Commissioners, tho' at three Miles distance, had granted a Warrand to the Sherriff, to apprehend one of her Tormenters: Her telling so perfect an account of the Sheriff, and of Mr *Guthrie* who was with him, while her Eyes were cieled and fast: Her being in excessive Torments (as she fore-told) till that Person was apprehended, and immediatly thereupon, tho' at many Miles distance, her telling that her Tormenters were now taken, betwixt Twelve and One a clock in the Morning; and the Sheriff when he returned, did declare the Seisure to have been about that time: Is so nottour and so well attested, that we need only to put you in mind thereof.

Her falling in Fits upon the sight, or touch of her Tormenters, was no effect of Imagination: For she was fully hood-winked[159] with a Cloak, so as

[159] 'hood-winked': blindfolded.

she saw no Body whatsomever; yet upon the approach of her Tormenter, she immediatly fell down dead: Whereas she remained no ways startled upon the touch of any other: Which Experiment was tried for ascertaining this *Mean* of Discovery.

Finally, she is naturally *Saggacious* and *Observant*: And discovered her integrity in face of Court. For when the President asked, Whether or not she knew one of the Pannals Name that was to be pricked? She answered, That tho' she knew her well enough of her self; yet *one had told* her the Name of this Pannal, when she was sent for to be confronted with her: So far did this Girle discover {*p. 6*} her aversion from any thing that might seem intended to aid unfairly the natural Evidence of Truth; and her Firmness to the outmost against Temptations of becoming a Witch; particularly against the last Assault of Satan, wherein he perswaded her at least to go to their Meetings; and she answered, that she would not follow such a base fallen Creature: And he rejoining, that she would go to Hell however for her other Sins; and she answering, that he was a Liar from the beginning, and the Blood of JESUS would cleanse her from all Iniquity: Whereupon he disappeared, and she perfitly recovered upon the Sabbath thereafter, was an happy End put to this fearful Tragedy of Witchcraft, and confirms to Conviction, the Reality of it.

As to the *Murdering of the Children* and the *Minister* libelled; you may observe several *extraordinary* things appearing in them; particularly the Witnesses depone, the Minister to have been in *excessive Torments*, and of an *unusual colour*, to have been of sound Judgement; and yet he did tell of several *Women* being *about him*, and that he heard the noise of the Door opening, when none else did hear it. The Children were *well* at Night, and found *Dead* in the Morning, with a little *Blood* on their Noses, and *Blaes*[160] at the roots of their Ears; which were obvious Simptoms of Stranglings: Besides that it is testified, that the Mother of one of them, cried out, *Matthew, Matthew, the Child is dead* – And the House of the other was *Whitened* within, with sifting of Meal the Night before. Both which Particulars were told and discovered, by the Confessants, *before* the Witnesses which now concur with them, in it, were examined.

2*do*. The *Second* part of the Probation consists of several *Adminicles*, proven by *unsuspected* Witnesses, which lead us to suspect those Pannals to be *Witches*, as so many Lines drawn from a Circumference to a Center, and as an *Avenue to the positive Probation* thereafter adduced: And these either strick at the whole Pannals in *general*, or some of them in *particular*. In general we need not enumerat all these Adminicles, but remit you to the Probation, which is so full thereanent; only you will be pleased to notice, that it is clearly proven, that *all* the Pannals have insensible *Marks*, and some of them in an extraordinary manner: That most of them have been long *Reputed* Witches, and some of them delated in 1687. by a Confessing Witch, whose subscribed Confession

160 'blaes': bruises or livid marks.

has been produced. You see that none of them do *shed* Tears, nor were they ever discovered to do it since their Imprisonment, notwithstanding of their frequent Howlings: So that it is not a sudden Grief or Surprise. And finally, that the Girle fell in Fits of Torment upon the Pannals approaches to her, and that she did name them all frequently, either out of, or in, her Fits.

In *particular*, you see how *Katharine Campbell* was provoked by this Girl's discovering her Thift; whereupon she has brought in the rest of her Confederets to act the following Mischiefs: How thereupon *Campbell* did *Curse* and *Imprecate* in a terrible manner: How she *stayed out of her Bed* at Night, and was frequently *drousie* in the Morning: How she was named by the Girle, particularly the two Nights that she was *out* of Prison: The Ball of Hair was taken out of her Pocket and burnt; whereupon the Girle's throwing out of Hair did *cease*: She could not express one word, even when on her Knees, of Prayer, for the Girl's Recovery: And the insensible Marks on her, were very remarkable.

Agnas Nasmith did not torment the Girl *after* she had prayed for her: She was *repute* a Witch, and hath the *Marks*. She came early in the Morning to *Bargarran*'s Closs, when by her refusing to go in, it appeared she had no *business*. {*p. 7*} Yea, it is plain, that she had a Resentment, for her not getting a greater *Alms* the last time she was there. The Girl declared *ex incontinenti*,[161] that *Nasmith asked* her Health and Age; which in these Circumstances was a shrewd Presumption of her evil Design: And she acknowledged herself to have done this, when she asked the Age of an other Child; wherein by Providence she was befooled, since that which she thought would have been an Excuse, tended to discover her Guilt. And lastly, after this appearance of *Agnes Nasmith*, the Girl did take her first Fit, and nominat her amongst the first Tormenters.

Margaret Laing, that great *imposter*, has been a Master-peice of the Devil: She has confessed *unnatural Lust*, which is known to some of your number: She sat near the Door where the *Charm* of Hair was found which the Girle declared did keep up her Tongue; and upon burning thereof it was loused. The Girle fell in Fits upon her approach: She has notable Markes; particularly one which the Confessants declare she lately received; and by Inspection it appears to be *Recent*. When she came from her private conversation (no doubt with the Devil.) she *Raged* as if she had been possest, and could not but declare, That she expected a *violent Death*: She *looked* in the face of *James Millar*'s Child, and asked her Age, whereupon that Child sickned the same Night, and named *Margaret Laing* on her Death-bed: It appears she was ready to show to *Janet Laird* a sight of her Mother, who had been three Years *Dead*. And finally, She has been taken in several *Lyes* and gross Prevarications; particularly you may remember, how six hours ago; when the Witnesses were examined on the Ball of Hair found with *Katharin Campbell*, a Gentleman (Mr. *Stewart* of [*1 word*

[161] 'without further ado'.

space blank])[162] heard her say to *Katharin* in the Ear; *This is well waird on you*[163] because ye would not put it away when I desired you &c. Which the said Mr. *Stewart* did openly testifie in Court upon Oath; notwithstanding whereof this impudent Wretch had the confidence to deny it, tho *Katharin Campbel* also *Confest*, That she had pulled at her, and had spoke some what to her, to which she did not advert. This was no wonder, the Witnesses deponing at the time being closs against *Katharin*.

Margaret Fulton was repute a Witch, has the Mark of it; and acknowledged in presence of her Husband, that she made use of a *Charm*; which appeared full of small Stones and Blood. That her Husband had brought her back from the *Faries*; and her Repute of being a Witch is of an old date; besides her being named often by the maleficiat Girl.

As to the *Lindsays* they all have the Mark: And were all of a long time reputed to be Witches. *John Lindsay* in *Barloch* was accidentally discovered by the Girles taking a *Fit* upon his coming to the House. *John* and *James Lindsays*, were dilated by a confessing Witch in *Anno* 1687, Which Confession is publickly read before you: And there was *Money* given to the Sheriff-depute for delaying of the pursute. *James Lindsay* appeared to *William Semple* suddenly, and *Flew about* like a Fowl, for an opportunity to strick him, in revenge of the quarrel mentioned in the Deposition, and at last prevailed to strick him dead over a Dyke. And finally which is a remarkable Indication both of Truth and Providence, the very Witnesses adduced in the *Exculpation* for the *Lindsays*, deponed so clearly against them, even *beyond* the Pursuers Witnesses, that their Advocate was stunned thereat; and thereupon *desisted* from craving any moe Witnesses to be examined on the *Exculpation*.

It is true, some of these Indications may be in *One*, and others of them in *Another*, either from Nature or Accident; and yet that person not be a Witch: {*p. 8*} But it was never heard or read, that all these indications, which are so many discoverys by Providence, of a crime that might other ways remain in the dark, did ever concur in one and the same *Individual Person* that was innocent: Yea on the contrary, they, by the Wisdom and Experience of all Nations, do als convincingly discover a Witch, as the Symptoms of a Leprosie confirmed by all Physicians, do unfold the Person affected with the same to be Leprous. But *Esto*,[164] They are not sufficient of themselves, yet their *Tendency* and *Meaning*, being cleared and applyed to their proper cause, by a liquid and positive Probation: There wants no more to determine you anent the Pannals guilt. And therefore,

3*tio*. As to the *Third* part of the Probation, we remit the *Positive Depositions* of the Confessants, and against whom they do concurr, wholly to your own

162 This blank also appears in the MS trial record, and in *SD*, p. 50.

163 *SD*, p. 50, has '*This is well bestow'd on you*'. The sense is: 'You deserve this.'

164 'suppose'.

Perusal and Examination: Only you would be pleased to notice. *1mo*. Some things which very much *Sustain* the *Credibility* of their Testimonies, arrising from their examination in Court. *2do*. We shall explain to you the import of the word *Nota*, which is added to the Interlocutor of the Judges admitting these last Witnesses.[165]

As to the *First*,

Elizabeth Anderson is of sufficient Age, being Seventeen; yet so young and pointed, that her Deposition appears no effect of *Melancholly*; She accused her *Father* to his face when he was a dying in the prison, as now there are two of her Aunts in the Pannal, which certainly must proceed from the strength of Truth, since even *Dives* retained a natural affection to his relations.[166] She went on *foot* to the Meetings with her Father, except only that the Devil transported them over the Water of *Clyde*, which was easy to the Prince of the Air who does far greater things by his *Hurri-canes*; she tells that *Montgomeries* House was *Meallie* when his Child was strangled: And she declares that she never renounced her *Baptism*; but was carried along by the Concussion[167] of a Parent: So that nothing can be objected against her testimony in any Judgement, much less in an *Excepted Crime*.[168]

James Lindsay it is true, is of less import: yet by his *Weeping* when he came in and was admonished of the greatness of his guilt, it appears that he had an *Sense* of it: he hath a natural *Precipitancy* in what he speakes, yet that is commonly the concomitant of Ingenuity, as importing his Expressions not to be fore-thought. He *Concurrs* in most things with the others, and yet he has declared, that he saw *Not Margaret Fulton* at *Dumbartoun*. &c. Which implys that he does not file the Pannals[169] all at Randome, but tells what occurred to his Senses. *&c*.

Janet and *Margaret Rodgers* are instances of a singular providence, for they did confess the same Morning that the Court did last sit, of their own proper motive, there being neither Ministers nor Judges beside them at the time. *Agnas Nasmith* is *Janets Relation*, and she tells that she never saw *Katharine Campbel*, as *Margaret* declares that she did not see *John Lindsay* in *Barloch*: which plainly demonstrats that they tell only the dictats of their *Natural Conscience* arrising from discretion and knowledge of the true matters of Fact: They both professed their Repentance last Sabbath in the Church: And do persist with a great Firmness, as you see their *Deportment* in deponing to be Congruous and Exact.

165 The judges had ordered that these witnesses should be received only *cum nota*, with some reservation.

166 Perhaps a reference to the parable of the rich man ('Dives' in the Vulgate) and Lazarus: Luke 16:19–31. The analogy seems strained, however.

167 'concussion': forcing by threats.

168 A rare instance of the explicit concept of *crimen exceptum* ('excepted crime') in Scotland.

169 'file the Pannals': declare the accused persons to be guilty.

Thomas Lindsay and *Christian Shaw*, being under Pupillarity, we did not press their being put to an *Oath*; yet you saw that they did declare in Court against {*p. 9*} these Pannals in such an *Harmony* with the rest of the Deponents, and gave such an cause of their knowledge, That it is certain their own youngness in years *Adds*, extreamly to the Credit of their Testimony: Because thereby it is incredible, that they could have contrived or executed the acting *of concert*.

As to the *Second*,

Since these Witnesses are admitted by the Judges; it necessarly implyes, that they meant them to be probative; only they adjected the words *Cum nota*: That is, you must notice, or *Notandum est*, That there must *something else* concurr to prove the Guilt of the Pannals, by and attour[170] the Depositions of *any two* such Witnesses: But so it is, that all the Adminicles on which you have seen Probation led, for more then Sixteen Hours of your time, are strengthening evidences, of those Witnesses Credebility, and cannot but have been *Notticed* by you as Illative[171] of the same things which they depone. Whereby the *Nota* is fully taken off by the concurrence of *four other positive Testimonys*, agreeing with that of two of these Witnesses: by the *Extraordinaryness* of the *corpora delicti*: by the *Probability* of the Adminicles: And finally by the whole *Chain* of this Affair, and the Sparkles of an Infernal Fire, which in every place have broke out of it.

It is true there are some few of the Adminicles that are proven only by one Witness. But, as to this, you may consider, 1*mo*. That a Witness deponing *de facto proprio*,[172] is in Law more credited than any other single Witness: And this is the present Case as to some of the Adminicles. 2*do*. The *Antecedent*, *Concomitant*, and *Subsequent*, circumstances of Fact, do sustain the Testimony and make the *Semi-plenary* Probation to become full;[173] But 3*tio*. The other Adminicles undoubtedly proven by concurring Witnesses, are *per se*, *sufficient*: And therefore you saw us, at the desire of the Judges, forbeare to call the far greatest part of our Witnesses; because the time had already run to so great a length, and it was thought that there was already enough proven of presumptions: For it may als reasonably be imagined, that the most Regular and Curious Scheme had emerged from the fortuitous concourse of Atoms roving without Rule, as that so many indications should *Concenter* against each of these Pannalls, and yet they remain Innocent of Witchcraft.

Now upon the whole, you will take notice, that Presumptions being vehement, make a more certain Probation then Witnesses: Because Presumptions are *Natural Emanations* of the thing it self, which cannot be brybed. Whereas Witnesses are obnoxious: So in our Law there was one condemned for Thift,

170 'by and attour': as well as.
171 'Illative': inferential.
172 'concerning his/her own deed'.
173 The Roman law of proof required two witnesses for full proof.

an other for falshood, and a third for Murdering of a Child, meerly upon Presumptions, as is related by *McKeinzie* in his Criminal Treatise:[174] much more may presumptions astruct the faith of,[175] and take off the *Nota* from, *positive Witnesses*: For it is a gross mistake, that several proofs, which have each of them *some* Import, may not be joyned to make a full Evidence, the same way as two small Candles in a Dark room, will not suffice; yet several others being added to them, will make a sufficient light, to discover the murderrer: Two Boys will be able to carry a Weight which one of them would not be able to sustain; as two units make a full number: One Witness of whatsoever dignity proves nothing; yet out of the Mouth of two or three Witnesses every Truth shall be established. And finally, Tho one Coal make nor a Fire that can do the work; yet several Coals added to it encrease the Flame; which is hoped will be sufficient for the operation. {*p. 10*}

We shall therefore leave you with this Conclusion, That as you ought to beware to condemn the innocent, and ought to incline to the safest side: so if these Pannals be proven legally guilty; Then *quoad bygones*, your Eye ought not to spare them, nor ought you to suffer a Witch to Live:[176] And, *as to the future*; you in doing otherways would be *Accessory* to all the Blasphemies, Apostacys, Murders, Tortures, and Seductions, *&c*. Whereof these Enemies of Heaven and Earth, shall hereafter be guilty, when they have got out. So than the question seems simply to come to this whether upon your Oath *de fideli*, you can swear, That the Pannals, notwithstanding of all that is proven against them, are not guilty of Witchcraft? In the Determination whereof we pray GOD may direct you to the right course.

The Inquest being inclosed near six Hours, brought in their Verdict to Court, that they found the Libel proven.

I am &c.

Letter Second

Sir, I Have Collected, according to my Promise, what appeared to me most *Specious*[177] in the Reasonings, either in Court, or private Conversation, anent the receiving of the Confessants as Witnesses. You are not to imagine, that the Pannals were Condemned on the *Faith of these*: For I do believe the Probation by unexceptionable witnesses, led antecedent to this last, was so pregnant, that the Pannals might have been Condemned on it, tho' these last had not been adduced.

174 Sir George Mackenzie, *The Laws and Customs of Scotland in Matters Criminal*, ed. Olivia F. Robinson (Edinburgh: Stair Society, 2012; originally published 1678), 378 (part 2, title 25, para 4).

175 *SD*, p. 51, has 'add to the credit of'.

176 Exodus 22:18, which Grant has evidently saved for his concluding passage.

177 'Specious': pleasing.

I may have missed the *Energy* of the Argument sometimes, in a Case which in it self is so *abstruse*: However, you have it in such manner as I was able to penetrat thereunto; as follows.[178]

In order to the more satisfactory Answering of the Objections made against these last Witnesses, we shall first, lay before you the *State* of the Case: And, then, clear up the *Determination* of it.

As to the First. The Question is not, whether *Partners in the Crime*, or others mentioned in the Objections, can be a Concluding Proof of *themselves*, tho' two of them would concur as to the same Act of Witchcraft: But whether the *Corpora delicti* appearing already to imply Witchcraft, and the extrinsick Adminicles being so pregnant, to infer that these Pannals are the Witches: there concurring such Characters, as by observance of all Nations and Ages, are the Symptoms of a Witch; particularly the *Marks*, *Fame*, not shedding of *Tears*, *&c.* which are Discoveries of Providence of so dark a Crime, that like Avenues lead us to the Secret of it. And finally, when six persons of different Ages and Stations, five Confessants, and the Girl, do, when *separatly examined*, agree in their Answers to every material Question that is put to them, even tho' it be *New*; so that it could not be concerted: We say, whether or not in such a Case may Witnesses be received to put the Cape-stone on the Evidence by a *positive* probation, of a Matter of Fact which is the Object of Sense, tho' otherways they be liable to exception, if such Extraordinariness of the *Corpora delicti*, Clearness of the Adminicles, and of the Diagnosticks of Witches; did not preceed them; as you have seen proven before you that they do? {*p. 11*}

The Case is not, whether these Witnesses would be Habile in an *Ordinarie* Crime, which *commonly* falls to be exposed to other Witnesses, then those concerned in it: But whether they can be received in this *Extraordinary*, *Occult*, and *Excepted Crime* of Witchcraft; wherein there are two special Cases to be noticed; *viz.* Sometimes the Acts thereof are open, and admitt the choise of Witnesses; such as Charmes used in the Day-time, when the Actor is visible. But that part of Witchcraft; whereby Witches meet in the Night-time, Adore their Lord, contrive their Malefices, and accordingly thereafter execute them, when other Witnesses are asleep, or the Witches themselves are covered from sight: We say, that this can be no otherways proven than by these that are Intimat to it, joyned to the *positive* Proof and Adminicles before-mentioned.[179]

We do not alledge, that Persons *altogether* destitute of Knowledge and *Natural Conscience* are to be admitted in any Case, such as Infants, Furious, Fatuous, *&c.* Neither do we contend, That *Thomas Lindsay* and *Christian Shaw*, who are under Pupillarity, should be put to an Oath; for they are only to

[178] The bulk of the following text is a version of Grant's actual speech in court. Although printed here as 'Letter Second', it was delivered as the *first* of his two speeches.

[179] These last nine words are additional to the MS version of the speech in the trial record.

be examined separatly before the Court, upon interrogators,[180] by which it may appear, whether or not they coincide with the four other Confessants,[181] that are to depone before them; and this is the *Pannal's Advantage* in case of Disagreement: But we insist, that any Person above Pupillarity; giving Evidences of considerable Knowledge and natural Conscience (which is a sufficient Fond[182] for all the Credit that we need in this Case, that is already almost fully proven) is to be received as a Witness.

As to the *2d.* we shall make this as clear as Noon. *1mo.* From *Reason* and the *Nature* of the thing. *2do.* The unanimous Judgment of *Lawiers* in all Nations and Ages. *3tio.* Our *own* Customs and Decisions. And *4to.* The *Singularity* of this Circumstantiat Case.

As to the *First.* The going to, and coming from Meetings, especially on *Foot*; the falling down, and worshiping the Devil there, under a *Corporeal* shape (which he had when he tempted our SAVIOUR to do it) The actual *Murdering* of Children by a Cord and Napkin; and the *Tormenting* of Others by Pins, *&c.* Are plain Objects of Sense: And therefore the Senses are to be beleived anent them. For as *Reason* hath Things Intelligible; and *Faith* Things Supernatural; so the Senses have Things Corporeal for their Object, whereanent they are to be trusted, ay and while[183] it be *Proven*, that the *Appearance* is *Impossible*, or that the Witness of it, is an *Impostor*. It is an part of the Witches Purchase from the Devil, that they cannot be seen at some occasions: So that the Abominations comitted *then* would remain unpunished, if such Witnesses were not admitted. It cannot be thought that Witches (who of all Criminals are the most *obstinat to Confess*) would venture the loss of their own Lives, by deponing against Others, against whom they have *no special picque*; yea, for whom they have particular *Affection*, as several of the Pannalls are some of the Witnesses Relations. Nor has the Devil any *peculiar* interest to Instigat them thereunto: For severals of the Pannalls have confessed *other execrable Crymes*: Whereby it cannot be supposed, That Satan would be divided against himself.[184] GOD in his ordinary Providence has taken such care of publick Judgments, that the Enemy of Justice[185] his *special Power* ceases thereabout, as appears by the Witches not being able either to do more Harm, or escape, after GOD's Ministers begin to counteract Satan's Instruments by Imprisonment. And finally, the oddness of the Malefices, the Concurrence of the {*p. 12*} Adminicles; and the existence of Matters of Fact, wherein these Confessants

180 'interrogators': questions asked formally in court.

181 These 'Confessants' were Elizabeth Anderson, James Lindsay, Janet Rodger and Margaret Rodger. (Thomas Lindsay was too young to testify on oath.)

182 'Fond': proof.

183 'ay and while': until.

184 Cf. Mark 3:23–6.

185 'the Enemy of Justice': the Devil. The point is that the Devil's power ceases in the face of the court, which executes God's justice.

(tho' not knowing the same otherways) do *agree with other* unexceptionable Witnesses, *&c.* Do sufficiently astruct their Credibility: For as Falshood being a Crime, is never presumed; so a person found true in many things, is still presumed to continue such, till the contrary be evinced.

As to the second, *Socius criminis &c. admittitur si delictum sit nefandum*[186] *Men: A: J: Q: l. 2d. i. C. cas*: 474. N. 27. *seq:*[187] *aut ocultum & veritas aliunde haberi non posit*[188] *Mas: vol:* 1. *Con:* 466. N. 6.[189] *aut difficilis probationis*[190] *Farin: lib.* 2. *Op: Criminalium. Tit.* 6 Q. 63. N. 28.[191] *Mas: vol. 3d. Con:* 1360. N. 4th. *Menoch. l. 2d. Cas:* 116. *l.* 1*st.* Q. 58. *nocturno tempore comissa quæ dificilis dicuntur probationis*[192] *Boer: decis.* 68 *N.* 6.[193] *Menoch D. Cas:* 116. N. 14. *Ideoque non solum presumptiva & conjecturata probatio sufficit, verum etiam in habiles admittuntur*[194] *farin.* I. 2d. Tit: 6. Q. 55. N. 40. *Masc.* l. 2. *Con:* 1124 N. 13. *idem in dilictis* [*sic*] *commissis in Eremo, Nemore, Monte alique loco secreto,*[195] *Gomez: Var: res, Tom: 3d.* C. 12. N. 21.[196] *Far: D.* Tit: 6. Q. 62. N. 55. *sed occultum non dicitur quod actu non intervenerint, at quod de Natura delicti vel ratione loci & temporis alii testes habitu intervenire non potuerint: ist est Maleficium in quo socius criminis* &c. *admittitur.*[197] *Men:* l. *2d. Cap.* 5. *Cas.* 474. N. 33 *Campeg: te* [*sic*] *test: Reg.* 86 *Fallen.* 6.[198] *Crotus de Test. part 4th.* N.

[186] 'Accomplices are admitted (as witnesses) if the crime was atrocious'.

[187] Possibly a reference to Giacomo Menochio (Jacobus Menochius) (1532–1607), an Italian jurist who published a number of works. This passage seems to have two further citations to him.

[188] 'or (if the crime is) hidden and the truth cannot be obtained in any other way'. For '*posit*' read '*possit*'.

[189] Probably a reference to Giuseppe Mascardi (Josephus Mascardus), *Conclusiones Probationum Omnium* ('Conclusions of All Proofs') (1584). This passage seems to have two further citations to this work.

[190] 'or (if the crime is) difficult of proof'.

[191] Probably a reference to Prospero Farinacci (Prosperus Farinacius), *Praxis et Theorica Criminalis* ('The Practice and Theory of Criminal Trials') (1616). This passage seems to have two further citations to this work.

[192] 'or (if the crime was) committed during the night, when probation is said to be difficult'.

[193] A reference to Nicolas Bohier (Nicolaus Boerius), *Decisiones Burdigalenses* ('Decisions from Bordeaux') (1547).

[194] 'therefore, proof merely presumptive or conjectural is not sufficient, but even things awkward are admitted'. For '*in habiles*' read '*inhabiles*'.

[195] 'the same with crimes committed in the wilderness, forest or mountains, or in any secret place'.

[196] A reference to Antonio Gómez, *Commentariorum Variorumque Resolutionum: Tomus Tertius* ('Commentaries and Various Resolutions, Book Three') (1555).

[197] 'but it is not said to be hidden because they may not have participated in the action, but because, on account of the nature of the crime or by reason of the place and time, other witnesses might apparently not have been able to intervene: this is (the case of) witchcraft in which accomplices are admitted (as witnesses)'.

[198] Possibly a reference to Lorenzo Campeggio (1474–1539), an Italian jurist and later cardinal.

97.[199] *Oldindorp. de Test. Til. de personis testium* N, 21.[200] In a word all Lawiers who wrot particular Treatises on Witchcraft in *Germany*, *Italie*, *Loven*, *France*, and *Spain*, &c.[201] Do conclude, that inhabile Witnesses; and particularly *Socii* are to be admitted in Witchcraft; only the strictest of them do think, that this Admission is to be *cum nota*; or as *Delrio* in the place cited for the Pannals expresses it *ex his solis*, the Judge is not to Condemn, nor do we require it.[202]

As to the Third. we have the Testimonie of our Famous *K. Ja: 6th. Demon: lib.* 3. C. *ult.* telling us, That it is *our* Law, that Boys, Girls, infamous Persons, *&c.* Are not to be rejected any more in Witchcraft, than in human lese Majesty,[203] even tho' they assert others to have been present at *Imaginary Meetings*:[204] Because this *Supposes* their having entred into a *Pre-contract*:[205] He sayes that Satan's Mark, and the want of Tears, are pregnant Aids to the Discovery, *Quod Deus praternatura ordinem voluit esse secretæ imanitatis judicium, & eo non permittente ut fedissimi criminis pertinaciam dissimulent.*[206] He gives an instance of a Girle, who having named several Witches in her Fitts; they were all Condemned upon other concurring Adminicles. This is not a common Author, but a Man who as Curious, was Exact: As Prudent did not publish such things without the Approbation of the best Divines and Lawiers; as a Prince, is to be Credited anent the Law of His own Countrey; and as a King

[199] A reference to Giovanni Crotto (Johannes Crotus), *Tractatus de Testibus* ('Treatise on Witnesses') (1523).

[200] A reference to Johann Oldendorp, *Tractatus de Testibus et Universa Testimoniorum Materia* ('Treatise on Witnesses and All Matters of Testimony') (1596).

[201] The only town in this list of places, 'Loven' (Leuven), was the original place of publication of Martin Delrio's treatise. Delrio cited other demonologists and jurists copiously, and, as we shall see further below, Grant probably borrowed many of his citations. There are numerous editions of Delrio; below I have used Martin Del Rio, *Disquisitionum Magicarum Libri Sex* ('Disquisitions on Magic, in Six Books') (Lyon [Lugduni]: Cardon, 1608) ('Delrio, *Disquisitiones Magicae*').

[202] Delrio, *Disquisitiones Magicae*, 382 (book 5, section 5, para 4). This passage is discussed further below. The phrase 'the place cited for the Pannals' is a reference to the speech made to the court by the defence advocate, James Roberton, which cited Delrio several times. This speech has been published with the other trial documents in Goodare and Willumsen (eds.), *Scottish Witchcraft Trials*, 580–8.

[203] 'lese Majesty' (*lèse-majesté*): treason.

[204] 'Imaginary Meetings': meetings attended in spirit rather than bodily.

[205] Grant argues here that, if a witness or confessing witch states that another person was present with them at the sabbat, then that other person must have made a pact with the Devil. He correctly states that James in *Daemonologie* had made this argument. All the citations from that work in this passage come from James VI, *Daemonologie*, in *Minor Prose*, 54–6 (book 3, chapter 6).

[206] This is a free translation of James's 'God having appoynted that secret super-naturall signe, for tryall of that secrete unnaturall crime ... God not permitting them to dissemble their obstinacie in so horrible a crime'. The MS trial record, more correctly, has '*indicii*' instead of the *True Narrative*'s '*judicium*', but has the less correct '*pater naturee*' instead of '*praeternatura*'.

has determined any Dubiety[207] that might have remained in this Point, alse farr as the Law of our Government will permitt.

But further our Judges and Lawiers have followed His Majesty: For in all the Processes in the Journals; Fame, and Delation, and the *Mark*, are still sustained, as most pregnant Presumptions; whereupon, and a very small Probation besides, Witches have been frequently Condemned. So in the Processes against the Bewitchers of Sir *George Maxwel of Pollock*, and *Hamilton* of *Barns*, *Anno*, 1677,[208] *Socius criminis*, tho' under Age, is sustained to be a Witness: And witnesses are adduced before the Inquest for proving, that the Mark was found upon some of the Witches. *Women* and *Minors* have been received by multitudes of Decisions cited by *McKenzie*. *Tit. prob: by Witnesses*, and *Tit: Witchcraft*. And he also cites Decisions, where, in paralel Cases, *Socii Criminis* and *{p. 13} others inhabile*, were admitted; particularly in Treason and in Falshood: And all Lawiers conclude, That witchcraft is as much an *excepted* crime as these.[209]

As to the *4th*. What ever inhability these witnesses might be under, it is fully made up, and they rendred unexceptionably Habile *by the Chain* of this whole Business. It is true *one* Man throw the concurrence of corrosive Humors, may have an insensible Mark; *another* be enviously defamed: A *Third* may through sudden Grief or Melancholy, not be able to weep, *&c.* A *Fourth* may be loaded with suspitious Circumstances, when extraordinary things fall out in the Countrey: And a *Fifth* may be deponed against by two false witnesses, tho' neither of these separatly be truely witches. But by the known Observation and Experience of *Mankind*, none except witches have had the unhappie Medley and Concurse of *All* or *Most* of these *Indicia*, and ordinarly, and for the *greater part*, Witches have them: So that since the Rules of Judgment are established upon that, *Quod plerumque sit*,[210] which does obtain *till an exception* be apparent in a special case, the Conjunction of these in *one person*, does as plainly give his Character, as the most certain symptoms of the plainest Disease, being universally concerted in all parts of the World, points out to us that the Haver of them is a person truely affected with that Desease, whereof he hath the concurrent Diagnosticks. In a word, one or other of these may concurr, in the Innocent; but no Writers do *Attest*, that *all of them* have concentred in any other person in the World but a witch: And on the other hand, they taking place in Witches, through *all parts of the World*, must proceed from a *common*, and not from a peculiar Humor or Cause.

207 'determined any Dubiety': ended any doubt.

208 For this case see Goodare and Willumsen (eds.), *Scottish Witchcraft Trials*, 504–28.

209 These arguments misrepresent Mackenzie in several particulars. He did not say that witchcraft was an excepted crime, and he expressed deep reservations about the evidence of the Devil's mark and testimony of other witches ('*socii criminis*'). Mackenzie, *Laws and Customs*, 66–86 (part 1, chapter 10).

210 'Which is generally the case'.

The *specifick Aptitude*; of some of the nicest of the *Indicia*, which appeared from the Probation already led, to discover a Witch, do serve to clear the ground of the Worldes Observation anent them. Particularly the Devil, as Aping GOD, imprints a Sacrament of his Covenant: Besides that, commonly this mark being given at the *first Meeting*, does by its intolerable Pain, force the Witch to a second Randevouz for curing it, at which the poor wretch being under this furious necessity, fixes the Paction by renewing it with deliberation, having been diverted in the mean time from considering the Horridness of the first Engagement by the Pain.[211] The inability to shed Tears may be a Charactristick of *Hardening*, tho' not always in the case of Christians; yet in these who have ceased to be such; lest the Devil giving them such words of Scripture and Prayer as many have, it should be impossible to discover their Hypocrisy; and that is not Satan's own interest, since by this Discovery occasion is given to Buffoon[212] the Profession of Holyness. A Report often arises without ground, but a *Constant Repute* that keeps footing, implyes for the most part a surer Cause; especially when it is of Persons below Envy; and by Persons above Calumny. The Girls falling in fitts at approach of the Pannalls might proceed from *Antipathie*, arriseing from the poisonous Steems of the witch accustom'd to produce that Effect through a vertue affixed thereto by the Devil, by Conjunction of natural Causes (the same way as the invisible Pestilence does operat)[213] or his *promise* of casting the Girl in Fitts at the Witches presence, might have been *General*; where by the Witch was eventually befooled and discovered, as it often falls out: For Satan envies even their temporal Felicity, and fears lest by continuing here, they should be reft out of his hands by Conversion: When they come to perceive the Delusion of his Promises to make them rich and the like, *&c.*

There was one thing further which was tried before your Lordships, *viz.* None of the Pannals that were tried (tho' most Saggacious and Knowing, and {*p. 14*} perfect in Memory, so that it could not proceed from Ignorance or Forgetfulness) could make out the attempt of saying the Lord's Prayer; which may either be a *secret Judgement* for Renuncing their first LORD, after whom it is peculiarly Denominat, or by *restraint* of their new lord, who may think that *too special an Homage* to his Adversary. But we have hindered you too long with that which is not necessary: For this being incontravertible *Law* and Custom, there needs no Philosophy to support it: Since Legislators do Reason, but Subjects must Obey: And both the Fool and the Lazie (who

211 The idea that the pain of the Devil's mark forces the witch to return for a second meeting may be an original idea in demonological thought.

212 'to Buffoon': to mock. Grant's argument seems to be that the Devil *wants* his witches to be discovered, so that the revelation of their existence will cause Christianity to suffer through this public mockery.

213 This argument about poisonous vapours, probably deriving from Glanvill, was also made by John Wilson in the introduction to the *True Narrative*, above.

have neither *Read* nor *Thought* enough to understand this Subject) are to be left to their own Chimera's: Yet lest they should *insult*, we shall Answer in their fashion, such of the Objections as the Pannals Advocate thought any ways worthy to be repeated in this place.

Whereas it is objected, that *Delrio Sect.* 5. § 4. says, That *Socii* are not to be admitted witnesses *ad condemnandum*; especially considering, that the Probation ought to be *luce meridiana clarior.*[214]

It is answered, that the place it self confutes this Inference in the present Case: For it says, *Ex* his solis *non est procedendum ad condemnationem, scio contrarium communius teneri & in praxi obtinere*, &c.[215] So that it is evident, 1*mo*. That the common Opinion and Custom is in the contrary, even when there is no other probation, but by the Partners of the Crime. Yet, 2*do*. we are not so straitned but subsume in his very words, *ex his solis* we do not desire the Pannals should be Condemned; but your Lordships see these Witnesses we are to adduce are not *soli* or *alone*; for the Probation led these last Sixteen Hours, are so many *Concomitants* and Discoveries of Providence, which astruct and make up any defect in their Credit that can be desiderat. Hence, 3*tio*. The Meaning of that Maxim (which is Metaphorical, as appears by the words, Clarior *luce meridiana*, an *equal* Clearness being sufficient) is fully Answered, and takes place in the present Case: For the Extraordinariness of the *Corpora delicti*, Pregnancy of the Adminicles, and Pointedness of the positive Probation, being conjoined; there is not a Clearer Proof upon Record in any Nation, than that to which, it's hoped, these will amount.

Whereas this Alledgance is enforced, by pretending it were of dangerous consequences to allow such witnesses to prove meeting with the Devil, since Satan might have represented others by their *false shapes*.

It is Answered.

1*mo*. That we are not straitned in this; because there are many other Articles proven, which could not have been falsified. But if we give some scope to Reasoning even in this point; it is to be considered, that[216] the Rules of Judgement are established upon that which for the most part does still obtain; and *Rules* are to be followed, till an *exception be proven* in a particular circumstantiat Case. But so it is, by the Experience and Observation of the wisest Divines, Lawiers, Philosophers, Phisicians, States-men, Judges and Historians, at Home and Abroad (that are too wise to be imposed upon, and too Ingenuous to deceive us, when they all concurr in the same matter of fact) beside the Testimony of Witches themselves every where; makes the

214 'Accomplices ... where sentence is to be passed ... clearer than noonday light'. Cf. Delrio, *Disquisitiones Magicae*, 382 (book 5, section 5, para 4).

215 'From these things alone one should not proceed to pass sentence, (although) I know the opposite to be more commonly believed and to be put into practice'.

216 The passage from 'That we are not straitned' to this point is additional to the MS version of the speech in the trial record.

Apparitions of Witches to be commonly and mostly *reall*; so *Delrio* tells us *lib.* 5. § 16. *Illusis rarissime contingit,*[217] *ita Jaqerius, Comensis, Sprengirus, Bienffeldus.*[218] &c. And therefore the Testimony of the Senses is always to be credited anent them, ay and while[219] it be canvelled.[220] For *single or few* instances of false Representations to the Senses esteeming them to be true, or a possibility of Appearances being false, can {*p. 15*} no ways invalidat the Rule established upon Experience, which is common, and for the *most* part, whereby no exception is to be presumed till it be proven in a *special* Case; since a *Wonder* does not subvert the Proof drawn from the *common course* of Nature;[221] Logick admits not to argue a *Particulari*, or from *possibility* to Existence; Law puts the burden of proving *Simulation* on the Affirmer, and that which *seldom* occurrs, is not considered by the Legislators.

For illustrating of which, it is further to be considered, that for the *most part* and *ordinarly*, the Witches are *personally existent* in the places where they appear; because it's more *easy* for the Prince of the Air to transport them in his Hurricanes which he can raise, as is plain in the instance of *Job* (who was put in his *power, i.e.* his *natural Power* without Delegation) forming a *Fence* upon their Face, whereby the violence of the Air may be diverted from chocking them: Than to form the curious *Miniatur* of such various Transactions on their Brain: The difficulty whereof is the greater, that all their *Fantacies* are not disposed at all times the *same* way; and they have not the *Seeds* of this work, unless they had once acted it in reality. It is both the greater *Cryme* and *Pleasure* to act in Truth; which therefore the Devil and Witches do rather choise (unless the Place be farr distant, or the Party indisposed,) and this *de facto* is attested to be so, by the Writers and Witches in all Nations and Ages, as said is.

2do. Notwithstanding that the *Rule* must hold, till an *Exception* of Exculpation be evinced, *quoad*[222] a particular Person, by evidencing that the reall *Appearance*

217 'It affects those deceived most seldom'. The substance of this point, though not the exact words, is found in Delrio, *Disquisitiones Magicae*, 400 (book 5, section 16).

218 'Jaqerius': Nicolas Jacquier, *Flagellum Haereticarum Fascinariorum* ('Scourge of Heretical Enchanters', 1458). 'Comensis': Bernard of Como (Bernardus Comensis), *Lucerna Inquisitorum Hæreticæ Pravitatis et Tractatus de Strigibus* ('Lamp of Inquisitors of Heretical Perversity and Treatise on Witches', 1584). 'Sprengirus': the *Malleus Maleficarum* ('Hammer of Witches', 1486), today considered to be the work of Heinrich Krämer alone, but usually attributed in this period jointly to Krämer and Jacob Sprenger, or even (as here) to Sprenger alone. 'Bienffeldus': Peter Binsfeld, *De Confessionibus Maleficorum et Sagarum* ('The Confessions of Witches and Magicians', first published in German 1589). The MS version of the speech in the trial record adds to this list 'Remigius': Nicolas Rémy, *Daemonolatreia* ('Demon-Worship', 1595). All these are probably second-hand citations via Delrio, *Disquisitiones Magicae*, 400 (book 5, section 16), which cites 'Iaquerius, Comensis, Sprenger, Michaëlius, Binsfeldius, Remigius'.

219 'ay and while': until.

220 'canvelled' (more commonly 'convelled'): refuted. *SD*, p. 55, has 'disprov'd'.

221 Grant is effectively arguing here that witchcraft is fully *natural*, and that it would be a 'wonder' – something beyond ordinary nature – if the events said by the prosecution to have occurred had been caused by any means *other* than witchcraft.

222 'as concerning'.

was in that special Case a true *Mistake*: yet this Exception is *sufficient* for safty of the *Misrepresented*; since the same providence which permitted the Affliction, will order the Out-gate and Exculpation; either by the Aeriall Bodies not byding the *toutch*, or some other *distinction*, as Providence commonly allowes the Devil to personat only with *cloven Feet*; or that the Apparition was solly[223] to one *single Witness*, who cannot be a Proof; or that the Innocent can prove *alibi*; or Finally the *Notour Charracter* of a Samuel, will *purge and dispel* the Aspersions of Satan, contrived of purpose to discredit the Evidence of *Sense*, by which alone his Instruments can be discovered. Especially this Charracter being joyned to the other Circumstances of the providence; such as, when good men are disguised[224] they are mostly *passive* in the Scene and out with thereof: Whereas Witches are personally *active* in their *common Life* by such Words and Deeds as (in conjunction with these Appearances) conspire to make us know and distinguish them from the truely Good; since these Witches open *Profanity*, *Naughtiness*, or *unvailed Hippocrisy*, being cleared by *Fame*, sealed by the *mark*, and confirmed by the other discoveries of the *Adminicles* that ly proven before you, do still make an Land-mark betwixt the Children of Darkness and Light. So *Delrio lib.* 5. *Sect.* 16. N. 5. tells of *Athanasius* and St. *Germanus*, against whom Probation was adduced for *Sorcery*, but Providence did canvel[225] it.[226] It's a famous instance of *Susanna*, *represented* by the Elders; which tho not in the Case of *spectre*, yet agrees in the *Rationale*.[227] The Representation by *Pharo's* Magicians had *Concomitants*, by which they were discovered and confounded.[228] But lastly, suppose that GOD in the deepths of His Wisdom (to Convince the Error of Nimious[229] *self Confidence*) should permitt all necessar Probation to concurr against an Innocent; yet the Judge following the Faith[230] of Proofs established by Divine and Humane Laws, is altogether Innoxious: Since this Case being very *Rare*, the *Evill is less* than the establishing a Principle, by which most of all these Monsters could not be cut off. {*p. 16*}

223 'solly': solely.

224 'when good men are disguised': when the apparitions of good men appear.

225 *SD*, p. 56, has 'disprove'.

226 Delrio, *Disquisitiones Magicae*, 405 (book 5, section 16).

227 Susanna was falsely accused of adultery, but was vindicated through the intervention of the prophet Daniel. In the Authorised Version of the Bible, the story appeared in the Old Testament Apocrypha, in the Book of Susanna. Grant seems to think that the story is relevant to his argument by showing that innocent people, falsely accused, will be vindicated. However, his main aim is to show that the Devil cannot cause the apparitions of innocent people to appear, and the story of Susanna, as he admits, did not involve apparitions.

228 In the biblical contest between Aaron and Pharaoh's magicians (Exodus 7:8–13), both contestants transformed their rods into serpents, but Aaron's serpent swallowed the magicians' serpents. The demonological understanding of this was that the magicians' serpents were demonic apparitions.

229 'Nimious': extravagant.

230 The MS version of the speech in the trial record has 'fouth' (abundance).

Upon the whole, It is certain, That as tho' oft times *false Witnesses* set on by the Devil, have taken away an harmless Life, by accusing it of *other Crimes*; yet the Testimony of Witnesses must still be credited till they be redargued;[231] so these Appearances of Witches with the other Specialities before exprest, being proven, ought to be esteemed *Real*, till the fallacy be established. Especially seing there are Examples in Ancient and Modern History of Satan's Representing the *best of Men*, as committing *Murther*, *Buggrie*, &c. In *effigie*; so *Delrio, lib.* 5. *Sect.* 16. N. 5. relats, That St. *Silvanus* was represented by the Devil, as committing a *common* Capital Crime:[232] And the like of a Monk: whereof there are several Modern paralel Instances; yet this cannot enervat the *Rule* and *Faith* of publick Judicaturs, founded on no more but upon the sight of the like Appearances; and any Argument against the Probation in Witchcraft, will equally hold against the Probation of any other Crime whatsomever: Wherefore the Rules of them both must be *common*, as to beleiving the Senses fortified, *ut supra*;[233] till their *Error be Individually discovered.*

Finally, the Certainty is no ways diminished by the *extraordinariness* of the Appearance to the Senses: For in *Law* and *Nature* Reality and not Simulation is presumed, till the contrair be made appear by proving the thing not possible in Nature, or tho' it be possible, that it is actually false. This is answer enough to those who place a great part of their small Wit in nonsensical arguing against all Divine Authority: But writers further illustrate that the extraordinariness of a Matter of Fact, does not exclude it's Reality's being the Subject of the Testimony of Witnesses, in our *Saviours Miracles*, Transfiguration, Walking on the Waters, standing in the midst of the Disciples while the Doors were shut, and arguing Assurance by Their Senses, That a Spirit had not *Flesh* and *Bones*, tho' indeed the *surer* Word of prophesy did put these beyond doubt.[234]

Nor could it be alledged for the Pannals (tho they had the last word, as perhaps they have not, in Objections against Witnesses, since therein *rei fiunt actores*[235] by attacquing the Witnesses presumed Hability)[236] That it's not conceiveable, how the Girl or Witnesses could *see* what the *bystanders could not behold*: Beside the impossibility of the real Bodies entering at *closs Doors and Windows*, or not *intercepting* the sight of what is at its back.

231 'redargued': questioned or disproved. *SD*, p. 56, has 'till they be made Evident'.

232 Delrio, *Disquisitiones Magicae*, 405 (book 5, section 16).

233 'as above'.

234 The MS version of the speech in the trial record has a shorter version of this paragraph: 'Finally the certainty is no wayes diminished by the extraordinaryness of the appearance to the senses: For as in law and nature, Realitie and not simulation is presumed till the contrary be made appear upon some evident ground: So this is plain (to all who place not a great part of their small will in nonesensicall argueing against the Divine authority) in our Saviours miracles, transfiguration, walking on water, standing in the midst of the Disciples when the Doors were shutt and yet argeueing assurance by their senses that a spirit had not flesh and bones.'

235 'the guilty are made into criminals'.

236 *SD*, p. 56, has 'the presumed hability, or *Legality* of the Witnesses'.

For to this it would be answered,

1mo. Proven facts must not be denyed, tho' Philosophers have not yet *certainly* reached the Invisible *manner* of their Existence: So in *Nature*, the Load-stone[237] draws the Iron, the Compass turns always to the Poles, &c. In *Scripture* the Angels (and the Devil was once such, retaining as yet his *Natural powers*) smote the *Sodomites*, that they could not *see the Door*; tho they saw the *House*.[238] *Balaam's* Ass perceived the Angel that stood *undiscovered* to himself;[239] and the Rod thrown down by the Magicians of *Ægipt*, was no doubt seen by themselves, tho invisible to the by-standers. Which *holding of their Eyes*, Interpreters explain to have been done by natural Means; and yet the Manner thereof is certainly difficult.

However, it is also certain, that if a *possible way* can be proposed, the Reality of a proved Fact is not to be contradicted: And this can be done in the the present Case: For,

2do. Satan's *Natural* Knowledge and *acquired* Experience, makes him perfect in *the Opticks* and *limning*:[240] Besides that, as a *Spirit* he excels in Strength and Agility; whereby he may easily bewitch the Eyes of others; to whom he intends {*p. 17*} that his instruments should not be seen in this manner as was formerly hinted: *viz*. He constricts the Pores of the Witches Vehicle,[241] which intercepts *a part* of the Rayes reflecting from her Body; he *condenses* the interjacent Air with grosser Meteors[242] blown into it, or other ways does violently *agitate* it, which drowns *another part* of the Rayes: And lastly he *obstructs* the optick Nerves with Humors stirred toward them: *All which joined together* may easily intercept the whole Rayes reflecting from these Bodies, so as to make no impression upon the common sense; and yet at the same time, by *refraction* of the Rayes, glydeing alongst the *fitted sides* of the Volatile Couch, wherein Satan transports them, and *thereby meeting* and coming to the eye, as if there were nothing interjacent, the wall or chair behind the same Bodies may be seen; as a peece of Money lying out of sight in a Cup becomes visible how soon the *medium* is altered by pouring in some water on it. Severals of your number do know, that the Girle declared, that she saw and heard the Doors and Windows open at the Witches entry, when no doubt the Devil had precondensed a *soft stopage* on the Eyes and Ears of others, to whom that was unperceived.

237 'Load-stone': magnet.
238 Cf. Genesis 8:11.
239 Cf. Numbers 22:22–34.
240 'limning': portrait-painting.
241 'Vehicle': the body (considered as a receptacle for the spirit).
242 'Meteors': atmospheric or airy phenomena.

So *Apolonius* escaped *Domitians sight*;[243] and *Giges* became *invisible* by his Magical Ring.[244] *John* of *Sarrisberrie*[245] tells us of a Witch, that could make any thing not to be seen: and *Mejerus*[246] relates another, that had the like power. Some *Italian* Witches of *greater then ordinary wit* confessed to *Grillandus* the *Devils* opening Doors and Windows for them, tho the more *Ignorant*, by a Fascination, think themselves *Actors* of this.[247] Whence it ought not to be doubted by any reasonable Man what in all Times and Places is so uncontestible Fact.

Finally the Pannals could not insist, that these Confessants are to depone only on their *Imagination*, which can prove no more against themselves or others then a *Dream*.

For still its to be minded, that there are other Proofs to which this is only necessary as a consonant adminicle. But further *Arg. causa*, It is answered, that the alledgeance is a mistake;[248] seeing they declare plain matters of fact obvious *not only* to *one*, but *several* of their Senses: *viz*. Some of them went the greatest part of the way to these meetings *on foot*: they there *saw* and *touched* their confederats; they heard their Combinations to Destroy and Torture the Infants, Girle and Ministers: They returned on *foot* again: and even when they were carried fore or back they knew on the next day that it was no Dream, the same way as all other Mortals discover the difference. But moreover this is adminiculate by some real effects of a personal Presence, as you have seen in the *probation*: And it is yet further cleared by the journal of *Bargarrens* daughters Sufferings; which was attested before the former Commissioners, and is nottour in the Countrey; particularly the Glass of Sack and *Orange pile*; the *peices* of the clouted Sleeves; the words expressed by the Keeper on the sudden Murder of the Child; which are constantly *told* by some of the Confessants; as also the Houses being *Meallie* that Night. The Girle tho *hood winked*, her falling in Fits at their approach, &c. And others, which shall be pointed at to the Assyse,[249] conjoyned together, can be ascrived to no other cause then the *real existence* of the Witches persons in the places Unless it be said, that Satan *might possibly* have *foisted* and *suborned* all these; and thence it

243 Apollonius of Tyan was a Greek sage who was said to have confronted the Roman Emperor Domitian (who reigned 81–96 CE).

244 Giges' ring of invisibility was discussed in Plato's *Republic*.

245 *Sic*. *SD*, p. 57, has '*Salisbury*'. John of Salisbury's *Policraticus* ('The Statesman') (1159) discussed various forbidden magical arts.

246 The MS version of the speech in the trial record gives this as 'Megerus'. *SD*, p. 57, has '*Mejerus*'. This name may well be the common German surname Meyer or Meier. No demonological or juristic writer of that name has so far been identified.

247 Paulo Grillando's *Tractatus de Hereticis et Sortilegis Eorumque Poenis* ('Treatise on Heretics and Witches and their Punishments') was first published in 1524 and often reprinted.

248 '*Arg[umentum] causa*': for the sake of argument. The MS version of the speech in the trial record has a shorter version of the opening of this paragraph: 'For it is answeared that this is a mistake'.

249 This phrase indicates that Grant's speech is addressed primarily to the judge rather than to the assize.

be concluded, that the Devill did *actually so*, in which case the *Objecters* are the Persons that bottom their Opinion on *Imagination without* any *positive* ground of the reality of what they fancy; yea *against* positive grounds of belief in the contrary; which arguing from *Possibility* to *Existence* is already sufficiently exploded. {*p. 18*}

Whereas for sustaining the Objection it is likewise alledged, That the confessants having been in the *Devils service*, and *renounced Christ*, they are not Capable of the Religion of an Oath,

It is answered,

1mo, In the rules of *Charity* &c. The Confessants tho once Witches, yet now they, at least the Majority of them have ceased to be such, having had the *use of means* by the Ministers and Word,[250] and *actually declared* their Repentance, and the Devils ceasing to molest them; particularly *Elizabeth Anderson* was only carried alongst violently by her Father, and *stood out* to the last against her renouncing to her baptism, or consenting to these Crimes which were contrived in their meetings. *Janet* and *Margaret Rodgers* do testifie a great remorse and avowed the same last Sabbath in *the face of the Congregation*. So those *three are sufficient* whatsoever might be said against the other two, especially if we join the *improbability* either of hazarding their own lives or the *Devils sending* them out against these Pannals, or their destroying their own *relations*: as was remarked before, But,

2do, Whether they remain Witches or not; It is certain by Reason and Experience that the Devils *peculiar influence* ceaseth in and about *judgement*: by the common course of providence: And therefore the Authors before cited admit Witches whether penitent or not.[251]

3tio. All the defects of their hability is supplied, and the intireness thereof compleated, by their testimonies being so wonderfully *adminiculat*; particularly the confessants are *constant* from the first discovery; *uniform* in so various circumstances not only with themselves, but with the *Girle*: They declare nothing but what is probable, most of the Pannals having been reputed Witches, all of them having the Mark; and one or other of them (to whom the associates *delighted* in mischief, never missed to join) having had particular *Irritations*[252] to take revenge by the torture and deaths libelled; Besides the *other adminicles* of guilt already proven before you. The confessants were *threatened* to retract by the Pannals themselves and their Friends: besides the *bad usage* from others in the Countrey. They concurr with the maleficats testimony, and amongst themselves, even when interrogatt *singly*: and upon *new things*: as severals of your number have tryed the experiment: on this head *Delrio. lib*

250 Having experienced the effects of prayer, in response to the prayers of the ministers and the preaching of the word of God.

251 They admit witches' testimony in court, whether penitent or not.

252 *SD*, p. 58, has 'Provocations'.

5. § 16. N, 5. wisely observes, *quamvis tam facile foret demoni plures decipere quam unum tamen non est censendus Deus hoc æque permittere ne omnis ratio probandi talia delicta occulta judicibus adimatur; hoc enim est dissentanium*[253] *providentiæ divinæ.*[254] The Reiteration of the Acts which they declare anent some persons whom they never saw except in these congresses, and yet whom *they know* now on the *first sight*, is unaccountable if they were falsaries:[255] And that they are not such is further astructed by some of the Pannals being delated by a confessing Witch in *Anno* 1687,[256] And you know that others delated by these confessants were lately brought in guilty by the Verdict of a former Inquest,[257] &c. which are so many *joint proofs* of these witnesses integrity, and makes an chain of evidence and moral demonstration both against Error in themselves and delusion in relation to others, &c.

There were some things objected out of the Law of *Scotland*, of which also I shall give you some touch.

Whereas it was alledged, That *irretiti criminibus capitalibus*,[258] and so under the Pursuers power, cannot be admitted to be Witnesses; Conform to a statute in *Regiam Majestatem*.[259] {*p. 19*}

To this it was answered, That we need not say, that these statutes have not the force of Law, except in so farr as they are received by Custom; unless conform thereto. A Laik cannot Witness against a Clerk,[260] or *e contra*, &c. Nor need we make use of that which is Obvious, *Viz.* That these Statutes are only common Rules in ordinary Crimes; which have their Exception in all Occult and excepted Crimes, such as Witchcraft, &c. *Nam omnis regula subverti potest*,[261] and particularly this Rule is actually so restricted in the Case of Witchcraft, by the Opinion of Lawiers and Customes before-mentioned, which are the *best interpreters* of Laws: For if this Application should hold,

253 *SD*, p. 58, more correctly, has '*dissentaneum*'.

254 'Although it might seem just as easy to a demon to deceive many as to deceive one, nevertheless God is not to be blamed for equally permitting this, lest all basis for investigating such hidden crimes be denied the judges; for this is a denial of divine providence.' Delrio, *Disquisitiones Magicae*, 405 (book 5, section 16).

255 *SD*, p. 58, has 'Cheats'.

256 The court had been informed that John Lindsay alias Bishop and James Lindsay alias Curate had been named in 1687 by Elspeth Aitken, a confessing witch in Kilmacolm: Goodare and Willumsen (eds.), *Scottish Witchcraft Trials*, 602–3. Aitken's case has not so far been traced in other records.

257 This may refer to the case of Janet Wodrow in Kilmacolm. On 3 March 1696, the privy council had granted a commission of justiciary to try her for witchcraft. See the introduction to *A Relation of the Diabolical Practices*, above in the present volume.

258 *SD*, p. 58, has '*Irretiti Criminibus Capitalibus*, those who are Indicted for Capital Crymes'.

259 The defence had cited to this effect 'Statutes of King William', chapter 11, in John Skene, *Regiam Majestatem: The Auld Lawes and Constitutions of Scotland* (Edinburgh, 1609), pp. 3–4 (2nd pagination).

260 'Laik': lay person; 'Clerk': clerical person, minister.

261 'for every rule may be overturned'.

socius criminis[262] could never be admitted: But we positively deny, that those Confessants are *under our Power* or Influence; seing *Elizabeth Anderson* is not Guilty of Witchcraft, for any thing that does appear: The *Lindsays* were never indicted for it; and the Dyet was deserted[263] against the *Rogers*; as the whole Commission is to Expyre against the first of *June*, betwixt and which time, they are to proceed no further then this particular tryal. So that this Objection evanishes to smoak.

Whereas it is pretended, That the *Rogers* cannot be received, because not given out in the List of Witnesses; conform to the Regulation, whereby the Pannals might have proven their Objection by their Exculpation.

It was answered, 1*mo*. This Objection ought to be repelled; because, besides that the Act speaks only of Criminal Lybells, and not indictments, which with the List of the Witnesses may be given in farr shorter time then the Additional List has been given to the Pannals, *being Prisoners*: This Act is interpreted by the *common Custom* of the Justice Court; of giving additional Lists after the first, upon shorter time then this has been given: As is particularly attested by *James Guthry* Macer, who has given them, and who being a *Person in Officio*, his Testimony is to be Credited in what relates to his Office: so that the old Custom confirmed by a Decision. 3. *August* 1661, where *Alexander Forrester* was cited *apud acta*[264] against a Witch, continues *quoad* this point,[265] as is related by *McKenzie, pag*. 529.[266] But 2*do*. Any Objection that the Pannals pretend against these Witnesses, is *injure*,[267] or may *instantly appear*. 3*tio*. The Case is altogether extraordinary and Circumstantiat: For these Witnesses had not Confessed: And so were not existent under that Reduplication when the principall List was given out: whereby the Act of Parliament can only be understood of Witnesses, that were then existent. And finally the Pannals got a *general warrand* of Exculpation for citing of any Witnesses they pleased, and they have had several Days since they got this additional List, so that they might have cited Witnesses to prove their Objections, were it not the truth is: they *have none*, besides these that are *common and before Answered*.[268]

Thus I have given you *hints* that your own *reasoning* (which I know to be refyn'd) may *improve* and *apply*, so as to dissolve the quibles which the *petty witts*, who have not *Soul enough* of themselves to penetrate into the true light of what is *recondite*; may raise against it: It being their common talent

262 *SD*, p. 58, has 'a *socius criminis*'. The phrase means 'an accomplice'.

263 'the Dyet was deserted': the prosecution was abandoned.

264 'in open court'.

265 *SD*, p. 59, has 'continues as to this point'.

266 Mackenzie, *Laws and Customs*, 381 (part 2, title 26).

267 *SD*, p. 59, has '*in jure*' ('in law').

268 At this point the *True Narrative* and *SD* both introduce an extra line space. The text that follows is not found in the MS version of the speech in the trial record, which instead continues with other material omitted from the *True Narrative*.

either to Skipp over the *Surface* of *Mines*, or, otherways, to tear assunder *some appurtenances* of a Scheme, and then presently pronounce it *Mortally Maimed.*[269]

I must confess that none could be more *sceptical* anent the Truth of such odd things as I had heard; nor inquisitive for canvassing the *Reality* and *Explications* of them; then I was *before* my attendances at *Bargarrans house*, and the several dyets of Court; and my *Conversation* with some of these concerned thereanent. But now, after all that I have *seen*, *reasoned*, and *heard*, I do acknowledge my self {*p. 20*} entirely captivate by the dictats of *natural understanding* and *common sense*, into a *sound mind* and perswasion, *that*, as there is such a thing as *Witchcraft*, so it was eminent in its forementioned *Effects*; and the seven Pannals were some of the *Witches*.

I have troubled you litle with my *proper Observations*;[270] yet lest you should think me either too *Lazie* or *Peevish*, I shall make one, *and it is*, that I do not think the greater part of the condemned prisoners will ever fully Confess: Of which Conjecture I have two chief grounds, *Viz*. That they are neither Ignorant nor Melancholick; but on the contrary, some of them would seem to have been once enlightned before they fell away, so that if this be a Sin unto Death, there is no appearance that they will glorify GOD by acknowledgment.

Severals of them are of singular *Knowledge* and *Acutness* beyond the common levell of their Station: Particularly *Margaret Lang* did make *Harangues* in her own defence, which neither *Divine* nor *Lawier* could reasonably *Mend*: Yet I thought that when they spoke in a matter of *any concern*, their *Eyes* stood *Squint* and *fix'd*, as if they had been turning their *Ears* and attentive to a *Dictator*. Their answers to the trying Interrogators put to them, were *Surprisingly subtile* and *Cautious*. Tho indeed, by the *industry* of some of the Judges and Lawiers, they were *at occasions* involved in *Lyes, Prevarications, and Contradictions*; which might have proceeded either from Natural or preternatural *Causes*. Some of them were esteemed in the *Country* very *Sagatious* and *Exact* in their Bussiness: *Margaret Lang* having been a *Mid-wife*, and one of the *Lindsays* having acquired a *considerable Fortune* by his *Tillage* and *Trade*: Yet it was noticed, that there did commonly break out of their *covered Course*, something *Odd* either of *Iniquity* or *Affectation*; and *Lindsay* did finely enough get off from the sherriff when he was formerly accused in 1687.

Melancholians are lovers of Solitude; *Witches* of Society, and Feasts: Those are commonly Pale and Heavy; many of these *Corpulent* and *Voluptuous*.[271] Witches are *Hard* to Confess as knowing their Guilt; Melancholians delight to discover their horridest Dampts,[272] because they think them *no Cryme*:

269 *SD*, p. 59, has 'to Skipp over things Superficially; or else to Attaque some of the slightest outworks, and then to Triumph as if they had obtain'd the Victory'.

270 'proper Observations': personal comments.

271 James VI drew the same distinction between melancholic persons and witches: *Daemonologie*, in *Minor Prose*, 21 (book 2, chapter 1).

272 'Dampts': stupefactions or trances.

The ones Confessions *Every where* are *Uniform*; the other's Phantasms are as *various* as their Humors. Finally, Witches teach their Trade; whereas *Conceits* would *Die* with them, and could be no more *conveyed* then the Humor which is the Specifick cause thereof. As these *distinguishing Characters* do hold in the General, so in this particular Case there are several *others*: Such as, most of the Pannals were of *Middle-age*, one of them not much above Twenty; and the first Confessants are known to be Young: Whereby *Dottage* or *Melancholy* are less to be suspected; yea was morally impossible in many of the Cases. For the *Facts* which the *Confessants* had *formerly declared* before the Commissioners for Enquiry were sworn to by *other unexceptionable Witnesses* before the Commissioners for the tryal; and the Circumstances were such, that the one *could not know* what was *to be* deponed by the other: As it's already manifest, that the *reall Effects* in several passages of *Bargarrans* Daughter were not possibly *producible* by any imagination or Humor; and it is speciall in this Case, that neither the *Pannals* nor *Confessants* were *Distempered* by being keept from *Sleep*, *tortured*, or the like, which were too usuall in former times;[273] but all the Measures were strictly observed, that are the requisits of a truely *impartial Judgment*.

I needed not to have sent unto you the Doubles of the Depositions themselves: Because it is *not deny'd* that the Depositions are such as they are represented in the Pleadings; the chief question being anent the Hability of the last Deponents. {*p. 21*} Neither was you to expect the *Defenders part* of the Debate, separatly by itself; in respect that what was *dispersed* here and there for them is faithfully *repeated* or *implyed* in what you have: As to those points which I thought worth the *Nottice*.[274]

Upon the whole I do believe; *that* there is scarcely a more rare providence of this nature in any true History; a more *exact caution* in any enquiry or Trial of this kind: A more clear *probation*, without confession of the Pannals themselves, or, a more *just sentence*, putting together all circumstances, upon record.

I am, what you have made me, Yours, &c. FINIS. {*final page, unnumbered, follows*}

273 This alludes to the excesses of previous witch-hunting, perhaps particularly the national panic of 1661–2. Pricking for the Devil's mark had also been a controversial practice in panics up to and including 1662, and this *had* been done in the Bargarran case, in a way that was quite unusual for 1697; Grant did not mention this. Grant was mainly drawing attention to the fact that sleep deprivation and other tortures had been important in extracting confessions from suspects in previous panics. In the Bargarran case the main accused persons (the '*Pannals*') had not confessed at all, but the '*Confessants*' – the former suspects like Elizabeth Anderson who had been converted into prosecution witnesses – had made statements resembling the confessions of guilty witches in some respects. It was thus relevant for Grant to argue (whether truthfully or not) that these statements had not been extorted by torture.

274 This passage explains why the *True Narrative* is not publishing the speech of the advocate for the defence, to which the present speech replies. The defence speech survives in the trial record, and has been published in Goodare and Willumsen (eds.), *Scottish Witchcraft Trials*, 580–8.

ADVERTISEMENT

After printing of what preceeds, there came Intelligence from the Countrey,[275] that a Person who is *Rich*, and stayes in a *publick place*, designed in the Narrative by the first Letters of her Name,[276] has, upon hearing that the Narrative was coming abroad, *hired* an *Hackney*[277] to *bring off* her *Repute*: whereby the Undertakers (who are of the Brutal Cabal of our *puny Wits*) are to take occasion of obscuring the Truth of the whole History. There was such regard had to the Fame[278] of those whom, as yet, there has not been *opportunity* to bring to their Trial, that commonly, there are only *initial Letters* for their Names: And there is such incontestible Evidence for the Facts here Narrated, that it is impossible, without the most effronted *impudence* and *falsehood*, to contradict them: Yet if the *Root of all Evil*, and *Spite* against Truth, shall so far prevail over *natural Ingenuity*, as to advance *bare-faced Lyes* against *Realitys*, and give the World *foppish Banter* in place of good *Reasoning*, thereby to delude the Opinion of those who were not Eye and Ear Witnesses; the Authors (whose Names, though told, are not here insert, because the Information may faill) may expect to be *Characteriz'd*, and otherways taken notice of, according to the demerit of such a Villanous project.

The Reader is intreated to excuse such Errors in the Printing, occasioned by the indistinctness of the writen Copie; which are easily corrigible by the Context.

[275] 'Intelligence from the Countrey': news from Renfrewshire.
[276] Probably Mary Morrison. See the introduction, above.
[277] 'Hackney': servile or mercenary writer.
[278] 'Fame': reputation.

8. FIVE PAMPHLETS ON THE PITTENWEEM CASE, 1704–5

INTRODUCTION

A witchcraft panic broke out in 1704 in Pittenweem, a small fishing town on the coast of Fife. It began with a case of demonic possession that resembled, and was influenced by, the Bargarran panic of 1696–7 that has featured above in the present volume. Aspects of the Pittenweem panic have been discussed in print from time to time, most fully in an excellent recent study by Brian Levack.[1] The briefer account that follows is intended to aid comprehension of the text of the five pamphlets edited below.

In March 1704, Patrick Morton, a 16-year-old apprentice blacksmith working for his father, had a dispute with Beatrix Laing. Laing was a small trader in her own right, while her husband, the tailor William Brown, was a former treasurer of the burgh. Laing asked Morton to make her some nails, but he refused, saying that he had a prior engagement to make nails for a ship. There was a quarrel; it was later alleged that Laing had threatened Morton with revenge. At any rate, Morton began to fear Laing's witchcraft. He probably had psychological problems of his own, though their nature would be hard to reconstruct. He became ill and refused to eat. In May, his condition worsened, and he began periodically to display what were described as 'fits' in which his body became uncontrollably contorted – and he declared that witches were afflicting him.

During this worsening of Morton's condition, Patrick Cowper, minister of Pittenweem, became involved. Cowper (1660–1740) was an influential presbyterian who had been imprisoned and exiled during the Restoration period.[2] He now guided Morton as to how to behave as a demoniac, by reading to him

1 Brian P. Levack, 'Witch-Hunting and Witch-Murder in Early Eighteenth-Century Scotland', in his *Witch-Hunting in Scotland: Law, Politics and Religion* (New York, 2008), 145–61. The following introduction draws frequently on this paper. There is another recent account in Lizanne Henderson, *Witchcraft and Folk Belief in the Age of Enlightenment: Scotland, 1670–1740* (Basingstoke, 2016), 213–24.

2 Hew Scott, *Fasti Ecclesiae Scoticanae: The Succession of Ministers in the Church of Scotland from the Reformation*, 2nd edn., 7 vols. (Edinburgh, 1915–28), v, 227–8.

the account of the possession of Christian Shaw – the *True Narrative* edited above in the present volume. Quite possibly the deterioration of Morton's condition in May might be attributed to this. It is not surprising, then, that the accounts of his possession resemble the accounts of Shaw's possession. The promoters of the panic initially commented on this similarity, which, they claimed, validated the genuineness of Morton's symptoms. However, the final pamphlet, the *Just Reproof*, backtracked on this claim after the panic collapsed.

Morton initially accused Beatrix Laing, but soon afterwards he also named at least three other women as witches: Janet Cornfoot (usually called 'Corphet', 'Corphat' or 'Corset' in the pamphlets), Nicolas Lawson ('Nicolas' was a woman's name) and Lilias Wallace. He named a further suspect, Isobel Adam, either at the same time or shortly afterwards.

Laing was tortured by sleep deprivation for five days and nights, a length of time that we may well believe to have been enough to force a confession. She was also pricked with pins to find the Devil's mark – a process that was not formally torture, but that was painful and degrading.[3] At least some of the other suspects were probably treated similarly; Janet Cornfoot later claimed that the minister had beaten her with his staff. Under pressure, four suspects – Isobel Adam, Janet Cornfoot, Beatrix Laing and Nicolas Lawson – confessed to bewitching Morton, and also to having made pacts with the Devil. Lilias Wallace never confessed. Nor did three further suspects who were brought into the case around this time: Thomas Brown, Janet Horsburgh and Margaret Jack.

The first two pamphlets, the *Account of Betty Laing* and the *True Relation*, were published around this time. Both named Adam, Cornfoot, Laing, Lawson and Wallace. They also mentioned (in the words of the *Account of Betty Laing*) 'a Sclater who is one of their accomplices, and was Piper to them at their Meetings', and implied that this suspect, evidently a man, had also been interrogated (p. 9). This was probably Thomas Brown, the only male suspect to be named.

The magistrates, minister and kirk session now petitioned the privy council, seeking a commission to try seven suspects: Adam, Brown, Cornfoot, Jack, Laing, Lawson and Wallace – all except Horsburgh.[4] Horsburgh's omission may have been because she had status and influence; her husband, Thomas White, would later serve as a bailie of the burgh, and she herself would

3 David Cook (ed.), *Annals of Pittenweem: Being Notes and Extracts from the Ancient Records of that Burgh, 1526–1793* (Anstruther, 1867), 125.

4 The list named 'Margaret Wallace', presumably an error for Lilias Wallace: SPCR, A1704/6/11; Cook (ed.), *Annals of Pittenweem*, 112–14. Levack, 'Witch-Hunting and Witch-Murder', points out this error. He discounts the accusation against Margaret Jack, saying that her name 'does not appear in any of the proceedings or the pamphlets' (p. 194, note 45); however, she is definitely named in the burgh's petition to the privy council, and 'Jack' is named in two of the pamphlets, the *Answer of a Letter* and the *Just Reproof*.

win a prosecution for wrongous imprisonment. There are hints in the later pamphlets of factional struggle within the burgh elite at this time, with Morton allegedly being willing to name some of the bailies' wives. Horsburgh was certainly imprisoned, and the intention may have been to prosecute her later. The panic may indeed have been at the point of spiralling outwards. The critical pamphlets spoke of an intention to prosecute members of the elite; the final pamphlet denied this, but admitted that 'a very few others of the meaner Sort' had been named (*Just Reproof*, p. 6).

The burgh authorities' petition requested that a commission of justiciary should be granted to local gentlemen to try the case locally, on the grounds that it would be troublesome and expensive to bring witnesses to Edinburgh. No doubt they also wanted more control over the outcome of the trial. However, the privy council decided on 13 June that the case should instead be heard before the court of justiciary in Edinburgh, and ordered the queen's advocate, Sir James Steuart of Goodtrees, to make arrangements for this.

On 12 August, the burgh magistrates freed 'the five women incarcerated' on bail.[5] The names of these five women were not given. As we have seen, six women had been in prison on 13 June: Adam, Cornfoot, Jack, Laing, Lawson and Wallace. It is possible that Cornfoot remained in prison at this stage; the later pamphlets said that she escaped from prison, though the date was not given.[6] The one male suspect, Thomas Brown, was later stated to have died in prison; his death seems already to have occurred before 12 August, to judge by the omission of mention of him on that date.

The reason for the freeing of the prisoners is unclear, since the burgh authorities still seem to have been committed to the prosecutions. However, the prosecution's case may already have been collapsing at this point. Problems seem to have begun when the earl of Rothes, sheriff of Fife, visited Pittenweem and was not convinced by Morton's fits or by the burgh authorities' account of them. It may have been Rothes' sceptical report to the privy council that led the latter to refuse to grant a commission for a local trial.

Matters continued to go badly for the prosecution. On 3 October, the queen's advocate reported to the privy council that he had examined Isobel Adam, 'said to be the most notorious witch', and Patrick Morton – 'And finding noe evidence from their Examinationes to be the ground of a proces,

5 Cook (ed.), *Annals of Pittenweem*, 117.

6 Levack regards the five women released on 12 August as having been Adam, Horsburgh, Laing, Lawson and Wallace: Levack, 'Witch-Hunting and Witch-Murder', 195, note 48. However, it is likely that Margaret Jack was one of the five. Exactly when Janet Horsburgh was imprisoned or released is unclear. Cowper reported to the presbytery on 15 November that 'the woman he was to summond from the pulpit is come to their bounds [i.e. has returned to the parish], and he expects she will be found': St Andrews University Library, Minutes of Presbytery of St Andrews, 1699–1705, CH2/1132/21, p. 324. This may have been one of the suspected witches.

Gave it as his oppinion That the Lords of privie Councill should allow him to sett the said Issobell Adam at liberty and lett the proces fall'. The privy council agreed to liberate Adam and to drop the case against her.[7]

We have a summary of events up to 19 November from a newsletter sent on that date from Edinburgh to Dublin. Its paragraph on the case is worth quoting in full:

> Our Presbyterian Ministers are showing great Zeal in discovering Witches, and they think they have fallen luckily on a cluster of them in Petinweem a Parish in the County of Fife. Some of them are brought over to Edinburgh to be examind, one of them who in her Ministers presence, confessed Witchcraft to the Queens Atturney Generall[8] did next time deny it to him, saying she had called her self a Witch to please the Minister, he having begd it of her, and assured her it should be for her good. I have this from Lyon King at Arms[9] who was witness to the examination, and assured me he had been with one of the confessing witches who swore to him the Minister did beat her severly while [i.e. until] she confessed, and now she denys all. The Ministers have used a great deal of barbarous severitys to extort confessions from those unhappy creaturs, for which many of them are subpenad[10] to Edinburgh. I had no inclination to trouble his Grace with these storys of Scotch Witches unless you should be pleasd to tell him them when you think fit. We are labouring under many sad Delusions, God deliver us from them, and from Presbytery and Poverty which are the occasion of many of them.[11]

It is not surprising that a letter sent to episcopal Dublin disapproved of the presbyterians, but this letter does lend support to the idea that presbyterians and episcopalians took opposite views of the case. The letter does not mention Morton or his possession.

We glimpse further prosecution efforts on 27 December, when Patrick Cowper raised a question before the presbytery about 'these women in

7 SPCR, A1704/10/4; Cook (ed.), *Annals of Pittenweem*, 117–18.

8 The queen's advocate, Sir James Steuart. The author, who is evidently not Scottish, uses English (or Irish) legal terminology.

9 Sir Alexander Erskine of Cambo (1663–1729) and his son, also Alexander Erskine, held the office of lord lyon jointly. Cambo in Fife was about eight miles from Pittenweem, but this 'examination' seems to have taken place in Edinburgh.

10 'Subpenad': formally summoned (another instance of non-Scottish terminology). The phrase 'many of them' appears to refer to the accused witches rather than the ministers.

11 The National Archives, London, [Anonymous] to Edward Southwell, Edinburgh, 19 November 1704, SP62/364, fos. 143r.–144r. The addressee, Edward Southwell, was chief secretary to the lord lieutenant of Ireland (James Butler, second duke of Ormonde, mentioned in the letter as 'his Grace') in Dublin. Levack cites what appears to be another version of this newsletter from a manuscript in the Folger Shakespeare Library, describing it as a letter from 'one Mr Miller … to a correspondent in Edinburgh': Levack, 'Witch-Hunting and Witch-Murder', 150. Manuscript newsletters were sometimes copied and recopied.

Pittenweem who had confessed themselves guilty of witchcraft, as also concerning a woman who had desired another to teach her to be a witch'. The presbytery decided that 'It is their opinion that the Kirk-session of Pittenweem call all these persons before them, and deal with their Consciences, to bring them to a Conviction of their guilt'. This may have been a plan to re-interrogate the accused witches who had retracted their confessions. Whether a renewed confession of guilt would have led to a revival of the criminal prosecution, or whether further actions would have been solely pastoral, was not stated. The presbytery instructed Cowper to report back at their next meeting (which would be on 17 January 1705), but no report was minuted.[12] Perhaps this effort came to nothing. And events would soon take a new and dramatic turn.

Janet Cornfoot was either not freed from prison in August, or else she was arrested again later. The events leading to her lynching began when she escaped from prison, apparently in January 1705. She fled from Pittenweem and went to nearby Leuchars. There, however, she was found by the local minister, George Gordon, who had her arrested and sent back to Pittenweem on 30 January. Arriving in the town, she begged the minister and magistrates to protect her, but they were either unwilling or unable to do so – one strand of the subsequent pamphlet controversy involved a dispute as to their responsibility at this point. Cornfoot sought lodging from another of the witchcraft suspects, Nicolas Lawson. However, that evening, she was seized by a crowd who ill-treated her and eventually killed her – a series of events narrated in gruesome and indignant detail by the next pamphlet to be published.

This pamphlet, *An Account of a Horrid and Barbarous Murder*, evidently appeared within weeks or even days of the killing. It was soon followed by another, *An Answer of a Letter from a Gentleman in Fife*, probably by the same author, giving further details and broadening the attack on the minister and magistrates. The fifth and final pamphlet, *A Just Reproof*, replied to these attacks in great detail. It defended the conduct of the magistrates and minister, and asserted the rightness of the prosecutions.

These shocking and tragic events led to various further recriminations and enquiries. There were attempts to prosecute the murderers, though these fizzled out. The magistrates and minister, too, escaped formal punishment for their role in the affair, although Janet Horsburgh won a case for wrongous imprisonment. This aftermath has been covered by Brian Levack.[13] Here, before reproducing the texts of the five pamphlets, a little more should be said about the pamphlets individually.

12 St Andrews University Library, Minutes of Presbytery of St Andrews, 1699–1705, CH2/1132/21, pp. 332–3.

13 Levack, 'Witch-Hunting and Witch-Murder', 157–61.

An Account of the Wicked and Terrible Confederacy of Betty Laing (1704)

This pamphlet is a tiny duodecimo of six leaves, smaller than the other pamphlets and with a smaller typeface. Because it focuses on Beatrix Laing, who is known to have been the first witch accused, and because it says less about prosecution proceedings, it seems to have been the first pamphlet to be published, before the *True and Full Relation*. However, this is not certain. It was evidently written during the proceedings, when Morton was still being possessed – 'his Picture is not yet found out, they allegding the Devil has taken it from them' (p. 9). It seems to assume that the reader is already familiar with events so far, since no full explanation of Morton is given. This might even suggest that it was the *second* pamphlet.

The *Account of Betty Laing* presents Laing as the principal witch, claiming that she is known to have committed several previous malefices. It implies that the case began when Laing's husband began to suspect her. However, it seems more likely that the stories it told about her husband were folkloric narratives attached retrospectively to her case. The pamphlet also narrates stories that had been told by Laing's 6-year-old granddaughter. The other witch who attracts attention in the pamphlet is Isobel Adam, who 'turned distracted' when the Devil propositioned her. She is intriguingly positioned between the status of a victim and the status of a witch.

The pamphlet's breathless narrative, partly in the present tense, seems to encourage the reader to await further developments – developments that would not be long in emerging. There are attempts at demotic speech, reported in the first person. A group of witches is called a 'Crew', a distinctive term that had been much used in the Bargarran case. The concluding moral, enjoining people to be content with their station in life and 'not to Repine and Grudge' at it, is couched in religious terms but seems almost commercial in its message.

A True and Full Relation of the Witches at Pittenweem (1704)

This pamphlet can be dated by its mention, in its final paragraph, of the privy council's recent decision to order the witches to be tried by the court of justiciary; this was on 13 June. It was issued by the same Edinburgh printer, John Reid, as the *Account of Betty Laing*.[14]

The first half of the pamphlet consists of a general introduction to demonology – in its own words, an 'Essay for proving the Existence of Good and Evil Spirits ... with Arguments against the Sadducism of the Present

[14] For Reid see Adam Fox, '"Little Story Books" and "Small Pamphlets" in Edinburgh, 1680–1760: The Making of the Scottish Chapbook', *Scottish Historical Review*, 92 (2013), 207–30, at p. 226.

Age'.[15] In its account of the Pittenweem witches themselves, it tells a similar story to the *Account of Betty Laing*, though in a very different way. It focuses on Patrick Morton and Isobel Adam rather than on Beatrix Laing, and is less detailed overall. It says that there are eight suspects altogether, of whom five have confessed. However, only four confessions (those of Adam, Cornfoot, Laing and Lawson) are individually specified by other sources.

An Account of a Horrid and Barbarous Murder (1705)

The *Just Reproof* hints (p. 14) that the author of this pamphlet was Andrew Bruce, the former episcopal minister, who had been deposed in 1692. Further research might well reveal more about his role, and about factional divisions among the local elite.

The pamphlet is largely self-explanatory, giving a detailed account of the murder that may well be broadly accurate. It was reprinted along with the next pamphlet shortly afterwards, and the opportunity was taken to revise the narrative at a crucial point. This may indicate that there was confusion as to exactly what had happened that night.

An Answer of a Letter from a Gentleman in Fife (1705)

This pamphlet may well have been by the same author as the *Account of a Horrid and Barbarous Murder*, though it claimed to be by a different hand. It was issued in a printed text that also included a revised version of the *Account of a Horrid and Barbarous Murder* itself. The revisions seem to have been made by the same author who had written the original, which lends support to the idea that this same author also wrote the *Answer of a Letter*. The author of the *Just Reproof*, in replying to both pamphlets, thought that both had been written by the same author.

A Just Reproof, to the False Reports … Dropt in Two Late Pamphlets (1705)

This final pamphlet replied to the two recent critical pamphlets, and defended the prosecutions. Its most likely author is Patrick Cowper, minister of Pittenweem. Certainly, if it was not him, it was someone closely connected with him. The pamphlet sometimes speaks in the minister's voice: 'the Minister … made use of no threatnings … and he dares the Author to give

15 A similar note would later be struck by the fifth pamphlet, the *Just Reproof*, in its conclusion. Henderson, *Witchcraft and Folk Belief*, 217, states that both pamphlets are by the same author. However, there is no specific evidence for this, and Henderson's statement that both pamphlets claim to be written by 'Lover of Truth' is incorrect. The *Just Reproof* does not use the term 'Sadducism', instead calling its opponents 'Atheistical', which may indeed suggest that the two pamphlets had different authors.

any evidence to the contrar' (p. 11); 'the Minister positively deny's' (p. 23); 'the Minister could give his Oath' (p. 24). The author of the pamphlet is extremely knowledgeable about the minister's correspondence, both letters he had sent and those he had not sent (p. 12). The minister's movements are most circumstantially detailed (p. 13). The author has access to the kirk session register (p. 20).

The pamphlet offers excuses for everyone involved in the affair: the minister, the burgh magistrates, the gaolers. Although the crowd who murdered Cornfoot are not exonerated as such, some of their doings are denied, and there is a claim that the crowd consisted of 'strangers', not inhabitants of the town (p. 14). However, it is Cowper himself whom the pamphlet is particularly concerned to exonerate. This may be because the charges against Cowper were particularly grave and detailed: he had read the narrative of Christian Shaw's bewitchment to Patrick Morton, he had beaten Janet Cornfoot to get her to confess, he had promised her immunity from prosecution, and he had usurped civil jurisdiction by ordering prisoners to be freed. But the pamphlet's focus on Cowper would make additional sense if he was its author.

The author passes over in silence the privy council's orders to submit the case to the court of justiciary in Edinburgh, though he regrets their decision not to grant a commission for a local trial (p. 6). He produces some extraordinary reasoning to avoid admitting directly that the earl of Rothes and the privy council had been unconvinced by the prosecution's case. Some of the admissions that he does make are therefore noteworthy. He admits that Patrick Morton committed some 'Extravagancies both in word and deed' (p. 17); admits that some of the suspects were ill-treated (pp. 8–9); admits that the suspects all retracted their confessions (pp. 9, 11); and even admits that the minister's servants were among the crowd who took part in Janet Cornfoot's murder – assuring readers that they were merely spectators and that they left early (p. 14).

The retraction of the suspects' confessions, a crucial event in the collapse of the prosecutions, is attributed to the meddling of unnamed people – it is hinted that the author of the anti-prosecution pamphlets and his friends were involved. They interfered with the suspects and 'induced' them or 'practised on' them to retract (pp. 9, 20). Concerning this, 'Strange Methods have been try'd both at *Pittenweem* and *Edinburgh*' (p. 23). There is an account of the opponents of prosecution interfering with the suspect Isobel Adam and the witchcraft victim Alexander MacGregor, allegedly without success (p. 24).

The author has evidently given up hope of reviving the prosecutions. He nevertheless continues to assert that Morton's fits were genuine and that the confessions of witchcraft were all true. He even adduces Cornfoot's confession as a justification for her having been denied Christian burial (p. 22).

These passages give a strong if unspecific impression of factional division among the town's elite, with Andrew Bruce, the former episcopal minister, involved in the struggle on the other side from Cowper. However, the pamphlet changes tack abruptly in its closing remarks, attributing the critical pamphlets instead to 'the Inconsiderate and Atheistical *Would-be-wits* of this Age', and claiming that the town's 'generous' episcopalians have supported the presbyterian Cowper (p. 25). This is a more conventional pro-witchcraft line of argument, indeed so conventional as to be stereotyped. The argument is that the anti-prosecution writers complain of improper prosecution procedure, but their real motive is that they do not believe in witchcraft and indeed do not believe in Christianity.

TEXTS

Pamphlet 1

An Account of the Wicked and Terrible Confederacy of Betty Laing[16]

The Grand Witch in Pittenweem, with her wicked conspiracy against *Peter Morton*, and her first contracting with the Devil her self, and her Causing *Isobel Adams*, *Nicolas Lawson*, *Janet Corset* and *Lillie Wallace* and others to become Witches, with her Terrible Actions at Sea and Land. Together with an Exhortation to all People to eschew such evil. &c.

Edinburgh *Printed* by John Reid *Younger*, *Printer in* Liberton's-Wynd, 1704. {*p. 2*}

An ACCOUNT of the Wicked and Terrible Actions of Betty Laing &c.

This *Beatie Laing* being come of mean Parentage, and having married meanly; was very poor. She used to Sell small Wair, and was scarce prosperous in any thing she took in hand; continually grudging and Repining at the Prosperity of her Neighbours.

The way and manner how she at first engaged in the Devils service, was thus; As she was going through *Magus* moor, towards *St. Andrews* to a Fair that was held there: she met with a Man who fell in discourse with her, amongst which she related to him her Poverty and Indigency; and that she had not, as she said, so good luck in Trading as others of her neighbours. To which the {*p. 3*} man (as she thought) very readily answered, that if she would do as he should desire her, she should hereafter have better Trading than any other whatsoever in that place of the Country: Yea, if that she would turn his Servant, and obey what he directed her, he promised that none should ever put their hand to her Goods, but should buy of her, and none other.

16 Source: *An Account of the Wicked and Terrible Confederacy of Betty Laing* (Edinburgh: John Reid, 1704: ESTC no. T183691).

And that he would furnish and pay her her Expenses at every Fair or Merkat she should go to: Whereupon he discovered himself to her, promising her that she should enjoy much Wealth, Long-life, Prosperity, and Revenge on all those her Enemies, *&c.* She hereupon engages, and throws her self out of the Fear of GOD, renouncing her Baptismal Vow, and receives the Devils mark. All which she confesses.

This *Beatie* proceeding in her Witchcrafts and Sorceries, she in short while came in so great a liking to her new Master, that for an Evidence of her promoting his Interest, she (having a Daughter short while after her Marriage) she proffered the Child her daughter to be for his Service; but the Devil answered her, that he would not accept of her, for he could have no power of her at all. However after several years, this Lass being come to Age, she was married to a Seaman in that place, and brought forth a Daughter, {*p. 4*} where her Mother attending her, and conveening with her wretched Crew, she there presents her Grandchild to the Devil, as a gift to him, in sign of her willingness to serve him. And no sooner is the Child nursed, than she takes it home to her, and so has brought it up in the Hellish Principles of Witchcraft, and takes her along with her to all her Meetings. This Child being at present not above six years old, gives Account that her Grand-Dame's Gentleman, as she calls him, takes her with them when he pleases, sometimes to torment *Peter Mortoun* the Smith, with scratching and nipping, and the like, telling her that if she do not perform it he will throw her in the Sea. She is likeways carried to several other places, particularly to *Norway*, where at present her Father is, whom she says she saw there.

Her Husband (who is repute a very honest man) had several times Suspicion of her, but one time he owns, that he did truly know that she acted not right, and it was thus: One time they were both at *Cyrus*-fair,[17] a little town in the East of *Fife*, where they staid in bargaining pretty late, till it was about nine at Night or more; her Husband was desirous that they might stay there all that Night, because it was upwards of nine miles they had to go before they could get home, {*p. 5*} but she told him that she would go home that Night, and that she had got a Horse saddled and ready with a Pad for her: He hardly condescends, but she at last prevails, and away they come, and find at the East-bridge, as its called, a Black Horse in Readiness for them, but no Body near that he could see to own the Horse; he after some Reluctancy mounts, and she behind him: Away they come, and in a short time are at home, the Horse having gone throw quickly; when they alight, her Husband asks her, where she would stable her horse. She answered, *Do not you fash your self, throw*

[17] 'Cyrus': Ceres. St Margaret's fair was held annually there on 13 June: *The Whole Yearly Faires and Weekly Mercats of this Ancient Kingdom of Scotland* (Aberdeen, 1684), sig. B3. Laing confessed on 19 June 1704 that she had met the Devil and renounced her baptism 'in Ceres Moor': St Andrews University Library, Minutes of Presbytery of St Andrews, 1699–1705, CH2/1132/21, p. 293.

up the Bridle on's head, he kens the gate[18] *to his own Stable well enough*. Upon which he was somewhat afraid, but for that Night said nothing at all.

At another time, They were to go to *Auchtermuchty* Fair, another little Town in *Fife*.[19] In the morning her Husband comes to her, saying, Beatie *will you rise and go to* Auchtermuchty *the day?* she answered, Not She was not well, and therefore she could not go; he makes pressing instances to her that they might both go together, but she tells him, that her Merchant had mistrysted her,[20] in not coming with the Packs of Wool that she had bargained for, and therefore she could not go, he answered, whats the Matter whether you have to sell or no, we may buy {*p. 6*} something to our selves at the Fair. However do what he list she would not rise to go with him: So away he goes alone, and takes neither House nor Hold by the way, but goes straight forward. He was no sooner there, but the very first that he sees in the Merkat, is his Wife with two Packs of Wool lying on the Ground before her; He comes to her, Beatie *how came ye here so soon, I am sure I saw you not by the way, and I did not halt but came streight forward?* Quoth she, Willie *Ye came the way about, but I came the streight Road; for just as you went away the Boat came in with the two Packs of Wool, and I immediatly got Horse and laid them on, and came here before You*. He was strangely surprised, but said nothing to her, but went and enquired at several People if they saw the Horses that carried his Wife's Packs of Wool, but none could give him any Account of them at all. The next day when he came home, he goes down to the Shore, and there enquires at the Waiters and several others, if they saw the Boat wherein his Wife's Wool came, but none could give him the least Notice of it. At which he was struck in a strange Consternation, but still kept his Mind to himself.

Now I leave the Reader to judge where, or from whom she had got them.

This *Beatie Laing* not only persisted in her {*p. 7*} damnable wicked Practices, but has also used means to make others as ill, if not worse with her self. There is one *Isabel Adams* a young Woman whom she hath brought over to these wicked practices, the way and manner was thus; This young Woman *Isobel Adams* being out of Service, *Beatie Laing* sends for her, and desires that she would come and spin to her, which the Lass refused; which Refusal *Beatie Laing* takes so ill out, that she vows to be revenged on the Lass cost what it will. She accordingly sends for the Lass, and then asks her, if she would serve any other since she would not serve her, to which the Lass made answer, that she would very willingly serve, providing she got a good Fee. Well then, quoth she, there is a Gentleman above stairs who will be very well contented to Fee you; So up stairs goes the Lass, where she finds *Nicolas Lawson* and *Lillie Wallace*, and the Devil like a Man of young years sitting together,

18 'on's head': on his head; 'kens the gate': knows the road.
19 A fair was held annually at Auchtermuchty on 2 July.
20 'mistrysted her': not kept his appointment with her.

who presently rose and kissed her, whereupon she immediatly fell in Love with him, as she confesses now, he desired her to sit down by him, which she did, then he drank to her, and asked her what Fee she would have? she asked Twelve Pounds a year, he answered, he would give her fifteen pound, because he would give her no Bounty.[21] The Lass finding him so kind, {*p. 8*} she agreed to serve him, upon which he drank to her on the concluding of the bargain, and she told him she was content to enter home to his Service as soon as he pleased. At length these Women *Nicolas Lawson* and *Lillie Wallace* were carried away, and then he and she committed Uncleanness together, and so for that time they parted. She continued for a long time in hopes of a kind Master, often requiring at *Beatie Laing* for her Master, but he did not return to her till New Years day, when he again commits Uncleanness with her; after which he told her that she must renounce her Baptism, and she should never want means wherewith to maintain her self, upon which she turned distracted, yet in the very time of her Distraction, she yeilded to his Commands: she Confesses that she never knew that he was the Devil till that time, but that she has several times seen him since.

Beatie Laing has long continued in this her most damnable Practices, yea, she is so full Revenge [*sic*], Malice and Devilry, that it it is fully known she Drown'd (together with her Accomplices) a ship belonging to *Pittenweem*; And that she was the Cause of hindering Captain *Gordon*'s taking a French prize on that Coast.[22] In brief, she has been the Cause of all the other Women's being Witches in that {*p. 9*} Place of the Country, so that it is unaccountable what Injuries she has done. For *Lillie Wallace*, *Nicolas Lawson*, *Janet Corset*, and all of them Confesses, that she was the only Author of their turning Witches.

Her actings and Practices might have gone a long course of time, and might have prov'd the Ruine of many innocent Souls; if it had not pleased GOD to detect them by the means of *Peter Mortoun* the Smith, whom they had Tormented by making his Image in Wax, Pricking and Nipping him at their meetings, so as he would be Pain'd in a hundred parts at once; his Picture is not yet found out, they allegding the Devil has taken it from them: But however, by the mercy of God, and the faithful Prayers of the Ministers thereabouts, this poor afflicted man is come to a far better State of health than formerly, and hopes in a short time to be fully liberat from it all.

There is a Sclater who is one of their accomplices, and was Piper to them at their Meetings: he would have denyed his being accessary to their Actings, but they made it good in his Face, particularly, for one instance they own that the last time the Devil and them were together, this Piper or Sclater, did not play right (it seems) to his pleasure, therefore he broke the End of his Pipe.

21 'Bounty': a payment to a servant in addition to regular wages.
22 Warfare between Britain and France had resumed in 1702.

There are several other things that might {*p. 10*} be said of them, but this being thought sufficient to Convince the World of their Malicious, Revengful, Despiteful and Damnable Practices I end.

It is therefore expected, that this Relation will be a Warning to all People of all Ranks, to be Content with the Dispensations that are allow'd them, and not to Repine and Grudge at the state wherein God has put them in [*sic*], seing that otherwise; those who do slight the Providencial Allowances which are bestowed on them, Seldom meet with better, but rather with Accidents that are in hazard to Ruine both Soul and Body. FINIS.

Pamphlet 2

A True and Full Relation of the Witches at Pittenweem[23]

To which is added by way of Preface,

An Essay for proving the Existence of Good and Evil Spirits, relating to the Witches at *Pittenweem*, now in Custody, with Arguments against the Sadducism of the Present Age.

Edinburgh. Printed by *John Reid Junior*, and are to be Sold at his Printing House in Libertouns Wynd. 1704. {*p. 2*}

To the Reader.

There being many People of this Age, who deny the Existence of Good and Evil Spirits, and who deny there are Wizards or Enchanters; I thought fit to give this small hint to convince the Judicious Reader, as well with Scripture Reasons, as others that have hapned before this, and in our Age. I have here inserted the way and manner of the Witches at *Pittenweem* as well as is come to my Hand, and their way and manner of Torturing and bewitching those People, against whom they bend their Designs. I had much more to add to this, but Referring the rest of this Relation, to such time, as we have the full of their Confessions

I Remain Yours, &c. {*p. 3*}

An Essay for proving the Existence of Good and Evil Spirits. Together with an Account of the Witches at *Pittenweem*.

Albeit it be evident from Scripture, and every Man's Experience, that there is a measure of God's good Spirit, given us to profit with all, exhorting to Righteousness, and whispering as it were behind us, *Here is the way, and walk ye in it*.[24]

23 Source: *A True and Full Relation of the Witches at Pittenweem* (Edinburgh: John Reid, 1704: ESTC no. T111617).

24 Cf. Isaiah 30:21.

So there are evil Spirits gone forth, Maliciously Tempting us to things quite contrary, even to Build up the Kingdom of Satan, promising the Possessions and Pleasures of this Lower World, to such as fall down and Worship this Tempter, such as, *Wealth to the Covetous, and to the Wrathful, Revenge.*

By which means the Devil hath prevailed with too many miserable Wicked creatures, to engage in an actual Confederacy with him, as appears by the Witchcrafts {*p. 4*} lately committed in the West,[25] and at this time by those in Custody at *Pittenweem*.

Yet notwithstanding that it was the Heresie of the Ancient Sadducees, to deny Angels and Spirits, *Acts* 8 and 23. There is a new sort of them Started up, who, as they deny the Existence of good Spirits, deny evil Spirits also, and the Possessing of, and Covenanting with Witches. Fools, who say, *That seeing with the Corporal Eye is Believing.*

But these People either believe the Scriptures, or not; if they believe, our proof is ready. What things were they of whom we read in *Jude* 6. *Angels that kept not their first estate, but left their Habitations, and were reserved in Chains, untill the Judgement of the Great Day.* Who was it that besought our Saviour? *If thou throw us out, suffer us to enter into the Herd of Swine.*[26] Who was it that Tempted *Job*?[27] What was the Legion that possessed one single Person? a Legion consisting of Twelve Thousand Six Hundred, but so many Spiritual Substances filled with wickedness against GOD, and Enmity against Man.[28] The Story of the Witch of *Endor*, is known to all.[29] We read how {*p. 5*} *Manasseh* used Enchantments, and Witchcrafts not a few, and dealt with Familiar Spirits.[30] So that those who believe the Scriptures, and the Powers of the Life to come, will be abundantly satisfied; *For Wisdom is justified of her Children.*[31]

But to convince the Infidel World, let us come to sensible Demonstration; To whom Seeing is Believing. And as to the Influence of Good Spirits, I've discoursed with many, but never found one, who denied that he found in himself something Spiritual, which, without Flattery or Hypocrisy, shew'd forthe the Mountain of Holiness, so as a wayfaring-man, tho' a Fool, could not mistake it, according to the Prophet.[32]

And as to the Influence of Evil Spirits, we have many thousand Witnesses, both in this, and the other side of the Hemisphere, I mean *America*, and the

25 Evidently the Bargarran case of 1697, which is mentioned later.
26 Cf. Mark 5:1–20.
27 'Satan' afflicted Job in the Book of Job.
28 This may be a second reference to the story in Mark 5:1–20 of the 'devils' whose name was 'Legion' and the Gadarene swine, alluded to earlier. The idea of 'a Legion consisting of Twelve Thousand Six Hundred' may have come from a Bible commentary.
29 Cf. 1 Samuel 28:7–25.
30 Cf. 2 Kings 21:6.
31 Cf. Matthew 11:19; Luke 7:35.
32 Cf. Jeremiah 31:23.

Plantations in *New-England*.[33] But why so far away, Have we not Witnesses here beside our selves at *Pittenweem*: The Person tortured,[34] and the Witches who do confess, and shew their Deeds; and own they did the mischief, telling how by Confederacy with the Devil, and by Images of Wax, and puting the Patient in Distortured[35] Figures {*p. 6*} and Shapes, as at sometimes his Joints will be so firm, that no Strength can bow his Wrists, or the Joints of his Legs: Dealing with him after the manner of their dealing with *Bargarran*'s Daughter, in the West, such Deeds being done on her and this Man, as is impossible any Disease or Deceit could produce. Some there are who are hardned, others penitent, and Owners of as much Reason, as those who laugh at all Conceit of Witchcraft.

The Exactest Scrutiny of Skilfull Phisicians, finding no Indispositions in their Bodies, nor Distraction in their Minds. These Confessions have also been made by those, who at the same time have produced the Ensigns and Engines of their Trade, and have given the Standers by Ocular Inspection, by Torturing, their Patients even before their Judges, shewing what they did, and how.

Besides all this, Witches in Different places here and in America, both in the last Ages and this, do concur in Witnessing the same things, viz. The Covenant 'twixt the Devil and them, their Renouncing their Baptismal Vows to GOD, and engaging to serve the Devil, and he promising them a better State of Living; {*p. 7*} as Satisfaction or Revenge on their Enemies, which is the principal point only he performs: For he promises Wealth, but as he is a liar, fails. Nor have we ever read or heard of any grown rich by Witchcraft. And in all Places they torture by Pictures and Images of Wax: For before Christianity, they worshipped a Ceraphim, which was the Devil speaking out of a Picture of Wax, as is yet practised by many of the *Laplanders*, in *Europe*, tho' after another manner. In fine, if such Evidences be redicul'd, there can be no Certainty in Human Affairs, all the Transactions of Mankind will be meerly Imaginations, since Proof can be of no moment.

Thus I have given you my sentiments, which I cut short, intending to shew forth the Relation of the Witchcrafts and Sorceries, at this time used in *Pittenweem*, which are as follows.

Peter Mortoun a Smith in *Pittinweem*, being desired by one *Beatie Laing*, to do some Work to her, which the said *Peter* did refuse, excusing himself, in respect he had been pre-engaged to serve a Ship with Nails, within a {*p. 8*} certain time; So that untill he had finished that Work, he could not engage in any other: Yet, notwithstanding of this Excuse, the said *Beatie Laing* declared her

[33] Evidently the panic at Salem, Massachusetts, in 1692.
[34] Patrick Morton.
[35] *Sic*. Read 'Distorted'.

self dissatisfied and disappointed, and threatned to be Revenged upon him for it. Shortly thereafter, the said *Peter* finding his Body in an Indisposition, and coming by the Dwelling house Door of this *Beatie Laing*, he sees there a small vessel full of Water, and therein a Coal of Fire Slockned[36] in the Water, so perceiveing an Alteration in his Health, and Remembring the said *Beatie Laings* threatnings and Menaces, and that she had been under no good Reputation, He presently Suspects, that there might be Devilrie in the matter, He quarrels the thing. And thereafter, finding his Indisposition to Encrease from worse to worse, being Tortured and Prickt, as it were with Bodkins and Pins; He openly throws the blame of all upon Witchcraft, whereof he principally Accuses this *Beatie Laing*, whereupon by Warrand she's apprehended, and several others in the Town of *Pittenweem*, but before apprehension no confession was made, and the Man still continued afflicted in such a manner as no Natural Reason could be given for it, his Countenance and *{p. 9}* Neck being so Distorted, his Back so prodigiously Rising of a Sudden, and falling as Suddenly, his Belly also Swelling up at another time, and presently drawing his Back to his Belly. His Joynts so plyable, at another time so Stiff and Firm, that no Strength could Bow them, and so as no Natural Distemper hath produced such Effects, and Phisicians Incapable to give him Cure or Ease, he particularizes the Names of those Tortoring him, as *Bargarrins* Daughter did in the West, and when those he Complains of, and now in Custody, are brought to the Room where he is, suppose in the mean time the afflicted person being in a Bed, Covered over with Cloaths, yet he tells his Tormenters are in the Room, and calls them by their Names, yet though no Confession was made formerly as said is, since their being taken in Custody; *Beatie Laing* now Confesses her own Crime, and Accuses several others as Accessary with her, *viz*.

Beatie Laing confesses her Compact with the Devil, and using Spells in prosecuting her Revenge against this *Peter Mortoun*; particularly the Slockning of the Coal of Fire in Water: And likeways, That she and her Associats, viz. *Janet Corset, Lillie {p. 10} Wallace*, and [*1 word blank*] *Lawson*,[37] had composed an Image or Picture of Wax; and each of the forenamed Persons having fastned in it their several Pins, in order to Torture. She likewise confessed, that one *Isobel Adams* a young Lass was likeways in compact with the Devil too.

Her foresaid Associats *Janet Corset* and the rest, do own, their being present at the making of the Image of Wax, but being examined where the Image was, and to deliver it up, they Declare they can give no account of it, but Complain, that the Devil hath stoln it from them, and say, that he appeared to them since they came to Prison.

This young woman *Isobel Adams* seems to be Penitent, and under great Remorse, acknowledging her Compact with the Devil, which she says was made up after this manner. *viz*.

36 'Slockned': quenched.
37 Nicolas Lawson.

That being in the House of the said *Beatie Laing*, and a Man at the end of the Table, *Beatie* Proposes to *Isobel*, that since she would not Fee and Hire with her, that she would do it, with the Man at the end of the Table; And, accordingly, *Isobel* agreed to it, and spoke with the Man at that time in General Terms. {*p. 11*}

Eight Days after, the same Person in Appearance comes to her, and owns that he was the Devil, desiring her to Engage in his Service, and to be Trustie therein; And that he would Procure her a far more Prosperous and Pleasant Life and Living in this World, than what her present was, as Wealth, Respect, Prosperity in all things: and thus the Confederacy being concluded, he committs Uncleanness with her, which no man ever did, as she pretends,[38] and put his mark in her Flesh, which was very painful; Sometime thereafter she was ordered to attend the Devil and the rest of the Company, together with a Piper, to go to the house of one *M^c^grigor* not far from thence, and to Murder him in the Night, but says that the Man Awakning with the Busle, and Blessing himself, they were forced to retire, and leave the thing undone.

And it is for certain, that *M^c^grigor* was Extreamly troubled in his Mind that very Night: However this Woman seems Ingenious[39] in her Acknowledgements, and very penitent for her Wickedness, and if she continue penitent, GOD who forgive *Manasseh* his Witchcrafts, and dealing with Familiar Spirits, may forgive her also. {*p. 12*}

Her case seems to be the same with one *Mary Johnston* in *Haitside*, who upon Confession of Witchcraft was Execute, and became very penitent. Who upon Discontentment and Repining at her present Condition, she Invocked the Devil to come to her Assistance, if none Else would[;] who appeared to her by the name of *Simon*, Rendering such Service as she Demanded. Her Master Reproved her one day, for not having the Chimny clear of Ashes, this *Simon* cleaned it ever after. Her Master Likeways having Ordered her to chase away a Herd of Swine out of Such a Park, it made her Laugh to see how the Devil Tossed them up and down, it seems they Run Hard whom the Devil Drives;[40] Notwithstanding she became penetent [*sic*], and shew such Remorse, that she Dyed Extreamly to the Satisfaction of all.[41]

Upon a Complaint given in to the Privy Council as is above, against those Witches at Pittenweem, *the Council have Ordered Her Majesty's Advocat to insist against them before the Justice General, where all Circumstances will be Examined, and Justice done. There are eight of them all, whereof only five have confessed.* FINIS.

38 'pretends': claims.

39 'Ingenious': perhaps meaning 'sensible', but more likely an error for 'ingenuous'.

40 A proverbial expression.

41 No documented Scottish witch called Mary Johnston has been found, nor even a place clearly called Haitside. This story seems to have been at least partly fictionalised; it may not be Scottish in origin, and it may not be traceable to a single documented case.

Pamphlet 3

An Account of a Horrid and Barbarous Murder[42]

In a LETTER from a Gentleman in *Fife*, to his Friend in *Edinburgh*, *Febr.* 5. 1705.

SIR, I doubt not of your being exceedingly Surpriz'd with this short and Just Account I give you, of a most Barbarous Murder committed in *Pittenweem* the 30*th* of *January* last. One *Peter Morton* a Blacksmith in that Town, after a long Sickness, pretended that Witches were Tormenting him, that he did see them and know them: And from time to time, as he delated[43] such and such Women to be Witches, they were by Order of the Magistrats and Ministers of *Pittenweem*, apprehended as such, to a very considerable Number, and put into Prison. This Man by his odd Postures and Fits, which seem'd to be very Surprising at first, wrought himself into such a Credit with the People of that Place; that unless the Earl of *Rothes*, our Sheriff, had discover'd his Villany, and discouraged that Practice, God knows how Fatal it might have prov'd to many Honest Families of Good Credit and Respect.[44] Sir, However, at first many were deceived, yet now all Men of Sense are asham'd for giving any Credit to such a Person. But how hard it is to Root out bad Principles once Espous'd by the Rabble; and how dangerous a Thing it is to be at their Mercy, will appear by the Tragical Account I give you of one of these poor Women, *Janet Corphat*. {*p. 2*}

After she was Committed Prisoner to the Tolbooth, upon a Suspicion of her being a Witch: She was well guarded with a Number of Men, who by Pinching her, and pricking her with Pins, keept her from Sleep many Days and Nights, threatning her with present Death, unless she would confess her self Guilty of Witchcraft, which at last She did. This Report spreading abroad, made People Curious to Converse with her upon the Subject, who found themselves exceedingly disappointed. The Viscount of *Primrose* being in *Fife* occasionally,[45] inclin'd to satisfy his Curiosity in this matter, the Earl of *Kellie*,[46]

42 Source: *An Account of a Horrid and Barbarous Murder* ([Edinburgh?] 1705: ESTC no. T183548).

43 'delated': accused. The reprint of this pamphlet, in *An Answer of a Letter* (hereafter *AL*), has 'declared'.

44 Rothes was a leading politician who had recently been appointed Lord Privy Seal. He was heritable sheriff of Fife. His seat was Leslie House near present-day Glenrothes. Andrew M. Lang, 'John Leslie, ninth earl of Rothes (1679–1722)', *ODNB*.

45 Sir James Primrose of Carrington (*c.*1680–1706), a commissioner to parliament from Edinburghshire, had been created Viscount Primrose in 1703. 'Being in Fife occasionally': having occasion to be in Fife.

46 Alexander Erskine, fourth earl of Kellie.

my Lord *Lyon*,[47] the Laird of *Scots-Tarvet*,[48] and the Laird of *Randerston*[49] were with his Lordship in *Pittenweem*. Three of the Number went to the Tolbooth and Discours'd her, to whom she said, that all that she had confessed, either of her self, or her Neighbours, were Lies, and cried out, *God forgive the Minister*, and said he had beat her one day with his Staff, when she was telling him the Truth. They ask'd her how she came to say any thing that was not true; she cried out, *Alas, alas, I behoved to say so, to please the Minister and the Bailies*: And in the mean time, she beg'd for Christ's Sake not to tell that She had said so, else she would be murdered. Another time, when the Laird of *Glenagies* and Mr. *Bruce* of *Kinross*,[50] were telling her, she needed not deny what they were asking her, for she had confessed as much as would infallibly burn her, she cried out, God Forbid! And to one of the two she said that, from which he might rationally conclude, she Insinuat she had Assurance from the Minister, her Life should not be taken.

A little before Harvest, Mr. *Ker* of *Kippilaw*[51] a Writer to the Signet being in *Pittenweem*, Mr. *Robert Cook* Advocat went with him to Prison, to see this poor Woman; Mr. *Cook* among other Questions ask'd her, if she had not Renounced her Baptism to the Devil; she answered, she never Renounc'd her Baptism but to the Minister. These were her Words, what she meant by them, I know not. The Minister having got Account of this from Mr. *Cook*, he sent for her, and in Presence of Mr. *Cook* and Mr. *Ker* in the Church, he threatn'd her very severely, and commanded the Keeper to put her into some Prison by her self under the Steeple, lest (as he said) she should pervert those who had Confessed. The Keeper put her into a Prison in which was a Low Window, out of which it was obvious {*p. 3*} that any Body could make an Escape, and accordingly she made her Escape that Night.

Next Day when they miss'd her, they made a very slight Search for her, and promised ten pound *Scots* to any Body that would bring her back.

Mr. *Gordon* Minister of *Leuchars*, hearing she was in his Parish, 8 Miles distant from *Pittenweem*, caused apprehend her, and sent her Prisoner, under Custody of two Men on the 30th of *January*, to Mr. *Cowper* Minister of *Pittenweem*, without giving any Notice to the Magistrates of the Place. When she came to Mr. *Cowper*, she ask'd him if he had any thing to say to her: he answered, No. She could get Lodging in no House, but with one *Nicolas Lowson*, one of the Women that had been called Witches. Some say a Bailie put her there.

47 Sir Alexander Erskine of Cambo.

48 David Scott of Scotstarvit.

49 James Balfour of Randerston.

50 *AL* has '*Glenagles*'. John Haldane of Gleneagles (1660–1721) was a commissioner to parliament from Perthshire. John Bruce of Kinross (d. 1711) was a commissioner to parliament for Kinross-shire.

51 Andrew Kerr of Kippilaw.

The Rabble hearing she was in Town, went to Mr. *Cowper*, and ask'd him what they should do with her? he told them he was not concern'd, they might do what they pleased with her. They took Encouragement from this, to Fall upon the poor Woman, those of the Minister's Family[52] going along with him, as I hear; they fell upon the poor Creature immediatly, and beat her unmercifully, tying her so hard with a Rope that she was almost strangl'd; they dragg'd her through the Streets, and alongst the Shoar by the heels. A Baillie hearing of a Rabble near his Stair, came out upon them, which made them immediatly disappear. But the Magistrats tho' met together, not taking Care to put her into closs Custody, for her Safety, the Rabble gathered again immediatly, and Streach'd a Rope betwixt a Ship and the Shoar, to a great height, to which they ty'd her fast; after which they swing'd her to and fro, from one side to another, in the mean time throwing Stones at her from all Corners, until they were weary: Then they loos'd her, and with a mighty Swing threw her upon the hard Sands; all about being ready in the mean time to Receive her with Stones and Staves, with which they beat her most cruelly.[53] Two of her Daughters came upon their Knees, begging to be allow'd one Word of their Mother, before she Expir'd; but that being Refus'd, and the Rabble threatning to Treat them in the same manner, they went off. The Rabble never gave over, till the poor Wretch was dead; and to be sure she {*p. 4*} was so, they call'd a Man with a Horse and a Sledge, and made him drive over her Corps backward and forward several times. When they were sure she was kill'd outright, they dragged her miserable Carcass to *Nicolas Lowson*'s House, where they first found her, laying on her Belly a Door of Boards, and on it a great heap of Stones.

There was a Motion, made to Treat Nicolas Lowson *after the same manner immediatly, but some of them being wearied with three hours Sport, as they call'd it, said it would be better to delay her for another Days Divertisement, and so they all went off.*

It's said, That Mr. Cowper, *in a Letter to Mr.* Gordon, *gave some Rise to all this: And Mr.* Cowper *to Vindicat hiself, wrote to* Mr. Gordon, *whose Return says,* If he were not going to *Edinburgh,* he would give him a Double of his

52 His servants, members of his household, are probably meant. The *Just Reproof* would later admit that the minister's servants were among the crowd.

53 *AL*, from this point until the end of the paragraph, has: 'Her Daughter in the time of her Mother's Agony, tho she knew of it, durst not adventure to appear, lest the Rabble had us'd her after the same manner, being in a House, in great Concern and Terror out of Natural Affection for her Mother: (About which the Author was misinform'd in the first Edition.) They laid a heavy Door upon her, with which they prest her so sore, that she cried out, to let her up for *Christ*'s sake, and she would tell the Truth: But when they did let her up, what she said could not satisfy them; and therefore they again laid on the Door, and with a heavy weight of Stones on it, prest her to Death: And to be sure it was so, they called a Man with a Horse and a Sledge, and made him drive over her Corp backward and forward several times. When they were sure she was killed outright, they dragged her miserable Carcass to *Nicolas Lowson*'s House, where they first found her.'

Letter. *It's strange he sent him not the Principal. In the Postscript he assures him he shall conceal it to Meeting.*

'Tis certain, that Mr Cowper *Preaching the Lord's Day immediatly after in* Pittenweem, *took no Notice of the Murder, which at least makes him guilty of sinful Silence.*[54] *Neither did Mr.* Gordon *in his Letter to Mr.* Cowper *make any Regrate for it: And this some construe to be a Justifying of the horrid Wickedness in both.*

We are perswaded the Government will Examine this Affair to the Bottom, and lay little Stress upon what the Magistrates or Minister of Pittenweem *will say, to smooth over the Matter: Seeing it's very well known, that either of them could have quash'd that Rabble, and prevented that Murder, if they had appeared Zealous against it.*

I am sorry I have no better News to tell You. GOD deliver us from those Principles that tend to such Practices.

I am, SIR, Your Humble Servant.

Pamphlet 4

An Answer of a Letter from a Gentleman in Fife, to a Nobleman, containing[55]

A brief Account of the Barbarous and illegal Treatment, these poor Women accused of Witchcraft, met with from the Baillies of *Pittenweem* and others, with some few Observations thereon.

To which is added

An Account of the horrid and Barbarous Murder, in a Letter from a Gentleman in *Fife*, to his Friend in *Edinburgh, February 5th.* 1705.

Printed in the Year 1705. {*p. 2*}

An Answer of a Letter from a Gentleman in Fife, *&c.*

MY LORD, I Reckon my self very much honoured by your Lordships Letter, desiring me to write you an Account of that horrible Murder committed in *Pittenweem*; I doubt not, but by this time, your Lordship has seen the Gentleman's Letter to his Friend thereanent: I refer you to it, the Author thereof being so well inform'd, and so ingenuous, that I'll assure you there is nothing in it, but what is generally talk'd, and believed to be true.

All I can contribute to your Lordship's further Information, shall be by way of a brief Narrative of the Baillies and Minister's unwarrantable imprisoning, and barbarous treating of the Poor Women.

I need not write your Lordship a Character of *Patrick Morton*, being now sufficiently known for a Cheat.

54 This was five days later. The day of the murder, 30 January, was a Tuesday.

55 Source: *An Answer of a Letter from a Gentleman in Fife to a Nobleman* ([Edinburgh?] 1705: ESTC no. N16460).

It was upon his Accusation allennarly[56] the Minister and Baillies imprisoned these poor Women, and set a Guard of drunken Fellows about them, who by pinching and Pricking some of them with Pins and Elsions,[57] kept them from sleep for several Days and Nights together; this cruel Usage made some of them learn to be so wise, as acknowledge every Question that was ask'd them; whereby they found the Minister and Baillies well pleas'd, and themselves better treated.

Notwithstanding of all this, some of the more Foolish, continued, as the Minister said, hardened in the Devil's Service, such as *White*, *Jack*, *Wallace*, *Patrick*, and others: All which, save the first, were ordered to the Stocks, where they lay for several Weeks. {*p. 3*}

All this, while *Patrick Morton*'s melancholly Fancy (to give it no harsher Term) being too much encouraged by severals, and particularly by the Minister's reading to him the Case of *Barrengarran*'s [*sic*] Daughter, continued roving after a wonderful manner, accusing for his Tormenters, some of the most considerable Mens Wives in the Town, but such as the Minister and Baillies durst not venture to imprison. By this your Lordship may see, it was only the weakest that went to the Walls.

My Lord *Rothes* accompanied with several Gentlemen of good Sense and Reputation, came to Pittenweem, where finding these poor Women's Confessions nowise satisfying, and *Patrick Morton* a Cheat, informed the Privy Council thereof, who sent an Order to send *Patrick* over to them.

This Turn being given; and *Patrick* finding, that things were not likely to go favourably with him as he before fancied, began to draw to his Breeches; and in a short time recovered his former Health, in which he still continues. By this time the Baillies began to be as earnest in emptying their Prisons, as ever they were forward in filling them: So after a long and serious Deliberation, they set them at Liberty: But that their last step might be as illegal as their first, obliged each of them to pay the Town-Officer, the Sum of 8 *lib. Scots*: To pay which, some of them were forced to sell some Linnen they had reserved for their Dead-Shirts and Wynding-Sheets.

I beg your Lordships further Patience to read these few following Observations. *Obs.* 1st. The Baillies and Minister sent and brought severals of these Women from Places without their Jurisdiction; one from *Anstruther*, and another from the Country at 6 Miles distance.

Obs. 2d. What Good could the Minister propose to *Patrick Mortoun* by reading to him the Book Intituled, *The Case of* Barrangarran*'s Daughter*.

Observ. 3d. After so much Unjustice done these poor Women, the Baillies and Ministers obliged them to pay the Town {*p. 4*} Officer eight Pounds *Scots*, is worthy of your Lordships, and the rest of the Lords of the Privy Council's

56 'allennarly': only.
57 'Elsions': bodkins or awls.

Considerations: And it would be the height of Charity, to fall on a method to oblige the Minister and Baillies to refound it seven-fold.

Obs. 5th. [*sic*] One *Thomas Brown* the only Man accused by *Patrick Mortoun*, and imprison'd by the Minister and Baillies, after a great deal of hunger and hardship, died in Prison. So as this poor Womans Murther was not the first, neither will it be the last, unless by severe Punishments prevented.

Obs. 5th. The Baillies in a manner justified these two Murthers by their not allowing them Christian Burial, but burying them like dogs, scarce covered them from the ravens.

Obs. 6th. You may wonder why all along I should say the Minister and Baillies? The reason is, because during all this Narrative he exercis'd more of the Civil Authority than any of the Baillies, and so continues to do, as you may see by this following late Instance.

The Baillies of *Pittenweem* being conveen'd before the Lords of Privy-Council on the 14th or 15th of *February*, I am inform'd, gave in to them a subscrived Account of the Murther; and to justify themselves, assert they had imprison'd severals of the Murtherers before they left *Pittenweem*. It is very true they did so, but they were not long from the Town, when the Minister set them at liberty: This I think is exercising the Office of a Civil Magistrate. Perhaps the Minister may say, he did it by the Magistrat's Order left behind them; then I think the Magistrats were mightily in the wrong to give in to the Lords of the Privy-Council an Account they knew to be false.

My Lord, This is not the tenth part of what may be said upon this Subject; I hope some other Person will be more particular.

I am, MY LORD, *Your Lordships most humble Servant*.[58]

Pamphlet 5

A Just Reproof, to the False Reports, Bold, & Unjust Calumnies, Dropt in Two Late Pamphlets[59]

The first entituled,

An account of a horrid and barbarous murder. In a letter from a gentleman in Fife, *to his friend in* Edinburgh.

And the other

An Answer of a Letter from a Gentleman in Fife *to a Nobleman, containing a brief Account of the Barbarous and Illegal Treatment, the Poor Woman accused of Witchcraft met with, from the bailies of* Pittinweem *and others.*

58 The remainder of the pamphlet, pp. 5–8, consists of a revised reprint of the previous pamphlet, the *Account of a Horrid and Barbarous Murder*. This is reproduced above in the present edition, with the variations noted.

59 Source: *A Just Reproof, to the False Reports, Bold, and Unjust Calumnies, Dropt in Two Late Pamphlets* (Edinburgh, 1705: ESTC no. N18477).

Prov. 10.18. *He that hideth hatred with Lying Lips, and he that uttereth Slander is a Fool.*

Prov. 12.19. *The Lip of truth shall be Establisht for ever: But a Lying tongue is but for a Moment.*

Prov. 17.4. *A Wicked doer giveth heed to false Lips: and a Lyer giveth Ear to a Naughty tongue.*

EDINBURGH. Printed in the Year M.DCC.V. {*p. 2 blank*} {*p. 3*}

A just reproof, to the false reports, bold, & unjust calumnies, dropt in two late pamphlets, &c.

The Triffling Pamphlet we are now to take under Correction, appeared several Weeks ago. The design of it was so palpably malicious, so discernible an Air of Partiality, Prejudice and ill nature, every where breath'd in the Paper; that all Persons of Judgment, Sobriety and Candor, how different soever in Principle from the Persons Traduc'd, Entertain'd it with Contempt. A Paper that carried its own Confutation so plainly in its Bosom, was scarce thought worthy of an Answer: Tho' the Impudence of the Author, in abusing the World with such scandalous Untruths, and his ignorance in managing his Malicious Design of blackening the Reputations of Persons, whom he durst not fairly attack in any Legal or Allowable way; by an Account of Matters of Fact that had not a Resemblance of Truth, were judged worthy of such a Reproof, as the Wise Man informs us, is *proper for fools.*[60] But the Author of this Pamphlet being either enraged by this Contempt, or growing bold because he met with no Opposition, has Impudently obtruded upon the World a second Impression of it, with Additions, of the same Temper and Alloy with the first Paper; since no Body thought fit to Answer his Letter He has Bless'd the World with an Answer of a Letter Stuft with more of the same Dirt that filled up the Lines of his former Paper: Our Author and his Accomplices have no Doubt heard their Friends read them that Lesson, *Calumniare audacter aliquid adherebis*. Throw Dirt some of it will Stick; and they have Conn'd it well, and in those two Papers have given Evidence of their Proficiency. But lest Silence should be Constructed an Evidence of Guilt, We are now in Compliance with the Wise Mans advice, that bids us in such Cases, *Answer a Fool according to his Folly, least he be wise in his own Conceit,*[61] Resolved to call those Pamphlets to Account for their Disingenuous Misrepresentations, Scandalous Falshoods, in matter of Fact their Malicious Insinuations, more bold Thrusts at the Reputation of innocent Persons, and other Miscarriages of an Alike nature.

[60] Perhaps a reference to Proverbs 23:9. The 'Wise Man' is Solomon.
[61] Cf. Proverbs 26:5. Again the 'Wise Man' is Solomon.

But before we take any Particular notice of this Pamphlet, it will be Necessary to Premit a short Hint of some Occurrences, that gave Rise to this whole matter.

About the Month of March last Year, on[e] *Beatrix Layng*, a Woman of very bad Fame, who had formerly been under Process for using Charms, and Refusing to be Reconcil'd to her Neighbours, was Debar'd from the Lord's Table, came to one *Patrick Mortoun* a Black Smith desireing him to make some Nails: which he refus'd to do, because otherwise Imploy'd at that time. Upon which She went off Muttering some Threatning Expressions; {*p. 4*} A little after the said *Patrick Mortoun*; with another Person in Company Carrying some Fish by the said *Beatrix Layng*'s Door, they saw a Vessel with Water plac'd at the Door, with a Burning Coal in it. Upon which he was presently Strucken with an Impression that it was a Charm Design'd against him; and upon this a little after he Sickn'd. In this Sickness he Languished for a long time: Physicians that saw him, could not understand his Distemper, yet try'd Various Medicines; till at length, his trouble Increas'd and he begun to be Seis'd with some Unusual Fits, which made them give over. He forbore all this while any Accusation of the Person whom he all along Suspected for his Trouble, at least he made no mention of it to the Minister, who frequently Visited him, while under it. But his trouble still increasing, he at length began to drop some Apprehensions of the Cause of it: Upon which *Beatrix Laing* was call'd, and by the Magistrats, in the said *Patrick Morton*'s Father's house, Examin'd in presence of a great Multitude of People; and own'd that she had plac'd that Vessel with Water, and the Coal in it there: But at that time would give no Account of the Reason of it. Being dismiss'd by the Magistrates, she went home; and that same Night when she was Challanged by *Katharine Marshal*, in her own house, before *Nicolas Lowson*, about the Lad's Trouble, she answered, *That he might blame his own ill Tongue, for what had befaln him, and that it was an Evil Spirit that was troubling him*: Which was in her Face maintained, by the said Persons next day, in Presence of the Magistrats. Then the Boy began to complain of her Tormenting him, and fell into grievous Fits of Trouble upon her Entring the House. Upon all which, she being imprison'd, after some time, did acknowledge to Magistrats and Minister, in Presence of many Witnesses, without Threat or Torture (of which we shall speak more afterwards). *That she was displeased with* Patrick Morton *for his refusing to make some Nails; that she designed to be avenged upon him for it: And that she used that Charm of the Coal in the Water against him: And that she renounced her Baptism, entred into a Compact with the Devil, some twelve years before; Condescending upon Time, Place, and her Inducements to engage in his Service: And that she, with* Nicolas Lowson, *had made a Wax Picture to Torment him, and put Pins in it; which the said* Nicolas *likewise confessed afterwards, and so Justified the Boy's Account of the Rise of his Trouble.*

After this the Boys trouble daily increas'd, in which there were many Strange things; first his Belly for some time, then his Breast frequently heav'd up to a Prodigious hight, and instantly sent off again, by a blowing at the Mouth like a Bellows, frequently he cried out that such Persons as he Nam'd were Pinching him in his Arms, Breast, or some other places of his Body, his Hands lying all the while above the Cloaths at distance from one another, in the view of many of the Spectators; and when they Look'd the places of which he complain'd, they saw distinctly the Print of Nails: Again {*p. 5*} he was frequently cast into Swooning Fits, became insensible, which was tryed by Exquisite Pinching the more sensible parts of his Body, of which he Complain'd afterwards, when he came out of the Fits, tho' he took no Notice of them, nor felt them in the time, while he was in these Fits; the Strongest who Essayed to lift his Head from the Pillow, were not able to move it, tho' both his Feet and Head were perfectly free of the Bed, which was exactly tried: Yea sometimes while the Trunk of his Body and his head were thus Rigid, and could not be rais'd from the Pillow, his Legs were loose, and any might move them as they pleas'd. Sometimes these Fits were not so great as at other times; and then, or when he was falling in, or coming out of them, several Persons lifted him with little Difficulty: But when he was in the Deepth of the Fit, the Strongest that essay'd it could not raise him up. Again when any of the Women whom he accused touched him, and sometimes on their coming into the Room, he fell into grievous Fits of Trouble, and cried out, That such a Person was Tormenting him, condescending on their Names: And this he did very frequently, before Multitudes of People of different Ranks, ready to attest the same. And commonly such Care was taken to prevent his having any Notice, either of the Womens Entry, or which of them was there, that there was no place left for any Rational Suspicion of Trick or Cheat in the Matter. He was carefully hoodwink'd[62] with several Plyes of Cloth: The Women were brought in with the utmost Secrecy, innocent Persons present in the Room laid their hands on him, but yet he never shew'd the least Concern, save when the accused Persons Touched him. Several Times Gentlemen that seem'd Jealous[63] that there was somewhat of an Imposture in the case, were allowed and Invited to make the Nicest Tryal, and found it hold. Several pitiful Cavils have been used about this, and other instances of the Boys trouble, which proceed either from Ignorance of the Circumstances of matter of Fact, or Gross inadvertancy in not observing the several Variations of the Boy's case; which had they been considered, they would have been so far from giving any Countenance to the Conclusion aimed at by these Objectors, that they would strongly have Enforced a Conviction of something Præter-Natural in the case: But we forbear to enter on the Detail of these Exceptions, because they are evidently Trifling, and Savouring rather of prejudice against the General Truth, that there is such a thing as Witchcraft, and the Persons who

[62] 'hoodwink'd': blindfolded.
[63] 'Jealous': suspicious.

profess to Believe it, than of Judgement or an Impartial Consideration of this particular case. Beside such as this Author sees meet to mention shall be afterward considered,

Further, In the time of his Trouble, he told, that severals of the Witches Tormenting him, were at their Meetings, condescending upon the time, Place, Persons present, in which the Confessing Witches did exactly concur with him, and Justified his Accounts.

These and many other Particulars of an alike Nature, might have been {*p. 6*} attested by the Oaths of many Witnesses, if the Wisdom of the Government had seen meet during the Lad's Trouble, to put this matter to an exact Tryal; which all concern'd much desired, whereof they gave sufficient evidence, by their Applications to all concern'd, to grant Commission to Try the whole matter on the place.

The design'd Brevity will not allow to enlarge in giving any further Account of this Boy's Troubles or of all Occurrences, with respect unto the Witches; Wherefore leaving this, we shall proceed to take this Pamphlet under Consideration, and begin with that part of it first Published.

In the first Paragraph, after a short hint of *Patrick Mortoun's* Trouble, our Author subjoins, *That this Man by his odd Postures and Fits, which seemed to be very Surprising at first, wrought himself into such a Credit with the People of that Place; that unless the Earl of* Rothes *our Sheriff had Discovered his Villany, and Discouraged that Practice, God knows how fatal it might have proved, to many honest Families of good Credit and Respect;* Sir, *However at first many were deceived, yet now all Men of Sence are Asham'd for giving any Credit to such a Person.*

To which its Replyd, 1*st*. As to the Boy's Trouble, we refer to the Account of the matters of Fact, just now given: and its left to unbyass'd Readers to Judge, whether Men of Sence had Reason to be Asham'd of giving any Credit to this Person, who is a Simple Boy, and uncapable of managing any Imposture, and it is not easie to understand, what might be his Inducement, if he had been Capable of it, since it did so much to ruine him and his Fathers Family.

2*ly*. Whereas our Author tells us, *That if a timely Discovery had not been made of the Imposture, it might have been of bad Consequence to many Honest Families of Good Credit and Respect*. We know no ground for the Authors fears; Its true many Reports have been blown about of Persons being Accus'd, who may come under this Character: But there was never any Ground for these Reports, for neither did the Boy drop any Accusation to Magistrats or Minister, nor the Confessing Witches ever delate any without the Bounds of the Parish of *Pittenweem*, nor any Person within the Town of note, or indeed any, save those who were imprison'd, and a very few others of the meaner Sort. 3. As to what our Author asserts of the Earl of *Rothes* detecting his Villany. We answer, that the Earl of *Rothes* is a Person, whom, on many Accounts we respect: But we must have better Ground than this Author's Word, before we can believe, that a Person of the Earl of *Rothes* Sense and Judgment, would conclude, from his not seeing any thing Remarkable, during half an hour, or an hours Stay. That there was nothing of Reality, in a Trouble carried on for a long Tract of Time, in a great Variety of Shapes, and which had various, and sometimes long Intermissions during which there was nothing observable to be seen. And who {*p. 7*} can believe, that, if the Earl of *Rothes* had discovered any manifest evidence of the Boy's villany, that he would have gone off the place where there was most need for this discovery, to undeceive the People, who, if we may believe this Author, had been wheedled by this Rogue, into a belief of the reality of his trouble, without giving these convincing evidences which this Pamphleter would have us believe he found. This is so manifestly unworthy of that Noble Lord, that we cannot entertain so mean thoughts of him upon so weak a ground, as the assertion of one, whose word shall be discovered to be of very little value before we have done with him. And if the Earl of *Rothes*, or any other, had offered any such evidence, the Magistrats or Minister, would have been as forward as any, to have him punished as an Imposture; besides, if any unquestionable evidence of Imposture had appeared, the known zeal and concern of that Noble Lord for the Execution of Justice, the punishment of Villany, and preventing such dangerous consequences, could not but have led him to use his utmost endeavours to have it punished in an Exemplary way.

Our Author in the next paragraph, proceeds to give us his History of *Janet Corphat*, the Woman who was murdered.

Before we take him to task, it will be needful, that we give some account of this Woman, not to extenuat the Murder, which we detest as much as he; she was a Woman of very bad fame, who of a long time was reputed a Witch, frequently used Charms, and was wont commonly to threaten persons who disobliged her, and such consequences some time followed, as made her the terror of many, both of the Town and Country, which might be verified by particular Instancs if it were necessary: she was not at first delated by *Patrick Mortoun*, tho' afterwards he complain'd of her as one of her Tormentors: But she with some several others in Company with the Devil, whereof *Isabel Adam* was one, in pursuance of a quarrel, which *Beatrix Laing* formerly mention'd, had with one *Alexander Mcgrigor*, a Fisher in the Town, made an Attempt to murder the said *Mcgrigor* in Bed; which was prevented by his awakning and wrestling against them. This Attempt was acknowledged by *Isabel Adam*, of whose Confession a more full Account shall be given afterwards, who had been taken up on that Man's Delation, and some other Informations against her, and not on the Lad's. As likeways, the said *Janet* was accused by *Nicolas Lowson*, another Person present at that Attempt. And *Nicolas* accus'd her of being at another Meeting in the Loan of *Pittenweem*; at both which Meetings they confess'd the Devil was present: All which she her self afterwards freely confess'd.

The manner of this Woman's Confession was very remarkable. After she had obstinatly some while denied, and with a subtility beyond what might be expected, from one of her Education, shifted all questions put to her, she with *Isobel Adam* aforesaid, being brought to the House where the tormented Lad lay, and he discovering her at her entry into the Room, notwithstanding the utmost precaution was used to conceal it from him, and he falling into grievous fits of trouble, {*p. 8*} did cry out of her as one of his Tormenters; at which she was so stunn'd, that instantly she fell a trembling. The Magistrats and Minister observing her in such a confusion, asked if she was willing to commune with them, in reference to the matters, whereof she had been accused, she declaring her self willing, went with them to another place, and when desired to be ingenuous, she again fell a trembling and said she would confess all, but was afraid the Devil would tear the Soul out of her Body if she did, and said if you will Pray, and cause all good Folk Pray for me, I will confess, and desired the Minister then to Pray, and, after Prayer, Confessed, *she was Bodily present at both the meetings aforesaid with the Devil and the Witches, and gave a circumstantiat account of the Renounciation of her Baptism, naming time, place, and inducements which led her to it, and the shape the Devil appeared to her in. She likeways told the reason of their attempt to Murder* M^c^griegor, *was, that he did not hire a House which belonged to* Beatrix Layng.

Again, on a Thursday after she had been hearing Sermon, she desir'd to speak with the Minister, and sent one to acquaint him with this Desire, on which he went to her; and she before several Witnesses, renewed her former Confession, and Condescended on all the Persons, the other Confessing Witches had Accused, as being present at the two foresaid Meetings, adding withal, that there were others present whom she knew not; This Confession she renewed before the Presbytrie, in presence of a great many Country Gentlemen, and many other Spectators, as likewise in face of a numerous Congregation on the Lord's day.

And now let us hear the Pamphleter's account of this Womans case, he tells us, *She was well guarded with a number of men, who by Pinching her*, &c. Here are almost as many Untruths, as Words, which a plain account of matters of Fact, which we offer to verify in all Points, if call'd to it, will make appear.

It is own'd, That when *Beatrix Laing* and *Nicolas Lawson* were first Imprisoned, they were ill us'd by some of the Guard, without the Knowledge of Magistrats or Minister, of which the Woman made Complaint to the Minister, whereof he presently acquainted the Magistrats, who with the Minister went to the Prison, and threatned the Guard, if they offered the least Disturbance to Persons in Custody: And the Minister on the Lord's day thereafter took occasion in Sermon, to discover the Wickedness of that practice, as being against the Light of Nature, Scripture, and the just Laws of the Land; after this, we heard of no more Disturbance they met with. Now it was not till after this precaution used to prevent their Trouble, that *Janet Corphat* was Imprisoned, and from the time of her Imprisonment, till the time that she Confessed, which was some Ten, or Twelve days after; she was not in the

Company with the rest, nor with the Guard, save one or two Days, but was alone in a separat Prison, and nothing to disturb her.

Now its Remarkable, that neither of these Persons who were ill us'd, of which *Janet Corphat* was none, did ever make any Acknowledgement to these {*p. 9*} persons who us'd them ill, nor till some days after they were quite freed of this Trouble. And when they did Confess, it was to Magistrates and Minister, whom they own'd to be careful to preserve them, from such Abuses; nor did Magistrats or Minister ever use any Threatning to extort a Confession, or any other Argument but what the Gospel requires to be made use of, to bring Impenitent Sinners to a Confession of their Sins: From all which its evident, how false our Authors Account is.

The Pamphlet toward the middle of this Paragraph, tells us, *That* Janet Corphet *said to some Noblemen and Gentlemen, who came to see her, that all she had confessed, &c. were lies, and cryed out, God forgive the Minister*, &c. To which its Answered, this Passage fell out a considerable time after their Confession, and also after the Story next mentioned, of which by and by, and before these Noblemen and Gentlemen came to see her, she had been prevailed with to retract her Confession, upon what Inducements, and upon whose means, and what were their Motives, we forbear to mention, being unwilling to drop any thing, that may Reflect on the Honour of Persons, to whose Character we owe some regard, if not driven to it by plain necessity. However litle regard they have to the reputation of Magistrats and Minister.

As to what she said to the Persons first mention'd in the Pamphlet, no Regard is to be had to it, For beside that we want evidence of the Truth of it, since the few Persons that entered the Prison, allowed none of the Place to be present, but thrust forth one of the Magistrates, that was going in: This Woman, as said is, having Retracted her confession before this, was now in Expectation of obtaining her Liberty immediatly, by means of one of these Persons, and when that Person by whom they Expected to be Liberate, did formerly visite her, she made use of this as an Argument with *Isobel Adam*, and *Nicolas Lowson* to Engage them to Retract their Confessions, and deny all; which the said *Isobel Adam*, and *Janet Corphet* did Confess afterwards before Witnesses; and *Isobel Adam* in the Confession she made in presence of the Magistrates, which is attested by their Subscriptions, and is now Lodg'd in the hands of my Lord Advocat acknowledges, that *Janet Corphet* practised on her and *Nicolas*, and induced her to Retract: And here it is not amiss to observe, that the said *Isobel Adam* while she stay'd in *Pittenweem*, never Retracted or varyed in her Confession, but this once upon the Inducement abovementioned, and she adher'd to her Confession before my Lord Advocat, one of the Lords of Justiciary, and several other Witnesses; It is true, she has since several times denyed all, as to which my Lord Advocat in a Letter to the Magistrates of *Pittenweem* say's, *he was very well Satisfy'd, she is perverted*:

As to what *Janet Corphet spake of the Ministers beating her with his Staff*. It is the most abominable untruth, and there was never the least shaddow of Ground for it: The Minister never spoke with her alone, when he was dealing with her to Confess; nor dare any Person say, that ever they saw the Minister {*p. 10*} treat her Rudely in the least, besides her former Confession was so free, and came so much of her self, as is evident from the Account above given, that there was no Tentation[64] to it.

As to what she said of her desire to have her Denyal Conceal'd, the former Account given of the Conduct of Magistrates and Minister, Demonstrates she had no Ground for any such fear, as she is pretended to have been under.

Next in the close of this Paragraph, we are Entertain'd with a Story of what she said to the Laird of *Glenagies* and Mr. *Bruce* of *Kinross*. The best way to Satisfie the Reader about this, is to give a plain Account of Matter of Fact, these Gentlemen came in Company with the Earl of *Rothes*, a considerable time before the last mentioned Story fell out: When the Earl came to the Prison where *Isobel Adam, Janet Corphet*, and *Nicolas Lowson* were, a Neighbouring Minister who was occasionally there, and had never spoke with *Isabel Adam* before, said to her before these persons, and a great many other Witnesses; *Isabel, My Lord* Rothes *is come here and desires to be Satisfi'd, as to the Truth of these Reports that are going of you, we shall not propose any Questions to you, but it will be most Satisfying to hear you give an Account of the whole matter your Self.* Upon which she presently began, and gave an Exact and Coherent Account how she was drawn to the Sin of Witch-craft, and of all she had so often before Confessed, with much seeming Concernedness. When she had done, the Minister said, *Isabel, this is a very Strange Story, has any Person by Torture or Threatnings, or any other violence Tempted you to accuse your self of such horrid Crimes*? To which she Answered, *None has done it, but it was a Truth she told*; whereupon *Glenagies* Standing at the end of the Table, said, *Woman, are you thinking long to be Burnt*? To which she with great concern and readiness Replyed instantly, *If it be GOD's will and Mans will. I desire it. Janet Corphet* did likewise own her Guilt to the Persons that Conversed with her, as is Confessed in the Pamphlet, for its Granted by our Author, that the Gentleman said to her, *she had confessed as much as would in infallibly Burn her*; to what purpose her Reply to this is mention'd, is not easy to understand, for nothing more can be inferr'd from her saying *God forbid*, when they spoke of Burning to her, than that she was unwilling to be Burnt; And this is Strange! As to what is Subjoin'd,

That, *to one of the two she said, that, from which he might rationally conclude, she had assurance from the Minister, her Life should not be taken*. Here we have a tast of Authors Candour, and how well he deserves the Character he assumes to himself of a Gentleman, what Man might he not abuse at this Rate? And if Men will follow such Courses, whose Reputation is safe? The Expression

64 'Tentation': coercion or inducement.

from which this Conclusion is alledged deduceable is not mention'd, and so there is no access for any to canvass the Words, and Judge what Construction they will bear, or what Conclusion may rationally be deduced from them. This is a convenient way of management for Persons that have a bad Cause, and whose pretended Consequences to the prejudice of others, cannot bear an Impartial Tryal. {*p. 11*} As to the matter it self, it's a downright untruth, for as the Minister never threatned Death, so he never promised Life to any of them, he knew very well the power of Life and Death was not in his hand: After all, it's a Question whether the Gentleman means, has really said so, we have only our Author's word for it, and any who reads this Paper, will be far from blaming us, if we refuse to take every thing he says for Truth. Many other stories have been told under these Gentlemens Names about what then occurr'd, which seem plainly intended to wrong the Reputation of others, which we forbear to mention, because we had them only upon vulgar report; And we can scarcely believe that Gentlemen of any Candour or Sense, could have been guilty of abusing the World with so foul Misrepresentations. A candid and impartial Representation of what was really matter of Fact, and could easily be evicted[65] to be so, would be sufficient to make the first reports asham'd of their disingenuity, and such as intertain'd them of their foolish Credulity: But the stories are really so ridiculous, that the Persons concerned, think them rather worthy of contempt than a Reply; especially since we have no other ground to fix them upon any Author, but common Fame. On which we Judge it unchristian to lay the stress, as this Pamphlet every where doeth, or to mention what may in the least prejudge the Reputation of others. But as to our Authors story, the short of the matter is, the Minister must be blackned, or his design is lost.

The Third Paragraph of this Pamphlet tells us a story of what *Janet Corphet* said to Mr. *Robert Cook* Advocat, and Mr. *Ker* of *Kippilaw* a Writer to the Signet, to whom we believe she did in part deny her Guilt, but this was after she had been influenced by the means abovementioned to retract her Confession; whether she used these words mentioned by our Author, we cannot tell, nor is it material. What might be the meaning of them, our Author says he knows not, and we know not to what purpose he has mentioned them, unless it be to perswade the World, that she was so simple that no regard is to be had to any Confession she made. As to which, we Answer, when she desired to be admitted publickly to renew her Baptismal Vows; The Presbytry of St. *Andrews*, after they had Examin'd her a considerable time in the presence of a multitude of Witnesses, found her a Person of no contemptible knowledge, and none who know the Woman, and how sagacious she was beyond many of her rank, would believe that her saying, *That she did never renounce her Baptism, but to the Minister*, was any other thing but a mistake in Expression occasion'd

[65] 'evicted': proved.

by the confusion she was in, upon her being closly urged as to her Guilt by them: For she acknowledged to them that she was at a meeting in the *Loan* with the rest of the Witches. Whereas it's said the Minister threatned her. It's Replyed, that the Minister, at this time, or any other time, made use of no threatnings, but such as every Minister of the Gospel is obliged to use when dealing with such Persons; and he dares the Author to give any evidence to the contrar.

In the close of this Paragraph, our Author tells us, *she was put in a low Prison, {p. 12} out of which it was obvious that any Body could make an escape, and accordingly she made her escape that night*. Here are but two assertions, and both of them False, for the Prison was the second story, and her escape was by breaking an old Iron Grate in the Window, nor was it that night after, that she broke the Prison, for it was on Friday these Gentlemen discours'd her, and on the Lord's Day at Night she broke Prison.

The Fourth Paragraph consists of two Assertions, and neither of them true, there was no search made for her, since the Magistrats thought it not probable she would Stay in the Town, only her Daughter Living in the place, was Examin'd about her accession to her Escape; who utterly denyed, she knew any thing of it, neither did they ever promise any Reward to such as should bring her back.

Our Author in his next Paragraph proceeds to his Account of the Murder. The Pamphlet has disjointed matters a little, and we must bring them together again, that we may give a distinct Reply. After he has told us, *That Mr. Gordon Minister of* Lewchars *sent* Janet Corphet *to* Pittenweem and told the hail Story of the Murder. He says in his last Page, *that its said Mr.* Couper *in a Letter to Mr.* Gordon *gave rise to it &c*. That the Reader may have a clear view of this, we must give a short Account of the matter of Fact, which we shall make good against this Author, or any that shall call it in Question. *Mr. Cowper* denyes that ever he gave any Encouragement, by Word or Write, direct or indirect to *Mr. Gordon*, to send her to *Pittenweem*; nor did *Mr. Couper* Write his first Letter to *Mr. Gordon*, till after the Murder, nor did Mr. *Gordon* ever mention to Mr. *Couper* that he had a design to send her back.

As for the Letter *Mr. Couper* wrote to *Mr. Gordon* after the Murder, it has never yet come into *Mr. Coupers* hands, but is Lodged in the hands of the Moderator of the Presbytrie of St. *Andrews*, It's manifest this which was the first Letter *Mr. Couper* wrote for many years to *Mr. Gordon*, could give no Rise to the sending of the Woman, or the Murder, since it was after both. As for what *Mr. Gordon* says in his Postscript *that he shall Conceal Mr. Coupers Letter; Mr. Gordon* has sent *Mr. Couper* a second Letter, *Which any that pleases may see, wherein he declares, the reason of that Postscript was, not anything he had found in the Letter; but that when Mr.* Cowper *sent for the Letter to him, he was going to his Horse for* Edinburgh, *and had not got time to peruse it.*

This Narrative shews how groundless our Author's uncandid Insinuations of the Rise of this Business are: Let us now see how he acquits himself in the Account of the Matter it self; there our Author has strangely jumbl'd Matters together. And therefore leaving his Confused Account, stuft with Falshoods, we shall give a short and true Account of it.

Janet Corphet *came to Town under Cloud of Night with two Men, and went straight to an Inn where her Daughter was Serving: After some Stay there, the two Men brought her to the Minister's House, who was Visiting a sick Child of one* James Cook, *a present Bailie, where his Servant came to him with Mr.* Gordon's *Letter; and as {p. 13} soon as he had perused it, he bid his Servant go tell them, he would have nothing to do with her; but since they had brought her to the Town, let them take her to the Magistrats: Which Answer, two Men then present have attested under their hands. On this, the Men brought her to Bailie* Cook's *House, where the Minister was; and the Men meeting him coming down stairs, pressed him to take her off their hands, which he refused to do; but call'd the two next Magistrats, and advised them instantly to set her off safe out of the Town: On which the two Bailies sent for their Officer immediatly; and the Minister went off straight to his own House, and saw no appearance of a Rabble, nor did hear of it, till the Rabble had gone a considerable length; and after a little, he heard that the Woman was got safe out of their hands, and the Rabble dissipat, and he knew nothing of her death till the next Morning.*

When the Officer came to the Magistrates, they, on Deliberation among themselves, Resolv'd to imprison her till the next Morning; and accordingly ordered their Officer to do it: And as the Officer was Executing the Magistrats Orders, the rabble gath'red upon them, attack'd the Officer, and took the Woman from him, with which, it's said, he did not acquaint the Magistrats, that they might have taken other Measures for the Woman's Safety. But we forbear to say any more of the Magistrats Conduct, because that matter is at present under the Cognition of the Lords of Her Majesty's most Honourable Privy Council.

This Rable did not flow from the Inclinations of the People of the Place, which is evident *from the Peaceable and Safe Residence, two confessing Witches had, two Months time in the Place, since they were set at Liberty*, but from an unhappy occasional concourse of a great many Strangers, some *Englishmen*, some from *Orkney*, and other parts who were forward in it, and have since taken guilt on them by their Flight.

It's needless to wast Paper, with a particular Account of the Actions of the Rable, and the Treatment they gave her, which was indeed Barbarous. A naked Representation of what was Truth in it, was sufficient to make it odious; so that our Author might well have spared a great many Falshoods, with which he has stuft his Account, some of which we shall briefly notice.

It's false, that *Janet Corphet* when she passingly saw Mr. *Cowper*, as said is, *moved any such Question, as that mention'd in this Pamphlet, nor did he give any such Answer*, as can be instructed by Witnesses beyond all Exception; it's false,

That she sought Lodging in Nicolas Lowsons, *or any where else, or that any put her there, till after the Rable had left her on the Sands: It's a most Abominable and Injurious Calumny, that never had any shadow of ground, that ever the Rable came near to Mr.* Cowper, *spoke to him, or he to them, or that he saw any Appearance of a Rable, when he was going home*; And the place where the Rable Murdered the Woman, lay at a great distance from Mr. *Cowper*'s House, the nearest place where they first fell on her, being on the Sands, in the Harbour, was not within the Loudest cry of it, where he abode all the time, and Mr. *Cowper* heard, *she was safe out of their Handes*, and knew nothing of her Death till eight a Clock {*p. 14*} the next Morning, as has been said, whence it's evident, what our Author says, *of the Rables taking Encouragement from Mr.* Cowper's *Words to fall on her*, is Groundless, untrue, and Malicious.

As to what the Pamphlet mentions of those of *Mr. Coupers* Family going along with the Rabble; Mr. *Couper* urged to have his Servants Examined *among the first, and they have declared before the Magistrates, that they Stole out in a Clandestine way, that their* Master *might not know of it, and he indeed knew nothing of it*, and they returned very quickly and made no stay. Nor do any of the Witnesses Examined insinuat any Accusation *of their having the least accession to any Injury she met with* nor were they any other way concerned, *than by Looking on a short while with some Hundred's of Spectators*, and Mr. *Bruce* the late Episcopal Incumbent his Daughter *Mary Bruce*, and his Servant Maid when examined by the Magistrates have declared *that they likewise were Onlookers at the Harbour where the Rable began, and at* Nicolas Lowsons *Door; where its said some few killed her*, but they did never accuse Mr. *Cowper*'s Women *as Accessory*. But it was not for our Authors purpose, to take notice of any concernment of those of Mr. *Bruce*'s Family in the Rable, though we dare boldly say, *there was more Reason for mentioning them, than any of* Mr. Cowpers *Servants*; nor is this strange, since Mr. *Bruce* (if we believe vulgar Report) our Authors best Informer, hath obliged the World with this Pamplet [*sic*]; It's true one of Mr. *Cowper*'s two Servants foresaid, being sent out late to the Post West-ward, out of her Curiosity went to *Nicolas Lawsons* door, *to see what was come of the Woman*, and she has declar'd before the Magistrats, what she saw, and knew of that mater, and return'd a Considerable time before it's said the Woman was Murdered.

The whole Story about the Womans Daughters is false, there are as many Untruths in it as Words, for it's well known there was but one of her Daughters in Town, and she came not near the Rable, which she is ready to declare, Which our Author has retracted in the second Edition of the Pamphlet.

As to what concerns *the Horse and Sledge*, it's altogether false, there was no Horse or Sledge near her that night, next morning a Horse and Sledge passed that way, to carry some Linnings to the Water, but she was dead a long time before, and there was no Rable *to call the Man, and make him drive over the Corps*.

Again what our Author subjoins of the Rables Treatment of the Woman, viz. *That they first found her at* Nicolas Lowsons *House, and that she was Killed out right, when they drag'd her there again*, is as ill grounded, as the rest of our Authors Assertions: For they found her not at *Nicolas Lowsons* House, and some of the Persons Examined have Declared, that after she was brought to that Door, she arose and put on Head Cloaths, and called to *Nicolas Lowson* to let her in; which if she had done, she, in all appearance, had met with no more Disturbance; but after this, we hear, *that some few of the Rable stole up secretly and Murdered her*. *{p. 15}*

As to what our Author tells us in a different Character, of the Language of the Rable, we can give no Account of it, nor are we to Justify their words, more than their Actions, but we have shewed sufficiently that our Authors Informations, are not much to be Depended on.

As to the next Paragraph that mentions Mr. *Couper's* Letter as giving rise to it, we have Answer'd the Substance of it before, and our Author himself seems not to be over Confident of the Truth of it, for he introduces it with a Remarkable Preface, *Its said*; But if this string fail him, he has another to his Bow, whereby he is confident to drive the Arrow home to Mr Coupar, for he tells us in the following Paragraph: *Its certain that Mr* Couper *took no notice of the Murder the next Lords day, which at least makes him guilty of Sinful silence*. Here is a home thrust indeed, but the happiness on't is our Author *say's*, and his *certainties* are much of a bind. Will it not absolve Mr. *Couper* with our Author, if he did in Prayer Regrate and Aggravat the Sin? If this will do, Mr. *Couper* is free to Appeal to his Hearers for the Truth of it; and besides the two next Lords day thereafter, did directly discover the Wickedness of Rables, which is yet Recent in the Memories of his Hearers. Where is then that Sinful silence our Author will have him certainly Guilty of?

Our Author in his last Paragraph save one, expresses his Confidence that *the Government will Examine the matter to the Bottom, and lay no stress on what the Magistrates of* Pittenweem, *or Minister, will say to Smooth over the matter*. We are not against the Governments Examining the matter to the bottom, and we are much perswaded, and on better Grounds, that the Wisdom and Justice of the Government, will lay no Stress on the Malicious Informations of one, who, to incense the Government against them, has abused the World with an Account Composed of a great many Palpable untruths, bold and Groundless Aspersions, and Spiteful Insinuations. The Minister is sufficiently vindicat by what is above said, and we hope the Magistrates will be able to give such an Account of themselves as may Satisfy the Government.

The Pamphlet is Concluded with a Prayer in which the Magistrates and Minister could cordially Join, if no more were meant by it, than the words abstracted from the foregoing Relation do natively[66] import: But when its considered as it Stands Related to the foregoing Narrative, any may see that it's design'd to put the Cop-stone on all the black Aspersions he has thrown

[66] 'natively': plainly.

on the Magistrates, and Minister; Before, he has said what his own prejudice, and that of his Informers Suggested against their *Practice*, here, he drives the matter further by an uncharitable Insinuation, that they may own *Principles*, that have a Tendency to such Practices as he has falsly Charged them with; and to make this Suggestion the more Solemn, he has addressed it to the GOD of Truth, who hates such untruths as this Paper is filled with, and has Discharged Persons of that Temper, which breaths in this uncharitable Prayer, to approach his Altar. It's not difficult to Conjecture, at whose Principles this is Levelled, and the Persons {*p. 16*} concern'd, who we take to be all, who own the present Government of Church or State, Espouse no principles that have the least Tendency to Favour Rables, or any such disorder; nor are they afraid to compare Principles or Practices in this Regard with the Author or the Party he seems to Favour; If we thought our Authors Example worth following, we might have given Representations of Rables, not a few no less odious, but more true; and that in a time of a fixed Regular Government; In which perhaps our Author and some of his Friends may think themselves concern'd; But we Scorn to Trace his Steps in so dirty a way: Let those who need, use such mean Shifts, and draw what inconsequential Conclusions they please, from Occurrences that have happened among all Parties, and in the best Regular Governments.

It's needless for this Pamphleter to excuse himself with the pretence of misinformation; One who pretends to give the World *a Just Account of Matters*, wherein the Reputation and Safety of others are concern'd, should have taken more care about his Information. It's unworthy of the Civility of a Gentleman, the Candour of a Man of Common Honesty, or the Charity of a Christian, *to take up ill grounded Reports of our Neighbours*, much more is it so, to spread them in Print; telling the World some of them are certain, and giving no better grounds for others of them, *than that it's said*. How would it please our Author, if we should now Print a great many odious stories about him, upon the Authority of a bare hear say? Would he not think himself very ill used to have such Calumnies thrown on his Name, by no body knows who, on the doubtfull *say* of Nameless Authors? I believe he would think he had a right to demand of the Government something more, than that meerly they should have no regard to such Reports; *Or lay little stress on what the Publishers of them would say to smoother over the matter*. Such as have any sense of Honour, regard their Reputation, as much as their Life, and to murder Mens Fames at this Rate, more especially that of Magistrats and Ministers, is not more justifiable than to Rable them, and have not we as good reason to pray to be delivered, from Principles that have a tendency to such practices, as he had.

Having dispatched this first Pamphlet, we shall likeways briefly call to an Account the other, which is prefixed to the second Impression of this Letter, and is Entituled, *An Answer of a Letter from a Gentleman in Fife to a Nobleman*.

This Second Letter vigorously pursues the same malicious design with the former, and has been written, either by the same Author, or one of the like Unchristian Spirit. He begins his Letter with a Complement, to the Nobleman he writes to, in which we are not concerned: But since this Author has been so kind, as to oblige us with his Judicious Observations on the Magistrats and Ministers Conduct; in requitance, we shall make this one, on his Complement: If this Nobleman did him Honour in desiring an Account of this Murder from him, he has made a sorry return, in abusing the World and him, with such a Scandalous and disingenous Account of matters of Fact. He refers this Noble Friend {*p. 17*} to the Pamphlet we have already Examined, Commending its Author for his Ingenuity and Information. How much ground there is for this Commendation, we have shewed above. But it is no ill Jest, to hear this Gentleman tell the World, *That the Writer of the foregoing Pamphlet, was well Informed*, and yet in the next line to acquaint us, *that he had his Information from the General Talk*. What he adds of the General belief of what is contain'd in that Pamphlet, it is an abominable Untruth. All unbyas'd Persons who know any thing of the matter, are sufficiently satisfied of the Falshood of the Reports blown about by that Scandalous Libel.

In his Second Paragraph, he proposes his design, which is to *give a Narrative of the Magistrats and Ministers unwarrantable Imprisoning, and barbarous treating of the poor Women*. This it seems he looks on as wanting to compleat his design of the former Pamphlet: We shall follow, where he leads the way, and I am jealous[67] before we have done with him, we shall make it evident, that he is guilty of more barbarity towards the Magistrats and Minister, than they to the Women.

He tells this Nobleman, *he needs not trouble him with a Character of* Patrick Mortoun, *who is sufficiently known for a Cheat*. One, by reading this would think *Patrick Mortoun* had been Try'd, and Convicted of Roguery and Imposture, in this matter. This is a heavy Charge against the poor Boy, and if our Author is not able to give very good proof for what he says, the Impartial Reader must look on this as a malicious Calumny; yea, were it true, we would desire our Author to satisfy us by his next; how he will reconcile his practice in this, with the Principles of the Christian Religion. Do's Christianity allow Men to load their Neighbours with the blackest Crimes, and that *publickly in Print* with such *confidence* and *assurance*, till they be found guilty by the Judge Competent?

If this clear sighted Author had been so kind, as to lend the Magistrats and Minister of *Pittenweem*, his Spectacles, they had acted a more Christian Part, and had brought this Rogue to a Trial, found him such, and taken care to have him punished in an Examplary way. And they do promise this Author,

[67] 'I am jealous': I suspect.

or any other who will undertake it, they shall improve[68] their Discoveries to the utmost against him.

But after all, we see no ground to conclude him an Imposture, we are not concerned to Justifie every thing he said, or did, under his Trouble, Persons of greater Sense and Judgement, when under the like trouble have been guilty of many Extravagancies both in word and deed. But as to the Principal things in the Boy's case, we could never, nor yet can see any Reason to conclude them Trick and Cheat.

Had he been a Rogue, we cannot see what could have induced him to attempt, to impose on the World, so much to his own Disadvantage, and that of his Fathers Family.

Nor do we see how he was Capable to carry on such an Imposture, for so {*p. 18*} long a tract of time, under the eyes of so many Curious Observers from all quarters, without being Convincingly Discovered.

Beside, Her Majesty's Advocat by order of the Privy Council, called him over in *September* last, and examined him, before one of the Lords of the Justiciary Court, and several other Witnesses.

And of late, again, by a new Order he was called over to *Edinburgh*, and Examined by a Committee of Her Majesty's most Honourable Privy Council, where the Right Honourable the Earl of *Rothes*, Lord Privy Seal presided, and after a strict Examination of him two several Diets; he was Dismissed, without being convict of Imposture. Now is it credible if there had been such Evidence of Imposture, as our Author pretends, that these Discerning Persons, could have overlooked it, *or suffer the Cheat to pass without Exemplary Punishment*?

Moreover, we leave it to any Impartial person, that peruses the short hint of the Boy's Trouble we have given, if it be probable that all this was Trick and Cheat; The Account of the rise of this Trouble, was Justified by *Beatrix Laing* her self, and that in part before she was Imprisoned, but more fully afterwards: Again how came he to know where and when the Witches had their Meetings, and who were present? and how came the Witches in their Confessions to Stumble on the same Account, and so Justify their Accuser? Or were they in a Consert together, the Witches acting a part to carry on their own Ruin.

Besides, it were easie to Demonstrat, that he could not deceive the Spectators, in the surprising particulars above mentioned, some of which could not possibly be done by Trick; but it belongs to our Author to Account for all these things others did, and do think still were Extraordinary in his Case; if our Author will convincingly prove that all these things were Cheat, we shall yeild to Light: But if he obtrude his Says on us, we crave to be Excused. If this Author will oblige the World with a Rational Solution of these *Phœnomena*,

68 'improve': substantiate.

we shall be glad to see it; but the Truth on't is, they who are wont to talk most confidently, of accounting for such Extraordinary Appearances from Natural Causes, are such as understand very litle about Nature.

But to proceed with our Author, he tells us next, *That it was one* [*sic*] Patrick Mortouns *Accusation allenerly that the Magistrats and Minister did Imprison the Women.* This so far from having a shadow of Truth, that none were Imprison'd on his simple Delation, and some were Imprisoned without any Delation from him. As to what he says of *Drunken Fellows Torturing the Women*, we have Answered it before, and shall not Trouble the Reader with a Repetition. After this Story of their being Tormented, he concludes this *Paragraph* thus, *This Cruel Usage made some of them be so wise, as to Acknowledge every Question that was asked them.* Leaving our Author to please himself with the Salt of his Malicious Scoff; To matter we Answer, It is altogether false, their Confessions were Extorted by Torment as was said already. *2dly*. It is false {*p. 19*} that *they acknowledged every question*, as he says, for some they Refused, other things they Confessed freely, as persons Ingenious [*sic*] are wont to do; *Isabel Adam* would never own that she was with the rest at their meeting in the Lone, tho' she confest *that she was at M'greigours House*; *Lilias Wallace* owned *that she was at that meeting in the Lone*, but Refused *that she was at M'greigours*; as likewise none of the confessing Witches did ever delate *Isabel Adam* to be at the meeting in the Lone.

Next he tells us *some of the more foolish, continued as the Minister said*, hardned in the Devils Service *such as, White, Jack, Wallace, Patrick and others; All which save the first were ordered for Stocks, where they lay several Weeks.* To which it's Answer'd. *1st*. Whereas our Author insinuates that all these Persons did still deny, it is false, for *Lilias Wallace* did freely confess *her Compact with the Devil, and Renouncing her Baptism to the Devil*, before several Gentlemen we can Name, and owned *her being at the meeting in the Lone with the Witches, and that* Nicolas Lowson *did take her thither*; but all that knew any thing of the Story, knew why she is shuffled in among these that never confessed, of which if occasion Require we shall give a more particular Account afterward. *2y*. It's false also that ever *Lilias Wallace* was put in the Stocks or was any way disturbed. *3ly*. The Reason why some of them were put in the Stocks was *their offering violence to Isabel Adam* for her delating of them, particularly *Thomas Brown* and *Beatrix Laing* after she had Confessed. Nor was any of them above a Day or two in the Stocks. Could any in so few words have Compacted more Lies?

In the following Paragraph, the Minister is directly accused of *Incouraging* Patrick Morton *in carrying on the Cheat, by Reading to him the case of Bargarrans Daughter*. In Answer to which, we shall give a short but Candid Account of matter of Fact; *In the Month of May last, the Minister with a Preacher, and a great many other People attending all Night in the Room where* Patrick Morton *lay, and he lying meanwhile, in a Swooning fitt, which was they tryed by Exquisite Pinching, the Minister and Probationer falling into some discourse about* Bargarrans *Daughter took out the Book, and for their own Satisfaction Read only two Sentences and stopt.*

Several weeks after, when the Minister was again attending in the Night time, the Lad being insensible, the Minister for his own diversion, Read the Preface and some part of the Process against the Witches; but had no Reason to think he heard any thing, but on the contrary: And it is to be observed, when the Committee of the Privy Council, did accuratly Examine the Boy, in Reference to this Story, he still declared he never heard anything of Bargarrans Daughter's case Read. By this Account it appears how unjust this Charge is against the Minister; the Minister, whatever this Author Suggests to the Contrar, is as far as he can be, from any inclination to Countenance and Incourage such Impostures, nor is there the least shaddow of Ground, to think this had any influence on the Boys trouble, or did Incourage him to Imitation; for beside what has been above hinted, before this was Read in the House, all that was most Extraordinary in his case had fall'n out, Nor was there any considerable Likeness betwixt his case and hers. {*p. 20*} After this he tells us, *The Boy accused for his Tormentors the most considerable Persons Wives in the Town.* The Falshood of this has been above evinced, and we challenge this Author to Name any one Person of Note in the Place, or else where, *whom the Boy accused of Tormenting him*: And the Magistrats and Minister, knew none he accused whom they durst not have Imprisoned, if they had seen cause: Our Author's Inference, *that it was only the weakest that went to the walls*, is Malicious and False; the most considerable accused by him, though not meerly on his Delation, were apprehended: And we shall only add this one Remark, *That if* Patrick Mortoun *had not been weak, our Author durst not have treated him at such a rate*: The story about my Lord *Rothes*, has been sufficiently Answer'd already. That this gave any turn to the Lad's trouble is altogether False, *My Lord* Rothes *came to see the Lad on the sixteenth day of* June, *and the Lad did not begin to recover till the beginning of* August, *nor was he able to go out till the beginning of* September.

As to *the Baillies emptying the Prisons of them*, the occasion of it was thus; *The Women after they had been practised on, began to retract their Confessions*, to tell any more of this story will no [*sic*] be for the Credit of our Author's Friends.

What he says of their obliging *them to pay Eight Pounds* Scots *to the Town Officer*, is many ways False; It's false they were ordered by the Magistrats to pay such a sum, it's false that they pay'd all alike, it is also untruth, that any of them gave *what they had provided for their winding sheets. Nicolas Lawson* one of the confessing Witches, her Husband voluntarly gave a *small piece of unbleeched Linning to the Officer for his Fees*, and this all the ground for the story of their winding-sheets.

And the Minister was so far from being concerned in this, that he challenged the Officer, for taking this piece of Cloath. Now we are come to our Author's remarkable Observations, the first Observation is, *The Baillies and Minister, sent and brought severals of these Women from Places without their Jurisdiction; one from* Anstruther, *and another from the Country at six miles distance.*

In Answer to this Observation, we shall give a short and Faithful Account of matter of Fact, for which we shall be Answerable. The Woman brought from *Anstruther* was one Mrs. *White* an Inhabitant of *Pittenweem*, who through fear of being Apprehended, fled thither to her Daughters House; This Woman whose cause is now so warmly espoused by some, with no advantage to their Reputation, and who is now Insisting against the Magistrats, in a Process for wrongous Imprisonment,[69] has been for many Years, a person of very bad Fame, some Eighteen Years ago, she pursued a Woman before the Session, in Mr. *Bruce* the late Episcopal Incumbents time, *for calling her a Witch*, and Succumbing in the Probation, Mr. *Bruce* urged her to be Reconciled with the Woman. She obstinatly refused, using most Unchristian and Revengeful Expressions, which are to be seen in the Session Register: Since the Revolution she desired Admission to the Sacrament of the Lord's Supper, which was denied, because she still refused to be Reconciled to {*p. 21*} that Woman; her Scandalous carriage in refusing to Co-habit with her Husband to this day, who is a sober honest Man, is generally known. This Woman being Accused by the Boy as one of his Tormentors, and Delated by two confessing Witches, and other presumptions of her Guilt, the Magistrats, one morning sent their Officer to the Magistrats of *Anstruther*, desiring them on these grounds to send Mrs. *White* to them, and the grounds of her Imprisonment were sent in write to her, in her Daughter Mrs. *Lindsays* House, and she being brought to *Pittenweem*, the two Women which Delated her, were confronted with her, in presence of the Magistrats, a great many Gentlemen and Ministers, where they did accuse her to her Face, and charged her particularly with being at a meeting in the Loan with the Devil and the Witches, and gave some binding tokens to convince her: By all which it appears, how little ground there is to accuse the Magistrats for Invading their Neighbours Jurisdiction, or load the Minister with any concernment in the matter.

As to the other instance, of one brought to *Pittinweem, at six miles Distance*, this was the young Woman *Isobel Adam*: about the middle of *May*, one *Alexander M^c^grigor* delated her, for an attempt to *Murder him in his House in the night time*, with several others whom he knew not; and there being some Surmises of other Presumptions of Witchcraft against her; The Minister hearing she was occasionally in the Town, called for her, and advised her before her Father, *If Innocent, to take proper Measures for her own Vindication*, which she undertook to do, *and promised to return for that end on Advertisement*, which her Father engaged to give. The noise about her still Increasing, her Father was desired according to promise, *to call her to the place*, which he declined, growing Jealous of her Guilt, on which the Minister Advertis'd her, but in case she Refused, *a Letter was sent to be delivered to the Gentleman in whose Ground she liv'd, desiring him to*

69 'Mrs. White' was Janet Horsburgh, who was married to Thomas White. She later won her case for wrongous imprisonment: Cook (ed.), *Annals of Pittenweem*, 128–9.

send her. So soon as the Advertisement was given, *she came Voluntarly, to her Father's House in* Pittinweem; and so there was no occasion for Force.

When she came, *she Confessed her Converse with the Devil at* Thomas Adamson's *House, on the first Day of* January 1704, she was confronted with *M^c^greigour*, and he accused her of the abovementioned attempt on him, which she then Refused; on which she was Imprison'd, and the two following days, she did with Tears and more than ordinary Concern, make a free and large Confession.

She told, *Beatrix Laing foresaid, a Confessing Witch, had been dealing with her, to Engage in her service, which she refused; and that sometime thereafter, this* Beatrix *came for her, and desir'd her to go along to her House, when she came there, they sat down at the fire, and she saw a Man in Black Cloaths, with a Hat on his head, sitting at the Table; and* Beatrix *said to her, since you will not engage with me, here is a Gentleman that will Fee you; whereupon he told her, he knew she was Discontented with her Lot, and if she would serve him, he promised she should want for nothing, to which she yeilded to serve him, and he came forward and Kiss'd her, and she said, he was fearsome like, and his Eyes Sparkled like Candle, on which she knew he was the Devil.* {*p. 22*}

Again she told, *That being Imploy'd to Spin in* Thomas Adamson's *House in* Pittinweem, *while she was lying awake in her Bed, in the Night time, The Devil appearing to her, where she did expressly renounce her Baptism to the Devil, by putting her Hand on her Head, and the other to her Feet, the other Maid lying in the Bed with her, being at the time Asleep*, as the Maid declar'd before the Session. *About a fortnight after this,* Beatrix Laing *came to Visite her, and asked her, if she had met with the Gentleman? she Answered, she had, and also engaged with him, on which* Beatrix *said, I have then got my Work wrought, and went away.* And she Confessed *she came to that Meeting at* Mcgreigours *with the Devil, and several Witches, viz.* Beatrix Laing, Nicolas Lowson, Janet Corphet, Thomas Brown, *and several others she knew not, designing to Murder* M^c^greigour*; But since the Man wakned and pray'd to God for himself, they could not do it.* She Confessed also, *Converse with the Devil at other times.* All which is in her two Confessions Sign'd by the Magistrats, and Transmitted to *Edinburgh*: As also My Lord Advocat, in his Letter to the Magistrats, says, *she freely own'd her Guilt before him*, and when afterwards she deny'd, says, *he was fully satisfied, she was perverted.* Now we desire to know what this Author can quarrel in the Magistrats or Minister's Conduct in this Matter.

As to the Pamphleters Second and Third Observation, they have been fully Answered above. *As for what he adds about Ministers Refounding the Imprisoned Womans Money seven fold.* We find the Author very charitable on other Mens Purses, but when the Magistrats and Minister, design'd to bestow their Charity, they will choose more observing Objects: And the Lords of Her Majesty's Privy Counsel understands themselves better, than to take their measures as to what is Just from the daring Prescriptions of this Author.

Our Authors 4*th* Observation is of a piece with the former, *Thomas Brown* was accused by the Lad, and Delated by three Confessing Witches, as being

Accessry to the the attempt on *M^c^greigour*; its false he was Starved, for his Daughter brought him his Dyet punctually. Our Authors Fears of moe Murders are altogether Groundless, as has been clear'd above, and we Appeal to all men of Candor, whither this Authors Impudent and unjust Accusation against Magistrates and Minister of Murdering *Thomas Brown*, deserves not Severer Punishment than any thing he can charge them with.

The *5th* Observation tells us, *The Baillies justified the Murder, by denying Christian Burial.* The Baillies gave no order thereabout; as for *Thomas Brown*, his own Son in Law, with some others Buried him: Our Author by his next may prove, that *Janet Corphet* a Woman that had so frequently, and so solemnly Confessed the Renounciation of her Baptism to the Devil, deserved Christian Burial.

Our Author in his last Observation tells us, *That the Minister all along Exercised more of the Civil Authority than any of the Baillies, which he pretends to clear by one instance,* which is this, *That the Magistrats, in the Acount of the {p. 23} Murder they gave in to the Privy Council, told they had Imprisoned severals of the Murderers, and that after they left the Town the Minister set them at liberty.* The matter of Fact is this in short, Application being made to have the Persons in Prison for the Rable Bail'd, the Bailies forgetting to Consult their Town Clerk the Night before they went off, came in the Morning to the Minister about five of the Clock, about other Affairs, and being loath to disturb their Clerk so Early, he being Aged and Sickly, desired the Minister to Consult him thereanent; which he Refused to do: Whereupon they call'd the Town Officer, and ordered him to acquaint the Clerk, that if they could be bailed in Law, he should do it, and the Officer was Ordered on this, to Liberat them; as also, they desired the Minister to attest to the Clerk, that they had given this Order to their Officer, which accordingly he did, after the Officer spoke to the Clerk, and was no further concerned in the Matter. Now we challenge this Author to shew wherein the Minister stept beyond his Sphere, in all this? But if our Author miss the Minister, he thinks he is sure to hit the Bailies; and therefore adds, *That if the Bailies Ordered before they went off to Liberat the Prisoners, they were mightily in the wrong in giving an Account to the Privy Council, which they knew to be false*; We desire to know where the falshood of their Account Lyes, it was not false they had Imprison'd them, it was not false that they left them in Prison; Nor was it false they were still Legally secure, being only Liberat on Bail; Besides it's false, that the Bailies in the Information call'd them the Murderers of the Woman, they were only Delated by the Witnesses, as being among the Rable. This Account we have given, we shall Justify by unexceptionable Witnesses if he dare attack it; But to speak a little Closser with our Author about the Justice of this Observation: With what Conscience durst our Author accuse the Minister *of exercising not only the Civil Authority, but more of it than any of the Bailies, and continuing to do so?* What a sore-head must he have to offer this one Scandalous instance as a proof of so base a Calumny. The Minister positively deny's that in any one instance he invaded the Office of the Civil Magistrat; can this Author prove it.

Our Authors Conclusion is Remarkable; *My Lord this is not the Tenth part, of what may be said on this Subject, I hope some other Person will be more particular*: We easily allow that if Men will assume a Liberty to Lye, to Slander, and Mis-Represent, they may blot Paper and abuse the World with Volumns: But if our Author had confin'd himself to Truth, instead of Abusing the World with ten times as many Lyes, the most part of this Pamphlet had been spared.

It were tedious here to Relate at length the many Artifices used to smother this discovery of Witch-craft, Strange Methods have been try'd both at *Pittenweem* and *Edinburgh*, with the Witches, to make them Retract their Confessions. The Boy has been Represented as a Notable Imposture, the {*p. 24*} Magistrates and Minister have been traduced as Encouragers and supporters of the Cheat: Upon what views and Inducements no body knows, nor can the spreaders of these Reports condescend on any colourable Inducement. The persons who seem'd any way convinced that there was Witchcraft in the case, not upon the triffling ground, some gave out they believed it, but from the joint Consideration of the Witches Confession, and the whole tract of the Boy's Trouble, as cloathed with all the particular Circumstances, have been exposed as Foolish and Credulous Men, who built their perswasion on ridiculous Grounds, whereon they never laid the least stress.

After the Boy was recovered, and going Abroad again, a Picture was Clandestinely conveyed into his bed on the Lord's Day by Persons, who, it seems, meant first to draw the Credulous vulgar into a conceit that this was the Picture, whereby the Boy was Tormented, that afterwards they might have a fair occasion to expose them for their Credulity; and rivet the suspicion of the Boys being a Cheat. When this took not, some gave it out, that the Minister had placed it there, which is a Story so Ridiculous that it cannot take with any person of Sobriety or Sence, and perhaps had he a great mind to it, he could find the Authors of this Sorry trick.

And of late again a certain person, who has done his utmost to stifle the whole Discovery of the Witchcraft did call out of Prison, the abovementioned *M^c^greigour*,[70] and threatned him with the severest Punishment, *If he did not deny his Accusation of* Isobel Adam, which we are able to prove by sufficient Testimonies.

Further, We know who told a certain Gentleman in the Neighbourhood, then at *Edinburgh*, that if he would discourse *Isobel Adam* then liberat, she would show him what Rogues and Villains the Magistrats and Minister were, In practising on the Woman, and alluring her with promises, to accuse many Honourable and Worthy Ladys, and that they named them expresly to her,

70 Alexander MacGregor has hitherto been presented as a victim of witchcraft. It is not clear why he was in prison.

which the Gentleman consented to hear, and accordingly she was sent to him, by this Persons order, who, it seems, knew well where to find her, for his designs, when she came, she told her Story in such sort, that the Gentleman declared to the Minister, he saw evidently it was put in her Mouth; As for the matter of this Calumny, we think it not worth the while to refute it at large: When the Baillies and Minister Conversed with her, they were never alone, we dare appeal to the Author of the Pamphlet, whether it be Credible that they, who, he says, *had not the Courage to attack the considerable Mens Wives in the Town*, would take such measures, to exasperat Persons of Quality, this is so far from being true, that the Minister did from the Pulpit discharge the People to ask the Women questions anent any: And if it were requisite, the Minister could give his Oath, That he never heard any of these Worthy and {*p. 25*} Honourable Persons Names mention'd to the Woman, or the Lad, or ever directly or indirectly accused by them; but all these Stories were spread on design to inrage Gentlemen, and to stifle this Discovery. When our Author or his Friends are pleas'd to Publish his ten parts more, of which he boasts, we shall then deal a little more plainly.

But we forbear now any particular Account of these, and others of the same Alloy, because we love not to touch the Reputation of others unless we are driven to it in Self Defence. But if necessity, which has extorted this Account, oblige us to be particular, we shall not spare to Narrate the Truth, and condescend without respect of Persons, on the Practices, Authors of them, Inducements, and the particular Circumstances, that are necessary to set them in a full Light. For all which we are able to give better Vouchers, than our Author's *Say's*.

And to conclude, whatever the Inconsiderate and Atheistical *Would-be-wits* of this Age may dream, Protestant Ministers of the Gospel, have no Temptation to be more easy than other Men in their belief, about particular stories of Which-craft [*sic*], or to obtrude them upon others, their Faith of the General Truth that there are Devils, and Witches, stands on no weaker Bottom, than the Faithful Word of GOD. Nor was it ever called in Question by any Persons that were sound in the Christian Religion, and the Truth of God needs no lie to support it. And this Truth is Safe, whatever come of this or any other particular Instance, when any such occurrences fall out in Ministers Congregations, it were more for there [*sic*] ease to suppress such Discoveries, by which they cannot propose so much as a shew of advantage to themselves, but on the contrar, such trouble, as might have, and has made them to be commiserat by generous Persons, that neither favour them nor their way; which the Minister of *Pittenweem* as he projected[71] from the beginning, has found to his sad Experience.

71 'projected': foresaw.

It's like some may wonder, why a full and circumstantiat Account, of the Witches Confessions, and this Boy's Trouble, has not been offered to the Publick: But waving other reasons, not a few, of this Omission; it's thought that there is no great need of this. Many well attested Narratives of try'd Instances of this sort, have been published of old and late, which are sufficient, to satisfy Persons, Sober, Ingenious, and Judicious; and to render the Atheistical pretenders of this or former Ages, who from their unbelief of the general Truth, in reference to the Being of Devils, or Witches, call in question all particular instances, without making any difference, altogether without Excuse: And there is no great hope of convincing by such Accounts, however attested, such as believe not *Moses*, the Prophets, nor even the SON, by whom GOD hath spoken to us in these last Ages: We know that the latest and best Attested Narratives of this sort, have been boldly called in Question, by many little *pretenders to Reason* in privat Companies.[72] But when they have assumed the courage publickly, and in Print to overthrow {*p. 26*} the Evidence of the matters of Fact, or offered a rational Account of them upon other Principles, there will then and not till then, be need of adding new instances, and Vindicating the former. This hitherto they have not thought fit to do, tho' they have been challenged oftner than once. Nor dare they attempt it, while the Witnesses, and Publishers of these Accounts are alive to speak for themselves; And while this is not done, the idle Cheat wherewith these Quacks in Philosophy entertain themselves, and abuse the simple, behind the Curtain, deserve not the regard of any Person of Sobriety. FINIS.

72 For the oral culture of freethinking in this period see Michael Hunter, *The Decline of Magic: Britain and the Enlightenment* (New Haven, 2020), 20–34.

9. [JOHN BELL,] *THE TRYAL OF WITCHCRAFT*, *c.*1705

INTRODUCTION

This tract, published anonymously and carrying neither place, date nor printer's name, has been shown by Christina Larner to be probably the work of John Bell (1676–1707).[1] Bell grew up in Glasgow and was educated at the University of Glasgow. From 1701 until his death he was minister of Gladsmuir in Haddingtonshire. Bell's autobiography, written in 1706, has recently been published. It is mainly about ecclesiastical politics, and it says nothing about witchcraft, but it shows Bell's strong commitment to presbyterianism and his determination to achieve his ends in the face of opposition.[2] As Larner showed, Bell may well also have written an earlier 'Treatise on Witchcraft' in the 1690s; this is now lost, with only three fragments surviving.[3] *The Tryal of Witchcraft* was probably printed in 1705.

Witchcraft trials had become rare by this period. Bell writes of 'witches of whom I have read' (p. 17), but he shows no sign of having encountered a witch or a witchcraft trial in person, even though he worked in Haddingtonshire, which in previous generations had prosecuted more witches than anywhere else in Scotland.

An unusual feature of Bell's reading is that it is mostly English. His main authorities are the treatises of William Perkins (1608) and Richard Bernard (1627). He also relies heavily on the anonymous narrative *The Witches of Warboys* (1593), about a case of demonic possession in the Throckmorton family in Huntingdonshire, and has one citation to a brief article from 1690 in the *Athenian Mercury* magazine. His only Scottish authority is the theologian

1 Christina Larner, 'Two Late Scottish Witchcraft Tracts: *Witch-Craft Proven* and *The Tryal of Witchcraft*', in Sydney Anglo (ed.), *The Damned Art: Essays in the Literature of Witchcraft* (London, 1977), 227–45, at pp. 227–32, 237.

2 'The Most Memorable Passages of the Life and Times of Mr J. B., Written by Himself, 1706', ed. Jeffrey Stephen, *SHS Miscellany XIV* (Edinburgh: SHS, 2010), 139–228.

3 This 'Treatise of Witchcraft' is discussed in the introduction to the 'Bargarran Witches' Manuscript, above in the present volume, in connection with its criticism of the Bargarran prosecutions.

James Durham, cited only once in the text. As will be seen in footnotes below, all Bell's other citations are probably second-hand ones via Bernard.

Bell's authorities are mostly old. The most recent English treatise that he knows about was published in 1627. To name just two of the many more recent English authors, Bell has not consulted John Webster (*The Displaying of Supposed Witchcraft*, 1677) or Joseph Glanvill (*Saducismus Triumphatus*, 1681), both of whom had been cited by the *Athenian Mercury*. As for recent Scottish authors, he might have paid attention to Sir George Mackenzie (for whom see an earlier chapter in the present volume) or to George Sinclair (for whom see the Introduction to the present volume), among others.

As a result of his English reading, Bell accepts ideas about witches' familiars without seeming to think that these are unusual. He seems to be thinking of animal familiars (calling them 'creatures', p. 20), which were common in England but almost unknown in Scotland. Were it not for Larner's investigations into its authorship, we might almost conclude from these citations that this was an English work. There is one distinctively Scots word in the text, 'thir' (pp. 13, 15).

Bell addresses Scottish issues more than English ones when he comes to the question of evidence in court. The range of evidence that he discusses would have been of less interest to an English court. He shows repeated interest in witches' confessions, and even in the idea that a confessing witch can implicate others (p. 21). He strongly emphasises the demonic pact, and, along with it, the Devil's mark. However, Bell is a minister, not a lawyer. His awkwardly-extended military metaphor for the making of the demonic pact evidently derives from preaching and pastoral practice, not from legal reasoning (p. 15).

Despite his antiquated authorities, some of Bell's ideas are up to date. In discussing malefice he emphasises victims' fits and possession. He cites the Throckmorton case from the 1590s, but he may have in mind the recent Salem, Bargarran or Pittenweem cases of possession – especially the Pittenweem case of 1704–5, since his opening paragraph speaks of the topicality of witchcraft. When he discusses the idea of suspected witches touching their victims, he initially has his enquirer suggest that such a touch may cure the victims, but he mixes into his reply to this a discussion of the more legally-relevant and topical question of whether a suspect is proven guilty if a demonically-possessed person has a fit when the suspect touches them.

Bell is also up to date in his scepticism about witches causing ordinary diseases, though it should be noted that his material mostly derives from Richard Bernard. He has an interesting idea of his own: the Devil may use ordinary diseases to cause innocent people to be accused of witchcraft by the over-credulous 'common person'. The Devil knows when someone is about to become ill, and stirs up someone else to quarrel with that person, so that the illness will look like the result of the other person's curse – yet that person is not a witch (p. 6). This ingenious deployment of demonological reasoning to produce an effectively anti-prosecution conclusion is perhaps characteristic of late-period demonology.

Overall, though, Bell's arguments are traditional ones, and he clearly envisages witches being prosecuted. He never brings this to the forefront of his discussion, but he shows repeated interest in the legal distinction between a 'presumption' and a 'proof' of guilt, and he regards the decision as a 'matter of life and death' (p. 13). Nevertheless he is cautious and even provisional in his arguments, professing to hope that other writers will do better than he has done, and admitting that others might legitimately disagree with him. For all his reliance on the dogmatic writers of middle-period demonology, Bell cannot quite recapture those writers' certainties, nor their aggressive advocacy of prosecutions.

TEXT[4]

The Tryal of Witchcraft, or, Witchcraft Arraign'd and Condemn'd,

In some Answers to a few Questions anent *Witches* and *Witchcraft*,

Wherein is shewed, how to know if one be a *Witch*, as also when one is bewitched: with some Observations upon the *Witches* Mark, their compact with the Devil, the White *Witches* &c.

Exod. 22.18. *Thou shalt not suffer a Witch to live.*

It is advantagious to have many engaged in writing on the same Subject, even though they should say little more then what is said by others. *Mr. Durham* on the *Revelation*. Digress. 3. Page 63.[5] {*p. 2 blank*} {*p. 3*}

A Letter from a Friend.

Sir, Having heard strange things reported of Witch-craft and Witches: I desire to know from you, what satisfaction you can give me in answer to the following *Queries*, wherewith the mouths of People are on that occasion so much filled: take them thus.

Query 1. How shall one know if a disease be the effect of Witch-craft, seeing all grant, that strange diseases may happen either to Man or Beast, which yet are neither the product of Devils or Witches.

Query 2, What meanes are best to be used for help to these thus bewitched. And here I would know 1. what is to be thought of causing the suspected *Witch*, touch the afflicted Party, 2. If this be not, then what other mean is best.

4 Source: [John Bell,] *The Tryal of Witchcraft, or, Witchcraft Arraign'd and Condemn'd* (n.p., n.d. [*c.*1705]; ESTC no. R172698).

5 Cf. James Durham, *A Commentarie upon the Book of the Revelation* (London: Company of Stationers, 1658), 63.

Query 3. I would further know, what will {*p. 4*} prove one to be a *Witch*? and here 1. If bitter cursing and imprecations with malefices following thereupon, will prove it? and if not that, then 2*d*. If a persons often enquiring into the disease of the tormented, or their coming to visite them unsent for; yea, after they have been discharg'd the house as being suspected persons, will do the business? Or 3*d*. if the afflicted person his or her seeing, in time of their tormenting fits, so as to know and name particular Persons; will prove the Person thus seen, known, and nominate, to be a *Witch*. Or 4*th*. If none of those, then (pray) what will do it? your answers agreeably to the mind of the best Writers you have seen, is earnestly intreated by,

Your Humble Servant.

An answer to the Letter.

Sir, Tho I am sensible,[6] that to speak on this head of witchcraft, is a very hard Task; considering especially the difficulty of discovering *Witches*; (the secrecy of the grounds of witchcraft, and the cunningness of some juggling counterfits, being so great and many) as also considering how Satan seeks to imitate God in his actions; as Scripture, and many strange {*p. 5*} (tho true) relations about *Witches* do abundantly make appear: for example, 2 *Kings* 5.27 we read that God by the Prophet makes *Naamans* leprosie cleave to *Gehazi*; so Satan does by the help of *Witches* at sometimes, take the disease from off one person, and layes it upon another. Also, we read *Acts* 8.39 of *Philips* being carried bodily out of the *Eunuchs* sight; so also can the Devil transport bodies from one place to another, as we find he took our blessed Saviour up unto the pinacle of the Temple, *Mat*. 4. And he often carries his own servants into the aire, as he did *Dr. Faustus*,[7] or over into forraign places;[8] as is usual for him to do with these *Witches*. Tho, I say, these with many moe things concurre to render the undertaking hard; yet I think it needs not be ill look't upon if an essay be made of this nature; considering especially how much light may be borrowed from the Writings of learned men both of old and of late, the direful experience of former ages, as well as of this, having afforded occasion for such questions as be proposed by you, and which are current with the common people. Adventuring therefore to obey your desire, take the Answers in the following Method. {*p. 6*}

6 'I am sensible': I am aware.

7 For an overview of the Faust legend, regarded as factual in the sixteenth and seventeenth centuries at least, see Wolfgang Behringer, 'Faust, Johann Georg (ca. 1480–1540)', in Golden (ed.), *Encyclopedia*, ii, 352–353.

8 The idea of witches flying long distances, or to foreign countries, seems to have become more common in the later seventeenth century: Julian Goodare, 'Witches' Flight in Scottish Demonology', in Julian Goodare, Rita Voltmer and Liv Helene Willumsen (eds.), *Demonology and Witch-Hunting in Early Modern Europe* (London, 2020), 147–67, at p. 162.

SECTION I.

How to know if one be bewitched.

In answer to your first *Query*, I would say; that no doubt most people may be thought too rash in attributing to Witchcraft every disease that seems strange and beyond ordinary, as is rightly insinuated, in your ground given for your first *Query*: famous writers instancing in their books many strange and wonderful diseases, yet no work of witchcraft, as are the *Apoplexy*, *Carum*, *Catalepsis*, *Cramp*, with many moe mentioned by *Dr. Cotta* in his *Emperiks*, and *Dr. Mason* in his practice of philosophy, and *R. Bernard* in his Guide to Grand jury men.[9] All which Authors do yet still affirm these to proceed from natural causes, and to be curable by natural remedies; tho scarce would a common person look on the party thus distempered, without concluding witchcraft to be there.

However, where the disease is more then natural, and no less then the effect of witchcraft {*p. 7*} it may be known by such signs as *Witches* themselves in their confessions, and learned Physicians have condescended upon as symptoms of Witchcraft, I only name a few which we may take thus, 1. When the disease is such as that wise and skilful Physicians can find no probable reason of any natural cause for it, as it was with *M. Throgmortons* child,[10] who would often have a great heaving and swelling of the belly, then a passing to the throat ready to stop the breath: as also thrusting out her leg or arm soas non could bow it, with other such like motions. 2. When the tormented Party in time of such fits vomite up crooked pins, coals, nails, needles, knoted hair, straw, &c. 3. When the tormented party in time of their fits tell truly many things; some past, others in doing, saying, &c. as hapened in the case of *Mr. Throgmorton's* elder daughter, *Mrs. Jean*, who could also tell some things to come, as how many in the house were to be bewitched, and who they were.

9 Richard Bernard, *A Guide to Grand-Jury Men* (London: Felix Kingston, 1627). The title of book 1, chapter 2, is: 'Strange diseases may happen either to man or beast, and the same originally from some naturall cause, and neither effected by Devils, nor yet proceede from Witches'. All four of the diseases mentioned by Bell are discussed in this chapter, and it is likely that Bell has not looked beyond Bernard. As for Bell's other citations: '*Dr. Cotta*' is John Cotta, *A True Discovery of the Empericke with the Fugitive, Physition and Quacksalver …* (London: William Jones, 1617). Cotta, a physician, denounced uneducated healers; Bernard had cited his book several times. '*Dr. Mason* in his practice of philosophy' is probably a garbled version of Bernard's citation, on the latter's p. 12, to 'D. Mason in his pract. of Phys.' Bell could have misread the long 's' of Bernard's 'Phys' as an 'l'.

10 The alleged bewitchment and demonic possession of members of the Throckmorton household took place in Warboys, Huntingdonshire, England, between 1589 and 1593, and resulted in three executions. This and later references come from *The Most Strange and Admirable Discoverie of the Three Witches of Warboys* (London: Thomas Man, 1593). For modern editions see Barbara Rosen (ed.), *Witchcraft in England, 1558–1618* (2nd edn., Amherst, 1991), 239–97 (abridged); Marion Gibson (ed.), *English Witchcraft, 1560–1736*, vol. ii: *Early English Trial Pamphlets* (London, 2003), 51–161. See also James Sharpe, 'Witches of Warboys', in Golden (ed.), *Encyclopedia*, iv, 1179–80.

4. When there is supernatural strength, so as that a very strong man should not be able to keep down a child of about 12. years of age as it was with one of *M. Throgmorton's* children. Other signs are given by Authors, but we pass them. {*p. 8*}

SECTION II.

Of Means to be used for helping the bewitched.

Various are the methods fallen upon for easing the afflicted: among which is that made mention of in the second *Query* of causing the suspected Witch touch the afflicted person as if their touch could cure them: Which yet seems not to be a mean on which we are to rely (though I find not the use of it simply condemned) as having neither a divine appointment, nor a natural reason for it. Add to this (which some have well taken notice of) that the suspected *Witches* either presence or absence, is a very uncertain thing, for 1. Their presence or absence as *Witches* takes it[s] force only from their league and covenant[11] with the Devil; which as they can renew at pleasure, so can they make their presence or *Touch* effectual accordingly; So as if the tormented party be bad, and take fits, they present, by indenting[12] with the Devil over again {*p. 9*} (God permitting) they may procure that in their presence they may take no more fits; and on the contrary, if in their presence and at their *Touch* they be well, so that their presence there will prove nothing, either for curing the diseased, or making them yet worse, and so thereby founding a presumption for By-standers to conclude them *Witches*, 2. Their touching is an uncertain thing, because (as writers on this head have sufficiently instructed) by *Touching* they even sometimes bewitch the afflicted party. Thus *Danaeus* in *Dialogis suis de Sortiariis*, witnesseth, that a *Witch* touched but the breasts of a woman that gave suck, and her milk dried up: and the forcited Rector of *Batcomb, R. Bernard* reports of one *Mary Suton* a *Bedfordshire Witch*, that having but touched the neck of one of *Mr. Engars* servants, with her finger, he was presently after her departure miserably vexed, how then can this touch cure the diseased?[13]

So then, the best mean is, fasting and prayer, for God only can best free us from Divels, and in the use of his means alone it is, that we are to expect a blessing: So that if we would prevent *Witches*, and whatever else the Devil

11 This phrase may be intended to echo the Solemn League and Covenant, the revolutionary treaty of 1643 that remained controversial in the eighteenth century. However, William Perkins had earlier written of a 'league or covenant made between the Witch and the Devill': William Perkins, *A Discourse of the Damned Art of Witchcraft* (Cambridge: Cantrel Legge, 1608), 42. Bell cites this book below.

12 'indenting': making an 'indenture' or contract.

13 As Larner pointed out, Bell's citation to Lambert Daneau (whose witchcraft treatise was published in French and Latin in 1574) was almost certainly a second-hand one via Bernard, *Guide to Grand-Jury Men*, 179. See Larner, 'Two Late Scottish Witchcraft Tracts', 241. Bernard was rector of Batcombe.

can do, let us always rely on God, who hath promised to such, that he will cover them under his wings, &c. *Psalms* 91.4. {*p. 10*}

SECTION III.

What will prove one to be a Witch.

Great is the Mystery of iniquity, and its hard to discover the Members of that Kingdom of darkness, where the King is Satan, the fiery Dragon, the roaring Lyon, and deceiver of the Nations; and where the subjects are faggots of hell, Deceivers and deceived: Yet thorough the Lords blessing on the means and methods fallen upon for detecting such, they may be known, let us then touch at these, and first negatively what will not prove one to be a *Witch*, and then positively, what will.

To begin then and go throw with the several particulars contained in the third *Query* let us consider the first particular which is it bitter cursings and imprecations, evil following thereupon, will prove one to be a *Witch*, and to this it is answered, that tho *Witches* have been known thus to bewitch people by *Cursing* them whereupon presently evil followed to the person {*p. 11*} thus *Cursed*, yet it is no more then a presumption of ones being a *Witch*, for first such *Cursings* and *Imprecations* are in some no other then the effect of a *natural constitution*, and so may be acted oftner than once or twice: Constitutions (in the Judgment of the learned) differing from habits mostly in name, when they come to any perfection; and habits being got by acts frequently repeated. 2. Because, as Satan may get a permission from God, to work *natural diseases* which do break forth upon cursing so doubtless he improves it subtily, of which some do thus conceive. They say, the Devil he knows when his power to do hurt is granted him of God; as also, he knows the growing, ripening, and breaking forth of a disease upon man or beast. Again, ere natures act thus break out, he stirs up some occasion to make the party against whom his design is, to fall out with some angry neighbour, which being gain'd, Satan stirs up people hereupon, because of one or two such practices, to pursue the neighbour to death, as becoming by her ill tongue a *Witch*; when as, tho she be otherwise pestilentious enough, yet possibly is no *Witch*. So then we conclude, that however this may be an *Item* to such ill natur'd cursers and railers to forbear further provocking of God by such practices to give them {*p. 12*} over to Satans power; yet I see not why cursings with harm following them are any other then a presumption (however great it be) that one is a *Witch*.

2. As to a persons often enquiring into the disease of the tormented, or their coming to visite them unsent for, yea perhaps after they have been discharg'd the house, as persons under suspicion, its answered in one word, that this is no other than a presumption, and that for this reason among others, that revengeful spirits (though they be no *Witches*) having once cursed, and hearing of some sudden mischance following in order of time thereupon, may inquire after the afflicted party, yea visite him or her, while under this

fit of cursed joy conceived in them at the hearing of such news, when yet for all this there is perhaps no league with the Devil; and as for their visiting undesir'd, yea, when prohibite and discharg'd, some have rightly imputed the same to the confidence, or rather impudence of the poorer, and unmannerly sort of people.

3. As to the afflicted persons seeing, knowing and naming diverse persons in time of their fits, as their tormentors; as it was with *Mr. Throgmortons* Children (as the Author of the Relation of *Warboys Witches* does attest) yet {*p. 13*} will not that prove the person or persons so known, and nominate, to be all *Witches*, for 1. as to their being *seen*, doubtless tho the Devil cannot create any inward *species* or representation, this being a work of *Omnipotencie* (as *Holy* and *learned Mr. Durham* hath observed)[14] yet God permitting him; he by working upon what is already within the person, may misrepresent objects, by disturbing inwardlie the Faculties and Organs: so that he can presentiate to the *Phantasie* such persons, as he knows the tormented party abhors to see, and useth to fear: for if he could represent a seeming *Samuel*,[15] much more a Graceless man or woman, to deceive the Fancy of disturbed minds of afflicted Persons; and yet these graceless persons may be no *Witches*, for doubtless in this the Devil may lie, as well as speak true. 2. As to their being named, its but the Devils Testimonie, which is not to be laid weight on, *in the matter of life and death*; seing he may accuse an innocent, as histories abundantly declare.

Sir, I perswade my self you take up my mind in this matter better then to think any favour to be intended or allowed, by what I have said of thir *Negative marks* (as I called them for distinctions sake) to any of these members of Satans Kingdom the *Witches*: God forbid any {*p. 14*} (far less I) should in the least Favour such for whom God hath told us in his word he hath no favor they continuing such; for however I have all alongst called these but *Presumptions*, in so doing, I say no other then what pious and learn'd Writers on this head have spoken, who withal are of opinion (as I also am) that such pregnant and shrewd presumptions sufficiently witnessed are just cause of imprisonment, and are worthy (after tryal) of most severe and condign punishment; but ere the life can be taken away from them, it will perhaps be found needful that a league with the Devil be once[16] proven, for understanding of this, let us premise these 4. or 5. things, 1. that the Devil seeks not to make any a *Witch* whom he finds not some way prepar'd either by impenitency and obduredness, distemperedness of passion, prophaness [*sic*], and the like: for he will not readily nor willingly attaque and surprize, where he thinks not to gain ground. 2. Finding man or woman thus prepared, he waits his opportunity

14 Durham, *Commentarie upon the Book of the Revelation*, 150.

15 An allusion to the case of the witch of Endor, who conjured up the apparition of the dead prophet Samuel. This biblical story (1 Samuel 28:7–25) was often discussed by demonologists.

16 'once': once for all, conclusively.

of appearing to them visibly, sometimes in one shape, sometimes in another, varying according to the nature, quality, and condition of the persons to whom he thus appears: thus he is said to have appeared to *Dr Faustus* in the habite of some religious person;[17] and now it is, that he works upon the {*p. 15*} poor creature, whom he at one time allures by many perswasives, at other times surprizing them, frights them into a complyance with his overtures, according as he finds them ignorant or witty: for he's a cunning Engineer, who attacks towns according to their fortification, situation or garrison: he understands who among men and women are weak, and on what side; and agreeably,[18] some are min'd, others bomb'd, some won by storm, others by composition, others again are starved into a surrender. 3. That which he aims at in all thir assaults, and in order whereunto he appears once, or oftner, as he finds need is, to draw the poor, impenitent, and obdured creature into a league with himself, which League or Covenant, Divines makes [*sic*] to be twofold: the one implicite, secret and closs; wherein is a mutual consent, but without any express terms on either side; *Mr. Perkins* in his discourse of Witchcraft, chap. 2 Explains this,[19] while he says that when a person desires in his heart to have such or such a thing effected by superstitious forms, &c. And the Devil consents thereunto, if he then do the business, there is a secret compact: thus such as by certain forms of words and prayers, call upon the Devil; and when tho they know it to be unwarantable, yet will do it, because they {*p. 16*} find an effect answerable to their expectation in using such charms and spells, they are in Covenant with the Devil, though they will not let themselves know or think it. Now this secret compact Satan sometimes, and as to some persons, rests satisfied with, as when the man or woman is of considerable knowledge, and hath much *Mother Wit* (as we commonly call it) and so is such as he knows will not be easily drawn into a more formal and express league with him; or when he is content they should be shinning professors[20] and such of whom he designs to serve himself mostly, if not only, in matters seemingly good. The other sort of league is that which is more express and formal, and when there be mutual conditions: the *Witch* on his or her part giving over their Soul (and sometimes also the body) into Sathans power,[21] he on the other part, promises great things to them, knowledge to the

17 This is from Bernard, *Guide to Grand-Jury Men*, 107.

18 'agreeably': accordingly.

19 Cf. Perkins, *Discourse*, 51–2. The two types of demonic pact (originally formulated by Thomas Aquinas) were often specified as 'tacit' and 'explicit', with the latter – the usual type for witches – being understood as an agreement in specific words, entered into on a specific occasion. See David Lederer, 'Pact with the Devil', in Golden (ed.), *Encyclopedia*, iii, 867–9.

20 'shinning professors': shining examples of Christian belief (though hypocritical).

21 This distinction between pledging the soul and pledging the body is unconventional in demonology. Bell may have been thinking of Perkins, *Discourse*, 48, which says that the witch gives the Devil 'either bodie, or soule, or both'. Neither Perkins nor Bell explain this

ignorant, revenge to the envious, and wrathful, &c. though he often breaks his promise to them, as he did to a *Hungarian Witch* of whom I have read, who being put in prison, and wanting food, she did eat her own flesh and so perished: Satan her Master never once helping her, if it was not to destroy her self, sooner then otherwise she might have done.[22] But then 4. the Covenant thus made, he {*p. 17*} proceeds to confirm it, which (some say) must be done by blood: therefore, some offer him a Sacrifice; perhaps of a cat, dog, &c., possibly he condescends thus far to some *Witches* of a more then ordinary station: but however I will not be positive in this; only I find it asserted by some, that he will not part thus with your ordinary *Witches*, but must needs *Suck Blood* of them which is done by *Spirits*, and that in several parts of the body, as the crown of the head, under the ear, the chin, &c. as witches of whom I have read, have confessed before the Judges. Next follows the *Witch Mark*, sometimes like a blew spot, or a little tate, or reid spots like flea-biting, sometimes also the flesh is sunk in, and hallow [*sic*], and this is put in secret places, as among the hair of the Head, or eyebrows, within the lips, under the arm-pits, and even in the most secret parts of the Body. 5. Thus the Devil and they becoming familiar, they get from him *Familiar Spirits*, some one, some moe, with whom they consult, and act, and over which Spirits he makes them believe they have all power, and can command them at pleasure: and in this they assume to themselves a kind of Glory, to think that they have *Spirits* at their nodd, to send forth for the torment of others; and herein they rejoyce, that they can {*p. 18*} keep others in awe by such thoughts of them or words to them, whereupon follows hurt and mischief. Some have so far run on in maintaining this point of it, anent the *Witches* getting familiar Spirits, at[23] that they think, that *Witches* do work all their malice and mischief by those cursed *Caytiffes*;[24] and so they make three things concure to the bewitching of a Person; *viz.* a Divine permission, a Devilish operation, and the evil Spirits working: and lastly, the *Witches* consent;[25] So that the Devil does all, and they consent to all, which to wit, is done in their behalf, for no doubt, Satan can go of and for himself, where he hath no league with the Witch, thus some define a *Witch* to be such *as do act beyond the ordinary power of Nature, by the help of wicked Spirits*. Athen. Merc. V. 1. N. 3. Q. 6.[26]

distinction, but it seems unlikely that they would have wished to challenge the orthodox Reformed Protestant doctrine that the soul of a witch or other reprobate person went immediately to hell on death, and that the body would follow at the Last Judgment and Resurrection. I am grateful to Martha McGill for advice on this topic.

22 This tale is from Bernard, *Guide to Grand-Jury Men*, 166–7.

23 *Sic.* Probably read 'as'.

24 'Caytiffes': wretches, villains.

25 As Larner pointed out, this passage echoed the opening words of the *Malleus Maleficarum* of 1486: Larner, 'Two Late Scottish Witchcraft Tracts', 242.

26 This is a quotation from the *Athenian Mercury* for March 1690, which carried a reader's question: 'Whether there be Witches? and what good Books have been written on that

Now, before we proceed further, we shall take notice of this one *Collorary*[27] that may be drawn from what we have now said anent the Covenant with the Devil. From hence possibly we may gather a reason, *why Witches themselves are not afraid to met [sic] with the Devil?* For one would think that *Humane Nature* might justly fright at the appearance, if not the *amusing*[28] name of *DEVIL*. We would say therefore, that we doubt nothing, but at sometimes the Devil appears even to his own in frightful {*p. 19*} shapes, to their great terror, especially if he be angry at them, and designs violence unto them, upon their refusing to do as he bids them, as *Bernard* reports he did to old *Dembdike*, whom he pusht into a Ditch, because she would not go help *Chattox* another *Witch*, (whom she could not abide) to make Picturs.[29] The same Author says, the Devil came sometimes to *Witch Chattox* gaping upon her in the Form of a *Beare*, with open mouth as if he would have worried her,[30] yet I think the reason why for ordinary they are not so much afraid to meet, speak to and keep Caballs with him; is, that they being now in Covenant with him, dream of no hurt in the business: yea, they fancy they have him at Command. And if it be said, its strange they have not checks of Conscience in the mean time because of their League with the Devil; We answer, that it is not so strange as sad, and to be lamented; For they being readily before that given up of God to a reprobate mind, have their Consciences seared, so as that they want all sense and feeling of sin.

But now, to come to the question more closely, and to shew how one may be convicted of this their league with the Devil; this compact how secretly so ever made, is to be searcht into, and all the presumptions hitherto spoken of, must tend to prove and discover {*p. 20*} this compact, which some think may be gotten done by a narrow scrutiny and search into these among other evidences of this Covenant,[31]

1. By a *Witches Mark*. We told already where this is to be found, it must therefore be again and again diligently searched for; and least it be mistaken for a Natural mark, it is to be observed, that this is Insensible, so that being pricked it will not bleed, as Natural marks will do. But what if they hide them? Or what if they find a way to remove them? We answer that God in his providence will scarce suffer it to be so; or if it so fall out, then it grows

Subject?' The answer was a conventional one: witches exist, and the good books on the subject are the Bible and the 'Histories of all Nations'. The biblical evidence was Exodus 22:18 and the witch of Endor. The author attacked Webster and cited Glanvill. *Athenian Mercury*, vol. 1, no. 3 (31 March 1690), Question 6.

27 *Sic*. Read 'Corollary'.

28 'amusing': cheating.

29 Bernard, *Guide to Grand-Jury Men*, 165. These cases, from the Lancashire witchcraft panic of 1612, became notorious. See James Sharpe, 'Lancashire Witches', in Golden (ed.), *Encyclopedia*, iii, 619–22.

30 Bernard, *Guide to Grand-Jury Men*, 166.

31 Paragraph breaks have been added editorially to Bell's six numbered points below.

again, and comes to its old Form, if we may credit the *Grand Witch Lewis Gaufridius* a rich and learn'd Priest,[32] as *Bernard* calls him:[33] So that, tho this mark be not found at first, it may be discovered at length.

2d. By *Witches* words, as their fortelling what shall happen to others the same found true, and their boasting thereof afterwards; as also, their speaking of transportation from home to forraign places, &c.

3d. Witches deeds; as their feeding creatures secretly, which some say they send their errands; their making of pictures, giving any thing to any Man which causes pains or death; as is, the perusing one [*sic*] shirt or cloaths, returning the same again, and the owner upon {*p. 21*} wearing them, and all the time of his or her wearing them, pained or tormented.

4th. The confession of Fellow-Witches, especially if appearing penitent, and being called one by one yet all agree in their Testimony; as their having seen, and been with them at their suspected Devilish meetings, plotings, &c. And here comes in the report of the *Good or white Witch* (as they call him or her) whereby is meant, these *Healers* or *Blessers* (as some call them) who pretend to know who are bad *Witches*, and where they dwell; and how to heal blasting, for-speaking &c. These being themselves *Witches* and in league with the Devil, best know who these are, and what be their practices.[34]

5. *A Divine witnese*, where God condescends to give it, as, when they pray for a token from God of displeasure against them if they be guilty; and it accordingly falls out. As it is reported to have been with one *Mother Samuel the Warboys Witch* that tormented *Mr. Throgmortons* children, who by bitter curses on her self if she were guilty; presently her *Chin* did *bleed*, the place (as afterwards she confest) where the *Spirits* did *Suck blood*.[35]

6th. And lastly, *The confession of the Witches themselves*. Sometimes the arraign'd *Witches* confess their being in Covenant with the Devil, {*p. 22*} partly upon being charg'd with the guilt, or of their own accord, or finally, being drawn thereto through terror of Conscience.

But now *Sir*, after all that is said, I desire not to be so understood, as if hereby I design'd to force any into a complyance with the Conclusions already laid down, further then the reasons brought by grave Authors already hinted will perswade; nor do I think the Opinions of Practices of others which may *seem* to run cross to something hitherto asserted are to be taxed by any; so

32 Louis Gaufridy was executed for witchcraft at Aix-en-Provence, France, in 1611. His case was often discussed in demonological works. See Sarah Ferber, *Demonic Possession and Exorcism in Early Modern France* (London, 2004), 70–88; Jonathan L. Pearl, 'Aix-en-Provence Nuns', in Golden (ed.), *Encyclopedia*, i, 25–6.

33 Bernard, *Guide to Grand-Jury Men*, 107.

34 Perkins condemned such so-called 'good witches' at particular length: Perkins, *Discourse*, 173–80, 255–7. It is noticeable that Bell does not use the common Scottish word 'charmers' for benevolent magical practitioners.

35 *The Most Strange and Admirable Discoverie of the Three Witches of Warboys*, sig. G1.

that what is here said is only to shew you what hath given the *Answerer* to your Questions most satisfaction in these Points. For a conclusion therefore I would say, that tho I have adventured on these few lines in answer to your *Queries*, therein I do not, nor indeed can I expect to satisfie all even of the more Judicious, but am apprehensive on the contrary, that I may displease some of them (for which I should yet be sorry) who may possibly think that the greatness of the Task might have forc'd me to a more awefull[36] distance, and a giving way to better and greater Undertakers; but finding none hitherto forward for allaying vulgar rude notions about your momentuous questions, I have (yet {*p. 23*} with all submission) adventur'd on this short essay [–] the questions handled therein, rather then the answers, being such as may push others forward to second and much better cares about them; which should much refresh,

Sir, Your Friend and Servant. *FINIS*.

[36] 'awefull': respectful.

10. APPENDIX: ALLOA AND RELATED WITCHES, CLACKMANNANSHIRE, 1658–61

INTRODUCTION

The document edited below relates to the trials of twelve accused witches in 1659, part of a wider panic in the Alloa area. It belongs with a much larger group of documents that were published in the companion volume to this one, *Scottish Witchcraft Trials*. It was omitted from that volume because the National Records of Scotland regarded the manuscript as in a fragile state, 'unfit for production', and the editors were unable to consult it. However, the NRS have since conserved it and made it available. The edition below should thus be read alongside the other documents about this case in the companion volume.[1]

The context for these trials was a local panic over witchcraft that arose in Alloa, near Stirling, in May 1658. Numerous witches were accused, and there were four executions in Edinburgh in August 1658. A second phase of the panic began shortly afterwards, and drew in further suspects from the town of Stirling and from the parish of Kippen to the west of the town. This second phase led to twelve trials in a circuit court in Stirling in March 1659. The document edited below was written in connection with these trials.

The document is a long roll of paper, endorsed 'Sterling Dittayes 1659'. A 'dittay', or indictment, listed the accused person's alleged crimes. The roll contains complete or fairly complete dittays (in order of appearance) for Bessie Stevenson, Isobel Bennett, Magdalen Blair and Katherine Black, and summary dittays for Elizabeth (Elspeth) Black, Barbara Erskine, Elizabeth Crockett, James Kirk, Isobel Keir, Margaret Gourlay, Margaret Harvie and Janet Miller. These twelve names fall into three groups. Bessie Stevenson, Isobel Bennett and Magdalen Blair were from Stirling; Katherine Black, Elizabeth Black, Barbara Erskine, Elizabeth Crockett and James Kirk were from Alloa, and had been under suspicion ever since the first phase of the panic; and Isobel Keir, Margaret Gourlay, Margaret Harvie and Janet Miller were from Kippen. In

[1] Julian Goodare and Liv Helene Willumsen (eds.), *Scottish Witchcraft Trials* (Woodbridge: SHS, 2025), 370–471. See particularly p. 383, with a note of the NRS's production of this document at the point when the volume had reached page proof stage.

the edition of the other documents we noted the absence of dittays from the court records, so it is good to have found these dittays – though they are not all complete, as we shall see.[2]

The four apparently complete dittays add to our knowledge of the case against these witches. There may well be further documents to be found among the justiciary court process papers, a mass of loose documents that have never been fully catalogued item by item. Most of the accusations in the dittays repeat and rephrase information that had previously been given in pre-trial confessions and witness statements, but we can now see what information the prosecutors selected from the pre-trial documents to convert into formal accusations. The lists of witnesses, too, are informative; most of the names (though not all) had been given in pre-trial documents, but here we see more clearly who was witnessing against whom. For several of the accused witches, individual malefices were crucial; the court minutes record arguments in court about many of the events.

The first dittay, that of Bessie Stevenson, lists the names of people whom she was alleged to have killed by witchcraft. Stevenson was a magical practitioner who sometimes used drastic kill-or-cure methods, and who sometimes transferred an illness from her client to another person – including herself, as her dittay makes clear. Folk healers were not usually blamed for the deaths of those whom they had tried to cure, but Stevenson's methods led, under hostile scrutiny, to a perception that she had killed several people.

Overall the document is neatly written, but it contains various crossings-out, annotations and gaps that give it an informal character. Katherine Black's dittay has been left unfinished, and all the later dittays are given in abbreviated form with references to other documents. Despite its sometimes scrappy compilation, though, this document may have been used in court, alongside other documents such as witnesses' written statements and lists of assizers. Phrasing like 'To read the depositions of the witnesses against the said Isabell, etc.' indicates that the prosecutor may have had this document in front of him as he 'read' the accusations out loud in court.

The twelve accused persons received various outcomes from the Stirling court. Barbara Erskine, Isobel Keir and Bessie Stevenson were convicted of witchcraft and executed. Isobel Bennett, Magdalen Blair, Margaret Gourlay, Margaret Harvie, James Kirk and Janet Miller were acquitted of witchcraft and survived, though Bennett, Blair and Gourlay were whipped for lesser offences. Elizabeth Black, Katherine Black and Elizabeth Crockett were convicted of witchcraft but sentenced to banishment from the country rather than execution. The banishments were never implemented, and the three women languished in prison for three years, but they were finally freed in 1661.[3]

2 Goodare and Willumsen (eds.), *Scottish Witchcraft Trials*, 385.
3 Goodare and Willumsen (eds.), *Scottish Witchcraft Trials*, 373–4.

Some notes should be given about the document and the editing process. The text of the roll is written in two columns. In the left-hand column are listed the names of accused criminals, a marginal note of the crimes of which they are accused, and sometimes a list of witnesses' names. In these lists of witnesses, an annotation, usually 'p[rese]nt' or occasionally 'abs[ent]', has been added immediately before most names. In the edition below, these annotations have been editorially placed *after* the name and enclosed in brackets, with abbreviations being extended. In the right-hand column are the accused criminals' dittays or summaries of their dittays. The edition below does not reproduce the columnar format, but instead places the left-hand material before the right-hand material for each case. Thus each case begins with the name of an accused witch, and ends with their dittay.

The witchcraft cases are preceded by a group of cases about adultery, theft and murder, written in a different hand. These cases are omitted here. However, halfway through these cases the heading 'Kathren Black, Elspeth Black, Witch' appears, written in the hand of the main scribe but crossed out, apparently when the other scribe later decided to use the space for non-witchcraft cases. This is one of several indications that this roll is a working document being compiled and used by several clerks in a busy office.

TEXT

Source: NRS, Court of Justiciary Process Papers, 1658–1659, JC26/26, roll labelled 'Stirling Court 1659 (Witchcraft)'.

[*Endorsed:*] Sterling Dittayes 1659

[*several non-witchcraft cases at the beginning, not transcribed*]

22 March 1659 Assyse convict[4]

Bessie Stevinsone relict of the deceast Alexander Lennox gairner [*sc.* gairdner] in Sterling prisoner

Witnessis
Jonet Henrie indueller in Sterling (present)
Margaret Mershell spous to Corporall Beggs (present)
Patrik Wright cordinare burges of Sterling (present)
Issobell Stewart spous to Malcome Ferguson at the brig of Turk (present)
Alexander Chrystesone younger in Craigforth (present)
Jonet Willison his spous (absent)

[4] This heading is a later addition.

Issobell Smart spous to George Wryght in Sterling (present)
George Wryght aforesaid (present)
Christiane Chrystesone spous to James Chrysteson in Sterling (present)
Jonet Chrystesone thair servant (present)
Margaret Matsone spous to Williame Lowrie in Sterling (present)
Bessie Burn spous to Robert Wingyet messenger (present)
Jonet Bennie relict of umquhile Thomas Gilfillane (present)
Jonet Gilfillane in Sterling (present)
Marjorie Wingyet spous to John Wilsone baxter thair (present)
Katharine Thomsone spous to Peter Easeman Englishman (present)
Katharin Wright spous to Thomas Mitchell maltman in Sterling (present)
Jean Watsone spous to John Moresone customer thair (present)
James Patersone in Corntoune (present)
Issobell Willisone his spous (present)
Helen Fergusone spous to Andrew Cowane wryght in Sterling (present)
John Gib cutler in Sterling (present)

Assise
[*a blank space is left here, perhaps for the assizers' names*]

Ye are indyted and accused for as much as by the divyne law of God and acts of parliament of this nation The comitters of the crymes of sorcerie, witchcraft and necromancie are punished by death. Nevertheles it is of veritie that ye the said Bessie hath shaken of[f] all feare of almightie God, reverence or regaird to his divyne law, and acts of parliament of this nation, and hes betaken yourself to the service of Sathan the enemie of mans salvation these 24 years past, and by your sorcerie, witchcraft and charming hes tane aff and layd on divers sicknessis and deseases upon sundrie his highnes subjects, namelie blasted or bewitched persones by taken thair shirts and mutches to St Ninians Well[5] and weeting the same thairin, and thairafter putting them on the deseased persone, as alsoe by makeing use of foxtree[6] leaves, and applying 2 of them under the deseased persons head, 2 under their midle and tua under their feet, and siclike for cureing of persones mawturned,[7] By leading them thrie tymes round about an oaken post, and useing this charme viz. oaken post stands thow, bairns maw turns thow, God and St Birnibane the bright turn my bairns maw right, in Gods name. Also for cureing of persons forspoken, useing this charme viz. thrie bitters hath thee bitten, heart and ill eye, tongue all the maist, the bitt must be In the name of the father, sone and holie ghost

5 St Ninian's Well is near Stirling. See the entry for it in the Canmore database (Historic Environment Scotland), at <http://canmore.org.uk/site/46210>.
6 'foxtree': foxglove.
7 'persones mawturned': persons (here assumed to be children) suffering from nausea or vomiting.

yee delyver all to him, In the useing of which charme, ye assume a pairt of the sike bodies desease But not so sore, which continowes with yow about the space of a quarter of an hower, And last for charmeing of the heart fevers, ye use this charme viz. ye take a belt with twa threeds putting one threed within and an other without the belt, and thairafter rolling it upe with the threed and putting it under the deseased persones arme holes, and if the pairtie be soe desesed both threeds turns to one side of the belt. By useing of which abovewrittene charmes yee takeing off diverse deseases aff some and putting it on uthers, ye have thairby occasioned divers of his highnes good subjects thair death by your sorcerie, witchcraft and charmeing, namelie \the death of/ Marie McKorer servitrix to Andrew Thomsone fleshor in Sterling, also the death of a young child of James Christisons wright in Sterling, and siclike the death of Margaret Ker servitrix to George Wright fisher thair, and als the death of Thomas Gilfillane weaver thair, as the depositiones of the witnesses underwrittine at lenth will manifest.

Pannell pleads not guiltie.[8]

22 March Assisse convict[9]

Issobell Bennet spous to William Mungall in Sterling prisoner[10]

Witnesses

Helen Ferguson spous to Andrew Cowan wryght in Sterling (present)
Isobell Smart spous to George Wright fisher in Sterling (present)
George Wright himself (present)
Thomas McAulay fleshor in Sterling (present)
Jonet Wright spous to James Buchannan wright (present)
James Patersone in Corntoun (present)
Isobell Willisone his spous (present)
Margaret Cowan spous to Edward Luckison cordiner in Sterling (present)
Elspet Miller spous to Robert Adame tayler (present)[11]
Thomas Miller merchand in Sterling (present)

Sworn.

Assise

[*a blank space is left here, perhaps for the assizers' names*]

Ye are indyted and accused Forasmuch as by the divyne law of God and acts of parliament of this nation The comitters of the crymes of sorcerie, witchcraft and charmeing are punished by death. Nevertheles it is of veritie that yee the

[8] This phrase is a later addition.
[9] This heading is a later addition.
[10] In margin: 'Witch'.
[11] 'Jonet Chrystesone servitrix to James Chrystesone' crossed out here.

said Issobell hath shaken off all feare of almightie God, reverence or regaird to his divyne law, and acts of parliament of this natione, hes betaken yourself to the service of Sathan the enimy of mans salvatione these [*1 word blank*] years past, \And/ By your sorcerie, witchcraft and charming, hes occasioned ather the death, or procured the death of divers his highnes good subjects in useing of thir charmes following viz. for blasted persons to end them or mend them of the siknes, washing such persons with water brought fra the how ground eb of the sea,[12] and takeing a litle meale and strawing it in the foure corners of their bed, alsoe laying under them the caker of a horse shooe[13] that has ridden ower our good neighbours viz. the fairie folkes, togither with a hooke[14] and a peece raw flesh, and uttering these words thrie tymes, The father, the sone and the holie ghost, which done the sike persone ather suddenlie recovers or dies of thair sikenes, And sicklike for the cureing of mawturned persones, viz. In leading them thrice round about an oken post, expressing these words, 'oaken post stands thow, bairns maw turns thow, God and St Birniebane the bright, turn the bairns maw right'.[15] And in likemaner by cureing one that is wronged by an other with whome they are at variance, Advyseing and counseling them to goe to such persons and crave thair health fra them for Gods sake and they wilbe weill, And lastlie for preserving persons from being wronged or bewitched of any uther persone, In advyseing and counselling them to take a quicke modiwort[16] and putt it in a box and burie it under the outside of the threshold of their doore.

By useing the which unlawfull charmes abovewritten ye have occasioned the death of divers deseased persons to whome ye used the same, As your owne confession and the depositiones of the witnesses given in against yow more amplie will manifest.

Confesses guiltie of all mentwned in her dittay, except witchcraft and sorcerie.[17]

22 March 1659 Assyse Clenged[18]
Magdalen Blair in Sterling prisoner[19]

Witnesses
James Andersone baxter in Sterling (present)
Helen Fergusone spous to Andrew Cowan wryght (present)
Margaret Paule spous to John Allan glover in Sterling (present)

12 'how ground eb of the sea': hollow seashore pool at low tide.
13 'hooke': sickle.
14 'caker of a horse shooe': iron pin inserted in a horseshoe to prevent slipping in icy conditions.
15 The words placed here in quotation marks have been written in a larger script.
16 'quicke modiwort': live mole.
17 This phrase is a later addition.
18 'convict' crossed out here, and 'Clenged' written after it. This heading is a later addition.
19 In margin: 'Witch'.

Williame Luckisone maltman in Sterling (present)
Katherin Luckison (present)

Assise
[*a blank space is left here, perhaps for the assizers' names*]

Ye are indyted and accused Forasmuch as by the divyne law of God and acts of parliament of this natione The comitters of the crymes of sorcerie, witchcraft and charming are punished by death. Nevertheles it is of veritie that yee the said Magdalen have shaken off all feare of God, reverence or regard to his divyne law, and of the saids acts of parliament, hes betane yourself to the service of Sathan the enemie of mans salvatione, these [*1 word blank*] years bypast, And by your sorcerie, witchcraft and fearfull imprecationes and threatenings, hes occasioned the \death and/ destruction of divers his highnes good subjects and of their bestiall and goods,[20] and als be the said airt advyseing persones wronged and bewitched by uthers to goe and seeke thair health frome them for Gods sake and they would be weill, As the depositions of the witnesses underwritten will clearlie manifest.

Pleads not guiltie.[21]

Kathren Black spouse to Thomas Measson in Alloway[22]

Witnesses
Barbara Arsken
Androw Thomsone (present)
James Lindsey (present)
William Moreis (present)
John Hunter (present)
Androw Arskein (present)
Robert Archibald (present)[23]
John McKenyie (ex.)
Agnes Aitken
Bessy Miller[24]
Margaret Herrine

Ye are indyted and accused Forsameikle as be the divyne law of almightie God and acts of parliament of this natione The committers of the cryms of sorcerie and witchcraft are punished by deathe. Nevertheles it is of verritie that

20 'bestiall and goods': livestock.
21 This phrase is a later addition.
22 In margin: 'Witch'.
23 'David Vertie' crossed out here.
24 'Sir Charles Arskein' crossed out here.

ye haveing shaken aff all feare of God, reverence or regaird to the lawes and acts of parliament, hes betaken your selfe to the service of Sathan the enemy of mans salvatione, entred in covenant and paction with him, renunced your baptisme, received his mark, and has had carnall copulation with him, Lykas ye have committed many malefices, layd on and taken aff sundrie disseases, alsweill upon men, wemen and children, as on their goods and bestiall, which will appeare by the depositions of the witnesses taken before the justices of peace, heirto annexed as a pairt of her dittay will testifie. And first, ye the said Kathren Black [*sic*]

Pleads not guiltie.[25]

Elspeth Black spouse to John Dempstertoun in Alloway[26]

Assise

[*no names are listed, nor is there space for them*]

Witnesses

Thomas Mitchell

Ye are indyted and accused Forasmuch as be the divyne law of almightie God Etc. as is in the former dittay, and to read the witnesses depositions against her.

Pleads not guiltie.[27]

Barbara Arskein prisoner[28]

Assise

[*a blank space is left here, perhaps for the assizers' names*]

Ye are indyted and accused Forasmuch etc., to read the narrative of Kathren Blackes dittay etc., as your owne confession heirto annexed as a pairt of your dittay more amplie will testifie etc., to read the first, second, thrid and fourth articles of her dittay, and 7th article thereof for sodrifying[29] her guiltines of the sin of witchcraft and charmeing.

Confesses.[30]

25 This phrase is a later addition.
26 In margin: 'Witch'.
27 This phrase is a later addition.
28 In margin: 'Witch'.
29 *Sic*. Perhaps this should be understood as 'solidifying'. The meaning is presumably 'confirming' or 'verifying'.
30 This phrase is a later addition.

Elizabeth Crocket[31]

Assise
[*a blank space is left here, perhaps for the assizers' names*]

Accused Forasmuch etc. to read the 2^{d} and 6th articles of her dittay for verifying her copulation with the Dewill and having his mark, etc.
Pleads not guiltie.[32]

James Kirk[33]

Witnesses
James Lindsey (present)
Androw Thomson (present)
John Kirk (present)

Assise
[*a blank space is left here, perhaps for the assizers' names*]

Accused Forasmuch etc., to read the 4th and 5th articles of his dittay anent his charming and of his receiving the Dewills mark, in quhich last article Margaret Tailyeor declaires the said James to be ane Warlock.

Also to read the 2^{d} article of his depositions anent[34] Kathren Rany for declaratione against the said James Kirk and his playing to them in Bodsmedowe.

Pleads not guiltie.[35]

Isabell Keir[36]

Witnesses
John Wryght (present)
Andro Dowgall (present)
Williame Ritchie (present)
Agnes Buchannane (absent)[37]
Janet Riach (absent)[38]
Agnes Denovan (present)

31 In margin: 'Witch'.
32 This phrase is a later addition.
33 In margin: 'Witch'.
34 'William Moreis' crossed out here.
35 This phrase is a later addition.
36 In margin: 'Witch'.
37 Annotated in later hand: 'Unlawed in 100 m[erks]'.
38 Annotated in later hand: 'Unlawed in 100 m[erks]'.

John Gow (present)
Jean Gillespie (present)
John Wre (present)
Marjorie Denoven (present)
John Harvie (present)
John Fairlie (absent)[39]
James Harvie (present)
Robert Foster (present)
John Harvie (present)[40]
John Mcilhoisch (present)[41]
Duncan Foster (present)
Janet Miller spouse to Androw Fairlie (exc.)[42]

Assise
[*no names are listed, nor is there space for them*]

Accused Forasmuch as by the divyne law of almightie God, lawes and acts of parliament of this natione, The committers of the crymes of sorcerie and witchcraft ar punished by death. Nevertheles it is of verritie that yee the said Isabell Keir, contrar the saids lawes and acts of parliament, hes given your selfe to the service of Sattan the enemy off mans salvatione these many years bygane, entred in pact and covenant with him, renunced your baptisme, and by the Dewill your masters help and assistance hes committed many malefices, layd on and taken aff sundrie sicknesses and disseases on sundrie his highnes good people, alsweill upon men, wemen and children, and upon their goods and bestiall, as the depositions of witnesses heirto annexed at more lenth will testifie. To read the depositions of the witnesses against the said Isabell, etc., etc., etc., etc.

Pleads not guiltie.[43]

39 Altered from 'present'.
40 *Sic.* This is the second instance of this name.
41 'Janet Miller, prisoner' crossed out here. This Janet Miller, one of the accused witches, should be distinguished from Janet Miller, wife of Andrew Fairlie, who appears as a witness later in this list.
42 This 'exc.' has been written in place of an illegible annotation (perhaps 'abs.'). In addition, a further annotation 'Unlawed in 100 m[erks]' has been written and then crossed out. Probably 'exc.' stands for 'excused'.
43 This phrase is a later addition.

Margaret Gourlay[44]
Janet Miller

Witnesses
Androw Wright (present)
James McKay (present)
Patrick Manoch (absent)
Janet Miller prisoner
Georg Wordie (present)
Christian Schaw (present)

Assise
[*no names are listed, nor is there space for them*]

Accused Forasmuch etc. To read as before in the former dittay, and to read the depositions of the witnesses against her etc.

Pleads not guiltie.[45]

Ye ar Indyted and accused for[46] contravening the acts of parliament, by wilfull raising of fyre within the dwelling house, barnes, byres and stables of Androw Wright sone in law to yow the said Margaret Gourlay.

Margaret Harvie[47]

Witnesses
Agnes Denovan
Janet Miller

Assise
[*no names are listed, nor is there space for them*]

Accused Forasmuch etc. To read as in the former dittay, and to read the depositions of the witnesses against her etc.

Pleads not guiltie.[48]

[44] In margin: 'Witch'. This annotation seems to apply to both names. Janet Miller was both an accused witch in her own right (her own summary dittay appears later), and a witness against Margaret Gourlay (she is named again in the witness list as 'Janet Miller prisoner').

[45] This phrase, and the paragraph that follows, are later additions.

[46] 'raising of fyre' crossed out here.

[47] In margin: 'Witch'.

[48] This phrase is a later addition.

Janet Miller prisoner[49]

Assise
[*no names are listed, nor is there space for them*]

Indyted Forasmuch etc. To read as before etc., and to read the depositions of the witnesses against her, etc., etc.

Pleads not guiltie.[50]

[49] In margin: 'Witch'.

[50] This phrase is a later addition. After it, the words 'Also accused for the ...' have been added and then crossed out. This may well relate to the accusation of fire-raising also made against Margaret Gourlay.

INDEX

Some persons have distinguishing letters in brackets added to their names, as follows: (c) for personnel of criminal courts; (d) for demonological writers; (i) for persons who took part in pre-trial investigations; (j) for juristic writers; (n) for neighbours, relatives and alleged victims of accused witches; (w) for persons accused of witchcraft.